Men's Lives

◆◆◆

MICHAEL S. KIMMEL
STATE UNIVERSITY OF NEW YORK
AT STONY BROOK

MICHAEL A. MESSNER
UNIVERSITY OF SOUTHERN CALIFORNIA

MACMILLAN PUBLISHING COMPANY
NEW YORK

Copyright © 1989 by Macmillan Publishing Company,
a division of Macmillan, Inc.

Macmillan Publishing Company
866 Third Avenue, New York, New York 10022

Collier Macmillan Canada, Inc.

   Library of Congress Cataloging-in-Publication Data
Men's lives / [compiled by] Michael S. Kimmel, Michael A. Messner.
      p.   cm.
   ISBN 0-02-364061-8
      1. Men — United States — Attitudes.   2. Masculinity (Psychology)
   3. Men — United States — Sexual behavior.   I. Kimmel, Michael S.
   II. Messner, Michael A.
   HQ1090.3.M465   1989
   305.3'1 — dc19   88-25877
                                       CIP

Printing: 1 2 3 4 5 6 7   Year: 9 0 1 2 3 4 5

For
John Lennon
(1940–1980)
and the kind of man he was
and
Daniel Hafkin Pleck
(born October 21, 1987)
and the kind of man he can become

Isn't it time we destroyed the macho ethic? . . . Where has it gotten us all these thousands of years? Are we still going to have to be clubbing each other to death? Do I have to arm wrestle you to have a relationship with you as another male? Do I have to seduce her — just because she's a female? Can we not have a relationship on some other level? . . . I don't want to go through life pretending to be James Dean or Marlon Brando.

— John Lennon, 1980

Preface

◆ ◆ ◆

Inspired by the growth of gender studies and by constant requests from our colleagues in women's studies for articles on men, we have assembled here some of the best social science and popular writings on men and masculinity. Our selections are based on the courses that we have taught at Rutgers University, California State University — Hayward, State University of New York at Stony Brook, and the University of Southern California. This anthology can, therefore, be used as a main or supplementary text in courses in men's studies, women's studies, sex roles, gender, sociology of men or women, and the psychology of women. It can be used as a supplement to the Macmillan text, *Thinking about Women*, by Margaret Andersen, or any similar text when an instructor wants to include readings on the male experience.

Over the past four years we have been teaching courses on the male experience, or "men's lives." Our courses have reflected our own education and recent research of feminist scholars and profeminist men in American society. (By profeminist men we mean active supporters of women's claims against male violence and for equal opportunity, political participation, sexual autonomy, family reforms, and equal education.) Gender, these scholars have demonstrated, is a general feature of social life, one of the central organizing principles around which our lives revolve. In the social sciences, women's studies courses and courses about women in traditional disciplines have explored the experiences of women's lives. But what does it mean to be a man in contemporary American society?

This anthology is organized around specific themes that define masculinity and the issues that men confront over their lifetimes. In addition, we incorporate a social constructionist perspective that examines how men actively construct their masculinity within a social and historical context. Related to this construction and integrated in our examination are the variations that exist among men in relation to class, race, and sexual preference.

We begin Parts I and II with issues and questions that unravel the "masculine mystique" and suggest various dimensions of men's position in society and their relationships with women and with other men. Parts III through X examine the different issues that emerge for men at different times of their lives and the ways in which their lives change over time. We touch on central moments in the lives of men related to boyhood and adolescence, sports, occupations, marriage, and fatherhood. Four of these parts deal with men's emotional and sexual relationships with women and with other men. The final part, "Men and the Future," explores some of the ways in which men are changing and possible directions in which men might continue to change.

Although a major component of the traditional, normative definition of masculinity is independence, we are pleased to acknowledge those colleagues and friends whose criticism and support have been a constant help throughout our work on this project. Christine Cardone, our editor at Macmillan, has been encouraging and supportive from the start. Tony English, editor in chief, was also helpful. Many other scholars who work on issues of masculinity, such as Bob Blauner, Robert Brannon, Harry Brod, Bob Connell, James Harrison, Jeff Hearn, Martin Levine, David Morgan, Don Sabo, and Peter Stein, have also contributed to a supportive general intellectual community in which we work. Joseph Pleck has been an ideal colleague and friend to this project — suggesting articles and authors, providing criticisms, and helping to shape the book as a whole. We also thank the following reviewers for their helpful comments and suggestions: Margaret L. Andersen, University of Delaware; Harold Brod, Kenyon College; Arlene Eskilson, Lake Forest College; Martin P. Levine, Bloomfield College; Susan E. Marshall, University of Texas at Austin; Borrie Thorne, University of Southern California; Carol S. Wharton, University of Richmond; Paul L. Wienir, Western Michigan University; and Kersti Yllo, Wheaton College.

Colleagues at the State University of New York at Stony Brook and the University of Southern California have also been supportive of this work. We are especially grateful to Paul Attewell, Lois Banner, Ruth Schwartz Cowan, John Gagnon, Norman Goodman, Helen Lefkowitz-Horowtiz, Carol Jacklin, and Barrie Thorne. A teaching fellowship from the Lilly Endowment has generously supported Kimmel's work on pedagogical issues of teaching about men and masculinity.

This book is also a product of the profeminist men's movement, a loose network of men who support a feminist critique of traditional masculinity and support women's struggles to enlarge the scope of personal autonomy and public power for women. These men are engaged in a variety of efforts to transform masculinity in order to allow men to live fuller, richer, and healthier lives. The editors of *Changing Men* (with whom we have worked as Book Review Editor and Sports Editor), Mike

Biernbaum and Rick Cote, have labored for a decade to provide a forum for antisexist men, and we acknowledge their efforts with gratitude and respect. In addition to many of the men listed above we also thank Jeff Beane, Tim Beneke, Sidney Miller, Geof Morgan, Tom Mosmiller, Fred Small, and John Stoltenberg.

Finally, our wider circle of friends and colleagues has provided that rare atmosphere that combines intellectual challenge and emotional support. We are grateful to Judith Brisman, Barbara and Herb Diamond, Bill Diamond, Martin Duberman, Kate Ellis, Judith Gerson, Frances Goldin, Cathy Greenblat, Pam Hatchfield, Sandi Kimmel, David Levin, Mary Morris, and Mitchell Tunick. We would also like to acknowledge our fathers — Edwin H. Kimmel and Russell J. Messner — who provided such important positive models of masculinity for us as we were growing up. Finally, Pierrette Hondagneu and Iona Mara-Drita have lived with this project since its beginnings, and we are grateful that they share these men's lives.

The two men to whom this book is dedicated bracket, for us, some of the central meanings of masculinity. Lennon's life was tragically cut short by an assassin's bullet, but he embodied the possibility of transformation and the linking of daily life with political vision and artistic creativity. And though Pleck's journey is just beginning, he carries our hopes for a new masculinity, enlarged and enriched by caring for himself and others.

M.S.K.
M.A.M.

Contents

◆ ◆ ◆

PART III *From Boys to Men*   YMCA   125

PART IV *Sports and War: Rites of Passage*   Little League
         in Male Institutions   181

PART V *Men and Work*   217

Introduction

◆ ◆ ◆

This is a book about men. But, unlike other books about men, which line countless library shelves, this is a book about men *as men*. It is a book in which men's experiences are not taken for granted as we explore the "real" and significant accomplishments of men, but a book in which those experiences are treated as significant and important for themselves.

Men as "Gendered Beings"

But what does it mean to examine men "as men"? Most courses in a college curriculum are about men, aren't they? But these courses routinely deal with men only in their public roles, so we come to know and understand men as scientists, politicians, military figures, writers, and philosophers. Rarely, if ever, are men understood through the prism of gender.

But listen to some male voices from some of these "ungendered" courses. Take, for example, composer Charles Ives, debunking "sissy" types of music; he said he used traditional tough guy themes and concerns in his drive to build new sounds and structures out of the popular musical idiom (cf. Wilkinson, 1986: 103). Or architect Louis Sullivan, describing his ambition to create "masculine forms": strong, solid, commanding respect. Or novelist Ernest Hemingway, retaliating against literary enemies by portraying them as impotent or homosexual.

Consider also political figures, such as Cardinal Richelieu, the seventeenth-century French First Minister to Louis XIII, who insisted that it was "necessary to have masculine virtue and do everything by reason" (cited in Elliott, 1984: 20). Closer to home, recall President Lyndon Baines Johnson's dismissal of a political adversary: "Oh him. He has to

1

squat to piss!" Or his boast that during the Tet offensive in the Vietnam War, he "didn't just screw Ho Chi Minh. I cut his pecker off!"

Democrats have no monopoly on unexamined gender coloring their political rhetoric. Richard Nixon was "afraid of being acted upon, of being inactive, of being soft, or being thought impotent, of being dependent upon anyone else," according to his biographer, Bruce Mazlish. And don't forget Vice-President George Bush's revealing claim that in his television debate with Democratic challenger Geraldine Ferraro he had "kicked ass." (That few political pundits criticized such unapologetic glee concerning violence against women is again indicative of how invisible gender issues are in our culture.) Indeed, recent political campaigns have revolved, in part, around gender issues, as each candidate attempted to demonstrate that he was not a "wimp" but was a "real man." (Of course, the few successful female politicians face the double task of convincing the electorate that they are not the "weak-willed wimps" that their gender implies in the public mind while *at the same time* demonstrating that they are "real women.")

These are just a few examples of what we might call gendered speech, language that uses gender terms to make its case. And these are just a few of the thousands of examples one could find in every academic discipline of how men's lives are organized around gender issues, and how gender remains one of the organizing principles of social life. We come to know ourselves and our world through the prism of gender. Only we act as if we didn't know it.

Fortunately, in recent years, the pioneering work of feminist scholars, both in traditional disciplines and in women's studies, and of feminist women in the political arena has made us aware of the centrality of gender in our lives. Gender, these scholars have demonstrated, is a central feature of social life, one of the central organizing principles around which our lives revolve. In the social sciences, gender has now taken its place alongside class and race as the three central mechanisms by which power and resources are distributed in our society, and the three central themes out of which we fashion the meanings of our lives.

We certainly understand how this works for women. Through women's studies courses and also in courses about women in traditional disciplines, students have explored the complexity of women's lives, the hidden history of exemplary women, and the daily experiences of women in the routines of their lives. For women, we know how gender works as one of the formative elements out of which social life is organized.

The Invisibility of Gender:
A Sociological Explanation

Too often, though, we treat men as if they had no gender, as if only their public personae were of interest to us as students and scholars, as if their interior experience of gender was of no significance. This became evident when one of us was in a graduate seminar on Feminist Theory several years ago. A discussion between a white woman and a black woman revolved around the question of whether their similarities as women were greater than their racial differences as black and white. The white woman asserted that the fact that they were both women bonded them, in spite of their racial differences. The black woman disagreed.

"When you wake up in the morning and look in the mirror, what do you see?" she asked.

"I see a woman," replied the white woman.

"That's precisely the issue," replied the black woman. "I see a black woman. For me, race is visible every day, because it is how I am not privileged in this culture. Race is invisible to you, which is why our alliance will always seem somewhat false to me."

Witnessing this exchange, Michael Kimmel was startled. When *he* looked in the mirror in the morning, he saw, as he put it, "a human being: universally generalizable. The generic person." What had been concealed — that he possessed both race and gender — had become strikingly visible. As a white man, he was able not to think about the ways in which gender and race had affected his experiences.

There is a sociological explanation for this blind spot in our thinking: the mechanisms that afford us privilege are very often invisible to us. What makes us marginal (unempowered, oppressed) are the mechanisms that we understand, because those are the ones that are most painful in daily life. Thus, white people rarely think of themselves as "raced" people, rarely think of race as a central element in their experience. But people of color are marginalized by race, and so the centrality of race is both painfully obvious and urgently needs study. Similarly, middle class people do not acknowledge the importance of social class as an organizing principle of social life, largely because for them class is an invisible force that makes everyone look pretty much the same. Working class people, on the other hand, are often painfully aware of the centrality of class in their lives. [Interestingly, upper class people are often more aware of class dynamics than are middle class people. In part, this may be the result of the emphasis on status within the upper class, as lineage, breeding, and family honor take center stage. In part, it may also be the result of a peculiar marginalization of the upper class in our society, as in the overwhelming number of television shows and movies that are ostensibly about just plain (i.e., middle class) folks.]

In this same way, men often think of themselves as genderless, as if gender did not matter in the daily experiences of our lives. Certainly, we can see the biological sex of individuals, but we rarely understand the ways in which *gender* — that complex of social meanings that is attached to biological sex — is enacted in our daily lives. For example, we treat male scientists as if their being men had nothing to do with the organization of their experiments, the logic of scientific inquiry, or the questions posed by science itself. We treat male political figures as if masculinity were not even remotely in their consciousness as they do battle in the political arena.

This book takes a position directly opposed to such genderlessness for men. We believe that men are also "gendered," and that this gendering process, the transformation of biological males into socially interacting men, is a central experience for men. That we are unaware of it only helps to perpetuate the inequalities based on gender in our society.

In this book, we will examine the various ways in which men are gendered. We have gathered together some of the most interesting, engaging, and convincing materials from the past decade that have been written about men. We believe that *Men's Lives* will allow readers to explore the meanings of masculinity in contemporary American culture in a new way.

Earlier Efforts to Study Men

Certainly, researchers have been examining masculinity for a long time. Historically, there have been three general models that have governed social scientific research on men and masculinity. *Biological models* have focused on the ways in which innate biological differences between males and females programmed different social behaviors. *Anthropological models* have examined masculinity cross-culturally, stressing the variations in the behaviors and attributes associated with being a man. And, until recently, *sociological models* have stressed how socialization of boys and girls included accommodation to a "sex role" specific to one's biological sex. Although each of these perspectives helps to understand the meaning of masculinity and femininity, each is also limited in its ability to fully explain how gender operates in any culture.

Relying on differences in reproductive biology, some scholars have argued that the physiological organization of males and females makes the differences we observe in psychological temperament and social behaviors inevitable. One perspective holds that differences in endocrine functioning are the cause of gender difference, that testosterone predisposes males toward aggression, competition, and violence, whereas estrogen predisposes females toward passivity, tenderness, and exaggerated emotionality. Others insist that these observed behavioral differences derive from the differences between the size or number of sperm

and eggs. Since a male can produce 100 million sperm with each ejaculation, whereas a female produce less than 20 eggs capable of producing
healthy offspring over the course of her life, these authors suggest that
men's "investment" in their offspring is significantly less than women's
investment. Other authors arrive at the same conclusion by suggesting
that the different size of egg and sperm, and the fact that the egg is the
source of the food supply, impels temperamental differences. Reproductive "success' to males means the insemination of as many females as
possible; to females, reproductive success means carefully choosing one
male to mate with and insisting that he remain present to care for and
support their offspring. Still other authors argue that male and female
behavior is governed by different halves of the brain; males are ruled by
the left hemisphere, which controls rationality and abstract thought,
whereas females are governed by the right hemisphere, which controls
emotional affect and creativity. (For examples of these works, see Wilson, 1976; Trivers, 1972; Goldberg, 1975; and Goldberg et al., 1986.)

   Observed normative temperamental differences between women and
men that are assumed to be of biological origin are easily translated into
political prescriptions. In this ideological sleight of hand, what is *normative* (i.e., what is prescribed) is translated into what is *normal*, and the
mechanisms of this transformation are the assumed biological imperative. George Gilder, for example, assembles the putative biological differences between women and men into a call for a return to traditional
gender roles. Gilder believes that male sexuality is, by nature, wild and
lusty, "insistent" and "incessant," careening out of control and threatening anarchic disorder, unless it can be controlled and constrained. This
is the task of women. When women refuse to apply the brakes to male
sexuality — by asserting their own or by choosing to pursue a life outside the domestic sphere — they abandon their "natural" function for
illusory social gains. Sex education, abortion, and birth control are all
condemned as facilitating women's escape from biological necessity. Similarly, he argues against women's employment, since the "unemployed
man can contribute little to the community and will often disrupt it, but
the woman may even do more good without a job than with one" (Gilder,
1986: 86).

   The biological argument has been challenged by many scholars on
several grounds. The implied causation between two observed sets of
differences (biological differences and different behaviors) is misleading,
since there is no logical reason to assume that one caused the other, or
that the line of causation moves only from the biological to the social.
The selection of biological evidence is partial, and generalizations from
"lower" animal species to human beings are always suspect. One sociologist asks if these differences are "natural," why their enforcement
must be coercive, why males and females have to be forced to assume
the rules that they are naturally supposed to play (see Epstein, 1986: 8).
And one primatologist argues that the evidence adduced to support the

current status quo might also lead to precisely the opposite conclusions, that biological differences would impel female promiscuity and male fragility (see Hrdy, 1981). Biological differences between males and females would appear to set some parameters for differences in social behavior, but would not dictate the temperaments of men and women in any one culture. These psychological and social differences would appear to be the result far more of the ways in which cultures interpret, shape, and modify these biological inheritances. We may be born males or females, but we become men and women in a cultural context.

Anthropologists have entered the debate at this point, but with different positions. For example, some anthropologists have suggested that the universality of gender differences comes from specific cultural adaptations to the environment, whereas others describe the cultural variations of gender roles, seeking to demonstrate the fluidity of gender and the primacy of cultural organization. Lionel Tiger and Robin Fox argue that the sexual division of labor is universal because of the different nature of bonding for males and females. "Nature," they argue, "intended mother and child to be together" because she is the source of emotional security and food; thus, cultures have prescribed various behaviors for women that emphasize nurturance and emotional connection (Tiger and Fox, 1984: 304). The bond between men is forged through the necessity of "competitive cooperation" in hunting; men must cooperate with members of their own tribe in the hunt and yet compete for scarce resources with men in other tribes. Such bonds predispose men toward the organization of the modern corporation or governmental bureaucracy.

Such anthropological arguments omit as much as they include, and many scholars have pointed out problems with the model. Why did not intelligence become sex linked, as this model (and the biological model) would imply? Such positions also reveal a marked conservatism: the differences between women and men are the differences that nature or cultural evolution intended, and are therefore not to be tampered with.

Perhaps the best known challenge to this anthropological argument is the work of Margaret Mead. Mead insisted that the variations among cultures in their prescriptions of gender roles required the conclusion that culture was the more decisive cause of these differences. In her classic study, *Sex and Temperament in Three Primitive Societies* (1935), Mead observed such wide variability among gender role prescriptions — and such marked differences from our own — that any universality implied by biological or anthropological models had to be rejected. And although the empirical accuracy of Mead's work has been challenged in its specific arguments, the general theoretical arguments remain convincing.

Psychological theories have also contributed to the discussion of gender roles, as psychologists have specified the specific developmental sequences for both males and females. Earlier theorists observed psychological distancing from the mother as the precondition for independence and autonomy, or suggested a sequence that placed the capacity for abstract reason as the developmental stage beyond relational reasoning. Since it is normative for males to exhibit independence and the capacity for abstract reason, it was argued that males are more successful at negotiating these psychological passages, and implied that women somehow lagged behind men on the ladder of developmental success. (Such arguments may be found in Freud, Erikson, and Kohlberg.)

But these models, too, have been challenged, most recently by sociologist Nancy Chodorow, who argued that women's ability to connect contains a more fundamentally human trait than the male's need to distance, and by psychologist Carol Gilligan, who claimed that women's predisposition toward relational reasoning may contain a more humane strategy of thought than recourse to abstract principles. Regardless of our assessment of these arguments, Chodorow and Gilligan rightly point out that the highly ideological assumptions that make masculinity the normative standard against which the psychological development of *both* males and females was measured would inevitably make femininity problematic and less fully developed. Moreover, Chodorow explicitly insists that these "essential" differences between women and men are socially constructed and thus subject to change.

Finally, sociologists have attempted to synthesize these three perspectives into a systematic explanation of "sex roles." These are the collection of attitudes, attributes, and behaviors that is seen as appropriate for males and appropriate for females. Thus, masculinity is associated with technical mastery, aggression, competitiveness, and cognitive abstraction, whereas femininity is associated with emotional nurturance, connectedness, and passivity. Sex role theory informed a wide variety of prescriptive literature (self-help books) that instructed parents on what to do if they wanted their child to grow up as a healthy boy or girl.

The strongest challenge to all these perspectives, as we have seen, came from feminist scholars, who have specified the ways in which the assumptions about maturity, development, and health all made masculinity the norm against which both genders were measured. In all the social sciences, these feminist scholars have stripped these early studies of their academic facades to reveal the unexamined ideological assumptions contained within them. By the early 1970s, women's studies programs began to articulate a new paradigm for the study of gender, one that assumed nothing about men or women beforehand, and that made no assumptions about which gender was more highly developed. And by the mid-1970s, the first group of texts about men appeared that had been inspired by these pioneering efforts by feminist scholars.

Thinking about Men: The First Generation

In the mid 1970s, the first group of works on men and masculinity appeared that was directly influenced by these feminist critiques of the traditional explanations for gender differences. Some books underscored the costs to men of traditional gender role prescriptions, exploring how some aspects of men's lives and experiences are constrained and under-developed by the relentless pressure to exhibit other behaviors associated with masculinity. Books such as Marc Feigen-Fasteau's *The Male Machine* (1974) and Warren Farrell's *The Liberated Man* (1975) discussed the costs to men's health — both physical and psychological — and the quality of relationships with women, other men, and their children of the traditional male sex role.

Several anthologies explored the meanings of masculinity in the United States by adopting a feminist-inspired prism through which to view men and masculinity. For example, Deborah David and Robert Brannon's *The Forty-Nine Percent Majority* (1976) and Joseph Pleck and Jack Sawyer's *Men and Masculinity* (1974) presented panoramic views of men's lives, from within a framework that accepted the feminist critique of traditional gender arrangements. Elizabeth Pleck and Joseph Pleck's *The American Man* (1980) suggested an historical evolution of contemporary themes. These works explored both the "costs" and the privileges of being a man in modern American society.

Perhaps the single most important book to criticize the normative organization of the male sex role was Joseph Pleck's *The Myth of Masculinity* (1981). Pleck carefully deconstructed the constituent elements of the male sex role, and reviewed the empirical literature for each component part. After demonstrating that the empirical literature did not support these normative features, Pleck argued that the male sex role model was incapable of describing men's experiences. In its place, he posited a "male sex role strain" model that specified the contemporary sex role as problematic, historically specific, and also an unattainable ideal.

Building on Pleck's work, a critique of the sex role model began to emerge. Sex roles had been cast as the static containers of behaviors and attitudes, and biological males and females were required to fit themselves into these containers, regardless of how ill-fitting these clusters of behaviors and attitudes felt. Such a model was ahistorical and suggested a false cultural universalism, and was therefore ill equipped to understand the ways in which sex roles change, and the ways in which individuals modify those roles through the enactments of gender expectations. Most telling, however, was the way in which the sex role model ignored the ways in which definitions of masculinity and femininity were based on, and reproduced, relationships of power. Not only do men as a group exert power over women as a group, but the definitions of masculinity and femininity reproduce those power relations. Power dynamics are an essential element in both the definition and the enactments of gender.

This first generation of research on masculinity was extremely valuable, particularly since it challenged the unexamined ideology that made masculinity the gender norm against which both men and women were measured. The old models of sex roles had reproduced the domination of men over women by insisting on the dominance of masculine traits over feminine traits. These new studies argued against both the definitions of either sex, and the social institutions in which those differences were embedded. A new model looked at "gender relations" and understood how the definition of either masculinity or femininity was relational, that is, how the definition of one gender depended, in part, on the understanding of the definition of the other.

In the early 1980s, the research on women again surged ahead of the research on men and masculinity. This time, however, the focus was not on the ways in which sex roles reproduce the power relations in society, but rather on the ways in which femininity is experienced differently by women in various social groups. Gradually, the notion of a single femininity — which was based on the white middle class Victorian notion of female passivity, langorous beauty, and emotional responsiveness — was replaced by an examination of the ways in which women differ in their gender role expectations by race, class, age, sexual orientation, ethnicity, region, and nationality.

The research on men and masculinity is now entering a new stage, in which the variations among men are seen as central to the understanding of men's lives. The unexamined assumption in earlier studies had been that one version of masculinity — white, middle age, middle class, heterosexual — was the sex role into which all men were struggling to fit in our society. Thus, working class men, men of color, gay men, and younger and older men were all observed as departing in significant ways from the traditional definitions of masculinity. Therefore, it was easy to see these men as enacting "problematic" or "deviant" versions of masculinity. Such theoretical assertions, however, reproduce precisely the power relationships that keep these men in subordinate positions in our society. It is not only that middle class, middle aged, heterosexual white masculinity becomes the standard against which all men are measured, but that this definition, itself, is used against those who do not fit as a way to keep them down. The normative definition of masculinity is not the "right" one, but it is the one that is dominant.

The challenge to the hegemonic definition of masculinity came from men whose masculinity was cast as deviant: men of color, gay men, and ethnic men. We understand now that we cannot speak of "masculinity" as a singular term, but must examine *masculinities:* the ways in which different men construct different versions of masculinity. Such a perspective can be seen in several recent works, such as Harry Brod's *The Making of Masculinities* (1987), Michael Kimmel's *Changing Men: New Directions in Research on Men and Masculinity* (1987), and Tim Carrigan, Bob Connell, and John Lee's "Toward a New Sociology of Masculinity" (1985). Bob Connell's *Gender and Power* (1987) and Jeff Hearn's *The Gender of Oppression* (1987) represent the most sophisticated theoretical statements of this perspective. Connell argues that the oppression of women is a chief mechanism that links the various masculinities, and that the marginalization of certain masculinities is an important component of the reproduction of male power over women. This critique of the hegemonic definition of masculinity as a perspective on men's lives is one of the organizing principles of our book, which is the first college-level text in this second generation of work on men and masculinities.

Now that we have reviewed some of the traditional explanations for gender relations, and have situated this book within the research on gender in general, and men in particular, let us briefly outline exactly the theoretical perspective we have employed in the book. Not only does our theoretical framework provide the organizing principle of the book as a whole, it also provided some of the criteria for the selection of the articles that are included.

The Social Construction of Masculinities

Men are not born, growing from infants through boyhood to manhood, to follow a predetermined biological imperative, encoded in their physical organization. To be a man is to participate in social life as a man, as a gendered being. Men are not born; they are made. And men make themselves, actively constructing their masculinities within a social and historical context.

This book is about how men are made and how men make themselves in contemporary American society. It is about what masculinity means, about how masculinity is organized, and about the social institutions that sustain and elaborate it. It is a book in which we will trace what it means to be a man over the course of men's lives.

Men's Lives revolves around three important themes that are part of a social scientific perspective. First, we have adopted a *social constructionist* perspective. By this we mean that the important fact of men's lives is not that they are biological males, but that they become men. Our sex may be male, but our identity as men is developed through a complex process of interaction with the culture in which we both learn the gender scripts appropriate to our culture, and attempt to modify those scripts to make them more palatable. The second axis around which the book is organized follows from our social constructionist perspective. As we have argued, the experience of masculinity is not a uniform and universally generalizable to all men in our society. Masculinity differs dramatically in our society, and we have organized the book to illustrate the *variations* among men in the construction of masculinity. Third, we have adopted a *lifecourse* perspective, to chart the construction of these various masculinities in men's lives, and to examine pivotal developmental moments or institutional locations during a man's life in which the meanings of masculinity are articulated. These three perspectives — social constructionism, variations among men, and the life course perspective — will define the organization of this book and the criteria we have used to select the articles included.

THE SOCIAL CONSTRUCTIONIST MODEL

The social constructionist perspective argues that the meaning of masculinity is neither transhistorical not culturally universal, but rather varies from culture to culture and within any one culture over time. Thus, males become men in the United States in the late twentieth century in a way that is very different from men in Southeast Asia, or Kenya, or Sri Lanka. The meaning of masculinity varies from culture to culture.

Men's lives also vary within any one culture over time. The experience of masculinity in the contemporary United States is very different from that experience 150 years ago. Who would argue that what it meant to be a "real man" in seventeenth-century France (at least among the upper classes) — high-heeled patent leather shoes, red velvet jackets covering frilly white lace shirts, lots of rouge and white powder makeup, and a taste for the elegant refinement of ornate furniture — bears much resemblance to the meaning of masculinity among a similar class of French men today?

A perspective that emphasizes the social construction of gender is, therefore, both *historical* and *comparative*. It allows us to explore the ways in which the meanings of gender vary from culture to culture, and how they change within any one culture over historical time.

VARIATIONS AMONG MEN

Masculinity also varies *within* any one society by the various types of cultural groups that compose it. Subcultures are organized around other poles, which are the primary way in which people organize themselves and by which resources are distributed. And men's experiences differ from one another in the ways in which social scientists have identified as the chief structural mechanisms along which power and resources are distributed. We cannot speak of masculinity in the United States as if it were a single, easily identifiable commodity. To do so is to risk positing one version of masculinity as normative, and making all other masculinities problematic.

In the contemporary United States, masculinity is constructed differently by class culture, by race and ethnicity, and by age. And each of these axes of masculinity modifies the others. Black masculinity differs from white masculinity, yet each of them is also further modified by class and age. A 30-year-old middle class black man will have some things in common with a 30-year-old middle class white man that he might not share with a 60-year-old working class black man, although he will share with him elements of masculinity that are different from the white man of his class and age. The resulting matrix of *masculinities* is complicated and often the elements are cross-cutting, but without understanding this, we risk collapsing all masculinities into one hegemonic version.

The challenge to a singular definition of masculinity as the normative definition is the second axis around which the readings in this book revolve.

The meaning of masculinity is not constant over the course of any man's life, but will change as he grows and matures. The issues confronting a man about proving himself, feeling successful, and the social institutions in which he will attempt to enact his definitions of masculinity will change throughout his life. Thus, we have adopted a *life course perspective* to discuss the ways in which different issues will emerge for men at different times of their lives, and the ways in which men's lives, themselves, change over time. The life course perspective we have employed will examine men's lives at various pivotal moments in their development from young boys to adults. Like a slide show, these points will freeze the action for a short while, to afford us the opportunity to examine in more detail the ways in which different men in our culture experience masculinity at any one time.

The book's organization reflects these three concerns. The first two sections, "Perspectives" and "Variations," set the context through which we shall examine men's lives. The next nine sections follow those lives through the life course, pausing at various central moments in the lives of men in the United States today. Specifically, the essays will touch on boyhood and adolescence, and discuss some of the institutions that are organized to embody and reproduce American masculinities, such as fraternities, the military, the Boy Scouts, and sports. A section on work explores the ways in which masculinities are constructed in relationship to men's occupations. The next sections describe men's emotional and sexual relationships with women and with other men. We deal with heterosexuality and homosexuality in the same section, mindful of the ways in which variations among men based on other lines (class, race, ethnicity) affect these sexual orientations. And the sections on "Men with Women" and "Men with Men" describe a variety of emotional and physical (but not necessarily sexual) relationships that men develop through their lives. The next section explores the construction of masculinities within the family, and discusses men as fathers and husbands, as well as aging. The final section, "Men in the Future," will examine some of the ways in which men are changing and points to some directions in which men might continue to change.

Our perspective, stressing the social construction of masculinities over the life course, will, we believe, allow a more comprehensive understanding of men's lives in the United States today.

References

Brod, Harry, ed. *The Making of Masculinities*. Boston: Allen and Unwin, 1987.

Carrigan, Tim, Bob Connell, and John Lee. "Toward a New Sociology of Masculinity" in *Theory and Society*, 1985, 5(14).

Chodorow, Nancy. *The Reproduction of Mothering*. Berkeley: University of California Press, 1978.

Connell, R. W. *Gender and Power*. Stanford, CA: Stanford University Press, 1987.

David, Deborah and Robert Brannon, eds. *The 49% Majority*. Reading, MA: Addison-Wesley, 1976.

Elliott, J. H. *Richelieu and Olivares*. New York: Cambridge University Press, 1984.

Epstein, Cynthia Fuchs. "Inevitability of Prejudice" in *Society*, Sept./Oct., 1986.

Farrell, Warren. *The Liberated Man*. New York: Random House, 1975.

Feigen-Fasteau, Marc. *The Male Machine*. New York: McGraw-Hill, 1974.

Gilligan, Carol. *In a Different Voice*. Cambridge, MA: Harvard University Press, 1982.

Gilder, George. *Men and Marriage*. Gretna, LA: Pelican Publishers, 1986.

Goldberg, Steven. *The Inevitability of Patriarchy*. New York: , 1975.

————. 1986. "Reaffirming the Obvious" in *Society*. Sept./Oct., 1986.

Hearn, Jeff. *The Gender of Oppression*. New York: St. Martin's Press, 1987.

Hrdy, Sandra Blaffer. *The Woman That Never Evolved*. Cambridge, MA: Harvard University Press, 1981.

Kimmel, Michael S., ed. *Changing Men: New Directions in Research on Men and Masculinity*. Newbury Park, CA: Sage Publications, 1987.

Mead, Margaret. *Sex and Temperament in Three Primitive Societies*. New York: McGraw-Hill, 1935.

Pleck, Joseph. *The Myth of Masculinity*. Cambridge, MA: M.I.T. Press, 1981.

———— and Elizabeth Pleck, eds. *The American Man*. Englewood Cliffs, NJ: Prentice-Hall, 1980.

———— and Jack Sawyer, eds. *Men and Masculinity*. Englewood Cliffs, NJ: Prentice-Hall, 1974.

Tiger, Lionel and Robin Fox. *The Imperial Animal*. New York: Holt, Rinehart & Winston, 1984.

Trivers, Robert. "Parental Investment and Sexual Selection" in *Sexual Selection and the Descent of Man* (B. Campbell, ed.). Chicago: Aldine Publishers, 1972.

Wilkinson, Rupert. *American Tough: The Tough Guy Tradition and American Character*. New York: Harper and Row, 1986.

Wilson, E. O. *Sociobiology: The New Synthesis*. Cambridge, MA: Harvard University Press, 1976.

PART ONE

◆ ◆ ◆

Perspectives

Jules Feiffer

"WHAT'S MANLY?"

A quick glance at any magazine rack or television talk show is enough to make you aware that these days, men are confused. What does it mean to be a "real man"? How are men supposed to behave? What are men supposed to feel? How are men to express their feelings? Who are we supposed to be like: Tootsie or Rambo? Clint Eastwood or Phil Donahue? Rhett Butler or Ashley Wilkes?

We are daily bombarded with images and handy rules to help us negotiate our way through a world in which all the rules seem to have suddenly vanished or changed. Some tell us to reassert traditional masculinity against all contemporary challenges. But a strength built only on the weakness of others hardly feels like strength at all. Others tell us that men are in power, the oppressor. But if men are in power as a group, why do individual men often feel so powerless? Can men change?

These questions will return throughout this book. In this section, several authors begin to examine some of the issues that define the depth of the question about men and masculinity. These articles begin to unravel the "masculine mystique" and suggest various dimensions of men's position in society, their power, their powerlessness, and their confusion.

Some authors offer a critique of traditional masculinity. Joe Jackson eloquently expresses men's confusion. Joseph H. Pleck explores contemporary masculinity and the way in which it shapes men's relations with women, other men, and in society in general. Gloria Steinem asks men to imagine how their world would be different if one small feature of their physiology were different.

On the other hand, Bruce Fierstein humorously defends traditional masculinity in this exerpt from his popular book *Real Men Don't Eat Quiche*. That this book was read by so many men not as a satiric look at men's confusion but as a perspective reassertion of an anachronistic masculinity itself indicates the depths of men's confusion. And all is not entirely utopian with today's "new man" either. Barbara Ehrenreich offers her suspicions that the new man may simply be a traditional man in a new guise, a form of consumerism with a masculine face. Finally, William Goode argues that to begin to understand contemporary men's responses — both their resistance and their "grudging acceptance" — of changing gender expectations, we must develop a "sociology of superordinates."

These selections indicate that the exploration of masculinities in the contemporary United States is a difficult one, and one that has only just begun. They provide some interesting perspectives from which to ask, as one recent author put it, "why men are the way they are."

Joe Jackson

REAL MEN

Take your mind back — I don't know when
Sometime when it always seemed
to be just us and them.
Girls that wore pink
    and boys that wore blue
Boys that always grew up better men
than me and you.

What's a man now — what's a man mean
Is he rough or is he rugged
Is he cultural and clean
Now it's all change — it's got to change more
'Cause we think it's getting better
But nobody's really sure.

Chorus: And so it goes — Go round again
                But now and then we wonder who
                    the real men are.

See the nice boys — dancing in pairs
Golden earring, golden tan
Blow-wave in their hair.
Sure they're all straight — straight as a line
All the gays are macho
Can't you see their leather shine.

You don't want to sound dumb — don't want to offend
So don't call me a faggot
Not unless you are a friend
Then if you're tall and handsome and strong
You can wear the uniform and I could play along.

Chorus

Time to get scared — Time to change plan
Don't know how to treat a lady
Don't know how to be a man
Time to admit — what you call defeat
'Cause there's women running past you now
And you just drag your feet.

1 cs. — Pleck
Ehrenreich
Boode
1/2 cs. — Pleck ;
Either Ecs D

Man makes a gun — Man goes to war
Man can kill and man can drink
and man can take a whore.
Kill all the blacks — kill all the reds
And if there's war between the sexes
Then there'll be no people left.

Chorus

Joseph H. Pleck

MEN'S POWER WITH WOMEN, OTHER MEN, AND SOCIETY:

A MEN'S MOVEMENT ANALYSIS

My aim in this paper is to analyze men's power from the perspective afforded by the emerging antisexist men's movement. In the last several years, an antisexist men's movement has appeared in North America and in the Western European countries. While it is not so widely known as the women's movement, the men's movement has generated a variety of books, publications, and organizations,[1] and is now an established presence on the sex role scene. The present and future political relationship between the women's movement and the men's movement raises complex questions which I do not deal with here, though they are clearly important ones. Instead, here I present my own view of the contribution which the men's movement and the men's analysis make to a feminist understanding of men and power, and of power relations between the sexes. First, I will analyze men's power over women, particularly in relation to the power that men often perceive women have over them. Then I will analyze two other power relationships men are implicated in — men's power with other men, and men's power in society more generally — and suggest how these two other power relationships interact with men's power over women.

1. See, for example, Deborah David and Robert Brannon, eds., *The Forty-Nine Percent Majority: Readings on the Male Role* (Reading, Mass.: Addison-Wesley, 1975); Warren Farrell, *The Liberated Man* (New York: Bantam Books, 1975); Marc Feigen Fasteau, *The Male Machine* (New York: McGraw-Hill, 1974); Jack Nichols, *Men's Liberation: A New Definition of Masculinity* (Baltimore: Penguin, 1975); John Petras, eds., *Sex: Male/Gender: Masculine* (Port Washington, N.J.: Alfred, 1975); Joseph H. Pleck and Jack Sawyer, eds., *Men and Masculinity* (Englewood Cliffs, N.J.: Prentice-Hall, 1974). See also the *Man's Awareness Network (M.A.N.) Newsletter*, a regularly updated directory of men's movement activities, organizations, and publications, prepared by a rotating group of men's centers (c/o Knoxville Men's Resource Center, P.O. Box 8060, U.T. Station, Knoxville, Tenn. 37916); the Men's Studies Collection, Charles Hayden Humanities Library, Massachusetts Institute of Technology, Cambridge, Mass. 02139.

MEN'S POWER OVER WOMEN, AND WOMEN'S POWER OVER MEN

It is becoming increasingly recognized that one of the most fundamental questions raised by the women's movement is not a question about women at all, but rather a question about men: Why do men oppress women? There are two general kinds of answers to this question. The first is that men want power over women because it is in their rational self-interest to do so, to have the concrete benefits and privileges that power over women provides them. Having power, it is rational to want to keep it. The second kind of answer is that men want to have power over women because of deep-lying psychological needs in male personality. These two views are not mutually exclusive, and there is certainly ample evidence for both. The final analysis of men's oppression of women will have to give attention equally to its rational and irrational sources.

I will concentrate my attention here on the psychological sources of men's needs for power over women. Let us consider first the most common and commonsense psychological analysis of men's need to dominate women, which takes as its starting point the male child's early experience with women. The male child, the argument goes, perceives his mother and his predominantly female elementary school teachers as dominating and controlling. These relationships *do* in reality contain elements of domination and control, probably exacerbated by the restriction of women's opportunities to exercise power in most other areas. As a result, men feel a lifelong psychological need to free themselves from or prevent their domination by women. The argument is, in effect, that men oppress women as adults because they experienced women as oppressing them as children.

According to this analysis, the process operates in a vicious circle. In each generation, adult men restrict women from having power in almost all domains of social life except child rearing. As a result, male children feel powerless and dominated, grow up needing to restrict women's power, and thus the cycle repeats itself. It follows from this analysis that the way to break the vicious circle is to make it possible for women to exercise power outside of parenting and parentlike roles and to get men to do their half share of parenting.

There may be a kernel of truth in this "mother domination" theory of sexism for some men, and the social changes in the organization of child care that this theory suggests are certainly desirable. As a general explanation of men's needs to dominate women, however, this theory has been quite overworked. This theory holds women themselves rather than men ultimately responsible for the oppression of women — in William Ryan's phrase, "blaming the victim" of oppression for her own oppression.[2] The recent film *One Flew over the Cuckoo's Nest* presents an extreme example of how women's supposed domination of men is used to justify sexism. This film portrays the archetypal struggle between a female figure depicted as domineering and castrating and a rebellious male hero (played by Jack Nicholson) who refuses to be emasculated by her. This struggle escalates to a climactic scene in which Nicholson throws her on the floor and

2. William Ryan, *Blaming the Victim* (New York: Pantheon, 1970).

nearly strangles her to death — a scene that was accompanied by wild cheering from the audience when I saw the film. For this performance, Jack Nicholson won the Academy Award as the best actor of the year, an indication of how successful the film is in seducing its audience to accept this act of sexual violence as legitimate and even heroic. The hidden moral message of the film is that because women dominate men, the most extreme forms of sexual violence are not only permissible for men, but indeed are morally obligatory.

To account for men's needs for power over women, it is ultimately more useful to examine some other ways that men feel women have power over them than fear of maternal domination.[3] There are two forms of power that men perceive women as holding over them which derive more directly from traditional definitions of adult male and female roles, and have implications which are far more compatible with a feminist perspective.

The first power that men perceive women having over them is *expressive power*, the power to express emotions. It is well known that in traditional male–female relationships, women are supposed to express their needs for achievement only vicariously through the achievements of men. It is not so widely recognized, however, that this dependency of women on men's achievement has a converse. In traditional male–female relationships, men experience their emotions vicariously through women. Many men have learned to depend on women to help them express their emotions, indeed, to express their emotions for them. At an ultimate level, many men are unable to feel emotionally alive except through relationships with women. A particularly dramatic example occurs in an earlier Jack Nicholson film, *Carnal Knowledge*. Art Garfunkel, at one point early in his romance with Candy Bergen, tells Nicholson that she makes him aware of thoughts he "never even knew he had." Although Nicholson is sleeping with Bergen and Garfunkel is not, Nicholson feels tremendously deprived in comparison when he hears this. In a dramatic scene, Nicholson then goes to her and angrily demands: "You tell him his thoughts, now you tell me *my* thoughts!" When women withhold and refuse to exercise this expressive power for men's benefit, many men, like Nicholson, feel abject and try all the harder to get women to play their traditional expressive role.

A second form of power that men attribute to women is *masculinity-validating power*. In traditional masculinity, to experience oneself as masculine requires

3. In addition to the mother domination theory, there are two other psychological theories relating aspects of the early mother–child relationship in men's sexism. The first can be called the "mother identification" theory, which holds that men develop a "feminine" psychological identification because of their early attachment to their mothers and that men fear this internal feminine part of themselves, seeking to control it by controlling those who actually are feminine, i.e., women. The second can be called the "mother socialization" theory, holding that since boys' fathers are relatively absent as sex-role models, the major route by which boys learn masculinity is through their mothers' rewarding masculine behavior, and especially through their mothers' punishing feminine behavior. Thus, males associate women with punishment and pressure to be masculine. Interestingly, these two theories are in direct contradiction, since the former holds that men fear women because women make men feminine, and the latter holds that men fear women because women make men masculine. These theories are discussed at greater length in Joseph H. Pleck's "Men's Traditional Attitudes toward Women: Conceptual Issues in Research" in *The Psychology of Women: New Directions in Research*, ed. Julia Sherman and Florence Denmark (New York: Psychological Dimensions, 1978).

that women play their prescribed role of doing the things that make men feel masculine. Another scene from *Carnal Knowledge* provides a pointed illustration. In the closing scene of the movie, Nicholson has hired a call girl whom he has rehearsed and coached in a script telling him how strong and manly he is, in order to get him sexually aroused. Nicholson seems to be in control, but when she makes a mistake in her role, his desperate reprimands show just how dependent he is on her playing out the masculinity-validating script he has created. It is clear that what he is looking for in this encounter is not so much sexual gratification as it is validation of himself as a man — which only women can give him. As with women's expressive power, when women refuse to exercise their masculinity-validating power for men, many men feel lost and bereft and frantically attempt to force women back into their accustomed role.

As I suggested before, men's need for power over women derives both from men's pragmatic self-interest and from men's psychological needs. It would be a mistake to overemphasize men's psychological needs as the sources of their needs to control women, in comparison with simple rational self-interest. But if we are looking for the psychological sources of men's needs for power over women, their perception that women have expressive power and masculinity-validating power over them is critical to analyze. These are the two powers men perceive women as having, which they fear women will no longer exercise in their favor. These are the two resources women possess which men fear women will withhold, and whose threatened or actual loss leads men to such frantic attempts to reassert power over women.

Men's dependence on women's power to express men's emotions and to validate men's masculinity has placed heavy burdens on women. By and large, these are not powers over men that women have wanted to hold. These are powers that men have themselves handed over to women, by defining the male role as being emotionally cool and inexpressive, and as being ultimately validated by heterosexual success.

There is reason to think that over the course of recent history — as male–male friendship has declined, and as dating and marriage have occurred more universally and at younger ages — the demands on men to be emotionally inexpressive and to prove masculinity through relating to women have become stronger. As a result, men have given women increasingly more expressive power and more masculinity-validating power over them, and have become increasingly dependent on women for emotional and sex-role validation. In the context of this increased dependency on women's power, the emergence of the women's movement now, with women asserting their right not to play these roles for men, has hit men with a special force.

It is in this context that the men's movement and men's groups place so much emphasis on men learning to express and experience their emotions with each other, and learning how to validate themselves and each other as persons, instead of needing women to validate them emotionally and as men. When men realize that they can develop in themselves the power to experience themselves emotionally and to validate themselves as persons, they will not feel the dependency on women for these essential needs which has led in the past to so much male fear, resentment, and need to control women. Then men will be emotionally more free to negotiate the pragmatic realignment of power between the sexes that is underway in our society.

MEN'S POWER WITH OTHER MEN

After considering men's power over women in relation to the power men per-ceive women having over them, let us consider men's power over women in a second context: the context of men's power relationships with other men. In recent years, we have come to understand that relations between men and women are governed by a sexual politics that exists outside individual men's and women's needs and choices. it has taken us much longer to recognize that there is a systematic sexual politics of male–male relationships as well. Under patriar-chy, men's relationships with other men cannot help but be shaped and pat-terned by patriarchal norms, though they are less obvious than the norms gov-erning male–female relationships. A society could not have the kinds of power dynamics that exist between women and men in our society without certain kinds of systematic power dynamics operating among men as well.

One dramatic example illustrating this connection occurs in Marge Piercy's recent novel *Small Changes*. In a flashback scene, a male character goes along with several friends to gang rape a woman. When his turn comes, he is impo-tent; whereupon the other men grab him, pulling his pants down to rape *him*. This scene powerfully conveys one form of the relationship between male–female and male–male sexual politics. The point is that men do not just happily bond together to oppress women. In addition to hierarchy over women, men create hierarchies and rankings among themselves according to criteria of "mas-culinity." Men at each rank of masculinity compete with each other, with what-ever resources they have, for the differential payoffs that patriarchy allows men.

Men in different societies choose different grounds on which to rank each other. Many societies use the simple facts of age and physical strength to stratify men. The most bizarre and extreme form of patriarchal stratification occurs in those societies which have literally created a class of eunuchs. Our society, re-flecting its own particular preoccupations, stratifies men according to physical strength and athletic ability in the early years, but later in life focuses on success with women and ability to make money.

In our society, one of the most critical rankings among men deriving from patriarchal sexual politics is the division between gay and straight men. This division has powerful negative consequences for gay men and gives straight men privilege. But in addition, this division has a larger symbolic meaning. Our society uses the male heterosexual–homosexual dichotomy as a central symbol for *all* the rankings of masculinity, for the division on *any* grounds between males who are "real men" and have power and males who are not. Any kind of powerlessness or refusal to compete becomes imbued with the imagery of ho-mosexuality. In the men's movement documentary film *Men's Lives*,[4] a high school male who studies modern dance says that others often think he is gay because he is a dancer. When asked why, he gives three reasons: because dancers are "free and loose," because they are "not big like football players," and because "you're not trying to kill anybody." The patriarchal connection: if you are not trying to kill other men, you must be gay.

Another dramatic example of men's use of homosexual derogations as weap-ons in their power struggle with each other comes from a document which

4. Available from New Day Films, P.O. Box 615, Franklin Lakes, N.J. 07417.

provides one of the richest case studies of the politics of male–male relationships to yet appear: Woodward and Bernstein's *The Final Days*. Ehrlichman jokes that Kissinger is queer, Kissinger calls an unnamed colleague a psychopathic homosexual, and Haig jokes that Nixon and Rebozo are having a homosexual relationship. From the highest ranks of male power to the lowest, the gay–straight division is a central symbol of all the forms of ranking and power relationships which men put on each other.

The relationships between the patriarchal stratification and competition which men experience with each other and men's patriarchal domination of women are complex. Let us briefly consider several points of interconnection between them. First, women are used as *symbols of success* in men's competition with each other. It is sometimes thought that competition for women is the ultimate source of men's competition with each other. For example, in *Totem and Taboo* Freud presented a mythical reconstruction of the origin of society based on sons' sexual competition with the father, leading to their murdering the father. In this view, if women did not exist, men would not have anything to compete for with each other. There is considerable reason, however, to see women not as the ultimate source of male–male competition, but rather as only symbols in a male contest where real roots lie much deeper.

The recent film *Paper Chase* provides an interesting example. This film combines the story of a small group of male law students in their first year of law school with a heterosexual love story between one of the students (played by Timothy Bottoms) and the professor's daughter. As the film develops, it becomes clear that the real business is the struggle within the group of male law students for survival, success, and the professor's blessing — a patriarchal struggle in which several of the less successful are driven out of school and one even attempts suicide. When Timothy Bottoms gets the professor's daughter at the end, she is simply another one of the rewards he has won by doing better than the other males in her father's class. Indeed, she appears to be a direct part of the patriarchal blessing her father has bestowed on Bottoms.

Second, women often play a *mediating* role in the patriarchal struggle among men. Women get men together with each other and provide the social lubrication necessary to smooth over men's inability to relate to each other noncompetitively. This function has been expressed in many myths, for example, the folk tales included in the Grimms' collection about groups of brothers whose younger sister reunites and reconciles them with their kingfather, who had previously banished and tried to kill them. A more modern myth, James Dickey's *Deliverance*, portrays what happens when men's relationships with each other are not mediated by women. According to Carolyn Heilbrun,[5] the central message of *Deliverance* is that when men get beyond the bounds of civilization, which really means beyond the bounds of the civilizing effects of women, men rape and murder each other.

A third function women play in male–male sexual politics is that relationships with women provide men a *refuge* for the dangers and stresses of relating to other males. Traditional relationships with women have provided men a safe place in which they can recuperate from the stresses they have absorbed in their daily struggle with other men, and in which they can express their needs with-

---

5. Carolyn G. Heilbrun, "The Masculine Wilderness of the American Novel," *Saturday Review* 41 (January 29, 1972), pp. 41–44.

out fearing that these needs will be used against them. If women begin to compete with men and have power in their own right, men are threatened by the loss of this refuge.

Finally, a fourth function of women in males' patriarchal competition with each other is to reduce the stress of competition by serving as an *underclass*. As Elizabeth Janeway has written in *Between Myth and Morning*,[6] under patriarchy women represent the lowest status, a status to which men can fall only under the most exceptional circumstances, if at all. Competition among men is serious, but its intensity is mitigated by the fact that there is a lowest possible level to which men cannot fall. One reason men fear women's liberation, writes Janeway, is that the liberation of women will take away this unique underclass status of women. Men will now risk falling lower than ever before, into a new underclass composed of the weak of both sexes. Thus, women's liberation means that the stakes of patriarchal failure for men are higher than they have been before, and that it is even more important for men not to lose.

Thus, men's patriarchal competition with each other makes use of women as symbols of success, as mediators, as refuges, and as an underclass. In each of these roles, women are dominated by men in ways that derive directly from men's struggle with each other. Men need to deal with the sexual politics of their relationships with each other if they are to deal fully with the sexual politics of their relationships with women.

Ultimately, we have to understand that patriarchy has two halves which are intimately related to each other. Patriarchy is a *dual* system, a system in which men oppress women, and in which men oppress themselves and each other. At one level, challenging one part of patriarchy inherently leads to challenging the other. This is one way to interpret why the idea of women's liberation so soon led to the idea of men's liberation, which in my view ultimately means freeing men from the patriarchal sexual dynamics they now experience with each other. But because the patriarchal sexual dynamics of male–male relationships are less obvious than those of male–female relationships, men face a real danger: while the patriarchal oppression of women may be lessened as a result of the women's movement, the patriarchal oppression of men may be untouched. The real danger for men posed by the attack that the women's movement is making on patriarchy is not that this attack will go too far, but that it will not go far enough. Ultimately, men cannot go any further in relating to women as equals than they have been able to go in relating to other men as equals — an equality which has been so deeply disturbing, which has generated so many psychological as well as literal casualties, and which has left so many unresolved issues of competition and frustrated love.

MEN'S POWER IN SOCIETY

Let us now consider men's power over women in a third and final context, the context of men's power in the larger society. At one level, men's social identity is defined by the power they have over women and the power they can compete for against other men. But at another level, most men have very little power over their own lives. How can we understand this paradox?

---

6. Elizabeth Janeway, *Between Myth and Morning* (Boston: Little, Brown, 1975); see also Elizabeth Janeway, "The Weak are the Second Sex," *Atlantic Monthly* (December 1973), pp. 91–104.

The major demand to which men must accede in contemporary society is that they play their required role in the economy. But this role is not intrinsically satisfying. The social researcher Daniel Yankelovich[7] has suggested that about 80 percent of U.S. male workers experience their jobs as intrinsically meaningless and onerous. They experience their jobs and themselves as worthwhile only through priding themselves on the hard work and personal sacrifice they are making to be breadwinners for their families. Accepting these hardships reaffirms their role as family providers and therefore as true men.

Linking the breadwinner role to masculinity in this way has several consequences for men. Men can get psychological payoffs from their jobs which these jobs never provide in themselves. By training men to accept payment for their work in feelings of masculinity rather than in feelings of satisfaction, men will not demand that their jobs be made more meaningful, and as a result jobs can be designed for the more important goal of generating profits. Further, the connection between work and masculinity makes men accept unemployment as their personal failing as males, rather than analyze and change the profit-based economy whose inevitable dislocations make them unemployed or unemployable.

Most critical for our analysis here, men's role in the economy and the ways men are motivated to play it have at least two negative effects on women. First, the husband's job makes many direct and indirect demands on wives. In fact, it is often hard to distinguish whether the wife is dominated more by the husband or by the husband's job. Sociologist Ralph Turner writes: "Because the husband must adjust to the demands of his occupation and the family in turn must accommodate to his demands on behalf of his occupational obligations, the husband appears to dominate his wife and children. But as an agent of economic institutions, he perceives himself as controlled rather than as controlling."[8]

Second, linking the breadwinner role to masculinity in order to motivate men to work means that women must not be allowed to hold paid work. For the large majority of men who accept dehumanizing jobs only because having a job validates their role as family breadwinner, their wives' taking paid work takes away from them the major and often only way they have of experiencing themselves as having worth. Yankelovich suggests that the frustration and discontent of this group of men, whose wives are increasingly joining the paid labor force, is emerging as a major social problem. What these men do to sabotage women's paid work is deplorable, but I believe that it is quite within the bounds of a feminist analysis of contemporary society to see these men as victims as well as victimizers.

One long-range perspective on the historical evolution of the family is that from an earlier stage in which both wife and husband were directly economically productive in the household economic unit, the husband's economic role has evolved so that now it is under the control of forces entirely outside the family. In order to increase productivity, the goal in the design of this new male work role is to increase men's commitment and loyalty to work and to reduce those ties to the family that might compete with it. Men's jobs are increasingly

7. Daniel Yankelovich, "The Meaning of Work," in *The Worker and the Job*, ed. Jerome Rosow (Englewood Cliffs, N.J.: Prentice-Hall, 1974).

8. Ralph Turner, *Family Interaction* (New York: Wiley, 1968), p. 282.

structured as if men had no direct roles or responsibilities in the family — indeed, as if they did not have families at all. But paradoxically, at the same time that men's responsibilities in the family are reduced to facilitate more efficient performance of their work role, the increasing dehumanization of work means that the satisfaction which jobs give men is, to an increasing degree, *only* the satisfaction of fulfilling the family breadwinner role. That is, on the one hand, men's ties to the family have to be broken down to facilitate industrial work discipline; but on the other hand, men's sense of responsibility to the family has to be increased, but shaped into a purely economic form, to provide the motivation for men to work at all. Essential to this process is the transformation of the wife's economic role to providing supportive services, both physical and psychological, to keep him on the job, and to take over the family responsibilities which his expanded work role will no longer allow him to fulfill himself. The wife is then bound to her husband by her economic dependency on him, and the husband in turn is bound to his job by his family's economic dependence on him.

A final example from the film *Men's Lives* illustrates some of these points. In one of the most powerful scenes in the film, a worker in a rubber plant resignedly describes how his bosses are concerned, in his words, with "pacifying" him to get the maximum output from him, not with satisfying his needs. He then takes back this analysis, saying that he is only a worker and therefore cannot really understand what is happening to him. Next, he is asked whether he wants his wife to take a paid job to reduce the pressure he feels in trying to support his family. In marked contrast to his earlier passive resignation, he proudly asserts that he will never allow her to work, and that in particular he will never scrub the floors after he comes home from his own job. (He correctly perceives that if his wife did take a paid job, he would be under pressure to do some housework.) In this scene, the man expresses and then denies an awareness of his exploitation as a worker. Central to his coping with and repressing his incipient awareness of his exploitation is his false consciousness of his superiority and privilege over women. Not scrubbing floors is a real privilege, and deciding whether or not his wife will have paid work is a real power, but the consciousness of power over his own life that such privilege and power give this man is false. The relative privilege that men gets from sexism and, more importantly, the false consciousness of privilege men get from sexism plays a critical role in reconciling men to their subordination in the larger political economy. This analysis does not imply that men's sexism will go away if they gain control over their own lives, or that men do not have to deal with their sexism until they gain this control. I disagree with both. Rather, my point is that we cannot fully understand men's sexism or men's subordination in the larger society unless we understand how deeply they are related.

To summarize, a feminist understanding of men's power over women, why men have needed it, and what is involved in changing it, is enriched by examining men's power in a broader context. To understand men's power over women, we have to understand the ways in which men feel women have power over them, men's power relationships with other men, and the powerlessness of most men in the larger society. Rectifying men's power relationship with women will inevitably both stimulate and benefit from the rectification of these other power relationships.

Gloria Steinem

IF MEN COULD MENSTRUATE —

A white minority of the world has spent centuries conning us into thinking that
a white skin makes people superior — even though the only thing it really does
is make them more subject to ultraviolet rays and to wrinkles. Male human
beings have built whole cultures around the idea that penis-envy is "natural' to
women — though having such an unprotected organ might be said to make men
vulnerable, and the power to give birth makes womb-envy at least as logical.

In short, the characteristics of the powerful, whatever they may be, are
thought to be better than the characteristics of the powerless — and logic has
nothing to do with it.

What would happen, for instance, if suddenly, magically, men could menstruate and women could not?

The answer is clear — menstruation would become an enviable, boast-wor-
thy, masculine event:

Men would brag about how long and how much.

Boys would mark the onset of menses, that longed-for proof of manhood,
with religious ritual and stag parties.

Congress would fund a National Institute of Dysmenorrhea to help stamp
out monthly discomforts.

Sanitary supplies would be federally funded and free. (Of course, some men
would still pay for the prestige of commercial brands such as John Wayne Tam-
pons, Muhammad Ali's Rope-a-dope Pads, Joe Namath Jock Shields — "For
Those Light Bachelor Days," and Robert "Baretta" Blake Maxi-Pads.)

Military men, right-wing politicians, and religious fundamentalists would
cite menstruation ("*men*-struation") as proof that only men could serve in the
Army ("you have to give blood to take blood"), occupy political office ("can
women be aggressive without that steadfast cycle governed by the planet
Mars?"), be priests and ministers ("how could a woman give her blood for our
sins?"), or rabbis ("without the monthly loss of impurities, women remain
unclean").

Male radicals, left-wing politicians, and mystics, however, would insist that
women are equal, just different; and that any woman could enter their ranks if
only she were willing to self-inflict a major wound every month ("you *must* give
blood for the revolution"), recognize the preeminence of menstrual issues, or
subordinate her selfness to all men in their Cycle of Enlightenment.

Street guys would brag ("I'm a three-pad man") or answer praise from a
buddy ("Man, you lookin' *good!*") by giving fives and saying, "Yeah, man, I'm
on the rag!"

TV shows would treat the subject at length. ("Happy Days": Richie and
Potsie try to convince Fonzie that he is still "The Fonz," though he has missed
two periods in a row.) So would newspapers. (SHARK SCARE THREAT-
ENS MENSTRUATING MEN. JUDGE CITES MONTHLY STRESS IN

PARDONING RAPIST.) And movies. (Newman and Redford in "Blood Brothers"!)

Men would convince women that intercourse was *more* pleasurable at "that time of the month." Lesbians would be said to fear blood and therefore life itself — though probably only because they needed a good menstruating man.

Of course, male intellectuals would offer the most moral and logical arguments. How could a woman master any discipline that demanded a sense of time, space, mathematics, or measurement, for instance, without that in-built gift for measuring the cycles of the moon and planets — and thus for measuring anything at all? In the rarefied fields of philosophy and religion, could women compensate for missing the rhythm of the universe? Or for their lack of symbolic death-and-resurrection every month?

Liberal males in every field would try to be kind: the fact that "these people" have no gift for measuring life or connecting to the universe, the liberals would explain, should be punishment enough.

And how would women be trained to react? One can imagine traditional women agreeing to all these arguments with a staunch and smiling masochism. ("The ERA would force housewives to wound themselves every month": Phyllis Schlafly. "Your husband's blood is as sacred as that of Jesus — and so sexy, too!": Marabel Morgan.) Reformers and Queen Bees would try to imitate men, and *pretend* to have a monthly cycle. All feminists would explain endlessly that men, too, needed to be liberated from the false idea of Martian aggressiveness, just as women needed to escape the bonds of menses-envy. Radical feminists would add that the oppression of the nonmenstrual was the pattern for all other oppressions. ("Vampires were our first freedom fighters!") Cultural feminists would develop a bloodless imagery in art and literature. Socialist feminists would insist that only under capitalism would men be able to monopolize menstrual blood. . . .

In fact, if men could menstruate, the power justifications could probably go on forever.

If we let them.

Bruce Feirstein

THE MODERN REAL MAN

In the past, it was easy to be a Real Man. All you had to do was abuse women, steal land from Indians, and find some place to dump the toxic waste.

But not anymore.

Society is much more complex today. We live with different threats and terrors. Robots are challenging us for spots on GM assembly lines. Women are demanding things like equality and respect. And instead of merely having to protect themselves against gunslingers and poker cheats, men today face a far more sinister crowd of predators: IRS agents, uninsured motorists, meter maids, carcinogenic food additives, and electronic banking machines.

So what, then, makes someone a Real Man today?

What sets him apart from the average Joe who can't find his car in the shopping-mall parking lot? Or the joker who takes his girl on her dream date — only to have the computer reject his credit card at the end of the meal?

How does he prove himself, now that things like barroom brawling, waging war, and baby-seal killing are frowned upon by polite society?

The answer is simple.

A Real Man today is someone who can triumph over the challenges of modern society.

Real Men, for example, do not cower and shake in the face of double-digit inflation.

Real Men do not worry about the diminishing ozone layer.

Real Men are not intimidated by microwave radiation; they're not afraid to fly DC-10s, drive Corvairs, or invest in the city of St. Louis municipal bonds.

In short, strength and bravery are still the hallmark of today's Real Man; but he's just found modern ways to show it.

Real Men carry cash. Never the American Express card.

Real Men don't buy flight insurance.

Real Men don't smoke low-tar cigarettes.

Real Men are not afraid of the communist threat.

Real Men don't cry during the "Mary Tyler Moore Show."

Going further, today's Real Man is still interested in the Spartan, simple life. He still believes in "roughing it"; he doesn't own a shower massage, remote-control TV, or an electric blanket.

Real Men don't floss.

Real Men don't use ZIP codes.

Real Men don't have telephones in the shape of Snoopy.

Real Men don't drive Volvos because they're supposedly safer; they don't have special jogging shoes or telephone answering machines. (Real Men, after all, are secure enough to know that if it's important, people will call back.)

Real Men don't itemize their tax deductions.

Real Men still pass in the no-passing lane.

A Real Man would never use a designated hitter.

But this is only the tip of the modern Real Man's psyche.

Today's Real Man is intelligent and astute; he's nobody's fool.

Real Men know that things don't really go better with Coke; he's not really in good hands with Allstate; and weekends were — in fact — not made for Michelob.

Real Men understand that using a Jimmy Connors tennis racquet will not improve a weak backhand; they realize that designer jeans, Paco Rabane and Riunite on ice will not help seduce any woman whose IQ is higher than the average number of a UHF television station.

Basically, today's Real Man is unaffected by fads or fashion.

Real Men don't disco.

Real Men don't eat brunch.

Real Men don't have their hair styled.

Real Men don't meditate, rolf, practice Tai Chi, or use hair thickeners.

Real Men don't advertise in the Personals section of the *Village Voice* for female companionship.

Real Men don't play games with wine in restaurants; they don't sniff the cork and say things like "It's a small, unpretentious, fruity red, with ambitious overtones of Bordeaux" about a four-dollar bottle of Ripple.

Real Men don't need water beds, lava lights, musk oil, mirrors on the ceiling, X-rated videocassettes, or Ravel's *Bolero*.

Real Men don't want Bo Derek.

Real Men don't use black condoms.

Real Men stop reading — and writing — letters to *Penthouse* when they're sixteen.

Real Men are secure enough to admit they buy *Playboy* for the women.

Politically, Real Men today are, well, realistic.

They don't trust the French.

The don't contribute to PBS.

They don't believe in bilingual education.

They don't belong to the National Rifle Association.

And Real Men don't believe in the United Nations.

("After thirty-five years," say Real Men, "all they've proved capable of doing is producing a marginally attractive Christmas card.")

Unlike his predecessors, today's Real Man actually can feel things like sorrow, pity, love, warmth, and sincerity; but he'd never be so vulnerable as to admit them.

All told, today's Real Man is probably closest to Spencer Tracy or Gary Cooper in spirit; he realizes that while birds, flowers, poetry, and small children do not add to the quality of life in quite the same manner as a Super Bowl and six-pack of Bud, he's learned to appreciate them anyway.

But perhaps there's one phrase that sums up his very existence, a simple declaration that he finds symbolic of everything in today's world that's phony, affected, limp, or without merit:

Real Men don't eat quiche.

Admittedly, this may seem — if you'll forgive the pun — a bit hard to swallow at first.

But think about it.

Could John Wayne ever have taken Normandy, Iwo Jima, Korea, the Gulf of Tonkin, and the entire Wild West on a diet of quiche and salad?

Barbara Ehrenreich

A FEMINIST'S VIEW OF THE NEW MAN

There have been waves of "new women" arriving on cue almost every decade for the last 30 years or so — from the civic-minded housewife, to the liberated single, to the dressed-for-success executive. But men, like masculinity itself, were thought to be made of more durable stuff. Change, if it came at all, would come only in response to some feminine — or feminist — initiative.

In the 1970's, for example, it had become an article of liberal faith that a new man would eventually rise up to match the new feminist woman, that he would be more androgynous than any "old" variety of man, and that the change, which was routinely expressed as an evolutionary leap from John Wayne to Alan Alda, would be an unambiguous improvement.

Today, a new man is at last emerging, and I say this as someone who is not much given to such announcements. A new man, like a new sexuality or a new conservatism, is more likely to turn out to be a journalistic artifact than a cultural sea change.

But this time something has happened, both to our common expectations of what constitutes manhood and to the way many men are choosing to live.

I see the change in the popular images that define masculinity, and I see it in the men I know, mostly in their 30's, who are conscious of possessing a sensibility and even a way of life that is radically different from that of their fathers. These men have been, in a word, feminized, but without necessarily becoming more feminist. In fact, I do not think that those of us who are feminists either can or, for the most part, would want to take credit for the change.

If we had not all been so transfixed by the changes in women in the last 15 or 20 years, far more attention would have been paid to the new man by this time. We can recall — with nostalgia or relief — the feminine ideal of less than a generation ago: the full-time homemaker who derived her status as well as her livelihood from her husband and considered paid employment a misfortune visited only on the opposite sex or the unwed. So sudden was her demise, at least as an ideal for most girls to aspire to, that we sometimes forget the notion of manhood that went along with that "feminine mystique."

I think of the men of my father's generation, men who came of age in the 1950's and who, like my own father, defined their masculinity, if not their identity, in terms of their ability to make a living and support a family. This was a matter of convention as much as of choice, for the man who failed to marry and become a reliable provider was considered a failure, and those who failed to marry at all (that is, by the age of 30 or so) were candidates for the stigma of "latent homosexual." Men of this generation were encouraged to equate effeminacy with un-Americanism and to use their leisure to escape — into sports, hunting or simply the basement — from women and all things feminine.

We recognize that for the most part men aren't like that anymore and those who are seem grievously out of style. Usually, we think of the change simply as a movement away from the old norm — an opening up of possibilities. But the new man emerging today is not simply the old one minus the old prohibitions and anxieties. There is a new complex of traits and attitudes that has come to define manhood and a kind of new masculine gentility.

Taking his mid-1950's progenitor as a benchmark, the most striking characteristic of the new man is that he no longer anchors his identity in his role as family breadwinner. He may *be* the family breadwinner, or imagine becoming one someday, but his ability to do so has ceased to be the urgent and necessary proof of his maturity or of his heterosexuality. In fact, he may postpone or avoid marriage indefinitely — which is why the women's magazines complain so much about the male "lack of commitment" and "refusal to grow up."

But if the old responsibilities have declined, the pressure is not off: The old man expressed his status through his house and the wife who presided over it; the new man expects to express his status through his own efforts and is deeply anxious about the self he presents to the world. Typically, he is concerned — some might say obsessed — with his physical health and fitness. He is an avid and style-conscious consumer, not only of clothes but of food, home furnishings and visible displays of culture. Finally, and in a marked reversal of the old masculinity, he is concerned that people find him, not forbearing or strong, but genuine, open and sensitive.

These traits do not always occur together; in individual men, in fact, we are probably more used to encountering them separately, scattered among men of the middle and upper-middle classes. For example, on a spring lunch hour in the nation's capital, you will find scores of ruddy, middle-aged men, jogging resolutely on the banks of the Potomac, and I doubt that many of them are practitioners of the new sensitivity. On the other hand, sensitivity is now fairly well dispersed throughout the male population, so that it is not uncommon to encounter it in married breadwinners with children, where it may take the form of a somewhat fatuous volubility on the subject of fathering. Then, too, rejection of the breadwinner role — at least as reflected in the scandalously high rate of default on child-support payments — is so endemic that it cannot be confined to a special new type of man. There are men who are otherwise old-fashioned but have taken up a formerly feminine activity like cooking; just as there must be (though I have not met one) upscale bachelors who eschew physical exercise and designer shirts.

But it is possible, increasingly, to find men who qualify as prototypical new males. They are likely to be from 25 to 40 years old, single, affluent and living in a city, for it is among such men that the most decisive break in the old masculine values is occurring. In these men, the traits that define the new masculinity are beginning to form a pattern and even to frame a new kind of conformity — one that is vastly different, however, from the gray-flannel blues that bedeviled an earlier generation of middle-class American men.

Jeffrey A. Greenberg was one of a number of young men interviewed by me and my assistant, Harriet Bernstein, a market researcher, who helped me locate single affluent men who were willing to discuss their interests and values. Greenberg is a 32-year-old resident in neurosurgery who lives and works in Washington. He puts in 80 to 100 hours a week as a doctor, works out in a gym three times a week and otherwise devotes himself to "the study and acquisition of art." Cooking is his latest enthusiasm: "I thought I wasn't creative in that aspect, but I found that I'm definitely O.K. I know what tastes good and I'm able to do that." He entertains at least once a week, which gives him a chance to show off his paintings and his eclectic music collection. He indicated that, while there were women in his life, he did not yet "have the ability to make a firm commitment."

Thirty or even 20 years ago, a man like Jeffrey Greenberg would have been in a self-conscious minority of "older" bachelors — probably envied by his married friends and, at the same time, faintly suspected for his "effeminate" tastes.

Today he is part of a demographic trend that fascinates market researchers and delights the purveyors of upscale consumer goods. There are 7.5 million men living alone (twice as many as there were in 1970). And as the home-furnishings expert Joan Kron observes in her recent book, "Home-Psych," single men are less likely today to view their condition as one of temporary deprivation, marked by canned-hash dinners and orange-crate furniture. They cook; they furnish; they may even decorate. Home Furnishings Daily has declared them the "New Target," and the magazines that guide their consumption decisions are proliferating and expanding. Significantly, the genre of men's magazine that has done the best in the last few years is the one (represented by Esquire, GQ and M) that does not depend on the lure of sexy female images, only page after page of slender, confident-looking male models.

What accounts for this change in men? Or, perhaps I should ask more broadly, for this change in our notion of masculinity — a change that affects not only single, affluent young men but potentially the married, middle-aged and financially immobile male? Sheldon Kotel, a Long Island accountant in his early 40's, who was my host on a local radio talk show, attributes any change in men to a prior revolution among women. From the early 1970's, he says, "you could see what was happening with women, and we had to get our act together, too. They didn't want to be in their traditional role anymore, and I didn't want to go on being a meal ticket for some woman."

Certainly the new man's unwillingness to "commit himself," in the old-fashioned sense, could be interpreted as a peevish reaction to feminist women — just as his androgynous bent could be interpreted as a positive adjustment, an attempt, as the advocates of men's liberation would say, to "get in touch with one's feminine side." Spokesmen for men's liberation, from Warren Farrell in the early 1970's to Donald H. Bell, whose book, "Being a Man: The Paradox of Masculinity," was published in 1982, depict themselves and their fellows as wrestling with the challenge of feminism — giving up a little privilege here, gaining a little sensitivity there, to emerge more "whole" and "self-nurturing."

But, for the most part, the new men one is likely to encounter today in our urban singles' enclaves (or on the pages of a men's fashion magazine) bear no marks of arduous self-transformation. No ideological struggle — pro- or anti-feminist — seems to have shaped their decision to step out of the traditional male role; in a day-to-day sense, they simply seem to have other things on their minds. Stephen G. Dent, for example, is a 29-year-old member of a private New York investment firm, who was also interviewed by Harriet Bernstein. Dent defines his goals in terms of his career and making money, "because that's how the score is kept." To this end, he rations his time carefully: More than 10 hours a day for work and approximately half an hour a day for calisthenics and running. Women definitely figure in his life, and he is pleased to have reduced the time spent arranging dates to an efficient five minutes a day.

Dent feels that "sensitivity is very important to being a man. It's easy for people to become so caught up in their career challenges that they don't stop to be sensitive to certain things." By that he said he meant "being able to appreciate things that girls appreciate. Like being able to window-shop, for example. An insensitive guy probably won't stop and look at a dress in a window."

For Brian Clarke, like Stephen Dent, the pressures of upward mobility have pushed marriage into the distant future. He is 33 and works 14 hours a day as a production assistant for a major network television show.

Feminism has not figured much in his life; he discussed it respectfully, but as if it were an idiosyncracy he had not encountered before. Yet he agreed enthusiastically to being identified as a new man. "I'm going uphill, and I don't see the top of the hill yet. So for now there is no one woman in my life. . . . I say it on the first date, 'No commitments!'" He is, furthermore, an ardent and tasteful consumer who remains au courant by reading GQ, M, Interior Design and Playboy — this last, he reassured me, "for the fashions."

So I do not think there is a one-word explanation — like feminism — for the new manhood. Rather, I would argue, at least a part of what looks new has been a long time in the making and predates the recent revival of feminism by many decades. Male resistance to marriage, for example, is a venerable theme in American culture, whether in the form of low humor (Li'l Abner's annual Sadie Hawkins Day escape from Daisy Mae) or high art (the perpetual bachelorhood of heroes like Ishmael or the Deerslayer). As Leslie Fiedler argued in 1955 in "An End to Innocence," the classics of American literature are, by and large, propaganda for boyish adventure rather than the "mature heterosexuality" so admired by mid-20th-century psychoanalysts.

The sources of male resentment are not hard to find: In a frontier society, women were cast as the tamers and civilizers of men; in an increasingly urban, industrial society, they became, in addition, the financial dependents of men. From a cynical male point of view, marriage was an arrangement through which men gave up their freedom for the dubious privilege of supporting a woman. Or, as H. L. Mencken put it, marriage was an occasion for a man "to yield up his liberty, his property and his soul to the first woman who, in despair of finding better game, turns her appraising eye upon him." After all, the traditional female contributions to marriage have been menial, like housework, or intangible, like emotional support. The husband's traditional contribution, his wage or at least a good share of it, was indispensable, measurable and, of course, portable — whether to the local tavern or the next liaison.

But before male resentment of marriage could become anything more than a cultural undercurrent of grumbling and misogynist humor, three things had to happen. First, it had to become not only physically possible but reasonably comfortable for men to live on their own. In 19th-century homes, even simple tasks like making breakfast or laundering a shirt could absorb long hours of labor. Bachelorhood was a privileged state, sustained by servants or a supply of maiden sisters; the average man either married or settled for boardinghouse life. As a second condition for freedom from marriage, men had to discover better ways of spending their money than on the support of a family. The historic male alternatives were drinking and gambling, but these have long been associated, for good reason, with precipitate downward mobility. Third, the penalties levied against the nonconforming male — charges of immaturity, irresponsibility and latent sexual deviancy — had to be neutralized or inverted.

Within the last few decades, all of these conditions for male freedom have been met. Domestic appliances, plus a rapid rise in the number of apartment dwellings and low-price restaurants made it possible for a man of average means to contemplate bachelorhood as something other than extended vagrancy. As Philip Roth observed of the 1950's in "My Life as a Man," it had become entirely feasible — though not yet acceptable — for a young man "to eat out of cans or in cafeterias, sweep his own floor, make his own bed and come and go with no binding legal attachments." In addition, that decade saw two innovations that boosted the potential autonomy of even the most domestically incompetent males — frozen foods and drip-dry clothes.

Perhaps more important, the consumer-goods market, which had focused on a bland assemblage of family-oriented products, began to show the first signs of serious segmentation. Playboy's success in the 1950's instigated a revival of sophisticated men's magazines (sophisticated, that is, compared with True, Police Gazette, or Popular Mechanics) that delivered an audience of millions of independent-minded men to the advertisers of liquor, sports cars, stereo equipment and vacations.

In Playboy's case, the ads were complemented by editorial exhortations to male revolt and feature articles portraying wives as "parasites" and husbands as "slaves." There were better ways to spend money than on power mowers and patio furniture, as Hugh Hefner insinuated in his magazine's very first issue: "We like our apartment. . . . We enjoy mixing up cocktails and an hors d'oeuvre or two, putting a little mood music on the phonograph and inviting in a female acquaintance for a quiet discussion of Picasso, Neitzsche, jazz, sex." And in case that sounded suspiciously effete for 1953, the centerfolds testified to an exuberant, even defiant, heterosexuality.

No sooner had the new, more individualistic male life style become physically possible and reasonably attractive than it began also to gain respectability. Starting in the 1960's, expert opinion began to retreat from what had been a unanimous endorsement of marriage and traditional sex roles. Psychology, transformed by the human-potential movement, switched from "maturity" as a standard for mental health to the more expansive notion of "growth." "Maturity" had been a code word, even in the professional literature, for marriage and settling down; "growth" implied a plurality of legitimate options, if not a positive imperative to keep moving from one insight or experience to the next. Meanwhile, medicine — alarmed by what appeared to be an epidemic of male heart disease — had begun to speak of men as the "weaker sex" and to hint that men's greater vulnerability was due, in part, to the burden of breadwinning.

The connection was scientifically unwarranted, but it cast a lasting shadow over conventional sex roles: The full-time homemaker, who had been merely a parasite on resentful males, became a potential accomplice to murder, with the hard-working, role-abiding breadwinner as her victim. By the 1970's, no salvo of male resentment — or men's liberation — failed to mention that the cost of the traditional male role was not only psychic stagnation and sexual monotony, but ulcers, heart disease and an early death.

Today, the old aspersions directed at the unmarried male have largely lost their sting. Images of healthy, hard-working men with no apparent attachments abound in the media, such as, for example, the genial-looking bicyclist in the advertisement for TV Guide, whose caption announces invitingly, "Zero Dependents."

Perhaps most important, a man can now quite adequately express his status without entering into a lifelong partnership with a female consumer. The ranch house on a quarter-acre of grass is still a key indicator of social rank, but it is not the only one. A well-decorated apartment, a knowledge of wines or a flair for cooking can be an equally valid proof of middle-class (or upper-middle-class) membership, and these can now be achieved without the entanglement of marriage or the risk of being thought a little "queer."

Certainly feminism contributed to the case against the old style of male conformity. On the ideological front, the women's movement popularized the sociological vocabulary of "roles" — a linguistic breakthrough that highlighted the social artifice involved in masculinity, as we had known it, as well as femininity. More practically, feminists envisioned a world in which neither sex would be automatically dependent and both might be breadwinners. Betty Friedan speculated that "perhaps men may live longer in America when women carry more of the burden of the battle with the world, instead of being a burden themselves," and Gloria Steinem urged men to support the cause because they "have nothing to lose but their coronaries." Yet feminism only delivered the *coup de grâce* to the old man, who married young, worked hard, withheld his emotions and "died in the harness." By the time of the feminist revival in the late 1960's and 70's, American culture was already prepared to welcome a new man, and to find him — not caddish or queer — but healthy and psychologically enlightened.

But if the new man's resistant to commitment grows out of longstanding male resentment, there are other features of the new manhood that cannot be explained as a product of the battle of the sexes, no matter which side is presumed to have taken the initiative. Married or single, the preoccupations of these men suggest anxiety rather than liberation, and I think the anxiety stems from very real and relatively recent insecurities about class.

The professional-managerial middle class, which is the breeding ground for social ideals like the new man or new woman, has become an embattled group. In the 1950's and 60's, young men of this class could look forward to secure, high-status careers, provided only that they acquired some credentials and showed up for work. Professional-level job slots were increasing, along with the expansion of corporate and governmental administrative apparatuses, and jobs in higher education increased to keep pace with the growing demand for managerial and "mental" workers.

Then came the long economic downturn of the 1970's, and whole occupations — from public administration to college history teaching — closed their ranks and lost ground. One whole segment of formerly middle-class, educated youth drifted downward to become taxi drivers, waiters or carpenters. As other people crowded into the most vocationally promising areas — medicine, law, management — those too became hazardously overpopulated. According to recent studies of the "disappearing middle class," the erstwhile middle-class majority is tumbling down and out (both because of a lack of jobs and because those that remain have not held their own against inflation), while a minority is scrambling up to become the new high-finance, high-tech gentry. Our new men are mainly in the latter category, or are at least holding on by their fingernails.

Times of rapid class realignment magnify the attention paid to class insignia — the little cues that tell us who is a social equal and who is not. In the prosperous 1960's and early 70's, the counterculture had temporarily blurred class lines among American men, mixing Ivy League dropouts with young veterans, hip professionals with unschooled street kids. Avant-garde male fashion

was democratic: Blue jeans, gold chains and shoulder-length hair could equally
well be affected by middle-aged psychiatrists, young truck drivers or off-duty
tax lawyers. Thanks to Army-surplus chic and its rock-star embellishments,
there was no sure way to distinguish the upward bound from the permanently
down and out.

In the insecure 1980's, class lines are being hastily redrawn, and many features of the new manhood can best be understood as efforts to stay on the right
side of the line separating "in" from "out," and upscale from merely middle class.
The new male consumerism, for example, is self-consciously elitist: Italian-knit
sweaters and double-breasted blazers have replaced the voluntary simplicity of
flannel shirts and denim jackets. Esquire announced a "return to elegant dressing" that excludes not only the polyester set but the rumpled professor and any
leftover bohemians.

Food fashions, too, have been steadily gentrified, and the traditional masculine culinary repertory of chili and grilled meats would be merely boorish today.
A recent issue of GQ magazine gave its readers the following advice, which I
would have thought almost too precious for the pages of Gourmet: To turn
dinner for two into "an affair," "break open the caviar again — this time over
oysters or spooned into baked potatoes with melted butter, a dollop of crème
fraîche and a sprinkling of minced green onion. Or offer truffles — black or
white . . . tossed with pasta, cream and butter." Real men may not eat
quiche — which has been adopted by the proletariat anyway — but new men
are enthusiasts of sushi and cold pasta salads, and are prepared to move on as
soon as these, too, find their way to more plebian palates. As M magazine half-
facetiously warned its readers, sushi may already be "out," along with pesto
dishes and white-wine spritzers.

Consumer tastes are only the most obvious class cues that define the new
man and set him off, not only from the old white-collar man but from the less
fortunate members of his own generation. Another is his devotion to physical
exercise, especially in its most solitary and public form — running. Running is
a new activity, dating from the 1970's, and it is solidly upscale. Fred Lebow,
the president of the New York Road Runners Club, describes the average marathon runner as a male, "34 years old, college educated, physically fit and well-
off," and a New York City Times poll found that 46 percent of the participants
in the 1983 New York City Marathon earned more than $40,000 a year (85
percent of the participants were male). The old man smoked, drank martinis to
excess and puttered at golf. The new man is a nonsmoker (among men, smoking
is becoming a blue-collar trait), a cautious drinker, and, if not a runner, a patron
of gyms and spas.

I would not argue that men run in order to establish their social status —
certainly not at a conscious level. Running is one manifestation of the general
obsession with fitness that gripped the middle class in the 1970's and for which
there is still no satisfactory sociological explanation. On one level, running is a
straightforward response to the cardiac anxiety that has haunted American men
since the 1950's; it may also be a response to the occupational insecurity of the
1970's and 80's. Then, too, some men run to get away from their wives —
transforming Rabbit Angstrom's cross-country dash in the final scene of John
Updike's "Rabbit Run" into an acceptable daily ritual. Donald Bell says he took
up running (and vegetarianism) "to escape somewhat from the pain and frustration which I felt in this less than perfect marriage."

But, whatever the individual motivations, running has become sufficiently identified as an upper-middle-class habit to serve as a reliable insignia of class membership: Running is public testimony to a sedentary occupation, and it has all but replaced the more democratic sports, such as softball and basketball, that once promoted interclass male mingling.

Finally, there is that most promising of new male traits — sensitivity. I have no hesitation about categorizing this as an upscale class cue if only because new men so firmly believe that it is. For more than a decade, sensitivity has been supposed to be the inner quality that distinguishes an educated, middle-class male from his unregenerate blue-collar brothers: "They" are Archie Bunkers; "we" are represented by his more liberal, articulate son-in-law. As thoughtful a scholar as Joseph H. Pleck, program director of the Wellesley College Center for Research on Women, who has written extensively on the male sex role, simply restates (in a 1976 Journal of Social Issues) the prejudice that blue-collar men are trapped in the "traditional" male role, "where interpersonal and emotional skills are relatively undeveloped."

No one, of course, has measured sensitivity and plotted it as a function of social class, but Judith Langer, a market researcher, reports that, in her studies, it is blue-collar men who express less "traditional" or "macho" values, both in response to products and in speaking of their relationships with women. "Certainly I'm not suggesting that *only* blue-collar men show such openness," she concludes, "but rather that the stereotype of blue-collar workers can be limited."

To the extent that some special form of sensitivity is located in educated and upwardly mobile males, I suspect it may be largely a verbal accomplishment. The vocabulary of sensitivity, at least, has become part of the new masculine politesse; certainly no new man would admit to being insensitive or willfully "out of touch with his feelings." Quite possibly, as sensitivity has spread, it has lost its moorings in the therapeutic experience and come to signify the heightened receptivity associated with consumerism: a vague appreciation that lends itself to aimless shopping.

None of these tastes and proclivities of the new man serves to differentiate him from the occasional affluent woman of his class. Women in the skirted-suit set tend to postpone marriage and childbearing; to work long hours and budget their time scrupulously; to follow fashions in food and clothing, and to pursue fitness, where once slimness would have sufficed. As Paul Fussell observes in "Class: A Guide Through the American Status System," the upper-middle class — and I would include all those struggling to remain in the upper part of the crumbling middle class — is "the most 'role-reversed' of all." And herein lies one of the key differences between the old and the new versions of the American ideal of masculinity: The old masculinity defined itself against femininity and expressed anxiety — over conformity or the rat race — in metaphors of castration. The new masculinity seems more concerned to preserve the tenuous boundary between the classes than to delineate distinctions between the sexes. Today's upper-middle-class or upwardly mobile male is less terrified about moving down the slope toward genderlessness than he is about simply moving down-scale.

The fact that the new man is likely to remain single well into his prime career years — or, if married, is unlikely to be judged by his wife's appearance and tastes — only intensifies his status consciousness. The old man of the middle class might worry about money, but he could safely leave the details of keeping up with the Joneses to his wife. He did not have to comprehend casseroles or canapés, because she would, nor did he have to feel his way through complex social situations, since sensitivity also lay in her domain. But our new man of the 1980's, married or not, knows that he may be judged solely on the basis of his own savoir-faire, his ability to "relate," his figure and possibly his muscle tone. Without a wife, or at least without a visible helpmeet, he has had to appropriate the status-setting activities that once were seen as feminine. The androgynous affect is part of making it.

The question for feminists is: Is this new man what we wanted? Just a few years ago, feminists were, on the whole, disposed to welcome any change in a direction away from traditional manhood. Betty Friedan, in "The Second Stage," saw "the quiet movement of American men" as "a momentous change in their very identity as men, going beyond the change catalyzed by the women's movement," and she suggested that it might amount to a "massive, evolutionary development."

That was written in a more innocent time, when feminists were debating the "Cinderella complex," as Colette Dowling termed women's atavistic dependencies on men, rather than the "Peter Pan syndrome," which is how one recent best seller describes the male aversion to commitment. In recent months, there has been a small flurry of feminist attacks on the new male or on assorted new-male characteristics.

The Washington City Paper carried a much-discussed and thoroughly acid article on "Wormboys," described by writer Deborah Laake as men who are "passive" in relation to women, who "shrink from marriage" and children, and cannot be depended on during tough times." According to one woman she quotes, these new men are so fearful of commitment that they even hesitate to ask a woman out to dinner: "They're more interested in saying, 'Why don't you meet me for a drink?' because it implies so much less commitment on their part." I wouldn't exaggerate the extent of the backlash, but it has been sufficient to send several male colleagues my way to ask, with nervous laughter, whether I was writing a new contribution to the "war on wimps."

I don't blame them for being nervous. My generation of feminists insisted that men change, but we were not always directive — or patient — enough to say how. We applauded every sign of male sensitivity or growth as if it were an evolutionary advance. We even welcomed the feminization of male tastes, expecting that the man who was a good cook and a tasteful decorator at 25 would be a devoted father and partner in midlife. We did not understand that men were changing along a trajectory of their own and that they might end up being less like what we *are* than like what we were once expected to be — vain and shallow and status-conscious.

But since these are times when any hint of revisionism easily becomes grist for conservatism, it is important to emphasize that if we don't like the new male, neither are we inclined to return to the old one. If the new man tends to be a fop, the old man was (and is) at worst, a tyrant and a bully. At best, he was merely dull, which is why, during the peak years of male conformity, when the test of manhood lay in being a loyal breadwinner, so many of us lusted secretly for those few males — from James Dean and Elvis Presley to Jack Kerouac — who represented unattainable adventure. In our fantasies, at least, we did not want to enslave men, as Playboy's writers liked to think, but to share the adventure.

Today, thanks to the women's movement, we have half a chance: Individualism, adventure — that "battle with the world" that Friedan held out to women more than 20 years ago — is no longer a male prerogative. But if it is to be a shared adventure, then men will have to change, and change in ways that are not, so far, in evidence. Up until now, we have been content to ask them to become more like women — less aggressive, more emotionally connected with themselves and others. That message, which we once though revolutionary, has gotten lost in the androgynous drift of the consumer culture. It is the marketplace that calls most clearly for men to be softer, more narcissistic and receptive, and the new man is the result.

So it is not enough, anymore, to ask that men become more like women; we should ask instead that they become more like what both men and women *might* be. My new man, if I could design one, would be capable of appreciation, sensitivity, intimacy — values that have been, for too long, feminine. But he would also be capable of commitment, to use that much-abused word, and I mean by that commitment not only to friends and family but to a broad and generous vision of how we might all live together. As a feminist, I would say that vision includes equality between men and women and also — to mention a social goal that seems almost to have been forgotten — equality among men.

William J. Goode

WHY MEN RESIST

Although few if any men in the United States remain entirely untouched by the women's movement, to most men what is happening seems to be "out there" and has little direct effect on their own roles. To them, the movement is a dialogue mainly among women, conferences of women about women, a mixture of just or exaggerated complaints and shrill and foolish demands to which men need not even respond, except now and then. When men see that a woman resents a common male act of condescension, such as making fun of women in sports or management, most males are still as surprised as corporation heads are when told to stop polluting a river.

For the time being, men are correct in this perception if one focuses on the short run only. It is not often that social behavior deeply rooted in tradition alters rapidly. Over the longer run, they are not likely to be correct, and indeed I believe they are vaguely uneasy when they consider their present situation. As against numerous popular commentators, I do not think we are now wit-

From *Rethinking the Family: Some Feminist Questions,* Edited by Barrie Thorne and Marilyn Yalom. Copyright © 1982 by Longman Inc.

nessing a return to the old ways, a politically reactionary trend, and I do not think the contemporary attack on male privilege will ultimately fail.

The worldwide demand for equality is voiced not only by women; many groups have pressed for it, with more persistence, strength, and success over the past generation than in any prior epoch of world history. It has also been pressed by more kinds of people than ever before: ethnic and racial groups, castes, subnational groups such as the Scots or Basques, classes, colonies, and political regimes. An ideal so profoundly moving will ultimately prevail, in some measure, where the structural bases for traditional dominance are weakened. The ancient bases for male dominance are no longer as secure as they once were, and male resistance to these pressures will weaken.

Males will stubbornly resist, but reluctantly adjust, because women will continue to want more equality than they now enjoy and will be unhappy if they do not get it; because men on average will prefer that their women be happy; because a majority of either sex will not find an adequate substitute for the other sex; and because neither will be able to build an alternative social system alone. When dominant classes or groups cannot rig the system as much in their favor as they once did, they will work within it just the same; to revise an old adage, if that is the only roulette wheel in town, they will play it even if it is honest and fair.

To many women, the very title of my essay is an exercise in banality, for there is no puzzle. To analyze the peculiar thoughtways of men seems unnecessary, since ultimately their resistance is that of dominant groups throughout history: They enjoy an exploitive position that yields them an unearned profit in money, power, and prestige. Why should they give it up?

The answer contains of course some part of the truth, but we shall move more effectively toward equality only if we grasp much more of the truth that bitter view reveals. If it were completely true, then the greater power of men would have made all societies male-vanity cultures, in which women are kept behind blank walls and forced to work at productive tasks only with their sisters, while men laze away their hours in parasitic pleasure. In fact, one can observe that the position of women varies a good deal by class, by society, and over time, and no one has succeeded in proving that those variations are the simple result of men's exploitation.

Indeed there are inherent socioeconomic contradictions in any attempt by males to create a fully exploitive set of material advantages for all males. Moreover, there are inherent *emotional* contradictions in any effort to achieve full domination in that intimate sphere.

As to the first contradiction, women — and men in the same situation — who are powerless, slavish, and ignorant are most easily exploitable, and thus there are always some male pressures to place them in that position. Unfortunately, such women do not yield much surplus product. In fact, they do not produce much at all. Women who are freer and are more in command of productive skills, as in hunting and gathering societies and increasingly in modern industrial ones, produce far more, but they are also more resistant to exploitation or domination. Without understanding that powerful relationship, men have moved throughout history toward one or the other of these great choices, with their built-in disadvantages and advantages.

As to emotional ties, men would like to be lords of their castle and to be loved absolutely — if successful, this is the cheapest exploitive system — but in real life this is less likely to happen unless one loves in return. In that case what happens is what happens in real life: Men care about the joys and sorrows of their women. Mutual caring reduces the degree to which men are willing to exploit their wives, mothers, and sisters. More interesting, their caring also takes the form of wanting to prevent *other* men from exploiting these women when they are in the outside world. That is, men as individuals know that *they* are to be trusted, and so should have great power, but other men cannot be trusted, and so the laws should restrain such fellows.

These large sets of contrary tensions have some effect on even those contemporary men who do not believe that the present relations between men and women are unjust. Both sets, moreover, support the present trend toward greater equality. In short, men do resist, but these and other tensions prevent them from resisting as fully as they might otherwise, while not so much as a cynical interpretation of their private attitudes would expect. On the other hand, they do resist somewhat more strenuously than we should predict from their public assertion in favor of, for example, equal pay, or slogans like "liberty and justice for all."

This exposition is necessarily limited. Even to present the latest data on the supposed psychological traits of males would require more space than is available here. I shall try to avoid the temptation of simply describing men's reactions to the women's movement, although I do plan to inform you of men's attitudes toward some aspects of equality. I shall try to avoid defending men, except to the extent that explaining them may be a defense. And, as is already obvious, I shall not assert that we are on the brink of a profound, sudden change in sex-role allocations, in the direction of equality, for we must never underestimate the cunning or the staying power of those in charge. Finally, because all of you are also observers of men, it is unlikely that I can bring forward many findings that are entirely unknown to you. At best, I can suggest some fruitful, perhaps new, ways of looking at male roles. Within these limitations, I shall focus on the following themes:

1. As against the rather narrow definition of men's roles to be found in the current literature on the topic, I want to remind you of a much wider range of traditionally approved role in this and other cultures.
2. As against the conspiracy theory of the oppression of women, I shall suggest a modest "sociology of the dominant group" to interpret men's behavior and thinking about male roles and thus some modest hypotheses about why they resist.
3. I shall point to two central areas of role behavior, occupations and domestic tasks, where change seems glacial at present and men's resistance strong.
4. As against those who feel that if utopia does not arrive with the next full moon, we should all despair, I shall point to some processes now occurring that are different from any in recorded history and that will continue to press toward more fundamental changes in men's social positions and roles in this as well as other countries of the world.

1. THE RANGE OF SEX ROLES

Let me begin by reminding you of the standard sociological view about the allocation of sex roles. Although it is agreed that we can, with only small error, divide the population into males and females, the biological differences between the two that might affect the distribution of sex roles — which sex is supposed to do which social tasks, which should have which rights — are much too small to determine the larger differences in sex-role allocation within any given society or to explain the curious doctrines that serve to uphold it. Second, even if some differences would give an advantage to men (or women) in some tasks or achievements, the overlap in talent is so great that a large minority of men (or women) could do any task as well as could members of the other sex. Third, the biological differences are too fixed in anatomy and physiology to account for the wide diversity of sex-role allocation we observe when we compare different societies over time and cultures.

Consequently, most of sex-role allocation must be explained by how we rear children, by the sexual division of labor, by the cultural definitions of what is appropriate to the sexes, and by the social pressures we put on the two sexes. Since human beings created these role assignments, they can also change them. On the other hand, these roles afford large advantages to men (e.g., opportunity, range of choices, mobility, payoffs for what is accomplished, cultivation of skills, authority, and prestige) in this and every other society we know. Consequently, men are likely to resist large alterations in roles. They will do so even though they understand that in exchange for their privileges, they have to pay high costs in morbidity, mortality, and failure.[1] As a consequence of this fact about men's position, it can be supposed that they will resist unless their ability to rig the system in their favor is somehow reduced. It is my belief that this capacity is in fact being undermined somewhat, through not at a rapid rate.

A first glance at descriptions of the male role, especially as described in the literature about mass media, social stereotypes, family roles, and personality attributes, suggests that the male role is definite, narrow, and agreed upon. Males, we are told, are pressed into a specific mold. For example, ". . . the male role prescribes that men be active, aggressive, competitive, . . . while the female role prescribes that women should be nurturant, warm, altruistic . . . and the like."[2] The male role requires the suppression of emotion, or "the male role, as personally and socially defined, requires men to appear tough, objective, striving, achieving, unsentimental. . . . If he weeps, if he shows weakness, he will likely be viewed as unmanly. . . ." Or: "Men are programmed to be strong and 'aggressive.'"[3]

We are so accustomed to reading such descriptions that we almost believe them, unless we stop to ask, first, how many men do we actually know who carry out these social presciptions (i.e., how many are emotionally anesthetized, aggressive, physically tough and daring, unwilling or unable to give nurturance to a child)? Second, and this is the test of a social role, do they lose their membership cards in the male fraternity if they fail in these respects? If socialization and social pressures are so all-powerful, where are all the John Wayne types in our society? Or, to ask a more searching question, how seriously should we take such sex-role prescriptions if so few men live up to them?

The key fact is not that many men do not live up to such prescriptions; rather, it is that many other qualities and performances are also viewed as acceptable or admirable, and this is true even among boys, who are often thought to be strong supporters of sex stereotypes. The *macho* boy is admired, but so is the one who edits the school newspaper, who draws cartoons, or who is simply a warm friend. There are at least a handful of ways of being an admired professor. Indeed a common feminist complaint against the present system is that women are much more narrowly confined in the ways they are permitted to be professors, or members of any occupation.

But we can go further. A much more profound observation is that oppressed groups are *typically* given narrow ranges of social roles, while dominant groups afford their members a far wider set of behavior patterns, each qualitatively different but each still accepted or esteemed in varying degrees. One of the privileges granted, or simply assumed, by ruling groups, is that they can indulge in a variety of eccentricities while still demanding and getting a fair measure of authority or prestige. Consider in this connection, to cite only one spectacular example, the crotchets and quirks cultivated by the English upper classes over the centuries.

Moreover, if we enlarge our vision to encompass other times and places, the range becomes even greater. We are not surprised to observe Latin American men embrace one another, Arab or Indian boys walk together hand in hand, or seminary students being gentle. The male role prescriptions that commonly appear in the literature do not describe correctly the male ideal in Jewish culture, which embodied a love of music, learning, and literature; an avoidance of physical violence; an acceptance of tears and sentiment, nurturance, and a sensitivity to others' feelings. In the South that I knew half a century ago, young rural boys were expected to nurture their younger siblings, and male–male relations were ideally expected to be tender, supporting, and expressed occasionally by embraces. Among my own kin, some fathers then kissed their school-age sons; among Greek-Americans in New York City, that practice continues many decades later. Or, to consider England once more, let us remember the admired men of Elizabethan England. True enough, one ideal was the violent, daring Francis Drake and the brawling poet Ben Jonson. But men also expressed themselves in kissing and embracing, writing love poems to one another, donning decorative (not to say gaudy and efflorescent) clothing, and studying flowers as well as the fiery heavens.

We assert, then, that men manage to be in charge of things in all societies but that their very control permits them to create a wide range of ideal male roles, with the consequences that large numbers of men, not just a few, can locate rewarding positions in the social structure. Thereby, too, they considerably narrow the options left for feminine sex roles. Feminists especially resent the narrowness of the feminine role in informal interaction, where they feel they are dealt with only as women, however this may be softened by personal warmth or affection.

We can recognize that general relationship in a widespread male view, echoed over the centuries, that males are people, individuals, while women are lumped together as an aggregate. Or, in more modern language: Women have roles, a delimited number of parts to play, but men cannot be described so simply.

Nor is that peculiar male view contradicted by the complaint, again found in all major civilizations, that women are mysterious, unpredictable, moved by forces outside men's understanding, and not controllable. Even that master of psychodynamics Sigmund Freud expressed his bewilderment by asking, "What do women want?" Men have found their women difficult to understand for a simple reason: They have continued to try to think of them as a set of roles (above all else, mothers and wives), but in fact women do not fit these roles, not only not now, but not in the past either. Some women were great fighting machines, not compliant; some were competitive and aggressive, not nurturant; many were incompetent or reluctant mothers. They have been queens and astronomers, moralists and nurturers, leaders of religious orders as well as corporations, and so on. At any point, men could observe that women were ignoring or breaking out of their social molds, and men experienced that discrepancy as puzzling. However, it is only recently that many have faced the blunt fact that there is no feminine riddle at all: Women are as complex as men are, and always will escape the confinements of any narrow set of roles.

2. THE SOCIOLOGY OF SUPERORDINATES

That set of relationships is only part of the complex male view, and I want to continue with my sketch of the main elements in what may be called the "sociology of superordinates." That is, I believe there are some general principles of regularities to be found in the view held by superordinates — here, the sex-class called males — about relations with subordinates, in this instance women. These regularities do not justify, but they do explain in some degree, the modern resistance of men to their new social situation.[4] Here are some of them:

1. The observations made by either men or women about members of the other sex are limited and somewhat biased by what they are most interested in and by their lack of opportunity to observe behind the scenes of each others' lives.[5] However, far less of what men do is determined by women; what men do affects women much more. As a consequences, men are often simply less motivated to observe carefully many aspects of women's behavior and activity because women's behavior does not usually affect what men propose to do. By contrast, almost everything men do will affect what women *have* to do, and thus women are motivated to observe men's behavior as keenly as they can.
2. Since any given cohort of men know they did not create the system that gives them their advantages, they reject any charges that they conspired to dominate women.
3. Since men, like other dominants or superordinates, take for granted the system that gives them their status, they are not aware of how much the social structure, from attitude patterns to laws, pervasively yields small, cumulative, and eventually large advantages in most competitions. As a consequence, they assume that their greater accomplishments are actually the result of inborn superiority.
4. As a corollary to this male view, when men weigh their situation, they are more aware of the burdens and responsibilities they bear than of their unearned advantages.
5. Superiors, and thus men, do not easily notice the talents or accomplishments of subordinates, and men have not in the past seen much wisdom in giving women more opportunities for growth, for women are not capable of much anyway, especially in the areas of men's special skills. Thus, in the past, women have embarrassed men by becoming superior in those areas. When they did, their superiority was seen, and is often still seen, as an odd exception. As a consequences, men see their superior position as a just one.
6. Men view even small losses of deference, advantages, or opportunities as large threats. Their own gains, or their maintenance of old advantages, are not noticed as much.[6]

Although the male view is similar to that of superordinates generally, as the foregoing principles suggest, one cannot simply equate the two. The structural position of males is different from that of superordinate groups, classes, ethnic populations, or castes. Males are, first, not a group, but a social segment or a statistical aggregate within the society. They share much of a common destiny, but they share few if any *group* or *collective* goals (within small groups they may be buddies, but not with all males). Second, males share with certain women whatever gain or loss they experience as members of high or low castes, ethnic groups, or classes. For example, women in a ruling stratum share with their men a high social rank, deference from the lower orders, and so on; men in a lowly Indian caste share that rank with their women, too. In modern societies, men and women in the same family are on a more or less equal basis with respect to "inheritance, educational opportunity (at least undergraduate), personal consumption of goods, most rights before the law, and the love and responsibility of their children."[7] They are not fully equal, to be sure, but much more equal than are members of very different castes or social classes.

Moreover, from the male view, women also enjoy certain exemptions: "freedom from military conscription, whole or partial exemption from certain kinds of heavy work, preferential courtesies of various kinds." Indeed, men believe, on the whole, that their own lot is the more difficult one.[8]

Most important as a structural fact that prevents the male view from being simply that of a superordinate is that these superordinates, like their women, do not live in set-apart communities, neighborhoods, or families. Of course, other such categories are not sequestered either, such as alcoholics, ex-mental patients, or the physically handicapped; but these are, as Goffman points out, "scattered somewhat haphazardly through the social structure." That is not so for men; like their women, they are allocated to households in a nonrandom way, for "law and custom allow only one to a household, but strongly encourage the presence of that one."[9]

A consequence of this important structural arrangement is that men and women are separated from their own sex by having a stake in the organization that gives each a set of different roles, or a different emphasis to similar roles; women especially come to have a vested interest in the social unit that at the same time imposes inequalities on them. This coalition between the two individuals makes it difficult for members of the same sex to join with large numbers of persons of their own sex for purposes of defense or exploitation. This applies equally to men and women.

One neat consequence may be seen in the hundreds of family law provisions created over the centuries that seem to run at cross-purposes. Some gave more freedom to women in order to protect them from predatory or exploitative males (i.e., in the male view, *other* men), and some took freedom away from women and put it in the hands of supposedly good and kindly men (i.e., heads of families, *themselves*). Or, in more recent times, the growing efforts of some fathers to press their daughters toward career competence so that they will not be helpless when abandoned by their future husbands, against those same fathers' efforts to keep their daughters docile and dutiful toward their protecting fathers.

You will note that male *views* are not contradictory in such instances, even though their *actions* may be. In coalition with their women, they oppose the exploitative efforts of outside men; within the family unit, however, they see little need for such protections against themselves, for they are sure of their own goodheartedness and wisdom.

That men see themselves as bound in a coalition with their families and thus with their daughters and wives is the cause of much common male resistance to the women's movement, while some have instead become angered at the unfair treatment their wives and daughters have experienced. The failure of many women to understand that complex male view has led to much misunderstanding.

3. RESPONSES OF SUPERORDINATES TO REBELLION[10]

First, men are surprised at the outbreak. They simply had not known the depth of resentment that many women harbored, though of course many women had not known it either. Second, men are also hurt, for they feel betrayed. They discover, or begin to suspect, that the previously contented or pleasant facade their women presented to them was false, that they have been manipulated to believe in that presentation of self. Because males view themselves as giving protection against anyone exploiting or hurting their women, they respond with anger to the hostility they encounter, to the discovery that they were deceived, and to the charge that they have selfishly used the dominant position they feel they have rightfully earned.

A deeper, more complex source of male anger requires a few additional comments, for it relates to a central male role, that of jobholder and breadwinner. Most men, but especially most men outside the privileged stratum of professionals and managers, see their job as not yielding much intrinsic satisfaction, not being fun in itself, but they pride themselves on the hard work and personal sacrifice they make as breadwinners. In the male view, men make a gift of all this to their wives and children.[11]

Now they are told that it was not a gift, and they have not earned any special deference for it. In fact, their wives earned what they received, and indeed nothing is owing. If work was a sacrifice, they are told, so were all the services, comforts, and self-deprivations women provided. Whatever the justice of either claim, clearly if you think you are giving or sacrificing much to make gifts to someone over a period of time, and then you learn he or she feels the gifts were completely deserved, for the countergifts are asserted to have been as great and no gratitude or special debt was incurred, you are likely to be hurt or angry.[12]

I am reasonably certain about the processes I have just described. Let me go a step further and speculate that the male resentment is the greater because many fathers had already come to suspect that their children, especially in adolescence, were indifferent to those sacrifices, as well as to the values that justified them.[13] Thus, when women too begin to assert that men's gifts are not worth as much as men thought, the worth of the male is further denied.

4. SOME AREAS OF CHANGE AND NONCHANGE

Although I have not heard specific complaints about it, I believe that the most important change in men's position, as they experience it, is a loss of centrality, a decline in the extent to which they are the center of attention. In our time, other superordinates have also suffered this loss: colonial rulers, monarchs and nobles, and U.S. whites both northern and southern, to name a few.

Boys and grown men have always taken for granted that what they were doing was more important than what the other sex was doing, that where they were, was where the action was. Their women accepted that definition. Men occupied the center of the stage, and women's attention was focused on them. Although that position is at times perilous, open to failure, it is also desirable.

Men are still there of course, and will be there throughout our lifetime. Nevertheless, some changes are perceptible. The center of attention shifts to women more now than in the past. I believe that this shift troubles men far more, and creates more of their resistance, than the women's demand for equal opportunity and pay in employment.

The change is especially observable in informal relations, and men who are involved with women in the liberation movement experience it most often. Women find each other more interesting than in the past, and focus more on what each other is doing, for they are in fact doing more interesting things. Even when they are not, their work occupies more of their attention, whether they are professionals or factory workers. Being without a man for a while does not seem to be so bereft a state as it once was. I also believe that this change affects men more now than at the time of the suffragist movement half a century ago, not only because more women now participate in it but also because men were then more solidary and could rely on more all-male organizations and clubs; now, they are more dependent on women for solace and intimacy.

As a side issue, let me note that the loss of centrality has its counterpart among feminist women too, and its subtlety should be noted. Such women now reject a certain type of traditional centrality they used to experience, because its costs are too great. Most women know the experience of being the center of attention: When they enter a male group, conversation changes in tone and subject. They are likely to be the focus of comments, many of them pleasurable: affectionate teasing, compliments, warmth. However, these comments put women into a special mold, the stereotyped female. Their serious comments are not welcomed or applauded, or their ideas are treated as merely amusing. Their sexuality is emphasized. Now, feminist women find that kind of centrality less pleasant — in fact, condescending — and they avoid it when they can. In turn, many men feel awkward in this new situation, for their repertory of social graces is now called boorish.

Although I have noted men's feelings of hurt and anger, I want to emphasize that I believe no backlash of any consequences has been occurring, and no trend toward more reactionary male attitudes exists. Briefly, there is a continuing attitude change on the part of both men and women, in favor of more equality. The frequent expressions of male objection, sometimes labeled "backlash" in the popular press, can be attributed to two main sources: (1) The discovery, by some men who formerly did pay lip service to the principle of equality, that they do not approve of its concrete application; and (2) active resistance by men and women who simply never approved of equality anyway and who have now begun to oppose it openly because it can no longer be seen as a trivial threat. Most of this is incorrectly labeled "backlash," which ought instead to refer only to the case in which people begin to feel negative toward a policy they once thought desirable, because now it has led to undesirable results. Those who oppose women's rights like to label any support they get as backlash because thereby they can claim that "women have gone too far."

It may surprise you to learn that it is not possible to summarize here all the various changes in public opinion about sex roles, as attitudes have shifted over the past generation, simply because pollsters did not bother to record the data.

They often did not try to find out about social trends and thus only rarely asked the same questions in successive decades. One unfortunate result is that one of the most fiercely debated events of this period, the women's liberation movement, almost does not appear in the polls.[14]

The single finding that seems solid is that no data show any backward or regressive trend in men's attitudes about women's progress toward equality. The most often repeated question is not a profound one: whether a respondent would vote for a qualified woman for President. Favorable answers rose from about one-fourth of the men in 1937 to two-thirds in 1971, and to four-fifths among men and women combined in 1975. Another repeated question is whether a married women should work if she has a husband able to support her, and here the answers of men and women combined rose from 18 percent in 1936 to 62 percent in 1975. In contrast to these large changes, a large majority favored equal pay, in principle at least, as early as 1942, and later data report no decrease.

In 1953, 21 percent of men said it made no difference whether they worked for a man or woman, and that figure rose slightly to 32 percent in 1975.[15] Polls in 1978 show that a large majority of the nation, both men and women, was in favor of the enforcement of laws forbidding job discrimination against women or discrimination in education; and most agreed that more women should be elected to public office.[16]

A plurality of only about 40 percent held such favorable opinions in 1970. On such issues, men and women do not differ by much, although, until recently, men's attitudes were somewhat more favorable. Divisions of opinion are sharper along other lines: The young are in favor more than the old, the more educated more favorable than the less educated, city dwellers more than rural people, blacks more than whites. Whatever the differences, clearly no substantial amount of male backlash has appeared. Through men's eyes, at least the *principle* of equality seems more acceptable than in the past. Their resistance is not set against that abstract idea. Modest progress, to be sure, but progress nonetheless.

I cannot forego making reference to a subvariety of the backlash, which has been reported in hundreds of articles, that is, that more men are impotent because of women's increased sexual assertiveness. This impotence, we are told, appears when women discover the delights of their own sexuality, make it clear to their men that they will play coy no more, and indeed look at their men as sexual objects, at least sometimes.

The widespread appearance of male impotence as an answer to, or an escape from, increased female willingness would certainly be news,[17] but it violates the sexual view of most men, and, much worse, it runs counter to the only large-scale data we have on the topic.[18] The male view may be deduced, if you will permit the literary reference, from traditional pornography, which was written by men and expressed male fantasies. Briefly, in such stories, but entirely contrary to real life, everything went smoothly: At every phase of the interaction, where women in real male experience are usually indifferent if not hostile, the hero encounters enthusiasm, and in response he himself performs miracles of sexual athleticism and ecstasy.

Nothing so embroidered is found in social science data, but it seems reasonably certain that in the five-year period ending in 1970, the married men of the

① Bumper stickers — Woman's place is in the home!
When she finishes at the office

GOODE   *Why Men Resist*   53

United States increased the frequency of their lovemaking with their wives. Doubtless, there were pockets of increased impotence, but with equal security we can assert that most husbands did not have that experience.

The reason is clear, I think: The message of permission had finally been received by women, and they put it into action. In millions of how-to-do-it books and articles, they were not only told to enjoy themselves but were urged to do so by seducing their men. Since the most important sex organ is the human mind, these changes in the heads of both men and women caused changes in the body. Without question, the simplest and most effective antidote to male impotence, or even lassitude and nonperformance, is female encouragement and welcome. Even if a few cases of the backlash of impotence have occurred, that has not, I think, been a widespread trend among males in our time, as a psychological response to women's move toward some equality in sexuality itself. To this particular change among women, men have offered little resistance.

5. DOMESTIC DUTIES AND JOBS

So far, the opinion data give some small cause for optimism. Nevertheless, all announcements of the imminent arrival of utopias are premature. Men's approval of more equality for women has risen, but the record in two major areas of men's roles — the spheres of home and occupation — gives but little reason for optimism. Here we can be brief, for though the voluminous data are very complex, the main conclusions can easily be summarized.[19] The striking fact is that very little has changed, if we consider the society as a whole and focus on changes in behavior.

Let us consider the domestic role of men. They have contributed only slightly more time to their duties in the home than in the past — although "the past" is very short for time budgets of men's child-care and homemaking activities. By contrast, the best record now indicates that homemakers without jobs spend somewhat less time at their domestic tasks then they did ten years ago. Working wives allocate much less time (26–35 hours a week) to the home than do stay-at-home wives (35–55 hours), but *husbands* of working wives do almost as little as husbands of stay-at-home wives (about 10–13 hours weekly). We hear much these days about Russian husbands who expect their wives to hold jobs and also take care of housework and child care, but so do American husbands. Moreover, that is as true of the supposedly egalitarian Swedish or Finnish husbands as it is of the German and French ones.[20]

Of course, there are some differences. If a child two years or younger is in the house, the father does more. Better-educated husbands do a bit more, and so do younger husbands. But the massive fact is that men's domestic contribution does not change much whether or not they work, and whether or not their wives work.[21] Still more striking is the fact that the past decade has shown little change in the percentage of women who want their husbands to take a larger share of domestic work, though once again it is the vanguard of the young, the educated, and the black who exhibit the largest increase. Studies have reported that only about 20 to 25 percent of wives express the wish for more domestic participation by their husbands, and that did not change greatly until the late 1970s.[22]

With reference to the second large area of men's roles, job holding, we observe two further general principles of the relations between superordinates and those at lesser ranks. One is that men do not, in general, feel threatened by competition from women if they believe the competition is fair and women do not have an inside track. Men still feel that they are superior and will do better if given the chance. Without actually trying the radical notion of genuinely fair competition, they have little reason to fear as yet: Compared with women, they were better off in wages and occupational position in the 1970s than in the 1950s.

The second principle is that those who hold advantaged positions in the social structure (men, in this case) can perceive or observe that they are being flooded by people they consider their inferiors — by women, blacks, or the lower classes — while the massive statistical fact is that only a few people are rising by much. There are several causes of this seeming paradox.

First, the new arrivals are so visible, so different from those who have held the jobs up to this time. The second cause is our perception of relative numbers. Since there are far fewer positions at higher job levels, only a few new arrivals constitute a fair-sized minority of the total at that level. Third, the mass media emphasize the hiring of women in jobs that seem not to be traditional for them, for that is considered news. Men's structural position, then, causes them to perceive radical change here, and they resist it.

Nevertheless, the general conclusion does not change much. The amount of sex segregation in jobs is not much different from the past.[23] More important, there is no decrease in the gap between the earnings of men and women; at every job level, it is not very different from the past, and in the period from 1955 to 1971 the gap actually became somewhat larger. That is, a higher percentage of women entered the labor force, and at better wages in the past, but men rose somewhat faster than they.

Although the mass figures are correct, we need not discount all our daily observation. We see women entering formerly masculine jobs from garbage collecting to corporate management. That helps undermine sex stereotypes and thereby becomes a force against inequality. For example, women bus drivers were hardly to be found in 1940, but they now make up 37 percent of that occupation; women bartenders now form 32 percent of that occupation, but a generation ago made up only 2.5 percent.[24] Although occupational segregation continued strong in the 1970s, it did decline in most professions (e.g., engineering, dentistry, science, law, medicine) between 1960 and 1970. That is, the percentage of women in these professions did rise.[25] Women now constitute over one-fourth of the law school classes in the higher-ranking law schools of the country. In occupations where almost everyone was once male, it is not possible to recruit, train, and hire enough women to achieve equality in a few years, but the trend seems clear.

A secondary effect of these increasing numbers should be noted. Percentages are important, but so are absolute numbers. If women lawyers increase from about seven thousand to forty thousand, they become a much larger social force, even though they may be only about 10 percent of the total occupation. When women medical students, while remaining a small percentage of their classes, increase in number so that they can form committees, petition administrators, or give solidarity to one another against the traditional masculine badgering and disesteem, they greatly increase their impact on discriminatory attitudes and behavior. That is, as their rise in numbers permits the formation of real groups, their power mounts faster than the numbers or even (except at the start) the percentages. Thus, changes occur even when the percentage of the occupation made up of women is not large.

6. BASES OF PRESENT CHANGES

Most large-scale, objective measures of men's roles show little change over the past decade, but men do feel now and then that their position is in question, their security is somewhat fragile. I believe they are right, for they sense a set of forces that lie deeper and are more powerful than the day-to-day negotiation and renegotiation of advantage among husbands and wives, fathers and children, or bosses and those who work for them. Men are troubled by this new situation.

The conditions we live in are different from those of any prior civilization, and they give less support to men's claims of superiority than perhaps any other historical era. When these conditions weaken that support, men can rely only on previous tradition, or their attempts to socialize their children, to shore up their faltering advantages. Such rhetoric is not likely to be successful against the new objective conditions and the claims of aggrieved women. Thus, men are correct when they feel they are losing some of their privileges, even if many continue to laugh at the women's liberation movement.

The new conditions can be listed concretely, but I shall also give you a theoretical formulation of the process. Concretely, because of the increased use of various mechanical gadgets and devices, fewer tasks require much strength. As to those that still require strength, most men cannot do them either. Women can now do more household tasks that men once felt only they could do, and still more tasks are done by repair specialists called in to do them. With the development of modern warfare, there are few if any important combat activities that only men can do. Women are much better educated than before.

With each passing year, psychological and sociological research reduces the areas in which men are reported to excel over women and discloses far more overlap in talents, so that even when males still seem to have an advantage, it is but a slight one. It is also becoming more widely understood that the top posts in government and business are not best filled by the stereotypical aggressive male but by people, male or female, who are sensitive to others' needs, adept at obtaining cooperation, and skilled in social relations. Finally, in one sphere after another, the number of women who try to achieve rises, and so does the number who succeed.

Although the pressure of new laws has its direct effect on these conditions, the laws themselves arise from an awareness of the foregoing forces. Phrased in more theoretical terms, the underlying shift is toward the decreasing marginal utility of males, and this I suspect is the main source of men's resistance to women's liberation. That is, fewer people believe that what the male does is indispensable, nonsubstitutable, or adds such a special value to any endeavor that it justifies his extra "price" or reward. In past wars, for example, males enjoyed a very high value not only because it was felt that they could do the job better than women but also because they might well make the difference between being conquered and remaining free. In many societies, their marginal utility came from their contribution of animal protein through hunting. As revolutionary heroes, explorers, hunters, warriors, and daring capitalist entrepreneurs, men felt, and doubtless their women did too, that their contribution was beyond anything women could do. This earned men extra privileges of rank, authority, and creature services.

It is not then as individuals, as persons, that males will be deemed less worthy in the future or their contributions less needed. Rather, they will be seen as having no claim to *extra* rewards solely because they are members of the male sex-class. This is part of a still broader trend of our generation, which will also increasingly deny that being white, or an upper-caste or upper-class person, produces a marginally superior result and thus justifies extra privileges.

The relations of individuals are subject to continuous renegotiation as people try to gain or keep advantages or cast off burdens. They fail or succeed in part because one or the other person has special resources or lacks that are unique to those individuals. Over the long run, however, the outcome of these negotiations depends on the deeper social forces we have been describing, which ultimately determine which qualities or performances are more or less valued.

Now, men perceive that they may be losing some of their advantages and that more aspects of their social roles are subject to public challenge and renegotiation than in the past. They resist these changes, and we can suppose they will continue to do so. In all such changes, there are gains and losses. Commonly, when people at lower social ranks gain freedom, those at higher ranks lose some power or centrality. When those at the lower ranks also lose some protection, some support, those at the higher ranks lose some of the burden of responsibility. It is also true that the care or help given by an dominant group in the past was never as much as members believed, and their loss in political power or economic rule was never as great as they feared.

On the other hand, I know of no instance when a group or social stratum gained its freedom or moved toward more respect and then had its members decide that they did not want it. Therefore, although men will not joyfully give up their rank, in spite of its burdens, neither will women decide that they would like to get back the older feminine privileges, accompanied with the lack of respect and material rewards that went with those courtesies.

I believe that men perceive their roles as being under threat in a world that is different from any in the past. No society has yet come even close to equality between the sexes, but the modern social forces described here did not exist before either. At the most cautious, we must concede that the conditions favoring a trend toward more equality are more favorable than at any prior time in history. If we have little reason to conclude that equality is at hand, let us at least rejoice that we are marching in the right direction.

NOTES

1. Herbert Goldberg, *The Hazards of Being Male* (New York: Nash, 1976); and Patricia C. Sexton, *The Feminized Male: Classrooms, White Collars, and the Decline of Manliness* (New York: Random House, 1969). On the recognition of disadvantages, see J. S. Chafetz, *Masculine/Feminine or Human?* (Itasca, Ill.: Peacock, 1974), pp. 56 ff.

2. Joseph H. Pleck, "The Psychology of Sex Roles: Traditional and New Views," in *Women and Men: Changing Roles, Relationship and Perceptions*, ed. Libby A. Cater and Anne F. Scott (New York: Aspen Institute for Humanistic Studies, 1976), p. 182. Pleck has carried out the most extensive research on male roles, and I am indebted to him for special help in this inquiry.

3. For these two quotations, see Sidney M. Jourard, "Some Lethal Aspects of the Male Role," p. 22, and Irving London, "Frigidity, Sensitivity and Sexual Roles," p. 42, in *Men and Masculin-*

ity, ed. Joseph H. Pleck and Jack Sawyer (Englewood Cliffs, N.J.: Prentice-Hall, 1974). See also the summary of such traits in I. K. Braverman et al., "Sex-Role Stereotypes: A Current Appraisal," in *Women and Achievement*, ed. Martha T. S. Mednick, S. S. Tangri, and Lois W. Hoffman (New York: Wiley, 1975), pp. 32–47.

4. Robert Bierstedt's "The Sociology of the Majority," in his *Power and Progress* (New York: McGraw-Hill, 1974), pp. 199–220, does not state these principles, but I was led to them by thinking about his analysis.

5. Robert K. Merton, in "The Perspectives of Insiders and Outsiders," in his *The Sociology of Science* (Chicago: University of Chicago Press, 1973), pp. 99–136, has analyzed this view in some detail.

6. This general pattern is noted at various points in my monograph *The Celebration of Heroes: Prestige as a Social Control System* (Berkeley: University of California Press, 1979).

7. Erving Goffman, "The Arrangement Between the Sexes," *Theory and Society* 4 (1977): 307.

8. Hazel Erskine, "The Polls: Women's Roles," *Public Opinion Quarterly* 35 (Summer 1971).

9. Goffman, "Arrangement Between the Sexes," p. 308.

10. A simple analysis of these responses is presented in William J. Goode, *Principles of Sociology* (New York: McGraw-Hill, 1977), pp. 359 ff.

11. See Joseph H. Pleck, "The Power of Men," in *Women and Men: The Consequences of Power*, ed. Dana V. Hiller and R. Sheets (Cincinnati: Office of Women's Studies, University of Cincinnati, 1977), p. 20. See also Colin Bell and Howard Newby, "Husbands and Wives: The Dynamic of the Deferential Dialectic," in *Dependence and Exploitation in Work and Marriage*, ed. Diana L. Barker and Sheila Allen (London: Longman, 1976), pp. 162–63; as well as Richard Sennett and Jonathan Cobb, *The Hidden Injuries of Class* (New York: Vintage, 1973), p. 125. On the satisfactions of work, see Daniel Yankelovich, "The Meaning of Work," in *The Worker and the Job*, ed. Jerome Rosow (Englewood Cliffs, N.J.: Prentice-Hall, 1974), pp. 19–49.

12. Whatever other sacrifices women want from men, until recently a large majority did *not* believe men should do more housework. On this matter, see Joseph H. Pleck, "Men's New Roles in the Family: Housework and Child Care," to appear in *Family and Sex Roles*, ed. Constantina Safilios-Rothschild, forthcoming. In the mid-1970s, only about one-fourth to one-fifth of wives agreed to such a proposal.

13. Sennett and Cobb, *The Hidden Injuries of Class*, p. 125.

14. To date, the most complete published summary is that by Erskine, "The Polls: Women's Roles," pp. 275–91.

15. Stephanie Greene, "Attitudes Toward Working Women Have 'A Long Way to Go,'" *Gallup Opinion Poll*, March 1976, p. 33.

16. *Harris Survey*, 16 February 1978; see also *Harris Survey*, 11 December 1975.

17. It is, however, in harmony with one view expressed by many women (as well as men), that men in the past were a bit necrophiliac (i.e., they preferred to hop on unresponsive women, take their quick crude pleasure, and hop off). It does not accord much with what we know of people generally (they gain more pleasure when their partner does) or even of bawds and lechers (they brag about the delirium they arouse in the women they seduce).

18. See Charles F. Westoff, "Coital Frequency and Contraception," *Family Planning Perspectives* 6 (Summer 1974): 136–41.

19. The most extensive time budget data on a cross-national basis are found in A. Szalai, ed., *The Use of Time* (The Hague: Mouton, 1972). The most useful summary of the data on the above points is in Joseph H. Pleck, "The Work-Family Role System," *Social Problems* 24 (1977): 417–27. See also his "Developmental Stages in Men's Lives: How Do They Differ From Women's?" (National Guidance Association, Hartland, Michigan, 1977), mimeo.

20. Elina Haavio-Mannila, "Convergences Between East and West: Tradition and Modernity in Sex Roles in Sweden, Finland, and the Soviet Union," in Midnick et al., *Women and Achievement*, pp. 71–84. Further data will appear in J. Robinson, *How Americans Use Time*, forthcoming.

21. Pleck, "Men's New Roles in the Family." For details on men's contribution to child care, see Philip J. Stone, "Child Care in Twelve Countries," in Szalai, *The Use of Time*.

22. These data are to be found in Pleck, "Men's New Roles in the Family." However, 1977 data show that in Detroit this figure has risen to over 60 percent. Arland Thornton and Deborah

S. Freedman, "Changes in the Sex Role Attitudes of Women 1962–1977," *American Sociological Review* 44 (October 1979): 833.

23. The expansion of women's jobs has occurred primarily in "female" jobs or through new occupations defined as female or (less frequently) by women taking over formerly male jobs. See Council of Economic Advisers, *Economic Report of the President*, 1973, p. 155; and Barbara R. Bergman and Irma Adelman, "The 1973 Report of the President's Council of Economic Advisors: The Economic Role of Women," *American Economic Review*, September 1973, pp. 510–11. In 1960, about 24 percent of the labor force was made up of women in occupations where women are predominant; in 1970, the figure was 27 percent according to Myra H. Strober, "Women and Men in the World of Work: Present and Future," in Cater et al., *Women and Men: Changing Roles, Relationships, and Perceptions*, pp. 128–33.

24. Jean Lipman-Blumen, "Implications for Family Structure of Changing Sex Roles," *Social Casework* 57 (February 1976): pp. 67–79.

25. Victor R. Fuchs, "A Note on Sex Segregation in Professional Occupations," *Explorations in Economic Research* 2, no. 1 (Winter 1975): 105–11.

◆ ◆ ◆

PART TWO

Variations among Men

"All men are alike," runs a popular wisdom. But are they really? Are gay men's experiences with work, relationships, love, and politics similar to those of straight men? Do black and chicano men face the same problems and conflicts in their daily lives that white men face? Do middle class men have the same political interests as blue-collar men? The answers to these questions, as the articles in this part suggest, are not simple.

Although earlier studies of men and masculinity focused on the apparently universal norms of masculinity, recent work has attempted to demonstrate how different the worlds of various men are. Men are divided along the same lines that divide any other group: race, class, sexual orientation, ethnicity, age, and geographic region. Men's lives vary in crucial ways, and to understand these variations, as Anthony Astrachan argues in his essay, will take us a long way toward understanding men's experiences.

In fact, the earlier studies that suggested a single universal norm of masculinity reproduced some of the problems they were trying to solve. To be sure, *all* men benefit from the inequality between women and men; for example, think of how rape jokes or male-exclusive sports cultures provide contexts for the bonding of men across class, race, and ethnic lines while denying full participation to women. But the single, seemingly universal masculinity obscured ways in which some men hold and maintain power over other men in our society, hiding the fact that all men do not share equally in the fruits of gender inequality.

Here is how sociologist Erving Goffman put it in his important book, *Stigma* (New York: Doubleday, 1963, p. 128):

> In an important sense there is only one complete unblushing male in America: a young, married, white, urban, northern, heterosexual Protestant father of college education, fully employed, of good complexion, weight, and height, and a recent record in sports. Every American male tends to look out upon the world from this perspective, this constituting one sense in which one can speak of a common value system in America. Any male who fails to qualify in any one of these ways is likely to view himself — during moments at least — as unworthy, incomplete, and inferior.

As Goffman suggests, the middle class, white, heterosexual masculinity is used as the marker against which other masculinities are measured, and by which standard they may be found wanting. What is *normative* (prescribed) becomes translated into what is *normal*. In this way, heterosexual men maintain their status by the oppression of gay men; middle aged men can maintain their dominance over older and younger men;

upper class men can exploit working class men; and white men can enjoy privileges at the expense of men of color.

The articles in this section explore the variations among men in contemporary United States. Following Astrachan's article, Robert Staples, Richard Majors, and Maxine Baca Zinn challenge popularly held negative stereotypes of black and chicano males as pathologically "macho." Instead, they suggest that an understanding of ethnic minority males must begin with a critical examination of how institutionalized racism, particularly (but not exclusively) in the economy, shapes and constrains the possibilities, choices, and personal life-styles of black and chicano males. Calls for "changing masculinities," these articles suggest, must involve far more emphasis on *institutional* transformation than the white middle class men's liberation literature has previously suggested.

The next article by Michael Kimmel gives us an illuminating glimpse of how ethnic identity informs our conceptions of masculinity in feminist politics. Seymour Kleinberg's discussion of gay politics highlights the dangers in assuming a universal "natural" heterosexuality when thinking about the politics of masculinities. The section closes with John Moreland's article on age and change in adult males. Men, we learn from this piece, not only vary across social class, race, and sexual preference lines, but throughout the life course as well.

Anthony Astrachan

DIVIDING LINES

Books and movies and advertisements, cultural artifacts of society, are part of the context in which the revolution in gender power and sex roles takes place. So are the various dividing lines that people see, or build, in a society.

I relied as much as possible in this book on individuals whose talk and actions would illuminate what happens at work and at home. They were all members of different groups defined by social dividing lines — class, race, region, age, and stage of adult development, sexual preference. Here I want to add some observations on those groups, those categories. My sample was not large enough or random enough to offer an opportunity for statistical comparisons, but I did form impressions.

CLASS

The class of gender crosses the boundaries of class defined by income, education, and power. Where the political and pyschological dimensions intersect, men and women are indeed class enemies at many moments in their lives. (The oppressed class always sees the struggle more clearly than the dominant; so far, women have seen this more clearly than men.) But the human condition is that these enemies must love each other and often do.

The ways they love each other, the ways through this contradiction, this paradox, vary according to the familiar categories of class. Income and education do affect men's feelings about women's demands for independence and equality. So does power. Men treat women as equals more easily when they are sure of themselves and their money and power, or when questions of power are diffuse.

Blue-collar men feel the contradiction between their physical power and their place at the bottom of the male hierarchy, and they are more obvious than men in other classes about their need to treat women as underlings to compensate. They are more honest, or quicker to voice their anger and their fear, about changes in the balance of power and in sex roles, at work and at home. They find it harder than men with higher incomes and more education to overcome the traditions of their culture that prohibit treating women as equals, but some do so; at least one market researcher finds that blue-collar men express fewer traditional and macho values than stereotypes suggest, that some express higher expectations of intimacy and emotional support in relationships with women than middle-class men do.[1] This sometimes translates from talk into action. Lower-income men in my small sample and in advertising surveys sometimes do more housework than middle-class men, I suspect for the simple reason that their wives work but they still can't afford maids.

Middle-class and upper-class men are more affected by the psychotherapy subculture and by commercial trends, both forces that make some try, and others pretend to try, to understand and accept what women are doing. A higher proportion of middle-class men than either blue-collar or upper-class men is genuinely supportive of women at work. A higher proportion is also more likely to take a real share in, or real responsibility for, child care and housework. In both cases it's still a small majority that reaches the stage of association. Many upper-class men talk about their devotion to equality, but few give it in business management and only slightly more in the professions. In both groups their economic, command, and prestige power is real and they don't want to lose it. They are probably sincere when they talk about equality in their personal lives, and the proportion who treat their wives as equals, while small, may be as great as in the middle-class. But with upper-class men, I can't escape the feeling that it's more a matter of principle than practice because they hire maids and nannies, almost always female.

Middle-class and upper-class men, I found in my interviews, are more likely than blue-collar men to sense that there is something wrong about our effort to monopolize power, to keep women powerless. (It's harder for blue-collar men because they are further from real power.) Part of it is cognitive dissonance between our preaching democracy, human rights, and social mobility, and our practicing a kind of power politics that transforms gender and race into class. But I think our sense of wrong goes deeper than that. We know that mastery produces satisfaction, that competence means power and self-esteem. Conversely, we know that failure in mastery produces dissatisfaction, which turns into rage. We know that powerlessness, which we have made congruent with incompetence, is synonymous with low self-respect. We restrict women's mastery and deny them power even as they force us to recognize their competence.

RACE

The black experience of the gender revolution is different from white and Hispanic for several reasons. Black women have been working outside the home for so many generations that the idea of women in the workplace was not as revolutionary for them or their men as it was for other groups. Black women in general are still at the bottom of the economic ladder, but the proportion with better education, higher-status jobs, and higher salaries than men have is higher than it is among whites. This means the balance of economic and work power between men and women did not shift as dramatically for blacks as for others in recent years. Black women have been heading families in larger proportions for at least sixty years, so the balance of power at home did not shift so dramatically there either. In addition, the women's movement originated in and focused on the white middle class; it was the creation of white women whom many blacks see as a threat to black progress. So it did not touch black women as deeply as white, did not stimulate them to offer as many challenges as quickly to black men as white women did to white men.

Despite this, the balance at work and home for blacks *has* been affected by the changes of the past fifteen years. Many black men identify with women's demands as an outgrowth of the civil rights movement. The proportion who strongly resist women's demands is probably greater than the proportion of whites, however, if only because they are more conscious of how little power they have and are therefore more sensitive to every erosion in it. Many middle-class black men think they see women with money and power all around them, and they are often more intensely hostile than their white counterparts. Many black women have come to recognize what they see as a double oppression, racial and sexual. So do many black men, like the Atlanta banking consultant who said, "Men have no control now, and they're looking for control. . . . You can't deal with your boss because he's white, and you can't control the home place because your wife is making as much as you do."[2]

Among poorer blacks, many men simply do not "feel like a man" because of their inability to find a good job, earn good money, and do even half the providing for a family. They may feel impotent (and sometimes turn sexually impotent), or they may abandon the families they start and then feel even less like a man. They may displace their anger and resentment from the economy and the white world onto women — and all the more so when they see black women who earn decent money and provide single-handedly for families. The men's economic disability has many causes. Thomas Sowell, an economist, and William Wilson, a sociologist, are black conservatives who argue that the psychological legacy of the past is more important than anything in the society as a whole in blacks' failure to advance economically. Most blacks who have looked at the problem disagree, blaming continuing racial discrimination, real if not always intentional, visible in an array of facts:[3] black men show greater increases in rates of chronic disease and mental illness than white men. Blacks are imprisoned at a rate four or five times higher than whites (and prison is not a place that trains men in sensitivity to women). The unemployment rate for black men officially is twice as high as the rate for white men and in fact may be much worse than that. (There is nearly a one-to-one correspondence in the increase in unemployment among black men and the increase in female-headed families over the years, according to Walter Allen, a sociologist at the University of Michigan.) Government welfare programs give no money to mothers and children if there is a man in the house. Yet many black men continue to maintain a connection with children even when they abandon the family in form or in reality — a sign that it may be possible to draw them into one of the main channels for men's participation in the gender revolution.

Hispanic attitudes resemble whites' more than blacks' because the place of *la mujer* was so unquestionably in the home that the movement of women into the workplace was a dramatic change for Latins as it was for Anglos, indeed even more revolutionary in most Hispanic communities than in the majority society. The myth that women are not in the labor force persisted far longer for Chicanas than for Anglos, though today the proportions for all women sixteen and over are similar. Hispanic men and women both insist that Latin machismo and the importance of the family are often misunderstood by Anglos, but their more accurate versions still emphasize the traditional importance of the father and the confinement of the mother to home, even if she demonstrates real strength there. A Hispanic woman who achieves an income or occupational level higher than her husband's arouses more agony in her spouse than occurs in any other ethnic group. Mexican-Americans often go on to say that the rebellion against the forces of machismo and family by Chicana women has created a change that may be greater in the long run than the changes among Anglos. But the forces of change are attenuated by the Hispanic birthrate, 75 percent higher than that of the rest of the population (25.5 births per thousand compared with 14.7 for non-Hispanics), with a higher percentage born to women under twenty, which keeps more women from finishing high school and from finding better jobs.

The birthrate of course reflects Catholic doctrine, but it also reflects the belief of many, perhaps most Hispanic males that manhood is demonstrated by the number of children a man has. My impression is that while the dynamics of power change among Hispanics resemble the Anglos', the proportion and the intensity of male resistance approach the blacks'.

REGION

I did the interviews for this book in cities and suburbs in four regions to make sure I did not fall into the trap of identifying any one place with the whole country. They were the East (New York and Washington), the Midwest (Chicago, Detroit, and two smaller cities), the South (Atlanta, Dallas, and two smaller cities), and California (Los Angeles and the San Francisco Bay area).

My impressions reflect the conclusions of experts on the census data that the United States is becoming ever more homogeneous in many respects though diversity is growing in others. I found the highest percentage of opponents of change in the South and a greater proportion in the Midwest than on the two coasts. There was a higher percentage of supporters in the East and West, but the Midwest came close to them in the proportion of pragmatics. I can't prove, but I imagine, that my impressions reflect such facts as the increasing similarity of all regions in education and per capita income, or the higher proportion of older people in the South. And the census data, of course, say nothing about differences in cultural values among the regions.

My overriding impression was that none of the differences was significant. Ambivalents were the biggest single group in every region. Anger, fear, and anxiety and relief, admiration, and identification can be found with equal ease or difficulty around the country.

AGE AND STAGES OF GROWTH

I did not find, as some of my friends expected, that older men uniformly tend to resist and younger men to support what women are doing, as though revolution depended primarily upon youth. It's true that men in their twenties today grew up with feminism in the air they breathed, and with an informality between the sexes that has many causes besides feminism. Many of them are freer of sex-role stereotypes than older men are. In surveys they profess more support for the equality of women than do older men or the male population as a whole, and a few studies say that (in much smaller proportions) they are more likely to live up to their professions. It's also true that men in their sixties are often more devoted to, or more the prisoner of, the habits that go with the old stereotypes. But in every season of a man's life from his twenties through his fifties, I found opponents, ambivalents, pragmatists, and supporters.

Looking at men under thirty, I found more who speak in terms of equality than those in any other age group, of equality within marriage and equality for women at work. But there are just as many in this group who assume power or privilege as there are true egalitarians. Many expect their wives to have careers, for instance, but also expect those careers to take second place to their own. Many become angry or fearful when they compete against women in the workplace. The under-thirties are traditional in tending to start relationships and initiate sex more often than the women they know, as the few women I interviewed confirm. They are often unsure how to treat single women and more cautious — from fear or anxiety — about marriage, so they postpone it. (The proportion of men between twenty-five and twenty-nine who are single grew from 23 to 38 percent between 1960 and 1984.[4]) But young men are better able to say no to a woman's initiative than are their elders, and better able to maintain nonsexual friendships with women.

There are also some who reject tradition without moving toward equality — young men who seem ready to let women assume the kind of dominance that used to be male. I met two who talked about being househusbands; half-consciously they expect their wives to support them in a mirror image of the old wage-earner ethic, and they have no idea how much labor is involved in child raising. Three had little idea of how they wanted to earn a living, little concept of a career — like women before the recent changes. They are no doubt responding to the changes women are making, but hardly in an egalitarian fashion.

The most traditional of the under-thirties are blue-collar men for whom the factory is the place where they pass from the worlds of home and school, which they see as being run by women, to a world run by men. A woman personnel manager in a heavy equipment plant, . . . who dealt every day with the workers, saw this, and I heard her thought echoed in many men's conversations. She said:

> Women who come to work in the factory are violating not only the man's sense of family but his sense of order in the world. Look at the world the man-child grows up in: up to the eighth grade it's run almost entirely by women — his mother and his teachers. Even in high school, there are a lot of women teachers — and the girl students affect the boys, whether they behave themselves or go wild. Graduation from high school and coming to work in the plant is graduation from a woman's world and coming into a man's world. When they see a woman at work on the line, it looks like, "Oh, Lord, here comes Mother back again."

Many of these men, even though they grew up in a world much influenced by feminist ideas, still see women primarily as sex objects, not as fellow workers. Many are more self-centered and less helpful than their elders to any peer; they give less support to women on the job than some older men who are uncomfortable with the female presence but have been conditioned both to help their buddies and to help ladies. And, as the personnel manager saw, many younger men think of the shop as the first place they will be members of a male world. Not all blue-collar men under thirty are like this, but many are — enough to remind people not to jump to conclusions or ignore the intersection of age with class.

Many men in their thirties, men born between 1945 and 1955, were closer to what had been predicted: old enough to have acquired traditional attitudes but young enough to have felt the impact of feminist charges and changes. Some tried to respond positively. Others were too unsure of themselves to resolve questions in a way that satisfied them or the women in their lives. Women looking at young men and at the thirties group often complain that they are getting neither what they asked nor the positive supports that accompanied the denial of equality in the old system.

Men in their late thirties and men in their forties were often in the position of marrying a homemaker and celebrating their tenth anniversary with a career woman. Some of these marriages ended in divorce, and the men in those that lasted probably struggled even harder to master the changing rules of the game. A *Ms.* magazine collective described both: "Some men who ran this gauntlet did not feel thanked enough. Some men who resisted change felt punished, angry, and occasionally guilty." That jibes completely with my interviews. *Ms.* added a point I didn't hear often, but which I find easy to believe: "Those feelings, once hidden, now surface as pained concern for the failures of feminism."[5]

Men under forty provide the members of two groups who have achieved prominence in the media, yuppies and new men. Both occupy a bigger place in middle-class consciousness than they do in the population. Yuppies account for only 4 percent of the baby boom, the seventy-six million people between the ages of twenty-one and thirty-nine. This figure comes from an advertising agency measure of the consumer population; what could be more appropriate? J. Walter Thompson U.S.A. defines yuppies as people in this age group who combine higher education (five years, on the average) and high income (a median of $39,100).[6] Despite the *u* for "urban" in yuppies, the agency finds that 56 percent of them live in the suburbs and only one in six is female. This figure may say more about their employers than about the yuppies themselves, but it provides an important reason for my observation that yuppies are unlikely to treat women as equals: they don't meet them as peers in large numbers.

Yuppies, by definition, are devoted to acquisitive and career pursuits, and appear (to me, at least) to be more selfish and narcissistic than the population as a whole. This may give them additional reason to postpone marriage and treasure the freedom of the single state. No doubt it also affects their behavior in marriage; I suspect that much of what I read about remodeling houses and finding new recipes for wholesome dishes reflects a yuppie attempt to substitute material ventures for some of the psychological effort needed to build intimacy and make a marriage last. I wonder if this makes for a more egalitarian marriage — it might, if the spouse were of the same kind — or a less. The first yuppies are now turning forty, and their behavior may change as they enter middle age and become more capable of thinking about others and integrating the masculine and feminine in themselves.

Thompson defines another 16 percent of the baby boom age group as would-bes, people with the same education as yuppies and presumably with yuppie values, but a median income of only $15,000 — teachers, clergy, social workers, paramedics, college instructors. There's obviously considerable overlap between Thompson's would-bes and my service occupations, and a much higher proportion of would-bes than yuppies are women. Those two facts should make more of the male would-bes treat women as equals.

When I'm asked about yuppies, however, I think not only about that low 4 percent proportion of the baby boomers, but also of the downward mobility of the whole generation, including elite workers, workers, and housewives. Real after-tax income for families headed by a person aged twenty-five to thirty-four declined 2.3 percent between 1961 and 1982. The combined takehome pay of a two-earner couple in this age group is probably less than what each of their respective fathers earned on his own at the same age.[7] Now, that's a good reason for having no, or fewer, children. But — thinking back to my expectations of a group with a high proportion of women and a lot of service jobs — a man may not treat his wife as an equal if he earns no more than she does; it may only fuel his anger and his anxiety.

The new man is someone whom feminists, social scientists, and advertisers all search for. Barbara Ehrenreich describes the prototype as twenty-five to forty years old, single, affluent, and living in a city, "for it is among such men that the most decisive break in the old masculine values is occurring."[8] (I disagree on the single and I have doubts about the affluent.) He is usually able to choose his clothes, decorate his apartment, and cook for himself — abilities that certainly distinguish him from traditional man, even if, as Ehrenreich says, he uses these skills to demonstrate his class status. They also enable him to stay independent of the women who used to take care of his domestic needs, and he does indeed tend to avoid commitment, in the current phrase. "Sensitivity" is a touchstone for the new man, who claims that he knows how to be "in touch with his feelings." Ehrenreich has her doubts. "Quite possibly," she says, "as sensitivity has spread, it has lost its moorings in the therapeutic experience and come to signify the heightened receptivity associated with consumerism: a vague appreciation that lends itself to aimless shopping."

That fits with marketing definitions of the new man. Playboy Marketing Services describes him as single, separated, divorced, widowed, living with someone who works or married with a working wife, and making purchasing decisions. It estimated in 1984 that 64.9 percent of all men meet this definition, rather different from my estimate of 5 to 19 percent who genuinely support women's demands for independence and equality.[9] . . . Advertising agencies describe him similarly, in terms of his willingness to do household chores and his propensity to make brand choices of products used in those chores, but they put him at 13 to 22 percent of all men.

All the surveys agree that men under thirty-five were more likely to show new-man characteristics than those over thirty-five. As I've said, I'm not so sure.

Hyatt & Esserman Research Associates did a poll for *Good Morning America* in 1980 that put the proportion of new men at 19 percent. They asked forty questions and defined the new man in terms of responses to the three that created the greatest division of opinion among the 752 men interviewed. The new man disagreed with the statement, "If women have children at home under six years of age, they should not work." He agreed that "when women marry, it's fine for them to keep their maiden names." And he agreed that "if both parents work, the wife and husband should take turns to stay home when the kids are sick."[10]

But two thirds of *all* men in the Hyatt & Esserman survey disagreed with the statement, "A man should never cry in public," and six out of seven agreed that men can be must as good at changing diapers as women. Those figures show how men in general have been affected by change. They are evidence for my feeling that it will be hard to reverse the revolution. But neither they nor the 19 percent of Hyatt & Esserman's definition of new men are going to make the revolution succeed. That will take another kind of man, or this kind of new man after he has gone through or been put through profound struggle with himself and society.

Some new men are certainly over thirty-five, even over forty. Older men do seem to find it harder than younger men to accept women on the job, but there are so many exceptions to this that I mention it only with reluctance. I found several older men who were genuinely supportive of women's demands for equality and choice. It takes a man who is relatively sure of his own competence, his own achievement, and his own masculinity to feel and behave positively about the changes women are making. Not every successful man is positive about these changes; many hate them as denials of their own lives and values, their own manhood. But a large proportion of those men who do like what women are doing are successful in their own terms. That means many of them are middle-aged.

Older men who are egalitarian and younger men who aren't don't constitute a historical anomaly as much as they illustrate the process of adult development that Daniel Levinson outlined.[11] A young man in his twenties, in early adulthood, is striving to take his place in the world as an adult male. He is apt to try to control or repress the feminine in himself. That often makes it harder for him to respond to women making changes, whom he sees as competing for places as adult "males." A man in his late thirties usually makes an intense effort to achieve a more senior, "manly" position in the world. That often makes him neglect or repress the feminine in himself and also makes him more hostile to women engaged in the same effort. In the forties, the period of the mid-life transition and the famous mid-life crisis, a man becomes more able to integrate the masculine and feminine in himself — and, if he is not too much the victim of tradition, more able to accept and support women's efforts to achieve independence and choice.

HOMOSEXUAL MEN

Many homosexuals, particularly gay activists, talk in convincing and fascinating detail about the ways that the women's movement gave them the courage to do two things: come out of the closet, and free themselves from the sexist culture in which they grew up. The two are intimately connected, but not identical; most gay men learn to accept and enjoy their sexual preferences before they discover the emptiness of conventional ideas of masculinity. Individual women inspired individual men to raise their consciousness (as happened to many straight men). Women's openness about sex encouraged gay men to be open about their sex lives. The collective militancy of the women's movement provided a model for the gay rights movement. The increasing numbers of gay men who have experienced these things identify strongly with women's demands for equality and independence. Steve Borst, an actor, spoke to me about the personal and political aspects:

> There was one woman, there was an enormous amount of love between me and her. It was through her consciousness, her struggle to perceive herself as a valid human being who didn't have to put up with heckling in the street and the vagaries of relationships with men and things like that, that I began to understand my situation and apply those principles to my gayness as something that was part of my self, that could make me stronger as a person and in society. And there's a political level on which

something like this happened to numbers of gay men. The development of the civil rights movements in this country started with blacks, went to women, then to gays, it was a progression from visibility to invisibility. The blacks were the most visible to straight white males, the women were harder for men to see, and before Stonewall in 1969 [the riot over police harassment that is usually considered the start of the gay liberation movement], the gays were invisible. Now we're visible, to ourselves and to everybody else.

Friendships like Borst's with straight women are very important to gay men. They seldom have deep friendships with straight men. Friendships with other gay men face problems and tensions similar to those of nonsexual friendships between heterosexual men and women: they might become sexual, which changes the nature of love and trust. Seymour Kleinberg believes from his own and others' experience that "the richest, least infantile, and most moral relationships gay men form are with women."[12] Both are struggling to realize their refusal to conform to the demands of traditional society. "Abandoning arbitrarily assigned, restrictive, sexual role-playing . . . she frees the male from an equally restrictive, equally arbitrary opposite role," John Rechy says, elaborating on the idea.[13] Women who have such friendships testify that the gay men neither patronize them nor treat them as objects as most straight men do.

Other gays say that it was their discovery, or rather their realization and fulfillment, of their homosexuality that enabled them to transcend traditional sex roles, to give up the efforts they had made since childhood to be "masculine" in the sense of repressing emotion or believing in "the system of leaders and followers," to "free the sister in ourselves" (and old slogan of the Gay Liberation Front).[14] They don't attribute this to friendship with a woman or the example of the women's movement. But a consciousness they think has been raised only through gayness still makes them identify with the changes of the gender revolution.

Gays learn early that they constitute an oppressed class, as women do. A few connect their oppression directly to their sexuality, which gives them something in common with a radical feminist like Ellen Willis. Kleinberg quotes a man who considered "the prodigality of gay promiscuity" as "a compensation for the injustices society has wished on us." Kleinberg says this struck him as more than mere defiance because it "implies that sexual obsession is not devoted exclusively to sensual pleasure but is much involved with an individual's sense of powerlessness."[15] Few straight men have reached an equivalent insight, which I think deserves to be included in revolutionary philosophy.

Homosexuals who give the women's movement credit for the start of their own liberation say that gays with other views probably make up a majority. Some compensate for their oppression by trying to dominate lesbians in gay activist groups, or women in their workplaces, acting very much like blue-collar workers or neurotically insecure men of any class in searching for people they can define as inferior — and finding women. An advertising man told me, "We want to be the equals of straight men, and if that means screwing women — figuratively — we'll do it."

Some gays would not care if they ever saw another woman. Some are clones who have adopted one variety or another of macho look, whether rigid Wall

Street or heavy leather, and oppressive images of physical strength, sexual violence, and dominance. These two groups overlap; "the macho gesture is prominent in those gay bars and resorts where women are entirely absent," Kleinberg notes. He offers another important insight:

> The homosexuals who adopt images of masculinity, conveying their desire for power and their belief in its beauty, are in fact eroticizing the very values of straight society that have tyrannized their own lives. . . . The perversity of imitating their oppressors guarantees that such blindness will work itself out as self-contempt. . . .
>
> While straight men define their ideas from a variety of sources (strength, achievement, success, money), two of those sources are always their attitudes toward women and toward paternity. It is no coincidence that the same decade that popularized liberation for women and announced that the nuclear family was a failure also saw men return to a long-haired, androgynous style. If straight men are confused about their maleness, what is the dilemma for gay men, who rarely did more than imitate these ideas?[16]

Kleinberg sees gays as tending toward one or another of two alternatives: the macho life, or a species of feminism that derives from recognition of "the common oppression" of homosexuals and women. Both tendencies show that sexual preference does not insulate a man from the forces of change or the question of gender power. Gay men are participants in the revolution and the fight against it, and they, like straight men, must pay the costs even or especially when they struggle to make it work.

NOTES

1. Barbara Ehrenreich, "A Feminist's View of the New Man," New York *Times Magazine*, 20 May 1984, and "Blue-Collar Lovers and Allies," *Ms.*, September 1985.

2. Diane Weathers, "A New Black Struggle," *Newsweek*, 27 August 1979.

3. See Ronald Smothers, "Concern for the Black Family: Attention Now Turns to Men," New York *Times*, 31 December 1983.

4. Census Bureau figures quoted in Alvin P. Sanoff et al., "The American Male," *U.S. News & World Report*, 3 June 1985.

5. Nancy Chodorow et al., "Feminism 1984: Taking Stock on the Brink of an Uncertain Future," *Ms.*, January 1984.

6. The study also lists elite workers, 3 percent of the total, with a median income of $34,852 but no higher education, and workers, 55 percent of the total, with no higher education and a median income of $10,036. Housewives and students account for the remaining 22 percent. Bert Metter and Peter Kim, "The New American Consumer" (Unpublished study by J. Walter Thompson U.S.A., New York, 1985).

7. Bureau of Labor Statistics and Census Bureau data quoted in Phillip Longman, "The Downwardly Mobile Baby Boomers," *The Wall Street Journal*, 12 April 1985.

8. Ehrenreich, "New Man."

9. Anthony Astrachan, "Overview: Marketing to Men," *Advertising Age*, 4 October 1984.

10. Ibid.

11. Daniel Levinson, *The Seasons of a Man's Life* (New York: Alfred A. Knopf, 1978).

12. Seymour Kleinberg, *Alienated Affections: Being Gay in America* (New York: St. Martin's Press, 1980).

13. John Rechy, *The Sexual Outlaw* (New York: Dell, 1977). Two books describe friendship between women and gay men: Rebecca Nahas and Myra Turley, *The New Couple: Women and Gay Men* (New York: Seaview, 1979); and John Malone, *Straight Women/Gay Men: A Special Relationship* (New York: Dial, 1981).

14. Jeff Keith, "My Own Men's Liberation" (Article distributed at a Men and Masculinity Conference).

15. Kleinberg, *Alienated Affections.*

16. Ibid.

See Clyde Franklin

Robert Staples

MASCULINITY AND RACE:
THE DUAL DILEMMA OF BLACK MEN

In recent years a great deal of attention has been given to the role of black women and their super-oppressed status in American society (Stack, 1974; Staples, 1973). This emphasis on black women was generated by the women's liberation movement and highlighted the domination of the society by men and the subordinate role of women. Most of the literature has focused on the privileges of masculinity in gaining access to the culture's values and goals. Males have begun to question, themselves, their own sex role expectations and to assess the negative consequences as well as the advantages of their gender.

In the case of black men, their subordination as a racial minority has more than cancelled out their advantages as males in the larger society. Any understanding of their experience will have to come from an analysis of the complex problems they face as blacks and as men. Unlike white males, they have few privileges in this society except vis-à-vis black women and even that advantage is being eroded by black women having a competitive edge over some black males for certain jobs (Epstein, 1973). Indeed, black men in comparison to white males find themselves on the negative side of social statistics in the area of health, employment, education, income, etc. As a result, we have to examine the sociocultural forces which have combined to create the increasing plight of black men in the United States (Wilkinson & Taylor, 1977).

The experiences of males and females — black and white — in their lives are critical and different from each other. Black men face certain problems related to institutional racism and environments which often do not prepare them very well for the fulfillment of masculine roles. In addition to the problems created

Reprinted from *Journal of Social Issues* 34(1), 1978.
I am deeply indebted to Leanor Johnson, Joseph Pleck, and Patricia Bell Scott for their comments and suggestions on an earlier draft of this paper.

by institutional and overt discrimination, they encounter the negative stereo-typing that exists on all levels, about them: being socially castrated, insecure in their male identity, and lacking in a positive self-concept. Most of these negative stereotypes have been perpetuated by the social science literature and have stemmed from a failure to understand the meaning and form of masculinity in black culture and as a result of the application of white norms to black behavior.

In the pre-slave era blacks lived in what can only be described as a patriarchal society on the African continent. It does not appear to have generated the total submission of women as was true of comparable European cultures. There are numerous cases where women in Africa exceeded their European counterparts in their authority and contribution to their respective social units (Paulme, 1971). Until recently, it had been assumed that slavery destroyed all vestiges of a black patriarchy by its suppression of the bondsman's authority over his fam-ily. The work of historian Stanley Elkins (1959) gave rise to a number of other theories that depicted the black man as a docile personality whose will had been broken by slavery. More recent historical research has presented us with a more balanced portrait of the male slave. Alex Haley's (1976) book, *Roots,* and the popular television production of that work most vividly illustrates the strong and resistant role of black men during the slavery era.

There were a variety of responses to the coercive institution, slavery. They ranged from the grinning, shuffling "Sambo" of pro-slavery lore to the revenge-ful runaways to many who used guile and humor to escape from work or to manipulate the slave owner (Blassingame, 1972). It is impossible to determine which response was dominant, only that all black men did not respond uni-formly to the same condition. A theory concomitant with the Elkins (1959) thesis was that under slavery black men abdicated their responsibility to their families (Frazier, 1939). Subsequent historical research has shown that most slave households had a male as head who fulfilled certain role prerequisites un-der the limited autonomy possible in a total institution. The fact that men did not have unlimited authority in the family, according to Genovese (1974), was "in fact a closer approximation to a healthy sexual equality than was possible for whites" (p. 16).

After slavery officially ended, the kind of role flexibility that existed during slavery continued for black families. Despite theories to the contrary, male-present households were the norm in poor black communities in the period between 1880–1925. Families headed by women were hardly, if at all, more common than among comparable whites (Gutman, 1976). These two-parent black households were often dual-worker families, as many wives worked along-side their husbands in order to obtain land and an education for their children. It was out of the harsh economic conditions of the late nineteenth century that a certain egalitarianism developed within black families and the sharp dichot-omy between male and female sex roles so common to antebellum Southern white families failed to develop.

THE MYTH OF THE MATRIARCHY

Although one-parent households have always been a minority of all black fam-ilies, a number of assumptions have been made about their effect on the acqui-sition of male identity patterns for the boys lodged in such households. Such notions have more relevance today since a near majority of black children presently live in female-headed households (U.S. Department of Labor, 1976a). Those who argue that male children can not learn the content of their masculine role make the erroneous supposition that there are no male role models available from whom those children can learn. In her study of matricentric households, Stack (1974) notes the striking fact that households almost always have men around: male relatives, in-laws, and boyfriends. Children have constant and close contact with these men and their relationships last over the years.

The fact that many black women head households has resulted in the stereotype of black men as castrated by their women, who have gained ascendency in the family through their greater education and economic contribution. Even in families where the husband is present, the wife is alleged to be the dominant figure in decision making. These pejorative stereotypes have persisted because black families are generally more equalitarian than comparable white families. Due to sexism in this society, few black women earn more than their husbands. Even in low-income families, 85% of the husbands have a higher income than the wife (Hill, 1973). Most black wives are not dominant matriarchs but share with their husbands the making of family decisions. With the special problems black women face — such as early pregnancies, the burdens of supporting children alone, and inadequate incomes and job opportunities — it is difficult to imagine them having castrated the slightly better-off male (Liebow, 1967; Staples, 1973).

Alongside these stereotypes of the black male extant in the social science literature is the lingering one of his negative self-concept, a subjective devaluation that derives from labelling processes in the family and his inferior status in the larger society (Rainwater, 1966). While this could be the logical outcome of minority status in this society, countervailing forces operate to maintain a high level of self-esteem for most black males (Staples, 1976). Among these forces are the insider–outsider dichotomy in selecting reference groups as guides for the expected level of achievement. Instead of using the higher standards of the majority group, many black males measure their worth by the achievement of others within their own culture. Being a member of an oppressed minority group also allows individual members to be extrapunitive in determining the reasons for their failures in life (Nobles, 1973; McCarthy & Yancey, 1971). Despite notions to the contrary, positive experiences in their families do serve as a source of positive self-identity in the developing male child (Halpern, 1973).

SOCIALIZATION INTO MANHOOD

As is true of majority youth, blacks have a variety of socializing agents and institutions upon which to draw for their male identity. Being exposed to the school, family, mass media, and peer group means a number of different values and roles are being conveyed to them at any point in time. Family structure and socioeconomic status are considered key factors in determining the kind of role models presented to the growing child. We have already noted the dominant— but unproven — theory that the content of the male role is not adequately conveyed to black youth because of absent or weak father figures. This ignores the fact that black boys learn the male role from a variety of sources. Even if there were not strong male role models available, women are able to transmit the male sex-role expectations symbolically, e.g., telling him how to walk, to carry his books, etc.

These children, however, are depicted as having different problems. It is not that they are unexposed to male role models, but the male role models present negative images of manhood and achievement to impressionable male children. Examples of such negative role images would be the pimp and hustler in low-income ghettos, who are the only successful men to whom many young boys are exposed. While this is a salient and somewhat valid point, it overlooks the fact that the pimp and hustler prototypes exist primarily in large Northern cities and are rare in the smaller towns and in the South. Moreover, as Taylor (1976) has noted, at any point in time, role model identifications can be observed to be closely related to the dominant concerns of youth at that time. What this means is that youth who are interested in a career, in developing interpersonal skills, or are preoccupied with a social or political issue focus on those environmental models assumed to be relevant and useful toward the resolution of those concerns.

It is difficult to single out a dominant force in the socialization process for black youth. The complexity of our society is such that they will be exposed to a number of models. Several key studies indicate that family background is an important — if not decisive — factor influencing the masculinity of young black males. For example, Benjamin (1971) discovered that male youth had a better conception of the socially accepted and prescribed model of the male familial role when their father had one or more years of college education. The implications of his finding is that a strong association exists between the opportunity to play a role and the actual playing of that role.

Questions might be raised about the tendency of many black youth to associate masculinity with hypersexuality and violence. It is true that many black youth are socialized and exposed to violence in their environments and in the mass media. Whether this becomes their only concept of masculinity depends on the opportunity to fulfill other concepts of masculinity. Violence as a means of status-conferral will continue to exist among black youths in the underclass as long as the opportunity structure for other expressions of their masculinity remain blocked by the forces of institutional racism. This is in reality a class, not a racial determination, and exists among lower-class groups of all races (Curtis, 1975).

PROBLEMS OF THE YOUNG BLACK MAN

Strongly related to the issue of black masculinity are the problems encountered on the path to manhood. Few Americans are unaware of the presence of young black men and they are generally regarded as a source of tension in the social structure. First, they are a large and, particularly in the inner city, quite visible group, relative to the total black population. Over 54% of the black population is under 24 years of age, compared to only 42% of whites (U.S. Bureau of the Census, 1975). Secondly, they are overrepresented in the statistics on violent crimes, a phenomena which has many Americans in a state of terror. What has happened to this group of young black males cannot be explained in simplistic terms of poor parenting or innate racial traits. It is the persistence of barriers to the expression of the masculine role that best explains their antisocial behavior.

The high school dropout rate is 25% for blacks in contrast to 15% for whites (More Women Enrolling in Graduate School, 1977). That means many black youth are without educational credentials or job skills and experience. The net result of this statistic is a 40% jobless rate for black males in the central cities (U.S. Department of Labor, 1976b). Unofficial, but no less authoritative, surveys of black teenage unemployment put the figure at close to 70% (National Urban League, Note 1).

What this means in very real terms is that the work function so closely associated with masculinity in this society is denied to the majority of black male youth. One finds a close correspondence between the joblessness of black male youth and their behavior patterns. It finds its most vivid manifestation in the crime statistics that show the largest number of crimes against a person and acts of theft were committed by black males below the age of 24. The largest group responsible for homicides in this country are black males in the 20- to 24-year age range. And their victims are similarly young black men — a fact which has as its most tragic consequence homicide being listed as the number one cause of death among black males aged 15–30. If there is any doubt that these young black men are members of the underclass, it can be relieved by the statistic which shows that almost 60% of young black prison inmates reported an annual income of less than $3000 (U.S. Bureau of the Census, 1975).

Not all of the response to failure to fulfill their manhood is expressed in antisocial behavior. Some of it is aggression turned inward. In New York City the highest cause of death is narcotic addiction among black male youth. Other symptoms of their feelings of powerlessness and hopelessness is a suicide rate among black youth that is higher than that of the total population of all ages. Others may seek to escape the fate of the criminal, the drug addict, and the suicide victim by joining the ranks of the volunteer army. More than a third of the new recruits into the new volunteer army were young black men (Staples, 1975).

It is patently clear that the central concerns of black men are not about relinquishing male privilege or forging new concepts of androgyny or sex-role egalitarianism. They must first and foremost deal with the issue of survival. It is not that they have abused the privileges accruing to men, but that they have never been given the opportunity to realize even the minimal perquisites of manhood — life sustaining employment and the ability to support a family. To a large extent, these problems are confined to a certain segment of the black population, but they constitute a very large proportion of all black men. We should also realize that the more these legitimate aspirations to manhood are retarded, the greater the tendency will be to assert it in other areas.

ROLE ASCRIPTION AND FULFILLMENT

Within the youth period attitudes are formed toward futuristic life styles and roles; hence it is necessary to assess how young black males see themselves — if at all — in the roles of lover, husband, and father. Are the roles of husband and father subordinate to the more glamorous and mass media portrayed ones of the free-wheeling bachelor and superstud? We need to analyze the role priorities among black men and the forces in their environment which facilitate or impede their fulfillment.

Lovers and Sexual Consorts   Folklore and research both depict the black male as preoccupied with his role as a lover and sexual partner. The concept of black male hypersexuality dates as far back as the sixteenth century, when Englishmen described Africans as beset by an unrestrained lustfulness. Until recently, the trait of black male sexual competency was pejoratively viewed as the sexuality of beasts and the bestiality of sex (Jordan, 1968). A less racist conception of black male sexuality is that it is a secondary symbol of manhood in a society that denies him the primary signs of masculinity, such as high status jobs (Vontress, 1971). Psychiatrists Grier and Cobbs (1968) have suggested that it is a symbol of power employed as an armament and used as a cautious and deliberate weapon against whites.

Such ascriptions of underlying motives and drives ignore the normative sexual socialization patterns of black men in this society (Hammond & Ladner, 1969). They, as well as females, are very early socialized into heterosexual relations by their culture and extended family system. A sexual orientation is well inculcated long before they become aware of the constraints on their other expressions of masculinity. Less rigid age and sex roles in the black community expose them to a more permissive sexual ethos at an early age. Because the restraints placed on black female sexual expression have not been as severe as for her white counterpart, this has liberated black male sexuality as well as provided a greater opportunity structure for sexual contacts. It is only in a puritanical culture such as the United States that male sexual interest is viewed with the disapprobation imposed on black male sexuality.

There is little doubt that black men are the most liberal of the sex-race groups. They start dating earlier, are more likely to have a romantic involvement in high school, have the most liberal sexual attitudes, and are most inclined to have nonmarital sex without commitment (Broderick, 1965; Larson, 1976; Reiss, 1964; Johnson, 1978). This does not mean that they have no sexual standards but only that the ones they have are less conservative than those of other sex-race groups. In particular there is a double standard in regards to what women should be allowed to do (Johnson, 1978). It should be noted that their double standard has not been as rigid or as oppressive as that of many white males. Black women are not labelled as "good" or "bad" girls on the basis of virginity or nonvirginity, but discretion in sexual affairs is expected, as is sexual exclusivity in a relationship where the male has an emotional investment.

Charges of black male hypersexuality have often come from white males, for reasons that many think are suspect. The sexual prowess of black men, whether true or not, has been seen as a threat to the white male's powerful status in this society. Such fears have been symbolically manifested in attempts to castrate black men as part of the lynchings and other acts of terror against them. This led Clark (1965) to suggest: "The white man in America has, historically, arranged to have both white and Negro women available to him. He has claimed sexual priority with both, and, in the process he has sought to emasculate Negro men." Others believe that black men still pose a sexual threat to white manhood although most whites would probably not admit it (Stember, 1976). One sociological experiment (Schulman, 1974) demonstrated that even liberal white males can be rankled to violence by the hint of black sexual competition.

Husbands   Clearly, the role of husband implies more responsibility and requires more than the role of lover and sexual consort. Black men who face uncertain futures see marriage as a risky undertaking. At an early age, many decide that they never want to take on the risk of marriage or be subjected to its requirements. This reluctance to marry is obviously associated with income and employment potential. Only 55% of black men earning less than $1000 a year marry, in comparison to 80% of those earning between $3000–$5000. As incomes rise so do the number of black men who marry (Glick & Mills, 1974). The fears of lower-class black men are rooted in an objective reality. They also have the highest divorce rate of any segment of the black population (U.S. Bureau of the Census, 1975).

While they may fear the responsibilities of marriage and the possibility of failure, black men do have an egalitarian attitude toward that institution. As early as adolescence, they expect egalitarian marriage roles concerning authority, housekeeping, and care of children (Rooks & King, 1973). In comparison to white males, black husbands are more accepting of a wife's employment outside the home (Axelson, 1970). Studies of familial decision-making processes reveal that black marriages are as egalitarian — or unegalitarian — as white ones. Where differences were found, they were related more to class than race. In general, blue-collar husbands of both races exercised more power in decisions in such areas as recreation, joint purchases, and household tasks than their white collar counterparts (Mack, 1974).

Fathers   The role of father is a vexatious one for many men in this society. It is a role that is ill-defined in terms of its function and, to many people, mostly means economic support of the growing child. Whatever the definition, it is evident that the physical care and socialization of children is a task that women primarily carry out. While women are assigned the basic caretaker role for children, men often define their masculinity in terms of the ability to impregnate women and to reproduce prolifically children who are extensions of themselves, especially sons. For many lower-income black males, there is an inseparable link between their self-image as men and their ability to have sexual relations with women and the subsequent birth of children from those sexual acts. At the root of this virility cult is the lack of role fulfillment available to men of the underclass. The class factor is most evident here if we note that middle-class black males sire fewer children than any other group in this society (McKay, 1978).

Once he has sired children, the black father is then faced with the problem of supporting them as well as helping them to cope with environmental forces. Neither of these tasks is very easy for a class of men subject to periodic periods of unemployment and low wages at jobs they do obtain. Some black men deal with this painful psychological dilemma by abdicating the official responsibility of fatherhood and leaving the home. Liebow (1967) found that some men found it easier to show concern and gentleness with the children of women with whom they were cohabiting since they did not have to face fear of failure and feelings of guilt, as was true of children to whom they had normatively defined obligations. However, many low-income fathers do maintain contact with their children and carry out normal paternal functions. Stack (1974) reports that a mother generally regards her children's father as a friend of the family whom she can recruit for help, rather than as a father failing his parental duties.

When black fathers are not beset by economic difficulties, their role as fathers is often not as marginal as imagined. Those social scientists who have studied ordinary black fathers have found them to be significant others to their children. The black father is not simply a shadowy figure who provides them with money or metes out punishment. He is a frame of reference, the person in general most respected and admired, and the most likely to be emulated by the children.

Scanzoni (1971) reports that the father was the male figure most admired by children of both sexes. However, black children are not uncritically accepting of the male parent. His salience to the child is often contingent on what he does or fails to do for him and his ability to provide critical resources such as teaching him coping skills and general value orientations (Taylor, 1976). Middle-class black fathers are more capable of this and, consequently, participate more in child care than do their white counterparts, are very child-oriented, and view their roles as different from the mothers' (Gillette, 1960; Daneal, 1975).

MALE SEXISM AND BLACK FEMINISM

Although black men represent one of the most powerless groups in America, this does not mean they are devoid of sexist feelings or practices. Their own lowly position has effectively prevented them from suppressing their women in the same manner that white males have dominated white females. They have been forced to adopt more egalitarian views towards the role of women as a result of certain historical and social forces. Moreover, as a result of the same intersection of forces, the gap in sex-role equality is not that great between black men and women. Not only is the disparity in income and occupational status less, but black women are actually better educated than black men at most levels (U.S. Bureau of the Census, 1975).

This, however, has not prevented black men from gaining ascendency over women by virtue of their gender. Despite having more education, black women consistently have a higher rate of unemployment and earn less income than black males. In addition, they suffer many of the liabilities of white women due to the pervasiveness of sexism in this society. The black woman is the victim of sexual stereotyping, forced in many cases to bear the responsibility for family planning alone, and expected to cater to male desires and assume a subordinate role. Whereas her main concerns relate to the practice of racism and economic survival, she is increasingly becoming preoccupied with the problems of gender per se. As a result we have witnessed a burgeoning of black feminist organizations to tackle women's issues (Staples, 1973).

At this point in time, black women are relatively uninvolved in the mainstream women's movement, but feminism as an ideology is beginning to take hold. It was manifest in the demands of coeds at predominantly black, all-female Spellman College that the new college president should be a black woman. It is symbolized in the manifesto of the National Black Feminist Organization (Note 2):

> "We will remind the Black Liberation Movement that there can't be liberation for half a race. We must, together, as a people, work to eliminate racism from without the Black community which is trying to destroy us as an entire people, but we must remember that sexism is destroying and crippling us from within.

Among the sexist acts they speak of are the subordinate roles black women are forced to play in black organizations and institutions, a practice best exemplified by a black civil rights leader's famous statement that the black woman's position in that movement "should be prone."

The black male's response to this charge has been slow in forthcoming. To a large extent he believes, as do many white males, that the women's demand for equal rights is a threat to whatever masculinity he's been allowed by the larger society. There is some resentment, particularly among middle-class black males, about what is considered the preferential treatment in jobs for black women who are used as a double minority in Affirmative Action hiring. It has not been overlooked that the only black named to President Carter's cabinet was a woman, with newspaper reports emphasizing that there were two women appointed to the cabinet (the other being white). Obviously, this pro-women attitude is forcing some changes in black male behavior. One notes a discernible erosion of the double sexual standard, more men participating in childcare and sharing of housework and decisions. One contingency in retarding these changes in male behavior is the excess number of women over men in the black community. Due to the severe competition for the low pool of eligible black males, many black women are still forced to take marriage on male terms (Wheeler, Note 3).

PROBLEMS AND PROSPECTS

In discussing the burden of masculinity and race for the black male, one has to assign priorities. It is quite clear that the problems caused by the legacy of racism are paramount. Although many middle-class black males will have to concentrate on the changing role of women, black males of the working class must continue to confront the challenge of economic survival. It is questionable how much emphasis should be placed on re-orienting their concept of traditional sex roles when they, in many cases, have not been allowed equal access to those roles. Sex-role equality for the poorest of the poor is a meager victory at best. The machination of social forces has placed black men in a position where one-fourth are without jobs, they are the only sex-race group whose life expectancy actually declined in the last decade, many are not keeping pace with the educational progress of other sex-race groups, and they have made less progress in white-collar areas relative to white males than black females have made relative to white females (Staples, 1975).

At the same time the changing role expectations of black women will necessitate some adjustments on the part of black males. These changes will be most pronounced in the middle class, since they have more resources to share, and it is among this group that the demands for sex-role equality will be heard. Such changes may be slow in coming due to countervailing forces. When men have a large pool of women to select from, they can afford to choose those who will conform to traditional sex-role norms; and women who are selecting from a limited pool of eligible males may opt to adhere to a subordinate role rather than do without. Many black women, however, will refuse to permit men to dominate the definitions of black womanhood and will demand parity in the home and in all aspects of black life.

What will happen in the future is hard to determine. Many black men will continue to fall behind black women in their educational and economic progress. The result may be a black female dominance of high-status positions. Some segments of white society will be pleased with this result because they perceive black women to be less threatening to their racial hegemony. At the same time, large numbers of black women — and men — will continue to occupy the bottom rung of the socio-economic strata. Whether either is better off than the other is an academic question, the need is for both black and women's liberation. The issues of masculinity and of race are too interwoven to separate at this time. What is necessary is a serious effort by this society to eliminate both racism and sexism from our lives.

NOTES

1. National Urban League. *Quarterly economic report on the black worker.* Washington, D.C.: National Urban League, Research Department, 1975.
2. National Black Feminist Organization. Statement, 1973.
3. Wheeler, W. *The sex ratio: Utopian ambience or catalytic agent to black female abuse.* Paper presented at the meeting of the American Personnel Guidance Association, Chicago, 1976.

REFERENCES

Axelson, L. The working wife: Differences in perception among Negro and white males. *Journal of Marriage and the Family,* 1970, *32,* 457–464.

Benjamin, R. *Factors related to conceptions of the male familial role by black youth.* State College, MI: Mississippi State University Press, 1971.

Blassingame, J. *The slave community.* New York: Oxford, 1972.

Broderick, C. Social heterosexual development among urban Negroes and whites. *Journal of Marriage and the Family,* 1965, *27,* 200–203.

Clark, R. *Dark Ghetto.* New York: Harper and Row, 1965.

Curtis, L. *Violence, race and culture.* Lexington, MA: Lexington, 1975.

Daneal, J. *A definition of fatherhood as expressed by black fathers.* Unpublished doctoral dissertation, University of Pittsburgh, 1975.

Elkins, S. *Slavery: A problem in American institutional and intellectual life.* Chicago: University of Chicago Press, 1959.

Epstein, C. Positive effects of the multiple negative: Explaining the success of black professional women. In J. Huber (Ed.), *Changing women in a changing society.* Chicago: University of Chicago Press, 1973.

Frazier, E. F. *The Negro family in the United States.* Chicago: University of Chicago Press, 1939.

Genovese, E. The slave family, women — A reassessment of matriarchy, emasculation, weakness. *Southern Voices,* 1974, *1,* 9–16.

Gillette, T. *Maternal employment and family structure as influenced by social class and role.* Unpublished doctoral dissertation, University of Texas, 1960.

Glick, P., & Mills, R. *Black families: Marriage patterns and living arrangements.* Atlanta: Atlanta University, 1974.

Grier, W., & Cobbs, P. *Black rage.* New York: Basic Books, 1968.

Gutman, H. *The black family in slavery and freedom, 1750–1925.* New York: Pantheon, 1976.

Haley, A. *Roots.* Garden City, NY: Doubleday, 1976.

Halpern, F. *Survival: Black/White.* New York: Pergamon, 1973.

Hammond, B., & Ladner, J. Socialization into sexual behavior in a Negro slum ghetto. In C. Broderick & J. Bernard (Eds.), *The individual, sex and society.* Baltimore: John Hopkins Press, 1969.

Hill, R. *The strengths of black families.* New York: Emerson-Hall, 1973.

Johnson, L. B. Sexual behavior of southern blacks. In R. Staples (Ed.), *The black family: Essays and studies (2nd ed.).* Belmont, CA: Wadsworth, 1978.

Jordan, W. *White over black: American attitudes toward the Negro 1550–1812.* Durham, N.C.: University of North Carolina Press, 1968.

Larson, D. Social factors in the frequency of romantic involvement among adolescents. *Adolescence,* 1976, *11,* 7–12.

Liebow, E. *Tally's corner.* Boston: Little, Brown and Company, 1967.

Mack, D. The power relationship in black and white families. *Journal of Personality and Social Psychology,* 1974, *30,* 409–413.

McCarthy, J., & Yancey, W. Uncle Tom and Mr. Charlie: Metaphysical pathos in the study of racism and personal disorganization. *American Journal of Sociology*, 1971, 76, 648–672.

McKay, R. One child families and atypical sex ratios in an elite black community. In R. Staples (Ed.), *The black family: Essays and Studies* (2nd ed.). Belmont, CA: Wadsworth, 1978.

Morse, R. Some factors influencing the masculinity of urban black male high school seniors. *Dissertation Abstracts, International*, 1975, 35.

More women enrolling in graduate school. *U.S. Department of Commerce News*, January 19, 1977.

Nobles, W. Psychological research and the black self-concept: A critical review. *Journal of Social Issues*, 1973, 291, 11–31.

Paulme, D. *Women of tropical africa*. Berkeley: University of California Press, 1971.

Rainwater, L. Crucible of identity: The lower class Negro family, *Daedalus*, 1966, 95, 258–264.

Reiss, I. Premarital sexual permissiveness among Negros and whites. *American Sociological Review*, 1964, 29, 688–698.

Rooks, E., & King, R. A study of the marriage role expectations of black adolescents. *Adolescence*, 1973, 8, 317–324.

Scanzoni, J. *The black family in modern society*. Boston: Allyn and Bacon, 1971.

Schulman, G. Race, sex and violence: A laboratory test of the sexual threat of the black male hypothesis. *American Journal of Sociology*, 1974, 79, 1260–1277.

Stack, C. *All our kin*. New York: Harper and Row, 1974.

Staples, R. *The black woman in America*. Chicago: Nelson-Hall, 1973.

Staples, R. To be young, black and oppressed. *The Black Scholar*, 1975, 6, 2–9.

Staples, R. *Introduction to black sociology*. New York: McGraw-Hill, 1976.

Stember, C. *Sexual racism*. New York: Elsevier Press, 1976.

Taylor, R., Psychosocial development of black youth. *Journal of Black Studies*, 1976, 6, 353–372.

U.S. Bureau of the Census. *The social and economic status of the black population in the United States*. Washington, D.C.: U.S. Government Printing Office, 1975.

U.S. Department of Labor. *Women who head families: A socioeconomic analysis*. Washington, D.C.: U.S. Government Printing Office, 1976. (a)

U.S. Department of Labor. *Youth in the labor force: An area study*. Washington, D.C.: U.S. Government Printing Office, 1976. (b)

Vontress, C. The black male personality. *The Black Scholar*, 1971, 2, 10–17.

Wilkinson, D., & Taylor, R. *The black male in America: Perspectives on his status in contemporary society*. Chicago: Nelson-Hall, 1977.

Richard Majors

COOL POSE:

THE PROUD SIGNATURE OF BLACK SURVIVAL

Just when it seemed that we black males were beginning to recover from past injustices inflicted by the dominant white society, we find once again that we are being revisited in a similar vein. President Reagan's de-emphasis of civil rights, affirmative action legislation and social services programs; the rise of black neoconservatives and certain black feminist groups; harshly critical media events on television (e.g., the CBS documentary "The Vanishing Family — Crisis in Black America") and in films (e.g., *The Color Purple*); and the omnipresent problems of unemployment and inadequate health care, housing, and education — all have helped to shape a negative political and social climate toward black men. For many black men this period represents a *New Black Nadir*, or lowest point, and time of deepest depression.

Black people in general, and the black man in particular, look out on a world that does not positively reflect their image. Black men learned long ago that the classic American virtues of thrift, perseverance and hard work would not give us the tangible rewards that accrue to most members of the dominant society. We learned early that we would not be Captains of Industry or builders of engineering wonders. Instead, we channeled our creative energies into construction of a symbolic universe. Therefore we adopted unique poses and postures to offset the externally imposed "zero" image. Because black men were denied access to the dominant culture's acceptable avenues of expression, we created a form of self-expression — the "Cool Pose."[13]

Cool Pose is a term that represents a variety of attitudes and actions that serve the black man as mechanisms for survival, defense and social competence. These attitudes and actions are performed using characterizations and roles as facades and shields.

COOL CULTURE

Historically, coolness was central to the culture of many ancient African civilizations. The Yorubas of Western Nigeria (900 B.C. to 200 A.D.) are cited as an example of an African civilization where cool was integrated into the social fabric of the community.[4] Uses of cool ranged from the way a young man carried himself before his peers to the way he impressed his elders during the initiation ritual. Coolness helped to build character and pride for individuals in such groups and is regarded as a precolonial cultural adaptation. With the advent of the modern African slave trade, cool became detached from its indigenous cultural setting and emerged equally as a survival mechanism.

Where the European saw America as the promised land, the African saw it as the land of oppression. Today, reminders of Black America's oppressive past continue in the form of chronic underemployment, inadequate housing, inferior schools, and poor health care. Because of these conditions many black men have become frustrated, angry, confused and impatient.

To help ease the pain associated with these conditions, black men have taken to alcoholism, drug abuse, homicide, and suicide. In learning to mistrust the words and actions of dominant white people, black males have learned to make great use of "poses" and "postures" which connote control, toughness, and detachment. All these forms arise from the mistrust that the black males feel towards the dominant society.

For these black males, particular poses and postures show the white man that "although you may have tried to hurt me time and time again, I can take it (and if I am hurting or weak, I'll never let you know). They are saying loud and clear to the white establishment, "I am strong, full of pride, and a survivor." Accordingly, any failures in the real world become the black man's secret.

THE EXPRESSIVE LIFE STYLE

On the other hand, those poses and postures that have an expressive quality or nature have become known in the literature as the "expressive life style."[5] The expressive life style is a way in which the black male can act cool by actively displaying particular performances that emphasize creative expression. Thus, while black people historically have been forced into conciliatory and often demeaning positions in American culture, there is nothing conciliatory about the expressive life style.

This dynamic vitality will not be denied even in limited stereotypical roles — as demonstrated by Hattie McDaniel, the maid in *Gone With the Wind* or Bill "Bojangles" Robinson as the affable servant in the Shirley Temple movies. This abiding need for creative self-expression knows no bounds and asserts itself whether on the basketball court or in dancing. We can see it in black athletes — with their stylish dunking of the basketball, their spontaneous dancing in the end zone, and their different styles of handshakes (e.g., "high fives") — and in black entertainers with their various choreographed "cool" dance steps. These are just a few examples of black individuals in their professions who epitomize this creative expression. The expressive life style is a dynamic — not a static — art form, and new aesthetic forms are always evolving (e.g., "rap-talking" and breakdancing). The expressive life style, then, is the passion that invigorates the demeaning life of blacks in White America. It is a dynamic vitality that transforms the mundane into the sublime and makes the routine spectacular.

A CULTURAL SIGNATURE

Cool Pose, manifested by the expressive life style, is also an aggressive assertion of masculinity. It emphatically says "white man, this is my turf. You can't match me here." Though he may be impotent in the political and corporate world, the black man demonstrates his potency in athletic competition, entertainment and the pulpit with a verve that borders on the spectacular. Through the virtuosity of a performance, he tips the socially imbalanced scales in his favor. "See me, touch me, hear me, but, white man, you can't copy me." This is the subliminal message which black males signify in their oftentimes flamboyant performance. Cool Pose, then, becomes the cultural signature for such black males.

Being cool is a unique response to adverse social, political and economic conditions. Cool provides control, inner strength, stability and confidence. Being cool, illustrated in its various poses and postures, becomes a very powerful and necessary tool in the black man's constant fight for his soul. The poses and postures of cool guard, preserve and protect his pride, dignity and respect to such an extent that the black male is willing to risk a great deal for it. One black man said it well: "The white man may control everything about me — that is, except my pride and dignity. That he can't have. That is mine and mine alone."

THE COST

Cool Pose, however, is not without its price. Many black males fail to discriminate the appropriate uses of Cool Pose and act cool much of the time, without regard to time or space.[6] Needless to say, this can cause severe problems. In many situations a black man won't allow himself to express or show any form of weakness or fear or other feelings and emotions. He assumes a facade of strength, held at all costs, rather than "blow his front," and thus his cool. Perhaps black men have become so conditioned to keeping up their guard against oppression from the dominant white society that this particular attitude and behavior represent for them their best safeguard against further mental or physical abuse. However, this same behavior makes it very difficult for these males to let their guard down and show affection, even for people that they actually care about or for people that may really care about them (e.g., girlfriends, wives, mothers, fathers, "good" friends, etc.).

When the art of being cool is used to put cool behaviors ahead of emotions or needs, the result of such repression of feelings can be frustration. Such frustrations sometimes cause aggression which often is taken out on those individuals closest to such men — other black people. It is sadly ironic, then, that the same elements of cool that allow for survival in the larger society may hurt black people by contributing to one of the more complex problems facing black people today — black-on-black crime.

Further, while Cool Pose enables black males to maintain stability in the face of white power, it may through inappropriate use render many of them unable to move with the mainstream or evolve in healthy ways. When misused, cool can suppress the motivation to learn, accept or become exposed to stimuli, cultural norms, aesthetics, mannerisms, values, etiquette, information or networks that could help them overcome problems caused by white racism. Finally, in a society which has as its credo, "A man's home is his castle," it is ironic that the masses of black men have no castle to protect. Their minds have become their psychological castle, defended by impenetrable cool. Thus, Cool Pose is the bittersweet symbol of a socially disesteemed group that shouts, "We are" in face of a hostile and indifferent world that everywhere screams, "You ain't."

COOL AND THE BLACK PSYCHE

To be fully grasped, Cool Pose must be recognized as having gained ideological consensus in the black community. It is not only a quantitatively measured "social reality" but a series of equally "real" rituals of socialization. It is a comprehensive, officially endorsed cultural myth that became entrenched in the black psyche with the beginning of the slave experience. This phenomenon has cut across all socioeconomic groups in the black community, as black men fight to preserve their dignity, pride, respect and masculinity with the attitudes and behaviors of Cool Pose. Cool Pose represents a fundamental structuring of the psyche of the black male and is manifested in some way or another in the daily activities and recreational habits of most black males. There are few other social or psychological constructs that have shaped, directed or controlled the black male to the extent that the various forms of coolness have. It is surprising, then, that for a concept that has the potential to explain problems in black male and black female relationships, black-on-black crime, and black-on-black pregnancies, there is such limited research on this subject.

In the final analysis, Cool Pose may represent the most important yet least researched area with the potential to enhance our understanding and study of black behavior today.

NOTES

1. Majors, R. G. Nikelly, A. G., "Serving the Black Minority: A New Direction for Psychotherapy." *J. for Non-white Concerns*, 11:142–151 (1983).
2. Majors, R. G., "The Effects of 'Cool Pose': What Being Cool Means." *Griot*, pp. 4–5 (Spring, 1985).
3. Nikelly, A. G. & Majors, R. G. "Techniques for Counseling Black Students," *Techniques: J. Remedial Educ. & Counseling*, 2:48–54 (1986).
4. Bascom, W., *The Yoruba of Southwestern Nigeria*. (New York: Holt, Rinehart & Winston, 1969).
5. Rainwater, L., *Behind Ghetto Walls*. (Chicago: Aldine, 1970).
6. Majors, R. G., "Cool Pose: A New Hypothesis in Understanding Anti-Social Behavior in Lower SES Black Males," unpublished manuscript.

Maxine Baca Zinn

CHICANO MEN AND MASCULINITY

Only recently have social scientists begun to systematically study the male role. Although men and their behavior had been assiduously studied (Pleck and Brannon, 1978), masculinity as a specific topic had been ignored. The scholar's disregard of male gender in the general population stands in contrast to the preoccupation with masculinity that has long been exhibited in the literature on minority groups. The social science literature on Blacks and Chicanos specifically reveals a long-standing interest in masculinity. A common assumption is that gender roles among Blacks are less dichotomous than among Whites, and more dichotomous among Chicanos. Furthermore, these differences are assumed to be a function of the distinctive historical and cultural heritage of these groups. Gender segregation and stratification, long considered to be a definitive characteristic of Chicanos, is illustrated in Miller's descriptive summary of the literature:

> Sex roles are rigidly dichotomized with the male conforming to the dominant–aggressive archetype, and the female being the polar opposite — subordinate and passive. The father is the unquestioned patriarch — the family provider, protector and judge. His word is law and demands strict obedience. Presumably, he is perpetually obsessed with the need to prove his manhood, oftentimes through excessive drinking, fighting, and/or extramarital conquests (1979:217).

The social science image of the Chicano male is rooted in three interrelated propositions: (1) That a distinctive cultural heritage has created a rigid cult of masculinity, (2) That the masculinity cult generates distinctive familial and so-

M. Baca Zinn, "Chicano Family Research: Conceptual distortions and alternative directions" appeared in the *JES* 7:3. Reprinted from *The Journal of Ethnic Studies* 10:2.

cialization patterns, and (3) That these distinctive patterns ill-equip Chicanos (both males and females) to adapt successfully to the demands of modern society.

The machismo concept constitutes a primary explanatory variable for both family structure and overall subordination. Mirande critically outlines the reasoning in this interpretation:

> The macho male demands complete deference, respect and obedience not only from the wife but from the children as well. In fact, social scientists maintain that this rigid male-dominated family structure has negative consequences for the personality development of Mexican American children. It fails to engender achievement, independence, self-reliance or self worth — values which are highly esteemed in American society. . . . The authoritarian Mexican American family constellation then produces dependence and subordination and reinforces a present time orientation which impedes achievement (1977:749).

In spite of the widely held interpretation associated with male dominance among Chicanos, there is a growing body of literature which refutes past images created by social scientists. My purpose is to examine empirical challenges to machismo, to explore theoretical developments in the general literature on gender, and to apply both of these to alternative directions for studying and understanding Chicano men and masculinity. My central theme is that while ethnic status may be associated with differences in masculinity, those differences can be explained by structural variables rather than by references to common cultural heritage.

THEORETICAL CHALLENGES TO CULTURAL INTERPRETATIONS: THE UNIVERSALITY OF MALE DOMINANCE

The generalization that culture is a major determinant of gender is widely accepted in the social sciences. In the common portrayal of Chicanos, exaggerated male behavior is assumed to stem from inadequate masculine identity.

> The social science literature views machismo as a compensation for feelings of inadequacy and worthlessness. This interpretation is rooted in the application of psychoanalytic concepts to explain both Mexican and Chicano gender roles. The widely accepted interpretation is that machismo is the male attempt to compensate for feelings of internalized inferiority by exaggerated masculinity. "At the same time that machismo is an expression of power, its origin is ironically linked to powerlessness and subordination." The common origins of inferiority and machismo are said to lie in the historical conquest of Mexico by Spain involving the exploitation of Indian women by Spanish men thus producing the hybrid Mexican people having an inferiority complex based on the mentality of a conquered people (Baca Zinn, 1980:20).

The assumption that male dominance among Chicanos is rooted in their history and embedded in their culture needs to be critically assessed against recent discussions concerning the universality of male dominance. Many anthropologists consider all known societies to be male dominant to a degree (Stockard and Johnson 1980:4). It has been argued that in all known societies male activities are more highly valued than female activities, and that this can be explained in terms of the division of labor between domestic and public spheres of society (Rosaldo, 1973). Women's child-bearing abilities limit their participation in public sphere activities and allow men the freedom to participate in and control the public sphere. Thus in the power relations between the sexes, men have been found to be dominant over women "and to the greater control of economic resources (Spence 1978:4).

While differing explanations of the cause of male dominance have been advanced, recent literature places emphasis on networks of social relations between men and women and the status structures within which their interactions occur. This emphasis is crucial because it alerts us to the importance of structural variables in understanding sex stratification. Furthermore, it casts doubt on interpretations which treat culture (the systems of shared beliefs and orientations unique to groups) as the cause of male dominance. If male dominance is universal, then it cannot be reduced to the culture of a particular category of people.

CHALLENGES TO MACHISMO

Early challenges to machismo emerged in the protest literature of the 1960s and 1970s and have continued unabated. Challenges are theoretical, empirical, and impressionistic. Montiel, in the first critique of machismo, set the stage for later refutations by charging that psychoanalytic constructs resulted in indiscriminate use of machismo, and that this made findings and interpretations highly suspect (1970). Baca Zinn (1975:25) argued that viewing machismo as a compensation for inferiority (whether its ultimate cause is seen as external or internal to the oppressed), in effect blames Chicanos for their own subordination. Sosa Riddell proposed that the machismo myth is exploited by an oppressive society which encourages a defensive stance on the part of Chicano men (1974). Delgado (1974:6) in similar fashion, wrote that stereotyping acts which have nothing to do with machismo and labeling them as such was a form of societal control.

Recent social science literature on Chicanos has witnessed an ongoing series of empirical challenges to the notion that machismo is the norm in marital relationships (Grebler, Moore and Guzman, 1970; Hawkes and Taylor, 1975; Ybarra, 1977; Cromwell and Cromwell, 1978; Cromwell and Ruiz, 1979; Baca Zinn, 1980a). The evidence presented in this research suggests that in the realm of marital decision making, egalitarianism is far more prevalent than macho dominance.

Cromwell and Ruiz find that the macho characterization prevalent in the social science literature is "very compatible with the social deficit model of Hispanic life and culture" (1979:355). Their re-analysis of four major studies on marital decision making (Cromwell, Corrales and Torsellio, 1973; Delchereo, 1969; Hawkes and Taylor, 1975 and Cromwell and Cromwell, 1978) concludes that "the studies suggest that while wives make the fewest unilateral decisions and husbands make more, joint decisions are by far the most common in these samples. . ." (1979:370).

Other studies also confirm the existence of joint decision making in Chicano families and furthermore they provide insights as to factors associated with joint decision making, most importantly that of wives' employment. For example,

Ybarra's survey of 100 married Chicano couples in Fresno, California found a range of conjugal role patterns with the majority of married Chicano couples sharing decision making. Baca Zinn (1980a) examined the effects of wives' employment outside of the home and level of education through interviews and participation in an urban New Mexico setting. The study revealed differences in marital roles and marital power between families with employed wives and nonemployed wives. "In all families where women were not employed, tasks and decision making were typically sex segregated. However, in families with employed wives, tasks and decision making were shared" (1980a:51).

Studies of the father role in Chicano families also called into question the authoritative unfeeling masculinized male figure (Mejia, 1976; Luzod and Arce, 1979). These studies are broadly supportive of the marital role research which points to a more democratic egalitarian approach to family roles. Luzod and Arce conclude:

> It is not our contention to say that no sex role differences occur within Chicano families, but rather demonstrate the level of importance which both the father and mother give to respective duties as parents as well as the common hopes and desires they appear to share equally for their progeny than was commonly thought. It therefore appears erroneous to focus only on maternal influences in the Chicano family since Chicano fathers are seen as being important to the children and moreover may provide significant positive influences on the development of their children (1979:19).

Recent empirical refutations of super-masculinity in Chicano families have provided the basis of discussions of the Chicano male role (Valdex, 1980; Mirandé, 1979, 1981). While these works bring together in clear fashion impressionistic and empirical refutations of machismo, they should be considered critical reviews rather than conceptual refutations. In an important essay entitled, "Machismo: Rucas, Chingasos, y Chingaderas" (1981), Mirandé critically assesses the stereotypic components of machismo, yet he asserts that it also has authentic components having to do with the resistance of oppression. While this is a significant advance, it requires conceptual focus and analysis.

UNANSWERED QUESTIONS, UNRESOLVED ISSUES AND UNRECOGNIZED PROBLEMS

The works discussed above provide a refutation of the simplistic, one-dimensional model of Chicano masculinity. As such they constitute important contributions to the literature. My own argument does not contradict the general conclusion that machismo is a stereotype, but attempts to expand it by posing some theoretical considerations.

In their eagerness to dispute machismo and the negative characteristics associated with the trait, critics have tended to neglect the phenomenon of male dominance at societal, institutional, and interpersonal levels. While the cultural stereotype of machismo has been in need of critical analysis, male dominance does exist among Chicanos. Assertions such as the following require careful examination:

> There is sufficient evidence to seriously question the traditional male dominant view (Mirandé, 1979:47).

Although male dominance may not typify marital decision making in Chicano families, it should not be assumed that it is nonexistent either in families or in other realms of interaction and organization.

Research by Ybarra (1977) and Baca Zinn (1980) found both egalitarian and male dominant patterns of interaction in Chicano families. They found these patterns to be associated with distinct social conditions of families, most notably wives' employment. The finding that male dominance can be present in some families but not in others, depending on specific social characteristics of family members, is common in family research.

The important point is that we need to know far more than we do about which social conditions affecting Chicanos are associated with egalitarianism and male dominance at both micro and macro levels of organization. Placing the question within this framework should provide significant insights by enlarging the inquiry beyond that of the culture stereotype of machismo. It is necessary to guard against measuring and evaluating empirical reality against this stereotype. The dangers of using a negative ideal as a normative guide are raised by Eichler (1980). In a provocative work, she raises the possibility that the literature challenging gender stereotypes, while explicitly attempting to overcome past limitations of the gender roles research may operate to reinforce the stereotype. Thus, it could be argued that energy expended in refuting machismo may devote too much attention to the concept, and overlook whole areas of inquiry. We have tended to assume that ethnic groups vary in the demands imposed on men and women. "Ethnic differences in sex roles have been discussed by large numbers of social scientists" (Romer and Cherry, 1980:246). However, these discussions have treated differences as cultural or subcultural in nature. Davidson and Gordon are critical of subcultural explanations of differences in gender roles because they "fail to investigate the larger political and economic situations that affect groups and individuals. They also fail to explain how definition of the roles of women and men, as well as those associated with ethnicity, vary over time and from place to place" (1979:124).

1. What specific social conditions are associated with variation in general roles among Chicanos?
2. If there are ethnic differences in gender roles, to what extent are these a function of shared beliefs and orientations (culture) and to what extent are they a function of men's and women's place in the network of social relationships (structure)?
3. To what extent are gender roles among Chicanos more segregated and male dominated than among other social groups?
4. How does ethnicity contribute to the subjective meaning of masculinity (and femininity)?

STRUCTURAL INTERPRETATIONS OF GENDER ROLES

There is a good deal of theoretical support for the contention that masculine roles and masculine identity may be shaped by a wide range of variables having less to do with culture than with common structural position. Chafetz calls into question the cultural stereotype of machismo by proposing that it is a socioeconomic characteristic:

> . . . more than most other Americans, the various Spanish speaking groups in this country (Mexican American, Puerto Rican, Cuban), . . .

stress dominance, aggressiveness, physical prowess and other stereotypical masculine traits. Indeed the masculine sex role for this group is generally described by reference to the highly stereotyped notion of machismo. In fact, a strong emphasis on masculine aggressiveness and dominance may be characteristic of most groups in the lower ranges of the socioeconomic ladder (1979:54).

Without discounting the possibility that cultural differences in male roles exist, it makes good conceptual sense to explain these differences in terms of sociostructural factors. Davidson and Gordon suggest that the following social conditions affect the development of gender roles in ethnic groups: (1) the position of the group in the stratification system, (2) the existence of an ethnic community, (3) the degree of self identification with the minority group (1978:120). Romer and Cherry more specifically propose that ethnic or subcultural sex role definitions can be viewed as functions of the specific and multiple role demands made on a given subgroup such as skilled or unskilled workers, consumers, etc., and the cultural prism through which these role expectations are viewed (1980:246). Both of these discussions underscore the importance of the societal placement of ethnics in the shaping of gender roles. This line of reasoning should not be confused with "culture of poverty" models which posit distinctive subcultural traits among the lower class. However, it can be argued that class position affects both normative and behavioral dimensions of masculinity.

The assumption that Chicanos are more strongly sex typed in terms of masculine identity is called into question by a recent study. Senour and Warren conducted research to question whether ethnic identity is related to masculine and feminine sex role orientation among Blacks, Anglos and Chicanos. While significant sex differences were found in all categories, Senour and Warren concluded that Mexican American males did not emerge as super masculine in comparison to Black and Anglo males (1976:2).

There is some support for this interpretation. In roles dealing with masculinity among Black males, Parker and Kleiner (1977) and Staples (1978) find that role performance must be seen in light of the structurally generated inequality in employment, housing, and general social conditions. Staples writes:

> . . . men often define their masculinity in terms of the ability to impregnate women and to reproduce prolifically children who are extensions of themselves, especially sons. For many lower income black males there is an inseparable link between their self image as men and their ability to have sexual relations with women and the subsequent birth of children from those sexual acts. At the root of this virility cult is the lack of role fulfillment available to men of the underclass. The class factor is most evident here, if we note that middle class black males sire fewer children than any other group in this society (1978:178).

What is most enlightening about Staples' discussion of masculinity is that it treats male behavior and male identity not as a subcultural phenomenon, but as a consequence of social structural factors associated with race and class.

A thoughtful discussion of inequality, race, and gender is provided by Lewis (1977). Her analysis enlarges upon Rosaldo's model of the domestic public split as the source of female subordination and male dominance discussed earlier. It has pertinent structural considerations. Lewis acknowledges the notion of a structural opposition between the domestic and public spheres which offers useful insights in understanding differential participation and evaluation of men and women. Nevertheless, she argues that its applicability to racial minority men and women may be questionable since historically Black men (like Black women) have been excluded from participation in public sphere institutions. Lewis asserts:

> What the black experience suggests is that differential participation in the public sphere is a symptom rather than a cause of structural inequality. While inequality is manifested in the exclusion of a group from public life, it is actually generated in the groups' unequal access to power and resources in a hierarchically arranged social order. Relationships of dominance and subordination, therefore, emerge from a basic structural opposition between groups which is reflected in exclusion of the subordinate group from public life (1977:342).

Lewis then argues that among racially oppressed groups, it is important to distinguish between the public life of the dominant and the dominated societies. Using this framework we recognize a range of male participation from token admittance to the public life of the dominant group to its attempts to destroy the public life within a dominated society. She points to the fact that Mexican American men have played strong public roles in their own dominated society, and as Mexican Americans have become more assimilated to the dominating society, sex roles have become less hierarchical. The significant feature of this argument has to do with the way in which attention is brought to shifts in power relationships between the dominant society and racial minorities, and how these shifts effect changes in relationships between the sexes. Lewis' analysis makes it abundantly clear that minority males' exclusion from the public sphere requires further attention.

CHICANO MASCULINITY AS A RESPONSE
TO STRATIFICATION AND EXCLUSION

There are no works, either theoretical or empirical, specifically devoted to the impact of structural exclusion on male roles and male identity. However, there are suggestions that the emphasis on masculinity might stem from the fact that alternative roles and identity sources are systematically blocked from men in certain social categories. Lillian Rubin, for example, described the martial role egalitarianism of middle class professional husbands as opposed to the more traditional authoritarian role of working class husbands in the following manner:

> . . . the professional male is more secure, has more status and prestige than the working class man, factors which enable him to assume a less overtly authoritarian role within the family. There are, after all, other places, other situations where his authority and power are tested and accorded legitimacy. At the same time, the demands of his work role for a satellite wife require that he risk the consequences of a more egalitarian family ideology. In contrast, for the working class men, there are few such rewards in the world outside the home. The family is usually the only place where he can exercise power, demand obedience to his authority.

> Since his work role makes no demands for wifely participation, he is un-
> der fewer and less immediate external pressures to accept the egalitarian
> ideology (rubin, 1976:99).

Of course, Rubin is contrasting behaviors of men in different social classes, but
the same line of thinking is paralleled in Ramos' speculation that for some Chicanos what has been called "machismo" may be a "way of feeling capable in a
world that makes it difficult for Chicanos to demonstrate their capabilities" (Ramos, 1979:61).

   We must understand that while maleness is highly valued in our society, it
interacts with other categorical distinctions in both manifestation and meaning.
As Stoll (1974:124) presents this idea, our society is structured to reward some
categories in preference to others (e.g., men over women) but the system is not
perfectly rational. First the rewards are scarce, second, other categories such as
race, ethnicity and other statuses are included in the formula. Furthermore, the
interaction of different categories with masculinity contributes to multiple societal meanings of masculinity, so that "one can never be sure this aspect of one's
self will not be called into dispute. One is left having to account for oneself,
thus to be on the defensive" (Stoll, 1974:124). It is in light of the societal importance attributed to masculinity that we must assess Stoll's contention that
"gender identity is a more profound personal concern for the male in our society
than it is for women, because women can take it for granted that they are female" (Stoll, 1974:105). This speculation may have implications for Chicanos as
well. Perhaps it will be found that ethnic differences in the salience of gender
are not only one of degree but that their relative significance has different meanings. In other words, gender may not be a problematic identifier for women if
they can take if for granted, though it may be primary because many still participate in society through their gender roles. On the other hand, men in certain
social categories have had more roles and sources of identity open to them.
However, this has not been the case for Chicanos or other men of color. Perhaps
manhood takes on greater importance for those who do not have access to socially valued roles. Being male is one sure way to acquire status when other
roles are systematically denied by the workings of society. This suggests that
an emphasis on masculinity is not due to a collective internalized inferiority,
rooted in a subcultural orientation. To be "hombre" may be a reflection of both
ethnic and gender components and may take on greater significance when other
roles and sources of masculine identity are structurally blocked. Chicanos have
been excluded from participation in the dominant society's political–economic
system. Therefore, they have been denied resources and the accompanying authority accorded men in other social categories. My point that gender may take
on a unique and greater significance for men of color is not to justify traditional
masculinity, but to point to the need for understanding societal conditions that
might contribute to the meaning of gender among different social categories. It
may be worthwhile to consider some expressions of masculinity as attempts to
gain some measure of control in a society that categorically denies or grants
people control over significant realms of their lives.

   Turner makes this point about the male posturing of Black men: "Boastful,
or meek, these performances are attempts by black men to actualize control in
some situation" (Turner, 1977:128). Much the same point is made in discussions
of Chicanos. The possibility has been raised that certain aggressive behaviors

on the part of Chicano men was "a calculated response to hostility, exclusion, and racial domination," and a "conscious rejection of the dominant society's definition of Mexicans as passive, lazy, and indifferent" (Baca Zinn, 1975:23). Mirandé (1981:35) also treats machismo as an adaptive characteristic, associated with visible and manifest resistance of Chicano men to racial oppression. To view Chicano male behavior in this light is not to disregard possible maladaptive consequences of overcompensatory masculinity, but rather to recast masculinity in terms of responses to structural conditions.

Differences in normative and behavioral dimensions of masculinity would be well worth exploring. Though numerous recent studies have challenged macho male dominance in the realm of family decision making, there is also evidence that patriarchal *ideology* can be manifested even in Chicano families where decision making is not male dominant. Baca Zinn's findings of *both* male dominant and egalitarian families revealed also that the ideology of patriarchy was expressed in all families studied:

> Patriarchal ideology was expressed in statements referring to the father as the "head" of the family as the "boss," as the one "in charge." Informants continually expressed their beliefs that it "should be so." Findings confirmed that while male dominance was a cultural ideal, employed wives openly challenged that dominance on a behavioral level (1979:15).

It is possible that such an ideology is somehow associated with family solidarity. This insight is derived from Michel's analysis of family values (cited in Goode, 1963:57). Drawing on cross cultural studies, she reports:

> . . . the concept of the strength or solidarity of the family is viewed as being identical with the father . . . the unity of the family is identified with the prerogatives of the father.

If this is the case, it is reasonable to suggest that the father's authority is strongly upheld because family solidarity is important in a society that excludes and subordinates Chicanos. The tenacity of patriarchy may be more than a holdover from past tradition. It may also represent a contemporary cultural adaptation to the minority condition of structural discrimination.

CONCLUSION

The assumption that male dominance among Chicanos is exclusively a cultural phenomenon is contradicted by much evidence. While many of the concerns raised in this paper are speculative in nature, they are nevertheless informed by current conceptualization in relevant bodies of literature. They raise the important point that we need further understanding of larger societal conditions in which masculinity is embedded and expressed. This forces us to recognize the disturbing relationship between the stratification axes of race, class and sex. To the extent that systems of social inequality limit men's access to societally valued resources, they also contribute to sexual stratification. Men in some social categories will continue to draw upon and accentuate their masculinity as a socially valued resource. This in turn poses serious threats to sexual equality. We are compelled to move the study of masculinity beyond narrow confines of subcultural roles, and to make the necessary theoretical and empirical connections between the contingencies of sex and gender and the social order.

REFERENCES

Baca Zinn, Maxine.

1975   "Political Familism: Toward Sex Role Equality in Chicano Families." International Journal of Chicano Studies Research. 6:13–26.

1980a "Employment and Education of Mexican American Women: The Interplay of Modernity and Ethnicity in Eight Families." Harvard Educational Review 50:47–62.

1980b "Gender and Ethnic Identity Among Chicanos." Frontiers: V(2)18–24.

Chafetz, Janet Saltzman.

1974   Masculine/Feminine or Human. F. E. Ithica, Ill.: Peacock Publishers, Inc.

Cromwell, Vicky L. and Ronald E. Cromwell.

1978   "Perceived Dominance in Decision-Making and Conflict Resolution Among Anglo, Black and Chicano Couples." Journal of Marriage and the Family. 40(Nov):749–759.

Cromwell, Ronald E. and Rene E. Ruiz.

1979   "The Myth of Macho Dominance in Decision Making Within Mexican and Chicano Families." Hispanic Journal of Behavioral Sciences. 1:355–373.

Davidson, Laurie and Laura Kramer Gordon

1979   "The Sociology of Gender." Rand McNally College Publishing Co.

Delgado, Abelardo.

1974   "Machismo." La Luz. (Dec.):6.

Eichler, Margrit.

1980   The Double Standard: A Feminist Critique of Feminist Social Science. St. Martin's Press.

Grebler, Leo, Joan W. Moore and Ralph C. Guzman.

1970   The Mexican American People: The Nation's Second Largest Minority. The Free Press.

Hawkes, Glenn R. and Minna Taylor.

1975   "Power Structure in Mexican and Mexican-American Farm Labor Families." Journal of Marriage and the Family. 37:807–811.

Hyde, Janet Shibley and B. G. Rosenberg.

1976   Half the Human Experience. The Psychology of Women. D. C. Heath and Company.

Lewis, Diane K.

1977   "A Response to Inequality: Black Women, Racism, and Sexism." SIGNS: Journal of Women in Culture and Society. 3:339–361.

Luzod, Jimmy A. and Carlos H. Arce.

1979   "An Exploration of the Father Role in the Chicano Family." Paper presented at the National Symposium on the Mexican American Child. Santa Barbara, California.

Mejia, Daniel P.

1976   Cross-Ethnic Father Role: Perceptions of Middle Class Anglo American Parents. Doctoral Dissertation, University of California, Irvine.

Miller, Michael V.

1975   "Variations in Mexican-American Family Life: A Review Synthesis." Paper presented at Rural Sociological Society, San Francisco, California.

Mirandé, Alfredo.

1977   "The Chicano Family: A Reanalysis of Conflicting Views." Journal of Marriage and the Family. 39:747–756.

1979   "A Reinterpretation of Male Dominance in the Chicano Family." Family Coordinator. 28(4), 473–497.

1981   "Machismo: Rucas, Chingasos, y Chingaderas." De Colores, Forthcoming.

Montiel, Miguel.

1970   "The Social Science Myth of the Mexican American Family." El Grito. 3:56–63.

Parker Seymour and Robert J. Kleiner.

1977   "Social and Psychological Dimensions of the Family Role Performance of the Negro

Male." Pp. 102–117 in Doris Y. Wilkinson and Ronald L. Taylor (editors), The Black Male in America. Nelson Hall.

Pleck, Joseph H. and Robert Brannon.
  1978 "Male Roles and the Male Experience: Introduction." Journal of Social Issues. 34:1–4.

Ramos, Reyes.
  1979 "The Mexican American: Am I Who They Say I Am?" Pp. 49–66 in Arnulfo D. Trejo (editor), The Chicanos as We See Ourselves. The University of Arizona Press.

Riddell, Adaljiza Sosa.
  1974 "Chicanas and El Movimiento." Aztlan. 5(1 and 2):155–165.

Romer, Nancy and Debra Cherry.
  1980 "Ethnic and Social Class Differences in Children's Sex-Role Concepts." Sex Roles. 6:245–263.

Rosaldo, Michelle and Louise Lamphere.
  1974 Woman, Culture, and Society. Stanford: Stanford University Press.

Rubin, Lillian.
  1976 Worlds of Pain. Basic Books.

Senour, Maria Neito and Lynda Warren.
  1976 "Sex and Ethnic Differences in Masculinity, Femininity and Anthropology." Paper presented at the meeting of the Western Psychological Association, Los Angeles, California.

Spence, Janet T. and Robert L. Helmreich.
  1978 Masculinity and Femininity: The Psychological Dimensions, Correlates and Antecedents. University of Austin Press.

Staples, Robert.
  1978 "Masculinity and Race: The Dual Dilemma of Black Men." Journal of Social Issues. 34:169–183.

Stockard, Jean and Miriam M. Johnson.
  1980 Sex Roles. Englewood Cliffs, New Jersey: Prentice-Hall.

Stoll, Clarice Stasz.
  1974 Male and Female: Socialization, Social Roles, and Social Structure. William C. Brown Publishers.

Taylor, Ronald L.
  1977 "Socialization to the Black Male Role." Pp. 1–6 in Doris Y. Wilkinson and Ronald L. Taylor (editors), The Black Male in America. Nelson Hall.

Turner, William H.
  1977 "Myths and Stereotypes: The African Man in America." Pp. 122–144 in Doris Y. Wilkinson and Ronald L. Taylor (editors), The Black Male in America. Nelson Hall.

Valdez, Ramiro.
  1980 "The Mexican American Male: A Brief Review of the Literature." Newsletter of the Mental Health Research Project, I.D.R.A. San Antonio: 4–5.

Ybarra-Soriano, Lea.
  1977 Conjugal Role Relationships in the Chicano Family. Ph.D. diss. University of California at Berkeley.

See Harry Brod!
a Monrch among Men

Michael S. Kimmel

JUDAISM, MASCULINITY AND FEMINISM

In the late 1960s, I organized and participated in several large demonstrations against the war in Vietnam. Early on — it must have been 1967 or so — over 10,000 of us were marching down Fifth Avenue in New York urging the withdrawal of all U.S. troops. As we approached one corner, I noticed a small but vocal group of counter-demonstrators, waving American flags and shouting patriotic slogans. "Go back to Russia!" one yelled. Never being particularly shy, I tried to engage him. "It's my duty as an American to oppose policies I disagree with. This is patriotism!" I answered. "Drop dead, you commie Jew fag!" was his reply.

Although I tried not to show it, I was shaken by his accusation, perplexed and disturbed by the glib association of communism, Judaism, and homosexuality. "Only one out of three," I can say to myself now, "is not especially perceptive." But yet something disturbing remains about that linking of political, religious, and sexual orientations. What links them, I think, is a popular perception that each is not quite a man, that each is less than a man. And while recent developments may belie this simplistic formulation, there is, I believe, a kernel of truth to the epithet, a small piece I want to claim, not as vicious smear, but proudly. I believe that my Judaism did directly contribute to my activism against that terrible war, just as it currently provides the foundation for my participation in the struggle against sexism.

What I want to explore here are some of the ways in which my Jewishness has contributed to becoming an anti-sexist man, working to make this world a safe environment for women (and men) to fully express their humanness. Let me be clear that I speak from a cultural heritage of Eastern European Jewry, transmuted by three generations of life in the United States. I speak of the culture of Judaism's effect on me as an American Jew, not from either doctrinal considerations — we all know the theological contradictions of a biblical reverence for women, and prayers that thank God for not being born one — nor from an analysis of the politics of nation states. My perspective says nothing of Middle-Eastern machismo; I speak of Jewish culture in the diaspora, not of Israeli politics.

The historical experience of Jews has three elements that I believe have contributed to this participation in feminist politics. First, historically, the Jew is an *outsider*. Wherever the Jew has gone, he or she has been outside the seat of power, excluded from privilege. The Jew is the symbolic "other," not unlike the symbolic "otherness" of women, gays, racial and ethnic minorities, the elderly and the physically challenged. To be marginalized allows one to see the center more clearly than those who are in it, and presents grounds for alliances among marginal groups.

Reprinted from *Changing Men*, Summer/Fall 1987.

This essay was originally prepared as a lecture on "Changing Roles for the American Man" at the 92nd Street Y in November, 1983. I am grateful to Bob Brannon and Harry Brod for comments and criticisms of an earlier draft.

But the American Jew, the former immigrant, is "other" in another way, one common to many ethnic immigrants to the United States. Jewish culture is, after all, seen as an ethnic culture, which allows it to be more oppressive and emotionally rich than the bland norm. Like other ethnic subgroups, Jews have been characterized as emotional, nurturing, caring. Jewish men hug and kiss, cry and laugh. A little too much. A little too loudly. Like ethnics.

Historically, the Jewish man has been seen as less than masculine, often as a direct outgrowth of this emotional "respond-ability." The historical consequences of centuries of laws against Jews, of anti-Semitic oppression, are a cultural identity and even a self-perception as 'less than men," who are too weak, too fragile, too frightened to care for our own. The cruel irony of ethnic oppression is that our rich heritage is stolen from us, and then we are blamed for having no rich heritage. In this, again, the Jew shares this self-perception with other oppressed groups who, rendered virtually helpless by an infantilizing oppression, are further victimized by the accusation that they are, in fact, infants and require the beneficence of the oppressor. One example of this cultural self-hatred can be found in the comments of Freud's colleague and friend Weininger (a Jew) who argued that "the Jew is saturated with femininity. The most feminine Aryan is more masculine than the most manly Jew. The Jew lacks the good breeding that is based upon respect for one's own individuality as well as the individuality of others."

But, again, Jews are also "less than men" for a specific reason as well. The traditional emphasis on literacy in Jewish culture contributes in a very special way. In my family, at least, to be learned, literate, a rabbi, was the highest aspiration one could possibly have. In a culture characterized by love of learning, literacy may be a mark of dignity. But currently in the United States literacy is a cultural liability. Americans contrast egghead intellectuals, divorced from the real world, with men of action — instinctual, passionate, fierce, and masculine. Senator Albert Beveridge of Indiana counseled in his 1906 volume *Young Man and the World* (a turn of the century version of *Real Men Don't Eat Quiche*) to "avoid books, in fact, avoid all artificial learning, for the forefathers put America on the right path by learning from completely natural experience." Family, church and synagogue, and schoolroom were cast as the enervating domains of women, sapping masculine vigor.

Now don't get me wrong. The Jewish emphasis on literacy, on mind over body, does not exempt Jewish men from sexist behavior. Far from it. While many Jewish men avoid the Scylla of a boisterous and physically harassing misogyny, we can often dash ourselves against the Charybdis of a male intellectual intimidation of others. "Men with the properly sanctioned educational credentials in our society," writes Harry Brod, "are trained to impose our opinions on others, whether asked for or not, with an air of supreme self-confidence and aggressive self-assurance." It's as if the world were only waiting for our word. In fact, Brod notes, "many of us have developed mannerisms that function to intimidate those customarily denied access to higher educational institutions, especially women."[1] And yet, despite this, the Jewish emphasis on literacy has branded us, in the eyes of the world, less than "real" men.

Finally, the historical experience of Jews centers around, hinges upon our sense of morality, our ethical imperatives. The preservation of a moral code, the commandment to live ethically, is the primary responsibility of each Jew, male or female. Here, let me relate another personal story. Like many other

Jews, I grew up with the words "Never Again" ringing in my ears, branded indelibly in my consciousness. For me they implied a certain moral responsibility to bear witness, to remember — to place my body, visibly, on the side of justice. This moral responsibility inspired my participation in the anti-war movement, and my active resistance of the draft *as a Jew*. I remember family dinners in front of the CBS Evening News, watching Walter Cronkite recite the daily tragedy of the war in Vietnam. "Never again," I said to myself, crying myself to sleep after watching napalm fall on Vietnamese villagers. Isn't this the brutal terror we have sworn ourselves to preventing when we utter those two words? When I allowed myself to feel the pain of those people, there was no longer a choice; there was, instead, a moral imperative to speak out, to attempt to end that war as quickly as possible.

In the past few years, I've become aware of another war. I met and spoke with women who had been raped, raped by their lovers, husbands, and fathers, women who had been beaten by those husbands and lovers. Some were even Jewish women. All those same words — Never Again — flashed across my mind like a neon meteor lighting up the darkened consciousness. Hearing that pain and that anger prompted the same moral imperative. We Jews say "Never Again" to the systematic horror of the Holocaust, to the cruel war against the Vietnamese, to Central American death squads. And we must say it against this war waged against women in our society, against rape and battery.

So in a sense, I see my Judaism as reminding me every day of that moral responsibility, the *special* ethical imperative that my life, as a Jew, gives to me. Our history indicates how we have been excluded from power, but also, as men, we have been privileged by another power. Our Judaism impels us to stand against any power that is illegitimately constituted because we know only too well the consequences of that power. Our ethical vision demands equality and justice, and its achievement is our historical mission.

NOTE

1. Harry Brod, "Justice and a Male Feminist" in *The Jewish Newspaper* (Los Angeles) June 6, 1985, p. 6.

Seymour Kleinberg

THE NEW MASCULINITY OF GAY MEN, AND BEYOND

WHERE HAVE ALL THE SISSIES GONE?: A VIEW FROM THE 1970'S

One week after Labor Day 1977, I made a trip to the Anvil Bar, a gay club in New York City. For a long time I had wanted to know whether the legends of debauchery one heard with some skepticism were accurate. No one I knew was a member, and I had been told by those who claimed to be informed that I was not a likely type to crash successfully. I presumed they meant that my only leather jacket, tailored like a blazer, would not pass muster. Then a close friend became enamored of a go-go boy who danced there, joined the Anvil, and took me along to meet Daniel.

The bar nearly lived up to its fame. The boys do dance continually on top of the four-sided bar, they do strip naked, not counting construction shoes or cock rings. There is a back room where no-nonsense, hard-core porno films silently and continually flicker, shown by a mesmerized projectionist wearily perched on the ledge of the back wall. A small pitch-dark cubicle called the fuck room opens off the rear wall. In the middle of the front-room bar is a stage raised five feet where fist-fucking demonstrations used to be held at 3 a.m. if the crowd was enthusiastic, but those spontaneous shows were stopped when they began to draw tourists from the uptown discos. Now it is used by the dancers, who take turns exhibiting their specialities in the limelight. The boys range from extraordinary to middling, from high-schoolers to forty-year-olds, from professionals (everything) to amateurs who move awkwardly but who are graceful and stunning when they don't move at all. There are types for every taste and some for none. Hispanic and black, WASP and Italian, the boys dance three hours of a six-hour stint for $25 a night, three or four times a week. There are always new faces, and the management is liberal about letting anyone with a good body try out. Usually, there is one dancer who has had some ballet training and is naive enough to make that clear; he is invariably the least favored by the clientele.

My friend's Daniel is unusual. He is one of the few boys who can use the trapeze bars bolted to the ceiling with real expertise. Without breaking the rhythm of his dance, he leaps for a trapeze and spends four or five minutes on or swinging from one bar to another in the most daring manner. When he alights, it is with a sure flip back onto the bar, where he continues to dance with an unbroken stride. Daniel has never fallen, as some of the boys have (a broken nose or a fractured arm is not unheard of), nor has he crashed into a customer since he holds his drugs well.

His other specialty is his ability to grab with his buttocks the folded one-

---

"The New Masculinity of Gay Men," written in 1978, was originally published as a chapter of Kleinberg's book *Alienated Affections* (New York: St. Martin's Press, 1980). "Life After Death: A View From the Late 1980s" is excerpted from an article in the *New Republic*, 11 and 18 Aug., 1986.

dollar or five-dollar tips the men at the bar hold between their teeth, a variation
on the skill of the Cotton Club girls of Harlem in the twenties and thirties. His
perfect behind descends in time to the music over the customer's uplifted face,
and there is a round of applause when the money disappears into those con-
stricted rosy cheeks.

Like most of the clientele, Daniel looks like a college athlete or construction
worker, two favored images these recent seasons. Clothed, he wears the uniform
of the moment: cheap plaid flannel shirts and jeans, or if it is really warm just
overalls, and boots or construction worker's shoes no matter what the weather
is. With the first signs of frost, boots and heavy leather bomber jackets are *de
rigueur.*

Daniel is also typical of one type of club client in that he is a masochist, a
"slave" who sleeps with other men with the permission of his master (who in-
structs him to charge a hefty fee). While Daniel's masochism has taken a pecu-
niary turn, he is not really a whore, for he is indifferent to money, keeping only
what he needs for his uppers and poppers, his grass and coke. He dances frenetically four nights a week and does what he is told because he finds that
exciting. There is little that he has not experienced sexually, and at twenty-two,
his tastes are now as perverse as any possibilities Western civilization has
devised.

To look at him, one would hardly suspect that this Irish kid from Queens
with his thatch of reddish hair, cowlick and all, this sweet-faced boy built like
a swimmer in his blue-collar uniform, lives a life more sexually extreme than
anything described by the Marquis de Sade. When he discusses his life, it appears to be an endless dirty movie, but the anecdotes tend to leave his listeners
in a moral vacuum. While it is possible to become erotically excited hearing his
adventures, it is difficult to judge them without feeling prudish. Conventional
moral standards are tangential, psychological ones almost as irrelevant. One is
not really shocked; rather, one feels adrift, puzzled, perhaps bemused. Most of
all, this nice boy seems very remote.

The values of his generation, acted out as theater of the absurd, are even more
histrionic in Daniel's life. Just as one does not expect experimental theater or
avant-garde art to live up to the standards of naturalism, one does not try to
understand Daniel's life from the lessons of one's own experience: the collective
sanity of the past is momentarily dumb.

What one struggled to learn and call "adult" as the final approbation now
looks somewhat priggish. If one wanted to use such standards, why go to the
Anvil at all? But once one *is* there or at the Mine Shaft or any of half a dozen
bars just like them, what does one use to understand this spectacle of men?
Some, like me, are clearly audience at a drama where only the actors understand
the play. Intuition is not trustworthy, and easy judgments make one feel like a
tourist. But whether or not one wishes to refrain from judgment, one thing is
clear, if not glaring. The universal stance is a studied masculinity. There are no
limp wrists, no giggles, no indiscreet hips swiveling. Walk, talk, voice, costume,
grooming are just right: this is macho country. It is a rigorous place where one
destroys oneself in drugs and sexual humiliation.

The same impulses are evident in other scenes. Fire Island Pines is as besotted
and extreme as the leather and Levis world, and often they overlap, but the
Pines is playful. Like its shabbier neighbor, Cherry Grove, the Pines enjoys the
long legacy of camp. It loves to dictate next year's chic to café society, for nov-

elty, flair, and sophistication are as paramount in this scene as they are in the world of women's fashion. For a time, the place seemed to veer toward egalitarianism; only youthful beauty was required if one were not rich. But with inflation, the freeloading beauty has to be spectacular indeed. The dance halls of the Pines and the Grove, like the waterfront bars, are filled with handsome men posing in careful costumes, and no matter how elegant or expensive, they are all butch.

As a matter of fact, young gay men seem to have abjured effeminacy with universal success. Muscular bodies laboriously cultivated all year round are standard; youthful athletic agility is everyone's style. The volleyball game on the beach is no longer a camp classic; now it takes itself as seriously as the San Francisco gay softball team. Hardness is in.

But talk to these men, sleep with them, befriend them, and the problems are the old familiar ones: misery when they are in love, loneliness when they are not, frustration and ambitiousness at work, and a monumental self-centeredness that exacerbates the rest. These have been the archetypes of unhappiness in homosexual America for as long as I can remember.

What is different from anything else I remember, however, is the relentless pursuit of masculinity. There are no limits; the most oppressive images of sexual violence and dominance are adopted unhesitatingly. Though the neo-Nazi adorations — fascinating fascism as Susan Sontag terms them — are more sinister than the innocuous ideals of the weight-lifting room, they are equally mindless. The offense is not aesthetic; it is entirely political. The homosexuals who adopt images of masculinity, conveying their desire for power and their belief in its beauty, are in fact eroticizing the very values of straight society that have tyrannized their own lives. It is the tension between this style and the content of their lives that demands the oblivion of drugs and sexual libertinism. In the past, the duplicity of closeted lives found relief in effeminate camping; now the suppression or denial of the moral issue in their choice is far more damaging. The perversity of imitating their oppressors guarantees that such blindness will work itself out as self-contempt.

Sex and Sexual Politics   This is the central message of the macho bar world: manliness is the only real virtue; other values are contemptible. And manliness is not some philosophical notion or psychological state; it is not even morally related to behavior. It lies exclusively in the glamorization of physical strength.

This idea of masculinity is so conservative it is almost primitive. That homosexuals are attracted to it and find it gratifying is not a total surprise. Gay male sexual preference has always favored a butch boyish beauty, and only in artistic or intellectual circles has beauty been allowed a certain feyness. Butchness is always relative; the least swishy man in the room is the most butch. It usually meant one looked straight, one could pass. In the past, an over-enthusiasm for butchness translated itself into a taste for rough trade. Those who were too frightened or sane to pursue that particular quarry could always find a gay partner who would accommodatingly act the part.

There is a special eroticism in the experience of pretending to be degraded that is by no means rare in adult sexual behavior of whatever persuasion. The homosexual whose erotic feelings are enhanced by the illusion that his partner holds him in contempt, who is thrilled when told his ass or mouth is just like a cunt, is involved in a complicated self-deception. What appears to be happening is a homosexual variation of masochism: the contempt of the "straight" partner emblazes gay self-contempt, which in turn is exploited as an aphrodisiac. Why this process works is less clear than how it does.

The complex tie between the need for degradation and sexual excitement has never been satisfactorily explored, though Freud began the effort over eighty years ago and writers and artists have always intuitively understood it. It seems to be prominent in societies that are advanced, where sexual mores are liberal or ambivalent, and where intellectual life is very sophisticated. In times like ours, when women are redefining their roles and images, men must also redefine theirs. As women forgo in dress and appearance the *style* of their oppression (it is the easiest to abandon and thus one of the first aspects to go), and as glamor falls under a suspicious light, men, increasingly accused of being the symbol of sexism, are forced to confront their own ideas of masculinity.

While straight men define their ideas from a variety of sources (strength, achievement, success, money), two of those sources are always their attitudes toward women and toward paternity. It is no coincidence that the same decade that popularized liberation for women and announced that the nuclear family was a failure also saw men return to a long-haired, androgynous style. If straight men are confused about their maleness, what is the dilemma for gay men, who rarely did more than imitate these ideas?

It is no accident that the macho gesture is always prominent in those gay bars and resorts where women are entirely absent. Certain gay locales have always catered exclusively to one sex: porno movie houses and bookstores, baths, public toilets. The new bars are often private clubs as much for the sake of legally barring women as for screening male customers. Their atmosphere is eerily reminiscent of the locker room. And, of course, while they are there, the men live as if there were no women in the world. This is a useful illusion. It allows some of them to get gang-banged in the back rooms and still evade the self-reproach that derives from the world's contempt for homosexual men who behave sexually like women. If there are no women in the world, some men simply must replace them. With women absent, whether one is sexually active or passive is no longer the great dividing issue.

In fact, some of the men who look most butch are the most liberated in bed, the least role-oriented. While there is still much role preference for passivity, it no longer has the clear quality it had in the past. Then, gay men made unmistakable announcements: those who liked to be fucked adopted effeminate mannerisms; those who were active tried to look respectable.

Quentin Crisp in his autobiography, *The Naked Civil Servant*, epitomized these attitudes. He documents the anger of an acquaintance railing at the misfortune of having picked up a young soldier who wanted to be fucked: "All of a sudden, he turned over. After all I'd done — flitting about the room in my wrap . . . camping myself silly. My dear, I was disgusted."[1] Today, to replace the usually reliable information that straight or campy behavior conveyed in the past, gay men at the leather bars have taken to elaborate clothing signals: key chains or handkerchiefs drooping from left or right pocket in blue or yellow or red all have coded meanings. Occasionally, some of the *cognoscenti* lie and misalliances occur. Of course, one could ask a prospective partner what his preferences are, but that is the least likely behavior between strangers.

If I am critical of the present style, it is not because I advocate a return to the denigrations of the past. Quentin Crisp's rebelliousness testifies to the hourly misery of gay life when all the sexual roles are petrified. He considered all his friends "pseudo men in search of pseudo women." That is not an improvement on pseudo men in search of nothing. Nor is his sense of inferiority: "I regard all heterosexuals, however low, as superior to any homosexual, however noble." Such estimates were commonplace for men subjected to lifelong ridicule because they could not or would not disguise their effeminacy.

But camping for Crisp and for the entire homosexual world until the end of the 1950s was not just the expression of self-contempt by men pretending to be women and feeling pseudo as both. Camping also gave homosexual men an *exclusive* form of behavior that neither women nor straight men could adopt. Some women and straight men are camp, but that is another story.

Camping in the gay world did not mean simply behaving in a blatantly effeminate manner; that was camp only when performed in the presence of those it irritated or threatened or delighted. Swishing is effective only if someone else notices, preferably registering a sense of shock, or ideally, outrage. In discreet bars like the Blue Parrot in 1950, men impeccably Brooks Brothers and as apparently WASP as one's banker could, in a flicker, slide into limpness. They had available a persona that mixed ironic distance, close observation, and wit, all allies of sanity.

Camping did express self-denigration, but it was a complex criticism. For example, the women whom these men imitated were themselves extraordinary; androgynous idols like Garbo or Dietrich symbolized an ambiguous and amoral sexuality. But more important, in their campy behavior, gay men revealed an empathic observation of women and feminine interests.

When camping also released for gay men some of their anger at their closeted lives, it became a weapon as well as a comment. The behavior chosen for imitation or ridicule was usually evidence of sexist attitudes, of positions women had taken or were forced to take that had effeminized them out of their humanity. It is for this reason that feminists object to drag queens who still try to resemble the slavish emblems of the past, and their criticism would be valid if the imitations were sincere. But men in drag are not swept up in the delusion that they are women; only insane men in drag believe that. The rest are committed to ambiguity; they are neither men nor women and are only rarely androgynous — the aura of drag is neuter.

When a gay man said, "Oh, Mary, come off it," he was sneering at pretension, self-deceit, or prudery. That it took the form of reminding one's fellow faggot that he was in reality no better than a woman, and often not as good with his "pseudo" sexual equipment, is not politically commendable, but why should gay men have had a special consciousness about sexism? At least they had a sure recognition of it: they imitated women because they understood that they were victims in sisterhood of the same masculine ideas about sexuality. Generations of women defined themselves entirely in men's terms, and homosexual men often seemed to accept the same values.

But there was also a chagrined recognition that they just could not live up to expectations. They could not be men as heterosexuals defined manhood; most of all they could not be men because they did not sleep with women or beget children. No amount of manliness could counterbalance that. Between the values of virility that they did not question and their rage at having no apparent alternatives, gay men would camp out their frustration. It was not a particularly effective means of ending oppression, but it was a covert defiance of a society that humiliated them.

With the political and social changes of the sixties, a new androgyny seemed to be on the verge of life. Heterosexual and homosexual suddenly became less interesting than just sexual. Getting out of the closet was more than announcing one was gay; it was a pronouncement that one was free of sexual shame. The new mood fostered this; even straight boys looked prettier than girls. The relief at seeing male vanity in the open, surrendered to and accepted, made it possible for homosexuals to reconsider some of their attitudes toward themselves. It was no longer extraordinary to look effeminate in a world where most sexual men looked feminine and where sexually liberated women were the antithesis of the glamorous and fragile.

Sexual style had become a clear political issue. Conventional manliness was properly identified with reaction and repression. The enemy had a crewcut, was still posturing in outmoded chivalric stances, while his wife and daughter and son embraced the revolutionary notion of rolelessness. To some extent, this is where American society still is: searching for a sense of what roles, if any, are appropriate for adult men and women. Only the betrayed patriarch still refuses to acknowledge the permanence of these changes, since for him they are pure deprivations, erosions of his long, long privilege.

Homosexuality and Masculinity   "Feminist" is a term that increasing numbers of gay men apply to themselves as they come to recognize the common oppression of homosexuals and women. The empathy of gay men in the past is the foundation for this newer understanding, and it is heartening to discover that a mutual sense of victimization need not always lead to self-denigration. If in the past women were less likely to self-contempt at being women than gay men felt at being homosexual, it was partly because women were rewarded for their acquiescence and partly because they did not have to experience the sense of having betrayed their birthright. Homosexual men usually gave up paternity as well as other prerogatives for their gayness and too often felt gypped for what they got. They exchanged the simplicity of being phallic oppressors for advantages much more dubious, and the sense that they had betrayed their best interests was haunting. As more gays come to realize the bankruptcy of conventional ideas of masculinity, it is easier for them to forgo the sexism they shared with heterosexual men.

Unfortunately, heterosexuals cling to their sexual definitions with even greater tenacity. For example, the Save Our Children slogan is not as banal as it sounds; the phobic hostility behind it expresses a genuine fear that some children will be lost, lost to patriarchy, to the values of the past, to the perpetuation of conventional ideas of men and women. There is a fear of homosexuality that is far beyond what the surface can explain.

Many gays, especially apolitical ones, are dismissive of Anita Byrant and what she represents. Remarks like "Straights will just have to hope that heterosexuality can hold its own on the open market" express a contempt for the fears, but not much understanding of them. It *is* puzzling: where does this idea of the frailty of heterosexuality come from, the assumption that a mere knowledge that teachers or ordinary people are gay will automatically seduce children? It comes from the panic about new sexual ideas, but most of all, about the identity of women.

It often sounds absurd when conservatives accuse feminist women of attempting to destroy the family, though it does not stop them from making the accusation. It is easier to appear sensible talking about the seduction of children by homosexuals. I suggest that much of the recent vehemence about the children is deflected from a much more central rage against women who are redefining their ideas about child rearing. The political issue is always hottest when women's connection with motherhood is raised. Thus, the issues of child rearing and anti-abortion gather a conservative support that puzzles liberal America. What these issues have in common is the attempt of women to free themselves from conventional roles, crucially their roles as mothers. That liberation is the first wave; the secondary one, far more perilous, lies beneath the surface: it demands that men liberate themselves from their notions as well, since the central ideas about masculinity have always been related to the unquestioned responsibilities of men as husbands and fathers.

It is curious that lesbians are never mentioned when child molestation is raised as an issue, and when lesbians are attacked, as they were at Houston, it is relation to their militant feminism, not in relation to their being school teachers. Lesbians have usually been exempt from heterosexual fears about seduction, partly because they are women and, like all women, traditionally powerless. When they are attacked, when the press notices lesbian issues, it is often in connection with custody cases. There the issue of saving the children for heterosexuality and precisely for patriarchy is clear. These lesbians who once lived as straight women, who married and had children, are objects of the most extreme wrath, and one that has used the judicial system as its instrument to punish them.

But most lesbians are not mothers, and most lesbian mothers do not end up, fortunately, as victims in custody hearings. Lesbians are usually dismissed as unimportant, as nuisances. It is the lowest rung on the ladder of social contempt. But gay men who have abdicated their privileges, who have made sexual desire a higher priority than power over women, are indeed not men at all.

Bryant's keynote is that homosexuals should return to the closet. That would solve the problem for straights, since it is *visibility* that is terrifying. To be openly gay without contrition or guilt or shame is to testify that there are viable alternative sexual styles. But the real alternative for the children is not necessarily homosexuality; it is to reject the old verities of masculine and feminine.

Ironically, the men at the Anvil have not rejected those verities at all. Their new pseudo-masculinity is a precise response to the confusions of a society venturing toward sexual redefinition. But it is in its way as reactionary as the hysteria that Anita Bryant's campaign consolidated.

The men of the macho bars will not buy Quentin Crisp's book, or if they do, they will not read it sympathetically, whereas they *are* part of the audience that made the story of football player David Kopay a best seller.[2] I do not want to belittle Kopay's modest effort, but its success depends more on his image than on his courage. Effeminate men like Crisp who have the courage to defy society are eccentric; butch men are heroic. Of course, what is left unsaid is that Kopay could have passed: no one would have known if he hadn't told them, and having once announced it, he can still pass. What could sissies like Crisp do even if they didn't flaunt it? Crisp's *life* is an act of courage.

Ex-soldier Leonard Matlovich is also a respectable image.[3] When media reporters treat him and Kopay just like the mainstream Americans they have always been, they make a point many gays approve of: homosexual men are really like everyone else. If beneath Matlovich's conservative, bemedalled chest beat aberrant yearnings, the public, if not the army, can accommodate them. What makes Kopay and Matlovich seem acceptable to gays and straights alike, while the Quentin Crisps remain pitiful?

Crisp was defiant and miserable, an acknowledged victim, and unrepentant: it was all agony, but it couldn't have been any other way. Even more, Crisp made his sexuality the obsession of his life. His whole existence was devoted to proclaiming his homosexuality; it is the meaning of his life. Today, his heir is Daniel, who is as absorbed in the same singular definition of himself. Daniel's life seems consecrated to pleasure while Crisp's was miserable, and that is an enormous difference. But the source of his pleasure in sexuality is as extreme, as dangerous and defiant as the quest for pleasure in Crisp's life. I may feel that Crisp is morally superior because he has suffered and Daniel refuses to, but that is only a sentimental notion. What is stunning in both their lives is the exclusivity of sexuality, and while Daniel is not heroic, his life demands that one refrain from easy judgment. The drama of such displays is filled with meaning for them and us. These lives are not like others'.

Kopay and Matlovich are fighting to be like everyone else. They claim that they are just like other football players or professional soldiers, and I do not dispute them. Compared to their conventionality, their homosexuality is almost incidental. Neither of them has gotten off quite free, nor have they seemed to expect to. For reasons they articulate with unquestionable credibility, they could not tolerate the duplicity of being conservative, rather ordinary men and secret homosexuals. Ironically, to some extent they have now become extraordinary men if somewhat commonplace homosexuals.

The men in leather watching naked go-go boys and having sex in back-room bars are not like Crisp or Daniel whom they regard as a kind of erotic theater; they are much closer to Kopay and Matlovich with whom they can identify. The rock-bottom premise of such sympathy is that all forms of traditional masculinity are respectable; all symptoms of effeminacy are contemptible. Real sexual extremism, like Daniel's, belongs to a netherworld; it is not regarded as liberated but as libertine. Daniel is the complete sexual object, and his presence makes the bar world the psychological equivalent of the brothel for the men who watch him. He turns them on, and then they can play whore or client or both.

Most men who are ardent for leather defend it as play. Dressing butch is another version of the gay uniform. What is the harm of walking through the world dressed like a construction worker? What does it matter what costume you wear to the ball? Go as Cinderella's fairy godmother, and you may break the law. But go as Hell's Angels, and you risk breaking your own spirit.

It is no coincidence that in the macho bar world and the libertine baths the incidence of impotence is so high that it is barely worth remarking, or that gay men increasingly rely on the toys and trappings of sadomasochism. It is not irrelevant that the new gay image of virility is most often illustrated in pornography.

Manly means hot, and hot is everything. Why then isn't it working better? Men tell me that I do not appreciate this new celebration of masculinity, that I am overlooking the important "fact": "We fell for masculinity when we were twelve; there must be something to it because it made us gay. Most of us didn't become gay because we fell in love with sissies; we became sissies because we fell in love with men, usually jocks."

It sounds familiar. And so what if one chooses to make one's life pornographic? Isn't that only the most recent version of sexual devotion, of incarnating Eros in one's life? Besides, it's too late to be a dogooder. Obviously, as soon as one sets up notions of propriety, no matter how well intended, they will be preempted by the worst, most coercive forces in our society. One is then forced to accept all choices of style; the alternative is to find oneself allied with oppression. In the arena of sexual politics, there is the left and the right. Those who think they are in the middle will ultimately discover that the center is the right.

But my feelings tell me that there is another version; that macho is somehow another closet, and not a new one — many have suspected that it's the oldest closet in the house. Macho cultures have always had more covert homosexuality. Without belaboring the analogy, there is one consistency. In those cultures, homosexuality is not a sexual identity; it is defined as role. Only the passive partner, which means anally passive or orally active, is homosexual; the other role is reserved for men, because one either is a man or one is not; that is, one is a woman, and a woman who cannot bear a child and attest to a man's virility is beneath contempt, at best a whore.

The men in the macho bars are not like this. They have adopted a style and abandoned its psychic origin in sexual role playing. Apparently they have rescued the best and discarded the worst. But it is an appearance that resonates with unexamined yearnings. It says I am strong and I am free, that gay no longer means the contemptibleness of being nelly, which is the old powerless *reactiveness* to oppression. Insofar as it does that — strong is better than weak, free is always good — it is an improvement on the past. But it claims more: it says that this is a choice, a proper fulfillment of those initial desires that led us to love men, and even at its oddest, it is only playful.

But it is not free, not strong, and it is dangerous play. It is dangerous to dress up like one's enemy, and worse, it can tie one to him as helplessly as ever. It still says that he, the powerful brute, is the definer, to which we then react. It is the other side of nelly, and more helpless because it denies that one is helpless at all. Effeminacy acknowledged the rage of being oppressed in defiance; macho denies that there *is* rage and oppression. The strength of those new bodies is a costume designed for sexual allure and for the discotheque. Passing for the enemy does not exempt one from the wrath. Men in leather are already the easiest marks for violent teenagers on a drunken rampage in Greenwich Village or on Mission Street on a Saturday night. Macho is another illusion. The lessons of Negroes who disliked blackness, or Jews who insisted they were assimilated, really *German*, are ignored. To some whites, everything not white is black; to Nazis, Jews are Jews, sidelocks or no. Telling the enemy one is as good as he is because one is like him does not appease him; often it makes him more vicious, furious because somehow his victim seems to approve his scorn. And the freedom — that too is illusory except as sexual taste. In that area alone, there has been real change. Compared to their counterparts in the past gay men today have found a freedom to act out their erotic tastes. But taste is not a choice; usually, it is a tyrant.

Homosexuals at their most oppressed have not been in love with men; they have been in love with masculinity. The politics of the New Left and the sexual aesthetics of androgyny have not lasted, but they seemed to be offering alternatives that were authentic, better choices than the ones we had. The new style seems both inauthentic and barely better than the old options. Sometimes it seems worse.

That is what is disturbing and enraging: to find it the growing choice in the 1980s. Does it seriously matter that some men choose to imitate their worst enemies? What is remarkable about such an old story? For one, it is so unnecessary. For the first time in modern history, there are real options for gays. The sissies in the Blue Parrot had little choice other than to stay home. They could only pretend their lives were ordinary. That pretense was survival, but one that led fatally to rage and self-contempt. The theatricality of camping helped to keep some sanity and humanity because it was an awareness of one's helplessness. Macho values are the architects of closeted lives, and adopting that style is the opposite of awareness. Whatever its ironies, they are not critical ones.

Fortunately, gay men are less helpless than they have ever been before, and because of that they are more threatened. What is worth affirming is not bravura, but political alliance with women and with a whole liberal America that is dedicated to freedom of personal choice. *That* is worth celebrating.

LIFE AFTER DEATH: A VIEW FROM THE LATE 1980s

These days the mood of the gay community ranges from cloudy optimism to crystal-clear despair, depending on whom you talk to. I've been talking to gay activists, journalists, academics, therapists and medical doctors, businessmen, poets and painters, working-class men, and men who don't work, either because they don't need to or because they can't find a job. Some are Marxists, some lesbian feminists, and some have no politics but sexual politics. The term "gay community" refers partly to a discernible group of homosexual men and lesbians in large cities, and partly to a political idea. The media made it a term to reckon with long before anyone could say what it was. In 1969 "gay community" was largely a political idea and a myth. Even then there was a community in the simplest sense of the word, but what it looked like, as in the case of the blind men describing the elephant, depended on what you touched.

Seventeen years later, there are listings in the Yellow Pages. Coherent and representative groups have emerged, particularly in San Francisco, Los Angeles, and New York. They differ enough to be unable to provide a national leadership, and persistent closetry makes estimates of their numbers and their members rough at best, but a gay man or woman would likely feel at home in any of those three cities. The real differences are geographical, not political or social, and there is no single lifestyle or even a dominant one. The promiscuous one that became the hallmark of urban gay life in the early seventies — newsworthy because it was commercial and outrageous and because it gradually became the self-defining image of so many gay men — no longer prevails as it once did.

Today the general mood is grim. Everyone is either melancholy or anxious, afraid not only of AIDS but of the growing signs of hostility toward gay men and women. It is chilling when the *New York Times*, purportedly in the interests of balanced journalism, publishes William F. Buckley in support of tatooing homosexual men and intravenous-drug users, while the word "quarantine" quivers between the lines of the article. (I naively waited for letters of protest from both the Jewish and gay communities. Wouldn't Jews be disgusted by the parodic horror of the suggestion?) Though Buckley is absurd, the fears he touches are not.

Helplessness about AIDS and uncertainty about the social future are exacerbated for gay men and women by their memories of the past. This is one reason so many are eager to be involved with gay organizations, to be tangibly connected to a real, not an ideological community. To be passive again is to stress one's helplessness, to be waiting for the next blow and wondering if the humiliation will be bearable.

Most of society is less concerned about who is responsible for the AIDS epidemic than with how gay men are going to behave in order to inhibit its spread. That issue, it should be said at once, arose in the gay community almost as soon as it was clear that AIDS was regarded as a gay disease. The closing of the bathhouses in San Francisco and New York was the occasion for raising the question in public. Publicly and privately it was admitted that the issue of accountability and social responsibility would have to be addressed. Obviously, this meant altering sexual behavior and style of life. Efforts were made in every large North American city with a gay community to inform and educate gay men about "safe sex," hoping that would be enough to halt the spread of AIDS. It is not yet clear how much deprivation this entails or how successful the educational campaign has been. History does not offer much ground for optimism: venereal epidemics of the past ended not with altered sexual behavior but with the discovery of penicillin.

But another issue, internal and not yet explored in any public way, has now arisen and needs attention, an issue that the symptoms of the crisis sometimes hint at: what does it mean to be homosexual in the modern world? This question is not about grievances and injustices, and it cannot be answered on the barricades, especially the barricade of rhetoric. As long as the subject of gay identity is argued in terms of whether it is good or bad, legitimate or illegitimate, there is no energy left to address the question of what it is. The new activism cannot address the more important internal questions the crisis has raised. The sources of change are elsewhere, in behavior and in thought about the homosexual condition that most men and women are reluctant to embrace.

Promiscuity and Liberation   Some have refused to change; they search for safe places to practice old pleasures. Latin America and the Caribbean have long accommodated homosexual men with their informal bordellos, their "muchachos" who are partners to passive men but who do not think of themselves as homosexual. It is only a question of time before these gay men spread AIDS to other islands near Haiti, from which they probably first brought it to the mainland. It is hard to gauge the state of mind of such men. They may be filled with rage and seeking revenge. They may fatalistically believe that their behavior doesn't matter. They don't feel they are doing anything wrong, or they don't care. They have no moral sense, or they are immoral. It's bad enough to live in dread of dying an awful premature death. Yet to be filled with desire for revenge, or to be without desire at all, even for ordinary dignity, is a terrible way to live or die. I assume that such men act less from conscious indecency than from pure evasion. To emphasize sexual desire and desirability is a very effective way to mask anxiety. The habit of promiscuity doesn't allow much room for introspection.

Promiscuity is a broad term. For some men, it means serial affairs or brief erotic relationships. For others, there are no relationships at all; sexual encounters begin and end with momentary arousal. And for some men, promiscuity is all of these — having a lover, and having someone else, and having anyone else. Promiscuity is time consuming and repetitious. Still, it also has another history and meaning for gay men; and it is that history, and that meaning, with which gay men in the shadow of AIDS must grapple.

In the last fifteen years or so, until AIDS appeared, promiscuity had been a rich if not invaluable experience for gay men, uniting a sense of liberation with a politics of resentment, a feeling of living at the modern edge with an outlet for aggressions created by long-held grievances. Such a combination is explosive, of course, and antiintellectual. But gay men did not invent sexual liberation. They merely stamped it with their hallmark of aggressive display. Casual sex, freed from commercialism, seemed a glamorous portent of a society free from sexism. After "Stonewall," the riot at a New York bar in which gay men successfully resisted arrest and inadvertently inaugurated gay liberation, gay activists felt they were going to redefine the old terms, junk the guilt and the remorse. They were already discarding with contempt the shrinks and the moralists, paying some of them back for the years of misery they had helped to create, the self-dislike they had urged gays to internalize for the sake of what now seemed merely propriety. Out the window went "sick" and "bad." Many could hardly believe they were jettisoning that dismal baggage.

Those years of sexual opportunism were a time of indifference to psychological inquiry. Description was a higher priority. After so much silence, the need to explain and the desire to shock were first on the agenda of gay writers and intellectuals, while the majority of gay men were exploring an exhilarating sense of relief in discos, bars with back room, and the baths. The politics of that eroticism had as much to do with ego as with eros: gay men said that sexuality did not diminish social status, to say nothing of intellectual or professional stature — no matter how vividly it was practiced.

In the early seventies, when movement politics was at the zenith of its popularity, the values it promoted were very seductive. It said the old romantic pieties were a slavish imitation of straight society, where they were already undergoing vigorous scrutiny from feminists. If women and blacks could use politics to demand that society acknowledge they had been unjustly treated, why not gay men? If the acknowledgment of that injustice took the form of striking down old laws and replacing them with better ones, then that, obviously, was the agenda. But for the most part, neither the victories nor the defeats changed the daily lives of gay men and women very much. With or without sodomy laws, most lived without concern for legality. It was understood that the principal struggle was psychological, a demand first for recognition, then for acceptance; the bold terms in which that demand was couched guaranteed the right to pursue a sexual lifestyle of their own choosing. After Stonewall, gays chose to be very visible.

Before Stonewall, promiscuous sex was illegal, but it was no particular threat to health. If the heart and heat of gay politics has been to ensure the right to fuck who, when, and where one pleases, then the consequences now for the movement have a rough poetic justice. The more that sex dominated the style of life, from discos to parades, with rights secured or not, the less need most men felt they had for politics — and the less others, such as lesbians, feminists, and minorities, felt the gay movement offered them. For gay men sexual politics became something oddly literal. Both before and after the movement, promiscuity was honored as the sign of an individual's aggressiveness (no matter how passive he was in bed). To fuck was to defy, as bad girls of the past did, dismantling some of society's dearest notions about virtue. But most homosexuals want to be conventional. They are no more imaginative, courageous, or innovative than their neighbors. They want a good life on the easiest terms they can get. Many regard as uninteresting the activism that a handful of men and women are devoted to.

By the late seventies, movement politics displaced flamboyant effeminacy. The piece of trade (a man who is fellated by another but pretends to be heterosexual) whose very pose of masculinity ensured his contempt for his homosexual partner, had been replaced by that formerly groveling queen himself, now looking more virile than his proletarian idol. The dominant image of rebellion was no longer the defiant queens with their merciless ironies but powerful, strong bodies modeled on working-class youth. This new image exposed the erotic ideal of gay male life more clearly and responsively than anything since classical Greece. It was a vast improvement. Liberation freed gays from a lot of burdens, and one of the biggest was to end the search for masculinity among the enemy.

But paralleling the rise of the macho body has been the decline of the health of the male community — a nasty coincidence, if you believe in coincidence. The deeper truth, however, is that the very values that motivated us to look strong rather than be strong are the same values that elevated promiscuity as the foundation of a social identity. AIDS is mobilizing many to work in agencies caring for the ill, allowing them opportunities for sympathy and generosity — but that, too, is not the basis of an identity. What is killing you is not likely to give you a sense of self.

Even if AIDS were cured tomorrow, the style and identity of gay life in the seventies and mid-eighties would be as dated as the sexual mores of closeted homosexual life are now. Many men may rush back to the baths, but it can no longer be the liberating experience it once was. AIDS has nullified promiscuity as politically or even psychologically useful and has replaced one set of meanings with another. It has now become mythic as the dark side of sexuality, Thanatos to Eros. The life force that is the sexual drive has always had its counterpart, and AIDS is the most dramatic juxtaposition of the need for another and the fear of the other, of pain and pleasure, of life and death, in modern medical history. From the ancient Greeks on down, without a moment's interruption, the interpretation has been the same: unfettered sexuality means death, whether through dishonor, the wrath of the gods, or nature itself. We are the heirs of those legends. AIDS, like a blotter, has absorbed those old meanings.

Life after Death   There is much, then, that gay men must give up. The loss of sexual life, nearly as much as the grief and fear, is a deprivation for which no amount of civic work or marching to banners of Gay Pride can compensate.

The most dramatic changes have occurred among those large numbers of men who have become abstinent, assuming a sense of responsibility to themselves if not to others. Not only must gay men refrain from what alone gave them a powerful enough identity to make a mark on the consciousness of society, a behavior that replaced society's contempt with the much more respectable fear and anger, but they must cease to think of themselves as unloved children. They must do both before they can have social acceptance or before their own behavior can have meaning for each other more nurturing than it has been. It is very hard to give up a sense of deprivation when little that created it has disappeared, and worse, when one is beset with fear.

One thing, however, is clear: gay men are not acting in concert. If gay men sensed they belonged to a recognized community, instead of struggling still to assert their legitimacy, the task would be simpler. If they felt the larger society was no longer so adamantly adversarial, they could give up the sense of injustice that makes talk of social responsibility seem hypocritical. And if their own experiences with each other had provided them with bonds deeper than momentary pleasure, they could trust themselves to act as a group in which members assumed responsibility for each other.

As long as the larger society continues to prefer the old homosexual invisibility, the nice couple next door to whom anyone can condescend, as long as that society fails to express its responsibilities to gay men, the harder it will be for gay men to give up their seductive sense of grievance. Those men who act irresponsibly in the midst of this crisis betray their isolation, their failure to feel they belong either to a gay community or to a larger one. They perceive the demand for accountability as a demand from strangers. Society has not acted as the surrogate family in which we all develop our loyalties and moral sense. In fact, too often it acts just like the family of gay men: filled with contempt or indifference.

Many gays are now relieved that sex is no longer a banner issue. It is not even so important that we all stand up to be counted; enough of us have stood up to satisfy the curious. Instead, much as other groups in U.S. society have done, the gay community has had to reassess more profoundly its relationship to the larger society. Customarily, that relationship has been adversarial. Now, for the first time in my memory, the gay community expects help. It hopes for sympathy from heterosexual society. It expects that those who are ordinarily silent will be uncomfortable with such neutrality when orthodox religious leaders proclaim AIDS the scourge of God upon homosexuals, or when politicians exploit and promote fear.

AIDS has made it necessary for gay men to begin questioning themselves. For too long we have lived as if we were driven, too impelled to know what we were doing and what, consequently, was happening to us. It takes perhaps half a lifetime before one is capable of the introspection (not self-absorption) necessary to make sense of the past and thus act as a morally free adult. The same is true of groups. There are moments in history when groups, too, must tell the truth about themselves.

NOTES

1. Quentin Crisp, *The Naked Civil Servant* (New York: New American Library, 1983).
2. David Kopay and Perry D. Young, *The David Kopay Story* (New York: Arbor House, 1980).
3. Leonard Matlovich was formerly a sergeant in the U.S. Army.

John Moreland

AGE AND CHANGE IN THE ADULT MALE SEX ROLE[1]

The present paper proposes that the male sex role cannot be adequately understood without adopting a developmental view of the adult years. Mussen (1962) has shown that possession of qualities stereotypically associated with the male sex role is more related to adjustment in adolescence than in adulthood. Terman (1938) demonstrated in his sample of gifted males that sex-typed interests were most highly endorsed in the 11th grade and that these men's interests were less restricted by the male sex-role stereotype as they grow older. Hartly (1959) and Knox and Kupfer (1971) have recognized that individuals' conceptions of male sex-role norms used to evaluate their own and others' masculinity are different in adulthood from those used in adolescence and childhood. While these authors have described a developmental change in sex-role norms between late adolescence and early adulthood, they have failed to recognize that such changes continue throughout adulthood. These modifications occur whenever a man's sexrole standards are contradicted by the age norms which are prevalent in his environment.

Jung (1960) presented one of the first discussions of a midlife shift in male sex-role standards when he proposed that men became more nurturant and other-centered around age 40. Neugarten and Guttman (1958) have provided empirical support for his assertion by showing that middle-aged subjects attribute more nurturant and affiliative qualities to middle-age targets than to younger male targets. These figures are not described as unmasculine. Rather, the standards used to define masculinity in a middle-aged male appear to be different from those used with a younger male. Jung and Neugarten and Guttman have described one time during adulthood when an individual modifies his sex-role standards. Recent research in the area of human life-span development suggests that adulthood can be divided into a number of distinct stable periods, each characterized by its own developmental tasks. Men in each of these periods have different conceptions of masculinity. These stable periods are separated from each other by transition periods in which men question and evaluate their sex-role standards. The stress frequently experienced during these transition periods is the consequence of a discontinuity between an individual's sex-role

Reprinted from *Sex Roles*, Vol. 6, No. 6, 1980.

1. The project presented or reported herein was performed pursuant to a grant from the National Institute of Education, Department of Health, Education, and Welfare. However, the opinions expressed herein do not necessarily reflect the position or policy of the National Institute of Education, and no official endorsement by the National Institute of Education should be inferred. The author wishes to thank his friends and colleagues Barb Benton, Laura Brown, Linda Gannon, Vince Harren, Steve Haynes, and Eileen Montague for their critical comments on earlier drafts of this manuscript.

standards and the age norms held by his social-cultural environment. Benedict (1938) has used the concept of discontinuity to explain the stress associated with the shift from child to adult in our culture. However, the concept is equally useful in understanding the stress experienced by men as they modify their conception of masculinity in response to changing age norms as they progress through adulthood.

Previous writers (Jourard, 1971; Fasteau, 1974; Nichols, 1975) have pointed out that male sex-role standards have served to inhibit the satisfaction of men's basic personality needs. It has been suggested that men must deny their needs for intimacy, support, and emotional expression if they are to view themselves as masculine. If men conceptualize masculinity solely in terms of instrumental-ity, competition, dominance, and control, they must deny themselves many growth-producing experiences. However, there are many men who have inte-grated qualities such as nurturance, emotional awareness and expressiveness, dependency, and sensuality into their personal lives. Their relationships with both men and women are characterized by emotional sensitivity, cooperation, and even playfulness. Yet these men neither view themselves nor are viewed by others as unmasculine. Such men are, however, usually older than the adoles-cent and college-age students who have most frequently been the subjects of our studies on the male sex role. By studying the male sex role from a devel-opmental perspective, we can more accurately understand what at first glance appear to be gross contradictions in the male sex-role literature.

Shostak (1972) has analyzed some of the sources of dissatisfaction experienced by middle-aged male blue collar workers. These men appear to be caught be-tween two contradictory sets of expectations. Shostak points out that histori-cally the male role expectations for manual workers have been characterized by such macho qualities as controlling one's spouse, sexual conquest, and authori-tarian rule in the home. With recent changes in women's role expectations, blue collar women are expecting more companionship, more emotional support, and more personal attention. Children in blue collar families are expecting more personal, emotional involvement from their fathers. The middle-aged male worker is caught in the middle of a painful transition in which his traditional model of masculinity is crumbling around him, and modern expectations appear vague and unnatural, Komarovsky (1973) has demonstrated that some college males are also experiencing a transition between two sets of contradictory norms. Traditionally, men have sought intellectual superiority over women, but newer norms require intellectual companionship between the sexes.

Pleck (1976) has described the transition between traditional and modern sex-role standards. He states,

> As contemporary culture has evolved, the modern male role has emerged, and its elements increasingly represent the dominant set of expectations and values against which males evaluate their behavior. Elements of the traditional male role still persist, both in culturally conservative groups and in the personalities of modern males, but these elements are increas-ingly less dominant.

While traditional male achievement was typically measured by physical prow-ess or concrete production, modern males' arenas for achievement frequently are based upon the cultivation of interpersonal and intellectual skills. Modern male standards require men to be interpersonally proficient, particularly in terms of promoting smooth collaboration with colleagues and supervisees. The traditional role, with its emphasis on instrumental behavior and suppression of affect, promoted benign neglect of interpersonal skills. Traditional standards allowed men to accumulate masculinity points based upon impulsive, brief explosions of anger, but prohibited expression of tenderness or vulnerability. The modern standard requires men to be tender and intimate in a small number of heterosexual relationships, yet in other contexts to be "cool" and controlled. In particular, anger expression and impulsiveness are strongly prohibited by modern standards. Two very discrepant sets of masculinity standards also exist as guidelines for appropriate behavior in marital relationships, male–male relationships, and the use of leisure time.

The existence of two sets of contradictory standards can produce considerable stress. However, most men do not continuously experience conflict about the appropriateness of sex-role standards. Rather, the stress resulting from the presence of two contradictory sets of standards will be most acutely experienced during the transition periods when men are questioning previous values and wrestling with the adoption of new ones. During the stable periods, most men are attempting to meet the personal commitments they have made to significant relations contained in their life structures and are not introspectively questioning their conception of masculinity. However, as they move into the next transition period, the presence of contradictory norms becomes more apparent and adds to the stress they experience.

What follows is a discussion of the life-span developmental literature. The author will demonstrate that men's conceptions of masculinity undergo a number of changes in response to social-culturally imposed discontinuities between sex-role standards and age norms throughout adulthood. Further, the existence of contradictory traditional and modern standards serves to exacerbate the stress which men experience at these times.

MODELS OF LIFE-SPAN DEVELOPMENT IN MEN

A number of different models of life-span development have been proposed (Valliant & McArthur, 1972; Gould, 1972; Haan, 1972; Peskin & Livson, 1972; and Crandall, 1972). Given the methodological problems inherent in comparing longitudinal studies, one must be struck by the similarity of the ideas expressed in these independently conducted projects. The present paper summarized and, at times, reinterprets the work of Levinson and his associates (Levinson, Darrow, Klein, Levinson, & McKee, 1976; Levinson, 1977). This group has presented the most comprehensive scheme for conceptualizing adult male growth between ages 18 and 45, and the findings of the other above mentioned investigators are consistent with their model.

The construct most central is that of "individual life structure." This term is used to describe the unique pattern or design of an individual's life at a given point in time. The major components of a life structure are the pattern of interpersonal relationships, institutional relationships, career activities, and leisure activities toward which the individual experiences a commitment.

This paper argues that the particular characteristics of a man's life structure are influenced by his conception of masculinity. In his 20s, a man measures his masculinity largely on the basis of successful competition and career advancement. The life structure he develops facilitates behavior consistent with these sex-role standards. Male sex-role standards for many men in their 40s give much greater weight to interpersonal skills, the establishment of intimacy in same- and opposite-sex relationships, as well as a temporal focus on the present instead of a constant striving for the future. The life structures for men in this period of their lives are consistent with these changes in their conceptualization of masculinity.

An individual's life structure progresses through an alternating series of stable and transition periods. Levinson et al. (1976) point out that no one life structure allows for the expression of all facets of one's "self." They argue that over time, suppressed aspects of the self increase their need for expression. This results in dissatisfaction with one's life structure and thus the individual moves into a transition period during which he reappraises his existing life structure and explores potential changes in both the self and the world. This critical reappraisal frequently results in a series of choices which will form the basis for a new life structure in the ensuing stable periods.

The present paper interprets the nature of these transition periods differently. Society expects certain kinds of behaviors from men just because of their age. Discontinuities exist in people's expectations for men at different ages. Stress from these discontinuities builds up gradually during an adult male's stable periods and finally reaches such intensity that the individual moves into what can be a rather tumultuous transition period. Each transition period represents a time during which a man cognitively and affectively reorganizes his conception of masculinity in order to meet more adequately the demands of the new age-related roles he accepts as he progresses through his adult years. This reconceptualization of the sex-role standards with which he evaluates his own masculinity requires changes in his life structure. As these modifications occur, the individual moves into his next stable period.

According to Levinson et al., the alternating sequence of transition and stable periods through which men progress between ages 18 and 45 is as follows:

a. Leaving the Family (LF): An individual's primary task is to distance himself psychologically, if not physically, from his immediate family. His self-concept becomes more firmly anchored in the external, nonfamilial world. This transition period ordinarily begins near the end of high school and continues into the early to mid-20s.
b. Getting Into the Adult World (GIAW): The primary task of this period is to gain legitimate entrance into the world of adults. The individual frequently embarks upon the implementation of his career/life style plans by establishing his first stable adult life structure.
c. Age Thirty Transition: Around age 30, many men, realizing they have ignored important needs, interests, and desires, begin questioning the validity of their past decisions. For some, this period may be characterized by turmoil and confusion, while for others it may be a rather intellectualized questioning of previous decisions.
d. Settling Down (SD): As the early life structure is questioned and modified, the in-

dividual moves into the next period of stability. He values order, stability, and security. He may appear to buttress his life structure by more strongly pursuing his goals or dreams. Levinson et al. characterize the end of this period as containing a surge for achievement and independence. They refer to this as "Becoming One's Own Man (BOOM)." The individual wants to be affirmed by society in those roles he values most.

e. Mid-Life Transition (MLT): The primary task during this transition period is to identify and incorporate into one's life structure previously suppressed and ignored aspects of one's self. Additionally, a man may recognize that many long-held beliefs or assumptions about himself and/or the world are not true. All aspects of his life structure may come into question.

f. Middle Age: Those individuals who allow themselves the time during the midlife transition to perform the necessary introspective work may find middle adulthood to be the fullest and most creative season of their life. Free from the distracting ambitions, illusions, and inhibitions of their earlier lives, men may actually become more creative and productive in ways reflecting a fuller understanding of themselves.

In order to examine the hypothesis that movement into transition periods is caused by the increasing awareness that male sex-role standards conflict with age-related standards, let us closely examine the three primary transition periods described by Levinson et al. (1976). The author agrees with Levinson et al. (1976) that these periods are crisis times. However, this paper interprets the nature of these crises differently.

Leaving the Family   Part of the stress associated with the LF transition period is caused by the need to develop new skills in response to new environmental demands. This stress is compounded because some of the new personal qualities being demanded by the environment are prohibited by the individual's traditional conception of masculinity. One of the tasks in which an individual must engage is that of questioning the basic model of masculinity which he developed in adolescence.

Adolescence is the time period in which the qualities described by Pleck (1976) as composing the traditional standards of masculinity are most uniformly endorsed as appropriate and desirable. At probably no other time in life are males quite as competitive with each other. This competition takes a variety of forms, but is expressed most graphically in physical competition. Adolescent males seem to continually test their physical instrumentality, not only on the athletic field, but in school hallways and on street corners. Status is conferred upon individuals for athletic success and/or physical toughness. The expression of vulnerability or positive feelings toward other males is particularly taboo. Even in heterosexual relationships there is an emphasis on doing rather than being, on action rather than feeling. For most adolescent males, intimacy is indistinguishable from sexuality; and sex, rather than being a modality for feeling expression, frequently becomes merely another arena for attaining success and achievement. Thus, the adolescent male enters this new transition period (LF) carrying with him a conception of masculine standards that is more traditionally stereotypic than any he will possess later in life. Concomitantly, there will probably be no time when he as adamantly rejects qualities stereotypically associated with femininity. These are the adolescent sex-role standards with which he assesses his own self-worth and his own normalcy.

As the male attempts to distance himself from his family and move into the adult world, he must confront a number of stress-producing discontinuities (Benedict, 1938). For most males, particularly those continuing with their education, the primary arena for competition and the attaining of status shifts from one requiring physical strength and prowess to one requiring a combination of intellectual and interpersonal skills. Such a shift in the valuing of skills by the environment must be confronted without the emotional support historically provided by his family and long-term familiar peer relations.

In response to this discontinuity, a young man must develop a new social/support network. For the first time in many men's lives they must independently acquire new personal relationships. However, in doing this, they are confronted with further discontinuities. The skills required to form new relationships in a strange environment may not only be different from those used in adolescence, but are frequently prohibited by adolescent sex-role standards for male behavior. During adolescence, male–male relationships were characterized by competition and an action orientation. In such relationships, males were occasionally aware of the emotional security they were obtaining, but typically this function remained covert. Support and acceptance were indirectly sought and indirectly given, strictly in accordance with the dictums of male sex-role standards. However, faced with the unfamiliar demands and requirements of the LF period, these kinds of relationships may prove less effective in meeting the individual's emotional needs. In at least a selected few male–male relationships most young men begin more explicitly sharing emotions, doubts, and indecisions. At first, such attempts to relate differently may be awkward and sporadic because these new behaviors are so explicitly prohibited by their traditional conceptions of masculinity.

Men in this period may also turn to women for support and acceptance. In high school, relationships with women typically served a number of functions, including opportunities for sexual conquest, means for acquiring new status, and companions with whom one could engage in activities in a less competitive manner than with other men. During the LF period, many men turn to women to express their doubts, concerns and fears. However, women are demanding new qualities and attributes from men in the LF period than they did during adolescence. They are less likely to accept sociability, action, and status in return for their nurturance and support. Women are looking for intimacy and are less willing to let men constantly translate this need into sexuality. Women are less likely to give emotionally to men without receiving emotionally in return. If males during the LF period are to establish mutually satisfying relationships with women, they cannot restrict their behaviors to those which worked so successfully in adolescence. Yet if they behave as demanded by women, they may feel emasculated, since these new qualities are so strongly prohibited by their adolescent male sex-role standards.

Once this adolescent conceptualization of masculinity is modified in a manner consistent with the new demands described above, one is able to respond in a more effective manner. Typically, these new standards differ from those developed in adolescence by allowing (1) greater feeling expression and, subsequently, more intimacy with women, (2) more appropriate expression of vulnerability, (3) a slight distinction between sexuality and intimacy with women, (4) more positive feeling expression with a small number of men, (5) more co-operation with a select few men, (6) less emphasis on physical instrumentality, and (7) more emphasis on intellectual productivity. This new conception of male sex-role standards is more consistent with environmental demands associated with young adulthood, thus allowing the individual to maximize the likelihood of positive self-evaluations. These new standards are then used as guidelines in the development of a new life structure which facilitates the individual's entry into the adult world. Levinson refers to this period as the GIAW (Getting Into the Adult World) years. Typically, men's life structures will emphasize career success and the acquisition of signs symbolizing status and achievement. Many men feel they can demonstrate their masculinity and adultness only by moving up their career ladder. While male sex-role standards allow for some feeling expression, men's interactions with significant others during this period are frequently superficial and designed not to "rock the boat."

Age 30 Transition   During the GIAW years the young man's evaluation of his success and normalcy has been based upon his ability to meet the standards derived from his conception of masculinity. As he has progressed through this period, he has experienced a gradual shift in environmentally originating expectations. In his career he has probably moved into a position in which his productivity is measured not by his own individual efforts, but by his ability to collaborate and cooperate with others. Thus, he experiences a seeming paradox that increasingly his ability to compete is facilitated by his ability to cooperate.

Sheehy (1974) has described the tendency in young couples for women to deemphasize their personal needs for emotional support, sharing, and spontaneity so as not to interfere with the man's task of achieving career-related success for himself and his family. During the GIAW years, she may become more willing to express these needs and demand more emotional involvement from her husband. In addition, if the couple has had children, she may experience new pressures which result in new needs for support and nurturance. By the time a man reaches his early 30s, his children are usually beyond the infant-toddler stages and are themselves making demands upon him for nurturance, support, and spontaneity.

All of these new demands require qualities which may be prohibited by the sex-role standards with which he assesses his masculinity. As the number and intensity of these new demands increase during the GIAW years, the individual experiences increasing discomfort and tension. This in turn contributes to the onset of questioning, self-doubt, and reassessment which characterizes the age 30 transition. Male sex-role standards must be questioned and the individual's conception of masculinity redefined before he can reduce the tension which arises from the conflict between his sex-role standards and the age-related demands he experiences from his environment.

This reconceptualization results in a new set of sex-role standards. The standards of the 20s are closer to traditional male sex role norms. The model which evolves during the age 30 transition incorporates some qualities typically associated with the female role during earlier life periods. The male who leaves this transition period (1) is more internally aware and emotionally expressive; (2) is able to relate on a more cooperative level with men, particularly insofar as he views this cooperation as facilitating his ability to compete in the area of career achievement; (3) is able to establish new levels of intimacy, although he may still restrict this to his relationships with a small number of significant women; (4) can assume new levels of nurturance with his children and with younger colleagues, although the ability to experience intimacy and provide nurturance is generally still not manifest in his relations with men with whom he still sees himself as competing; and (5) distinguishes between sexuality and intimacy much more clearly. He can tolerate significant others depending on him, but not his dependence on them. This new model of masculinity is utilized during the ensuing stable period, labeled by Levinson et al. (1976) as Settling Down (SD), in his self-evaluation and his evaluation of other men's masculinity and normalcy.

Midlife Transition   Although most men in their mid- to late 30s allow themselves a greater range of experience than during earlier periods, they still define a significant aspect of their maleness in terms of achievement and status. The latter part of the SD period for men is characterized by a surge for achievement and independence which Levinson describes as the BOOM period. BOOM refers to "Becoming One's Own Man." During this period, the man wants to be affirmed by society as successful in those roles he most values. These roles are usually career-related. During this period, the individual feels that if the outcome is favorable, the future is assured, and if unfavorable, then he as an individual is without value. The goal-directed nature of man's BOOM period activities may be motivated both by his desire to demonstrate that he can work in an independent and responsible manner and by his need to acquire the symbols of success, i.e., promotion, raises, and reputation. Irrespective of whether men receive the validation they so desperately seek during the BOOM period, they gradually begin moving into the midlife transition period. Men who succeed in acquiring the much sought-after signs of successful achievement frequently find their attainment hollow and empty. However, few men obtain the degree of success manifest in their youthful fantasies. This failure, or at least partial failure, is discrepant with the male standard of "reaching the top" and contributes to the need for another reformulation of their male sex-role standards. Many men in this period are also confronted with evidence that they have not been as successful in their roles of husband and father as they had hoped to be. These failures are less discrepant with their male sex-role standards than perceived career failure. They also contribute to the need to further examine and modify their model of masculinity.

A number of other factors add to the need to reassess the standards with which men evaluate themselves. Since leaving adolescence, most men have broadened their definition of performance to include interpersonal and intellectual skills and qualities. However, most men have still maintained an image of themselves as physically capable. By the late 30s it becomes increasingly difficult to believe that they are as strong, tough, manly, and sexually attractive as in their younger years. This initial awareness may precipitate crash diets and exercise programs or sexual encounters with significantly younger women. Eventually they realize that physical youthfulness is an illusion. This insight may be coupled with an awareness that the end of one's life is steadily approaching. Physicians may be warning of the need to change one's life style or friends and colleagues may be suffering their first life-threatening physical disorders.

Each of these factors contributes to men's need to find meaning in their lives. Values which they had previously attached to their careers, marriages, families, religion, and social involvements are called into question.

This examination frequently results in the incorporation of a number of qualities which are not only discrepant with traditional male sex-role standards, but also with the more modern model of masculinity described by Pleck (1976), which evolved during the two previous transition periods. This transition period is the time when many men may begin fully to experience the intensity and range of their affective life. They may discover feelings which had previously been suppressed. They realize that contradictory feelings toward the same person such as love and hate, caring and anger, jealousy and respect can coexist. These awareness may lead to a desire to experience and share more of their lives with significant others.

Men also begin to realize that life is to be lived now and not postponed until after certain tasks or goals have been successfully conquered. This temporal reorientation leads to a decrease in achievement strivings and feelings of competition. Men not only can become more cooperative with other men, but may actively seek out other men for companionship and intimacy. Men's relationships with women frequently grow more meaningful as women are viewed less as distractions from, or supporters of, their achievement strivings. Men can become more nurturant to their primary partners and their children since they now view them less as extensions of their achieving, striving selves and more as individuals in their own right. A 41-year-old man once commented to me that several years earlier his first internal response to his teenage daughter's announcement that she was pregnant was "Will this affect my promotion." Now several years later he feels embarrassed and disappointed in his reaction.

The incorporation of these new personal qualities and consequent reweighting of priorities necessitate further modification in the individual's conception of masculinity. It is important to realize that old standards are not thrown out, but rather new dimensions are incorporated and old norms modified. Men who successfully negotiate the midlife transition are still invested in being competent, successful, respected, and sexually attractive. However, they can now more realistically assess their strengths and accept their weaknesses; they are aware of previously suppressed interests and feelings and engage in activities which allow for greater expression and growth of these qualities. The successive modification at each transition period of their sex-role standards has allowed them gradually to incorporate more personal qualities into their self-images without losing self-esteem or considering themselves unmasculine.

In short, the middle-age man who has confronted the issues at each transition point in a positive, growth-oriented manner has an internal model of masculinity which can be described as androgynous. The sex-role standards with which he evaluates himself are composed of both traditional and modern components which have evolved over time in response to ever-changing environmental demands and expectations.

SUMMARY

The present paper proposed that the male sex role cannot be adequately understood without adopting a developmental orientation of the adult years. An alternating sequence of transition and stable periods was described. The author demonstrated that the onset of each transition period is elicited by the presence of conflict between a man's conception of male sex-role standards and expectations associated with the age-related roles he has assumed. The primary task in each transition period is to cognitively and affectively reorganize personal conceptualizations of the construct, masculinity. This new conception is more consistent with age-related demands and allows the individual to modify his life structure in ways consistent with his new sex-role standards. This process leads into the next stable period, which typically lasts between 5 and 7 years, after which the process repeats itself.

REFERENCES

Benedict, R. Continuities and discontinuities in cultural conditioning. *Psychiatry*, 1938, 2, 161–167.

Crandall, V. The Fels Study: Some contributions to personality development and achievement in childhood and adulthood. *Seminars in Psychiatry*, 1972, 4, 383–397.

Fasteau, M. *The male machine.* New York: McGraw-Hill, 1974.

Gould, R. The phases of adult life: A study in developmental psychology. *American Journal of Psychiatry*, 1972, 126, 33–43.

Haan, N. Personality development from adolescence to adulthood in the Oakland Growth and Guidance Studies. *Seminars in Psychiatry*, 1972, 6, 399–414.

Hartley, R. Sex role pressures in the socialization of the male child. *Psychological Reports*, 1959, 5, 457–468.

Hourard, S. Some lethal aspects of the male sex role. In S. Jourard, *The transparent self.* New York: D. Van Nostrand Company, 1971.

Jung, C. G. The stages of life. In R. F. C. Hill (Trans.), *The collected works: Structure and dynamics of the psyche* (Vol. 8). New York: Pantheon, 1960.

Knox, W., & Kupferer, H. A discontinuity in the socialization of males in the United States. *Merrill-Palmer Quarterly*, 1971, 17, 251–261.

Komarovsky, M. Cultural contradictions and sex roles: The masculine case. *American Journal of Sociology*, 1973, 4, 873–884.

Levinson, D. Mid-life transition: A period of adult psychosocial development. *Psychiatry*, 1977, 40, 99–112.

Levinson, D., Darrow, C., Klein, E., Levinson, M., & McKee, B. Periods of adult development in men: Ages 18–44. *The Counseling Psychologist*, 1976, 6, 21–25.

Mussen, P. Long term consequences of masculinity of interests in adolescence. Journal of Consulting Psychology, 1962, 26, 435–440.

Neugarten, B., & Guttman, D. Age-sex roles and personality in middle age: A thematic-apperception study. *Psychological Monographs*, 1958, 72, No. 17 (Whole No. 470).

Nichols, J. *Men's liberation: A new definition of masculinity.* New York: Penguin, 1975.

Peskin, H., & Livson, N. Pre- and post-pubertal personality and adult psychological functioning. *Seminars in Psychiatry*, 1972, 4, 343–353.

Pleck, J. The male sex role: Definitions, problems, and sources of change. *Journal of Social Issues*, 1976, 32, 155–164.

Sheehy, G. *Passages: Predictable crises of adult life.* New York: Dutton, 1974.

Shostak, A. Middle-aged working class Americans at home: Changing expectations of manhood. *Occupational Mental Health*, 1972, 3, 2–7.

Terman, L. *Psychological factors in marriage happiness.* New York: McGraw-Hill, 1938.

Valliant, G., & McArthur, C. Natural history of male psychologic health: The adult life cycle from 18–50. *Seminars in Psychiatry*, 1972, 4, 415–427.

PART THREE

♦ ♦ ♦

From Boys to Men

Matt Groening

THE ROAD TO MANHOOD

Men are not born, they are made. And the social processes by which boys become men are complex and important. How does early childhood socialization differ for boys and girls? What specific traits are emphasized for boys that mark their socialization as different. What types of institutional arrangements reinforce those traits? How do the various institutions in which boys find themselves — school, family, and friends — influence their development? What of the special institutions that promote "boy's life" or an adolescent male subculture?

During their childhood and adolescence, masculinity becomes a central theme in a boy's life. *New York Times* editor A. M. Rosenthal put the dilemma this way: "So there I was, 13 years old, the smallest boy in my freshman class at DeWitt Clinton High School, smoking a White Owl cigar. I was not only little, but I did not have longies — long trousers — and was still in knickerbockers. Obviously, I had to do something to project my fierce sense of manhood" (*New York Times*, 26 April 1987). That the assertion of manhood is part of a boy's natural development is suggested by Roger Brown, in his textbook, *Social Psychology* (NY: Free Press, 1965, p. 161):

> In the United States, a *real* boy climbs trees, disdains girls, dirties his knees, plays with soldiers, and takes blue for his favorite color. When they go to school, real boys prefer manual training, gym, and arithmetic. In college the boys smoke pipes, drink beer, and major in engineering or physics. The real boy matures into a "man's man" who plays poker, goes hunting, drinks brandy, and dies in the war.

The articles in this section address the question of a boy's development. Joseph H. Pleck provides an interesting discussion of how the rules of traditional masculinity shape the kinds of behaviors that we expect of boys. Barrie Thorne discusses the consequences of separate play for both boys and girls.

The next three articles examine distinctly male institutions. Robert Bly provides an anthropological overview of the centrality of male initiation rituals. Jeffrey P. Hantover gives an historical account of the creation of the Boy Scouts of America as an attempt to develop an institution to rescue boys from the dangers of "feminization." And if the Boy Scouts have historically been a "boy's liberation movement," the contemporary fraternity, as Peter Lyman shows, continues to provide a homosocial haven for young men, away from women, an island of brotherhood in an enervating sea. Finally, Gary Alan Fine shows how masculinity is socially constructed through the development of preadolescent male subcultures.

Joseph H. Pleck

PRISONERS OF MANLINESS

TRUE OR FALSE?

___ Boys need a father figure when they are growing up in order to become secure men.

___ Boys are harmed academically and psychologically because so many teachers in the early grades are women.

___ Male homosexuality reflects a man's confusion over his masculine role.

___ Men who have not developed a secure masculine identity are more likely than other men to be violent, hostile to women, and irrationally afraid of homosexuality.

___ Black men are especially vulnerable to problems with masculinity.

The macho image of the male may have softened recently; many men now realize that they can express tender feelings without jeopardizing their performance in business or in bed. However, the belief that it is essential for men to acquire a "sex-role identity" — expressed by masculine traits, attitudes, and interests — remains firmly entrenched. So does the belief that it is hard for men to develop this secure sense of masculinity, especially now that women are becoming more assertive.

If you answered true to all or most of the above statements, the chances are that you are still hold to the belief that a strong sex role identity is crucial to male psychological health. The notion is not just a popular prejudice. It is the creation of decades of research in psychology, including the work of some of the most prominent investigators — among them Alfred Adler, Lewis Terman, Talcott Parsons, Jerome Kagan, and E. Mavis Hetherington. It has been disseminated by other writers, notably by Benjamin Spock and by the psychologist Fitzhugh Dodson, who advised fathers in his 1974 book, *How to Father:* "Your preschool boy needs contact with you so that he can imitate you and stabilize his gender identity as a male."

Psychologists have been preoccupied with masculinity over the past several decades. Research on sex roles actually has focused primarily on men and has been dominated by two insistent questions: what makes males less masculine than they should be and what can we do about it? The answers given, both by psychologists and by other social scientists, are based on the theory of male sex-role identity, whose key assertions are summarized in the true/false statements that appear above.

My own examination of the evidence suggests that the theory is unsubstantiated and has damaging consequences for men, women, and society as a whole. The conventional expectations of what it means to be a man are difficult to live up to for all but a lucky few and lead to unnecessary self-deprecation in the rest when they do not measure up. Even for those who do, there is a price; they may be forced, for example, to inhibit the expression of many emotions.

The emergence of male-identity theory since the 1930s can best be interpreted as a response to the gradual breakdown of social and institutional structures that supported traditional sex roles — for example, the decline of the large family, which kept a woman home having babies. With industrialization and urbanization, these structures waned, leaving doubts about just what it meant to be female or male. The vacuum was neatly filled by the "discovery" that masculinity and femininity had deep psychological bases. It is no accident that the work that founded male-identity theory, *Sex and Personality*, by the Stanford psychologists Lewis Terman and Catherine Miles, was published in 1936, at the depths of the Depression, which posed the single greatest threat to the male role in U.S. history by taking away men's ability to support their families, traditionally their most important responsibility. If holding a job could no longer be counted on to define manhood, perhaps a masculinity/femininity test could.

To understand how poorly substantiated the theory of male sex-role identity is, it is important to examine the psychological research underlying each of the five basic assertions above.

Boys need a father figure when they are growing up in order to become secure men.   At issue here is not *whether* it is good for a boy to have positive relationships with his father or other adult males, but *why*. This notion implies that the most important result of a boy's contact with his father is the boy's sex-role identity — and that view raises several problems.

The research that people most often think demonstrates the point above has examined the effects on boys of having fathers who were not present. Between 1945 and 1975, this topic was more popular than almost any other in sex-role research. Many studies found no differences. Others produced conflicting results. In one experiment, Mavis Hetherington of the University of Virginia compared boys with fathers and boys without them by giving them a test in which children guessed the preferences for toys of an imaginary child named "It" (represented by a stick figure), who was supposed to be sexually neutral. Hetherington found that boys whose fathers were absent beginning in the first four years of life made fewer "masculine" choices, saying that "It" liked to play with a necklace rather than a dumptruck, for example. She interpreted this as a sign that they were having difficulty in thinking of themselves as male. Another study, by psychologists David Lynn and William Sawrey, found that the sons of Norwegian sailors who were away at least nine months a year were *more* masculine than average. The investigators interpreted the boys' behavior as indication that they were overcompensating — trying to make up for inner sexual insecurities.

These findings may indicate that father absence causes identity problems, but they may also indicate that researchers stack the deck in favor of the hypothesis: they interpret both *low* and *high* masculinity as signs of sexual insecurity. Proponents of the boys-need-male-models hypothesis explain these inconsistent results by claiming that father absence can make boys either more or less masculine depending on their personalities and circumstances.

In my view, these arguments are feeble attempts to make recalcitrant data fit the theory.

In their 1971 report, *Boys in Fatherless Families*, Elizabeth Herzog and Cecilia Sudia of the federal Office of Child Development concluded that the evidence "offers no firm basis for assuming that boys who grow up in fatherless homes are more likely, as men, to suffer from inadequate masculine identity as a result of lacking a resident male model." In school performance, Herzog and Sudia also found that if factors like class and education were equal, boys with absent fathers appeared to turn out as well as boys whose fathers were present. They did show slightly more delinquent behavior.

Other research on fathers and sons concerns the impact on a son's masculinity of variations in the father's characteristics, especially his power, his warmth, and his own degree of masculinity. Some important studies, such as the 1965 work *Identification and Child Rearing* by Stanford psychologists Robert Sears, Lucy Rau, and Richard Alpert, have found that almost no relationship exists. Other research, such as the studies conducted by Paul Mussen in the Berkeley psychology department in the 1950s and 1960s, for example, has found some relationship. However, Mussen's studies require a greater degree of faith in his measures than is usually the case in psychological research. His oft-cited findings of relationships between fathers' warmth and sons' masculinity assume, for example, that a father is friendly if a boy depicts a male character in a doll-play game as friendly and that a boy is masculine if he declares that the stick figure named "It" likes to play with a dumptruck rather than a necklace. (Those who cite Mussen's studies also usually fail to report his further finding that males who were ranked high on masculinity scales as youths displayed considerable maladjustment in adulthood.)

Today, a new generation of research is focusing on a broader range of questions: when a father is close to his children, how does his presence affect his children's thinking, how does childrearing affect his feelings about himself? As part of the contemporary reappraisal, many people now believe that if fathers are more involved in raising children than they were, children, and sons in particular, will learn that men can be warm and supportive of others as well as be high achievers. Thus, fathers' involvement may be beneficial not because it will help *support* traditional male roles, but because it will help break them down.

Boys are harmed academically and psychologically because so many teachers in the early grades are women.   Most current attention to sex role issues in education concerns the disadvantages that girls seem to face in schools. But an older elaboration of the boys-need-male-models hypothesis is still around: the theory that boys are damaged by the predominance of women in the educational system.

In her 1969 study, *The Femininized Male*, New York University sociologist Patricia C. Sexton argued: "Though run at the top by men, schools are essentially feminine institutions, from nursery school through graduate school. In the school, women set the standards for adult behavior, and many favor students, male and female, who most conform to their own behavior norms — polite, clean, obedient, neat, and nice." Sexton concluded, then, that "if the boy absorbs school values, he may become feminized himself."

The "feminization" argument involves three hypotheses: (1) boys do better with male teachers, (2) teachers "reinforce" (respond to and/or encourage) femininity in boys, and (3) boys perceive school as feminine. The evidence for all three is weak.

Studies of academic performance do not show that boys with male teachers do any better academically than boys with female teachers. On measures of social adjustment, many studies find no differences and others find only weak or inconsistent ones. For example, Dorothy J. Sciarra, now a professor of child development at the University of Cincinnati, hypothesized that male models in the early years of school would enhance boys' self-esteem, thereby decreasing both their aggression and their susceptibility to peer-group influence. When she compared boys with adult males in the classrooms and boys without, however, she found a tendency for boys with male models to be *more* susceptible to peer-group influences, although statistical tests showed that the result could have been due to change.

Sciarra handily transformed the trend disconfirming the feminization thesis into one confirming it by redefining, after the fact, the meaning of what she measured: she argued that susceptibility to peer-group pressure (a negative characteristic) was actually peer-group *cooperation* (a desirable one) and thus showed the positive effect that male models had on boys.

Reviewing the research on boys with male teachers, psychologists Dolores Gold of Concordia University and Myrna Reis of the Jewish Vocational Service of Montreal concluded that "increasing the number of male teachers in the early school grades is a proposed panacea to alleviate boys' school difficulties which . . . appeals to common sense as well as to widespread bias. However, it is an alternative which likely will not be effective."

The evidence that teachers encourage femininity in boys is also weak. Researchers often cite a 1969 study by Beverly Fagot and Gerald Patterson, psychologists at the University of Oregon, showing that teachers reinforce feminine behaviors in boys more often than masculine ones. Detailed examination of this study — which includes only two nursery school classes and four teachers — reveals, however, that the major "feminine' behaviors being reinforced were art activities and listening to stories. Perhaps more interesting than the finding that teachers reinforced those behaviors is the psychologists' interpretation of art and listening to stories as feminine.

A study that may be closer to the truth is a 1973 survey of preschool through second-grade teachers by developmental psychologist Patrick Lee and Annie Wolinsky at Columbia Teachers College. They classified only 14 percent of the activities that female teachers reinforced as female-typed; 17 percent were male-typed, and the vast majority were neutral.

Another study that is widely cited as showing teachers' alleged reinforcement of femininity was done in 1972 by psychologists Teresa Levitin and David Chananic at the University of Michigan. It found that teachers approved more of obedient and dependent fifth-grade boys than of disobedient and aggressive ones (though they reported liking the disobedient boys no less). But there too, the cards were stacked by selecting male traits that are socially undesirable and female ones that are desirable. Given such a bias, it comes as no surprise that teachers disapproved of the undesirable ones — but they disapproved of them regardless of the child's sex and because they are socially undesirable, not because they are masculine.

The idea that boys perceive school as feminine originated in an ingenuous study done in the 1960s by developmental psychologist Jerome Kagan at Harvard. Kagan's second and third graders were taught to pair sexually neutral nonsense syllables with objects pertaining to men and women — "DEP" with men's trousers and a baseball bat, "ROV" with a women's shoe and lipstick. After learning the associations, the children were then asked to guess the category, whether DEP or ROV, of each of a new set of objects, including eight related to schools, for example, a pencil, a school building, a blackboard, a page of arithmetic.

It is by no means clear from the results of Kagan's study that boys perceive school as feminine. Of the eight school-related objects, the second-grade boys rated only two (blackboard, page of arithmetic) as feminine significantly more often than masculine, but they saw two others (map, book) as masculine more often than feminine — and more strongly so. In the third grade, the boys perceived the arithmetic page as masculine, the blackboard as neutral. Thus, far from demonstrating that boys see school as feminine, Kagan's study actually found that second-grade boys perceived a minority of school objects as feminine, but they viewed an equal minority of other objects as even more strongly masculine, and that only one grade later they had discarded or even reversed their perceptions of the feminine school objects.

Male homosexuality reflects a man's confusion over his masculine role.   As psychologist Donald Brown of the U.S. Air Force Academy put it in 1957, "The male invert psychologically perceives himself as a female, and accordingly looks to the 'opposite' sex for sexual gratification. . . . Inversion has its roots in the earliest years of life when the child forms, at first involuntarily and later consciously, an identification attachment to the parent of the opposite sex and thereby internalizes the sex role of the opposite sex."

Homosexuality has always been a central preoccupation of those concerned about male identity. A major portion of Terman and Miles's *Sex and Personality* is devoted to studies of homosexuals — primarily male homosexuals. When people say they are concerned about how "male identity" is affected by whatever it is they see it threatened by (single parent families, a mother's employment, girls in school sports, and so forth), very often what they have in mind is an increased rate of male homosexuality. Homosexuality, especially in men, is thus viewed as the quintessential failure in development of normal sex-role identity.

One kind of evidence that might support this interpretation is data showing that male homosexuals emerge as more feminine than heterosexuals on tests of masculinity and femininity. The tests place people on a scale ranging from masculine to feminine according to their answers to such questions as "I prefer a shower to a bath" (Yes = masculine); "I would like to be a singer" (Yes = feminine); and "I like artichokes" (Yes = feminine). These items have distinguished men from women in at least some samples.

Data showing male homosexuals as more feminine than heterosexuals on these tests exist, but whatever they mean, much of the research is based on prisoners, who are hardly typical of all heterosexuals and homosexuals. One study actually used heterosexual rapists as the control group against whose masculinity the masculinity of homosexuals was compared!

A second problem with interpreting homosexuality as a failure to develop a masculine identity is that many studies completely fail to find significant differences in masculinity between male homosexuals and male heterosexuals.

Three recent studies, with samples of college students and improved measures that assess masculinity and femininity as separate dimensions that can coexist in anyone, yield completely inconsistent results.

In response to the empirical failings, male-identity theorists like Donald Brown and British psychiatrist D. J. West now argue that there are actually two kinds of male homosexuals: "passive" ones, who are psychologically feminine and therefore fit the original theory, and "active" ones, who are not and therefore don't. This interpretation assumes a distinction that most authorities now reject. It also has the interesting implication, quite troubling for a larger theory of male identity, that there are no differences in sex-role identity between heterosexual males and "active" homosexual males. Such intellectual surgery may reconcile the theory with the data, but it amputates a vital spot in the patient. In short, whatever does cause homosexuality, there is little evidence to show that the factors involve an inadequate sense of a masculine identity.

Men who have not developed a secure masculine identity are more likely than other men to be violent, hostile to women, and irrationally afraid of homosexuality. Weakness in sex-role identity may be reflected in too much masculinity as well as too little. The notion is that male crime, misogyny, and homophobia represent overcompensations for underlying male insecurity. To describe that phenomenon, Alfred Adler in 1927 coined the term "masculine protest." Harvard sociologist Talcott Parsons proposed in 1947 that the Western pattern of close mother–child relationships causes boys to have an unresolved feminine identification against which they psychologically defend themselves through aggression and delinquency. The idea has been further developed by numerous theorists and researchers.

In the 1950 study *The Authoritarian Personality*, Theodor Adorno and other psychologists at Berkeley suggested that this character type was, in part, the result of male insecurity. The researchers interpreted authoritarianism, which included rigidity, contempt for weakness, and intolerance of deviance — especially sexual deviance — as the underlying psychological basis of World War II fascism. (Adorno and one of his coinvestigators, Else Frenkel-Brunswick, had earlier fled from Hitler.) Nevitt Sanford, another of the investigators, wrote later that the researchers "became convinced that one of the main sources of this personality syndrome was ego-alien femininity — that is to say, underlying femininity that had to be countered by whatever defenses the subject had at his disposal." In effect, they linked men's insecure sex-role identities to the rise of Hitler and to the Holocaust.

Researchers have applied the "hypermasculinity" hypothesis most often to the relationship between delinquency and father absence, especially in black males. There, too, the evidence is thin. Herzog and Sudia concluded that in studies in which social class is controlled (a relative rarity), father absence may have a weak effect on delinquency, but that the effect is too small to have any practical significance. For example, in a 1969 study, Lawrence Rosen, a sociologist at Temple University, surveyed a probability sample of 1,098 black male youths in a 10-square-mile area of Philadelphia and found that having an absent father was connected to only 1.2 percent of the variation in the amount of delinquency among the youths. More intensive studies examining variations among delinquents, such as those conducted in 1970 by Charles Harrington at Columbia Teachers College and in 1974 by Ohio State University sociologists Ira Silverman and Simon Dinitz, find few differences among subgroups of delinquents and other institutionalized males, with or without fathers, in hypermasculinity and sex-role identity. Harrington concludes that his study "throws into some question the view of aggression as 'protest masculinity.'"

The idea that many men fear women, a fear rooted in insecure masculinity, has attracted a number of feminist scholars. Nancy Chodorow, a psychoanalytic sociologist at the University of California, Berkeley, argued in 1974 that "in his attempt to gain an elusive masculine identification . . . the boy tries to reject his mother and deny the deep personal identification with her that has developed during his early years. He does this by repressing whatever he takes to be feminine inside himself, and, importantly, by denigrating whatever he considers to be feminine in the outside world (that is, women)."

It is unclear what kind of data might provide a definitive test of this theory. Some studies find that men who say they have the closest relationships with their mothers report the most favorable attitude toward women — not the least favorable, as the theory predicts. Or do those data actually *support* the theory, because the men's profemale attitudes prove how much they are identified with their mothers? The theory's protean ability to interpret both profemininst and antifeminist attitudes as signs that a man is identified with his mother makes it possible to interpret any data as supporting the hypothesis.

There are, no doubt, some men who hate and fear women because of complex psychological dynamics deriving from their relationship with their mothers. But it is questionable whether those dynamics in the few should be invoked as the basis of the far more common, garden-variety male sexism so evident in our culture. Simpler theories can account for much, if not most, male antipathy to women: for example, negative male attitudes toward women may justify male social privilege.

Male dispositions to crime and violence, fear of women, and extreme fear of homosexuality are profoundly undesirable and cause serious social problems. Many men do indeed try to act "masculine." The question is how best to interpret their behavior. The hypermasculinity approach assumes that men have a natural inner urge to learn the male role, that many fail to attain it and therefore overcompensate, and that they — and their mothers — are ultimately at fault.

An alternative view is that people are not born with an inner psychological need to take on roles or traits different from those of the other sex, but that their culture strongly inculcates this need. If they do not spontaneously fit the cultural mold, they may try to force themselves into it. Thus, exaggerated masculinity, rather than being a reaction to inner insecurities, may reflect an over-learning of the externally prescribed role or an overconformity to it. The alternative interpretation, part of the emerging new theory of sex-role strain, puts the burden of responsibility for destructive, extreme male behavior on society's unrealistic male-role expectations — where it belongs — and not on the failings of individual men and their mothers.

Hypermasculinity arguments narrowmindedly ignore the direct role psychology has played in fostering hypermasculinity. After decades of psychological pronouncements about the deficiencies of women and the psychopathology of homosexuals, it seems a self-serving evasion of moral responsibility for psychologists to claim that the real reason that men dislike women and homosexuals is because of a sex-role identity problem caused by identifying too closely with their mothers.

Black men are especially vulnerable to problems with masculinity.   According to this idea, acquiring a secure sense of masculinity is more difficult for blacks than for whites because black fathers are absent more often and because many of them, even when present, are poor role models for their children.

Identity problems are then supposedly compounded in adulthood by higher rates of unemployment and overrepresentation in low-paying, low-prestige jobs among black men, especially such "feminine" service jobs as waiting on tables. As Harvard's social psychologist and race-relations expert Thomas F. Pettigrew expressed it in 1964, among black males "the sex-identity problems created by the fatherless home are perpetuated in adulthood." In their 1968 best-seller, *Black Rage*, psychiatrists William Grier and Price Cobbs asserts that "whereas the white man regards his manhood as an ordained right, the black man is engaged in a never-ending struggle for its possession."

Pettigrew based his conclusions about blacks' greater sex-role identity problems (as shown by masculinity/femininity measures) on only two studies — one involving a sample of Alabama convicts, the other a sample of tubercular working-class veterans in Wisconsin — hardly a broad base of evidence. More recent studies, with both more representative samples and better sex-role measures, have not found the same differences between blacks and whites.

The "black emasculation" hypothesis was in vogue in the late 1960s and early 1970s. Its appeal to liberals arguing for equal rights is obvious: it holds that the racial oppression of blacks, in addition to producing the obvious consequences of poverty, shorter life expectancy, and so forth, has an even more insidious and subtle effect — the destruction of black men's masculinity. That apparently radical critique of racism conceals a patronizing view of blacks as psychological cripples and masks as well a deeply conservative notion of what proper sex roles ought to be.

Nowhere is that more evident than in Daniel Patrick Moynihan's 1967 work, *The Negro Family: The Case for National Action*, the famous "Moynihan Report." Moynihan argued for the worthy objective of a federal policy to promote full employment targeted especially at black males. But his justification for it hinged on the hypothetically devastating consequences of unemployment on black males' sex-role identities. In Moynihan's view, "the very essence of the male animal, from the bantam rooster to the four-star general, is to strut." Writing as America mobilized for a war in Vietnam, he praised military service as an almost ideal solution to black men's frustrated masculinity: "Given the strains of the disorganized and matrifocal family life in which so many Negro youth come of age, the Armed Forces are a dramatic and desperately needed change: a world away from women, a world run by strong men of unquestioned authority."

Another example of the patronization inherent in the black-emasculation hypothesis occurred in a popular book on fatherhood, *Father Power*, published in 1965 by University of Rhode Island psychologist Henry Biller and journalist Dennis Meredith. Material on black fathers appears in a chapter titled "Fathers with Special Problems." The only other example given there is the physically handicapped father.

Like the hypermasculinity hypothesis, the black-emasculation hypothesis ultimately blames the victim of a social problem for having it. Many critics have responded to this idea in narrow terms, arguing that black men have other role models, that their sexual identities are not impaired, or even that they actually are more masculine than white men. Few critics, unfortunately, have questioned the concept of sex-role identity itself. Few have asked just how much the notion of sex-role identity really does add to our understanding of the more basic issues — issues involving the negative impact of poverty, unemployment, or unsatisfying jobs on black (or any other) men.

On the basis of the evidence, we cannot go so far as to say that these five assertions have been proven false; in research, negative findings can never conclusively prove that a relationship does not exist, but can only show that a relationship has not been confirmed. We can say, however, that many popular ideas about masculinity that are widely thought to be backed up by decades of research have not been substantiated.

Unsubstantiated theories of masculinity have negative consequences for both sexes. In making women responsible for male insecurity and hostility, traditional male sex-role identity theory has made women both villains and victims in a male struggle for masculinity. The theory also holds that sex roles cannot change substantially because male identity is so fragile, a belief that leads to policies and strategies for imprisoning men in traditional roles, just as exaggerated ideas of women's fragility support restrictions on them. When a school district in West Virginia introduced a home economics curriculum that included homemaking skills for boys, members of the community opposed it on the grounds that it would turn their sons into homosexuals. The argument, typical of many, implies that the only way to make a man secure in his sex-role identity is to lock him up within it.

At last, a new approach to understanding masculinity and femininity is emerging, based on quite different assumptions — the theory of sex-role strain. In this view, there is no special need to encourage men and women to take different roles. If women and men do differ biologically in ways that cause different psychological traits (researchers are still debating), this approach says these differences will express themselves without help from parents and psychologists anxious about their children's sex-role identity. The point is not that we have to make men and women the same, but rather, that we do not have to strive so hard to make them different.

Researchers taking the new approach are investigating how traditional cultural standards for men and women create feelings of inadequacy if those standards are not achieved and other problems if they are. For example, what are the consequences of raising women to inhibit their achievement and men to inhibit their emotions? How does perceiving a difference between oneself and a cultural ideal for one's sex impair well-being? In the new view, the problem of sex roles is not how to learn a predetermined sex-role identity but rather how to avoid the strain built into traditional roles.

The feminist journalist Letty Cottin Pogrebin recently noted that feminist parents often find it easier to understand what nonsexist childrearing means for their daughters than for their sons. They support nontraditional activities and interests for daughters, but are often concerned if their sons are not aggressive and competitive or are sensitive or artistic ("They eventually have to face the real world, don't they?"). The journalists Lindsy Van Gelder and Carrie Carmichael reported in *Ms.* magazine in 1975 that when they asked a sample of feminist parents what they were doing to make their sons less like typical males, parents either had no response or expressed fears that any changes in traditional childrearing would make their sons homosexual. Van Gelder and Carmichael suggest that unless something is done to support change in men's roles, when today's daughters "reach womanhood in the 1990s, they will be confronted with a new generation of perfectly preserved 1960s males." So, indeed, they will — unless we demystify psychological myths of masculinity.

FURTHER READINGS

Gold, Dolores, and Myrna Reis, *Do Male Teachers in the Early School Years Make a Difference?* ERIC Clearinghouse, 1978.

Herzog, Elizabeth and Cecilia Sudia, "Children in Fatherless Families," in *Review of Child Development Research.* Vol. 3. Bettye Caldwell and Henry N. Ricciult, eds., University of Chicago Press, 1973.

Pogrebin, Letty Cottin, *Growing Up Free.* McGraw Hill, 1980.

Barrie Thorne

GIRLS AND BOYS TOGETHER . . .
BUT MOSTLY APART:
GENDER ARRANGEMENTS IN ELEMENTARY SCHOOLS

Throughout the years of elementary school, children's friendships and casual encounters are strongly separated by sex. Sex segregation among children, which starts in preschool and is well established by middle childhood, has been amply documented in studies of children's groups and friendships (e.g., Eder & Hallinan, 1978; Schofield, 1981) and is immediately visible in elementary school settings. When children choose seats in classrooms or the cafeteria, or get into line, they frequently arrange themselves in same-sex clusters. At lunchtime, they talk matter-of-factly about "girls' tables" and "boys' tables." Playgrounds have gendered turfs, with some areas and activities, such as large playing fields and basketball courts, controlled mainly by boys, and others — smaller enclaves like jungle-gym areas and concrete spaces for hopscotch or jumprope — more often controlled by girls. Sex segregation is so common in elementary schools that it is meaningful to speak of separate girls' and boys' worlds.

Studies of gender and children's social relations have mostly followed this "two worlds" model, separately describing and comparing the subcultures of girls and of boys (e.g., Lever, 1976; Maltz & Borker, 1983). In brief summary: Boys tend to interact in larger, more age-heterogeneous groups (Lever, 1976; Waldrop & Halverson, 1975; Eder & Hallinan, 1978). They engage in more rough and tumble play and physical fighting (Maccoby & Jacklin, 1974). Organized sports are both a central activity and a major metaphor in boys' subcultures; they use the language of "teams" even when not engaged in sports,

and they often construct interaction in the form of contests. The shifting hierarchies of boys' groups (Savin-Williams, 1976) are evident in their more frequent
use of direct commands, insults, and challenges (Goodwin, 1980).

Fewer studies have been done of girls' groups (Foot, Chapman, & Smith,
1980; McRobbie & Garber, 1975), and — perhaps because categories for description and analysis have come more from male than female experience —
researchers have had difficulty seeing and analyzing girls' social relations. Recent work has begun to correct this skew. In middle childhood, girls' worlds are
less public than those of boys; girls more often interact in private places and in
smaller groups or friendship pairs (Eder & Hallinan, 1978; Waldrop & Halverson, 1975). Their play is more cooperative and turn-taking (Lever, 1976). Girls
have more intense and exclusive friendships, which take shape around keeping
and telling secrets, shifting alliances, and indirect ways of expressing disagree-
ment (Goodwin, 1980; Lever, 1976; Maltz & Borker, 1983). Instead of direct
commands, girls more often use directives which merge speaker and hearer,
e.g., "let's" or "we gotta" (Goodwin, 1980).

Although much can be learned by comparing the social organization and subcultures of boys' and of girls' groups, the separate worlds approach has eclipsed
full, contextual understanding of gender and social relations among children.
The separate worlds model essentially involves a search for group sex differences, and shares the limitations of individual sex difference research. Differences tend to be exaggerated and similarities ignored, with little theoretical attention to the integration of similarity and difference (Unger, 1979). Statistical
findings of difference are often portrayed as dichotomous, neglecting the considerable individual variation that exists; for example, not all boys fight, and
some have intense and exclusive friendships. The sex difference approach tends
to abstract gender from its social context, to assume that males and females are
qualitatively and permanently different (with differences perhaps unfolding
through separate developmental lines). These assumptions mask the possibility
that gender arrangements and patterns of similarity and difference may vary by
situation, race, social class, region, or subculture.

Sex segregation is far from total, and is a more complex and dynamic process
than the portrayal of separate worlds reveals. Erving Goffman (1977) has observed that sex segregation has a "with-then-apart" structure; the sexes segregate
periodically, with separate spaces, rituals, groups, but they also come together
and are, in crucial ways, part of the same world. This is certainly true in the
social environment of elementary schools. Although girls and boys do interact
as boundaried collectivities — an image suggested by the separate worlds approach — there are other occasions when they work or play in relaxed and
integrated ways. Gender is less central to the organization and meaning of some
situations than others. In short, sex segregation is not static, but is a variable
and complicated process.

To gain an understanding of gender which can encompass both the "with"
and the "apart" of sex segregation, analysis should start not with the individual,
nor with a search for sex differences, but with social relationships. Gender
should be conceptualized as a system of relationships rather than as an immutable and dichotomous given. Taking this approach, I have organized my research on gender and children's social relations around questions like the following: How and when does gender enter into group formation? In a given
situation, how is gender made more or less salient or infused with particular

meanings? By what rituals, processes, and forms of social organization and conflict do "with-then-apart" rhythms get enacted? How are these processes affected by the organization of institutions (e.g., different types of schools, neighborhoods, or summer camps), varied settings (e.g., the constraints and possibilities governing interaction on playgrounds vs. classrooms), and particular encounters?

METHODS AND SOURCES OF DATA

This study is based on two periods of participant observation. In 1976–1977 I observed for 8 months in a largely working-class elementary school in California, a school with 8% Black and 12% Chicana/o students. In 1980 I did fieldwork for 3 months in a Michigan elementary school of similar size (around 400 students), social class, and racial composition. I observed in several classrooms — a kindergarten, a second grade, and a combined fourth-fifth grade — and in school hallways, cafeterias, and playgrounds. I set out to follow the round of the school day as children experience it, recording their interactions with one another, and with adults, in varied settings.

Participant observation involves gaining access to everyday, "naturalistic" settings and taking systematic notes over an extended period of time. Rather than starting with preset categories for recording, or with fixed hypotheses for testing, participant-observers record detail in ways which maximize opportunities for discovery. Through continuous interaction between observation and analysis, "grounded theory" is developed (Glaser & Strauss, 1967).

The distinctive logic and discipline of this mode of inquiry emerges from: (1) theoretical sampling — being relatively systematic in the choice of where and whom to observe in order to maximize knowledge relevant to categories and analysis which are being developed; and (2) comparing all relevant data on a given point in order to modify emerging propositions to take account of discrepant cases (Katz, 1983). Participant observation is a flexible, open-ended and inductive method, designed to understand behavior within, rather than stripped from, social context. It provides richly detailed information which is anchored in everyday meanings and experience.

DAILY PROCESSES OF SEX SEGREGATION

Sex segregation should be understood not as a given, but as the result of deliberate activity. The outcome is dramatically visible when there are separate girls' and boys' tables in school lunchrooms, or sex-separated groups on playgrounds. But in the same lunchroom one can also find tables where girls and boys eat and talk together, and in some playground activities the sexes mix. By what processes do girls and boys separate into gender-defined and relatively boundaried collectivities? And in what contexts, and through what processes, do boys and girls interact in less gender-divided ways?

In the school settings I observed, much segregation happened with no mention of gender. Gender was implicit in the contours of friendship, shared interest, and perceived risk which came into play when children chose companions — in their prior planning, invitations, seeking-of-access, saving-of-places, denials of entry, and allowing or protesting of "cuts" by those who violated the rules for lining up. Sometimes children formed mixed-sex groups for play, eating, talking, working on a classroom project, or moving through space. When adults or children explicitly invoked gender — and this was nearly always in ways which separated girls and boys — boundaries were heightened and mixed-sex interaction became an explicit arena of risk.

In the schools I studied, the physical space and curricula were not formally divided by sex, as they have been in the history of elementary schooling (a history evident in separate entrances to old school buildings, where the words "Boys" and "Girls" are permanently etched in concrete). Nevertheless, gender was a visible marker in the adult-organized school day. In both schools, when the public address system sounded, the principal inevitably opened with: "Boys and girls . . . ," and in addressing clusters of children, teachers and aides regularly used gender terms ("Heads down, girls"; "The girls are ready and the boys aren't"). These forms of address made gender visible and salient, conveying an assumption that the sexes are separate social groups.

Teachers and aides sometimes drew upon gender as a basis for sorting children and organizing activities. Gender is an embodied and visual social category which roughly divides the population in half, and the separation of girls and boys permeates the history and lore of schools and playgrounds. In both schools — although through awareness of Title IX, many teachers had changed this practice — one could see separate girls' and boys' lines moving, like caterpillars, through the school halls. In the 4th–5th grade classroom the teacher frequently pitted girls against boys for spelling and math contests. On the playground in the Michigan school, aides regarded the space close to the building as girls' territory, and the playing fields "out there" as boys' territory. They sometimes shooed children of the other sex away from those spaces, especially boys who ventured near the girls' area and seemed to have teasing in mind.

In organizing their activities, both within and apart from the surveillance of adults, children also explicitly invoked gender. During my fieldwork in the Michigan school, I kept daily records of who sat where in the lunchroom. The amount of sex segregation varied: It was least at the first grade tables and almost total among sixth graders. There was also variation from classroom to classroom within a given age, and from day to day. Actions like the following heightened the gender divide:

> In the lunchroom, when the two second grade tables were filling, a high-status boy walked by the inside table, which had a scattering of both boys and girls, and said loudly, "Oooo, too many girls," as he headed for a seat at the far table. The boys at the inside table picked up their trays and moved, and no other boys sat at the inside table, which the pronouncement had effectively made taboo.

In the end, that day (which was not the case every day), girls and boys ate at separate tables.

Eating and walking are not sex-typed activities, yet in forming groups in lunchrooms and hallways children often separated by sex. Sex segregation assumed added dimensions on the playground, where spaces, equipment, and activities were infused with gender meanings. My inventories of activities and groupings on the playground showed similar patterns in both schools: Boys controlled the large fixed spaces designated for team sports (baseball diamonds, grassy fields used for football or soccer); girls more often played closer to the building, doing tricks on the monkey bars (which, for 6th graders, became an area for sitting and talking) and using cement areas for jumprope, hopscotch, and group games like four-square. (Lever, 1976, provides a good analysis of sex-divided play.) Girls and boys most often played together in kickball, and in group (rather than team) games like four-square, dodgeball, and handball. When children used gender to exclude others from play, they often drew upon beliefs connecting boys to some activities and girls to others:

> A first grade boy avidly watched an all-female game of jump rope. When the girls began to shift positions, he recognized a means of access to the play and he offered, "I'll swing it." A girl responded, "No way, you don't know how to do it, to swing it. You gotta be a girl." He left without protest.

Although children sometimes ignored pronouncements about what each sex could or could not do, I never heard them directly challenge such claims.

When children had explicitly defined an activity or a group as gendered, those who crossed the boundary — especially boys who moved into female-marked space — risked being teased. ("Look! Mike's in the girls' line!" "'That's a girl over there,' a girl said loudly, pointing to a boy sitting at an otherwise all-female table in the lunchroom.") Children, and occasionally adults, used teasing — especially the tease of "liking" someone of the other sex, or of "being" that sex by virtue of being in their midst — to police gender boundaries. Much of the teasing drew upon heterosexual romantic definitions, making cross-sex interaction risky, and increasing social distance between boys and girls.

RELATIONSHIPS BETWEEN THE SEXES

Because I have emphasized the "apart" and ignored the occasions of "with," this analysis of sex segregation falsely implies that there is little contact between girls and boys in daily school life. In fact, relationships between girls and boys — which should be studied as fully as, and in connection with, same-sex relationships — are of several kinds:

1. "Borderwork," or forms of cross-sex interaction which are based upon and reaffirm boundaries and asymmetries between girls' and boys' groups;
2. Interactions which are infused with heterosexual meanings;
3. Occasions where individuals cross gender boundaries to participate in the world of the other sex; and
4. Situations where gender is muted in salience, with girls and boys interacting in more relaxed ways.

Borderwork   In elementary school settings boys' and girls' groups are sometimes spatially set apart. Same-sex groups sometimes claim fixed territories such as the basketball court, the bars, or specific lunchroom tables. However, in the crowded, multifocused, and adult-controlled environment of the school, groups form and disperse at a rapid rate and can never stay totally apart. Contact between girls and boys sometimes lessens sex segregation, but gender-defined groups also come together in ways which emphasize their boundaries.

"Borderwork" refers to interaction across, yet based upon and even strengthening gender boundaries. I have drawn this notion from Fredrik Barth's (1969) analysis of social relations which are maintained across ethnic boundaries with-

out diminishing dichotomized ethnic status.[1] His focus is on more macro, eco-
logical arrangements; mine is on face-to-face behavior. But the insight is similar:
Groups may interact in ways which strengthen their borders, and the maintenance of ethnic (or gender) groups can best be understood by examining the
boundary that defines the group, "not the cultural stuff that it encloses" (Barth,
1969, p. 15). In elementary schools there are several types of borderwork: contests or games where gender-defined teams compete; cross-sex rituals of chasing
and pollution; and group invasions. These interactions are asymmetrical, challenging the separate-but-parallel model of "two worlds."

Contests   Boys and girls are sometimes pitted against each other in classroom
competitions and playground games. The 4th–5th grade classroom had a boys'
side and a girls' side, an arrangement that re-emerged each time the teacher
asked children to choose their own desks. Although there was some within-sex
shuffling, the result was always a spatial moiety system — boys on the left,
girls on the right — with the exception of one girl (the "tomboy" whom I'll
describe later), who twice chose a desk with the boys and once with the girls.
Drawing upon and reinforcing the children's self-segregation, the teacher often
pitted the boys against the girls in spelling and math competitions, events
marked by cross-sex antagonism wand within-sex solidarity:

> The teacher introduced a math game; she would write addition and sub-
> traction problems on the board, and a member of each team would race
> to be the first to write the correct answer. She wrote two score-keeping
> columns on the board: 'Beastly Boys' . . . 'Gossipy Girls.' The boys yelled
> out, as several girls laughed, 'Noisy girls! Gruesome girls!' The girls sat
> in a row on top of their desks; sometimes they moved collectively, pushing
> their hips or whispering 'pass it on.' The boys stood along the wall, some
> reclining against desks. When members of either group came back victo-
> rious from the front of the room, they would do the 'giving five' hand-
> slapping ritual with their team members.

On the playground a team of girls occasionally played against a team of boys,
usually in kickball or team two-square. Sometimes these games proceeded matter-of-factly, but if gender became the explicit basis of team solidarity, the interaction changed, becoming more antagonistic and unstable:

> Two fifth-grade girls against two fifth-grade boys in a team game of two-
> square. The game proceeded at an even pace until an argument ensued
> about whether the ball was out or on the line. Karen, who had hit the
> ball, became annoyed, flashed her middle finger at the other team, and
> called to a passing girl to join their side. The boys then called out to other
> boys, and cheered as several arrived to play. 'We got five and you got
> three!' Jack yelled. The game continued, with the girls yelling, 'Bratty
> boys! Sissy boys!' and the boys making noises — 'weee haw' 'ha-ha-ha' —
> as they played.

Chasing   Cross-sex chasing dramatically affirms boundaries between girls and
boys. The basic elements of chase and elude, capture and rescue (Sutton-Smith,

---

1. I am grateful to Frederick Erickson for suggesting the relevance of Barth's analysis.

1971) are found in various kinds of tag with formal rules, and in informal episodes of chasing which punctuate life on playgrounds. These episodes begin with a provocation (taunts like "You can't get me!" or "Slobber monster!"; bodily pokes or the grabbing of possessions). A provocation may be ignored, or responded to by chasing. Chaser and chased may then alternate roles. In an ethnographic study of chase sequences on a school playground, Christine Finnan (1982) observes that chases vary in number of chasers to chased (e.g., one chasing one, or five chasing two); form of provocation (a taunt or a poke); outcome (an episode may end when the chased outdistances the chaser, or with a brief touch, being wrestled to the ground, or the recapturing of a hat or a ball); and in use of space (there may or may not be safety zones).

Like Finnan (1982), and Sluckin (1981), who studied a playground in England, I found that chasing has a gendered structure. Boys frequently chase one another, an activity which often ends in wrestling and mock fights. When girls chase girls, they are usually less physically aggressive; they less often, for example, wrestle one another to the ground.

Cross-sex chasing is set apart by special names — "girls chase the boys"; "boys chase the girls"; "the chase"; "chasers"; "chase and kiss"; "kiss chase"; "kissers and chasers"; "kiss or kill" — and by children's animated talk about the activity. The names vary by region and school, but contain both gender and sexual meanings (this form of play is mentioned, but only briefly analyzed, in Finnan, 1981; Sluckin, 1981; Parrott, 1972; and Borman, 1979).

In "boys chase the girls" and "girls chase the boys" (the names most frequently used in both the California and Michigan schools) boys and girls become, by definition, separate teams. Gender terms override individual identities, especially for the other team ("Help, a girl's chasin' me!"; "C'mon Sarah, let's get that boy"; "Tony, help save me from the girls"). Individuals may call for help from, or offer help to, others of their sex. They may also grab someone of their sex and turn them over to the opposing team: "Ryan grabbed Billy from behind, wrestling him to the ground. 'Hey, girls, get 'im,' Ryan called."

Boys more often mix episodes of cross-sex with same-sex chasing. Girls more often have safety zones, places like the girls' restroom or an area by the school wall, where they retreat to rest and talk (sometimes in animated postmortems) before new episodes of cross-sex chasing begin.

Early in the fall in the Michigan school, where chasing was especially prevalent, I watched a second grade boy teach a kindergarten girl how to chase. He slowly ran backwards, beckoning her to pursue him, as he called, "Help, a girl's after me." In the early grades chasing mixes with fantasy play, e.g., a first-grade boy who played "sea monster," his arms outflung and his voice growling, as he chased a group of girls. By third grade, stylized gestures — exaggerated stalking motions, screams (which only girls do), and karate kicks — accompany scenes of chasing.

Names like "chase and kiss" mark the sexual meanings of cross-sex chasing, a theme I return to later. The threat of kissing — most often girls threatening to kiss boys — is a ritualized form of provocation. Cross-sex chasing among sixth graders involves elaborate patterns of touch and touch avoidance, which adults see as sexual. The principal told the sixth graders in the Michigan school that they were not to play "pom-pom," a complicated chasing game, because it entailed "inappropriate touch."

Rituals of Pollution   Cross-sex chasing is sometimes entwined with rituals of pollution, as in "cooties," where specific individuals or groups are treated as contaminating or carrying "germs." Children have rituals for transfering cooties (usually touching someone else and shouting "You've got cooties!"), for immunization (e.g., writing "CV" for "cootie vaccination" on their arms), and for eliminating cooties (e.g., saying "no gives" or using "cootie catchers" made of folded paper) described in Knapp & Knapp, 1976). While girls may give cooties to girls, boys do not generally give cooties to one another (Samuelson, 1980).

In cross-sex play, either girls or boys may be defined as having cooties, which they transfer through chasing and touching. Girls give cooties to boys more often than vice versa. In Michigan, one version of cooties is called "girl stain"; the fourth-graders whom Karkau, 1973, describes, used the phrase "girl touch." "Cootie queens," or "cootie girls" (there are no "kings" or "boys") are female pariahs, the ultimate school untouchables, seen as contaminating not only by virtue of gender, but also through some added stigma such as being overweight or poor.[2] That girls are seen as more polluting than boys is a significant asymmetry, which echoes cross-cultural patterns, although in other cultures female pollution is generally connected to menstruation, and not applied to prepubertal girls.

Invasions   Playground invasions are another asymmetric form of borderwork. On a few occasions I saw girls invade and disrupt an all-male game, most memorably a group of tall sixth-grade girls who ran onto the playing field and grabbed a football which was in play. The boys were surprised and frustrated, and, unusual for boys this old, finally tattled to the aide. But in the majority of cases, boys disrupt girls' activities rather than vice versa. Boys grab the ball from girls playing four-square, stick feet into a jumprope and stop an ongoing game, and dash through the area of the bars, where girls are taking turns performing, sending the rings flying. Sometimes boys ask to join a girls' game and then, after a short period of seemingly earnest play, disrupt the game:

> Two second-grade boys begged to "twirl" the jumprope for a group of second-grade girls who had been jumping for some time. The girls agreed, and the boys began to twirl. Soon, without announcement, the boys changed from "seashells, cockle bells" to "hot peppers" (spinning the rope very fast), and tangled the jumper in the rope. The boys ran away laughing.

Boys disrupt girls' play so often that girls have developed almost ritualized responses: They guard their ongoing play, chase boys away, and tattle to the aides. In a playground cycle which enhances sex segregation, aides who try to spot potential trouble before it occurs sometimes shoo boys away from areas where girls are playing. Aides do not anticipate trouble from girls who seek to join groups of boys, with the exception of girls intent on provoking a chase sequence. And indeed, if they seek access to a boys' game, girls usually play with boys in earnest rather than breaking up the game.

2. Sue Samuelson (1980) reports that in a racially mixed playground in Fresno, California, Mexican-American, but not Anglo children gave cooties. Racial, as well as sexual inequality may be expressed through these forms.

A close look at the organization of borderwork — or boundaried interactions between the sexes — shows that the worlds of boys and girls may be separate, but they are not parallel, nor are they equal. The worlds of girls and boys articulate in several asymmetric ways:

1. On the playground, boys control as much as ten times more space than girls, when one adds up the area of large playing fields and compares it with the much smaller areas where girls predominate. Girls, who play closer to the building, are more often watched over and protected by the adult aides.
2. Boys invade all-female games and scenes of play much more than girls invade boys. This, and boys' greater control of space, correspond with other findings about the organization of gender, and inequality, in our society: compared with men and boys, women and girls take up less space, and their space, and talk, are more often violated and interrupted (Greif, 1982; Henley, 1977; West & Zimmerman, 1983).
3. Although individual boys are occasionally treated as contaminating (e.g., a third grade boy who both boys and girls was "stinky" and "smelled like pee"), girls are more often defined as polluting. This pattern ties to themes that I discuss later: It is more taboo for a boy to play with (as opposed to invade) girls, and girls are more sexually defined than boys.

A look at the boundaries between the separated worlds of girls and boys illuminates within-sex hierarchies of status and control. For example, in the sex-divided seating in the 4th–5th grade classroom, several boys recurringly sat near "female space": their desks were at the gender divide in the classroom, and they were more likely than other boys to sit at a predominantly female table in the lunchroom. These boys — two nonbilingual Chicanos and an overweight "loner" boy who was afraid of sports — were at the bottom of the male hierarchy. Gender is sometimes used as a metaphor for male hierarchies; the inferior status of boys at the bottom is conveyed by calling them "girls":

> Seven boys and one girl were playing basketball. Two younger boys came over and asked to play. While the girl silently stood, fully accepted in the company of players, one of the older boys disparagingly said to the younger boys, 'You girls can't play.'[3]

In contrast, the girls who more often travel in the boys' world, sitting with groups of boys in the lunchroom or playing basketball, soccer, and baseball with them, are not stigmatized. Some have fairly high status with other girls. The worlds of girls and boys are assymetrically arranged, and spatial patterns map out interacting forms of inequality.

Heterosexual Meanings   The organization and meanings of gender (the social categories "woman/man," "girl/boy") and of sexuality vary cross-culturally (Ortner & Whitehead, 1981) — and, in our society, across the life course. Harriet Whitehead (1981) observed that in our (Western) gender system, and that of many traditional North American Indian cultures, one's choice of a sexual object, occupation, and one's dress and demeanor are closely associated with gen-

---

3. This incident was recorded by Margaret Blume, who, for an undergraduate research project in 1982, observed in the California school where I earlier did fieldwork. Her observations and insights enhanced my own, and I would like to thank her for letting me cite this excerpt.

der. However, the "center of gravity" differs in the two gender systems. For Indians, occupational pursuits provide the primary imagery of gender; dress and demeanor are secondary, and sexuality is least important. In our system, at least for adults, the order is reversed: heterosexuality is central to our definitions of "man" and "woman" ("masculinity"/"femininity"), and the relationships that obtain between them, whereas occupation and dress/demeanor are secondary.

Whereas erotic orientation and gender are closely linked in our definitions of adults, we define children as relatively asexual. Activities and dress/demeanor are more important than sexuality in the cultural meanings of "girl" and "boy." Children are less heterosexually defined than adults, and we have nonsexual imagery for relations between girls and boys. However, both children and adults sometimes use heterosexual language — "crushes," "like," "goin' with," "girlfriends," and "boyfriends" — to define cross-sex relationships. This language increases through the years of elementary school; the shift to adolescence consolidates a gender system organized around the institution of heterosexuality.

In everyday life in the schools, heterosexual and romantic meanings infuse some ritualized forms of interaction between groups of boys and girls (e.g., "chase and kiss") and help maintain sex segregation. "Jimmy likes Beth" or "Beth likes Jimmy" is a major form of teasing, which a child risks in choosing to sit by or walk with someone of the other sex. The structure of teasing, and children's sparse vocabulary for relationships between girls and boys, are evident in the following conversation which I had with a group of third-grade girls in the lunchroom:

> Susan asked me what I was doing, and I said I was observing the things children do and play. Nicole volunteered, 'I like running, boys chase all the girls. See Tim over there? Judy chases him all around the school. She likes him.' Judy, sitting across the table, quickly responded, 'I hate him. I like him for a friend.' 'Tim loves Judy,' Nicole said in a loud, sing-song voice.

In the younger grades, the culture and lore of girls contain more heterosexual romantic themes than that of boys. In Michigan, the first-grade girls often jumped rope to a rhyme which began: "Down in the valley where the green grass grows, there sat Cindy (name of jumper), as sweet as a rose. She sat, she sat, she sat so sweet. Along came Jason, and kissed her on the cheek . . . first comes love, then comes marriage, then along comes Cindy with a baby carriage . . ." Before a girl took her turn at jumping, the chanters asked her "Who do you want to be your boyfriend?" The jumper always proffered a name, which was accepted matter-of-factly. In chasing, a girl's kiss carried greater threat than a boy's kiss; "girl touch," when defined as contaminating, had sexual connotations. In short, starting at an early age, girls are more sexually defined than boys.

Through the years of elementary school, and increasing with age, the idiom of heterosexuality helps maintain the gender divide. Cross-sex interactions, especially when children initiate them, are fraught with the risk of being teased about "liking" someone of the other sex. I learned of several close cross-sex friendships, formed and maintained in neighborhoods and church, which went underground during the school day.

By the fifth grade a few children began to affirm, rather than avoid, the charge of having a girlfriend or a boyfriend; they introduced the heterosexual courtship rituals of adolescence:

> In the lunchroom in the Michigan school, as the tables were forming, a high-status fifth-grade boy called out from his seat at the table: 'I want Trish to sit by me.' Trish came over, and almost like a king and queen, they sat at the gender divide — a row of girls down the table on her side, a row of boys on his.

In this situation, which inverted earlier forms, it was not a loss, but a gain in status to publically choose a companion of the other sex. By affirming his choice, the boy became unteasable (note the familiar asymmetry of heterosexual courtship rituals: the male initiated). This incident signals a temporal shift in arrangements of sex and gender.

Traveling in the World of the Other Sex   Contests, invasions, chasing, and heterosexually-defined encounters are based upon and reaffirm boundaries between girls and boys. In another type of cross-sex interaction, individuals (or sometimes pairs) cross gender boundaries, seeking acceptance in a group of the other sex. Nearly all the cases I saw of this were tomboys — girls who played organized sports and frequently sat with boys in the cafeteria or classroom. If these girls were skilled at activities central in the boys' world, especially games like soccer, baseball, and basketball, they were pretty much accepted as participants.

Being a tomboy is a matter of degree. Some girls seek access to boys' groups but are excluded; other girls limit their "crossing" to specific sports. Only a few — such as the tomboy I mentioned earlier, who chose a seat with the boys in the sex-divided fourth–fifth grade — participate fully in the boys' world. That particular girl was skilled at the various organized sports which boys played in different seasons of the year. She was also adept at physical fighting and at using the forms of arguing, insult, teasing, naming, and sports-talk of the boys' subculture. She was the only Black child in her classroom, in a school with only 8% Black students; overall that token status, along with unusual athletic and verbal skills, may have contributed to her ability to move back and forth across the gender divide. Her unique position in the children's world was widely recognized in the school. Several times, the teacher said to me, "She thinks she's a boy."

I observed only one boy in the upper grades (a fourth grader) who regularly played with all-female groups, as opposed to "playing at" girls' games and seeking to disrupt them. He frequently played jumprope and took turns with girls doing tricks on the bars, using the small gestures — for example, a helpful push on the heel of a girl who needed momentum to turn her body around the bar — which mark skillful and earnest participation. Although I never saw him play in other than an earnest spirit, the girls often chased him away from their games, and both girls and boys teased him. The fact that girls seek, and have more access to boys' worlds than vice versa, and the fact that girls who travel with the other sex are less stigmatized for it, are obvious asymmetrices, tied to the asymmetries previously discussed.

Relaxed Cross-Sex Interactions   Relationships between boys and girls are not always marked by strong boundaries, heterosexual definitions, or by interacting

on the terms and turfs of the other sex. On some occasions girls and boys interact in relatively comfortable ways. Gender is not strongly salient nor explicitly invoked, and girls and boys are not organized into boundaries collectivities.
These "with" occasions have been neglected by those studying gender and children's relationships, who have emphasized either the model of separate worlds
(with little attention to their articulation) or heterosexual forms of contact.

Occasions where boys and girls interact without strain, where gender wanes,
rather than waxes in importance, frequently have one or more of the following
characteristics:

1. The situations are organized around an absorbing task, such as a group art project
   or creating a radio show, which encourages cooperation and lessens attention to
   gender. This pattern accords with other studies finding that cooperative activities
   reduce group antagonism (e.g., Sherif & Sherif, 1953, who studied divisions between boys in a summer camp; and Aronson et al., 1978, who used cooperative activities to lessen racial divisions in a classroom).
2. Gender is less prominent when children are not responsible for the formation of the
   group. Mixed-sex play is less frequent in games like football, which require the
   choosing of teams, and more frequent in games like handball or dodgeball which
   individuals can join simply by getting into a line or a circle. When adults organize
   mixed-sex encounters — which they frequently do in the classroom and in physical
   education periods on the playground — they legitimize cross-sex contact. This removes the risk of being teased for choosing to be with the other sex.
3. There is more extensive and relaxed cross-sex interaction when principles of grouping other than gender are explicitly involved — for example, counting off to form
   teams for spelling or kickball, dividing lines by hot lunch or cold lunch, or organizing a work group on the basis of interests or reading ability.
4. Girls and boys may interact more readily in less public and crowded settings.
   Neighborhood play, depending on demography, is more often sex and age integrated than play at school, partly because with fewer numbers, one may have to
   resort to an array of social categories to find play partners or to constitute a game.
   And in less crowded environments there are fewer potential witnesses to "make
   something of it" if girls and boys play together.

Relaxed interactions between girls and boys often depend on adults to set up
and legitimize the contact.[4] Perhaps because of this contingency — and the
other, distancing patterns which permeate relations between girls and boys —
the easeful moments of interaction rarely build to close friendship. Schofield
(1981) makes a similar observation about gender and racial barriers to friendship
in a junior high school.

IMPLICATIONS FOR DEVELOPMENT

I have located social relations within an essentially spatial framework, emphasizing the organization of children's play, work, and other activities within specific settings, and in one type of institution, the school. In contrast, frameworks
of child development rely upon temporal metaphors, using images of growth
and transformation over time. Taken alone, both spatial and temporal frameworks have shortcomings; fitted together, they may be mutually correcting.

---

4. Note that in daily school life, depending on the individual and the situation, teachers and
aides sometimes lessened, and at other times heightened sex segregation.

Those interested in gender and development have relied upon conceptualizations of "sex role socialization" and "sex differences." Sexuality and gender, I have argued, are more situated and fluid than these individualist and intrinsic models imply. Sex and gender are differently organized and defined across situations, even within the same institution. This situational variation (e.g., in the extent to which an encounter heightens or lessens gender boundaries, or is infused with sexual meanings) shapes and constrains individual behavior. Features which a developmental perspective might attribute to individuals, and understand as relatively internal attributes unfolding over time, may, in fact, be highly dependent on context. For example, children's avoidance of cross-sex friendship may be attributed to individual gender development in middle-childhood. But attention to varied situations may show that this avoidance is contingent on group size, activity, adult behavior, collective meanings, and the risk of being teased.

A focus on social organization and situation draws attention to children's experiences in the present. This helps correct a model like "sex role socialization" which casts the present under the shadow of the future, or presumed "endpoints" (Speier, 1976). A situated analysis of arrangements of sex and gender among those of different ages may point to crucial disjunctions in the life course. In the fourth and fifth grades, culturally defined heterosexual rituals ("goin' with") begin to suppress the presence and visibility of other types of interaction between girls and boys, such as nonsexualized and comfortable interaction, and traveling in the world of the other sex. As "boyfriend/girlfriend" definitions spread, the fifth-grade tomboy I described had to work to sustain "buddy" relationships with boys. Adult women who were tomboys often speak of early adolescence as a painful time when they were pushed away from participation in boys' activities. Other adult women speak of the loss of intense, even erotic ties with other girls when they entered puberty and the rituals of dating, that is, when they became absorbed into the institution of heterosexuality (Rich, 1980). When Lever (1976) describes best-friend relationships among fifth-grade girls as preparation for dating, she imposes heterosexual ideologies onto a present which should be understood on its own terms.

As heterosexual encounters assume more importance, they may alter relations in same-sex groups. For example, Schofield (1981) reports that for sixth- and seventh-grade children in a middle school, the popularity of girls with other girls was affected by their popularity with boys, while boys' status with other boys did not depend on their relations with girls. This is an asymmetry familiar from the adult world; men's relationships with one another are defined through varied activities (occupations, sports), while relationships among women — and their public status — are more influenced by their connections to individual men.

A full understanding of gender and social relations should encompass cross-sex as well as within-sex interactions. "Borderwork" helps maintain separate, gender-linked subcultures, which, as those interested in development have begun to suggest, may result in different milieux for learning. Daniel Maltz and Ruth Borker (1983) for example, argue that because of different interactions within girls' and boys' groups, the sexes learn different rules for creating and interpreting friendly conversation, rules which carry into adulthood and help account for miscommunication between men and women. Carol Gilligan (1982) fits research on the different worlds of girls and boys into a theory of sex differences in moral development. Girls develop a style of reasoning, she argues, which is more personal and relational; boys develop a style which is more positional, based on separateness. Eleanor Maccoby (1982), also following the insight that because of sex segregation, girls and boys grow up in different environments, suggests implications for gender differentiated prosocial and antisocial behavior.

This separate worlds approach, as I have illustrated, also has limitations. The occasions when the sexes are together should also be studied, and understood as contexts for experience and learning. For example, asymmetries in cross-sex relationships convey a series of messages: that boys are more entitled to space and to the nonreciprocal right of interrupting or invading the activities of the other sex; that girls are more in need of adult protection, and are lower in status, more defined by sexuality, and may even be polluting. Different types of cross-sex interaction — relaxed, boundaried, sexualized, or taking place on the terms of the other sex — provide different contexts for development.

By mapping the array of relationships between and within the sexes, one adds complexity to the overly static and dichotomous imagery of separate worlds. Individual experiences vary, with implications for development. Some children prefer same-sex groupings; some are more likely to cross the gender boundary and participate in the world of the other sex; some children (e.g., girls and boys who frequently play "chase and kiss") invoke heterosexual meanings, while others avoid them.

Finally, after charting the terrain of relationships, one can trace their development over time. For example, age variation in the content and form of borderwork, or of cross and same-sex touch, may be related to differing cognitive, social, emotional, or physical capacities, as well as to age-associated cultural forms. I earlier mentioned temporal shifts in the organization of cross-sex chasing, for mixing with fantasy play in the early grades to more elaborately ritualized and sexualized forms by the sixth grade. There also appear to be temporal changes in same and cross-sex touch. In kindergarten, girls and boys touch one another more freely than in fourth grade, when children avoid relaxed cross-sex touch and instead use pokes, pushes, and other forms of mock violence, even when the touch clearly couches affection. This touch taboo is obviously related to the risk of seeming to *like* someone of the other sex. In fourth grade, same-sex touch begins to signal sexual meanings among boys, as well as between boys and girls. Younger boys touch one another freely in cuddling (arm around shoulder) as well as mock violence ways. By fourth grade, when homophobic taunts like "fag" become more common among boys, cuddling touch begins to disappear for boys, but less so for girls.

Overall, I am calling for more complexity in our conceptualizations of gender and of children's social relationships. Our challenge is to retain the temporal sweep, looking at individual and group lives as they unfold over time, while also attending to social structure and context, and to the full variety of experiences in the present.

ACKNOWLEDGMENT

I would like to thank Jane Atkinson, Nancy Chodorow, Arlene Daniels, Peter Lyman, Zick Rubin, Malcolm Spector, Avril Thorne, and Margery Wolf for comments on an earlier version of this paper. Conversations with Zella Luria enriched this work.

REFERENCES

Aronson, E. et al. (1978). *The jigsaw classroom*. Beverly Hills, CA: Sage.

Barth, F. (Ed.). (1969). *Ethnic groups and boundaries*. Boston: Little, Brown.

Borman, K. M. (1979). Children's interactions in playgrounds. *Theory into Practice, 18,* 251–257.

Eder, D., & Hallinan, M. T. (1978). Sex differences in children's friendships. *American Sociological Review, 43,* 237–250.

Finnan, C. R. (1982). The ethnography of children's spontaneous play. In G. Spindler (Ed.), *Doing the ethnography of schooling* (pp. 358–380). New York: Holt, Rinehart & Winston.

Foot, H. C., Chapman, A. J., & Smith, J. R. (1980). Introduction. *Friendship and social relations in children* (pp. 1–14). New York: Wiley.

Gilligan, C. (1982). *In a different voice: Psychological theory and women's development*. Cambridge, MA: Harvard University Press.

Glaser, B. G., & Strauss, A. L. (1967). *The discovery of grounded theory*. Chicago: Aldine.

Goffman, E. (1977). The arrangement between the sexes. *Theory and Society, 4,* 301–336.

Goodwin, M. H. (1980). Directive-response sequences in girls' and boys' task activities. In S. McConnell-Ginet, R. Borker, & N. Furman (Eds.), *Women and language in literature and society* (pp. 157–173). New York: Praeger.

Greif, E. B. (1980). Sex differences in parent-child conversations. *Women's Studies International Quarterly, 3,* 253–258.

Henley, N. (1977). *Body politics: Power, sex, and nonverbal communication*. Englewood Cliffs, NJ: Prentice-Hall.

Karkau, K. (1973). *Sexism in the fourth grade*. Pittsburgh: KNOW, Inc. (pamphlet)

Katz, J. (1983). A theory of qualitative methodology: The social system of analytic fieldwork. In R. M. Emerson (Ed.), *Contemporary field research* (pp. 127–148). Boston: Little, Brown.

Knapp, M., & Knapp, H. (1976). *One potato, two potato: The secret education of American children*. New York: W. W. Norton.

Lever, J. (1976). Sex differences in the games children play. *Social Problems, 23,* 478–487.

Maccoby, E. (1982). *Social groupings in childhood: Their relationship to prosocial and antisocial behavior in boys and girls*. Paper presented at conference on The Development of Prosocial and Antisocial Behavior. Voss, Norway.

Maccoby, E., & Jacklin, C. (1974). *The psychology of sex differences*. CA: Stanford University Press.

Maltz, D. N., & Borker, R. A. (1983). A cultural approach to male-female miscommunication. In J. J. Gumperz (Ed.), *Language and social identity* (pp. 195–216). New York: Cambridge University Press.

McRobbie, A., & Garber, J. (1975). Girls and subcultures. In S. Hall and T. Jefferson (Eds.), *Resistance through rituals* (pp. 209–223). London: Hutchinson.

Ortner, S. B., & Whitehead, H. (1981). *Sexual meanings*. New York: Cambridge University Press.

Parrott, S. (1972). Games children play: Ethnography of a second-grade recess. In J. P. Spradley & D. W. McCurdy (Eds.), *The cultural experience* (pp. 206–219). Chicago: Science Research Associates.

Rich, A. (1980). Compulsory heterosexuality and lesbian existence. *Signs, 5,* 631–660.

Samuelson, S. (1980). The cooties complex. *Western Folklore, 39,* 198–210.

Savin-Williams, R. C. (1976). An ethological study of dominance formation and maintenance in a group of human adolescents. *Child Development, 47,* 972–979.

Schofield, J. W. (1981). Complementary and conflicting identities: Images and interaction in an interracial school. In S. R. Asher & J. M. Gottman (Eds.), *The development of children's friendships* (pp. 53–90). New York: Cambridge University Press.

Sherif, M., & Sherif, C. (1953). *Groups in harmony and tension*. New York: Harper.

Sluckin, A. (1981). *Growing up in the playground*. London: Routledge & Kegan Paul.

Speier, M. (1976). The adult ideological viewpoint in studies of childhood. In A. Skolnick (Ed.), *Rethinking childhood* (pp. 168–186). Boston: Little, Brown.

Sutton-Smith, B. (1971). A syntax for play and games. In R. E. Herron and B. Sutton-Smith (Eds.), *Child's Play* (pp. 298–307). New York: Wiley.

Unger, R. K. (1979). Toward a redefinition of sex and gender. *American Psychologist, 34*, 1085–1094.

Waldrop, M. F., & Halverson, C. F. (1975). Intensive and extensive peer behavior: Longitudinal and cross-sectional analysis. *Child Development, 46*, 19–26.

West, C., & Zimmerman, D. H. (1983). Small insults: A study of interruptions in cross-sex conversations between unacquainted persons. In B. Thorne, C. Kramarae, & N. Henley (Eds.), *Language, gender and society*. Rowley, MA: Newbury House.

Whitehead, H. (1981). The bow and the burden strap: A new look at institutionalized homosexuality in Native America. In S. B. Ortner & H. Whitehead (Eds.), *Sexual meanings* (pp. 80–115). New York: Cambridge University Press.

Robert Bly

MEN'S INITIATION RITES

The ancient rites of male initiation were complicated and subtle experiences which could be imagined better as a continual spiral than as a walk down a road. The spiral could be described as a year which repeats itself in seasons. The four seasons of male development amount to four stages, four steps and four events, though we all know that seasons run into each other, and repeat.

The four seasons, or stages, I'll discuss here are bonding with and separation from the mother; bonding with and separation from the father; finding of the male mother; and the interior marriage or marriage with the Hidden Woman.

BONDING WITH AND SEPARATION FROM MOTHER

The first event is bonding with the mother and separation from the mother. Bonding of the son with the mother usually goes quite well in this country, though we could distinguish between instantaneous birth-bonding and a later, slower emotional bonding. The medical profession has adopted birth practices involving harsh lights, steel tables, painful medicines and, most harmful of all, the infant's isolation for long periods, all of which damage the birth bond. Joseph Chilton Pearce has written of that movingly in *The Magical Child* (Dell). Mothers can sometimes repair that bonding later by careful attention to their sons' needs, by praise, carrying, talking, protecting, comforting — and many mothers do exactly that. Most American men achieve a successful bonding with the mother. It is the *separation* from the mother that doesn't go well.

When the world of men is submerged in the world of technology and business, it seems to the boy that cool excitement lies there, and warm excitement

From the *Utne Reader*, April–May 1986. Copyright © 1986 by Robert Bly. Reprinted with his permission.

with the mother; money with the father, food with the mother; anxiety with the father, assurance with the mother; conditional love with the father, and unconditional love with the mother. All over the United States we meet women whose 35-year-old sons are still living at home. One such woman told me that her divorce brought her freedom from the possessiveness of her husband, who wanted her home every night, etc. But she had noticed last week that her son said, "Why are you going out so much in the evenings?" In recent years the percentage of adult sons still living at home has increased; and we can see much other evidence of the difficulty the male feels in breaking with the mother: the guilt often felt toward the mother; the constant attempt, usually unconscious, to be a nice boy; lack of male friends; absorption in boyish flirtation with women; attempts to carry women's pain, and be their comforters; efforts to change a wife into a mother; abandonment of discipline for "softness and gentleness"; a general confusion about maleness. These qualities are all simple human characteristics, and yet when they, or a number of them, appear together, they point toward a failure in the very first stage of initiation. Ancient initiation practices, still going on in many parts of the world, solve this problem decisively through active intervention by the older males. Typically, when three or four boys in a tribe get to be eight to 12 years old, a group of older men simply appears at the houses one night, and takes them from their mothers, with whom the boys never live again. They may return, but often with faces covered with ash, to indicate that they are now "dead" to their mothers, who in their part return this play by crying out in the mourning when they see their sons again, and acting out rituals otherwise done for the dead.

BONDING WITH AND SEPARATION FROM FATHER

The second season of initiation is bonding with the father and separation from the father. Before the Industrial Revolution this event took place with most sons. But this bonding requires many hours in which the bodies of the father and son sit, stand or work close to each other, within a foot or two. The average father in the United States talks to his son less than 10 minutes a day. And that talk may be talk from a distance, such as "Is your room cleaned up?" or "Are you on drugs?" As we know, the psyche of the child interprets the death of a parent personally; that is, the psyche regards it as a failure on the child's part: "If I had been worthy, my parent would not have died." So the psyche of the small son interprets without question the father's absence from the house for hours and hours each day as evidence of the same unworthiness. The German psychiatrist Alexander Mitscherlich in his book *Society Without the Father* (Tavistock Publications) gives an image still more startling. He declares that when a son does not witness his father at work through the day and through the year, a hole develops in the son's psyche, and that hole fills with demons. Dustin Hoffman played such a son in *Marathon Man:* The son does not bond with the father then, but on the contrary a magnetic repulsion takes place, for by secret processes the father becomes associated in the son's mind with demonic energy, cold evil, Nazis, concentration camp guards, evil capitalists, agents of the CIA, powers of world conspiracy. Some of the fear felt in the '60s by young leftist men ("Never trust anyone over 30") came from that well of demons.

The severance that the Norwegian immigrant male, for example, experienced when he lost his old language in which feelings naturally expressed themselves — and the Polish immigrant, and the German immigrant — affected the ability of these men to talk to their sons, and their sons to their sons. We might add to that the frontier mentality, whose pressure of weather, new land, building, plowing, etc. left almost all feeling activities — music appreciation, novel reading, poetry recital — to women. This request to women that they carry on "feeling" activities obviously deepened the crisis, because the boy then learns cultural feeling, verbal feeling, discrimination of feeling almost entirely from his mother. Bonding requires physical closeness, a sense of protection, approval of one's very being, conversation in which feelings and longings can step out, and some attention which the young male can feel as *care for the soul*. The boy in the United States receives almost all of these qualities, if he receives them at all, from the mother, and so his bonding takes place with her, not with the father. If bonding with the father does not take place, how can separation from the father take place? There are many exceptions to this generalization, of course, but most of the exceptions I met were in men who worked in some physical way with their fathers, as carpenters, woodcutters, musicians, farmers, etc.

American men in general cannot achieve separation from the father because they have not achieved bonding with the father; or more exactly, our bonding with the father goes on slowly, bit by bit, often beginning again, after the remoteness of adolescence, at the age of 35 or so; and of course this gradual bonding over many years slows up the separation as well, so that the American man is often 40 or 45 before the first two events of initiation have taken place completely enough to be felt as events. The constant attempt by young males working in popular music to play a music their fathers never played or heard suggests an inability to bond with their fathers. The fathers in their turn feel puzzled, rejected, inadequate and defeated. So many American fathers if they answer the phone when a son or daughter calls will usually say after a moment: "Here is your mother."

MALE MOTHER

A third event in the ancient male initiation was the appearance of the male mother, and we'll call that the essential event. John Layard, who gained much of his knowledge of male initiation from his years with the Stone-Age tribes of Malekula, declares in his study called *The Celtic Quest* (Spring Publications) that Arthur was a male mother. "Arthur" may have been the name traditionally given to such an initiator centuries before he came King Arthur. In the ancient Mabinogion story "Culhwch and Olwen," Arthur is the keeper of a castle to which the young male initiate gains entry. Though male, Arthur's kingdom, Layard says, "has to be 'entered' as though it were a woman." Layard continues: "This entry into the male world which is a 'second mother' is what all initiation rites are concerned with." When Arthur has accepted the invader, he details the things he will not give to the young man, which are ship, cloak, sword, shield, dagger and Guinevere, his wife. He then asks the boy, "What do you want?" Culhwch says, "I want my hair trimmed." Then "Arthur took a golden comb and shears with loops of silver, and combed his head." The younger male places his head, or his consciousness, into the hands of an older man he trusts, and by that act he is symbolically freed from his bonds both to his mother and to his father.

Our culture lacks the institution of the male mother: The memory of its seems to have dropped into forgetfulness. We receive only one birth, from the mother, even though Jesus insisted on the importance of a second birth. We lose the meaning of his metaphor by interpreting it as a conversion experience. It was a new birth from the male, and it is possible that Jesus himself provided this second birth to young men. The Australian aborigines to this day arrange an experience of male birth that the sons do not forget: They construct a sort of tunnel of sticks and brush 20 to 30 feet long, and at the proper moment put the boys in at one end, and receive them, surrounded by the tremendous male noise of the bullroarers, at the other end, and immediately declare them to be born out of the male body for once and for all — a new boy, a new body, a new spirit, a man at last.

This experience, of course, implies the willingness of the older males to become male mothers, and so exhibit the protectiveness, self-sacrificing generosity and soul-caring that the female mother traditionally shows. In Africa, males of the Kikuyu tribe take boys who are hungry and terrified, after a day's fasting, and sit them down among adult males around a fire late at night. Each adult male then cuts his arm with a knife and lets his blood flow into a gourd which is passed on to the young boys to drink, so that they can see and taste the depth of the older males' love for them. By this single ceremony, the boy is asked to shift from female milk to male blood.

It is Arthur's kindness, savvy, spiritual energy, his store of psychic knowledge, his willingness to lead, guide and welcome the young male which we lack in American ritual, when, for example, the initiating power is held by sergeants, priests or corporate executives. The qualities I've mentioned above cannot appear together, or only rarely, in those three roles because we have forgotten the male mother role. We need to rethink the purpose of a male mother and how he achieves that purpose. The old apprentice system in crafts and arts through the Middle Ages and Renaissance accomplished initiation for some young men, but the mass university lectures of today cannot provide it — nor can workshop classes of 20. Pablo Casals was a male mother to some young men; William Carlos Williams to others, and there are always a few marvelous teachers or woodsmen here and there who understand the concept and embody it. By and large, however, one would say that if the American male does achieve the first two events — bonding with and separation from the mother, bonding with and separation from the father — he will come up short on this third step. A man needs to look decisively for a male mother, but he cannot look if the culture has not even retained the concept in its storehouse of possibilities. The men around Arthur were healthy because he nourished them, and they expected it.

THE INVISIBLE CZARINA

We notice that the male mother, or primary initiator, is not one's personal father; so by this third step, the male passes beyond the realm of his personal mother and father. He also expands his conception of women beyond the roles of wife, girlfriend, mistress, chick, movie actress, model. The predominant figure in the fourth stage is the Invisible Czarina, or Elena the Wise, as some Russian fairy tales call her, and in the fourth season it is the man's task to marry her. Edward Schieffel, in *Rituals of Manhood*, writing about contemporary male rituals in

New Guinea, reports that in the Kaluli tribe the young boys sometimes find in the pool below a waterfall during ceremonies a "stone bride," which they can identify because it moves on its own. We see here again a connection being made with a secret, powerful and usually helpful woman who is not a living woman. The fourth step does not aim then at a hardening or intensification of maleness, but rather at a deepening of feeling toward the religious life. We can immediately see the connection with the worship of the woman in Arthurian legend, the image of Mona Lisa in Italy, "Diotima" in Socrates' Greece, and lunar substance that contributes to the creation of "gold" that is the aim of alchemy. The "woman by the well" preserves in many European fairy tales and in the New Testament the memory of the Hidden Woman. In Celtic initiation, Arthur guides the young male toward the marriage with her; she is in fact the Olwen ("white trace" or "track of the moon") mentioned in the title of the Celtic story, "Culhwch and Olwen."

The fourth season therefore represents an astonishing leap into the other world and a love for the radiance of the yin. Initiation results in less dependence on living women or "strong" women, less fear of the feminine and creation of the more balanced older man that Zen and Tibetan traditions, to name only these two, aim at. Western culture has retained a dim memory of this fourth stage; and when most men today imagine initiation, a fourth stage like this is probably not a part of their imaginative scenario, even though the Wild Man story or "Iron Hans" ends like so many Grimm Brothers tales, in a marriage. The 20th-century Spanish poet Antonio Machado retained a very lively memory of Elena or the Hidden Woman, about whom he wrote a number of poems. This poem he wrote around 1900:

> Close to the road we sit down one day,
> our whole life now amounts to time, and our sole concern
> the attitudes of despair that we adopt
> while we wait. But She will not fail to arrive.

I want to emphasize that the ancient view of male development implies a spiral movement rather than a linear passage through clearly defined stages, with a given stage finished once and for all. As men, we go through all stages in a shallow way, then go back, live in several stages at once, go through them all with slightly less shallowness, return again to our parents, bond and separate once more, find a new male mother, and so on and so on. The old initiation systems having been destroyed, and their initiators gone, no step is ever done cleanly, just as we don't achieve at 12 a clean break with our mothers. So a quality of male initiation as we live it in the culture is a continual returning. Gradually and messily over many years a man achieves this complicated or subtle experience; it is very slow.

Jeffrey P. Hantover

THE BOY SCOUTS AND THE VALIDATION
OF MASCULINITY

The Boy Scouts of America was formally incorporated in 1910 and by 1916 had received a federal charter, absorbed most of the organizations which had claimed the Scouting name, and was an accepted community institution. The President of the United States was the organization's honorary president, and Scouting courses were offered in major universities. At the end of its first decade, the Boy Scouts was the largest male youth organization in American history with 358,573 scouts and 15,117 scoutmasters.

The Boy Scouts' rapid national acceptance reflected turn-of-the-century concern over the perpetuation and validation of American masculinity. The widespread and unplanned adoption of the Scout program prior to 1916 suggests that Scouting's message, unadorned by organizational sophistication, spoke to major adult concerns, one of which was the future of traditional conceptions of American masculinity.

This paper will argue that the Boy Scouts served the needs of adult men as well as adolescent boys. The supporters of the Scout movement, those who gave their time, money, and public approval, believed that changes in work, the family, and adolescent life threatened the development of manliness among boys and its expression among men. They perceived and promoted Scouting as an agent for the perpetuation of manliness among adolescents; the Boy Scouts provided an environment in which boys could become "red blooded" virile men. Less explicitly, Scouting provided men an opportunity to counteract the perceived feminizing forces of their lives and to act according to the traditional masculine script.

THE OPPORTUNITY TO BE A MAN:
RESTRICTION AND ITS CONSEQUENCES

Masculinity is a cultural construct and adult men need the opportunity to perform normatively appropriate male behaviors. Masculinity is not affirmed once and for all by somatic change; physical development is but a means for the performance of culturally ascribed behaviors. American masculinity is continually affirmed through ongoing action. What acts a man performs and how well he does them truly make a male a man.

However, the availability of opportunities is not constant. Anxiety about the integrity and persistence of the male role can result from a restriction of opportunities experienced by the individual and the groups with which he identifies. Adult experiences produce adult anxieties. Masculine anxiety can arise when adult men know the script and wish to perform according to cultural directions but are denied the opportunity to act: The fault lies in social structuring of opportunities and not in individual capabilities and motivations.

Reprinted from *Journal of Social Issues* Volume 34, Number 1, 1978.
The author wishes to thank Joseph Pleck and Mayer Zald for their constructive comments.

The anxiety men increasingly exhibited about the naturalness and substance of manliness in the period 1880 to World War I flowed from changes in institutional spheres traditionally supportive of masculine definitional affirmation. Feminism as a political movement did raise fears of feminization but, as Filene (1975) suggests, in relation to preexistent anxiety about the meaning of manliness. Changes in the sphere of work, the central institutional anchorage of masculinity, undercut essential elements in the definition of manliness. Men believed they faced diminishing opportunities for masculine validation and that adolescents faced barriers to the very development of masculinity.

Masculine anxiety at the turn of the century was expressed in the accentuation of the physical and assertive side of the male ideal and in the enhanced salience of gender in social life. The enthronement of "muscularity" is evident in leisure activities, literary tastes, and cultural heroes. In the early nineteenth century, running and jumping were not exercises befitting a gentleman (Rudolph, 1962), but now men took to the playing fields, gyms, and wilderness in increasing numbers. Football, baseball, hiking, and camping became popular and were defended for their contribution to the development of traditional masculine character. Popular magazine biographies of male heroes in the period 1894 to 1913 shifted from an earlier idealization of passive traits such as piety, thrift, and industry to an emphasis on vigor, forcefulness, and mastery (Greene, 1970). Literary masculinization extended beyond mortals like Teddy Roosevelt to Christ who was portrayed as "the supremely manly man": attractive to women, individualistic, athletic, self-controlled, and aggressive when need be — "he was no Prince of Peace-at-any-price" (Conant, 1915, p. 117).

Sex-role distinctions became increasingly salient and rigid. The birth control issue became enmeshed in the debate over women's proper role; diatribes against expanded roles for women accompanied attacks on family limitation. The increased insistence on sexual purity in fiction and real life was a demand for women to accept the traditional attributes of purity, passivity, and domesticity. The emphasis on the chivalrie motif in turn-of-the-century youth organizations (Knights of King Arthur, Order of Sir Galahad, Knights of the Holy Grail) can be interpreted as an expression of the desire to preserve male superordination in gender relations.

PERCEIVED FORCES OF FEMINIZATION

Men in the period 1880 to World War I believed that opportunities for the development and expression of masculinity were being limited. They say forces of feminization in the worlds of adults and adolescents. I will concentrate on changes in the adult opportunity structure. However, the forces of feminization that adolescents were thought to face at home and school should be mentioned, for they contributed to the anxiety of men worried about the present and wary of the future.

For the expanding urban middle class, the professionalization and sanctification of motherhood, the smaller family size, the decline in the number of servants who could serve as buffers between mother and son, and the absence of busy fathers from the home made the mother–son relationship appear threatening to proper masculine socialization. The expansion of the public high school took sons out of the home but did not allay fears of feminization. Female students outnumbered males, the percentage of female staff rose steadily between 1880 and World War I, and the requirements of learning demanded "feminine" passivity and sedentariness. Education would weaken a boy's body and direct his mind along the "psychic lines" of his female instructors. Finally, let me suggest that G. Stanley Hall's concept of adolescence may have generated sex-role anxiety by extending and legitimating dependency as a natural stage in the developmental cycle. A cohort of men who had reached social maturity before the use and public acceptance of adolescence as an age category, who had experienced the rural transition to manhood at an early age, and who had fought as teenagers in the Civil War or knew those who had were confronted with a generation of boys whose major characteristics were dependency and inactivity.

Changes in the nature of work and in the composition of the labor force from 1880 to World War I profoundly affected masculine self-identity. From 1870 to 1910 the number of clerical workers, salespeople, government employees, technicians, and salaried professionals increased from 756 thousand to 5.6 million (Hays, 1957). The dependency, sedentariness, and even security of these middle-class positions clashed with the active mastery, independence, self-reliance, competitiveness, creativity, and risk-taking central to the traditional male ideal (Mills, 1951). In pre-Civil War America, there were opportunities to approach that ideal: It is estimated that over 80% of Americans were farmers of self-employed businessmen (Mills, 1951). They owned the property they worked; they produced tangible goods; and they were not enmeshed in hierarchical systems of "command and obedience."

Industrialization and bureaucratization reduced opportunities to own one business, to take risks, exercise independence, compete, and master men and nature. The new expanded middle class depended on others for time, place, and often pace of work. The growth of chain stores crowded out independent proprietors, made small business ventures shortlived, and reduced the income of merchants frequently below the level of day laborers (Anderson & Davidson, 1940). Clerical positions were no longer certain stepping stones to ownership; and clerical wages were neither high enough to meet standards of male success nor appreciably greater than those of less prestigious occupations (Filene, 1975; Douglas, 1930).

This changed occupational landscape did not go unnoticed. College graduates were told not to expect a challenging future:

> The world is steadily moving toward the position in which the individual is to contribute faithfully and duly his quota of productive or protective social effort, and to receive in return a modest, certain, not greatly variable stipend. He will adjust his needs and expenses to his income, guard the future by insurance or some analogous method, and find margin of leisure and opportunity sufficient to give large play to individual tastes and preferences. (Shaw, 1907, p. 3)

Interestingly for this paper's thesis, these graduates were to seek fulfillment in activities outside work.

The increased entry of women into the labor force raised the specter of feminization as did the changed character of work. In terms of masculine anxiety, the impact was two-fold: the mere fact of women working outside the home in larger numbers and their increased participation in jobs which demanded non-masculine attributes. From 1870 to 1920, there was a substantial increase in the percentage of women aged 16 and over in nonagricultural occupations — from 11.8% to 21.3% (Hill, 1929). Men expressed concern over the entrance of women into a previously exclusive domain of masculine affirmation. (Women's occupations were not enumerated in the federal census until 1860.) Magazine and newspaper cartoons showed women in suits, smoking cigars, and talking business while aproned men were washing dishes, sweeping floors, and feeding babies (Smuts, 1959). Sex-role definition, not simple income, was at stake. Only one-third of employed men in 1910 worked in occupations where women constituted more than 5% of the work force (Hill, 1929). The actual threat posed by working women was more cultural than economic. Women doing what men did disconfirmed the naturalness and facticity of sex-role dichotomization.

Imposed on this general concern was the anxiety of men in white-collar positions. It was into these "nonmasculine" jobs that women entered in large numbers. Women were only 3% of the clerical work force in 1870, but 35% in 1910 (U.S. Department of Commerce, 1870; Hill, 1929). The increase for specific occupations between 1910 and 1920 is even more dramatic, especially for native white women of native parentage: female clerks increased 318%; bookkeepers, accountants, and cashiers, 257%; stenographers and typists, 121%; and sales personnel, 66% (Hill, 1929). It is to be argued that men in these occupations, feminine in character and composition, sought nonoccupational means of masculine validation, one of which was being a scoutmaster.

SCOUTING AND THE CONSTRUCTION OF MANLINESS

The Boy Scouts of America responded explicitly to adult sex-role concerns. It provided concerned men the opportunity to support "an organized effort to make big men of little boys . . . to aid in the development of that master creation, high principled, clean and clear thinking, independent manhood" (Burgess, 1914, p. 12). At the turn of the century, manliness was no longer considered the inevitable product of daily life; urbanization appeared to have removed the conditions for the natural production of manliness. Scouting advertised itself as an environmental surrogate for the farm and frontier:

> The Wilderness is gone, the Buckskin Man is gone, the painted Indian has hit the trail over the Great Divide, the hardships and privations of pioneer life which did so much to develop sterling manhood are now but a legend in history, and we must depend upon the Boy Scout Movement to produce the MEN of the future. (Daniel Carter Beard in Boy Scouts of America, 1914, p. 109)

Scouting's program and structure would counter the forces of feminization and maintain traditional manhood. Following the dictates of Hall's genetic psychology, boys were sexually segregated in a primary group under the leadership of an adult male. The gang instinct, like all adolescent instincts, was not to be repressed but constructively channeled in the service of manhood. By nature boys would form gangs, and the Boy Scouts turned the gang into a Scout patrol. The gang bred virility, did not tolerate sissies, and would make a boy good but not a goody-goody; in short, he would "be a real boy, not too much like his sister" (Puffer, 1912, p. 157; also see Page, 1919).

The rhetoric and content of Scouting spoke to masculine fears of passivity and dependence. Action was the warp and woof of Scouting, as it was the foundation of traditional American masculinity. After-school and summer idleness led to and was itself a moral danger, and scouts were urged to do "anything rather than continue in dependent, and enfeebling, and demoralizing idleness" (Russell, 1914, p. 163). "Spectatoritis" was turning "robust, manly, self-reliant boyhood into a lot of flat-chested cigarette smokers with shaky nerves and doubtful vitality" (Seton, 1910, p. xi). So Scout activities involved all members, and advancement required each boy to compete against himself and nature. Scouting stands apart from most nineteenth-century youth organizations by its level of support for play and its full acceptance of outdoor activities as healthy for boys.

The Scout code, embodied in the Scout Oath, Law, Motto, and requirements for advancement, was a code for conduct, not moral contemplation. It was "the code of red blooded, moral manly men" (Beard, Note 1, p. 9). The action required by the code, not one's uniform or badges, made a boy a scout and differentiated a scout from a non-scout. The British made a promise to act, but the Americans made a more definite commitment to action: they took an oath. More than the British, Americans emphasized that theirs was a "definite code of personal purposes," whose principles would shape the boy's total character and behavior.

The Scout code would produce that ideal man who was master of himself and nature. The American addition to the Scout oath, "To keep myself physically strong, mentally awake, and morally straight," was a condition for such mastery. In pre-Civil War America, "be prepared" meant being prepared to die, having one's moral house in order (Crandall, 1957). The Scout motto meant being prepared to meet and master dangers, from runaway horses to theater fires and factory explosions. In emergencies, it was the scout who "stood firm, quieted those who were panic stricken and unobtrusively and efficiently helped to control the crowds" (Murray, 1937, p. 492). American Scouting added the tenth law: "A Scout is Brave." Bravery meant self-mastery and inner direction, having the courage "to stand up for the right against the coaxing of friends or the jeers or threats of enemies."

The linchpin of the Scout code was the good deed. Boys active in community service reassured males that the younger generation would become manly men. To Scout supporters, the movement provided a character building "moral equivalent to war." The phrase was used by William James in 1910 to suggest a kind of Job Corps for gilded youths. They would wash windows, build roads, work on fishing boats, and engage in all types of manual labor. This work would knock the childishness out of the youth of the luxurious classes and would produce the hardiness, discipline, and manliness that previously only war had done (James, 1971). As a result, young men would walk with their heads higher, would be esteemed by women, and be better fathers and teachers of the next generation. Scouts would not accept payment for their good deeds. To take a tip was un-American, un-masculine, and made one a "bit of a boot lick" (Eaton,

1918, p. 38). Adherence to the Scout code would produce traditional manliness in boy's clothing:

> The REAL Boy Scout is not a "sissy." He is not a hothouse plant, like little Lord Fauntleroy. There is nothing "milk and water" about him; he is not afraid of the dark. He does not do bad things because he is afraid of being decent. Instead of being a puny, dull, or bookish lad, who dreams and does nothing, he is full of life, energy, enthusiasm, bubbling over with fun, full of ideas as to what he wants to do and knows how he wants to do it. He has many ideals and many heroes. He is not hitched to his mother's apronstrings. While he adores his mother, and would do anything to save her from suffering or discomfort, he is self-reliant, sturdy and full of vim. (West, 1912, p. 448)

THE SCOUTMASTER AND MASCULINE VALIDATION

Scouting assuaged adult masculine anxiety not only by training boys in the masculine virtues. The movement provided adult men a sphere of masculine validation. Given the character and composition of their occupations and the centrality of occupation to the male sex role, young men in white-collar positions were especially concerned about their masculine identity. They were receptive to an organization which provided adult men the opportunity to be men as traditionally defined.

At the core of the image of the ideal scoutmaster was assertive manliness. Scoutmasters were "manly" patriots with common sense and moral character who sacrificially served America's youth (Boy Scouts of America, 1920). Scouting wanted "REAL, live men — red blooded and righthearted men — BIG men"; "No Miss Nancy need apply" (Boy Scouts of America, n.d., p. 9). Scoutmasters by the force of their characters, not by their formal positions (as in a bureaucracy), would evoke respect. They were portrayed as men of executive ability who took decisive action over a wide range of problems and were adroit handlers of men and boys. An analysis of the social characteristics and motivation of all the Chicago scoutmasters for whom there are records — original applications — through 1919 ($N = 575$) raises questions about the veracity of this portrayal (Hantover, 1976).

The first scoutmasters were men of educational, occupational, and ethnic status, but they did not serve solely from a sense of *noblesse oblige* and a disinterested commitment to all boys. They were more concerned about saving middle-class boys from the effeminizing forces of modern society than with "civilizing" the sons of the lower classes. Only four scoutmasters singled out the lower class for special mention; just 8% of the over 700 experiences with youth listed by scoutmasters were with lower-class youth. The typical Chicago scoutmaster was white, under 30, native born, Protestant, college educated, and in a white-collar or professional/semi-professional occupation. Scoutmasters were more Protestant, better educated, and in higher prestige occupations than the adult male population of Chicago. Many teachers, clergymen, and boys' workers were scoutmasters because Scouting was part of their job, was good training for it, or at least was congruent with their vocational ideology. If we exclude those men drawn to Scouting by the requirements of their occupations, Scouting disproportionately attracted men who had borne longer the "feminine" environment of the schools and now were in occupations whose sedentariness and dependence did not fit the traditional image of American manliness.

Though the motivational data extracted from the original scoutmaster applications are limited, there does emerge from the number and quality of responses a sense that clerical workers were concerned about the development of masculinity among adolescents and its expression by adults. Clerical workers were more concerned than other occupations unrelated to youth and service about training boys for manhood, filling a boy's time with constructive activities so he would not engage in activities detrimental to the development of manhood, and about the sexual and moral dangers of adolescence.

It is not simply chance, I believe, that clerical workers gave elaborate and individualistic responses which evince a sense of life's restrictedness and danger. A 26-year-old stenographer, "always having lived in Chicago and working indoors," felt Scouting was a way to get outdoors for himself, not the scouts. A 21-year-old clerk, implying that his career had reached its apogee, praised Scouting for its development of initiative and resourcefulness and admitted that lack of these qualities had handicapped him greatly. A draftsman, only 27, thought "association with the boys will certainly keep one from getting that old and retired feeling." Another young clerk evokes a similar sense of life's restrictedness when he writes that Scouting "affords me an opportunity to exercise control over a set of young men. I learn to realize the value of myself as a force as a personality."

The masculine anxiety that clerical workers felt may not have been generated by their occupations alone. They brought to the job achievements and attributes which at the turn of the century could have exacerbated that anxiety. Clerical workers had the highest percentage of high school educated scoutmasters of any occupational group. They were subject to the perceived feminine forces of high school without the status compensation of a college education and a professional position. With education controlled, Protestants and native Americans were more likely to be clerical workers. It was the virility and reproductive powers of the native American stock which were being questioned after the Civil War. Women in the better classes (native and Protestant) denied men the opportunity to prove their masculinity through paternity. Albion Small complained, "In some of the best middle-class social strata in the United States a young wife becomes a subject of surprised comment among her acquaintances if she accepts the burdens of maternity! This is a commonplace" (Small, 1915, p. 661). The fecundity and alleged sexuality of the immigrants raised turn-of-the-century fears about the continued dominance of the native Protestant stock. The experiences of key reference groups as well as one's own individual experiences were factors contributing to a sense of endangered masculinity.

CONCLUSION

Adult sex-role anxiety is rooted in the social structure; and groups of men are differentially affected, depending on their location in the social system and the opportunity structure they face. Critics of men's supposed nature can be dismissed as misguided by medical and religious defenders. But when the opportunity structure underlying masculinity begins to restrict, questioning may arise from the ranks of the men themselves. When taken-for-granted constructs become the objects of examination, anxiety may arise because elements in a cultural system are defended as natural, if not transcendant, rather than convenient or utilitarian. Under the disconfirming impact of social change, men may at first be more likely to reassert the validity of traditional ends and seek new avenues for their accomplishment than to redefine their ends.

"Men not only define themselves, but they actualize these definitions in real experience — *they live them*" (Berger, Berger, & Kellner, 1974, p. 92). Social identities generate the need for self-confirming action. The young men in the scoutmaster ranks were the first generation to face full force the discontinuity between the realities of the modern bureaucratic world and the image of masculine autonomy and mastery and the rhetoric of Horatio Alger. They found in the Boy Scouts of America an institutional sphere for the validation of masculinity previously generated by the flow of daily social life and affirmed in one's work.

NOTE

1. Beard, D. C. Untitled article submitted to *Youth Companion*. Unpublished manuscript, Daniel Carter Beard Collection, Library of Congress, 1914.

REFERENCES

Anderson, H. D., & Davidson, P. E. *Occupational trends in the United States.* Stanford: Stanford University Press, 1940.

Berger, P., Berger, B., & Kellner, H. *The homeless mind.* New York: Vintage Press, 1974.

Boy Scouts of America. Fourth annual report. *Scouting*, 1914, *1*.

Boy Scouts of America. *Handbook for scoutmasters* (2nd ed.). New York: Boy Scouts of America, 1920.

Boy Scouts of America. *The scoutmaster and his troop.* New York: Boy Scouts of America, no date.

Burgess, T. W. Making men of them. *Good Housekeeping Magazine*, 1914, *59*, 3–12.

Conant, R. W. *The virility of Christ.* Chicago: no publisher, 1915.

Crandall, J. C., Jr. *Images and ideals for young Americans: A study of American juvenile literature, 1825–1860.* Unpublished doctoral dissertation, University of Rochester, 1957.

Douglas, P. *Real wages in the United States, 1890–1926.* New York: Houghton Mifflin, 1930.

Eaton, W. P. *Boy Scouts in Glacier Park.* Boston: W. A. Wilde, 1918.

Filene, P. G. *Him, her, self: Sex roles in modern America.* New York: Harcourt Brace Jovanovich, 1975.

Greene, T. P. *America's heroes: The changing models of success in American magazines.* New York: Oxford University Press, 1970.

Hantover, J. P. *Sex role, sexuality, and social status: The early years of the Boy Scouts of America.* Unpublished doctoral dissertation, University of Chicago, 1976.

Hays, S. P. *The response to industrialism: 1885–1914.* Chicago: University of Chicago Press, 1957.

Hill, J. A. *Women in gainful occupations 1870 to 1920* (Census Monograph No. 9, U.S. Bureau of the Census). Washington, D.C.: U.S. Government Printing Office, 1929.

James, W. The moral equivalent of war. In J. K. Roth (Ed.), *The moral equivalent and other essays.* New York: Harper Torchbook, 1971.

Mills, C. W. *White collar.* New York: Oxford University Press, 1951.

Murray, W. D. *The history of the boy scouts of America.* New York: Boy Scouts of America, 1937.

Page, J. F. *Socializing for the new order of educational values of the juvenile organization.* Rock Island, Ill.: J. F. Page, 1919.

Puffer, J. A. *The boy and his gang.* Boston: Houghton Mifflin, 1912.

Rudolph, F. *The American college and university.* New York: Knopf, 1962.

Russell, T. H. (Ed.). *Stories of boy life.* No location: Fireside Edition, 1914.

Seton, E. T. *Boy Scouts of America: A handbook of woodcraft, scouting, and life craft.* New York: Doubleday, Page, 1910.

Shaw, A. *The outlook for the average man.* New York: Macmillan, 1907.

Small, A. The bonds of nationality. *American Journal of Sociology,* 1915, *10*, 629–83.

Smuts, R. W. *Women and work in America.* New York: Columbia University Press, 1959.

U.S. Department of Commerce. *Ninth census of the United States, 1870: Population and social statistics* (Vol. 1). Washington, D.C.: U.S. Government Printing Office, 1870.

West, J. E. The real boy scout. *Leslie's Weekly,* 1912, 448.

Peter Lyman

THE FRATERNAL BOND AS A JOKING RELATIONSHIP

One evening during dinner, 45 fraternity men suddenly broke into the dining room of a nearby campus sorority, surrounded the 30 women residents, and forced them to watch while one pledge gave a speech on Freud's theory of penis envy as another demonstrated various techniques of masturbation with a rubber penis. The women sat silently staring downward at their plates listening for about ten minutes, until a woman law student who was the graduate resident in charge of the house walked in, surveyed the scene, and demanded, "Please leave immediately!" As she later described that moment, "There was a mocking roar from the men, 'Its tradition.' I said, 'That's no reason to do something like this, please leave!' And they left. I was surprised. Then the women in the house started to get angry. And the guy who made the penis envy speech came back and said to us, 'That was funny to me. If that's not funny to you I don't know what kind of sense of humor you have, but I'm sorry.'"

That night the women sat around the stairwell of their house discussing the event, some angry and others simply wanting to forget the whole thing. They finally decided to ask the University to require that the men return to discuss the event. When University officials threatened to take action, the men agreed to the meeting. I was asked by both the men and the women involved to attend the discussion as a facilitator, and was given permission to write about the event as long as I concealed their identities.

A longer analysis of this research material was published as "The Fraternal Bond as a Joking Relation: A Case Study of the Role of Sexist Jokes in Male Group Bonding," published in Michael Kimmel (ed.), *Changing Men: New Directions in Research on Men and Masculinity.* Newbury Park: Sage Publications, 1987:148–163.

In the women's view, the joke had not failed because of its subject; they considered sexual jokes to be a normal part of the erotic joking relationship between men and women. They criticized its emotional structure, the mixture of sexuality with aggression and the atmosphere of physical intimidation in the room. Although many of the men individually regretted the damage to their relationship with women friends in the group, they argued that the special group solidarity created by the initiation was a unique form of masculine friendship that justified the inconvenience caused the women.

Fraternal group bonding in everyday life frequently takes the form of *joking relationships,* in which men relate to each other by exchanging insults and jokes in order to create a feeling of solidarity that negotiates the latent tension and aggression they feel toward each other (Radcliffe-Brown, 1959). The humor of joking relationships is generally sexual and aggressive, and frequently consists of sexist or racist jokes. As Freud (1960:99) observed, the jokes men direct *toward* women are generally sexual, tend to be clever (like double entendres), and have a seductive purpose; but the jokes that men tell *about* women in the presence of other men tend to be sexist rather than intimate or erotic, and use hostile and aggressive rather than clever verbal forms. In this case study, joking relationships will be analyzed to uncover the emotional dynamics of fraternal groups and the impact of fraternal bonding upon relationships between men and women.

THE GIRLS' STORY

The women had frequently been the target of fraternity initiation rites in the past, and generally enjoyed this joking relationship with the men, if with a certain ambivalence. "There was the naked Christmas Carol event, they were singing 'We wish you a Merry Christmas,' and 'Bring on the hasty pudding' was the big line they liked to yell out. And they had five or six pledges who had to strip in front of the house and do naked jumping jacks on the lawn, after all the women in the house were lined up on the steps to watch." The women did not think these events were hostile because they had been invited to watch, and the men stood with them watching, suggesting that the pledges, not the women, were the targets of the joke. This defined the joke as sexual, not sexist, and part of the normal erotic joking relation between "guys and girls." Still, these jokes were ritual events, not real social relationships. One woman said, "We were just supposed to watch, and the guys were watching us watch. The men set up the stage and the women are brought along to observe. They were the controlling force, then they jump into the car and take off."

At the meeting with the men, 2 of the women spoke for the group while 11 others sat silently in the center, surrounded by about 30 men. The first woman began, "Your humor was pretty funny as long as it was sexual, but when it went beyond sexual to sexist, then it became painful. You were saying 'I'm better than you.' When you started using sex as a way of proving your superiority, it hurt me and made me angry."

The second woman said that the fraternity's raid had the tone of a rape. "I admit we knew you were coming over, and we were whispering about it. But it went too far, and I felt afraid to say anything. Why do men always think about women in terms of violating them, in sexual imagery? You have to understand that the combination of a sexual topic with the physical threat of all of you standing around terrified me. I couldn't move. You have to realize that when men combine sexuality and force, it's terrifying to women."

Many of the women began by saying, "I'm not a feminist, but . . . ," to re-assure the men that although they felt angry, they hoped to reestablish the many individual friendships that had existed between men and women in the two groups. In part the issue was resolved when the women accepted the men's construction of the event as a joke, although a failed joke, transforming a dis-cussion about sexuality and force into a debate about good and bad jokes.

For an aggressive joke to be funny, and most jokes contain some hostility, the joke teller must send the audience a cue that says "this is meant as a joke." If accepted, the cue invokes special social rules that "frame" the hostile words that are typical of jokes, ensuring they will not be taken seriously. The men had implicitly sent such a cue when they stood *next* to the women during the naked jumping jacks. Verbal aggression mediated by the joke form will generally be without later consequences in the everyday world, and will be judged in terms of the formal intention of jokes, shared play and laughter.

In accepting the construction of the event as "just a joke" the women absolved the men of responsibility for their actions by calling them "little boys." One woman said, "It's not wrong, they're just boys playing a prank. They're little boys, they don't know what they're doing. It was unpleasant, but we shouldn't make a big deal out of it." In appealing to the rules of the joke form (as in saying "that was funny to me, I don't know what kind a sense of humor you have"), the men sacrificed their personal friendships with the women in order to protect the feelings of fraternal solidarity it produced. In calling the men "little boys" the women were bending the rules of friendship, trying to preserve their rela-tionships to the guys by playing a patient and nurturing role.

THE GUYS' STORY

Aside from occasional roars of laughter, the men interrupted the women only once. When a woman began to say that the men had obviously intended to intimidate them, the men loudly protested that the women couldn't possibly judge their intentions, that they intended the whole event only as a joke, and the intention of a joke is, by definition, just fun.

At this point the two black men in the fraternity intervened to explain the rules of male joking relationships to the women. In a sense, they said, they agreed with the women, being the object of hostile jokes is painful. As they described it, the collective talk of the fraternity at meals and group events was entirely hostile joking, including many racist jokes. One said, "I've had to listen to things in the house that I'd have hit someone for saying if I've heard them outside." The guys roared with laughter, for the fraternal joking relation con-sisted almost entirely of aggressive words that were barely contained by the convention that joke tellers are not responsible for what they say.

One woman responded, "Maybe people should be hit for saying those things, maybe that's the right thing to do." But the black speaker was trying to explain the rules of male joke culture to the women, "If you'd just ignored us, it wouldn't have been any fun." To ignore a joke, even though it makes you feel hurt or angry, is to be cool, one of the primary masculine ideals of the group.

Another man tried to explain the failure of the joke in terms of the difference between the degree of "crudeness" appropriate "between guys" and between "guys and girls." He said, "As I was listening to the speech I was both embarrassed and amused. I was standing at the edge of the room, near the door, and when I looked at the guys I was laughing but when I looked at the girls I was embarrassed. I could see both sides at the same time. It was too crude for your sense of propriety. We have a sense of crudeness you don't have. That's a cultural aspect of the difference between girls and guys."

The other men laughed as he mentioned "how crude we are at the house," and one of the black men added, "You wouldn't believe how crude it gets." Many of the men later said that although they individually found the jokes about women vulgar, the jokes were justified because they were necessary for the formation of the fraternal bond. These men thought that the mistake had been to reveal their crudeness to the women, this was "in bad taste."

In part the crudeness was a kind of "signifying" or "dozens," a ritual exchange of intimate insults that creates group solidarity. "If there's one theme that goes on its the emphasis on being able to take a lot of ridicule, of shit, and not getting upset about it. Most of the interaction we have is verbally abusing each other, making disgusting references to your mother's sexuality, or the women you were seen with, or your sex organ, the size of your sex organ. And you aren't cool unless you can take it without trying to get back." Being cool is an important male value in other settings as well, like sports or work; the joking relationship is a kind of training that, in one guy's words, "teaches you how to keep in control of your emotions."

But the guys themselves would not have described their group as a joking relationship or fraternal bond, they called it friendship. One man said that he had found perhaps a dozen guys in the house who were special friends, "guys I could cry in front of." Another said, "I think the guys are very close, they would do nearly anything for each other, drive each other places, give each other money. I think when they have problems about school, their car, or something like that, they can talk to each other. I'm not sure they can talk to each other about problems with women though." Although the image of crying in front of the other guys was often mentioned as an example of the intimacy of the fraternal bond, no one could actually recall anyone in the group ever crying. In fact crying would be an admission of vulnerability which would violate the ideals of "strength" and "being cool."

The women interpreted the sexist jokes as a sign of vulnerability. "The thing that struck me the most about our meeting together," one said, "was when the men said they were afraid of trusting women, afraid of being seen as jerks." One of the guys added, "I think down deep all the guys would love to have satisfying relationships with women. I think they're scared of failing, of having to break away from the group they've become comfortable with. I think being in a fraternity, having close friendships with men is a replacement for having close relationships with women. It'd be painful for them because they'd probably fail." These men preferred to relate to women as a group at fraternity parties, where they could take women back to their rooms for quick sex without commitments.

Sexist jokes also had a social function, policing the boundaries of the group, making sure that guys didn't form serious relationships with girls and leave the fraternity (cf. Slater, 1963). "One of the guys just acquired a girlfriend a few weeks ago. He's someone I don't think has had a woman to be friends with, maybe ever, at least in a long time. Everybody has been ribbing him intensely the last few weeks. It's good natured in tone. Sitting at dinner they've invented a little song they sing to him. People yell questions about his girlfriend, the size of her vagina, does she have big breasts." Thus, in dealing with women, the group separated intimacy from sex, defining the male bond as intimate but not sexual (homosocial), and relationships with women as sexual but not intimate (heterosexual).

THE FRATERNAL BOND IN MEN'S LIFE CYCLE

Men often speak of friendship as a group relationship, not a dyadic one, and men's friendships often grow from the experience of shared activities or risk, rather than from self-disclosing talk (cf. Rubin, 1983:130). J. Glenn Gray (1959:89–90) distinguishes the intimate form of friendship from the comradeship that develops from the shared experience of suffering and danger of men at war. In comradeship, he argues, the individual's sense of self is subordinated to a group identity, whereas friendship is based upon a specific feeling for another that heightens a sense of individuality.

In this case, the guys used joking relationships to suspend the ordinary rules and responsibilities of everyday life, placing the intimacy of the fraternal group in competition with heterosexual friendships. One of the men had been inexpressive as he listened to the discussion, but spoke about the fraternity in a voice filled with emotion, "The penis envy speech was a hilarious idea, great college fun. That's what I joined the fraternity for, a good time. College is a stage in my life to do crazy and humorous things. In ten years when I'm in the business world I won't be able to carry on like this. [loud laughter from the men] The initiation was intended to be humorous. We didn't think through how sensitive you women were going to be."

This speech gives the fraternal bond a specific place in the life-cycle. The joking relationship is a ritual bond that creates a male group bond in the transition between boyhood and manhood: after the separation from the family where the authority of mothers limits fun; but before becoming subject to the authority of work. One man later commented on the transitional nature of the fraternal bond, "I think a lot of us are really scared of losing total control over our own lives. Having to sacrifice our individuality. I think we're scared of work in the same way we're scared of women." The jokes expressed hostility toward women because an intimate friendship with a woman was associated with "loss of control," namely the risk of responsibility for work and family.

Most, but not all, of the guys in the fraternity were divided between their group identity and a sense of personal identity that was expressed in private friendships with women. Some of the guys, like the one who could "see both sides" as he stood on the edge of the group during the initiation, had reached a point of leaving the fraternity because they couldn't reconcile the tension between his group identity and the sense of self that he felt in his friendships with women.

Ultimately the guys justified the penis envy joke because it created a special kind of male intimacy. But although the fraternal group was able to appropriate the guys' needs for intimacy and commitment it is not clear that it was able to satisfy those needs, because it defined strength as shared risk taking rather than a quality of individual character or personality. In Gray's terms, the guys were constructing comradeship through an erotic of shared activities with an element of risk, shared danger, or rule breaking such as sports, paramilitary games, wild parties, and hostile jokes. In these contexts, strength implied the substitution of a group identity for a personal code that might extend to commitment and care for others (cf. Bly 1982).

In the guys' world, aggression was identified with strength, and defined as loss of control only if it was angry. The fraternal bond was built upon an emotional balance between aggression and anger, for life of the group centered upon the mobilization of aggressive energies in rule-governed activities, especially sports and games. In in each arena aggression was defined as strength (toughness) only when it was rule governed (cool). Getting angry was called "losing control," and the guys thought they were most likely to lose control when they experienced themselves as personally dependent, that is, in relationships with women and at work. The sense of order within fraternal groups is based upon the belief that all members are equally dependent upon the rules, and that no *personal* dependence is created within the group. This is not true of the family or of relations with women, both of which are intimate, and, from the guys' point of view, are "out of control" because they are governed by emotional commitments.

The guys recognized the relationship between their male bond and the work world by claiming that "high officials of the University know about the way we act, and they understand what we are doing." Although this might be taken as evidence that the guys were internalizing their father's norms and thus inheriting the rights of patriarchy, the guys described their fathers as slaves to work and women, not as patriarchs. It is striking that the guys would not accept the notion that men have more power than women; to them it is not men who rule, but work and women that govern men.

REFERENCES

Bly, Robert (1982) "What men really want: An interview with Keith Thompson." *New Age* 30–37, 50–51.

Freud, Sigmund. (1960) *Jokes and Their Relation to the Unconscious.* New York: W. W. Norton.

Gray, Glenn J. (1959) *The Warriors: Reflections on Men in Battle.* New York: Harper.

Radcliffe-Brown, Alfred. (1959) *Structure and Function in Primitive Society.* Glencoe: The Free Press.

Rubin, Lillian. (1983) *Intimate Strangers.* New York: Harper & Row.

Slater, Phillip. (1963) "On Social Regression." *The American Sociological Review* 28: 339–364.

Gary Alan Fine

THE DIRTY PLAY OF LITTLE BOYS

The tormented Earl of Gloster moaned in *King Lear:* "As flies to wanton boys, are we to gods; they kill us for their sport." These mordant lines may tell us more about the interests of boys than gods. Why do boys kill flies for their sport? Why, as Plutarch noted, do they throw stones at frogs; or why, as Swift depicted, do they pour salt on sparrows' tails? What are boys like or, more to the point, what do boys do? While mountains of tomes have been devoted to scientific, development studies of boys, few researchers have spent time with them on their own turf.

My chosen site was around the world of sport. For three years I spent springs and summers observing ten Little League baseball teams in Minnesota, Rhode Island, and Massachusetts as they went through their seasons. I observed at practice fields and in dugouts, remaining with the boys after the games and arriving early to learn what they did when adults were not present. As I came to know these boys better, I hung out with them when they were "doing nothing."

My goal was to elucidate the process by which the rich veins of preadolescent male culture are developed — particularly those areas considered morally unacceptable by adults. In sport and in informal male activity, sex role development and display are crucial — certainly in the view of the participants. If we hope to understand how adult sex roles are shaped, we must observe the blossoming of these roles in childhood peer groups.

Preadolescence is a difficult period to define, covering the twilight zone between the perils of the Oedipus complex and the *Stürm und Drang* of puberty. Yet preadolescence is more than a way station to puberty. Child psychologists Fritz Redl once cleverly suggested that preadolescence is the period in which "the nicest children begin to behave in the most awful way." This pithy description captures the basic split personality of this period. By preadolescence, the boy is a part of several social worlds: same-sex groups, cross-sex interaction, school, and family life. Each of these settings requires a different standard of behavior. Because there is not total segregation of the child's life with friends from that with parents, parents tend to be aware of boys' awfulness, even if they are unaware of the details.

The conflict derives from the fact that the preadolescent has neither the right nor the ability to keep these two spheres of social life separate. When removed from peers, juveniles may be sweet, even considerate, and sometimes tender. Yet, placed in a social situation in which they do not have to be on their best behavior and given situational constraints which militate against proper behavior, they may engage in aggressive sexuality, prejudice, and destructiveness. These are "good boys" engaging in "dirty play." These patterns of behavior reflect both biological and social factors, and provide internal and external constraints on a child's behavior. These factors constitute the child's imperatives of development.

In examining the social lives of these middle-class, suburban white preadolescent baseball players, I focused on their friendships. For these boys, as for most of us, friendship constitutes a staging area in which activities improper elsewhere can be tested in a supportive environment. The moral choices children are experimenting with are played out with their chums. Boys are "boys" only when they are with their peers.

How is it that these boys are willing to engaged in activities so abhorrent to adults — what I have called "dirty play." The concept of dirty play is borrowed loosely from sociologist Everett Hughes's discussion of "dirty work." Hughes asked how it is that some in our society become involved and them become satisfied with what the rest of society consider to be dirty work — those activities that no "decent" person would do. Hughes's focus was on the occupational order, but the issue applies equally to the world of preadolescent play. Why do our children do these things? Hughes noted that some people had to engage in some very unpleasant behaviors to keep the social order functioning, and that other members of the society did not wish to know about this in order to "keep their hands clean." In some of Hughes's formulations these dirty work activities were behaviors no decent person should agree to, such as the behavior of Nazi SS officers. But Hughes recognized that some dirty workers (grave diggers, janitors) are necessary for all smoothly functioning social systems. Because of the "pollution" of the work, the rest of society closes its eyes and the dirty workers remain a closed society. A membrane protects the rest of society from contamination from these dirty workers.

The same membrane may be necessary in regard to children's dirty play. Dirty play may well be necessary for effective socialization (at least to our society as it currently exists), but it may be best for adults not to know what their offspring are doing. Children's play, perhaps, should remain in the closet. The dirty play of children seems to be a natural outpouring of some of the developmental imperatives of growing up, but how it is handled depends very much on the situations in which children and the adult guardians find themselves. I begin my analysis by describing some forms that this preadolescent dirty play takes. Specifically I focus on: aggressive pranks, sexual talk and activity, and racist remarks.

Some children's pranks can, on occasion, be elaborate and distressing. Consider the following: A group of boys wraps dog feces in newspaper, lights the newspaper on fire, rings a homeowner's doorbell, and runs away to watch. When the victim comes to the door, he stomps on the flaming package. At that point another boy rings the back doorbell and the man, not thinking, rushes through the house, tracking it with dog excrement.

AGGRESSIVE PRANKS

Such accounts suggest that children are continually engaging in troublesome behavior. However, we need to be careful not to overgeneralize this behavior. Talk about these legendary pranks is far more common than their doing. After their original occurrence, the story is told and retold. Talking about the prank conveys the meaning of the event with far less danger to the participants. Pranks represent an attempt by preadolescents to explore the boundaries of moral propriety. In their talk, preadolescents place a premium on daring behavior as expressed through what they term "mischief."

Pulling a prank is a form of social behavior, both in that pranks vary from community to community and because preadolescents who play these pranks invariably do them with those closest to them. In one suburb, "mooning" cars (pulling down one's trousers while facing away from the traffic) was the most common prank; in another "egging" cars and houses was most common, and in the others the most frequent prank was to ring doorbells and run away. Virtually all of the boys who play these pranks do so in the company of their best friends. In one community, of the forty-eight boys who named their prank partners, 89 percent of these were described as "best" or "close" friends. Friendship, therefore, serves as the staging area in which this type of ritualized dirty play occurs. Given the value placed on taking chances, the copresence of friends is likely to promote the performance of aggressive pranks in defining the action as legitimate, providing status for the boy if he succeeds, and goading him if his fear of adults threatens to stand in his way.

Rather than defining pranks as expressions of an aggressive instinct directed at those who control them — the traditional psychiatric approach — I see pranks as social action designed to shape a boy's public identity. The dirty play has something of a status content about it, where the goal is not to do harm, but to gain renown for being daring. The prank is but the set-piece that provides the basis of identity attributions — not an aggressive end in itself.

SEXUAL TALK

Whatever latency might have been during Freud's childhood, in contemporary America preadolescence is a period of much sexual talk and some sexual behavior. This sexual talk, among boys in particular, with its aggressive overtones is worrying to parents who are unable to understand how their sons could possibly talk that way about each other and about girls. Yet, however much we might object, boys strive to be "masculine" and they talk about girls in terms both unflattering and too explicit for what their parents expect them to know.

Males maturing in our sexualized society quickly recognize the value of being able to talk about sexual topics in ways that bring them credit. As with pranks, sexual talk is a social activity and is a form of presenting oneself in desirable ways. In fact, given the reality that many of the talkers have not reached puberty, we can assume that their sexual interests are more social than physiological. Boys wish to convince their peers that they are sexually mature, active, and knowledgeable.

One means by which a person can convince others that he has an appropriate sexualized self is through sexualized behavior. This can include behavior among same-sex peers (mutual masturbation, homosexual experimentation, or autosexual activities such as measuring the length of one's penis) or behavior with girls. These behaviors, like pranks, although not frequent for any one child, may be notable and remembered. One public kiss, if done well, can serve for a thousand private caresses. The second "proof" of sexuality is talk — both talk that has a behavioral referent and talk that is in itself an indication of a sexualized self. In the first instance, the talk presents behavior that should, by rights, remain private ("kiss and tell"), and must be convincing as narrative; the latter serves as an end in itself — such as sexualized insults and talk about biological and physiological processes. This indicates that the child knows, in the words of one preadolescent, "What's a poppin'." These expectations are primarily social, and are based on the desire to reveal what preadolescents consider adult competences, although adults will consider these same things to be dirty when performed by preadolescents.

A boy must walk a narrow line between not showing enough involvement with girls, in which case he may be labeled effeminate, immature, or gay, and showing too much serious, tender attention, in which case he may be labeled "girl crazy." For these reasons, much talk indicates that boys are interested in girls sexually, but they are not so interested that they find any to their liking. While preadolescent boys have girlfriends, they must be careful about what they say about them to other boys. Girls can easily break the bonds of brother-hood among boys.

A related fear among boys is that of being tarred as homosexual or gay. During my research (in the late 1970s) boys attempted to define their sexualized selves in contrast to "improper" sexual activity. To be sure, most of these boys have never met anyone whom they believe really is a homosexual, and they have, at best, a foggy vision of gay sexual behaviors. Despite this, it is common to hear boys saying things like "You're a faggot," "What a queer," and "Kiss my ass."

Being gay has little to do with homosexual behavior; rather it suggests that the target is immature. Indeed, some homosexual behavior (for example, mutual masturbation) occurs among high-status boys who would never be labeled gay. Being gay is synonymous with being a baby and a girl. In each instance the target has not comported himself in accord with the traditional male sex role. Homosexual rhetoric has an additional benefit for the speaker in that its use suggests that the speaker is mature himself, and can be differentiated from the boy who is scorned.

RACIST INVECTIVE

When I inform white audiences that I found considerable racial invective in the middle-class suburban communities I studied, many are surprised; most of the blacks I tell are not. These boys had little direct contact with blacks, but as they lived near major metropolitan areas, they were well aware of racial tensions.

One of the Little League teams, a team in southern Rhode Island, was particularly notable for the racial epithets uttered by players. The team was lily-white, but there were four black children on other teams in the league and this team had a black coach two seasons before. The talk by one of the star players was particularly virulent, and his hatred was particularly reserved for two of the black children in the league, Roger and Bill Mott: "I was talking with some players about the best home-run hitters in the League, and I mentioned that Billy Mott was pretty good. Justin replies with disgust: 'That dumb nigger.' He immediately described how 'two niggers tried to jump me.'" Most racial talk was not serious in intent, but was joking. In driving some boys home one day in a Massachusetts suburb we passed two black youths walking quietly through town. One boy leaned out of my car window and yelled "Get out of here, you jungle bunnies." The other boys broke up in gales of laughter. Or: "One of the groundskeeper's helpers is a swarthy adolescent. Justin playfully tells his friends Harry and Whitney that the boy is a Puerto Rican and, therefore, is 'half nigger and half white.' Justin calls him a 'punk' and Justin and Whitney both call him 'half and half.' The boy, within earshot, is becoming angry: Justin, Harry, and Whitney run away laughing."

Remember that most times this rhetoric occurs it is not spoken in anger, but in play — although play of a rather nasty disposition. Preadolescents, emphasizing status and position among peers, are very concerned about group boundaries. It should be no surprise that they draw lines between those who are part of the group and those who must remain outsiders. This explains some of the concerns about sexuality and gender at this period and also explains the concern with race, class, nationality, and geographical affiliation (school, town, etc.). Further, during preadolescence children learn the adult significance of these boundary issues. Even if parents do not tell white children that blacks are inferior, the children still learn that race is a crucial division in our society, and preadolescents will assume that those who are not "us" are suitable subjects for attack. Although such an analysis does not work equally well for all children with regard to each demographic or social category, it is fair to emphasize that social differentiation is common to the period and is reflected in remarks adults find disquieting and offensive.

WHY DIRTY PLAY?

The prevalence of dirty play in the lives of children, and their evident enjoyment of it, should give pause to all adults. Rarely do children behave fully in accord with adult moral standards. This is particularly dramatic in societies such as our own in which adults believe in the innocence of children. The existence of these forms of play suggests either that children are not really innocent or that they have been corrupted. Either charge is troubling.

I suggest four rationales for these "disturbing" behaviors : (1) control, (2) status, (3) social differentiation, and (4) socialization to perceived adult norms. These four themes do not apply equally well to all examples of play. If asked, most preadolescents would admit to engaging in these activities because they are "fun," but this sidesteps the question of why these sorts of things are seen as fun. Thus, we must go beyond this simple explanation.

Dirty play can be seen as a claim-making behavior. Each instance attempts implicitly to make a statement about the rights of preadolescents to engage in a set of activities and have a set of opinions in the face of adult counter-pressures. When children behave in accord with adult prescriptions, which they often do, their play causes little comment, but when a preadolescent chooses to play in a way contrary to adult authority the play becomes an issue. Preadolescents recognize this problem and are typically sophisticated enough to engage in their dirty play out of the eyesight and earshot of their adult guardians. They are claiming for themselves the right to make public statements about race, sex, or authority. This play is remarkably sophisticated in that it deals with those areas of adult social structure adults typically wish to preserve for themselves.

These acts are sociopolitical, although playful. While the content of this dirty play is troubling to many, it is also troubling that our children feel competent to make judgements and act on them. They reflect a judgment on adult social order and, typically, one different from that which adults officially put forward, although one that (especially in the case of racial and sexual remarks) they may privately believe.

The adult emphasis on decorum and politeness is significant in light of the age-graded power structure. Politeness is a tactic used by those in power to keep those without power subservient. Politeness and decorum structure collective action so as to preserve order and process. If all that children can do to "get their way" is to request things politely from adults, then adults have full power to make their own decisions without consequences from those who are asking. Once a request has been rejected by the authorities there is nothing the requester can do, under this model, other than accept this decision gracefully. The implicit benefit for those without power is that on the next polite request the authority might be more willing to accede. However, there is not certainty of this and, even so, authority still remains unchallenged.

It may be apt to speak of these examples of dirty play that question the adult authority structure through the metaphor of playful terrorism. Ultimately such "terrorism" is politically impotent because of the lack of organization of the "terrorist groups," their lack of commitment and uniformity of beliefs, the tight control adults have over them, and the rewards that can be offered to those who conform. Still, it is hard to miss the potential threat to the authority structure inherent in some of this play which tests boundaries and legitimacy.

The dirty play I have described is important in shaping relationships within the group, as well as outside. Its performance is a technique for gaining status within a peer group. Preadolescent interaction can be seen, in part, as a status contest at an age at which status really matters. Status matters at all ages, but during preadolescence, with its change in orientation toward adult status symbols and a social world outside of the eyes of adults, the evaluation of peer position is of particular importance.

Boys gain renown from participating in these actions. There is a premium on being willing to do things that other boys wish to do but are afraid to. If there is some consensus that the prank is desirable, the boy who performs it or leads the group gains status for breaking through the barrier of fear in which others are enveloped. There is risk involved in throwing eggs at houses or at moving cars; one could get caught, beaten, grounded, or even arrested.

The costs, coupled with the lack of status rewards, suggest why it is apparently so rare for preadolescents to engage in these behaviors when alone. It is not that they have a personal, destructive impulse but, rather, they want to show off in the presence of friends. To think of these children as bad misses the point; they are, more or less, amoral — in that enforcing the dictates of morality is not one of their primary goals; rather, their aim is to get by with as much interpersonal smoothness as possible. The concern with those wonderful Goffmanlike images of "presentation of self," "teamwork," and "impression management" is omnipresent.

One of the collective tasks of preadolescents is to define themselves in contrast to other groups that share some characteristics. In my empirical discussion of dirty play among white middle-class boys I focused on racial and sexual differentiation. Whites are not blacks, and boys are not girls. Also, there is the belief held to fiercely by many of those whom I have studied that whites are better than blacks, and that boys are better than girls. Given the stance of today's tolerant, egalitarian society and particularly those social scientists who choose to write about it, such beliefs are heresy, morally repugnant, and represent a social problem. Yet, from the standpoint of the preadolescent white boy they seem perfectly natural. Ethnocentrism always does. Indeed, when we look over the lengthy landscape of human history we see that social differentiation has been more the rule than the exception. People always wish to make their own group special and distinct. This basic need of humanity is sometimes (particularly) overcome, but surely the desire for differentiation is not a mark of Cain.

When boys torment girls or jeer at blacks, we may see this as a kind of dirty play that does not necessarily adhere to the moral selves of these social actors. The positive side of such group actions is that the preadolescents are learning some measure of communal feeling, even though it is directed at another group. It is significant that much of what we consider to be dirty or cruel play is at the

178

PART III   *From Boys to Men*

expense of some other group or members of another group. Even disagreeable play that is internally directed typically is focused on a boy who is to be differentiated from the group in some significant way: such as because of some physical handicap or because of the belief that he can be morally differentiated (for example, as "gay").

Preadolescent dirty play does not simply appear from nowhere. It is a transformation of things that boys see enacted by older boys or by adults, or learn about through the media. The content does matter. Yet, this is often material that many adults sincerely wish they had not communicated. Unfortunately we cannot shield preadolescents from that which we do not want them to learn. They are information vacuum cleaners and, of the information gained, will selectively use that which fits their purposes.

The themes of preadolescent dirty play are far from unrecognizable. Aggression, sexism, and racism are found in adult activity. These themes are also indicated in dramatic media representations, even when the themes are ostensibly being disparaged. Still, audiences can choose to select whatever information they wish from a media production, even if this material is incompatible with the official morality of the society. The best example of this during the research project was the reaction to the film, *The Bad News Bears*. Although the film ostensibly warned against the dangers of over-competition and excessive adult involvement in youth sports, the images that preadolescents took from the film were techniques of talking dirty and acting grossly ("stick this where the sun never shines").

We all know that often a moral message is but the sugar coating for sexual or aggressive doings that the producers use to capture an audience. This technique is as applicable to media productions aimed at adults as those aimed at children. In the case of children this may be compounded by the fact that preadolescents often attempt to act mature. Maturity does not have a clearly defined meaning; however, maturity as a concept implies a change in behavior. To validate that we are acting maturely, we need to act differently from the ways we have acted before. This typically takes the form of doing those things we had not known about or had not been allowed to do under the watchful eyes of adults. As a consequence, many of these markers of maturity will be precisely those things that adults see as dirty play. It is not that the children are being childish or immature in their view, but the contrary. They are attempting to live up to adult standards of behavior, and address adult issues from which they had previously been excluded.

Socialization to society's expectations has been well established as one important feature of children's play; yet, what is learned through play is diverse and some of what is learned may be formally offensive to those given the task of guiding children's development. The agenda for children's development is not always set by adults, although it typically is based on a reflection of what they do.

TAMING DIRTY PLAY?

Each of these four component motivations of dirty play should help us understand that playing dirty, by adult standards, is not identical to being morally bad. The issue, as Everett Hughes raised it in light of adult "dirty work," is the extent to which a person can get away with doing dirty work without that dirtiness adhering to his public self. In some cases that would appear to be relatively easy; in other cases, almost impossible.

The connection of a boy's dirty play with his moral self is a matter of negotiation, with different ideologies prevailing at different times, places, among different groups, and depending on the relationship of the judger to the person judged. The likely intention of the actor, the presence of others supporting the action, the social supports for the action, and the actual expected outcome influence the way in which children's dirty play will be evaluated.

Children's dirty play is virtually inevitable. There are so many needs and traditions connected with the doing of these actions that we would be hard pressed to visualize a serious program that would eradicate these behaviors. These are play forms we must live with. We do have one weapon — a long-term weapon, but a dramatically effective one as many of us can testify: guilt. In planting the seeds that this type of behavior is morally objectionable, we may recognize that these teachings will not work when given. Yet, often they will eventually be effective when reward structures change and when social needs alter. The seed of morality will (imperfectly) bloom at some later date and in some other place. As children grow older, and their needs for presentation of self change, they come to believe that such behaviors they used to delight in are morally offensive. While we object to children playing concentration camp guards, holding mock lynchings, or simply torturing their peers in the name of fun, we should recognize that this too may pass. Although sometimes morality does not change, if the new "improved" morality is supported by the subtle reward structures of adult society, we can say with a fair measure of confidence that dirty payers emerge into saintly adults — at least adequately saintly adults. Children, in dealing with a transformed version of the raw, emotional issues of life, distress adults but they need not permanently smudge the very core of their angelic souls.

SUGGESTED READINGS

Glassner, B. "Kid Society." *Urban Education* 11 (1976):5–22.

Hughes, E. "Good People and Dirty Work." *Social Problems* 10 (1962):3–11.

Knapp, M. and Knapp, H. *One Potato, Two Potato . . . : The Secret Education of American Children*. New York: Norton, 1976.

Sutton-Smith, B. *A History of Children's Play*. Philadelphia: University of Pennsylvania Press, 1981.

PART FOUR

♦♦♦

Sports and War: Rites of Passage in Male Institutions

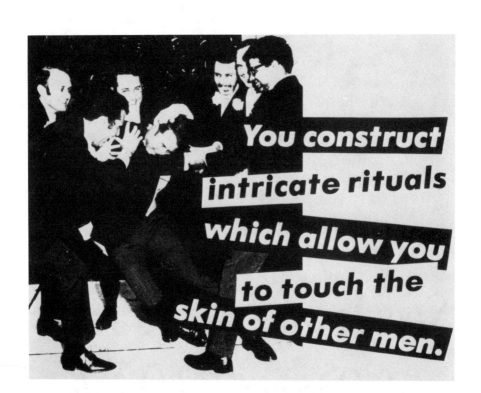

Are men naturally more competitive, aggressive, and violent than women? Why are so many cultural heroes males who have been victors on the playing fields or the battle fields? Why do men so often feel that their closest relationships with other men are those that developed "in the heat of battle?" And how do men's battles with each other connect to men's domination of women? The articles in this section shed light on these questions by focusing our attention on two very male-dominated institutions: organized sports and the military.

Recently, largely because of the women's movement, sport sociologists and historians have begun to reconceptualize the meaning of sport as a social institution. Clearly, a major role of sports in the twentieth century has been to provide an institutional context for "masculinity-validation" in a rapidly changing world. Much of the experiential and ideological prominence of sports can be attributed to the fact that it is a male-created homosocial world that provides dramatic symbolic "proof" of the "natural superiority" of men over women. But as the first few articles in this section show, there is nothing "natural" about the connection between sports and what we think of as masculinity. In fact, as the first article by Don Sabo shows, organized sports is an important institutional context in which certain types of masculinity are produced and "naturalized." Here boys learn to overvalue competition and winning, to take physical pain and control their emotions, to view aggression and violence as legitimate means to achieve one's goals, to uncritically accept authority and hierarchy, and to devalue women as well as any "feminine" qualities in males. The next two articles by Mike Messner suggest how the narrow definitions of masculinity that boys learn in sports connect with other forms of social domination — social class and ethnic inequalities among men and the marginalization of gay men.

The athletic experience can act as a training ground for the construction of an even narrower form of masculinity: the soldier. The article by Connell demonstrates that violent aggression is not *the* "natural" form of masculinity. In fact, it takes a very intense process of socialization to make killers out of most men. Levy shows how racism, mysogyny, and homophobia are utilized by the military to dehumanize the enemy in order to rationalize killing him or her. Together, these articles show how in patriarchal society, values concerning militarism and war have permeated the very fabric of social life. Challenging the form of masculinity that so dominates our society (and that brings us wars) will involve more than simply changing the ways we raise young boys — it must involve a basic rethinking of many of our most fundamental social institutions.

Don Sabo

PIGSKIN, PATRIARCHY AND PAIN

I am sitting down to write as I've done thousands of times over the last decade. But today there's something very different. I'm not in pain.

A half-year ago I underwent back surgery. My physician removed two disks from the lumbar region of my spine and fused three vertebrae using bone scrapings from my right hip. The surgery is called a "spinal fusion." For seventy-two hours I was completely immobilized. On the fifth day, I took a few faltering first steps with one of those aluminum walkers that are usually associated with the elderly in nursing homes. I progressed rapidly and left the hospital after nine days completely free of pain for the first time in years.

How did I, a well-intending and reasonably gentle boy from western Pennsylvania ever get into so much pain? At a simple level, I ended up in pain because I played a sport that brutalizes men's (and now sometimes women's) bodies. *Why* I played football and bit the bullet of pain, however, is more complicated. Like a young child who learns to dance or sing for a piece of candy, I played for rewards and payoffs. Winning at sport meant winning friends and carving a place for myself within the male pecking order. Success at the "game" would make me less like myself and more like the older boys and my hero, Dick Butkus. Pictures of his hulking and snarling form filled my head and hung above my bed, beckoning me forward like a mythic Siren. If I could be like Butkus, I told myself, people would adore me as much as I adored him. I might even adore myself. As an adolescent I hoped sport would get me attention from girls. Later, I became more practical-minded and I worried about my future. What kind of work would I do for a living? Football became my ticket to a college scholarship which, in western Pennsylvania during the early 'sixties, meant a career instead of getting stuck in the steelmills.

THE ROAD TO SURGERY.

My bout with pain and spinal "pathology" began with a decision I made in 1955 when I was eight years old. I "went out" for football. At the time, I felt uncomfortable inside my body — too fat, too short, too weak. Freckles and glasses too! I wanted to change my image, and I felt that changing my body was one place to begin. My parents bought me a set of weights, and one of the older boys in the neighborhood was solicited to demonstrate their use. I can still remember the ease with which he lifted the barbell, the veins popping through his bulging biceps in the summer sun, and the sated look of strength and accomplishment on his face. This was to be the image of my future.

That fall I made a dinner-table announcement that I was going out for football. What followed was a rather inauspicious beginning. First, the initiation rites. Pricking the flesh with thorns until blood was drawn and having hot peppers rubbed in my eyes. Getting punched in the gut again and again. Being forced to wear a jockstrap around my nose and not knowing what was funny. Then came what was to be an endless series of proving myself: calisthenics until my arms ached; hitting hard and fast and knocking the other guy down; getting hit in the groin and not crying. I learned that pain and injury are "part of the game."

I "played" through grade school, co-captained my high school team, and went on to become an inside linebacker and defensive captain at the NCAA Division I level. I learned to be an animal. Coaches took notice of animals. Animals made first team. Being an animal meant being fanatically aggressive and ruthlessly competitive. If I saw an arm in front of me, I trampled it. Whenever blood was spilled, I nodded approval. Broken bones (not mine of course) were secretly seen as little victories within the bigger struggle. The coaches taught me to "punish the other man," but little did I suspect that I was devastating my own body at the same time. there were broken noses, ribs, fingers, toes and teeth, torn muscles and ligaments, bruises, bad knees, and busted lips, and the gradual pulverizing of my spinal column that, by the time my jock career was long over at age thirty, had resulted in seven years of near-constant pain. It was a long road to the surgeon's office.

Now surgically freed from its grip, my understanding of pain has changed. Pain had gnawed away at my insides. Pain turned my awareness inward. I blamed myself for my predicament; I thought that I was solely responsible for every twinge and sleepless night. But this view was an illusion. My pain, each individual's pain, is really an expression of a linkage to an outer world of people, events, and forces. The origins of our pain are rooted *outside*, not inside, our skins.

THE PAIN PRINCIPLE

Sport is just one of many areas in our culture where pain is more important than pleasure. Boys are taught that to endure pain is courageous, to survive pain is manly. The principle that pain is "good" and pleasure is "bad" is crudely evident in the "no pain, no gain" philosophy of so many coaches and athletes. The "pain principle" weaves its way into the lives and psyches of male athletes in two fundamental ways. It stifles men's awareness of their bodies and limits our emotional expression. We learn to ignore personal hurts and injuries because they interfere with the "efficiency" and "goals" of the "team." We become adept at taking the feelings that boil up inside us — feelings of insecurity and stress from striving so hard for success — and channeling them in a bundle of rage which is directed at opponents and enemies. This posture toward oneself and the world is not limited to "jocks." It is evident in the lives of many nonathletic men who, as "workaholics" or success-strivers or tough guys, deny their authentic physical or emotional needs and develop health problems as a result.

Today, I no longer perceive myself as an *individual* ripped off by athletic injury. Rather, I see myself as just *one more man among many men* who got swallowed up by a social system predicated on male domination. Patriarchy has two structural aspects. First, it is an hierarchical system in which men dominate women in crude and debased, slick and subtle ways. Feminists have made great progress exposing and analyzing this dimension of the edifice of sexism. But it is also a system of *intermale dominance*, in which a minority of men dominates the masses of men. This intermale dominance hierarchy exploits the majority of those it beckons to climb its heights. Patriarchy's mythos of heroism and its morality of power-worship implant visions of ecstasy and masculine excellence in the minds of the boys who ultimately will defend its inequities and ridicule its victims. It is inside this institutional framework that I have begun to explore the essence and scope of "the pain principle."

TAKING IT

Patriarchy is a form of social hierarchy. Hierarchy breeds inequity and inequity breeds pain. To remain stable, the hierarchy must either justify the pain or explain it away. In a patriarchy, women and the masses of men are fed the cultural message that pain is inevitable and that pain enhances one's character and moral worth. This principle is expressed in Judeo-Christian beliefs. The Judeo-Christian god inflicts or permits pain, yet "the Father" is still revered and loved. Likewise, as chief disciplinarian in the patriarchal family, the father has the right to inflict pain. The "pain principle" also echoes throughout traditional western sexual morality; it is better to experience the pain of *not* having sexual pleasure than it is to have sexual pleasure.

Most men learn to heed these cultural messages and take their "cues for survival" from the patriarchy. The Willie Lowmans of the economy pander to the prophets of profit and the American Dream. Soldiers, young and old, salute their neo-Hun generals. Right-wing Christians genuflect before their idols of righteousness, affluence, and conformity. And male athletes adopt the visions and values that coaches are offering: to take orders, to take pain, to "take out" opponents, to take the game seriously, to take women, and to take their place on the team. And if they can't "take it," then the rewards of athletic comraderie, prestige, scholarships, pro contracts, and community recognition are not forthcoming.

Becoming a football player fosters conformity to male-chauvinistic values and self-abusing lifestyles. It contributes to the legitimacy of a social structure based on patriarchal power. Male competition for prestige and status in sport and elsewhere leads to identification with the relatively few males who control resources and are able to bestow rewards and inflict punishment. Male supremacists are not born, they are made, and traditional athletic socialization is a fundamental contribution to this complex social-psychological and political process. Through sport, many males, indeed, learn to "take it" — that is, to internalize patriarchal values which, in turn, become part of their gender identity and conception of women and society.

My high school coach once evoked the pain principle during a pre-game pep-talk. For what seemed an eternity, he paced frenetically and silently before us with fists clenched and head bowed. He suddenly stopped and faced us with a smile. It was a though he had approached a podium to begin a long-awaited lecture. "Boys," he began, "people who say that football is a 'contact sport' are dead wrong. Dancing is a contact sport. Football is a game of pain and violence! Now get the hell out of here and kick some ass." We practically ran through the wall leaving the locker room, surging in unison to fight the coach's war. I see now that the coach was right but for all the wrong reasons. I should have taken him at his word and never played the game!

Mike Messner

SPORTS AND THE POLITICS OF INEQUALITY

Our town had two high schools. Ours was mostly the poor and blue collar workers, and the rich kids all went to Northside. They always beat us in sports, but my senior year we had a good basketball team, we all really hoped we could beat Northside. Well, by the middle of the first half our team was just totally *dominating* them — it was amazing — and the crowd on our side did this cheer: IN YOUR *FACE* NORTHSIDE! After a couple of minutes, the Northside crowd yelled back: THAT'S ALL RIGHT, THAT'S OK, YOU'LL BE WORKING FOR *US* SOMEDAY!

This story, told by a young man about his own high school experience in a small midwest town, illuminates some of the complex and contradictory aspects of sports in a society which is stratified along ethnic and class lines. It appears on the surface that the sporting contest exists *outside* the realm of everyday social experience in that it can bring together people of diverse cultural and economic backgrounds. Here every person (theoretically) has the same opportunity to excel, is judged by the same standards, must conform to the same set of rules under the watchful eye of a neutral authority (referees) and the community. The game thus reinforces the myth of fairness, equal opportunity, meritocracy and democracy.

But simmering just below the surface of this seemingly egalitarian contest are the hatreds, prejudices and antagonisms that result from social inequality. In a stratified society, when participation in sport is opened up to all, the sporting arena often becomes a "contested terrain" where intergroup antagonisms are played out. For the "blue collar" kids (and for their fans and families in the stands) the game becomes a place to prove that "we're just as good as they are — indeed, perhaps *better* than they are." For a fleeting moment in this arena, they can achieve this victory and shove it in the faces of their superiors. But this victory is immediately shoved back into their faces as meaningless and hollow in terms of life *outside* the sporting arena: inequality still exists after the final buzzer sounds, and the privileged classes have the luxury of pooh-poohing the importance of a mere game when compared to real life where you'll be working for *us* someday!

From the point of view of many who are concerned with dealing with the problems of the poor, the under-privileged, the oppressed in this society, the experience of athletes is often seen as meaningless. Sports are regarded by some as an "opiate" which keeps vital attentions and energies diverted away from the real political and economic tasks at hand. But there is another point of view which is not so immediately obvious. What goes on in the sporting arena is meaningful in understanding the making and re-making of social reality. When poor people, working class people, black or brown people participate with the dominant classes and achieve some success in sports, this does not automatically eliminate poverty and inequality, but it does change the context in which class and race relations take place.

REINFORCING RACISM

Organized sports were originally set up in Britain and in the U.S. by white upper class males to measure themselves against each other and to "build character" in an expanding entrepreneurial environment. As long as a system of "sports apartheid" existed, the athletic accomplishments of white males from the upper classes could be used as an ideological justification for the existence of inequality. Blacks, women and other oppressed groups, it was argued, could not compete with white males in sports or in the economy because they would surely lose, given their "obvious" inherent inferiority.

But as some color bars began to fall in professional and amateur sports — Satchel Paige striking out top white professional baseball players in an exhibition, Jesse Owens capturing the Olympic Gold in Munich in 1936, Jackie Robinson excelling in the previously all-white professional baseball leagues — the old myths of white superiority were challenged. Today, athletes still symbolically embody the hopes, dreams — and prejudices — of different communities. For example, many whites hope that Gerry Cooney will be the "Great White Hope" who finally wins the heavyweight boxing championship. And a black friend tells me that Boston Celtics' star Larry Bird is the second most hated man in the black community (after Ronald Reagan) for daring to be among the best in a "black sport."

Behind the symbolic meaning of the mythological giants of professional sports are millions of people who compete in high schools, recreation leagues, and on playgrounds. Sociologist Harry Edwards argues that hundreds of thousands of black youth are "channeled" into sports by role models in the media, by peer group and family encouragement, and by the denial of access to white-dominated schools and professions. Thus, far from being an indicator of "black progress," the predominance of blacks in many sports is an indicator of the persistence of racism in society. And, as Edwards and others have pointed out, the "carnage" that results can be staggering due to the incredibly small number of people who actually ever make a living through sports. In Edwards' words,

> Despite the fact then that American basketball, boxing, football, and baseball competitions have come more and more to look like Ghana playing Nigeria, sport nonetheless looms like a fog-shrouded minefield for the overwhelming majority of black athletes. It has been a treadmill to oblivion rather than the escalator to wealth and glory it was believed to be. There is today disturbingly consistent evidence that the black athlete who blindly sets out to fill the shoes of Dr. J., Reggie J., Magic J., Kareem Abdul-J., or O.J. is destined to end up with "No J." — no job whatsoever that he is qualified to do in our modern, technologically sophisticated society. At the end of his career, he is not running through airports like O.J. He is much more likely to be sweeping up airports — if he has the good fortune to land even that job.[1]

Is the institution of sport simply a social mechanism through which existing social inequalities are reproduced and justified? Are there perhaps moments in sports — especially for the majority of participants who never come close to making it "big" — which might lead to the opposite tendencies? Specifically, does the day-to-day interaction of males "playing together" on the nation's play-

grounds lead to a breakdown of racism and to a discovery of our common humanity with which we can challenge the inequities of the larger society?

<h2>IN YOUR FACE!</h2>

I drove the lane and put up what I thought was a pretty good-looking jumphook
in heavy traffic when, seemingly from nowhere, a large black hand swatted the
ball away. "Try to come in here again with that weak shit and I'll kick your
white ass!" Such was my introduction to Ron, who appeared to me the epitome
of the black playground player: with his gangly 6'4" frame, his shaved head, his
quickness and style, his aggressive intensity, and his frequent verbal intimidation, he would usually dominate play at this mostly-white playground which I
came to frequent.

After playing in pickup games with Ron for three years (yet rarely speaking
with him), I decided he would be an interesting person to interview for my
research on athletes. He quickly agreed ("You gonna make me *famous?*"). Although my goal was to learn about "The Black Athlete," my interview with this
good-humored and thoughtful thirty-year-old "professional gym-rat" ultimately
taught me more about my own deeply-ingrained attitudes and assumptions concerning black males. I admitted to Ron that his verbal and physical aggressiveness had certainly intimidated me. When playing against him I found myself
playing a much more "passive" game, simply out of fear that if I "took the ball
to the hoop," he would embarrass me — or even hurt me. Ron laughed and told
me that much of his style is a persona which he has consciously constructed to
intimidate "white boys" like me and get the edge.

> I'm tall, I'm thin, I'm a black person with a shaved head, and I'm fearful.
> You have to intimidate mentally, because that's the advantage you have.
> But you're not really out to hurt that individual — it's competitiveness —
> the whole realization is that you've *gotta* talk shit in this game, you *have*
> to say, you know, "If you come close to me, I'm gonna *hurt* you!"

I asked Ron if he had ever had to back up that bluster with his fists, and his
answer was a real revelation to me: "No, never. Are you kidding? Never.
(laughs) — I would run. I would *run*. I'd be scared to fight." Now, I've played
basketball since I was old enough to count to two, and it had never occurred to
me that the black players might be a bit scared too. It's fascinating to me to
realize that I have always been a little more tentative — even passive — when
playing against black guys, and underlying this tentativeness was my fear of
what I assumed to be a potential for violence simmering just below the surface
of that black skin. Where did this assumption come from? Certainly not from
personal experience — I never have had overt violence committed against me
by a black player in a game! But the fear was there nonetheless. And on some
(semiconscious) level, I always felt that winning a particular game just wasn't
so important if it meant that I had to get my face smashed in for it. If it's so
important to him that he has to threaten me, then by God he can *have* the
damned game! (Am I mistaken, or is there a faint echo of "You'll be working
for *us* someday," here?)

Interestingly, even though my talk with Ron was disturbing to me in that it
made me aware of how deeply-ingrained my own racist attitudes are, it also
raised my hopes that sports can be an activity in which racism is under-

mined. Ron spent a good deal of time talking to me about how he met his best friend — a white man — on a basketball court, and when they play on the same team together, he told me, "We know each other's moves so well it's like magic sometimes."

SPORTS AND THE POLITICS OF INEQUALITY

If this discussion of sports and inequality seems to make contradictory points, it is because sports plays a contradictory role in the larger politics of inequality. On an ideological level, sports strengthens and legitimates class and ethnic inequalities in society while simultaneously providing cultural space where ideologies supporting inequalities can be challenged and debunked. And for participants, sports offers a place where class and ethnic antagonisms and prejudices can be destructively played out *and* it can offer a space where participants can experience transcendent moments of play which are relatively free from the larger social inequities. In this space, it is possible to discover ourselves and each other as human beings. What all this means is that the role sports will play in the politics of inequality will be determined by "how we play the game," both individually and collectively.

REFERENCE

1. Harry Edwards, "The Collegiate Athletic Arms Race," *J. of Sport and Social Issues*, 8 (1) Winter/Spring 1984.

Mike Messner

GAY ATHLETES AND THE GAY GAMES:
AN INTERVIEW WITH TOM WADDELL

In 1982, a history-making event took place in San Francisco when 1300 athletes from 12 different nations gathered for the first-ever Gay Games. The story of the Games is the story of the growth of a community. It is also the story of the evolution of a gay man, Tom Waddell, who for years lived a closeted existence while competing as a world-class decathlete in the highly homophobic world of organized sports.

When I was a kid, I was tall for my age and I was very thin, but very strong. And I was usually faster than most other people. But I discovered rather early that I liked gymnastics and I liked dance. I was very interested in being a ballet dancer, and I studied with my mother until I was about 17 and she said "I can't teach you any more — you need to go to New York now." I had lived in New Jersey, so I started studying in New York. And something became obvious to me right away: that male ballet dancers were effeminate, that they were what most people would describe as faggots. And I thought, I just couldn't handle that. It suddenly occurred to me that this was real dangerous territory for me — I'm from a small town and I was totally closeted and very concerned about being male . . . This was in the 50s, a terrible time to live, and everything was stacked against me. Anyway, I realized that I had to do something to protect my image of myself as a male — 'cause at that time, homosexuals were thought of primarily as men who really preferred to be women. And so I threw myself into athletics — I played football, gymnastics, track and field. I went to college on a gymnastics scholarship, was a nine-letter man through college, and I won all sorts of athletic awards and what-have-you. And I tried out for the Olympic team in 1960 and finished 6th in the tryouts. . . . I was a *jock* — that's how I was viewed, and I was comfortable with that, except that I suddenly realized in my junior year, I don't want to be a jock all my life — just a jock. So then I went to medical school.

During medical school he "literally forgot about athletics." He completed his internship, did a stint in the Army, and then at age 34, he finished an impressive 6th in the decathlon at the stormy 1968 Olympics in Mexico City. At this time,

I felt that I hadn't really achieved my peak yet. I was still concerned about, somewhere in my mind, wanting to protect a male image — I mean I was very much aware of that.

When you talk about protecting a male image, are you talking about the self that you're presenting to the world, or are you talking about how you feel about yourself?

How people viewed me. I was very comfortable with how I felt about myself. I had met a man a few years earlier who taught me internally to be at peace with myself, that being homosexual is okay.

I'm interested in that transition you went through from dance to sports.

I think ballet dancers are the greatest athletes in the world — far and away — it takes such coordination, strength, endurance. . . . In the past 20 years, it's changed here — boys get into it fairly young and it's okay to be a dancer now. You don't have to be queer to be a dancer. I just liked dancing. I mean, I liked moving, I liked the motion. I liked the finiteness of the motions in ballet — that there was a historical significance to all the moves, and they were labelled, and different people could execute them in different ways. To me, track and field is that same kind of beauty. When I watch runners, I just see motion in its most beautiful form — someone running for speed. Or a pole-vaulter or a high jumper — here's someone propelling their body through the air to achieve a particular thing. Now whether it's a jeté or a world record in the high jump doesn't make any difference — it's that particular kind of motion, it's very beautiful to me.

Did you feel sad when you left ballet?

No, I felt sad much later when I felt, hey, I could have been a dancer — I could have handled all this. See, I grew up thinking that I was the only gay person in the world.

During his athletic career, he struggled with his identity as a closeted gay man in the world of organized sports where homophobia is "rampant."

You see, I think a lot of athletes go into athletics for the same reason that I did. They need to prove their maleness. I did, I readily admit it. I wanted to be viewed as male, otherwise I would be a dancer today. I wanted the male, macho image of an athlete. So I was protected with a very hard shell. And I was *clearly* aware of what I was doing.

When people associated gayness with femininity, it seems like that really bothered you.

Yeah it did. I didn't feel that their reference points, as far as femininity, applied to me.

Did you feel an attachment to more traditional male traits?

Yeah, I mean athletically I was just as aggressive and hostile on the football field as anybody else. I loved knocking people down — I mean, I *liked* running over people — the whole thing was *fun*. And, uh, I've examined that often. I've examined my whole competitiveness in the Olympics, for example. . . . I often felt compelled to go along with a lot of locker room garbage because I wanted that image — and I know a lot of others who did too. And I think many athletes are attracted to athletics because they're fighting their feminine qualities — they don't want to be seen that way. I know a lot of football players who very quietly and secretly like to paint, or play piano. And they do it quietly because this to them is threatening if it's known by others.

Toward the end of his athletic career, living in the closet became "so uncomfortable, so hot" he finally decided to come out.

I had wanted to come out earlier and my friends always discouraged me — you know, "That'll create problems for you." Well, I already had problems, and the problems had to do with hiding. I was willing to face the new problems. To me, they were preferable to the ones I was having. . . . So I did come out publicly in 1976, in *People Magazine*. I didn't do it in any small way! And you know, it's interesting, of the hundreds of people that I wrote to before I came out, only two people stopped talking to me. Both of them were world class athletes — both of whom I think have real problems with their own sexual identities . . . it just scared the hell out of them when I came out — they didn't want to be guilty by association, so they just cut me off completely.

Tom Waddell became a very active member of the San Francisco Bay Area community. He re-kindled his interest in the arts and in dance. He also remained very active in athletics. In 1982, Tom Waddell's brainchild, the Gay Games, took place in San Francisco. Waddell's vision is a radical break from the traditional notion of the role of sports in society, and the Gay Games reflected his values and his vision of building an "exemplary community" based upon equality and universal participation. Despite, or perhaps because of, this vision, the United States Olympic Committee (U.S.O.C.) went to court to see that the word "Olympics" was not used by gays to denote their Games. As Waddell explains,

See, there's a "Police Olympics" occurring now. Yeah, and they use the same symbol, the flame, and the five rings — the bottom two are handcuffs, but it's still the five rings.

That's a nice touch.

Yeah, and *they've* never been touched by the U.S. Olympic Committee, 'cause that's "mom and apple pie." But we're queer. The whole thing is that they have a real problem with homosexuality — and they don't want to see the words "gay" and "olympics" in any combination. "Police," okay. "Special," okay. "Senior," okay. "Xerox," okay. "Armenian," okay. I mean, these are all Olympics that exist. "Crab cooking" okay, but not "Gay." Why don't they attack the Armenians, for instance? Because they don't do nasty things in bed. The whole thing's just stupid, you know. Here the courts are just knuckling under because of the power of the U.S.O.C. I mean, we're fighting corporate America here — a lot of special interest groups are involved in this. I'm sure the Coca Cola company says to the U.S.O.C.: "Hey! We're sponsoring the Olympics! We don't want 'Gay' out there!"

In terms of your personal involvement, what do the Games mean to you?

To me, it's one of those steps in a thousand-mile journey to try and raise consciousness and enlighten people — *not* just people outside the gay community, but within the gay community as well. When they come to the ghetto, they bring all the prejudices that they learned from the dominant society. We have 'em all there: we're just as racist, and ageist, sexist, nationalistic and chauvinistic as anybody else. So it seems to me if a subculture's gonna form, that somehow we've gotta make ourselves exemplary. And how do we do that? Let's use that same process of self-liberation that we learned through coming out to get at other issues. Let's get at the sexism issue. Let's get at the ageism issue. Let's make ourselves an exemplary community.

So that's my vision of what the Games are about — it's just a step — it's a way of bringing a lot of people together and specifically addressing all those issues with these Games. We have age-group competition, so all ages are involved. We have parity — if there's a men's sport, there's a women's sport to complement it. And we go out and recruit in Third World and minority areas. All of these people are gonna get together for a week, they're gonna march in together, march out together, they're gonna hold hands, and they'll say "Jesus Christ! this is wonderful!" There's this *discovery:* "I had no idea women were such fun!" and "God! Blacks are okay . . . I didn't do anything to offend him, and we became *friends!*" and "God, that guy over there's in his 60s, and I had no idea they were so sexually *active!*"(laughs) Maybe it's simplistic to some people, but you know, why does it have to be complicated? Put people in a position where they can experience this process of discovery, and here it is!

Every time I speak, people go "Oh, God, here he goes with his visions again!" Well, I realize that I might die before I see any of these things really grab — and most likely that'll be the case . . . but I just hope that this is something that'll take hold and a lot of people will get the idea. Everybody's welcome! Let's get together and have a *festival* — a *People's Games.*

Bob Connell

MASCULINITY, VIOLENCE AND WAR

ONE

In 1976 there were 22 million people under arms in the world's 130-odd standing armies. The figure today may be a little higher. Probably 20 million of them are men. I have not seen any global totals by sex, but there are figures for particular countries which serve as pointers. In the major NATO forces in 1979–80, for instance, 92% of the US military forces were men; 95% of the French and British; 99.93% of the German. From what is commonly known about other countries, these are not likely to be exceptional figures. The vast majority of the world's soldiers are men. So are most of the police, most of the prison warders, and almost all the generals, admirals, bureaucrats and politicians who control the apparatus of coercion and collective violence. Most murderers are men. Almost all bandits, armed robbers, and muggers are men; all rapists, most domestic bashers; and most people involved in street brawls, riots and the like.

The same story, then, appears for both organised and unorganised violence. It seems there is some connection between being violent and being male. What is it? And what light can an analysis of masculinity, apparently a question of individual psychology, throw on the question of violence on a world scale?

There is a surprisingly widespread belief that this is all "natural." Human males are genetically programmed to be hunters and killers, the argument runs. The reason is that ape-man aggression was a survival need in the prehistoric dawn, while the ape-women clustered passively round their campfires suckling and breeding.

Right-wing inflections of this argument thus explain and justify aggression, competition, hierarchy, territoriality, patriarchy, and by inference private property, national rivalry, armies and war. Crude versions of this doctrine are part of the stock rhetoric of modern fascism. More sophisticated versions are developed by "sociobiologists" in the universities.

Remarkably, there is now a feminist version of this argument too. The line of thought is that human males are naturally predatory and violent; patriarchal power is thus an expression of men's inner nature. Rape and war become synonymous. A poster slogan reads: RAPE IS WAR, WAR IS RAPE. Even serious and thoughtful attempts to reckon with the connection between sexual dominance and war, like Penny Strange's pamphlet *It'll Make a Man of You*, talk freely of "male cosmology," "male violence," "male values" and so on.

Two things have gone wrong here. One is that biological speculation has substituted for hard analysis. A critical examination shows practically no grounding in evidence. The sociobiologists' pre-history is speculative, their anthropology highly selective, and their mechanisms of selection and inheritance simply imaginary. By equally convincing evolutionary speculation one can "prove" that men are naturally co-operative and peaceful. In fact it has been done, by Kropotkin in *Mutual Aid*.

Reprinted from *War/Masculinity*, P. Patton and R. Poole, eds. Intervention Publishers.

More important, perhaps, is the confusion of concepts in phrases like "male power," "male violence," "male culture," "malestream thought," "male authority." In each of these phrases a social fact or process is coupled with, and implicitly attributed to, a biological fact. The result is not only to collapse together a rather heterogeneous group (do gays suffer from "male cosmology," for instance; or boys?). It also, curiously, takes the heat off the open opponents of feminism. The hard-line male chauvinist is now less liable to be thought personally responsible for what he says or does in particular circumstances, since what he says or does is attributable to the general fatality of being male.

That this is a point where argument and emotion have got tangled is not accidental. There is a basic theoretical problem here. The social categories of gender are quite unlike other categories of social analysis, such as class, in being firmly and visibly connected to biological difference. It is therefore both tempting and easy to fall back on biological explanation of any gender pattern. This naturalisation of social processes is without question the commonest mechanism of sexual ideologies. That biological difference underpins and explains the social supremacy of men over women is the prized belief of enormous numbers of men, and a useful excuse for resisting equality. Academic or pseudo-academic versions of this argument, male-supremacist "sociobiology" from Tiger's *Men in Groups* through Goldberg's *The Inevitability of Patriarchy* to the present, find a never-failing audience.

If we cannot do better than this in getting to grips with the connection between masculinity and violence, then the left might as well pack its bags and go home, turn on the VCR and play *Threads* until the missiles arrive. For if it all stems from the biological fact of maleness, there is nothing that can be done.

We can do better, and the basis for doing so is well known. It is to recognise that war, murder, rape and masculinity are social and cultural facts, not settled by biology. The patterns we have to deal with as issues of current politics have been produced within human society by the processes of history. It is the shape of social relations, not the shape of genes, that is the effective cause. "Male" and "masculine" are very different things. Masculinity is implanted in the male body, it does not grow out of it.

This argument implies a very different approach to the nature of gender from the natural categories appealed to by both sociobiology and cultural (or eco-) feminism. Such an understanding has been emerging from the work of other groups of feminists (in Australia, research such as Game and Pringle's *Gender at Work* and Burton's *Subordination*), theorists of gay liberation (such as Fernbach's *The Spiral Path*), and others. Broadly, gender is seen as a structure of social practice, related in complex ways to biological sex but with a powerful historical dynamic of its own.

That general framework suggests two lines of approach to the question of masculinity and war. One is to investigate the social construction of masculinity. The other is to undertake a social analysis of war. In what follows I'll suggest some points about both.

TWO

Given a framework of social analysis, we can look at the familiar images and archetypes of manliness in a clearer light. They are parts of the cultural process of producing particular types of masculinity. What messages they convey are important because they help to shape new generations.

One of the central images of masculinity in the Western cultural tradition is the murderous hero, the supreme specialist in violence. A string of warrior-heroes — Achilles, Siegfried, Lancelot and so on — populate European literature from its origins. The twentieth century has steadfastly produced new fictional heroes of this type: Tarzan, Conan, James Bond, the Jackal, the Bruce Lee characters. If you walk into a shop selling comics you will find a stunning array of violent heroes: cops, cowboys, supermen, infantry sergeants, fighter pilots, boxers and so on. The best of the Good Guys, it seems, are those who pay evil-doers back in their own coin.

This connection between admired masculinity and violent response to threat is a resource that governments can use to mobilise support for war. The most systematic case in modern history was the Nazis' cult of Nordic manhood, reaching its peak in the propaganda image of the SS-man during World War II. In a different context, a cult of masculinity and toughness flourished in the Kennedy and Johnson administrations in the USA, and helped commit that country to war in Vietnam. Fasteau documents this in one of the early books to come out of the American "men's movement," *The Male Machine*. I can remember the process operating on young men of my generation in Australia, whose conservative government sent troops to support the Americans in Vietnam. Involvement in the war was presented as standing up to threat, and opponents were smeared as lily-livered effeminates. In the fullness of time support for napalm raids and carpet bombing by B-52s became the test of manliness. In the aftermath of the TWA jet hijacking, Reagan has been playing this tune again, trying to rouse American feeling against the threat of terrorism to provide a cover for his own military operations in central America.

Yet there is a good deal of scepticism in response to Reagan. And in the previous case, Western opposition to the Vietnam war did grow. Together with the Vietnamese resistance it eventually forced the American military to withdraw. The cult of masculine toughness is not all-powerful. This should alert us to some complexities in masculinity and its cultural images.

It is striking that the *Iliad* centres not on Achilles' supremacy in violence, but on his refusal to use it. And what changes his mind is not his reaction to threat, but his tenderness — his love for his friend Patroclus. Siegfried and Lancelot, not exactly gentle characters, are likewise full of hesitations, affection, and divided loyalties.

The image of heroism in modern figures like Tarzan and James Bond is a degraded one. The capacity for tenderness, emotional complexity, aesthetic feeling and so on has been deleted. More exactly, they are split off and assigned only to women, or to other, inferior types of men — such as the wimps, poofters and effeminates who evaded the Vietnamese war. (Part of the legend of Achilles was that he put on a dress and lived among women in order to evade the Trojan war.)

We know very little of the history of masculinity as distinct from the history of men; the detailed research has not been done. We know enough to understand that such changes in images of heroism are part of the historical process by which different kinds of masculinity are separated from each other, some exalted and some spurned. A crucial fact about men is that masculinity is not all of a piece. There have always been different kinds, some more closely associated with violence than others. This is why one should not talk of "male violence" or of "males" doing this and that — phrasing which smuggles back in the idea of a biological uniformity in social behaviour.

At any given moment some forms of masculinity will be hegemonic — that is, most honoured and most influential — and other forms will be marginalized or subordinated. The evidence about these forms is very scattered, as the question is only just coming into focus as a research issue. Some points are clear. Modern hegemonic masculinity is defined as heterosexual (not true of all societies or all periods of history), and sharply contrasted with homosexual masculinity (in our society the type case of subordinated masculinity). Some other forms of subordinated masculinity are temporary — like that of apprentices in a strongly-masculinized trade. There are kinds of masculinity that are not directly subordinated but rather marginalized by a process of social change that undermines their cultural presuppositions — the patriarchal masculinity of many immigrant men from Mediterranean countries is an important case in Australia at present. And there are struggles about what form of masculinity should be hegemonic — for instance the contest going on in the ruling classes of the capitalist world between professional/managerial and entrepreneurial/authoritarian masculinities. (The victory of Reaganism in the US is an important shift in the style of American patriarchy as well as in the precise locus of class power.)

THREE

In some civilisations the hegemonic forms of masculinity stress restraint and responsibility rather than violence. I believe that was true, for instance, of Confucian China. In contemporary Western society, hegemonic masculinity is strongly associated with aggressiveness and the capacity for violence. Modern feminism has shown us one of the bases for this: the assertion of men's power over women. This relationship itself has a strong component of violence. Wife-bashing, intimidation of women in the street, rape jealousy-murder, and other patterns of violence against women are not accidental or incidental. They are widespread and systematic, arising from the tensions of a power struggle. This struggle has many turns and twists. Even in a society that defines a husband as the "head of the household," there are many families where wives actually run the show. Bashings may then result from an attempt to re-assert a damaged masculine ego. In other cases domestic violence is a direct expression of the husband's power, his belief that he can get away with anything, and his contempt for women in general or his wife in particular.

So there are many complexities and contradictions. The main axis, however, remains the social subordination of women, and men's general interest in maintaining it. The masculinity built on that bedrock is not necessarily violent — most men in fact do not bash women — but it is constructed, so to speak, with a door open towards violence.

Gay liberation has shown us another dimension: hegemonic masculinity is aggressively heterosexual. It defines itself in part by a vehement rejection of homosexuality. This rejection very often takes violent forms: arrests, frequent bashings, and occasional murders. Homosexual men seem to arouse particular fear and loathing among tough "macho" men. This fact has led many to think the violence is an attempt to purge the world of what one suspects in oneself.

In psychoanalytic terms, there is a current of repressed homosexual feeling buried somewhere in hegemonic masculinity. This, again, suggests the importance of the tensions and contradictions within masculinity. It is by no means a neat package.

In much of the writing about men produced by the "men's liberation movement" of the 1970s it was assumed that violence was simply an expression of conventional masculinity. Change the macho image, stop giving little boys toy guns, and violence would be reduced. We can now see that the connection of masculinity and violence is both deeper and more complex than that. Violence is not just an expression; it is a part of the process that divides different masculinities from each other. There is violence within masculinity; it is constitutive. Once again, this is not to imply that it is universal. Real men don't necessarily bash three poofters before breakfast every day. For one thing, TV does it for them. Part of the pattern of contemporary masculinity is the commercial production of symbolic violence on an unprecedented scale, from Tarzan movies to Star Wars, Space Invaders, World Series Cricket, and now Rambo.

FOUR

It is very important that much of the actual violence is not isolated and individual action, but is institutional. Much of the poofter-bashing is done by the police; much of the world's rape is done by soldiers. These actions grow readily out of the "legitimate" violence for which police forces and armies are set up. The state is an instrument of coercion; this remains true whatever else about it varies. It uses one of the great discoveries of modern history, rational bureaucratic organization, to have policy-making centralized and execution down the line fairly uniform. Given this, the state can become the vehicle of calculated violence based on and using hegemonic masculinity. Armies are a kind of hybrid between bureaucracy and masculinity.

But to make this connection with an undifferentiated "masculine violence" — as, say, Fernbach does in *The Spiral Path* — is to misunderstand the way armies work. Generals, notoriously, die in bed. They are not themselves "violent men," and would be bad generals if they were. Of course they need violent men under their command as front-line troops, or at least as organisers of front-line troops — men like the grim Sergeant Croft of *The Naked and the Dead* (a novel that strikingly makes the point about different masculinities).

It is the *relationship* between forms of masculinity — physically violent but subordinate to orders on the one hand, dominating and organisationally competent on the other — that is the basis of military organisation. The two need not overlap at all. Heinrich Himmler, the commander of one of the most brutal military organisations in recent history, never killed anyone personally. When present at any execution where some brains splattered on his neat SS uniform, he threw a screaming fit.

Even this is to understate the matter. In modern armies the majority of soldiers are not combatants at all. Most are in support services, as transport workers, administrators, technicians, maintenance workers, cooks, etc., and have no competence as fighters at all. The proportion of this kind of worker in armies has grown markedly over the last century and a half with the increasing technologisation of warfare, as several major developments have reduced the need for cannon-fodder and increased the need for supply workers. The US made two great contributions to the art of war in the 1940s — nuclear weapons and logistics. Logistics was certainly more militarily effective at the time. And you don't want Rambo types driving your jeeps and supply trucks.

Automatic weapons (machine-guns and quick-firing artillery), self-propelled military vehicles (tanks and aircraft), and ultimately long-distance weapons that eliminate the 'front' (strategic bombers, nuclear missiles) have successively intensified the trend. They have made more and more important in military organisations a third kind of masculinity, the professionalised, calculative rationality of the technical specialist.

The first stage of this was the rise of the "General Staff" to a central position in European military organisation by the early twentieth century. The idea of a General Staff was a group of planners, separate from the command of combat units, who worked out overall strategies as well as technical issues of supply. The "Schlieffen Plan" for the German attack on France in 1914 marked the ascendancy of staff over line commanders. In no sense did this mean a shift away from violence — the violence of war was growing on an unprecedented scale. The man who was the 20th century's most successful general, the Soviet Chief of Staff Georgi Zhukov, was notorious for his disregard for human life. He accepted huge casualties in order to gain advantage in battles of attrition at Moscow, Stalingrad and Kursk (the battles responsible for the ultimate defeat of Hitler).

The second stage was the mobilisation of physical scientists on a large scale into weapons research, culminating in the Manhattan Project. The friction within the Manhattan Project, and the crisis of conscience suffered by the nuclear physicists immediately after the explosion of the Hiroshima and Nagasaki bombs, are measures of the difficulty of integrating this kind of worker into the military. But the huge growth of nuclear weapons research establishments in the USA and USSR since then shows that the initial difficulties have been overcome. The end of the world has been made technically possible by this achievement in human relations.

FIVE

In the past, as well as being the main actors of war, men have also been the main victims. Napoleon's wars killed mainly soldiers. The harnessing of high technology to the bureaucratic state has steadily changed this. Hitler's mass extermination campaigns, and the Anglo-American firebombing of Hamburg, Dresden and Tokyo, were an organised turning of conventional weapons to the killing of whole populations. The nuclear arsenal has been directed against whole populations from the start.

It has thus become a matter of urgency for humans as a group to undo the tangle of relationships that sustains the nuclear arms race. Masculinity is part of this tangle. It will not be easy to alter. The pattern of an arms race, i.e., mutual threat, itself helps sustain an aggressive masculinity.

Nor can the hegemonic pattern of masculinity be rejected totally. To achieve disarmament in reality means conducting a long and difficult struggle against an entrenched power structure. This calls for some of the qualities hegemonic masculinity exalts — toughness, endurance, determination and the like. It is no accident that hegemonic masculinity has been important in radical movements in the past: in unionism, in national liberation movements, and in socialist parties.

Yet we know masculinity is not fixed. It is at least conceivable that we can re-work masculinity in a way that sustains a struggle without reproducing the enemy. In much this sense feminism has been re-working femininity. In doing this it will be useful to remember the hidden riches of masculinity, as well as its horrors. There are cultural resources in subordinated masculinities, and in patterns lost or bypassed in recent history.

REFERENCES

Burton, C., *Subordination: Feminism and Social Theory*, Sydney, Allen and Unwin, 1985.

Carrigan, T., Connell, R. W. & Lee, J. "Hard and Heavy Phenomena: the Sociology of Masculinity," *Theory & Society*.

Chapkis, W., Ed., *Loaded Questions: Women in the Military*, Amsterdam, Transnational Institute, 1981.

Clark, A., *Barbarossa: The Russian-German Conflict 1941–1945*, Harmondsworth, Penguin, 1966.

Connell, R. W., "Men's bodies" in *Which Way Is Up?*, Sydney, Allen and Unwin, 1983.

Fernbach, D., *The Spiral Path: A Gay Contribution to Human Survival*, London, Gay Mens' Press, 1981.

Fasteau, M. F., *The Male Machine*, New York, McGraw-Hill, 1974.

Game, A. & Pringle, R., *Gender at Work*, Sydney, Allen and Unwin, 1983.

Goldberg, S., *The Inevitability of Patriarchy*, New York, William Morrow, 1973.

Irving, D. J. C., *The Destruction of Dresden*, London, Kimber, 1963.

Kropotkin, P., *Mutual Aid* (1902), Boston, Extending Horizons, n.d.

Mailer, N., *The Naked and the Dead* (1949), London, Deutsch, 1964.

Strange, P., *It'll Make a Man of You: A Feminist View of the Arms Race*, Nottingham, Peace News/Mushroom, 1983.

Tiger, L., *Men in Groups*, New York, Random House, 1969.

Zhukov, G. K., *Marshal Zhukov's Greatest Battles*, London, Sphere, 1971.

Charles J. Levy

ARVN AS FAGGOTS:
INVERTED WARFARE IN VIETNAM

The way in which civilians often view Vietnam from the United States suggests that too much perspective can be just as distorting as too little. For it seems to be popularly believed that the actions of American troops there have resulted from racism and depersonalization of the enemy. But racism would not explain why there has been a high regard for the Viet Cong and North Vietnamese Army (VC/NVA) who are racially indistinguishable from the Army of the Republic of (South) Vietnam (ARVNs) for whom there has been a low regard.

Published by permission of Transaction Publishers, from "ARVN as Faggots: Inverted Warfare in Vietnam," *Society*, Vol. 8, No. 12, 1971. Copyright © 1971 by Transaction Publishers.

Nor would depersonalization of the enemy explain why there was substantial hostility directed against the ARVNs with whom there was personal contact, and little or no hostility toward the more remote VC/NVA.

In the case of American marines, the beginning of an explanation could be found in boot camp. Homosexuality appeared in two contradictory themes of basic training. On the one hand, homosexuals were the enemy. Referring to navy corpsmen in general, and one in particular, a former marine explained:

> A lot of them were like prissy. I mean looked on the faggoty-type side. You could tell they were corpsmen. But I mean if that guy was in marine boot camp he'd of got bounced out. Or he'd have so many problems within the system that he fucking wouldn't be able to hack it. He'd go out of his mind. He'd be called "a faggot."

On the other hand, marine recruits were called "faggots" by their drill instructors during boot camp. By compelling these men to accept such labels, the drill instructors achieved on a psychological level the same control that they had on a physical level when, for example, the men were not permitted a bowel movement for the first week of boot camp.

As defined by the boot camp experience, homosexuality was only incidentally a sexual condition. More important, it represented a lack of all the aggressive characteristics that were thought to comprise masculinity. The connection between passivity and homosexuality was made vivid to the marines in boot camp inasmuch as they were unable to combat either the label or the activities surrounding it. When a recruit mentioned that he and a friend had been separated in violation of the "buddy system" under which they joined, the drill instructor is reported to have asked, "Do you like Private R?" The next question is, "Do you want to fuck him?"

After sending six men into a small shower room, the drill instructor, in another account, shouted, "Everybody on your back."

> We're all nude. So you fall on top of each other. You get assholes in your face. And then they turn on cold water and they make you run out and stand there.

This ritual, like most others in boot camp, was coupled with violence. As the men left the showers, the drill instructors "beat your fucking head in."

The violence towards trainees was merged with their learning how to do violence, so that "We used to be disgusted with the other services because we considered them unaggressive." Aggression meant learning how to protect not only their lives, but also their masculinity. Accordingly, after boot camp they referred to the Marine Corps as "the crotch," while the other military branches were called "the sister services."

The overreaching lesson of boot camp had been that combat must be on the marines' terms. This point was made by the drill instructors in a way that led one veteran to recall: "You just get shit on all the time if you don't live by their rules. If you don't they'll screw you any way they can." One of these accepted rules involved the rationale for this training, "They have to do it to protect your lives if you're going in combat." Boot camp training was continually linked to Vietnam by such means as reminding the recruits of the date they would be arriving there and by indicating the number of casualties that would result "if you don't take the training seriously." It was made clear that submission to the drill instructors would provide the recruits with the training that was necessary to in turn make the VC/NVA submit.

Yet, in Vietnam, the marines discovered that the VC/NVA "fight on their fucking terms, not on ours," according to another veteran. Much effort was aimed at getting the VC/NVA to fight on the marine terms. "What we tried to do is fucking chase them around so they don't know what's going on. But it's never that way." The VC/NVA not only refused to fight on the marines' terms, by fighting on their own terms they made the marines' terms inoperable. The link that was established between boot camp and Vietnam reappeared to hinder rather than help morale. For instead of the promised discontinuity between the two settings, the marines vis-à-vis the VC/NVA bore an unexpected similarity to the recruits who were called "girl" by the drill instructors.

The ascendance of the VC/NVA's terms was possible in large part because these terms were unknown to the marines. Even after locating the VC/NVA, their intentions were unclear:

> It depends on where they want to fight. You never know if they want to fight there and get that one company and consider it a day. Or if they want to just really get out of there. You can't tell. Or if they're just sucking you into one big mob scene.

The last of these possibilities, that there were other VC/NVA waiting in ambush, was the governing one. It meant that the marines were never able to assume a correspondence between the VC/NVA they saw and the ones that saw them.

Because the marines were seen in their totality, their intentions were open. Their terms were correspondingly weakened. For the VC/NVA were given an opportunity to develop counter-terms: "They know every map square where they can hold a good defense. Where there's a lot of heavy brush that would be tough for us to move our heavy equipment in."

Some of the problems that arose from trying to prepare men who were still in the United States for Vietnam were inherent to using a low risk artificial setting to anticipate the high risk real one. Training in the United States did not pass for combat in Vietnam: "When they used to send us out we used to go make believe. We set up an ambush and make believe someone walked by. You knew when all this shit was over you got to get to bed. So I mean it's not good." Just as combat in Vietnam does not pass for training in the United States: "You're not sitting there in 'Nam saying to yourself: 'Let me think now, the instructor told me to do it this way.' What the hell!"

The deeper problems that arose had less to do with training for wars in general than with this war in particular. Booby traps caused a majority of deaths in Vietnam. But booby trap training was regarded as a contradiction in terms:

> They show you all the booby traps and stuff. What's good showing you the booby trap. I mean, if you find a booby trap, the odds are good you ain't going to see it 'til after it blows up.

Efforts to simulate a Vietnam in the United States suffered from a more general handicap: "How can you train a person to fight someone that they've been fighting for so long that they haven't done good enough a job to find out anything about them?" Training in the United States, then, was futile for the same principal reason that combat in Vietnam was to be futile for the marines. So the difficulty of anticipating the VC/NVA through training in the United States was at least one authentic reconstruction of the setting to be found in Vietnam. Also the apparent unreality of training in the United States may not have been entirely inappropriate preparation for Vietnam. The above example of marines setting ambushes for other marines was said to be "make believe." But it anticipated the internecine character of the war.

The military techniques of the VC/NVA compelled the marines to violate their own traditions. These traditions were not abstractions. They were reasons for being. They also provided a set of expectations for Vietnam. But after arriving there, it turned out they had no application when "You can't go in and kick ass like you could in other wars." Here is the process of discovery:

> When I first got there, two VC held down the whole platoon just by firing over our heads. Then word was passed out, 'Stay down. Don't waste rounds. They'll just do this for fifteen minutes and leave.' And being a new guy and thinking how the marines are supposed to be so tough, I said, 'Why don't we go get them?' But, of course, they [the experienced marines] knew what they were doing. We probably would've went and got them, there probably would've been booby traps all over the place and we would've probably lost another 20 guys getting two. So we just sit there and stay for 15 minutes, 20 minutes, until they got tired.

When they arrived in Vietnam, these men had belonged to the Marine Corps for about eight months. This is a short time to become deeply involved in traditions — even allowing for the intensity of the boot camp experience. The commitment to the traditions of the Marine Corps was largely a result of their coinciding with the traditions of the street corners to which these men had belonged before their enlistment. The interchangeability of the traditions could be seen when the same marine who was "thinking how the marines are supposed to be so tough" later described his Vietnam experience through a street corner analogy: "That's like some guy walking up to you and punching you in the face every night and then before you have time to turn around or put up your hands he's gone."

ORIENTAL SMILES

The previously clear and central distinction between aggressiveness and passivity was lost for the marines when they arrived in Vietnam. They found themselves using aggressive means which had passive results. Meantime, the VC/NVA used passive means which had aggressive results.

The passive aspects of the VC/NVA took a variety of forms. To begin with, the VC/NVA did not fit any of the traditional American notions of what a formidable adversary should look like. They were the wrong size. Sometimes they were the wrong sex. They wore the wrong clothes, since the VC and occasionally the NVA lacked uniforms. They even wore the wrong expression: "It's hard to look through an Oriental person. They could probably hate your guts and stab you in the back, but they'll always smile at you." As it turned out, the more passive they appeared, the more difficult it was to defend against their aggression.

The marines heard lectures about Vietnamese men expressing friendship among themselves and with other men through physical contact. But this behavior became all the more inexplicable as a result of the lectures. For if hand-holding between men was a custom, it meant — as far as the marines were concerned — that these gestures were not aberrations within the Vietnamese society: rather the whole society was an aberration. A marine recalled that

> we had classes before we went over: that's just their way of life. Like them holding their arm on another guy means they're friends. It don't mean — that's what we were told anyways.

Nevertheless, in Vietnam, "most of us" believed it did mean they were homosexuals.

The marines needed an explanation that would enable them to relate these male gestures to their own culture, not that of the Vietnamese. This was possible by defining it as homosexuality, since it was a familiar category to marines. By placing the ARVN in it, his behavior ceased to be strange. Equally important, the marines understood what their own behavior ought to be in response:

> I had been in the country a year by this time. We were going back to regiment in Danang. We pulled the truck over and the ARVN engineer stopped us at a roadblock. And they bore you to death. They make you sick. They're trying to be military. So they've got this roadblock up. And they stopped the truck. And the driver is saying, "Get out of our way, you little slopes." And they come out and they said, "We have a wounded veteran." We said, "So what?" They said, "He doesn't have one leg. Could you give him a ride up to the hospital?" So everybody's saying, "Let him hop." I was in charge of the detail so I said, "Let him on." I was in the back of the truck. It was a PC three-quarter. So he comes over on his crutches. I said, "Throw your crutches up." So he passed up the crutches. And I grabbed him under the arms and I pick him up and I set him in the seat. The little slope grabbed me by the leg. And I had been in the country long enough to know that most of them are queer. They hold hands and stuff. And this sort of irks most marines and soldiers. And we're told that it's a Vietnamese custom, when you're really friendly you should hold hands. So they try to hold a lot of guys' hands. So they end up getting beat bloody. The guy grabbed my leg. So I got mad. I wasn't in a good mood that morning and I whacked him. And my buddies grabbed his crutches. And I said "Go!" So we took off. We threw his crutches in the rice paddy one time and went about another 150 yards and threw the other crutch and then out he went. He was screaming and crying and begging us. "Out you go." We all had a good laugh about that.

In more important ways, the classification of ARVNs as homosexuals was not based on their presumed sexual activity. The fact that ARVNs were living at bases with their wives contributed to the belief that they were homosexuals. For the presence of wives meant the ARVNs led a soft life. Hence they were not, to use a common marine term, "hard."

In the same way, the fact that ARVNs did not attempt to engage in homosexual activity with the marines was taken as proof that the ARVNs were homosexual. For it was thought that fear, a sign of homosexuality, kept them from making advances: "They wouldn't fool around with us anyway. They wouldn't even look at us the wrong way. 'Cause they knew how good we were, which I thought we were."

A literal interpretation of the war by the marines, among other results, would have made them allies of the ARVNs. But the ARVNs provided the model for a less literal approach that released the marines from whatever obligations remained to define them as allies. It was thought they interpreted the war out of existence: "They don't want nothing to do with the war, but yet it's their war."

The reluctance of the ARVNs to engage in combat was treated as interchangeable with fighting on the side of the VC/NVA. A marine who regarded the ARVNs as homosexuals, "every one of them," cited as evidence: "They're just too scared where there is gooks. Where the gooks are, they go in the opposite direction. They don't want to go out and make contact with them at all." A related assumption was expressed by another marine who considered it just as likely they would go in the same direction as the VC/NVA: "I heard if you get a patrol of ARVNs with you, and if they're getting beat, they'll just go right on the opposite side. And they'll shoot at you instead of with you. They kind of get scared."

UNRELIABLE ALLIES

The marines considered the ARVNs to be so far removed from the war that in the process of preventing their lives from being disrupted they were able to augment them. As one former marine observed "I think they got a good thing going for them because of the black market." Further, this remoteness from the war while in the midst of it often meant that the marines saw themselves being made more vulnerable to attacks from the VC/NVA:

> The ARVNs felt that being in the army was great. They used to wear starched utilities. Everything was so nice. And like the marines were all slobs, because we had our clothes washed in rice paddy water and everything else. Nothing starched. And they looked like they should be in recruiting posters all the time. We had ARVN security and it started to rain. They went in houses — into their buddy's house — until the rain stopped, so they wouldn't get their uniforms wet. And left us out there with no security.

Official ethnology was the response of the Marine Corps to a feeling among the marines that "We didn't like the idea of us fighting for an army of faggots." Specifically,

> You hear the propaganda report, you know, our bullshit, like public relations between us and the Vietnamese. Well our public relations give us propaganda material telling us how the Vietnamese are a proud, simple people and courageous. And give us history of the country and how they fought the Chinese and everybody. And the Vietnamese war heroes and all this other shit. To impress upon us the fact that they're really not fucking gutless bastards. But we all knew better and we used to just hate them all the more. The more they tried to justify the Vietnamese the more we didn't like them.

The troops were not in a situation that they thought lent itself to this or any other form of intellectualizing. What did matter was that where the marines were vulnerable to attack from the VC/NVA they became the passive party, and the ARVNs were seen contributing to this vulnerability. In at least one sense, moreover, the marines were more passive vis-à-vis the VC/NVA than the ARVN were. The marines had their passivity imposed upon them by the VC/NVA, while the ARVNs acted passively through their own volition.

At times, the marines worked almost as hard at making themselves the enemy of the ARVNs as they did at making the ARVN their enemy. The first process recreated the theme of boot camp that violence should be done *for* one group so that they might do violence *to* a second group. There was a consensus among marines that ARVNs had nothing to fight for: "They didn't give a shit." The marines tried to give them something to fight against by making themselves the foremost enemy of the ARVNs.

As the marines found it increasingly difficult to establish a direct link between means and intended ends, they resorted to these indirect links. The assumption was that a marine offense against the VC/NVA required an offense against the ARVN that would result in an ARVN defense against the marines that would take the form of an ARVN offense against the VC/NVA. The mechanics of this sequence appear in the following episode:

> The marines were in there putting out the fire but unbeknownst to them, they were stomping to death a three-week-old baby. So this caused uncontrollable laughter among the marines when they found they had accidentally killed a baby. There's nothing else they could do. And they've got to keep up this pretense of being fucking raving maniacs in order to keep the respect of the Montagnards. The gooks think that we're fucking lunatics. And you've got to keep this. As long as they're afraid of us, they won't give you a hard time. If they're afraid you'll shoot them in any minute and you don't find anything wrong in killing. So the guys start laughing. First, it was sort of a nervous laugh and then they just had a fucking grand time.

However, it soon became clear to these marines that an indirect linkage of means and ends was at least as unattainable as a direct one. When they were ambushed soon afterwards, the marine squad leader

> yelled to the commander of the Vietnamese to bring on line assaults. So the four marines get up and they're pumping away. And all the eight gooks just sat there and watched them. And then they withdrew in disorganized retreat. What they do is they ran like hell while the marines were on line shooting. What they [marines] had to do is pull some escape and evasion maneuvers to get away. They were pissed.

In other words, the sequence that materialized consisted of a VC offense that resulted in an ARVN defense that resulted in a marine defense.

In short, one reason the ARVNs became the enemy was that the marines were, after all, bound to them as allies. For the ineffectiveness of the ARVNs in combat meant the task of the marines was that much greater and more dangerous: "Most of the time when they did get into contact they always got their ass kicked. And we usually had to come in and help them out."

The marines were bound to the ARVNs in a more immediate way. They provided the marines with a means of trying to salvage a disrupted frame-of-reference. For the ARVNs were proof that there was, after all, a connection between passivity and homosexuality. The marines were not only able to focus on them as passive targets, they could act against them aggressively.

Locating homosexual ARVNs was a welcome relief from having to cope with an often unrecognizable and always evasive VC/NVA. There were no problems identifying the homosexuality of the readily available ARVNs. The identification was based on criteria that did not require interrogation or scrutiny. The proof was an impression:

> We thought a lot of them were queer, because of the way they act. They were so I don't know, prissy like, and awkward. And just the way they laughed and looked at you.

This imprecise definition is appropriate considering that "prissy" owes its first two letters to precise.

However, the assaults against assumed homosexuals were in no sense a charade. They were more a form of warfare than an alternative to it. All that kept the beatings from escalating was a lack of resistance. The exceptions illuminated the usual case:

> They'll come up to you and they'll rub your leg and you sucker them. Because as far as we're concerned, they're queer. So the ARVN lieutenant told his men, "The next time a marine hits you, I want you to shoot him." So our lieutenant heard about it and he says, "As soon as you see an ARVN pick up a weapon, first I want you to kill the lieutenant, and then I want you to wipe out all his men." We continued to beat them up and nobody shot anybody.

Meantime, the VC/NVA imposed the ultimate passivity on marines by making them the instruments of their own death. For the VC/NVA were "good at skills that we didn't even know — like booby traps." Most booby traps are arranged to have the victim act as his own executioner. And there is a mockery involved which accounts for the term. It is a trap for the booby. The only aggression permitted the marine was against himself. The more aggressive the marine tried to be, the more susceptible he was to booby traps.

Marines continued to be their own victims when they tried to fight on the terms of the VC/NVA. The marines began using a highly sophisticated mine called the Claymore that they expected to be far more effective than the relatively crude booby traps of the VC/NVA. The Claymore has pellets in the front that are fired by an explosive in the back. However, the VC/NVA were able to carry the Claymore one step further:

> They can sneak right up and turn your Claymore around. And then you start moving around there so you'll hit the Claymore and it's turned around. You'll be the one that gets it.

Booby trapped by their own booby traps. As the marines sought a new means of becoming more aggressive, they were made still more passive.

The invisibility of the VC/NVA and the visibility of the marines were the underlying reasons for the success of one and the failure of the other with booby traps. For there are two conditions that must be met if a booby trap is to operate successfully. First, the hunter must know where his prey will be. Second, the prey must not know where the hunter has been.

There is an interval between planting and detonating a booby trap. The aggressor is removed in both time and space from his aggression. But the marines (and the corner boys before them) were unaccustomed to aggression that was not spontaneous. This was another reason they had both a problem setting booby traps and a propensity for tripping them.

The ambush is closely related to the booby trap. It relies on one's own invisibility and the other's visibility. There are, in addition, elaborate preparations that require deferred aggression. For these reasons, the ambushes prepared by marines were subject to the same problems as the booby traps they set:

> Every night these NVA or VC used to come down and they used to screw up marine ambushes. And they always used to get away. They'd know where the ambush was set up and killer teams were set up. They'd sneak by them when they go into the village to get their rice and what they needed and leave. And then they'd screw them up on the way back. They'd fire on the ambush. And they'd take off up into the mountains. They did this every night. And they [marines] never got any of them.

Hiding entails actively seeking invisibility. It is ordinarily considered a passive act, because it is seen as the avoidance of action. More important, it is seen as the avoidance of being acted upon. But in the context of Vietnam, both these components were redefined when they became the means by which the VC/ NVA were able to act aggressively. To speak of a means and end suggests a break that did not exist. Instead, the means and end were part of the same process. When the VC/NVA hid, it was not only a way to avoid disadvantageous encounters with the marines, it was preparation for engaging the marines on advantageous terms:

> A lot of times you don't see them. They suck you into some type of ambush situation where there's a lot of them and a lot of you's. And they've already preregistered the area. Like two weeks before that they'll lie in the same position and fire their weapons for effect.

Not only was the means not entirely passive because it was part of an aggressive end, but the end was not entirely aggressive because it was part of a passive means. That is, the VC/NVA strategy was all the more difficult for the marines to sort out because it was cyclical. The marines found that the VC/ NVA "aren't staying and fighting." Instead, "they hit you and run." But the running could not be classified as passive, because in addition to being the last stage of an aggressive act, it was the first stage of the next aggressive act. The confusion that resulted from trying to classify the tactics of the VC/NVA is reflected in the following account where the VC are shuttled between categories of offense and defense:

> The VC was more or less on a defense all the time. Always hiding and coming out at night. But he still had to move around, unless he was in a large group. But he always had to be the aggressor. And he was always under cover and stuff. So when he did come out and you did get in contact with him, he was determined that either he was going to die or he was going to get one of us.

When the VC/NVA hid, it was an aggressive act even if it did not lead to an engagement with the marines. For the marines had an aggressive mission in Vietnam. They were there to eliminate the VC/NVA. A status quo meant failure. The objective of the Marine Corps was summed up by the name given their "search and destroy missions." The VC/NVA could thwart these missions simply by hiding.

> You'd go in there for three days; you'd pull out. And if they were there anyways, they weren't there when we got there. I imagine they must have come back after we left. So those are the most useless operations I ever heard of. If they seen a hole they'd start saying, "Oh, I bet there's weapons down there. I bet there's rice down there." We'd dig it up and there'd be nothing there. We never found nothing. I went on three of those, never found nothing.

The only result of these operations would be "carrying a couple of dead guys back — our own," men who encountered booby traps.

Catching those who hide is a form of aggressiveness, except in Vietnam. The contradiction of being permitted by the enemy to take the initiative was described by a former marine: "You catch them when they want you to catch them. They have all their bunkers and everything all set for you."

Traditionally, setting the time and place of battle has been another aggressive characteristic. The marines found themselves helping to set these terms because the VC/NVA "just wait 'til I guess they think they have you at your weakest, then they hit you." Another veteran provides an illustration:

> Usually they'll hit the areas that are most secure. The lines are never checked. There won't be much bother about falling to sleep on watch. The platoon commander didn't care because we were never hit. Everyone gets to not caring.

Here too the apparent passivity of the VC/NVA was the means to an aggressive act. For they were able to make the camp vulnerable by not attacking it.

The marines had a sense of being objects that comes from being continually visible while those viewing them remain for the most part invisible. But they had not adapted to the dangers that follow from this condition. It was only in retrospect, that the marine veteran just quoted saw that the more secure they felt, the less secure they were in fact. In Vietnam, when the VC/NVA abstained from an attack it was regarded as security not as a forewarning. There was less stress for the marines in facing a disaster that would be observable than in admitting to themselves that they were living with an unseen threat.

Telescoped examples of this dilemma could occur several times a day to the same men. A former marine tells of walking at the head of a patrol along a trail:

> You see a shell case. So you start to step over this way. But you think: "Maybe it was put there on purpose so I'd step over that way." So it really screws your head up. The hell with it. I'd step over this way. And if it blows, it'll blow.

The weakness of the marines was maximized by not only the behavior but more particularly through the attitudes with which they were provided by the VC/NVA. The invisibility of the VC/NVA provided them with a safe view of marines as a prelude to safe action against them: "They could be hiding under a rock or in a tunnel. We could walk right over them so they could see everything you have. What the hell can you do? They're watching you all the time, you never see them."

All this means that the marines were less visible to themselves than they were to the VC/NVA. Until the marines set off a mine or walked into an ambush, they did not usually know where they were in relation to the VC/NVA. In one way or another, "You wait to get hit; wait for them to come to you." But there was more involved than the VC/NVA seeing precisely what dangers the marines were exposed to. For the VC/NVA saw into the operations of the marines as well as the context in which they were held. It amounted to the marines having to rely on the VC/NVA in order to view themselves. The VC made this reliance explicit:

> They talk to us all the time and shit — loud-speakers. In fact they told us one night, before anyone that was with us knew it, that we were going to move up to Phu Bai. Imagine that! They told us over a loud-speaker that they were pulling us out, because they knew if we stayed there that the VC were going to annihilate us. So the squad leader went to the CO and they checked on it and we *were* going to move out about three weeks later. So they knew it before we did. That kind of fucked up your mind a little, you know.

(The announcement by the VC was in English — which served to tell the marines that their language, too, was visible.) Even a formal statement of defeat by the VC/NVA could be made into an aggressive act by them:

> One day eight of them [NVA] turned themselves in. You could see their white flag. They had me walking up. I felt like an asshole. They're fucking clean. New uniforms. Spotless. Their boots were shined. Haircuts. And they're supposed to be living in the mud? They're doing better than we are. And they're walking up. They're clean as a whistle. They had tailored uniforms. So everyone's there wondering: What's going on out there?

In describing the episode, this former marine wonders if "they just sent them out there to turn themselves in to make us look like they were doing good out there." But he dismisses this possibility. It is a reassuring one insofar as it indicates the prisoners were not typical. Yet, to accept this explanation would be an acknowledgment that the NVA were capable of deliberately redefining the terms of war by turning surrender on its head. Further, it would mean that the marines had accommodated the NVA.

Where the marines did succeed in killing, they often discovered that this could not be considered a form of domination, particularly when the victims were civilians. These deaths were both a cause and effect of the marines' passivity. For killing civilians usually meant the marines had lost control. The particular kind of control varied, but every case included a loss of control over the VC/NVA. When the marines were acting in rage, the civilians they killed served as surrogates for elusive VC/NVA. They were acting spontaneously at the time, but afterwards the marines saw their action as a loss of control over themselves:

> You see a guy you're really tight with for a period of months getting killed. We got really pissed off about it. You don't just say, "Well, fuck it." You go like kind of nutty. Anybody that even looked at you the wrong way

you'd probably shoot. I think the American fighting man can be the most vicious ever. People don't realize this.

When civilians were killed through mistaken identity, it was a more direct reminder that the VC/NVA were beyond control, to the point of being unidentifiable. The misplaced aggressiveness of these acts sometimes resulted in ridicule, as when a marine shot a village elder one night and was afterwards nicknamed "killer" by his fellow marines. His death was the outcome of a curfew rule that required the shooting of any violators. The curfew was imposed as a means of assuring that the VC/NVA would be identifiable.

Whatever the circumstances, killing civilians weakened the position of the marines. For it meant the villagers became still more dedicated to the VC/NVA, as seen in the following episode about the death of another elder:

> There's a killer team out one night. They were outside this village. This old man, he was a villager, was going out to do a crap in the rice paddy. And he was killed. That was right at the edge of the village. He was mistaken for a VC. Immediately after that happened the villagers turned VC sympathizers. After that, there was always a build up of VC coming in. Along Highway 1, on the other side of the village, it was always mined. After this happened there was like a triple amount of mines planted in the road. And there was a road going up to the top of the hill. It was never really combed for any mines. Two days later a jeep went over a mine and blew up. That never happened before. But I imagine it was the villagers.

There were other ways in which the marines discovered that killing might not after all be the ultimate measurement of domination after all. For example, the VC/NVA were seen demonstrating a greater control of the situation when they abstained from killing. This realization by the marines made the control of the VC/NVA over them still greater:

> This [NVA soldier] goes "Good morning, marines." A lot of shit they did just to fuck up your head. I mean, they must have had a chance before that to really fucking zap someone. They did this shit just to fucking scare the fuck out of you. Just to let you know that they were on the ball and they weren't fucking around. Everyone fucking flies out of the trenches with their rifles. They're expecting attack. Fucking gook is probably laughing his ass off in the bushes. That's fucked up though.

The marines had finally recognized hiding as a means of killing. But here it was seen as a more subtle form of aggression — a means of killing morale. The VC/NVA directed the attention of marines to the importance of a psychological assault through their constant practice of it. However, the marines were as unable to cope with this sophisticated approach as they were with an apparently unsophisticated agrarian approach to combat.

The marines found that more than themselves was being relegated to passivity. The same thing was happening to the previously inviolate technology that had permitted the United States to maintain an aggressive stance in the world. Here, too, the victim brought on his own undoing, for the aggressiveness of this technology in Vietnam was often self-destructive. The following episode is typical of what could happen when technological superiority was invoked instead of dealing with the VC/NVA on equal terms:

> Say you had 30 gooks in the open. And you were too far away from them. Instead of losing men over them, artillery was the best bet. But we had too many restrictions on us. Like when we had to call an artillery mission. They had to get air clearance which is make sure there wasn't any helicopters flying around in the area or any jets, any Phantoms, flying over the area. So by the time we got that clearance then we'd have to get a ground clearance making sure that there wasn't any friendly troops around that area. So by the time the clearance came in, they were walking away. I mean they were just gone.

This failure had much to do with the characteristics of technology that were expedient or tolerated when they appeared in the United Sates. Its massiveness was inappropriate for the intimacy of combat in Vietnam where no one group was at a great distance from any other group. The bureaucracy attached to the technology was intended to make it manageable, but in the fluidity of this combat the bureaucracy made it all the more unmanageable.

Moreover, the futility of technology was carefully engineered by the VC/NVA. They were skilled at bringing out its limitations. Just as they made the visibility of marines a disadvantage by emphasizing the opposite characteristic among themselves, so they were able to turn technology into a disadvantage by not trying to fight it with technology. Again they stressed an opposite; this time, nature. It was a matter of building a strategy out of both their strength and the marines' weaknesses. Americans were unaccustomed to nature being used aggressively. When necessary, the land was used as a weapon:

> In valleys where you're pinned down — a lot of times we've had jets come in over the top of us, when it was hard to hit them any other way. They couldn't come across because of the mountains and stuff. They release the bombs right over our heads. And you can see the bombs. They'd be going towards us. And we're saying, "Ooh, fucking things just don't drop." But they like carried on the momentum of the speed they're going. They go in front of you. They blow up. That takes a lot of skill on an estimate. And a lot of fucking luck. The gooks choose this type of thing because they know that our jets can't come into a valley this way and make it, because there's a mountain there and they can't get up. So they set up their defenses so they can shoot down the planes as they're coming in.

The rationale for much of American technology had been the conquest of nature. But in Vietnam, the VC/NVA used nature for the conquest of technology.

Technological futility led to occasional attempts at de-emphasizing technology. But this only made way for problems that were more subtle and therefore less predictable. It brought out the other levels on which American culture was not transferable. These problems were subtle to the Americans, but they were obvious to everyone else. For example, a program was established to work with the villagers in a manner that minimized technology.

> We had an outfit that was called CAC — Combined Action Company. But cac in Vietnamese means prick. So they had to change it to Combined

Action Platoons. They called it CAP. It was a laughing stock of the villages. And the VC played it to the hilt.

The extent to which the ethos of this war disoriented the marines was reflected in their way of trying to cope with it. For they engaged in a classification of the VC/NVA that was in itself disorienting. While the ARVNs represented what the marines feared they were becoming, the VC/NVA represented what the marines would like to have been. It was typically thought that in contrast to the ARVNs, the VC "have a lot of balls." Such metaphors of courage assisted in linking cowardice to a lack of masculinity, which is a short conceptual distance from homosexuality.

Through relating to the VC/NVA, the marines were seeking a way to offset their inability to relate to the terms of the war. Their approval of the VC/NVA was reflected in the narrative of a former marine whose unit had suffered heavy casualties on several occasions, leading to its being known as "the walking dead." Eventually they found themselves at Khe Sanh. The NVA had them surrounded and were again inflicting substantial damage without being damaged. The siege was so thorough that the NVA were tunneling underneath the marine positions. During the excavation, a marine used a stethoscopic device to overhear the conversation of the NVA digging below:

> Scared as everybody was, you had to fucking laugh hearing them swearing and shit. 'Cause they were like us really. I figured the grunts [NVA] were there exactly like us. They didn't like the fucking shit more than we did. They're probably down there swearing about their fucking officers and fucking shit like that. It was funny. We were really laughing.

There was another way in which the marines benefited from thinking of the VC/NVA in personal terms. It made them visible — only to a slight degree — but it was that much of an improvement over invisibility. The contrasting visibility of the marines was indicated when "They'd shoot at you at midnight. You'd light up a smoke and he'd shoot at you." The unseen sniper was made visible insofar as he received a name from the marines: "Bed-Check Charley."

While the personalization of the VC/NVA operated in a way that introduced positive feelings, the impersonalization of the VC/NVA was invoked to prevent negative feelings. The fact that the NVA were trying to kill marines was explained away by one former marine who recalled that "you don't dislike them, because no one NVA ever did anything to you."

In other words, the marines did not suppose that the VC/NVA, on such occasions, were acting personally toward them. Clearly, the same could not be said about the ARVNs. The marines had no trouble relating specific grievances to specific ARVNs. Moreover, they had a sense that homosexuality was more personal than death.

HOW THE MARINE VETERANS' STUDY WAS MADE

In a working class Irish neighborhood of Boston, the community boasts of having the highest proportion of marine enlistees in the country. This claim, repeated to the point of being a cliché, is characteristic of the community's intensely patriotic attitudes. This preoccupation with patriotism became the subject of research three years ago when the study reported in the accompanying article was undertaken. As the marines from the neighborhood began arriving home from Vietnam the following year, the researcher concentrated on getting acquainted with them in order to explore the process of becoming a veteran. Over a period of several years he gradually got to know 60 marine veterans who represented a cross section of the neighborhood to the extent that there are economic and educational variations in such a homogeneous community.

Since the veterans' frame of reference was still the war, it was necessary to reconstruct as far as possible their experiences in Vietnam. The most formal part of this reconstruction was extensive tape-recorded interviews. However, the interviews did not occur until the researcher had established an informal relationship with the men during a year spent on their corners, at their bars and wherever else they "hung." The veterans guided the interviews. Although they were held individually, the interviews produced recurring themes. It was these themes that guided the writing of the essay.

Some of the same themes have reappeared in the veterans' civilian life, particularly in connection with the violence that now characterizes their lives. In its broadest terms, this dependence on violence reflects their having fought an unrequited war. Not only had the war not been won, but the men had been unable to establish a satisfactory working relationship with it. Because they are still trying to achieve the dominance that had been denied them in Vietnam (without any of this necessarily being a conscious process), the war remains alive for them in civilian life. Their threshold for feeling threatened is markedly lower than in the case of men whose civilian life was uninterrupted by the war.

This is not to say that these veterans were nonviolent before their enlistment. But in the past, there were informal rules that limited the amount of damage to the other party. These limits no longer bind them. Another difference, also related to Vietnam, is that this violence is likely to be directed at those who are nominally allies. For example, a group that some veterans rejoined was particularly known for its mutual assistance. But one night there was a fire fight between these veterans. The casualties included one dead. As a consequence, the formerly cohesive group reappeared as two factions, led by veterans, that have been involved in additional combat against each other — resulting in another murder.

The connection with Vietnam may be camouflaged when the victim is a veteran's mother and his weapon is a hurled television set. But the underlying parallels remain, beyond her being a nominal ally. Here, in common with most cases, the violence is spontaneous. For the veterans are still responding to the initiatives of others. And the intentions of these others are still likely to be misperceived. There are times when the continuity with Vietnam is more explicit, as when a veteran destroyed a restaurant in Boston's Chinatown after attacking the waiter who put a hand on his shoulder.

For every boy aged 5 - 12 in the U.S.,
2 G.I. Joe products are sold yearly.

DEMILITARIZE THE PLAYGROUND

PART FIVE

◆ ◆ ◆

Men and Work

BUILDING THE GOLDEN GATE BRIDGE, 1937

In what ways is work tied to male identity? Do men gain a sense of fulfillment from their work, or do they view it as necessary drudgery? How might the organization of workplaces play on, reinforce, or sometimes threaten the types of masculinity that males have already learned as youngsters? How does the experience of work (or of not having work) differ for men of different social classes, ethnic, and sexual preference groups? And how do recent structural changes in society impact upon the masculinity–work relationship? The articles in this section address these issues and more.

As Jesse Bernard points out, the rise of urban industrial capitalism saw the creation of separate "public" and "domestic" spheres of social life. As women were increasingly relegated to working in the home, men were increasingly absent from the home, and the male "breadwinner role" was born. The sexual division of labor, this gendered split between home and workplace, has led to a variety of problems and conflicts for women and for men. Since World War II, as Anthony Astrachan points out in his article, profound structural changes — among them, women's continued movement into the paid labor force, higher levels of structural unemployment, and the rise of a more service-oriented economy — have led to dramatic shifts in the quality and quantity of men's experiences in the paid labor force.

These changes in the economy have had a different impact on various groups of men. Robert Zussman traces recent changes in the work and family roles in "the new middle class." John Ceely's article outlines some of the important dynamics of blue-collar work, male identity, and male bonding at the worksite. Ben Fong-Torres shows how racist stereotypes can limit the kinds of occupations that are available to Asian males. Similarly, Martin Levine outlines the ways in which gay men have been discriminated against in the workworld, both historically and today.

The section ends with a thoughtful piece by Harry Brod, in which he challenges the emergent men's movement (see Part XI) not only to recognize the importance of work to men, but to develop a politics around a recognition of the very different issues that often face the blue-collar, poor, or ethnic minority males, as opposed to those issues that might face the mostly college-educated white males who make up the men's movement. Personal life-style transformations (breaking away from compulsive workaholism, getting more into parenting, etc.) are important goals, Brod agrees, but, if the majority of men's lives are going to change for the better, there is also a need for basic institutional transformations — especially in the economy and in workplaces.

Garry Trudeau

"DOONESBURY" CARTOON

Jessie Bernard

THE GOOD-PROVIDER ROLE:
ITS RISE AND FALL

The Lord is my shepherd, I shall not want. He sets a table for me in the very sight of my enemies; my cup runs over (23rd Psalm). And when the Israelites were complaining about how hungry they were on their way from Egypt to Canaan, God told Moses to rest assured: There would be meat for dinner and bread for breakfast the next morning. And, indeed, there were quails that very night, enough to cover the camp, and in the morning the ground was covered with dew that proved to be bread (Exodus 16:12–13). In fact, in this role of good provider, God is sometimes almost synonymous with Providence. Many people like Micawber, still wait for him, or Providence, to provide.

Granted, then, that the first great provider for the human species was God the Father, surely the second great provider for the human species was Mother, the gatherer, planter, and general factotum. Boulding (1976), citing Lee and deVore, tells us that in hunting and gathering societies, males contribute about one fifth of the food of the clan, females the other four fifths (p. 96). She also concludes that by 12,000 B.C. in the early agricultural villages, females provided four fifths of human subsistence (p. 97). Not until large trading towns arose did the female contribution to human subsistence decline to equality with that of the male. And with the beginning of true cities, the provisioning work of women tended to become invisible. Still, in today's world it remains substantial.

Whatever the date of the virtuous woman described in the Old Testament (Proverbs 31:10–27), she was the very model of a good provider. She was, in fact, a highly productive conglomerate. She woke up in the middle of the night to tend to her business; she oversaw a multiple-industry household; *her* candles did not go out at night; there was no ready market for the high-quality linen girdles she made and sold to the merchants in town; and she kept track of the real estate market and bought good land when it became available, cultivating vineyards quite profitably. All this time her husband sat at the gates talking with his cronies.

A recent counterpart to the virtuous woman was the busy and industrious shtetl woman:

> The earning of a livelihood is sexless, and the large majority of women . . . participate in some gainful occupation if they do not carry the chief burden of support. The wife of a "perennial student" is very apt to be the sole support of the family. The problem of managing both a business and a home is so common that no one recognizes it as special. . . . To bustle about in search of a livelihood is merely another form of bustling about managing a home; both are aspects of . . . health and livelihood. (Zborowski & Herzog, 1952, p. 131)

In a subsistence economy in which husbands and wives ran farms, shops, or businesses together, a man might be a good, steady worker, but the idea that

From *American Psychologist*, Vol. 36, No. 1 (January 1981), pp. 1–12. Copyright 1981 by the American Psychological Association. Reprinted by permission of the publisher and author.

he was *the* provider would hardly ring true. Even the youth in the folk song who listed all the gifts he would bestow on his love if she would marry him — a golden comb, a paper of pins, and all the rest — was not necessarily promising to be a good provider.

I have not searched the literature to determine when the concept of the good provider entered our thinking. The term *provider* entered the English language in 1532, but was not yet male sex typed, as the older term *purveyor* already was in 1442. Webster's second edition defines the good provider as "one who provides, especially, colloq., one who provides food, clothing, etc. for his family; as, he is a good or an adequate provider." More simply, he could be defined as a man whose wife did not have to enter the labor force. The counterpart to the good provider was the housewife. However the term is defined, the role itself delineated relationships within a marriage and family in a way that added to the legal, religious, and other advantages men had over women.

Thus, under the common law, although the husband was legally head of the household and as such had the responsibility of providing for his wife and children, this provision was often made with help from the wife's personal property and earnings, to which he was entitled:

> He owned his wife's and children's services, and had the sole right to collect wages for their work outside the home. He owned his wife's personal property outright, and had the right to manage and control all of his wife's real property during marriage, which included the right to use or lease property, and to keep any rents and profits from it. (Babcock, Freedman, Norton, & Ross, 1975, p. 561)

So even when she was the actual provider, the legal recognition was granted the husband. Therefore, whatever the husband's legal responsibilities for support may have been, he was not necessarily a good provider in the way the term came to be understood. The wife may have been performing that role.

In our country in Colonial times women were still viewed as performing a providing role, and they pursued a variety of occupations. Abigail Adams managed the family estate, which provided the wherewithal for John to spend so much time in Philadelphia. In the 18th century "many women were active in business and professional pursuits. They ran inns and taverns; they managed a wide variety of stores and shops; and, at least occasionally, they worked in careers like publishing, journalism and medicine" (Demos, 1974, p. 430). Women sometimes even "joined the menfolk for work in the fields" (p. 430). Like the household of the proverbial virtuous woman, the Colonial household was a little factory that produced clothing, furniture, bedding, candles, and other accessories, and again, as in the case of the virtuous woman, the female role was central. It was taken for granted that women provided for the family along with men.

The good provider as a specialized male role seems to have arisen in the transition from subsistence to market — especially money — economies that accelerated with the industrial revolution. The good-provider role for males emerged in this country roughly, say, from the 1830s, when de Tocqueville was observing it, to the late 1970s, when the 1980 census declared that a male was not automatically to be assumed to be the head of the household. This gives the role a life span of about a century and a half. Although relatively short-lived, while it lasted the role was a seemingly rock-like feature of the national landscape.

As a psychological and sociological phenomenon, the good-provider role had wide ramifications for all our thinking about families. It marked a new kind of marriage. It did not have good effects on women: The role deprived them of many chips by placing them in a peculiarly vulnerable position. Because she was not reimbursed for her contribution to the family in either products or services, a wife was stripped to a considerable extent of her access to cash-mediated markets. By discouraging labor force participation, it deprived many women, especially affluent ones, of opportunities to achieve strength and competence. It deterred young women from acquiring productive skills. They dedicated themselves instead to winning a good provider who would "take care of" them. The wife of a more successful provider became for all intents and purposes a parasite, with little to do except indulge or pamper herself. The psychology of such dependence could become all but crippling. There were other concomitants of the good-provider role.

EXPRESSIVITY AND THE GOOD-PROVIDER ROLE

The new industrial order that produced the good provider changed not so much the division of labor between the sexes as it did the site of the work they engaged in. Only two of the concomitants of this change in work site are selected for comment here, namely, (a) the identification of gender with work site as well as with work itself and (b) the reduction of time for personal interaction and intimacy within the family.

It is not so much the specific kinds of work men and women do — they have always varied from time to time and place to place — but the simple fact that the sexes do different kinds of work, whatever it is, which is in and of itself important. The division of labor by sex means that the work group becomes also a sex group. The very nature of maleness and femaleness becomes embedded in the sexual division of labor. One's sex and one's work are part of one another. One's work defines one's gender.

Any division of labor implies that people doing different kinds of work will occupy different work sites. When the division is based on sex, men and women will necessarily have different work sites. Even within the home itself, men and women had different work spaces. The woman's spinning wheel occupied a different area from the man's anvil. When the factory took over much of the work formerly done in the house, the separation of work space became especially marked. Not only did the separation of the sexes become spatially extended, but it came to relate work and gender in a special way. The work site as well as the work itself became associated with gender; each sex had its own turf. This sexual "territoriality" has had complicating effects on efforts to change any sexual division of labor. The good provider worked primarily in the outside male world of business and industry. The homemaker worked primarily in the home.

Spatial separation of the sexes not only identifies gender with work site and work but also reduces the amount of time available for spontaneous emotional give-and-take between husbands and wives. When men and women work in an economy based in the home, there are frequent occasions for interaction. (Con-

ABNEGATION- *rejections, renunciation, denial*

sider, for example, the suggestive allusions made today to the rise in the birth rate nine months after a blackout.) When men and women are in close proximity, there is always the possibility of reassuring glances, the comfort of simple physical presence. But when the division of labor removes the man from the family dwelling for most of the day, intimate relationships become less feasible. De Tocqueville was one of the first to call our attention to this. In 1840 he noted that

> almost all men in democracies are engaged in public or professional life; and . . . the limited extent of common income obliges a wife to confine herself to the house, in order to watch in person and very closely over the details of domestic economy. All these distinct and compulsory occupations are so many natural barriers, which, by keeping the two sexes asunder, render the solicitations of the one less frequent and less ardent — the resistance of the other more easy. (de Tocqueville, 1840, p. 212)

Not directly related to the spatial constraints on emotional expression by men, but nevertheless a concomitant of the new industrial order with the same effect, was the enormous drive for achievement, for success, for "making it" that escalated the provider role into the good-provider role. De Tocqueville (1840) is again our source:

> The tumultuous and constantly harassed life which equality makes men lead [becoming good providers] not only distracts them from the passions of love, by denying them time to indulge in it, but it diverts them from it by another more secret but more certain road. All men who live in democratic ages more or less contract ways of thinking of the manufacturing and trading classes. (p. 221)

As a result of this male concentration on jobs and careers, much abnegation and "a constant sacrifice of her pleasures to her duties" (de Tocqueville, 1840, p. 212) were demanded of the American woman. The good-provider role, as it came to be shaped by this ambience, was thus restricted in what it was called upon to provide. Emotional expressivity was not included in the role. One of the things a parent might say about a man to persuade a daughter to marry him, or a daughter might say to explain to her parents why she wanted to, was not that he was a gentle, loving, or tender man but that he was a good provider. He might have many other qualities, good or bad, but if a man was a good provider, everything else was either gravy or the price one had to pay for a good provider.

Lack of expressivity did not imply neglect of the family. The good provider was a "family man." He set a good table, provided a decent home, paid the mortgage, bought the shoes, and kept his children warmly clothed. He might, with the help of the children's part-time jobs, have been able to finance their educations through high school and, sometimes, even college. There might even have been a little left over for an occasional celebration in most families. The good provider made a decent contribution to the church. His work might have been demanding, but he expected it to be. If in addition to being a good provider, a man was kind, gentle, generous, and not a heavy drinker or gambler, that was all frosting on the cake. Loving attention and emotional involvement in the family were not part of a woman's implicit bargain with the good provider.

By the time de Tocqueville published his observations in 1840, the general outlines of the good-provider role had taken shape. It called for a hard-working man who spent most of his time at his work. In the traditional conception of the role, a man's chief responsibility is his job, so that "by definition any family behaviors must be subordinate to it in terms of significance and [the job] has priority in the event of a clash" (Scanzoni, 1975, p. 38). This was the classic form of the good-provider role, which remained a powerful component of our social structure until well into the present century.

COSTS AND REWARDS OF THE GOOD-PROVIDER ROLE FOR MEN

There were both costs and rewards for those men attached to the good-provider role. The most serious cost was perhaps the identification of maleness not only with the work site but especially with success in the role. "The American male looks to his breadwinning role to confirm his manliness" (Brenton, 1966, p. 194).[1] To be a man one had to be not only a provider but a *good* provider. Success in the good-provider role came in time to define masculinity itself. The good provider had to achieve, to win, to succeed, to dominate. He was a bread*winner.* He had to show "strength, cunning, inventiveness, endurance — a whole range of traits henceforth defined as exclusively 'masculine'" (Demos, 1974, p. 436). Men were judged as men by the level of living they provided. They were judged by the myth "that endows a money-making man with sexiness and virility, and is based on man's dominance, strength, and ability to provide for and care for 'his' woman" (Gould, 1974, p. 97). The good provider became a player in the male competitive macho game. What one man provided for his family in the way of luxury and display had to be equaled or topped by what another could provide. Families became display cases for the success of the good provider.

The psychic costs could be high:

> By depending so heavily on his breadwinning role to validate his sense of himself as a man, instead of also letting his roles as husband, father, and citizen of the community count as validating sources, the American male treads on psychically dangerous ground. It's always dangerous to put all of one's psychic eggs into one basket. (Brenton, 1966, p. 194)

The good-provider role not only put all of a man's gender-identifying eggs into one psychic basket, but it also put all the family-providing eggs into one basket. One individual became responsible for the support of the whole family. Countless stories portrayed the humiliation families underwent to keep wives and especially mothers out of the labor force, a circumstance that would admit to the world the male head's failure in the good-provider role. If a married woman had to enter the labor force at all, that was bad enough. If she made a good salary, however, she was "co-opting the man's passport to masculinity" (Gould, 1974, p. 98) and he was effectively castrated. A wife's earning capacity diminished a man's position as head of the household (Gould, 1974, p. 99).

---

1. Rainwater and Yancey (1967), critiquing current welfare policies, note that they "have robbed men of their manhood, women of their husbands, and children of their fathers. To create a stable monogamous family we need to provide men with the opportunity to be men, and that involves enabling them to perform occupationally" (p. 235).

Failure in the role of a good provider, which employment of wives evidenced, could produce deep frustration. As Komarovsky (1940, p. 20) explains, this is "because in his own estimation he is failing to fulfill what is the central duty of his life, the very touchstone of his manhood — the role of family provider."

But just as there was punishment for failure in the good-provider role, so also were there rewards for successful performance. A man "derived strength from his role as provider" (Komarovsky, 1940, p. 205). He achieved a good deal of satisfaction from his ability to support his family. It won kudos. Being a good provider led to status in both the family and the community. Within the family it gave him the power of the purse and the right to decide about expenditures, standards of living, and what constituted good providing. "Every purchase of the family — the radio, his wife's new hat, the children's skates, the meals set before him — all were symbols of their dependence upon him" (Komarovsky, 1940, pp. 74–75). Such dependence gave him a "profound sense of stability" (p. 74). It was a strong counterpoise vis-à-vis a wife with a stronger personality. "Whether he had considerable authority within the family and was recognized as its head, or whether the wife's stronger personality . . . dominated the family, he nevertheless derived strength from his role as provider" (Komarovsky, 1940, p. 75). As recently as 1975, in a sample of 3,100 husbands and wives in 10 cities, Scanzoni found that despite increasing egalitarian norms, the good provider still had "considerable power in ultimate decision-making" and as "unique provider" had the right "to organize his life and the lives of other family members around his occupation" (p. 38).

A man who was successful in the good-provider role might be freed from other obligations to the family. But the flip side of this dispensation was that he could not make up for poor performance by excellence in other family roles. Since everything depended on his success as provider, everything was at stake. The good provider played an all-or-nothing game.

DIFFERENT WAYS OF PERFORMING THE GOOD-PROVIDER ROLE

Although the legal specifications for the role were laid out in the common law, in legislation, in legal precedents, in court decisions, and, most importantly, in custom and convention, in real-life situations the social and social-psychological specifications were set by the husband or, perhaps more accurately, by the community, alias the Joneses, and there were many ways to perform it.

Some men resented the burdens the role forced them to bear. A man could easily vent such resentment toward his family by keeping complete control over all expenditures, dispensing the money for household maintenance, and complaining about bills as though it were his wife's fault that shoes cost so much. He could, in effect, punish his family for his having to perform the role. Since the money he earned belonged to him — was "his" — he could do with it what he pleased. Through extreme parsimony he could dole out his money in a mean, humiliating way, forcing his wife to come begging for pennies. By his reluctance and resentment he could make his family pay emotionally for the provisioning he supplied.

At the other extreme were the highly competitive men who were so involved in outdoing the Joneses that the fur coat became more important than the affectionate hug. They "bought off" their families. They sometimes succeeded so well in their extravagance that they sacrificed the family they were presumably providing for to the achievements that made it possible (Keniston, 1965).[2]

The Depression of the 1930s revealed in harsh detail what the loss of the role could mean both to the good provider and to his family, not only in the loss of income itself — which could be supplied by welfare agencies or even by other family members, including wives — but also and especially in the loss of face.

The Great Depression did not mark the demise of the good-provider role. But it did teach us what a slender thread the family hung on. It stimulated a whole array of programs designed to strengthen that thread, to ensure that it would never again be similarly threatened. Unemployment insurance was incorporated into the Social Security Act of 1935, for example, and a Full Employment Act was passed in 1946. But there proved to be many other ways in which the good-provider role could be subverted.

ROLE REJECTORS AND ROLE OVERPERFORMERS

Recent research in psychology, anthropology, and sociology has familiarized us with the tremendous power of roles. But we also know that one of the fundamental principles of role behavior is that conformity to role norms is not universal. Not everyone lives up to the specifications of roles, either in the psychological or in the sociological definition of the concept. Two extremes have attracted research attention: (a) the men who could not live up to the norms of the good-provider role or did not want to, at one extreme, and (b) the men who overperformed the role, at the other. For the wide range in between, from blue-collar workers to professionals, there was fairly consistent acceptance of the role, however well or poorly, however grumblingly or willingly, performed.

First the noncomformists. Even in Colonial times, desertion and divorce occurred:

> Women may have deserted because, say, their husbands beat them; husbands, on the other hand, may have deserted because they were unable or unwilling to provide for their usually large families in the face of the wives' demands to do so. These demands were, of course, backed by community norms making the husband's financial support a sacred duty. (Scanzoni, 1979, pp. 24–25)

Fiedler (1962) has traced the theme of male escape from domestic responsibilities in the American novel from the time of Rip Van Winkle to the present:

> The figure of Rip Van Winkle presides over the birth of the American imagination; and it is fitting that our first successful home-grown legend should memorialize, however playfully, the flight of the dreamer from the shrew — into the mountains and out of time, away from the drab duties

2. Several years ago I presented a critique of what I called "extreme sex role specialization," including "work-intoxicated fathers." I noted that making success in the provider role the only test for real manliness was putting a lot of eggs into one basket. At both the blue-collar and the managerial levels, it was dysfunctional for families. I referred to the several attempts being made even then to correct the excesses of extreme sex role specialization: rural and urban communes, leaving jobs to take up small-scale enterprises that allowed more contact with families, and a rebellion against overtime in industry (Bernard, 1975, pp. 217–239).

of home . . . anywhere to avoid . . . marriage and responsibility. One of
the factors that determine theme and form in our great books is this strategy of evasion, this retreat to nature and childhood which makes our literature (and life) so charmingly and infuriatingly "boyish." (pp. xx–xxi)

Among the men who pulled up stakes and departed for the West or went
down to the sea in ships, there must have been a certain proportion who, like
their mythic prototype, were simply fleeing the good-provider role.

The work of Demos (1974), a historian, offers considerable support for Fiedler's thesis. He tells us that the burdens thrust on men in the 19th century by
the new patterns of work began to show their effects in the family. When "the
[spatial] separation of the work lives of husbands and wives made communication so problematic," he asks, "what was the likelihood of meaningful communication?" (Demos, 1974, p. 438). The answer is, relatively little. Divorce and
separation increased, either formally or by tacit consent — or simply by default,
as in the case of a variety of defaulters — tramps, bums, hoboes — among them.

In this connection, "the development of the notorious 'tramp' phenomenon is
worth noticing," Demos (1974, p. 438) tells us. The tramp was a man who just
gave up, who dropped out of the role entirely. He preferred not to work, but
he would do small chores or other small-scale work for a handout if he had to.
He was not above begging the housewife for a meal, hoping she would not find
work for him to do in repayment. Demos (1974) describes the type:

> Demoralized and destitute wanderers, their numbers mounting into the
> hundreds of thousands, tramps can be fairly characterized as men who
> had run away from their wives. . . . Their presence was mute testimony
> to the strains that tugged at the very core of American family life. . . .
> Many observers noted that the tramps had created a virtual society of their
> own [a kind of counterculture] based on a principle of single-sex compan-
> ionship. (p. 438)

A considerable number of them came to be described as "homeless men" and,
as the country became more urbanized, landed ultimately on skid row. A large
part of the task of social workers for almost a century was the care of the
"evaded" women they left behind.[3] When the tramp became wholly demoral-

3. In one department of a South Carolina cotton mill early in the century, "every worker was
a grass widow" (Smuts, 1959, p. 54). Many women worked "because their husbands refused to
provide for their families. There is no reason to think that husbands abandoned their duties
more often than today, but the woman who was burdened by an irresponsible husband in 1890
usually had no recourse save taking on his responsibilities herself. If he deserted, the law-en-
forcement agencies of the time afforded little chance of finding and compelling him to provide
support" (Smuts, 1959, p. 54). The situation is not greatly improved today. In divorce child
support is allotted in only a small number of cases and enforced in even fewer. "Roughly half
of all families with an absent parent don't have awards at all. . . . Where awards do exist they
are usually for small amounts, typically ranging from $7 to $18 per week per child" (Jones, 1976,
abstract). A summary of all the studies available concludes that "approximately 20 percent of
all divorced and separated mothers receive child support regularly, with an additional 7 percent
receiving it 'sometimes'; 8 percent of all divorced and separated women receive alimony regularly or sometimes" (Jones, 1976, p. 23).

ized, a chronic alcoholic, almost unreachable, he fell into a category of his own — he was a bum.

Quite a different kettle of fish was the hobo, the migratory worker who spent several months harvesting wheat and other large crops and the rest of the year in cities. Many were the so-called Wobblies, or Industrial Workers of the World, who repudiated the good-provider role on principle. They had contempt for the man who accepted it and could be called conscientious objectors to the role. "In some IWW circles, wives were regarded as the 'ball and chain.' In the West, IWW literature proclaimed that the migratory worker, usually a young, unmarried male, was 'the finest specimen of American manhood . . . the leaven of the revolutionary labor movement'" (Foner, 1979, p. 400). Exemplars of the Wobblies were the nomadic workers of the West. They were free men. The migratory worker, "unlike the factory slave of the Atlantic seaboard and the central states, . . . was most emphatically 'not afraid of losing his job.' No wife and family cumbered him. The worker of the East, oppressed by the fear of want for wife and babies, dared not venture much" (Foner, 1979, p. 400). The reference to fear of loss of job was well taken; employers preferred married men, disciplined into the good-provider role, who had given hostages to fortune and were therefore more tractable.

Just on the verge between the area of conformity to the good-provider role — at whatever level — and the area of complete noncomformity to it was the non-good provider, the marginal group of workers usually made up of "the under-educated, the under-trained, the under-employed, or part-time employed, as well as the under-paid, and of course the unemployed" (Snyder, 1979, p. 597). These included men who wanted — sometimes desperately — to perform the good-provider role but who for one reason or another were unable to do so. Liebow (1966) has discussed the ramifications of failure among the black men of Tally's corner: The black man is

> under legal and social constraints to provide for them [their families], to be a husband to his wife and a father to his children. The chances are, however, that he is failing to provide for them, and failure in this primary function contaminates his performance as father in other respects as well. (p. 86)

In some cases, leaving the family entirely was the best substitute a man could supply. The community was left to take over.[4]

At the other extreme was the overperformer. De Tocqueville, quoted earlier, was already describing him as he manifested in the 1830s. And as late as 1955 Warner and Ablegglen were adding to the considerable literature on industrial leaders and tycoons, referring to their "driving concentration" on their careers and their "intense focusing" of interests, energies, and skills on these careers, "even limiting their sexual activity" (pp. 48–49). They came to be known as workaholics or work-intoxicated men. Their preoccupation with their work

---

4. Even though the annals of social work agencies are filled with cases of runaway husbands, in 1976 only 12.6% of all women were in the status of divorce and separation, and at least some of them were still being "provided for." Most men were at least trying to fulfill the good-provider role.

even at the expense of their families was, as I have already noted, quite acceptable in our society.

Poorly or well performed, the good-provider role lingered on. World War II initiated a challenge, this time in the form of attracting more and more married women into the labor force, but the challenge was papered over in the 1950s with an "age of togetherness" that all but apotheosized the good provider, his house in the suburbs, his homebody wife, and his third, fourth, even fifth, child. As late as the 1960s most housewives (87%) still saw breadwinning as their husband's primary role (Lopata, 1971, p. 91).[5]

INTRINSIC CONFLICT IN THE GOOD-PROVIDER ROLE

Since the good-provider role involved both family and work roles, most people believed that there was no incompatibility between them or at least that there should not be. But in the 1960s and 1970s evidence began to mount that maybe something was amiss.

De Tocqueville had documented the implicit conflict in the American businessman's devotion to his work at the expense of his family in the early years of the 19th century; the Industrial Workers of the World had proclaimed that the good-provider role which tied a man to his family was an impediment to the great revolution at the beginning of the 20th century; Fiedler (1962) had noted that throughout our history, in the male fantasy world, there was freedom from the responsibilities of this role; about 50 years ago Freud (1930/1958) had analyzed the intrinsic conflict between the demands of women and the family on one side and the demands of men's work on the other:

> Women represent the interests of the family and sexual life, the work of civilization has become more and more men's business; it confronts them with ever harder tasks, compels them to subliminations of instinct which women are not easily able to achieve. Since man has not an unlimited amount of mental energy at his disposal, he must accomplish his tasks by distributing his libido to the best advantage. What he employs for cultural [occupational] purposes he withdraws to a great extent from women, and his sexual life; his constant association with men and his dependence on his relations with them even estrange him from his duties as husband and father. Woman finds herself thus forced into the background by the claims of culture [work] and she adapts an inimical attitude towards it. (pp. 50–51)

In the last two decades, researchers have been raising questions relevant to Freud's statement of the problem. They have been asking people about the relative satisfactions they derive from these conflicting values — family and work. Among the earliest studies comparing family–work values was a Gallup poll in 1940 in which both men and women chose a happy home over an interesting job or wealth as a major life value. Since then there have been a number of such polls, and a considerable body of results has now accumulated. Pleck and Lang

5. Although all the women in Lopata's (1971) sample saw breadwinning as important, fewer employed women (54%) than either nonemployed urban (63%) or suburban (64%) women assigned it first place (p. 91).

(1979) and Hesselbart (Note 1) have summarized the findings of these surveys. All agree that there is a clear bias in the direction of the family. Pleck and Lang conclude that "men's family role is far more psychologically significant to them than is their work role" (p. 29), and Hesselbart — however critical she is of the studies she summarizes — believes they should not be dismissed lightly and concludes that they certainly "challenge the idea that family is a 'secondary' valued role" (p. 14).[6] Douvan (Note 2) also found in a 1976 replication of a 1957 survey that family values retained priority over work: "Family roles almost uniformly rate higher in value production than the job role does" (p. 16).[7]

The very fact that researchers have asked such questions is itself interesting. Somehow or other both the researchers and the informants seem to be saying that all this complaining about the male neglect of the family, about the lack of family involvement by men, just is not warranted. Neither de Tocqueville nor Freud was right. Men do value family life more than they value their work. They do derive their major life satisfactions from their families rather than from their work.

It may well be true that men derive the greatest satisfaction from their family roles, but this does not necessarily mean they are willing to pay for this benefit. In any event, great attitudinal changes took place in the 1960s and 1970s.

Douvan (Note 2), on the basis of surveys in 1957 and 1976, found, for example, a considerable increase in the proportion of both men and women who found marriage and parenthood burdensome and restrictive. Almost three fifths (57%) of both married men and married women in 1976 saw marriage as "all burdens and restrictions," as compared with only 42% and 47%, respectively, in 1957. And almost half (45%) also viewed children as "all burdens and restrictions" in 1976, as compared with only 28% and 33% for married men and married women, respectively, in 1957. The proportion of working men with a positive attitude toward marriage dropped drastically over this period, from 68% to 39%. Working women, who made up a fairly small number of all married women in 1957, hardly changed attitudes at all, dropping only from 43% to 42%. The proportion of working men who found marriage and children burdensome and restrictive more than doubled, from 25% to 56% and from 25% to

6. Pleck and Lang (1979) found only one serious study contradicting their own conclusions: "Using data from the 1973 NORC [National Opinion Research Center] General Social Survey, Harry analyzed the bivariate relationship of job and family satisfaction to life happiness in men classified by family life cycle stage. In three of the five groups of husbands . . . job satisfaction had a stronger association than family satisfaction to life happiness" (pp. 5–6).

7. In 1978, A Yankelovich survey on "The New Work Psychology" suggested that leisure is now becoming a strict competitor for both family and work as a source of life satisfactions: "Family and work have grown less important than leisure; a majority of 60 percent say that although they enjoy their work, it is not their major source of satisfaction" (p. 46). A 1977 survey of Swedish men aged 18 to 35 found that the proportion saying the family was the main source of meaning in their lives declined from 45% in 1955 to 41% in 1977; the proportion indicating work as the main source of satisfaction dropped from 33% to 17%. The earlier tendency for men to identify themselves through their work is less marked these days. In the new value system, the individual says, in effect, "I am more than my role. I am myself" (Yankelovich, 1978). Is the increasing concern with leisure a way to escape the dissatisfaction with both the alienating relations found on the work site and the demands for increased involvement with the family?

58%, respectively. Although some of these changes reflected greater willingness in 1976 than in 1957 to admit negative attitudes toward marriage and parenthood — itself significant — profound changes were clearly in process. More and more men and women were experiencing disaffection with family life.[8]

"ALL BURDENS AND RESTRICTIONS"

Apparently, the benefits of the good-provider role were greater than the costs for most men. Despite the legend of the flight of the American male (Fiedler, 1962), despite the defectors and dropouts, despite the tavern habitué's "ball and chain" cliché, men seemed to know that the good-provider role, if they could succeed in it, was good for them. But Douvan's (Note 2) findings suggest that recently their complaints have become serious, bone-deep. The family they have been providing for is not the same family it was in the past.

Smith (1979) calls the great trek of married women into the labor force a subtle revolution — revolutionary not in the sense of one class overthrowing a status quo and substituting its own regime, but revolutionary in its impact on both the family and the work roles of men and women. It diluted the prerogatives of the good-provider role. It increased the demands made on the good provider, especially in the form of more emotional investment in the family, more sharing of household responsibilities. The role became even more burdensome.

However men may now feel about the burdens and restrictions imposed on them by the good-provider role, most have, at least ostensibly, accepted them. The tramp and the bum had "voted with their feet" against the role; the hobo or Wobbly had rejected it on the basis of a revolutionary ideology that saw it as enslaving men to the corporation; tavern humor had glossed the resentment habitués felt against its demands. Now the "burdens-and-restrictions" motif has surfaced both in research reports and, more blatantly, in the male liberation movement. From time to time it has also appeared in the clinicians' notes.

Sometimes the resentment of the good provider takes the form of simply wanting more appreciation for the life-style he provides. All he does for his family seems to be taken for granted. Thus, for example, Goldberg (1976), a psychiatrist, recounts the case of a successful businessman:

> He's feeling a deepening sense of bitterness and frustration about his wife and family. He doesn't feel appreciated. It angers him the way they seem to take the things his earnings purchase for granted. They've come to expect it as their due. It particularly enrages him when his children put him down for his "materialistic middle-class trip." He'd like to tell them to get someone else to support them but he holds himself back. (p. 124)

Brenton (1966) quotes a social worker who describes an upper-middle-class woman: She has "gotten hold of a man who'll drive himself like mad to get money, and [is] denigrating him for being too interested in money, and not interested in music, or the arts, or in spending time with the children. But at

---

8. Men seem to be having problems with both work and family roles. Veroff (Note 3), for example, reports an increased "sense of dissatisfaction with the social relations in the work setting" and a "dissatisfaction with the affiliative nature of work" (p. 47). This dissatisfaction may be one of the factors that leads men to seek affiliative-need satisfaction in marriage, just as in the 19th century they looked to the home as shelter from the jungle of the outside world.

the same time she's subtly driving him — and doesn't know it" (p. 226). What seems significant about such cases is not that men feel resentful about the lack of appreciation but that they are willing to justify their resentment. They are no longer willing to grin and bear it.

Sometimes there is even more than expressed resentment; there is an actual repudiation of the role. In the past, only a few men like the hobo or Wobbly were likely to give up. Today, Goldberg (1976) believes, more are ready to renounce the role, not on theoretical revolutionary grounds, however, but on purely selfish ones:

> Male growth will stem from openly avowed, unashamed, self-oriented motivations. . . . Guilt-oriented "should" behavior will be rejected because it is always at the price of a hidden build-up of resentment and frustration and alienation from others and is, therefore, counterproductive. (p. 184)

The disaffection of the good provider is directed to both sides of his role. With respect to work, Lefkowitz (1979) has described men among whom the good-provider role is neither being completely rejected nor repudiated, but diluted. These men began their working lives in the conventional style, hopeful and ambitious. They found a job, married, raised a family, and "achieved a measure of economic security and earned the respect of . . . colleagues and neighbors" (Lefkowitz, 1979, p. 31). In brief, they successfully performed the good-provider role. But unlike their historical predecessors, they in time became disillusioned with their jobs — not jobs on assembly lines, not jobs usually characterized as alienating, but fairly prestigious jobs such as aeronautics engineer and government economist. They daydreamed about other interests. "The common theme which surfaced again and again in their histories, was the need to find a new social connection — to reassert control over their lives, to gain some sense of freedom" (Lefkowitz, 1979, p. 31). These men felt "entitled to freedom and independence." Middle-class, educated, self-assured, articulate, and for the most part white, they knew they could talk themselves into a job if they had to. Most of them did not want to desert their families. Indeed, most of them "wanted to rejoin the intimate circle they felt they had neglected in their years of work" (p. 31).

Though some of the men Lefkowitz studied sought closer ties with their families, in the case of those studied by Sarason (1977), a psychologist, career changes involved lower income and had a negative impact on families. Sarason's subjects were also men in high-level professions, the very men least likely to find marriage and parenthood burdensome and restrictive. Still, since career change often involved a reduction in pay, some wives were unwilling to accept it, with the result that the marriage deteriorated (p. 178). Sometimes it looked like a no-win game. The husband's earlier career brought him feelings of emptiness and alienation, but it also brought financial rewards for the family. Greater work satisfaction for him in lower paying work meant reduced satisfaction with life-style. These findings lead Sarason to raise a number of points with respect to the good-provider role. "How much," he asks, "does an individual or a family need in order to maintain a satisfactory existence? Is an individual being responsible to himself or his family if he provides them with little more than the bare essentials of living?" (p. 178). These are questions about the good-provider role that few men raised in the past.

Lefkowitz (1979) wonders how his downwardly mobile men lived when they left their jobs. "They put together a basic economic package which consisted of government assistance, contributions from family members who had not worked before and some bartering of goods and services" (p. 31). Especially interesting in this list of income sources are the "contributions from family members who had not worked before" (p. 31). Surely not mothers and sisters. Who, of course, but wives?

WOMEN AND THE PROVIDER ROLE

The present discussion began with the woman's part in the provider role. We saw how as more and more of the provisioning of the family came to be by way of monetary exchange, the woman's part shrank. A woman could still provide services, but could furnish little in the way of food, clothing, and shelter. But now that she is entering the labor force in large numbers, she can once more resume her ancient role, this time, like her male counterpart the provider, by way of a monetary contribution. More and more women are doing just this.

The assault on the good-provider role in the Depression was traumatic. But a modified version began to appear in the 1970s as a single income became inadequate for more and more families. Husbands have remained the major providers, but in an increasing number of cases the wife has begun to share this role. Thus, the proportion of married women aged 15 to 54 (living with their husbands) in the labor force more than doubled between 1950 and 1978, from 25.2% to 55.4%. The proportion for 1990 is estimated to reach 66.7% (Smith, 1979, p. 14). Fewer women are now full-time housewives.

For some men the relief from the strain of sole responsibility for the provider role has been welcome. But for others the feeling of degradation resembles the feelings reported 40 years earlier in the Great Depression. It is not that they are no longer providing for the family but that the role-sharing wife now feels justified in making demands on them. The good-provider role with all its prerogatives and perquisites has undergone profound changes. It will never be the same again.[9] Its death knell was sounded when, as noted above, the 1980 census no longer automatically assumed that the male member of the household was its head.

THE CURRENT SCENE

Among the new demands being made on the good-provider role, two deserve special consideration, namely, (1) more intimacy, expressivity, and nurturance — specifications never included in it as it originally took shape — and (b) more sharing of household responsibility and child care.

As the pampered wife in an affluent household came often to be an economic parasite, so also the good provider was often, in a way, a kind of emotional parasite. Implicit in the definition of the role was that he provided goods and material things. Tender loving care was not one of the requirements. Emotional

9. Among the indices of the waning of the good-provider role are the increasing number of married women in the labor force; the growth in the number of female-headed families; the growing trend toward egalitarian norms in marriage; the need for two earners in so many middle-class families; and the recognition of these trends in the abandonment of the identification of head of household as a male.

× Bumper stickes "Woman's place is in the home; just as soon as she finishes at the office."

BERNARD   *The Good-Provider Role*   237

ministrations from the family were his right; providing them was not a corresponding obligation. Therefore, as de Tocqueville had already noted by 1840, women suffered a kind of emotional deprivation labeled by Robert Weiss "relational deficit" (cited in Barnard, 1976). Only recently has this male rejection of emotional expression come to be challenged. Today, even blue-collar women are imposing "a host of new role expectations upon their husbands or lovers. . . . A new role set asks the blue-collar male to strive for . . . deep-coursing intimacy" (Shostak, Note 4, p. 75). It was not only vis-à-vis his family that the good provider was lacking in expressivity. This lack was built into the whole male role script. Today not only women but also men are beginning to protest the repudiation of expressivity prescribed in male roles (David & Brannon, 1976; Farrell, 1974; Fasteau, 1974; Pleck & Sawyer, 1974).

Is there any relationship between the "imposing" on men of "deep-coursing intimacy" by women on one side and the increasing proportion of men who find marriage burdensome and restrictive on the other? Are men seeing the new emotional involvements being asked of them as "all burdens and restrictions"? Are they responding to the new involvements under duress? Are they feeling oppressed by them? Fearful of them?

From the standpoint of high-level pure-science research their may be something bizarre, if not even slightly absurd, in the growing corpus of serious research on how much or how little husbands of employed wives contribute to household chores and child care. Yet is is serious enough that all over the industrialized world such research is going on. Time studies in a dozen countries — communist as well as capitalist — trace the slow and bungling process by which marriage accommodates to changing conditions and by which women struggle to mold the changing conditions in their behalf. For everywhere the same picture shows up in the research: an image of women sharing the provider role and at the same time retaining responsibility for the household. Until recently such a topic would have been judged unworthy of serious attention. It was a subject that might be worth a good laugh, for instance, as when an all-thumbs man in a cartoon burns the potatoes or finds himself bumbling awkwardly over a diaper, demonstrating his — proud — male ineptness at such female work. But is is no longer funny.

The "politics of housework" (Mainardi, 1970) proves to be more profound than originally believed. It has to do not only with tasks but also with gender — and perhaps more with the site of the tasks than with their intrinsic nature. A man can cook magnificently if he does it on a hunting or fishing trip; he can wield a skillful needle if he does it mending a tent or a fishing net; he can even feed and clean a toddler on a camping trip. Few of the skills of the homemaker are beyond his reach so long as they are practiced in a suitably male environment. It is not only women's work in and of itself that is degrading but any work on female turf. It may be true, as Brenton (1966) says, that "the secure man can wash a dish, diaper a baby, and throw the dirty clothes into the washing machine — or do anything else women used to do exclusively — without thinking twice about it" (p. 211), but not all men are that secure. To a great many men such chores are demasculinizing. The apron is shameful on a man in the kitchen; it is all right at the carpenter's bench.

The male world may look upon the man who shares household responsibilities as, in effect, a scab. One informant tells the interviewer about a conversation on the job: "What, are you crazy?" his hard-hat fellow workers ask him

SCAB – workman who refuses join labor union, act with union; one who takes place of strikers, crosses picket line when he speaks of helping his wife. "The guys want to kill me. 'You son of a bitch! You are getting us in trouble.' . . . The men get really mad" (Lein, 1979, p. 492). Something more than persiflage is involved here. We are fairly familiar with the trauma associated with the invasion by women of the male work turf, the hazing women can be subjected to, and the male resentment of admitting them except into their own segregated areas. The corresponding entrance of men into the traditional turf of women — the kitchen or the nursery — has analogous but not identical concomitants.

Pleck and Lang (1979) tell us that men are now beginning to change in the direction of greater involvement in family life. "Men's family behavior is beginning to change, becoming increasingly congruent with the long-standing psychological significance of the family in their lives" (p. 1). They measure this greater involvement by way of the help they offer with homemaking chores. Scanzoni (1975), on the basis of a survey of over 3,000 husbands and wives, concludes that at least in households in which wives are in the labor force, there is the "possibility of a different pattern in which responsibility for households would unequivocally fall equally on husbands as well as wives" (p. 38). A brave new world indeed. Still, when we look at the reality around us, the pace seems intolerably slow. The responsibilities of the old good-provider role have attenuated far faster than have its prerogatives and privileges.

A considerable amount of thought has been devoted to studying the effects of the large influx of women into the work force. An equally interesting question is what the effect will be if a large number of men actually do increase their participation in the family and the household. Will men find the apron shameful? What if we were to ask fathers to alternate with mothers in being in the home when youngsters come home from school? Would fighting adolescent drug abuse be more successful if fathers and mothers were equally engaged in it? If the school could confer with fathers as often as with mothers? If the father accompanied children when they went shopping for clothes? If fathers spent as much time with children as do mothers?

Even as husbands, let alone as fathers, the new pattern is not without trauma. Hall and Hall (1979), in their study of two-career couples, report that the most serious fights among such couples occur not in the bedroom, but in the kitchen, between couples who profess a commitment to equality but who find actually implementing it difficult. A young professional reports that he is philosophically committed to egalitarianism in marriage and tries hard to practice it, but it does not work. He even feels guilty about this. The stresses involved in reworking roles may have an impact on health. A study of engineers and accountants finds poorer health among those with employed wives than among those with nonemployed wives (Burke & Wier, 1976). The processes involved in role change have been compared with those involved in deprogramming a cult member. Are they part of the increasing sense of marriage and parenthood as "all burdens and restrictions"?

The demise of the good-provider role also calls for consideration of other questions: What does the demotion of the good provider to the status of senior provider or even mere coprovider do to him? To marriage? To gender identity? What does expanding the role of housewife to that of junior provider or even coprovider do to her? To marriage? To gender identity? Much will of course depend on the social and psychological ambience in which changes take place.

A PARABLE

I began this essay with a proverbial woman. I close it with a modern parable by William H. Chafe (Note 5), a historian who also keeps his eye on the current scene. Jack and Jill, both planning professional careers, he as doctor, she as lawyer, marry at age 24. She works to put him through medical school in the expectation that he will then finance her through law school. A child is born during the husband's internship, as planned. But in order for him to support her through professional training as planned, he will have to take time out from his career. After two years, they decide that both will continue their training on a part-time basis, sharing household responsibilities and using day-care services. Both find part-time positions and work out flexible work schedules that leave both of them time for child care and companionship with one another. They live happily ever after.

That's the end? you ask incredulously. Well, not exactly. For, as Chafe (Note 5) points out, as usual the personal is also political:

> Obviously such a scenario presumes a radical transformation of the personal values that today's young people bring to their relationships as well as a readiness on the part of social and economic institutions to encourage, or at least make possible, the development of equality between men and women. (p. 28)

The good-provider role may be on its way out, but its legitimate successor has not yet appeared on the scene.

NOTES

1. Hesselbart, S. *Some underemphasized issues about men, women, and work.* Unpublished manuscript, 1978.

2. Douvan, E. *Family roles in a twenty-year perspective.* Paper presented at the Radcliffe Pre-Centennial Conference, Cambridge, Massachusetts, April 2–4, 1978.

3. Veroff, J. *Psychological orientations to the work role: 1957–1976.* Unpublished manuscript, 1978.

4. Shostak, A. *Working class Americans at home: Changing expectations of manhood.* Unpublished manuscript, 1973.

5. Chafe, W. *The challenge of sex equality: A new culture or old values revisited?* Paper presented at the Radcliffe Pre-Centennial Conference, Cambridge, Massachusetts, April 2–4, 1978.

REFERENCES

Babcock, B., Freedman, A. E., Norton, E. H., & Ross, S. C. *Sex discrimination and the law: Causes and remedies.* Boston: Little, Brown, 1975.

Bernard, J. *Women, wives, mothers.* Chicago: Aldine, 1975.

Bernard, J. Homosociality and female depression. *Journal of Social Issues,* 1976, *32,* 207–224.

Boulding, E. Familial constraints on women's work roles. *SIGNS: Journal of Women in Culture and Society,* 1976, *1,* 95–118.

Brenton, M. *The American male.* New York: Coward-McCann, 1966.

Burke, R. & Wier, T. Relationship of wives' employment status to husband, wife and pair satisfaction and performance. *Journal of Marriage and the Family,* 1976, *38,* 279–287.

David, D. S. & Brannon, R. (Eds.). *The forty-nine percent majority: The male sex role.* Reading, Mass.: Addison-Wesley, 1976.

Demos, J. The American family in past time. *American Scholar,* 1974, *43,* 422–446.

Farrell, W. *The liberated man.* New York: Random House, 1974.

Fasteau, M. F. *The male machine.* New York: McGraw-Hill, 1974.

Fiedler, L. *Love and death in the American novel.* New York: Meredith, 1962.

Foner, P. S. *Women and the American labor movement.* New York: Free Press, 1979.

Freud, S. *Civilization and its discontents.* New York: Doubleday-Anchor, 1958. (Originally published, 1930.)

Goldberg, H. *The hazards of being male.* New York: New American Library, 1976.

Gould, R. E. Measuring masculinity by the size of a paycheck. In J. E. Pleck & J. Sawyer (Eds.). *Men and masculinity.* Englewood Cliffs, N.J.: Prentice-Hall, 1974. (Also published in *Ms.,* June 1973, pp. 18ff.)

Hall, D. & Hall, F. *The two-career couple.* Reading, Mass.: Addison-Wesley, 1979.

Jones, C. A. *A review of child support payment performance.* Washington, D.C.: Urban Institute, 1976.

Keniston, K. *The uncommitted: Alienated youth in American society.* New York:Harcourt, Brace & World, 1965.

Komarovsky, M. *The unemployed man and his family.* New York: Dryden Press, 1940.

Lefkowitz, B. Life without work. *Newsweek,* May 14, 1979, p. 31.

Lein, L. Responsibility in the allocation of tasks. *Family Coordinator,* 1979, *28,* 489–496.

Liebow, E. *Tally's corner.* Boston: Little, Brown, 1966.

Lopata, H. *Occupation housewife.* New York: Oxford University Press, 1971.

Mainardi, P. The politics of housework. In R. Morgan (Ed.), *Sisterhood is powerful.* New York: Vintage Books, 1970.

Pleck, J. H. & Lang, L. Men's family work: Three perspectives and some new data. *Family Coordinator,* 1979, *28,* 481–488.

Pleck, J. H. & Sawyer, J. (Eds.), *Men and masculinity.* Englewood Cliffs, N.J.: Prentice-Hall, 1974.

Rainwater, L. & Yancy, W. L. *The Moynihan report and the politics of controversy.* Cambridge, Mass.: M.I.T. Press, 1967.

Sarason, S. B. *Work, aging, and social change.* New York: Free Press, 1977.

Scanzoni, J. H. *Sex roles, life styles, and childbearing: Changing patterns in marriage and the family.* New York: Free Press, 1975.

Scanzoni, J. H. An historical perspective on husband-wife bargaining power and marital dissolution. In G. Levinger & O. Moles (Eds.), *Divorce and separation in America.* New York: Basic Books, 1979.

Smith, R. E. (Ed.), *The subtle revolution.* Washington, D.C.: Urban Institute, 1979.

Smuts, R. W. *Women and work in America.* New York: Columbia University Press, 1959.

Snyder, L. The deserting, non-supporting father: Scapegoat of family non-policy. *Family Coordinator,* 1979, *38,* 594–598.

Tocqueville, A. de. *Democracy in America.* New York: J. & H. G. Langley, 1840.

Warner, W. L. & Ablegglen, J. O. *Big business leaders in America.* New York: Harper, 1955.

Yankelovich, D. The new psychological contracts at work. *Psychology Today,* May 1978, pp. 46–47; 49–50.

Zborowski, M. & Herzog, E. *Life is with people.* New York: Schocken Books, 1952.

Anthony Astrachan

MEN AND THE NEW ECONOMY

Pete used to be proud of the work he did as a machinist in an auto parts factory. Now he's just tired — and scared. Half the workers in his plant have been laid off because carmakers have been buying parts from Japan. On top of that, his company is automating in order to compete. "That means they only need a quarter of the workers they used to," Pete says, "and if they move the plant or write new job descriptions that get around the union and seniority, they can hire women. With the computer running the operation they don't need my muscle. And they don't need my skill with the lathe and the drill presses anymore. Work gets simple enough and they turn it over to the girls."

Pete is one of the many men in the United States who see themselves as casualties of the changes occurring in the workplace over the past 30 years. Some, like Pete, string together complaints about imports, automation, and women as though they were all part of the same great shift.

In fact, men are facing very different kinds of change. One thing these changes have in common, however: They alter the nature of work itself. In the United States more than in other countries, and for men more than for women, what you do defines who you are. A man's work is an important part of his identity as a man.

ECONOMICS VS. MAN THE PROVIDER

Historically, men grew up expecting to provide for themselves and for their family. Providing was a man's job — whether he did it as doctor or lawyer, merchant or corporate executive, cop or soldier, auto worker or miner.

Today the role of man as provider is being transformed, and economic change is the main force responsible. Note the measure of the shift: In 1960, 83.3 percent of all men over the age of 16 were in the labor force; in 1985, it was 76.2 percent. By contrast, 37.7 percent of women 16 and over were in the labor force in 1960, but the figure had risen to 54.4 percent by 1985.

Men are no longer the sole providers for their families. The traditional family — a husband who goes out to work while his wife stays home and raises children — now accounts for only 10.7 percent of U.S. households. Now, more than 32 percent of all households are two-earner families in which the wife shares the role of provider.

There are two reasons for these changes. First, the cycle of inflation and recession and the shift from manufacturing to services have produced an economy in which the family needs more than one income to live decently or even survive. Second, rising competition from imports, dwindling jobs in manufacturing, the high Reagan budget, and growing trade deficits occurring over the past five years have helped to destroy thousands of the jobs that enabled men to provide.

IMPORTS AND JOBS

The boom in imports has had so much impact in everyday life and in the media recently that we may forget it's part of a broader decline in manufacturing and connected with the switch from smokestack to high-tech industry over the past 20 years. Economists estimate that we have lost about 2 million jobs, 30,000 of them in the textile industry alone, since the U.S. dollar and U.S. imports started to climb in 1981. The rise in imports and the fall in manufacturing seem like statistical abstractions, but the abstract soon becomes concrete: Brown Shoe Company of St. Louis closed eight of its 30 domestic shoe plants and bought a company that imports Italian shoes; Caterpillar Tractor cut its total work force by a third; Dixie Yarns in Chattanooga spun 45 percent less yarn in 1985 than the year before.

Then the statistics hit home: Theodore McBryar, a 43-year-old Dixie Yarns dye-machine operator, made only half as much in 1985 as he did the year before and couldn't afford to replace his 1973 Chevrolet, which had 213,000 miles on it when *U.S. News* reported his plight. Kevin Englert, 30, a roving tender at the same mill, couldn't buy his three children new clothes for last school year. That kind of hardship undermines a man's faith in himself. A man unable to "do his job" as provider has lost more than just money.

Ironically, the economic policies that have hurt traditional men (and traditional corporations) by bringing on the import crisis came from the conservative administration of Ronald Reagan, whose supporters labor so hard — and most fruitlessly — in behalf of traditional values in both personal and economic life.

TECHNOLOGY VS. A "MAN'S JOB"

Automation, like economics, brings losses beyond jobs or money. "A man's job" once required skill, strength, and the ability to work long hours — all admirable qualities that used to be thought of as exclusively male. Thanks to technological advances, many such jobs now require less and less skill in the use of a worker's hands, eyes, and judgment. Pride and craftsmanship become irrelevant.

This seems brand new, something very modern. In fact, it's the latest stage in a long historical process that began with the Industrial Revolution and the development of factories 200 years ago and gathered force with the invention of the assembly line in the early years of this century.

Today's jobs require more and more obedience to company rules and the tyranny of electronic monitoring. Management often translates these new conditions to mean that the work has become suitable for women, whom they see as reliable, punctual workers who like repetitive work and believe that they profit when the company does. Male managers, in fact, do not try to hide this. Most technological changes in one factory "were of a type that would tend to increase the percentage of women. For example, we have broken down the alignment of components and simplified [the] job, and as the jobs called for less skill, they became women's work." That was one New Jersey executive quoted in Georgina Smith's study of the job market, which cited many more.

WOMEN IN MEN'S JOBS

The arrival of women in the workplace, particularly in what were once labeled masculine occupations, is a social and psychological shift that is more significant and far reaching than the economic changes caused by the five-year boom in imports or by automation, though these may have higher and more visible immediate costs.

A woman employed in what was once called a man's job is a more radical departure from tradition because she violates a division of labor that goes back millennia. She is also more universal. Imports hurt some industries, automation primarily affects factory workers, but we all meet this working woman, whether or not we are employed. She is in every kind of work and from every racial and ethnic group.

The idea that a woman can and should do "a man's job" is the product of social and psychological forces that are reshaping both the male role as provider and the male monopoly on certain occupations.

These powerful traditions deprived women of independence and equality, confining them to low-paid work that brought few of the satisfactions of mastery and achievement that many of us find so necessary for happiness. For the past 20 years women have been fighting to do away with these restrictions on equality and power. Their struggle has produced changes in U.S. politics, culture, and psychology. They have shown that the old strengths and skills and the ability to work long hours that were needed for what used to be seen as a man's job are not exclusively male — or even often required now. The number of women has increased in many occupations, from factory worker to police officer to corporate manager to physician — 18 percent of blue-collar workers and 16 percent of doctors and lawyers, for example, are now women.

Frequently overlooked, however, is the part economic forces have played in these changes. Women have been pushed in this direction by the same shifts that have done so much to change the role of work in men's lives.

This affects both men's acceptance of change and their resistance to it. Most men recognize the injustice of the old division of labor and have learned to live with some of the ways women are changing that division. Our acceptance reflects recognition of many realities — a family needs two incomes to survive; women perform as well as men in many jobs; women have the right to equal opportunity in any occupation they choose.

But for most men, I believe, resistance is still stronger than acceptance. The very economic necessities that bring women into "a man's job" underline the erosion of the male role as provider and thus produce conflict. Polls that show acceptance must be seen in this context. It appears that many men give pollsters views that they think are socially acceptable, but behave differently. A recent survey by the *Harvard Business Review*, for instance, shows that only 5 percent of male executives have an unfavorable view of female executives, compared to 41 percent in 1965. But more than half the men surveyed made $100,000 or more a year, while only 10 percent of the women did. However low the expressed bias, many women attribute such measurable discrimination to male resistance.

Most men can't accept that a woman no longer devotes herself primarily to housekeeping and childcare, even though they know it's true and still value her as a partner. It is hard to welcome change when the myths and emotions of the traditional system remain strong. It's especially hard when men are confronted at the same time with such economic and technological changes, just described, that damage or destroy many of the satisfactions of work that might otherwise survive the introduction of women into the workplace. Generally, men find it more difficult to feel support for the women they work with than a wife or daughter going out to face a similar situation.

My own research indicates that most men also feel some combination of anger, fear, and anxiety toward women in traditionally masculine jobs, often treating women co-workers in any or all of three ways. They show *hostility*; *deny* their competence, sometimes their very presence; or *transform* them in fantasy — into nuns, whores, lovers, mothers, wives, daughters, sisters — any role that allows them to treat women as traditional females rather than peers.

These behaviors take different forms in different occupations. Hostility is often expressed sexually. Some factory workers, for instance, put porn pictures in their tool chests and display them when women workers walk by. Suggestive propositions and other forms of sexual harassment directed at women are common occurrences in offices. Recruiters from the investment banking firm Goldman, Sachs asked women at Stanford University if they would have an abortion rather than jeopardize their careers, thus attacking both their right and their ability to combine motherhood and career.

Denial is what's being expressed by the committee of men who direct all their comments to the man from the ad agency, though the woman on the team, sitting next to him at the table, is his boss and the designer of the campaign. It's denial also when men insist that most women are not as career-oriented as men, despite statistics showing that in many industries women in technical, professional, supervisory, and managerial positions have the same rate of turnover as men.

Transformation can take forms as nasty as a sexual assault on a woman coal miner or as "innocent" as a request by a male executive that his female colleague sew on an errant button for him, thus transforming her into a mother.

THE BRIGHT SIDE

The fearsome changes discussed here are changes in work that alter the shape of society and of individual lives, that change the very way we see ourselves as men. The answer to these threats isn't to block imports, stop automation, or deny women the right to work. It's to find ways that government, corporations, and individuals can cushion the effects of change.

One way is to remember that in every change there's a bright side as well as a dark side. In every case, the promise can alter our lives as much as the threat does.

On the economic front, for instance, the threat of imports has been accompanied by the arrival of foreign firms to build factories here that may make up for some of the jobs lost, like Komatsu, the Japanese manufacturer of earthmoving machines, in Chattanooga.

Technology has improved living standards for everyone and working conditions for the people who master new tools. It can lead to increased responsibility and demand higher skills in operators, as Paul Adler points out in his book

Dollars and Sense. Responsibility increases because machines cost more and produce more. Operators need higher skills because they must understand the control program logic well enough to correct errors on the line or help write new programs. When the Communications Workers of America polled members in 1979, about 78 percent said technological change had increased the skill requirements of their jobs.

A woman in "a man's job" constitutes a more personal challenge to a man than economic or technological change. It's a challenge he meets at home as well as at work, in his gut, often in his crotch, as well as in his head. Despite or because of the challenge she represents, a man can probably enrich his life more by learning to work with women in his kind of job than by switching jobs to escape the threat of imports or mastering automation.

Men can start by seeking the positive emotions that are generated by the arrival of women in the workplace, and by their assertion of equality. These emotions are admiration, identification, and pleasure. Such feelings produce positive behavior — acceptance, support, and association.

I also believe a man can work with a woman in "her kind" of job. A small but increasing number of men are now sharing the work of raising their children. They find it enriches both their own and their children's lives.

Few men, however, even those who welcome women as peers, do literally half the household work. There will always be economic crises and technological changes that alter our work patterns, but society will truly be transformed only when men do half the work of childcare and take half the responsibility for it from the moment of birth. Unhappily, we can't take more than a small step toward this day until individuals and trade unions, government and corporations, change the way work is organized.

Robert Zussman

WORK AND FAMILY IN THE NEW MIDDLE CLASS

Few developments have been so momentous for the ways in which we think about the relationship between work and family as the great transformation from an economy of farms and shops to one dominated by bureaucratic employment. For the old middle class of independent farmers, small shopkeepers, and fee-for-service professionals, a way of work was also a way of life. For the salaried employees of the new middle class — engineers, accountants, technicians, officials, administrators, and middle managers of all sorts — work may do little more than provide the wherewithal for a style of life. Only when work and family are distinct, as they are among salaried employees, does the relationship between them become problematic.

In the old middle class, the relationship between work and family was often intimate. Blending together in the form of unpaid family labor, the exercise of authority at work on the basis of parenthood or husbandhood, and the use of a single location as both residence and business, work and family formed a well-integrated whole. All this is captured neatly in terms like the "family farm" or "mom and pop grocery store." In such situations, there undoubtedly were — and where such situations persist, undoubtedly still are — pervasive conflicts: between sons anxious to take over the family business and fathers holding on to parental authority; between husbands and wives; between brothers and brothers-in-law and cousins. Yet such conflicts were not between work and family; they were, put simply, all in the family.

For the new middle class the situation is different. Home and office are separated by time and space. If the salaried employee exercises authority over a subordinate, it is as a manager, not as a parent: and if he or she exercises authority over a child, it is as a parent, not as an employer. Where, for the old middle class, the relationship between work and family was diffuse and pervasive, for the new middle class it is specific and limited.[1]

It is precisely the separation between work and family in the salaried middle class that has led many sociologists to see a potential tension between them. Do one's obligations as a husband or wife or parent conflict with one's obligations as an employee? Is work a "central life interest"? Or is the family? How is this tension experienced?

Certainly, for many members of the salaried middle class, the tension between work and family is both real and difficult, particularly for those women who have entered the labor force while maintaining the full burden of motherhood and domestic duties. Yet it is the contention of this paper that the men of the new middle class experience few tensions between work and family. Although work and family do not blend together as they did in the old middle class, these men see them as fitting together neatly, like the pieces of a carefully constructed jigsaw puzzles, as the obligations of fatherhood and husbandhood are met in the very course of meeting one's obligations as an employee.

Over a period of eight months in 1977, I studied engineers at two New England corporations, observing them at work, interviewing them, and, when invited, joining them for dinner or other casual social occasions. One of the companies ("Precision Metals") is in the metal-working industry. Founded just after the Civil War, it is still located in the small industrial town that was its original site. The other ("Contronics") is in consumer electronics. Founded after World War II, it is located in the suburb of a middle-sized city, roughly a twenty-minute drive from Precision Metals.[2]

Engineering is the prototypical occupation of the new middle class: in contrast to the old middle-class professions, engineering has from its very origins been characterized by salaried employment. It is also one of the most male-dominated occupations: according to the 1970 census, only 2 percent of American engineers were women, and even by 1980 that figure had risen only to 4 percent.[3] Engineers are well-paid: salaries for new college graduates started at an average of $26,000 in 1984 and, if the past is any guide, will continue to rise steadily (though in some cases slowly) over the remainder of a working life.[4] Engineering is also a secure occupation: although layoffs have been common in the more volatile advanced industries like aeronautics and electronics (and have affected a number of the engineers who worked at Contronics), extended unemployment is rare. Even during the much publicized aerospace cutbacks of the early 1907s, rates of unemployment in engineering have never reached even half that of the labor force as a whole.[5]

FAMILIES

Engineers' families are notable only for their conventionality. Sixty-five of the 80 engineers I interviewed were married; only 4 were divorced, and 1 widowed. Of the 70 engineers who had ever been married, 86 percent had at least one child. Only 2 of the married engineers lived in an extended household, one sharing his home with his mother, the other with his mother-in-law. When the younger engineers, representing an earlier stage in the life cycle, are excluded, there is even less variation. Of the 61 engineers over thirty, only 2 had never been married, and only 3 were childless.

Roughly half of the engineers' wives work outside the home, and many more either have worked or probably will work over the course of their marriages. Most of the engineers support, and some actively encourage, their wives' employment, though typically only after their children are in school:

> I love it for the extra income. She's not bored, and it gets her out. I didn't want her to work when the kids were younger. She agreed.

> Terrific, as soon as the youngest is in school. I wouldn't want to deprive her. The emphasis has changed in the last twenty years.

Thus, although most of the engineers' wives have had some experience in the labor force, only a few have had careers in the sense of continuous, full-time employment with orderly movement through a sequence of related positions. This, to the engineers, seemed as it should be.

The engineers themselves were their families' main providers. Although there are occasional hints of change, especially among the younger engineers, this, too, seemed to most as it should be. On the duties of husbands and wives, the engineers are still traditionalists. Virtually all mentioned love and companionship as essential to marriage. Many spoke of the relationship between husband and wife as a partnership. However, less than a third made no distinction between the "partners'" obligations. For the rest, love is expressed and partnership realized through a division of labor. If some might see a tension in these ideas, the engineers themselves do not:

> I believe in a marriage of equal partners with the man ruling the roost. Although I may be the primary breadwinner, I can use help and I can help around the house. My major responsibility is going to work every day and being a father to my children. I should be a companion to my wife, but we should be allowed to grow as individuals. She's responsible for the upbringing of the children, for the mundane chores of the house. She should be a companion to the children. She should have time to grow as an individual.

Most of the engineers expect their wives to care for their homes: "she should cook and clean," do "the mundane chores." But they also expect their wives to provide a home life: "see the family runs smoothly"; "provide an atmosphere I can come home to"; and "create harmony." In return, almost all the engineers believe that it is their obligation to "earn money to support a family," "feed and clothe and take care of the family," "provide a decent home and a decent income," and make sure that their children have "bikes and food and education." In order to be reliable husbands and fathers, they must be reliable workers. But the emotional life of their families remains the primary responsibility of their wives. As one engineer put it, "My job is to provide a home. Her job is to keep it happy."

<h2>WORK AND FAMILY</h2>

Beyond the income that it provides, however, the engineers' work has little to do with their family lives. "It's a separate thing," said one engineer, "There are no integral activities." Indeed, a formal separation between work life and family life is a striking, and distinguishing, characteristic of the salaried middle class: families play no official part either in finding work or in its practice.[6]

There is, of course, a considerable difference between the formal separation of work from family and the realities of corporate life. In fact, in the higher reaches of salaried employment, demands of families may be quite frequent: according to many reports, both scholarly and journalistic, a wife's willingness to share in her husband's career (for example, by entertaining business guests) is often an unspoken requirement of executive positions. So, too, many executive and professional positions require long hours of "overtime" and in some cases (particularly for employees in concerns dependent on public favor) participation in community service.[7]

But the engineers at Contronics and Precision Metals are largely free even of these demands. Work typically begins within a few minutes of the official opening time and ends within a few minutes of the official closing time. Only a few of the engineers take work home more than occasionally. Only in the manufacturing departments of the two companies, where production schedules are often tight, do any of the engineers come in on weekends. The entertainment of clients, rare in any event, is typically limited to lunch at restaurants close to the plant. Moreover, managers at both companies carefully avoid even the suggestion of imposing on private lives. This, like many policies, becomes clearest through its near violation. A personnel officer at Precision Metals found out, apparently quite by accident, that a newly hired, unmarried, young engineer was living with a woman friend. An older man, the personnel officer was taken aback by this arrangement. But he was also insistent on explaining that, whatever his personal feeling, he understood that the company had no legitimate concern in this area. In another case, two German engineers planning to visit Contronics asked to stay in private homes rather than in a hotel, in order to get a better feel for life in America. The appropriate manager called all his engineers into his office, explained the request, and asked for volunteers to put up the German guests — but only after apologizing and explaining, with great elaboration, that compliance was entirely voluntary and that neither he nor the company believed that any engineer should feel obligated to respond.

The separation of work and family is further reinforced by a pattern of residential dispersion that is particularly strong at Contronics. Of the 40 engineers I interviewed at Precision Metals, 16 lived in the town in which the company is located. The remaining 24 lived in a total of 13 towns within a radius of roughly twenty miles from the worksite. At Contronics, located in a suburb and in this respect altogether atypical of postwar industrial development, the pattern is more pronounced. Only 2 of the 40 engineers I interviewed lived in the suburb in which their company is headquartered, and only 4 more in the neighboring middle-sized city. The remaining 34 were scattered among no less than 24 towns and villages. This pattern has far-reaching consequences.

Most important, the engineers' work contributes little to a public identity. For the old middle class of shopkeepers, farmers, and fee-for-service professionals, this was not the case. Living and working in the same community, with diverse clients or customers, and often active in community affairs, they were known by what they did: their work became a way of life. But the engineers' work is hidden, invisible not only to neighbors, who may have only the vaguest conception of what an engineer is, but even to their own families. The engineers are known not by their work but as husbands and fathers, as homeowners, and as participants in a residential community.[8]

A few of the younger engineers at Contronics and Precision Metals do argue that who they are and what they do at work inevitably affected who they are and what they do at home. One told me, "It's made me think better and straighter — to slow down and take my time." Another said:

> My job requires a certain amount of ability just like a lot of life situations. The practice I get here helps me out at home. Like, contrast it to the shop. I don't run around goosing everyone like they do down there. Everything here is on a more elite level, a more adult level. I try to treat everyone with respect and consideration.

This describes work's effect on personality, on an inner life, and on behavior. But such effects are largely a private matter, carrying none of the institutionalized obligations associated with the family life of the old middle class: they do not amount to a public identity.

To be sure, most of the engineers acknowledged that their work might have some effect on their family life — for example, the amount of time they have for their families: "It gets me home after eight hours." And: "The biggest thing is I don't have to spend a lot of time traveling." And work might affect their moods:

> Compared to some other jobs I've had, this is a good one. At my other job I was ready to go home and punch the wall after work. This job doesn't detract as much. I've separated my career from my personal life.

> The atmosphere here isn't depressing. I go home in a fair frame of mind. It's not bad financially, either, but the atmosphere's the most important thing. I don't have all that much to talk about when I go home. I'm not mad at my boss or anything like that, so I try to leave my work here.

> Knowing that a man has some peace of mind, that he's accomplishing what he wants. I can talk about other things at home. I leave my problems at work so we can enjoy each other.

But these effects are transitory: they may last for a day or a week or even a month, but no longer than the duration of a particular situation. They may affect the family, but they are not fundamental to it. And they will not be integrated, in any permanent way, into a personality.

We should not, of course, read the engineers' claims as statements of fact. Undoubtedly, as Melvin Kohn and others have argued for many years, the kind of work that people do does affect their personalities, even if these effects are not recognized.[9] Yet even if the engineers' statements cannot be read as literal descriptions, they can be read profitably for the values implicit in them. In this sense, they are an ideology of family life.

Above all, the engineers see the relationship between work and family as an exchange in which they give time in return for income to support their families. This exchange is seen as altogether fair and appropriate so long as the demands of work are limited to a "normal" working day of eight hours, five days a week. This image of an exchange excludes the idea that work may influence the quality of family life in any but a material sense: work and family are linked by what a husband takes from and brings to the family, not by what he does within the family itself.

Insofar as the engineers do see any effects of work on the internal life of their families, they see it negatively. When work is going well, the employee does not bring it home with him ("I can talk about other things than work at home"); when work is not going well, and only then, bad moods may spill over into family time ("If I was unhappy, it would come home with me"). Whereas the bad job generates tensions that cannot be contained within the workplace, the good job is marked merely by the absence of any effect. Thus, the separation of work from family becomes a virtue, and the statement that "I've never brought my problems home" becomes a mark of pride. In short, the best situation, as the engineers see it, is one in which the relationship between work and family is limited to an exchange of resources; in all other respects, particularly in regard to emotional life, they should be kept separate.

The engineers see themselves as having successfully contained work within its proper boundaries. They are satisfied with the terms of exchange they have established: very few say that their income is insufficient to meet their families; needs; more are pleased that work does not make excessive demands on family time than complain that it does; considerably more are satisfied that work creates no problems at home than are concerned about the tensions it might generate.[10]

CONCLUSION

The rebirth of feminism over the last two decades and the concomitant entrance of large numbers of married women into the labor force have been widely announced as sources of new tensions between work life and family life. Perhaps, for women, this has been the case. Yet among the men of the American middle class, these tensions are not apparent. Shaped by the structure of salaried employment, the values of engineers at Contronics and Precision Metals have proven surprisingly resistant to change: possible tensions between work and family continue to be resolved by a conception of the "good provider" that has been a familiar presence in American life at least since the rise of a corporate economy.[11]

For the engineers at Contronics and Precision Metals — and perhaps for middle-level male employees more generally — there is a rather easy harmony between the demands of work and the demands of family. Salaried employees do not face the strains on family lives created by either an insufficiency of income or difficult working conditions, both frequently reported as endemic to contemporary working-class life.[12] Nor do they, as a rule, face the strains associated with excessive demands on their time, strains quite common in the lives of many professionals and upper-level managers. This harmony, though, is based on a strict compartmentalization of work and family: each is a distinct sphere of experience, with its own satisfactions and its own logic.

At the same time, however, work and family are part of a single whole. Work and family are not competing "central life interests."[13] Rather, the engineers meet what they see as the obligations of husbandhood and fatherhood precisely by meeting their obligations as employees.

But harmony is rarely achieved without cost or compromise. The engineers keep a distance from their work. They do not see it as a source of identity, and certainly not as a source of public identity. They work so that they can support their families. But what are the consequences for their lives in those families in whose name they work? The engineers' work is hidden from their families. And whether by choice or necessity elevated to principle, they prefer to keep it hidden. They are good providers but abdicate full participation in the emotional life of their families to their wives. The engineers themselves express contentment with this arrangement, and we have no reason to doubt them. Yet we may well wonder if they have not become strangers in their own homes.

NOTES

1. For discussions of the relationship between work and family in a number of settings, see Rosabeth Moss Kanter, *Work and Family in the United States: A Critical Review and Agenda for Research and Policy* (New York: Russell Sage Foundation, 1977), and Stanley R. Parker, *The Future of Work and Leisure* (New York: Praeger, 1971).

2. For a full discussion of this research, see my *Mechanics of the Middle Class: Work and Politics Among American Engineers* (Berkeley: University of California Press, 1985).

3. U.S. Bureau of the Census, *1980 Census of Population, Supplementary Reports* (PC80-S1-15) (Washington, D.C.: Government Printing Office).

4. Engineers Joint Council, Engineering Manpower Commission, *Professional Income of Engineers* (New York: Engineers Joint Council, 1984).

5. U.S. National Science Foundation, *Unemployment Rates and Employment Characteristics for Scientists and Engineers, 1971* (Washington, D.C.: Government Printing Office, 1971).

6. Although a father and a son both work as engineers at Precision Metals, engineering is among the occupations in which formal qualifications are likeliest to count more than family connections in finding employment. See Mark Granovetter, *Getting a Job* (Cambridge: Harvard University Press, 1974).

7. On executives, see, for example, Rosabeth Moss Kanter, *Men and Women of the Corporation* (New York: Basic Books, 1977), and Diane Margolis, *The Managers: Corporate Life in America* (New York: Morrow, 1977). On professionals, see, for example, Martha R. Fowlkes, *Behind Every Successful Man: Wives of Medicine and Academe* (New York: Columbia University Press, 1980), and Jerome Carlin, *Lawyers on Their Own* (New Brunswick, N.J.: Rutgers University Press, 1962).

8. For a more general discussion of this issue, see John Alt, "Beyond Class: The Decline of Industrial Labor and Leisure," *Telos*, no. 28 (1976): 55–82, and Christopher Lasch, *Haven in a Heartless World: The Family Besieged* (New York: Basic Books, 1977).

9. Melvin Kohn, *Class and Conformity*, 2d ed. (Chicago: University of Chicago Press, 1977).

10. For discussion of what happens to engineers and their families when the accustomed income and security are disrupted, see Paula Goldman Leventman, *Professionals Out of Work* (Glencoe, Ill.: Free Press, 1981).

11. On the history of the conception of the good provider, see Jessie Bernard, "The Good-Provider Role: Its Rise and Fall," *American Psychologist* 36 (1981):1–12.

12. See, for example, Lillian Breslow Rubin, *Worlds of Pain: Life in the Working-Class Family* (New York: Basic Books, 1976).

13. For discussions of "central life interests," see Robert Dubin, "Industrial Workers' Worlds: A Study of the Central Life Interests of Industrial Workers," *Social Problems* 3 (1956):3–42, and Robert Dubin, R. Alan Hedley, and Thomas C. Taveggia, "Attachment to Work," in Robert Dubin (ed.), *Handbook of Work, Organization, and Society* (Chicago: Rand McNally, 1976).

John Ceely

ON THE JOB:
EXCERPTS FROM A WORKINGMAN'S JOURNAL

Sunday, January 28, 1973   The first week Shelby and I were hired — we're the two newest men — Big Hal grabbed Shelby into the air and rocked him like a baby in the void over the sewer pipe ditch. Had he let go, Shelby would have dropped 20 feet onto bedrock. Everybody laughed.

Monday, June 4, 1973   The wall they were starting was only about 10 feet from the sidewalk, and some of the bricklayers were saying "Hi!" to the pretty girls that walked past. One stunningly beautiful young student, braless, long hair and healthy, smiled shyly and chirped back, "Hi!"

The guys melted. Nobody said, "How'd ya like ta come home with me?" No one muttered, "Now ain't *she* a loose one!"

She was too close and personal.

Tuesday, January 16, 1973   Shelby and I came on the job the same day and we both got Hal's heavy kidding treatment: "Hey John, ya got a picture of yer wife naked?" "No, and if I did, you think I'd show it to you?" "Well *I* got a picture of her naked. How much ya gimme for it?"

Pretty soon I learned to be more aggressive (with a big grin on my mug). "Hey John, does yer wife bite yer cock when she blows ya?" "No, but *your* wife does. That's why I quit going with her. But she told me she had a guy lined up that liked to have his cock bit. Name was Hal, she said."

Hal would smile, and we'd razz-ma-tazz back and forth. When Hal gave Shelby the same treatment Shelby sulked. If he kept at it long enough, Shelby got mad. A stylized kind of mad — Hal being 6 foot 5 and solid as a crowbar.

Wednesday, January 27, 1971 — Don
Fingernails fractured and purple
bruised knuckles

tanned hide to his hand
battered animal claw
   nicks, scabs.
Even stacking steel beams
   he won't wear gloves.

Monday, March 28, 1982   Two guys stand at a power buggy loaded with
cement, one guy on either side, and they race each other shoveling the concrete
out of the buggy and into the wall forms. Their shoulders start to ache, they're
panting at the edge of swoon, and the buggy's only half empty. The older guy
is matching the younger guy dive for dive, but he wants to yell, "Jesus, we're
on the same side! Aren't we? Why the fuck don't we shovel this stuff out at a
reasonable speed?" But the kid's 25 and worried about getting laid off, and the
older guy is 45 and even more worried. They try to kill each other.

Tuesday, September 12, 1972   At 8:00 A.M., I get to the house where we're
going to work. We're going to pour the basement and garage this morning. The
cement truck's here, but the driver's looking at the motor. He walks over to
where we're standing in a group. "The fuel pump's busted. I'm gonna put in a
call to the mechanic."

There's nothing we can do till the mechanic comes, so Ted, Bob, Fred, Doug,
and I stand or squat near our cars and shoot the shit.

Bob's talking about his pickup, "I never knew a Ford transmission to fuck up
the way this one does. I seen plenty o' lousy International transmissions but
this is the first Ford I ever seen it happen."

"Oh, you get lemons in every brand."

Bob again: "Remember that Chevy Tom Berger used to drive to work? Ja-
hee-zus! The goddamned stick for the stick shift broke off one day, so he takes
my vise-grips out o' my tool box and clamps *them* things on there. *For three
goddamned months* we had to shift that thing with them vise-grips. By Jesus, the
day I quit I took them vise-grips home with me. I dunno how the fuck he drove
his truck home. I didn't *give* a fuck, neither."

Quiet, warm rattle of talk. Getting to know one another. It's okay, it's okay.
Each in effect is saying to the others, "I feel pretty okay being here working
with you guys."

Tuesday, January 30, 1973   Everybody snapping at everyone else. Fred our
foreman was Snapper Number One. We didn't see who was snapping down on
him, probably somebody in the office. Fred made it seem like we were doing
everything wrong, and us flunkies below tried to shift the blame onto each
other's head.

Snapping is uncontrollable jitters wanting out. You walk around with a
shovel in your hand wondering what you're supposed to do, and Fred barks at
you, "Get the goddamned cable around the pipe, so I can at least get it into the
air." (Whereas yesterday he told us be sure and have the rings and gaskets on
before you raise 'em up.) You wonder if maybe Fred thinks you're a dumb cluck
and ought to get fired at the first layoff; after all, manholes aren't all that special
a situation, and probably Fred feels you ought to *know* the pipe's got to be raised
up first when it's going into a manhole; so you're worried the rest of the morning
that you'll make the fatal false move, some *really* dumb, absent-minded move.

So when you and Shelby are driving over to pick up cement block and Shelby makes a wrong turn in full view of the whole crew you yell at the dumb son of a bitch because Fred might be watching and think it's *your* fault.

Snapping at your co-workers comes from fear. It's usually not premeditated or malicious. I try to let snaps wash off my back. No need to add another link in the chain. After getting snapped at (except by Fred) I find it best to answer the person, tell him plainly why I did what I did. Let him know I am accepting no blame for petty human fallibility.

Thursday, June 24, 1971   Mel's a big, swaggering student, a 220 pounder. Blue eyes, blond short hair. He's a zoology major, has a wife and kid. His hips are wide like a chopping block, his torso sits above them like a barrel. He's not muscular, he's beefy. A corn-fed Wisconsin boy. Works construction every summer to get through the University.

On the job Mel undergoes a transformation. Every other word becomes "fuckin." He throws himself into the work, rushes for what he takes to be the manliest jobs — cement hose operator, power buggy operator — anything involving phallic locomotive machinery.

Comes a lull in the work, Mel begins his reminiscences. Flat-footed, arched back, belly sticking out: "*Jee-sus* kee-*riist*! You shudda seen that dumb cock sucker. Why, the sonovabitch couldn't even get the fuckin Bobcat started." His assumed stud voice is an oily singsong, almost a whine. He speaks through tightly pursed lips, and if he pauses he leaves his upper teeth showing, as he absently gazes at other workers in distant corners of the job site. Then he'll start again, not loud, that same oily singsong (restrained, modest); he's a big man taking his break, a nice guy who likes to talk with the boys and can back up all his claims.

Friday, December 5, 1981   Hank is 60, the oldest guy on the job. I worked with him all day. He looks straight at me out of clear blue eyes. His face is round and firm, with deep creases but no wrinkles. His hair is thin but still dark, dark brown, and crew cut. Hank is burly, and he walks stoop-shouldered, hunched a little forward. Long, loping strides with plenty of armswing.

"I'm a Irish Swede. How do ya like that? My mother was Irish and my dad was a Swede . . .

"I never got much schoolin', really. I learned figures, though. Nobody can bluff me at figurin'. Readin'? Not so good. I can read, but I'm slow. I like it better when somebody reads *to* me . . .

"I quit school when I was fourteen, went to work in a loggin' camp. It was on the bluffs, north of the Wisconsin River. That was the Depression, you know. I *had* ta work. The truck come and got us Sunday night and took us to the camp. We provided our own blankets. We slept, worked, and et up there. We worked Saturday, too. We worked six days a week in them days. Then the truck would take us home Saturday night. . . .

"I worked on a two-man crosscut saw. They didn't start usin' chainsaws, really, 'til after the war. She was 6 foot long. You didn't push on 'er, you pulled. You didn't bear on 'er, neither. The guy I was teamed up with was about forty. Nice fella. You end up settin' on your knees and sawin' in the snow. Now do you understand why we was wet all the time? And coldern a sonovabitch! We never took no clothes off to sleep.

"All winter long we worked. At night we'd sit around in the sleepin' shack filin' our saws — we had a pot bellied stove in there — and some a the men would tell stories. We was too pooped to do much else . . .

"Summers, I worked around, on farms mostly. 'Til the war come . . .

"Yep, I was in the service. North Africa. Then they shipped me home. Then they shipped me to the Pacific. All them islands: Iwo Jima, Okinawa . . . I was in the infantry. Even today, I see a Jap and my back goes up. After all that time . . .

"When I got outa the service, I joined the union. Oh, I was farmin', too, for awhile. But that's awful fuckin' tough tryin' ta run a farm *and* go to a job every day. I finally give up farmin'. . . .

"I been a foreman for a couple outfits. If they let me work 'longside the men, it wasn't so bad; but when they'd tell me I can't work, I just gotta watch the men, that's when I'd get tired . . . Shit, yes, I get tired now! After 4 o'clock if I stop movin', I fall right ta sleep. But it was worse when I was foreman and just watchin' the men. I ain't shittin' ya!"

Wednesday, May 19, 1976   Mark sent Toby and me out to the boneyard this morning. We were piling 4 by 4's all day. Thank God. I could never have faced those beams.

I can't write my way out of this impasse. Somehow I've got to walk my way out — on the beams.

Yesterday as I stood 25 feet under Spike and watched him hopping along the 5-inch wide beams overhead, I began to understand. The big-mouthed practitioners of yoga, the hip young businessmen, all the poets and squabbling professors: they are physical and spiritual babies compared to this high school dropout, this unliterate loner who has learned to live with the fear of death.

It's a mistake to imagine Spike is "insensitive" to fear. When he was going up the freight elevator with me for lunch-break last Friday, Spike told me, "I fell last year. I cracked 3 ribs and cut my neck. I missed a month and a half of work. I landed on a 4 by 4, that's the trouble, otherwise I probably wouldn't have cracked my ribs. For two fucking weeks I had to sleep sitting up. It hurt every time I breathed. When I got back to work I wouldn't go up on the beams for five weeks. Even now I don't like to do it. If somebody else'll go up, I always work on the ground. I go up when Mark tells me to, but otherwise . . ."

Spike admits to feeling fear. And yet, as I watched him up there yesterday I was awed by his slow, unwobbling precision. No trembling, no grabbing, no fast moves.

Monday, August 27, 1973   I used to dread being around when a mason yells, "O.K. boys, it's about time to raise us up." I used to tighten up, secrete adrenalin, and invariably end up confused and overpowered by their 16-foot feeder plank. Yesterday Smitty helped me raise their plank.

"It works easier if you stand on the outrigger and just lift the plank straight up."

"Stand on the outrigger!" Christ. That ain't much holding you. I'll try it." We were working 25 feet above the ground, and I was shaky.

Smitty was right. It puts your feet higher so you get that extra 16 inches of lift.

Now, whenever the call comes to raise the plank, I know I can do it. I move deliberately.

Friday, May 28, 1976   Orange disk in the sky. Sun just before setting. Long, slanting distance of atmosphere filters out the injurious, high-energy rays, so I can look directly at the huge exploding ball. It sits 2 inches above our horizon. Every movement on earth; every warm, lubricated, re-combination of sliding molecules; every growth; every expenditure or transfer of energy: the power for all this movement comes from that exploding, burning, shearing, fusing sun.

A guy with a paunch walks down the sidewalk trailing his little black dog on a leash. Evening piss. Those two creatures, their energy, their consciousness, the metabolic smokestacks that their bodies are — all of this was and is from the sun.

The sun gives Sara and I our flash when we make love.

What about gravity? I was scared to the point of shame today up on the beams. Bernie did the plank-carrying work that was clearly mine, and he did it because I was too slow, too hesitant.

If I were to slip on the wet gypsum that coated some of those beams I'd flash 12 feet down to hard concrete floor. It would do more than just "hurt."

The mass of earth below was yanking at me to come down. Like I was meant to walk on ground, not balancing on sticks of steel 12 feet above concrete floor which itself was 100 feet above earth's dirt. This whole building is cold, hard, heartless greed and calculation, and we build it at our peril.

Wasting our sun-loaned energy erecting this rigid stack of pennies. Sun and earth have *already* established their natural balance. Sun's gravity pulls earth around and around and never lets go. Earth forever facing and softening to the light.

What am I doing up on slippery steel beams? I should be home with Sara.

Ben Fong-Torres

WHY ARE THERE NO MALE ASIAN ANCHOR*MEN* ON TV?

Connie Chung, the best-known Asian TV newswoman in the country, is a co-anchor of *1986*, a primetime show on NBC. Ken Kashiwahara, the best-known Asian TV newsman, has been chief of ABC's San Francisco bureau for seven years; his reports pop up here and there on ABC's newscasts and other news-related programs.

Wendy Tokuda, the best-known Asian TV newswoman in the Bay Area, is a co-anchor of KPIX's evening news. David Louie, the most established Asian TV newsman, is a field reporter, covering the Peninsula for KGO.

This article is a revised version of an article that appeared in the "Datebook" section of the *San Francisco Chronicle* July 13, and is printed with their permission.

And that's the way it is: among Asian American broadcasters, the glamor positions — the anchor chairs, whose occupants earn more than $500,000 a year in the major markets — go to the women; the men are left outside, in the field, getting by on reporters' wages that top out at about $80,000.

The four Bay Area television stations that present regular newscasts (Channels 2, 4, 5 and 7) employ more than 40 anchors. Only two are Asian Americans: Tokuda and Emerald Yeh, a KRON co-anchor on weekends. There is no Asian male in an anchor position, and there has never been one. (Other Asian women who have anchored locally are Linda Yu [KGO] and Kaity Tong [KPIX], now prime-time anchors in Chicago and New York.)

None of the two dozen broadcasters this reporter spoke to could name a male Asian news anchor working anywhere in the United States.

Don Fitzpatrick, a TV talent headhunter whose job it has been for four years to help television stations find anchors and reporters, maintains a video library in his San Francisco office of 9000 people on the air in the top 150 markets.

There are, in fact, several reasons proposed by broadcasters, station executives, talent agents and others.

- Asian men have been connected for generations with negative stereotypes. Asian women have also been saddled with false images, but, according to Tokuda, "In this profession, they work for women and against men."
- Asian women are perceived as attractive partners for the typical news anchor: a white male. "TV stations," says Henry Der, director of Chinese for Affirmative Action, "have discovered that having an Asian female with a white male is an attractive combination." And, adds Sam Chu Lin, a former reporter for both KRON and KPIX, "they like the winning formula. If an Asian woman works in one market, then another market duplicates it. So why test for an Asian male?"
- Asian women allow television stations to fulfill two equal-opportunity slots with one hiring. As Mario Machado, a Los Angeles-based reporter and producer puts it, "They get two minorities in one play of the cards. *They* hit the jackpot."
- Asian males are typically encouraged by parents toward careers in the sciences and away from communications.
- Because there are few Asian men on the air, younger Asian males have no racial peers as role models. With few men getting into the profession, news directors have a minuscule talent pool from which to hire.

And, according to Sumi Haru, a producer at KTLA in Los Angeles, the situation is worsening as stations are being purchased and taken over by large corporations. At KTTV, the ABC affiliate, "The affirmative action department was the first to go." At her own station, he public affairs department is being trimmed. "We're concerned with what little Asian representation we have on the air," said Haru, an officer of the Association of Asian-Pacific American Artists.

HONORS THESIS

Helen Chang, a communications major at UC Berkeley now working in Washington, DC, made the missing Asian anchorman the subject of her honors thesis. Chang spoke with Asian anchorwomen in Los Angeles, Chicago and New York as well as locally. "To capsulize the thesis," she says, "it is an executive decision based on a perception of an Asian image. On an executive decision level, the image of the Asian woman is acceptable."

"It's such a white bread medium; it's the survival of the blandest," says a male Asian reporter who asked to remain anonymous. A native San Franciscan, this reporter once had ambitions to be an anchor, but after several static years at his station, "I've decided to face reality. I have a white man's credentials but it doesn't mean a thing. I'm not white. How can it not be racism?"

"Racism is a strong word that scares people," says Tokuda.

"But whatever's going on here is some ugly animal. It's not like segregation in the south. What it is is very subtle . . . bias."

To Mario Machado, it's not that subtle. Machado, who is half Chinese and half Portuguese, is a former daytime news anchor in Los Angeles who's had the most national television exposure after Kashiwahara. Being half-Chinese, he says, has given him no advantage in getting work. "It's had no bearing at all. There's a move on against Asians, period, whether part-Asian or full-Asian."

TV executives, he charges, "don't really want minority males to be totally successful. They don't want minority men perceived as strong, bright, and articulate. We can be cute second bananas, like Robert Ito on *Quincy*. But having an Asian woman — that's always been the feeling from World War II, I guess. You bring back an Asian bride, and she's cute and delicate. But a strong minority man with authority and conviction — I don't think people are ready for that."

WAR IMAGE

Bruno Cohen, news director at KPIX, agrees that "for a lot of people, the World War II image of Japanese, unfortunately, is the operative image about what Asian males are all about."

That image, says Serena Chen, producer and host of *Asians Now!* on KTVU, was one of danger. "They may be small, but they're strong. So watch out, white women!"

The Vietnam war and recent movies like *Rambo*, Machado says, add to the historic negativity. "You never went to war against Asian women," he says. "You always went to war against Asian men."

Today, says Tokuda, Asian men are saddled with a twin set of stereotypes. "They're either wimpy — they have real thick glasses and they're small and they have an accent and they're carrying a lot of cameras — or they're a murderous gangster." "Or," says Les Kumagai, a former KPIX intern now working for a Reno TV station, "they're businessmen who are going to steal your jobs."

"The Asian woman is viewed as property, and the Asian male has been denied sexuality," says Chen. "Eldridge Cleaver created a theory of the black male being superglorified in the physical and superdecreased in the mental. It's very difficult for people to see a successful black male unless he's an athlete or a performer. If he's in a corporate situation, everyone says, 'Wow, he's the product of affirmative action.' That theory holds that in this society, people who have potential to have power have to be male, and have both mental and physical [strength] to be the superior male. In this society, they took away the black male's mental and gave him his physical. The Asian male has been denied the physical and given the mental."

Veteran KRON reporter Vic Lee listens to a tally of stereotypes and images associated with Asian men. "All those reasons limit where an Asian American

can work. I've always said to my wife, if I'm fired here, there're only a couple of cities I can go to and get a job based on how well I do my work, not how I look or what color my skin is. There are cities with Asian American populations, and you can count them on one hand: Seattle, Los Angeles, New York, Boston, and possibly Washington.

"The rest of the country? You might as well forget Detroit. They *killed* a [Chinese] guy just 'cause he looked Japanese." Lee is referring to Vincent Chin, who was beaten to death by two white auto workers who mistook him for a Japanese and blamed him for their unemployment.

'EXOTIC' FEMALES

In contrast to the threatening Asian male, says Les Kumagai, "Females are 'exotic.' They're not threatening to non-Asian females and they're attractive to non-Asian males. You're looking to draw the 18-to-45-year-old female demographic for advertising. You just won't get that draw from an Asian male."

To Tokuda, the Asian woman's persisting stereotype is more insidious than exotic. "It's the Singapore girl: not only deferential but submissive. It's right next to the geisha girl."

At KGO, says one newsroom employee, "somebody in management was talking about [recently hired reporter] Janet Yee and blurted out, 'Oh, she's so cute.' They don't care about her journalistic credentials. . . . That type of thinking still persists."

AGGRESSIVE

Janet Yee says she can take the comment as a compliment, but agrees that it is "a little dehumanizing." Yee, who is half Chinese and half Irish-Swedish, says she doesn't get the feeling, at KGO, that she was hired for her looks. Stereotypes "are the things I've fought all my life," she says, adding that she isn't at all submissive and deferential. "I'm assertive and outgoing, and I think that's what got me the job."

Emerald Yeh, who worked in Portland and at CNN (Cable News Network) in Atlanta before joining KRON, says she's asked constantly about the part being an Asian woman played in her landing a job. "The truth is that it's a factor, but at the same time, there is absolutely no way I can keep my job virtually by being Asian."

Despite the tough competition for jobs in television, Yeh, like Tokuda and several peers in Los Angeles, is vocal about the need to open doors to Asian men. "People think Asians have done so well," she says, "but how can you say that if one entire gender group is hardly visible?"

George Lum, a director at KTVU who got into television work some 30 years ago at Channel 5, has a theory of his own. "The Asian male is not as aggressive as the Asian female. In this business you have to be more of an extrovert. Men are a little more passive."

Headhunter Don Fitzpatrick agrees. "Watching my tapes, women in general are much more aggressive than men. . . . My theory on that is that — say a boy and girl both want to get into television, and they have identical SATs and grade point averages. Speakers tell them, you'll go to Chico or Medford and start out making $17,000 to $18,000 a year. A guy will say, 'This is bull. If I stay in school and get into accounting or law . . .' And they have a career change. A woman will go to Chico or Medford and will get into LA or New York."

"In Helen Chang's paper," recalls Tokuda, "she mentions the way Asian parents have channeled boys with a narrow kind of guidance."

"With Japanese kids," says Tokuda, "right after the war, there was a lot of pressure on kids to get into society, on being quiet and working our way back in." In Seattle, she says, "I grew up with a whole group of Asian American men who from the time they were in junior high knew they were going to be doctors — or at least that they were gonna be successful. There was research that showed that they were very good in math and sciences and not good in verbal skills. With girls there's much less pressure to go into the hard sciences."

Most of the men who do make it in broadcasting describe serendipitous routes into the field, and all of them express contentment with being reporters. "Maybe I'm covering my butt by denying that I want to anchor," says Kumagai, "but I do get a bigger charge being out in the field."

Still, most Asian male reporters do think about the fame and fortune of an anchor slot. Those thoughts quickly meet up against reality.

David Louie realizes he has little chance of becoming the 6 o'clock anchor. "I don't have the matinee idol look that would be the most ideal image on TV. Being on the portly side and not having a full head of hair, I would be the antithesis of what an anchorman is supposed to look like."

Kind of like KPIX's Dave McElhatton? Louie laughs. "But he's white," he says, quickly adding that McElhatton also has 25 years of experience broadcasting in the Bay Area.

At least Louie is on the air. In Sacramento, Lonnie Wong was a reporter at KTXL (Channel 40), and Jan Minagawa reported and did part-time anchoring at KXTV (Channel 10). Both have been promoted into newsroom editing and production jobs. And neither is thrilled to be off the air.

Wong, who says he was made an assignment editor because, among reporters, he had "the most contacts in the community," says his new job is "good management experience. But I did have a reservation. I was the only minority on the air at the station; and I know that's valuable for a station."

Minagawa's station, KXTV, does have an Asian on the air: a Vietnamese woman reporter named Mai Pham. "That made the decision easier," says Minagawa, who had been a reporter and fill-in anchor for seven years. A new news director, he says, "had a different idea of what should be on the air" and asked him to become a producer. "I didn't like it, but there was nothing I could do."

Mitch Farris rejects any notion of a conspiracy by news directors against Asian American men. In fact, he says, they are "desperate" for Asian male applicants. "Just about any news director would strive to get an Asian on the air and wouldn't mind a man."

To which Machado shouts, "We're here! We're here! We're looking for work."

Martin P. Levine

THE STATUS OF GAY MEN IN THE WORKPLACE

Work poses manifold meanings in modern American life (Julian and Kornblum, 1983:489–492). On one hand, it denotes the quality of our economic well being. For most of us, our job determines how much money we make, and this in turn affects how well we live. Work also signifies our social status. What we do for a living strongly influences how other people evaluate and rank us. And finally, work affects how we think about ourselves. What we do often determines how we feel about who we are.

Jobs hold additional meanings for men. For them, work demonstrates manliness (Pleck, 1982; Doyle, 1983). To prove their masculinity, men attempt to be breadwinners. This test applies most strongly for men, typically blue collar workers, who adhere to the traditional male role (Le Masters, 1975). These men demonstrate their manliness by earning enough to support a wife and family. Men who follow the modern male role, usually white collar workers or "yuppies," emphasize professional success (Ehrenreich, 1983; Gould, 1974). These men prove their masculinity by achieving corporate power, professional recognition, and high earnings.

Gay men experience great difficulty in meeting this manly test. The deep-seated cultural antipathy towards men who love men, called homophobia, prevents homosexuals from obtaining good jobs. Homophobia drives gay men into nonprestigious, low paying, white collar or service jobs, which are commonly regarded as unsuitable for men (Harry, 1982:181–183; Harry and DeVall, 1978:159–160). This, in turn, reinforces the popular impression of homosexuals as effeminate.

This article explores the status of homosexuals in the work force. After examining the prevailing stereotypes of gay men, I will consider the effect of these stereotypes on attitudes towards the hiring of homosexuals, and then examine how these attitudes provoke employment discrimination against gay men.

STEREOTYPES OF HOMOSEXUALS

Americans view homosexuals as "failed men."[1] Most of us equate masculinity with heterosexuality and believe that "real men" love women. We accordingly associate homosexuality with a spoiled masculinity—with a lack of the physical, emotional, or social characteristics of real men.[2]

The stereotypes of homosexuals incorporate these assumptions and include several interrelated images of gay men: (1) the swishy pansy, (2) the cultivated fop, (3) the diseased pervert, and (4) the immoral degenerate. The first two stereotypes link homosexuality with unmasculine behaviors and interests. As swishy pansies, gay men prance with mincing gaits, shriek in lisping voices, and dress in womanly garb. Their physiques, moreover, are puny and thin.[3] As cultivated fops, gays revel in haute cuisine, couture, and culture. They adore trendy food and nightspots, decorate and dress in the latest styles, and flock to the ballet, opera, and theater.[4] The last two stereotypes link homosexuality with unmanly illnesses and vices. As diseased perverts, gay men suffer from twisted erotic desires and illnesses. Their deranged upbringing fosters unnatural sexual interests, compulsive promiscuity, and susceptibility to AIDS.[5] As immoral degenerates, gay men are sex crazed, substance abusing, molesters of children. Their twisted emotions provoke uncontrollable urges for sex, liquor, and drugs, which prompts them to drink, snort cocaine, and molest young boys.[6]

ATTITUDES TOWARDS THE EMPLOYMENT OF HOMOSEXUALS

These stereotypes account for our conflicting attitudes towards the employment of gay men. On one hand, we endorse the principle of equal job opportunities for homosexuals (Schneider and Lewis, 1984:18). Americans have recently accepted the doctrine of equal opportunity in the work place, which by extension fosters support for equal job opportunities for racial, religious, and sexual minorities (Schneider and Lewis, 1984:18). A recent poll, for instance, found that nearly two-thirds of the public favored equal rights in the labor force for homosexuals (Gallup, 1982). On the other hand, we also favor banning gay men from particular lines of work. Americans oppose employing homosexuals for either jobs typically done by men, or jobs involving maternal duties (Schneider and Lewis, 1984:18).

Homophobic stereotypes account for these attitudes. Americans perceive homosexuals as swishy pansies and cultivated fops, and therefore consider gay men as unfit for the jobs traditionally assigned to men (Harry, 1982:181–183). "Men's work" expresses stereotypically masculine traits like rationality, toughness, and aggressiveness, which tend to be concentrated in high status, better paying, blue or white collar fields (Davidson and Gordon, 1979:72–75). Public opinion polls record extensive opposition to homosexuals doing men's work. By large pluralities, we disapprove of gay men working as judges, doctors, policemen, and government officials (Levitt and Klassen, 1974; Scheider and Lewis, 1984:18).

The stereotypes foster the belief that homosexuals *are* suitable for traditionally feminine jobs, "women's work" (Davidson and Gordon, 1979:72–75). These jobs embody traditionally feminine attributes like domesticity, compassion, and dependency. All of these jobs tend to be in low status, poorly paying, white collar or service fields (Benokratis and Feagin, 1985:52–53). Polls indicate widespread support for gay men doing nutrient, decorative, or expressive forms of women's work. By overwhelming majorities, we approve of homosexuals working as artists, beauticians, musicians, florists, and retail clerks (Schneider and Lewis, 1984:18; Levitt and Klassen, 1974). These jobs can be classified as "sissy work."

We do not, however, regard gay men as fit for all kinds of women's work. Americans also believe that homosexuals are diseased perverts and immoral degenerates, which evokes strong opposition to gay men doing jobs involving such maternal responsibilities as intimate contact, moral training, and the care of children. We believe that homosexuals are too "sick" for these jobs — their perverted nature will lead them to corrupt or molest young people. By huge pluralities, we disapprove of homosexuals working as clergy, teachers, principals, and camp counselors (Schneider and Lewis, 1984:18; Gallup, 1987).

EMPLOYMENT DISCRIMINATION AGAINST GAY MEN

Homophobic stereotypes provoke discriminatory practices against gay men in the work place (National Gay Task Force, 1981). Work associates share the cultural stereotypes of gay men, which cause them to hold extremely negative perceptions of homosexual workers. For example, employers and co-workers view gay men as swishy pansies and debauched lechers and they therefore believe that homosexual workers would dress like women and sexually harass people on the job (Maddocks, 1969:101–102). Employers also regard gay men as diseased perverts and they consequently believe that homosexual workers would be emotionally unstable, which would result in high rates of absenteeism and low rates of productivity (Weinberg and Williams, 1974:223–228; Bellard Weinberg, 1978:141–142).

These images affect the attitudes of workplace associates towards the employment of gay men in particular jobs. Employers and co-workers hold similar attitudes towards this issue as the general public, believing gay men to be unsuitable for traditionally masculine or maternal lines of work but fit for "sissy" jobs.

AIDS fosters additional negative perceptions of gay employees. Misconceptions about the nature of this disease appear to be fairly widespread. Despite all the evidence that AIDS cannot be spread by casual contact, many Americans believe that AIDS can be spread through such casual means as handshakes, bathroom facilities or shared work spaces (Institute of Medicine, 1988:67; Jennings, 1988:66).

This misconception influences the attitudes of workplace associates toward homosexual workers. Employers and co-workers view gay men as diseased perverts who are infected with the AIDS virus and consequently fear that homosexual employees will give them AIDS. In addition, employers worry about the high medical costs and lost productivity incurred by people afflicted with this disease (Leonard, 1975; Smothers, 1988; Hamilton et al., 1987).

These attitudes prompt job discrimination against gay men. This victimization can be either direct or indirect (Harry and De Vall, 1978:159). In direct job discrimination, workplace associates either harass gay men or discriminate against them in hiring, retention, and advancement. In indirect job discrimination, fear of victimization drives homosexuals into stereotypically "sissy" lines of work.

Direct Job Discrimination   This form of employment discrimination occurs primarily in jobs considered unsuitable for gay men. Many employers, in typically male or maternal fields, consider homosexuality grounds for not hiring, promoting, or retaining otherwise qualified individuals (Maddock, 1969). They consequently refuse to employ, advance, or retain gay men.

The practice of direct job discrimination varies according to openness about sexual orientation. Homosexuals differ in their ability to hide their sexual preference from work associates (Bell and Weinberg, 1978). Sociologists use the terms "discredited" and "discreditable" to describe these differences (Goffman, 1963:4). Discredited gay men are unable to hide their sexual orientation from work associates. The reasons for this are twofold: First, discredited men may be labeled homosexual in the official records of the courts, armed forces, and medical facilities. Employers regularly check these records, and consequently discover the homosexuality of discredited men (Levine, 1979). These men are involuntarily discredited.[7] Second, feelings of pride, self-affirmation or intimacy may compel discredited men to reveal their sexual preference to work associates (Troiden, 1988). These men are voluntarily discredited. Discreditable gay men are able to hide their sexual orientation from work associates. Employers and coworkers consequently are unaware of their sexual preference. Discredited and discreditable gay men are victimized differently during hiring procedures and after employment.

Hiring Procedures   Employers do not want to hire homosexuals. They therefore routinely ask questions during the hiring process that expose the homosexuality of discredited and discreditable men. These questions appear on standard application and interview forms. Nearly all forms ask prospective employees about their personal interests and background. More specifically, they inquire about prior criminal, military, medical, marital, and residential experiences. They also ask about hobbies and community service.

These questions place involuntarily discredited men in a classic double bind. If they answer the questions truthfully, they will disclose their sexual orientation and lose the job:

> I applied for a job at G.E. and told them about my discharge. He said he could have hired me if I had served my time in prison for murder but not with that discharge. The department stores told me, we're sorry but we don't employ homosexuals (Williams and Weinberg, 1971:116).

If they lie and hide their homosexuality, they will be terminated once the records are checked.

The questions concerning personal interests threaten the hiring of voluntarily discredited men. These men typically reveal their sexual preference while discussing pastimes or community service. To illustrate, they may state that they volunteer for a local gay charity. The effects of voluntary disclosure are documented in two recent studies. Adam (1982) investigated the hiring practices of law firms in Ontario, Canada. He sent each firm an application form and resume for an entry level position known as articling, which is open to recent law school graduates. The applications and resumes were identical except for the sex and sexual preference of the applicant. Sexual orientation was indicated by listing "active in local Gay People's Alliance" under the Personal Background section of the resume. The findings reveal that homosexual applicants were the least likely to obtain interviews; heterosexual men received 1.6 times more interview offers than gay men. The American Sociological Association's Task Group on Homosexuality investigated the employment practices of American sociology departments (Huber, 1982). The Task Group asked the heads of these departments about their ability to hire sociologists who were self-proclaimed gay or lesbian rights activists. More than half of the chairs reported that employing such activists would cause serious problems or that it just could not be done.

The questions about marital status, living arrangements, medical histories, and personal interests jeopardize the employment of discreditable gay men. Employers regard particular answers to these questions as evidence of homosexuality. They assume that men who state that they have never married, live with a male roommate, or dwell in a gay neighborhood are homosexual, as are men who report frequent exposures to sexually transmitted diseases or interest in the arts. These statements typically cost men the position.

Job interviews also endanger the hiring of discreditable gay men. Employers commonly check the applicant's demeanor and appearance for signs of homosexuality during the interview. They presume that men who are effeminate, well dressed, or slightly built are gay, and consequently refuse to employ them.

Placement agencies further threaten employment (Brown, 1976:163; Zoglin, 1974). These agencies regularly scrutinize prospective employees' application forms and interviews for evidence of homosexuality. Men evincing these signs are thought to be gay, and their forms are coded with a letter or number signifying homosexuality. Most agencies will not refer suspected homosexuals to potential employers because they believe that such referrals would damage business with these employers.

After Employment   Workplace associates, moreover, do not want to retain or promote gay men. They consequently ask questions after hiring that reveal the homosexuality of discredited and discreditable gay men. These questions appear in either standard personnel investigations or on-the-job conversations. Almost all employees conduct periodic investigations into the background of their staff, usually for purposes of promotion or retention. These investigations commonly inquire about arrest records, sexual orientation, and personal life.

The arrest questions expose the homosexuality of involuntarily discredited men. Many of these men have been arrested after hiring for such homosexual offenses as sodomy, solicitation for illegal sexual conduct, or loitering for purposes of engaging in deviant sexual intercourse (Boggan, et al., 1983).[8] Employers discover these arrests while checking police records, and therefore detect the men's homosexuality, which may cost them the job or promotion.

The questions about sexual preference jeopardizes the employment of discreditable men. Many employers require these men to answer direct questions about their sexual orientation during polygraph (lie-detector) tests that disclose false replies to the questions. Employers frequently fire or deny promotions to men whose test results indicate that they lied about being gay.

Polygraph tests put discreditable gay men in a "no-win" situation. If they take the test, they will disclose their homosexuality and lose their job or promotion. If they refuse to be tested, they will also be fired or denied promotion:

> I had to turn down a job offer which was conditional on my agreement to take a lie-detector test, because I was afraid they would ask The Question (Jay and Young, 1979:706).

The questions about personal lives further threaten the jobs of discreditable men. Employers typically question these men about their living arrangements, recreational interests, and friendship circles. They perceive certain kinds of answers to these questions as evidence of homosexuality. They presume that men who report living with other men, attending cultural events, or associating with gay people, organizations or gathering places are homosexual. These answers cost men the job or promotion.

Industrial intelligence agencies are often used to verify the answers concerning personal lives (Levine, 1979). These agencies frequently utilize investigative procedures that encroach upon constitutional rights to privacy. Some of these procedures include secretly monitoring daily activities and interrogating family, friends, and neighbors:

> Lloyd, at age fifty-three, had worked his way up from a door-to-door salesman for a large insurance company to the point where in 1973, he was about to be promoted to a vice-presidency. . . . Lloyd was a homosexual who had been living for twelve years with a man he told neighbors and visitors was his cousin. In 1968 Lloyd's lover was crippled in an automobile accident and confined for the rest of his life to a wheelchair. Lloyd made him the beneficiary of his own life insurance policy, explaining to the company that he had an obligation to provide for a relative who was no longer able to work.
>
> As part of a final check on the man they were about to promote, the senior officers sent an investigator to speak with Lloyd's neighbors and to interview people in his "cousin's" hometown. The investigator used the standard ploy — the young man was about to become the beneficiary of an $80,000 insurance policy. His former neighbors talked freely, and the investigator soon learned that the man was in fact not related to Lloyd. Back in Lloyd's town, he learned that the two men had been living together for years. With the investigator's report in hand, the company officials called Lloyd in and demanded his immediate resignation. The word homosexual was not mentioned; they were too polite for that (Brown, 1976:151–152).

The media also informs employers about discreditable men's homosexuality. In many localities, news editors regard arrests for homosexual offenses and gay rights demonstrations as major news features. They consequently spotlight these arrests and demonstrations as front page or lead stories. These stories, moreover, usually include the names, addresses, occupations, and occasionally pictures of the offenders and demonstrators. Employers see these stories, discover an employee's homosexuality, and fire or deny this man a promotion:

> I was fired from my job I held for thirteen years (engineering management) because I am homosexual. They discovered this when a letter I wrote decrying oppression was published in the local newspaper (Jay and Young, 1979:705).

Co-workers also endanger the employment of discreditable men. Work associates are often the first to recognize that a colleague is gay (Harry and DeVall, 1978:161–162). Their suspicions arise from the disclosures men make about their private lives during on-the-job conversations.[9] For example, the men may show little interest in sports, dating or sex talk, or they may receive frequent telephone calls from male friends or roommates. Co-workers discriminate against men they presume to be gay. They either harass them into quitting or pressure employers into firing them:

> On the job I was ridiculed and made the butt of jokes until I retaliated by losing my head and temper over something minor, resulting in my dismissal (Jay and Young, 1979:705).

The other people used to abuse me because of it. Finally I got tired of pussyfooting around and complained about it and they told me I was through (Bell and Weinberg, 1978:144).

In addition, they may use this knowledge to advance their career at the expense of the man thought to be gay:

The guy was after my job. He suspected I was gay and started to spread it through the office, making all sorts of wisecracks, trying to damage my reputation. Eventually, the atmosphere in the office grew very hostile (Interview with author).

Homosexuals are further victimized in terms of job responsibilities. Many gay men find their work assignments curtailed after employers discover their homosexuality. They may be demoted to a less responsible position or transferred to a job beneath their qualifications (Zoglin, 1974):

The owner of a Portland-based international firm recruited a 44-year-old man for a position as director of marketing. The owner found out that this man was homosexual and wanted to fire him immediately, but because the company was in financial difficulty he was kept on. After a year his responsibilities were gradually taken from him until he resigned (Task Force on Sexual Preference, 1978:47).

Special Cases of Direct Job Discrimination: Occupational Licenses and Security Clearances   A wide range of jobs, in both private industry and the civil service, demand occupational licenses or security clearances. According to one count (Boggan, et al., 1983:25), over 350 different fields require occupational licenses, including such diverse trades as doctor, teacher, and barber — and about 7 million people work in licensed jobs. In addition, many positions within the Defense and State Department demand security clearances, as do thousands of jobs in security-related research and manufacturing industries. Approximately 2.2 million people work in these industries (Boggan, et al., 1983:53).

The agencies authorized to grant occupational licenses routinely discriminate against gay men. Virtually every jurisdiction has created special boards for administering occupational licensing. These boards issue licenses, which are certificates stating that an individual is authorized to engage in a particular occupation, on the basis of legally proscribed professional and moral standards. The professional standards specify certain skill levels, age requirements, work experiences, and educational backgrounds. The moral standards prohibit licensing people who either lack "good moral character" or have committed criminal offenses or unprofessional conduct. The boards construe homosexuality as evidence of "moral failure" and consequently revoke or refuse to grant licenses to gay men, which prevents them from working in their field:

My chief of service, a well-meaning but misguided man who had used me as a resident for four years, had a delayed guilt reaction for having "harbored" a homosexual. He decided that he must tell the truth for the good of all concerned. So he informed the ACS (American College of Surgeons) and my specialty board that I was a homosexual. To their credit, the ACS approved my membership, making me an FACS (Fellow of the American College of Surgeons). The specialty board, however, turned down my request to take the exam on the grounds of "poor moral character. . . . This lack of formal certification meant I might not be reappointed to my hospital and raised questions about my competency. It delayed my career as a neurosurgeon (Brown, 1976:154).

My arrest record [for a homosexual offense] caused my California teacher's license to be rescinded. I'm not allowed to teach in the public schools because of it (Bell and Weinberg, 1978:144).

Homosexuals are also regularly victimized in the awarding of security clearances. A handful of government agencies (such as the federal Defense Industrial Security Office and the Civil Service Commission) grant such clearances, which are documents permitting the holder access to classified information about matters pertaining to the national security. These agencies perceive homosexuality as a threat to the national security. First, they believe that gay men are too emotionally unstable to keep classified information secret. Second, they believe that gay men can be easily blackmailed into divulging official secrets through threats of exposing their homosexuality (Walters, 1986). The agencies thus revoke or refuse to issue security clearances to gay men, which prevents them from working in their field:

I lost my security clearance and am unable to get one. My field was industrial health, radioactive stuff. It requires a security clearance. Anyone that could use me has defense contracts and because they have defense contracts they can't use me. I applied for three or four jobs and they asked for my discharge [Undesirable discharge for homosexuality] and said, "Sorry, we can't use you" (Williams and Weinberg, 1971:118).

The rationale for such discriminatory actions is seriously flawed. There is no evidence that gay men are more emotionally disturbed that straight males. Studies of matched samples of homosexual and heterosexual men show equal rates of psychopathology in both groups (Bell and Weinberg, 1978). Furthermore, gay men are not uniformly vulnerable to blackmail. Voluntarily discredited men cannot be blackmailed about something that is evident. In addition, discreditable men are susceptible only because disclosure of their homosexuality would cost their job. Employment discrimination not homosexuality makes them vulnerable to blackmail.

Coping Strategies   Sociologists classify the tactics homosexuals use to cope with direct job discrimination as techniques for avoiding stigmatization (Goffman, 1963; Humphreys, 1972; ch 8). These strategies enable gay men to evade or lessen victimization. The most widely used tactics include passing, covering, and minstrelization.

Passing as heterosexual is probably the most commonly utilized technique, and is favored mainly by discreditable men (Troiden, 1988:52; Humphreys, 1972:28). In passing, homosexuals conceal their sexual orientation from work associates, which leads employers and co-workers to think that they are heterosexual. Gay men hide their sexual preference through subterfuge, suppression, and nondisclosure. Subterfuge involves overt pretenses of heterosexuality. To convince work associates that they are straight, homosexuals actively pretend to be heterosexual. For example, they may comment about the physical attractiveness of female associates, participate in the traditional lunch-time pastime of "girl-watching," or bring female dates to job-related social events:

> I will often be eating lunch with one of the vice presidents or the controller or somebody, and the talk will get to sex — as it always does. I will play along. For example, when we comment on girls, they all know what my type is (Zoglin, 1974:27).

Dates, moreover, usually pose as girl-friends, fiancees, and even wives:

> I work in an extremely homophobic organization. To protect myself, I married a woman. She was an illegal alien and married me to stay in the country. I married her for a cover. Everyone at work thinks I am straight because I am married (Interview with author).

Suppression entails concealment of evidence of homosexuality. To keep their sexual orientation secret, gay men consciously hide features of their private lives that are considered signs of homosexuality. For example, they purposefully avoid telling work associates that they have male roommates, vacation in gay resorts, or attend the opera. Finally, nondisclosure involves covertness about erotic preference. In this strategy, gay men stop either pretending to be straight or concealing signs of their homosexuality. They instead behave as naturally as they can without revealing their sexual orientation.

Covering constitutes the second most widely used tactic for evading discrimination. In covering, homosexuals convince work associates that they are "normal" by dressing and acting like conventionally masculine men. This strategy enables discredited men to show employers and co-workers that they are not like stereotypical homosexuals, which hopefully thwarts victimization. It also allows discreditable men to deflect any suspicions about their sexual orientation:

> My image at work is decidedly conservative. I always wear dark Brooks Brothers suits, with cuffed pants, button-down shirts, and tortoise shell glasses. I always talk about sports. My act is so straight that no one would think that I am gay (Interview with author).

Passing and covering entail significant psychological and occupational costs. Both techniques involve careful, even tortuous, monitoring of behavior and talk, which generates tremendous feelings of strain and inauthenticity. Anxiety over the possibility of exposing one's homosexuality and then being discriminated against further heightens the anguish (Weinberg and Williams, 1974:226–228). In addition, these techniques require social distance from employers and co-workers, which impedes advancement because promotion often depends on socializing or being friendly with work associates.

Discredited men also avoid victimization through mistrelization. In this strategy, gay men either seek jobs or form businesses (typically small retail establishments) in culturally approved fields dubbed sissy work (Whitam and Marthy, 1986:84–86). These occupations embody traditionally feminine behaviors and are considered suitable for homosexuals (Table 1):

> Women usually expect a hairdresser to be homosexual. They aren't threatened by it (Bell and Weinberg, 1978:145).

TABLE 1   SISSY WORK

Feminine Field	Occupations
Nurturient Jobs	
Helping professions	Nurse, librarian, secretary
Domestic work	Cook, counterman, airline steward, bellhop, bartender, waiter, orderly
Decorative Jobs	
Home-related	Interior decorator, florist
Grooming	Fashion designer, hairdresser, model
Commercial arts	Graphic designer, window display
Expressive Jobs	
Arts	Dancer, musician, artist
Entertainment	Actor, singer

Note. The listed occupations are illustrative not exhaustive.

There are a number of gays in interior decorating, and it makes things easier in terms of the rest of society. They kind of expect it (Bell and Weinberg, 1978:145).

Furthermore, being gay is generally an asset in these fields because homosexuals actively hire and advance one another (Harry and De Vall, 1978:156):

Most people in display are queer. It's been easier at times to get ahead because I am homosexual (Bell and Weinberg, 1978:145).

Indirect Job Discrimination   Minstrelization constitutes a form of indirect job discrimination and negatively affects the occupational position of gay men. To shield themselves from possible discrimination, some homosexuals avoid jobs in which they anticipate victimization, and instead choose fields in which they are tolerated:

My whole goals are affected. I have to choose a job where I won't be discriminated against (Bell and Weinberg, 1978:144).

They accordingly shun higher-status, better-paying lines of men's work for lower-status, poorly-paying forms of sissy work:

Homosexuality forced me out of the service and caused me to become a hairdresser because here only I could be myself (Saghir and Robins, 1973:174).

Moreover, these jobs tend to be below their educational qualifications (Harry and DeVall, 1978:157–160):

There are plenty of gay Ph.D's waiting tables in San Francisco (Interview with author).

The unusual occupational distribution of gay men flows from indirect discrimination (Levine, 1979). Researchers consistently report high levels of educational attainment among gay men (Harry and DeVall, 1978:155). For example, more than two thirds of Harry and DeVall's (1978:155) homosexual respondents — and about three quarters of Bell and Weinberg's (1978:277) had at least some college education. Yet gay men are often unable to convert their educational qualifications into high income and status jobs. Indirect discrimination forces them to cluster in marginal white collar or service jobs (Harry and DeVall, 1978:156–157).

Extent of Discrimination   No one knows exactly how often gay men are victimized in the workplace. Our inability to do representative sampling in the homosexual community prevents us from obtaining precise measures of this problem (Levine, 1979). Representative sampling requires knowing the size and location of the population under investigation. These parameters are unknown for the gay community. (No exhaustive listings of the homosexual population are presently available.)

There are, however, some empirical studies of homosexual behavior that provide limited data on the magnitude of this problem. (These studies are listed in Table 2.) All of these studies used questionnaires to investigate the social and psychological adjustment of gay men. The questionnaires, moreover, included a few items about employment discrimination. For example, four of the 145 questionnaire items in Weinberg and William's (1974) research — and three out of the 528 items in Bell and Weinberg's (1978) study pertain to job discrimination.

The picture that emerges from these data shows that gay men anticipate and encounter significant victimization in the workplace. More than three quarters of the homosexuals interviewed in Weinberg and William's (1974:106) research feared that there would be problems at work if it became known that they were gay. The men worried primarily about punitive reactions from work associates. Almost half felt that their employers would be intolerant or rejecting; about two fifths expected co-workers to behave similarly.

The studies that uncovered actual instances of discrimination demonstrated that such fears are not groundless. In Williams and Weinberg's (1971:98) work, 16 percent of the respondents lost or were refused jobs because of their homosexuality. Similar figures appear in other studies. Saghir and Saghir (1973:174) discovered that 16 percent of their sample was fired or asked to resign after detection of their sexual orientation. In a later study, Weinberg and Williams (1974:109) found that 16 percent of their respondents lost a job after their homosexuality became known. Finally, Bell and Weinberg (1978:362) reported somewhat lower figures — 7 percent of their sample lost or almost lost a job due to erotic preference, and 6 percent were denied better work assignments.

The studies also showed that a considerable percentage of homosexuals believed that their sexual orientation has adversely affected their careers by making them vulnerable to discrimination. Nearly one third of Weinberg and Williams' (1974:108) sample felt that their homosexuality caused them problems on the job. This proportion holds in two other studies. Approximately one third of Saghir and Robin's (1973:172) sample believed that their sexual preference limited their choice of work or their career advancement. In addition, almost a third of William's and Weinbergs' (1971:98) respondents felt that their sexual orientation negatively influenced their economic lives. Likewise, one quarter of Bell and Weinberg's (1978:361) sample believed that their homosexuality adversely affected their careers.

Two of the studies collected data on coping strategies among homosexual workers. Most gay men passed for heterosexual on the job. Nearly three quarters of Weinberg and Williams' (1974:106) respondents — and more than half of Bell and Weinberg's (1978:96) concealed their sexual orientation from employers. Passing appears to be less common with co-workers. Only two fifths of Weinberg and Williams' (1974:106) sample — and one third of Bell and Weinberg's (1978:296) hid their homosexuality from all of their co-workers.

When taken together, these studies afforded a somewhat muddled picture of the scope of employment discrimination. We can, however, obtain a clearer image through a secondary analysis of the data presented in all four studies. We can reanalyze this data to compute approximate measures of victimization because all of the studies posed similar questions about job discrimination and looked at similar samples. (All of the researchers used large but nonrepresentative samples recruited from gay organizations and gathering places, and all of the samples came from urban areas.)

In determining the overall extent of the victimization, we defined perceived adverse consequences as the belief that homosexuality negatively affected careers, and actual discrimination, as firing, nonhiring, or nonpromotion. We calculated the percentages of gay men who perceived adverse consequences or experienced discrimination by dividing the number of respondents in all of the studies which asked questions about these factors by the number who answered these questions affirmatively (Tables 2 and 3).

Nearly one third of the homosexuals surveyed felt that their sexual preference had negatively affected their careers, and almost one sixth of the men had actually experienced job discrimination. The only comparable estimates for lesbians are quite similar, with 31 percent of the lesbians surveyed anticipating victimization in the workplace and 13 percent actually encountering discrimination (Levine and Leonard, 1984).

Although certainly imposing, these figures offer only an imprecise measure of the extent to which gay men are victimized in employment, and most likely represent a low estimate. There are three reasons for making this claim. First, all the data come from self-report studies in which gay men are queried about their experiences with job discrimination. Yet homosexuals are often unaware

TABLE 2   EXTENT OF PERCEIVED ADVERSE CAREER CONSEQUENCES OF HOMOSEXUALITY AMONG GAY MEN

Studies	Gay Men Perceiving Adverse Career Consequences (%)
Williams and Weinberg (N = 63)	29
Saghir and Robins (N = 89)	32
Weinberg and Williams (N = 1057)	30
Bell and Weinberg (N = 665)	25
All four studies (N = 1874)	30

TABLE 3   EXTENT OF ACTUAL EMPLOYMENT DISCRIMINATION
AMONG GAY MEN

Studies	Gay Men Experiencing Discrimination (%)
Williams and Weinberg (N = 63)	16
Saghir and Robins (N = 89)	16
Weinberg and Williams (N = 1057)	16
Bell and Weinberg (N = 665)	7
All four studies (N = 1874)	13

of being discriminated against on the job (Harry and DeVall, 1978:161). Employers may be too frightened of adverse public reaction or may be too embarrassed to acknowledge that sexual orientation is the reason for not hiring, promoting, or retaining a gay man. They therefore conceal the real motive for taking discriminatory actions by stating that, for example, the position has already been filled or that the homosexual employee was incompetent or unqualified. Second, the gay men participating in these studies lived in cities where, according to various polls, residents are far more accepting of homosexuality than nonurban dwellers (Schneider and Lewis, 1984; Gallup, 1987). In fact, all of these studies included men who lived in San Francisco or New York, cities well known for their acceptance of homosexuality.

CONCLUSION

Whatever the precise statistic may be, homosexuals are clearly victimized in the workplace. Homophobic stereotypes cause employers and co-workers to routinely discriminate against gay men in traditionally masculine lines of work. To cope with this victimization, homosexuals use psychologically taxing or professionally damaging tactics. Moreover, fear of discrimination drives many gay men away from men's work and into sissy jobs, which functions to reinforce prevailing images of gay men as effeminate.

Not only does this discrimination waste promising talents, it also seriously reduces life chances of homosexuals. Many talented and qualified gay men are working at positions far beneath their capabilities because of job discrimination, which robs our society of their potential contributions. In addition, discrimination erodes the ability of homosexuals to earn a living which adversely affects their life-style and self-esteem.

Anti-discrimination laws and policies are needed to curtail the victimization of gay men. A handful of localities have passed laws — and a number of companies have formulated personal policies barring employment discrimination on the basis of sexual orientation. It is time that these laws and policies become commonplace.

NOTES

1. I am indebted to Michael S. Kimmel for the concept of homosexuals as failed men.

2. Many Americans believe that homosexuals lack the genetic, hormonal, or familial makeup of real men, which is why they become gay. Familial explanations are perhaps the most popular of these perceptions. It is commonly believed that gay men grow up in households in which parents fail to follow traditional roles. Their mothers are overbearing and dominating; and their fathers, weak and passive, which causes homosexuals to hate women, love men and turn gay. Bell, et al. (1981) found no relationship between this kind of upbringing and adult homosexuality. Approximately equal number of homosexuals and heterosexuals grew up in such family settings.

3. Research indicates that most gay men are appropriately masculine in demeanor and appearance. Saghir and Robins (1973:106–8) evaluated the effeminacy of their homosexuals respondents, and found that only one sixth of their sample manifested womenly attributes.

4. The extent to which gay men display these interests is presently unknown. As best we can tell, such interests are not typical of all gay men. Saghir and Robins (1973:175) found that about two thirds of their respondents were interested in individual sports (e.g., swimming, tennis). About half were interested in the arts; a quarter in constructional hobbies like carpentry, and one tenth, in domestic pursuits (e.g., cooking, sewing).

5. Mental health professionals no longer classify homosexuality as an emotional disorder. In 1973, the American Psychiatric Association removed homosexuality from its official listing of mental illnesses. Heterosexuals are also vulnerable to AIDS; men and women can get AIDS from unprotected (without a condom) vaginal or anal intercourse.

6. Research demonstrates that homosexuals are not hypersexual pedophiles. Bell and Weinberg (1978) found that their homosexual sample was not overly interested in sex. DeFrancis (1976) reports that most instances of child molestation involve heterosexual men and young girls.

7. The evidence suggests that considerable numbers of gay men are involuntarily discredited. Forty one percent of the homosexuals questioned by Weinberg and Williams (1974:108) stated that they had been officially labeled as gay. The police and the military appear to be the most frequent labelers. Twenty five percent of the men reported being arrested for reasons related to their homosexuality. Saghir and Robins (1973:161) found, in a different study, that 20 percent of their sample had received a draft deferment or less than honorable discharge from the military for being gay.

8. The legal problems of homosexuals flow from the criminalization of the same-sex contact. Sexual relations between two men is considered a crime in nearly half the states. Moreover, many states criminalize solicitation or loitering for purposes of same-sex contact. These laws make gay men vulnerable to arrest (Boggan, et al., 1983).

9. Co-workers routinely share or overhear information about each other's lives. For example, they may regularly discuss their families, relationships, and pastimes with one another during coffee breaks or lunch hours. Such disclosures may cause them to suspect that an associate is homosexual.

REFERENCES

Adam, Barry D. 1981. "Stigma and Employability: Discrimination by Sex and Sexual Orientation in the Ontario Legal Profession." *Canadian Review of Sociology and Anthropology* 18(2):216–221.

Bell, Alan P., and Martin S. Weinberg. 1978. *Homosexualities: A Study of Diversity Among Men and Women*. New York: Simon & Schuster.

———, Martin S. Weinberg, and Sue Kiefer Hammersmith. 1981. *Sexual Preference: Its Development in Men and Women*. Bloomington, IN: Indiana University Press.

Benodraitis, Nijole V., and Joe R. Feagin. 1986. *Modern Sexism: Blatant, Subtle, and Covert Discrimination*. Englewood Cliffs, N.J.: Prentice-Hall.

Boggan, E. Carrington, Marilyn G. Haft, Charles Lister, John P. Rupp, and Thomas Stoddard. 1983. *The Rights of Gay People: Revised Edition.* New York: Bantam Books.

Brown, Howard. 1976. *Familiar Faces, Hidden Lives.* New York: Harvest/HBJ.

Chafetz, Janet Saltzman. 1974. *Masculine/Feminine or Human? An Overview of the Sociology of Sex Roles.* Itasca, IL: F.E. Peacock.

Davidson, Laurie, and Laura Kramer Gordon. 1979. *The Sociology of Gender.* Chicago: Rand McNally.

DeFrancis, Vincent. 1976. *Protecting the Child Victim of Sex Offenders.* Denver: The American Humane Association Children's Division.

Doyle, James A. 1983. *The Male Experience.* Dubuque, Iowa: Wm. C. Brown.

Ehrenreich, Barbara. 1983. *The Hearts of Men: American Dreams and the Flight From Commitment.* Garden City, N.Y.: Anchor.

Gallup, 1982. "Homosexuality." *The Gallup Report* 205 (October): 3–19.

———. 1987. "Homosexuality." *The Gallup Report* 258 (March): 12–18.

Goffman, Erving. 1963. *Stigma: Notes on the Management of Spoiled Identity.*

Gould, Robert. 1976. "Measuring Masculinity by the Size of a Paycheck." In *The Forty-Nine Percent Majority: The Male Sex Role,* edited by Deborah S. David and Robert Branan, 113–117. Reading, MA: Addison-Wesley.

Hamilton, Joan O.C, Julie Flynn, Patrick Houston, and Reginald Rhein, Jr. "The AIDS Epidemic and Business." *Business Week* March 23, 1987:122–126.

Harry, Joseph. 1982. *Gay Children Grown Up: Gender Culture and Gender Deviance.* New York: Praeger.

——— and William B. De Vall. 1978. *The Social Organization of Gay Males.* New York: Praeger.

Huber, Joan, Chair. 1982. "Report of the American Sociological Association's Task Group on Homosexuality." *American Sociologist* 17(3):164–88.

Humphreys, Laud. 1972. *Out of the Closets: The Sociology of Homosexual Liberation.* Englewood Cliffs, N.J.: Prentice-Hall.

Institute of Medicine. 1988. *Confronting AIDS: Update 1988.* Washington, D.C.: National Academy Press.

Jay, Karla, and Allen Young. 1979. *The Gay Report.* New York: Summit Books.

Jennings, Chris. 1988. *Understanding and Preventing AIDS: A Book for Everyone, Second Edition.* Cambridge, MA: Health Alert Press.

Julian, Joseph, and William Kornblum. 1983. *Social Problems: Fourth Edition.* Englewood Cliffs, N.J.: Prentice-Hall.

Le Masters, E.E. 1975. *Blue-Collar Aristocrats: Life Styles of a Working-Class Tavern.* Madison, WI: University of Wisconsin Press.

Leonard, Arthur S. 1985. "Employment Discrimination Against Persons with AIDS." *University of Dayton Law Review* 10(681):689–96.

Levine, Martin P. 1979. "Employment Discrimination Against Gay Men." *International Review of Modern Sociology* 9(5–7):151–63.

——— and Robin Leonard. 1984. "Discrimination Against Lesbians in the Work Force." *Signs* 9(4):700–710.

Levitt, Eugene E., and Albert D. Klasser, Jr. 1974. "Public Attitudes Toward Homosexuality: Part of the 1970 National Survey of the Institute for Sex Research." *Journal of Homosexuality* 1(1):131–134.

Maddocks, Lewis I. 1969. "The Law and the Church vs. the Homosexual." In *The Same Sex: An Appraisal of Homosexuality,* edited by Ralph W. Weltge, 95–112. Philadelphia: United Church Press.

National Gay Task Force. 1981. "You and Your Job — A Gay Employee's Guide to Discrimination." New York: National Gay Task Force.

Pleck, Joseph R. 1981. *The Myth of Masculinity.* Cambridge, MA: MIT Press.

Saghir, Marcel T., and Eli Robins. 1973. *Male and Female Homosexuality.* Baltimore: William L. Wilkens.

Schneider, William, and I.A. Lewis. 1984. "The Straight Story on Homosexuality and Gay Rights." *Public Opinion* 7(1):16–21.

Smothers, Ronald. 1988. "Survey Finds a Clash on AIDS in the Workplace." *The New York Times*. (February 7, 1988).

Task Force on Sexual Preference. 1978. *State of Oregon, Department of Human Resources, Final Report of the Task Force on Sexual Preference.*

Troiden, Richard R. 1988. *Gay and Lesbian Identity: A Sociological Analysis*. Dix Hills, NY: General Hall.

Walter, Dave. 1986. "NSA/CIA/FBI: Gays Need Not Apply." *The Advocate* 438 (January 21, 1986):10–12.

Weinberg, Martin S., and Colin J. Williams. 1974. *Male Homosexuals: Their Problems and Adaptations*. New York: Oxford University Press.

Whitam, Frederick L., and Robin M. Mathy. 1986. *Male Homosexuality In Four Societies: Brazil, Guatemala, the Philippines and the United States*. New York: Praeger.

Williams, Colin J., and Martin S. Weinberg. 1971. *Homosexuals and the Military*. New York: Harper and Row.

Zoglin, Richard. 1974. "The Homosexual Executive." *MBA* (July–August):26–31.

Harry Brod

WORK CLOTHES AND LEISURE SUITS: THE CLASS BASIS AND BIAS OF THE MEN'S MOVEMENT

The men's movement is predominantly made up of men who are middle class and white, with a large percentage having professional careers. Before we strategize about how to respond to that indictment, if it really is one, we had best understand the origins of that fact.

When movement men are asked about the reasons for the movement's class composition, and the impact of that composition on the goals of the movement and its position in the larger society, a pattern emerges in the responses. The dominant self-understanding of the men's movement on these questions can be summarized in the following distinct but related ideas:

1. Middle class men predominate in the movement because their greater access to financial resources, leisure time, and education gives them greater opportunities to entertain new ideas and break out of traditional roles. But the ideas and values of the movement — cooperation instead of competition, nurturing of self and others instead of exploitation of women's nurturing, expression rather than denial of positive emotions, sensitive, egalitarian relationships instead of aggressive domination, etc. — are in principle equally applicable and available to all men simply as men.
2. We are a minority vanguard, whose consciousness is in fundamental opposition to and in advance of the society around us. We are engaged in the task of giving up our male privileges and freeing ourselves from an oppressive system.

3. The reasons for seeking to broaden the class composition of the movement are essentially altruistic and moral. Middle class men must compensate for their greater privilege, and a movement whose values are as universal as ours should be representative of the population as a whole.
4. The basic issue in improving our outreach techniques is finding ways to bring the ideas current in the movement to other men. Probably the chief vehicle for this is individual consciousness-raising.

I believe that all of the above — the explanation of predominance of middle class men in terms of enlightened consumerism in the marketplace of ideas, the image of ourselves as a vanguard divesting itself of power, the moralistic basis of our outreach work, and the idealist emphasis on individual consciousness-raising in that work — are wrong.

ROOTS OF IDEOLOGY

To begin to understand why this outlook is wrong, we need to dispel the myth that the ideology of the men's movement arises apart from or outside the economic class system. What the movement likes to think of as a *counter*-culture is really a *sub*-culture which fits into a certain niche in American society. Rather than arising in fundamental opposition to the system, the men's movement develops from changes taking place within that system. Despite some rhetoric to the contrary, this has always been true of radical movements and ideologies. For example, the slogan "the personal is political" was not created out of thin air. It was a response to the pattern of twentieth century industrialization in which more and more of everyone's personal life is directly dominated by economic and political forces beyond their personal control. It was an attempt to meet this greater factual politicization of daily life on its own terms. The battleground is not chosen by the opposition, but by the dominant structures.

To situate men's movement ideology within the system does not lessen the radical potential of the movement. Rather, it increases it. It is a long-established truth of radical social theory that the system produces its own gravediggers. Were the movement not grounded in the internal dynamics of the system itself, it would not have the potential it does have. To understand this, we need to examine the relevant structural changes in the U.S. economy.

The economic system of the United States in the late twentieth century has shifted from manufacturing (e.g., steel, plastics, etc.) to service (e.g., information processing, public services, etc.), with a corollary transition from a work to a consumer ethic. These changes have especially affected the work and life styles of the middle classes. The values espoused by the "new male" — cooperation, self-expression, sensitivity, etc., — fit smoothly into this new economic reality. In the first place, the office or service worker, in contrast to the factory worker, must be more congenial, thoughtful, and presentable in appearance, because these jobs have a public relations component.

Equally important, the shift to a consumer ethic has meant that the performance principle of the older work ethic, which required men to repress their needs for gratification in order to channel their energy and resources into productive labor, has been replaced by an ethic of self-gratification through leisure pursuits outside of work. This loosens some of the restrictions and rigidities of traditional masculinity. The movement for sexual liberation is perhaps the most conspicuous result of this development.

Workers now define themselves less through their work itself, and more in terms of the consumer goods their wages purchase. Workers who once would have identified with their work and defined themselves as working class (i.e., those who work for a wage and do not control their working conditions) now identify with their standard of living (as defined by the purchasing power of their wages), and define themselves as middle class. Given this consumerism and lack of class consciousness of American society, it is only natural that men's movement rhetoric be filled with talk of "life-styles," "options," and "choices." We do not relate our ideas to the work we must do, but to the life-styles we choose to lead outside of work.

But we cannot go beyond the system or its ideology if we perpetuate its blindness to the material roots of our ideology. The men's movement must recognize that this new consciousness results from large-scale structural changes in economic life, not from the inspired enlightenment of a few individuals. Our strategies must be aimed not simply at individual ideological transformation, but at producing the concrete material transformations which can alone sustain this ideological growth. We must take this new consciousness back into the workplaces which produced it, and extend it into those which did not.

CRITIQUE OF STYLE

There are serious dangers in conceptualizing the movement as revolving around issues of "life-styles." "Styles" inevitably pass. This is the primary mechanism of co-optation. In the early 60s, for example, in revolt against artificiality and hypocrisy, some women rejected makeup, elaborate hair styling, constricting clothing, etc. in order to remain true to their natural selves. But when "looking natural" became "The Natural Look," complete with appropriate cosmetics, hair styles, and clothing now sanctioned by the fashion industry, the way was paved for this "New Look" to pass in a few years with a return to traditional fashions. Our economy is built on such periodic changes in style. Similarly, if men's new sensibilities are seen simply as part of the packaging of the "New American Man," it practically guarantees that we shall see a return to traditional styles of masculinity in a few years.[1] For this reason, the frequency of media appearances by movement superstars is not a reliable measure of the success of the movement.

The ambiguity of some current life-style changes is reflected in the growing industry in male cosmetics and jewelry. On the one hand, this represents a move away from thinking of the male body solely as a productive machine and toward an aesthetic sense of self, which is all to the good. On the other hand, however, under current market conditions it also represents an extension of commercial sexual exploitation and objectification from the female to the male body. To answer the question of whether this is really progress, the concept of "repressive desublimation" developed by philosopher Herbert Marcuse can be helpful. That is to say, this kind of aestheticization of the male body *does* liberate previously repressed erotic impulses (i.e., it "desublimates" them), but it does so in a way which extends the oppressive domination of the social order as a whole (i.e., potential liberation becomes greater confinement). Gay pornography would be another example of the same dynamics. The ambiguities here were captured by a remark Marcuse made in response to a comment by an interviewer that the guillotine, which quickly came to be regarded with horror, was originally invented as a more humane method of execution: "Such is the nature of progress in bourgeois society."[2]

WORK VS. LEISURE ETHICS

Over-emphasis on individual consciousness-raising promotes inattention to the social basis of change. This makes it more difficult to change the institutions which give rise to the values we want to be fighting, and it prevents large numbers of men from joining the movement. The split between male feminist leisure and work ethics is made clear in the following excerpts from Ross Wetzsteon's "The Feminist Man?":

> "To the extent that I'm able to learn from feminism in my private life," a Wall Street broker told me, "I'm a happier and freer person, but all those new values not only have no bearing on my work, they'd actively hamper me. I mean if I tried to 'relate' to a client 'humanely' instead of treating him as a dollars-and-cents abstraction, I'd be eaten alive."
>   . . . "One of the things feminism has done, in fact," an account manager told me, "is to make me feel schizophrenic. My home and work values are no longer of a piece."
>   . . . . "So it often happens in work situations that men who take their feminism seriously end up implicitly damaging their careers. After they've left for the day-care center, someone else remains to do that crucial piece of extra work on the big case, account, sale."[3]

Wetzsteon is acutely aware of the problem. Yet his response is typical of men's movement consciousness. Rather than attempting to develop a politics of workplace-oriented social change, he counsels retreating ever more deeply into consciousness alone.

A LIMITED CLASS PERSPECTIVE

The only way to prevent the men's movement from passing as just another fad, or remaining a retreat for a privileged minority, is to sink much deeper roots into the daily context of the majority of men's lives, and that means, above all, the workplace. The middle class men who make up the majority of the movement must move in two related directions: bridging the gap between work and leisure, in order to more thoroughly ground the movement in material life, and bringing feminism into men's workplaces at all levels of society, and not solely in their own strata. The movement can then reach the majority needed to bring about lasting social change.

Unfortunately, even when the movement addresses issues of work, it usually does so from a limited class perspective. The chapter on "Work" in Jack Nichols' *Men's Liberation: A New Definition of Masculinity*, one of the basic movement texts, exemplifies this. Nichols' criticisms of "big business" and "the corporate state" are made from the perspective of "the corporation employee" to whom "the rugged individualism projected in capitalist lore is lost as he sits in lushly carpeted offices where the faint clacking of typewriters can barely be heard above Muzak."[4] The entire discussion deals with men who take "business lunches," not men who are allowed only a lunch break. Insofar as he has anything to say about changing the structure of the economy, he idealizes an earlier stage of entrepreneurial capitalism where men "were not only risk-takers but also risk-creators."[5] He wants to enlighten, but ultimately retain, class hierarchy. He says nothing about collective organizing to give workers more control over their work, and hence greater possibilities of finding satisfaction in it. Rather than suggesting activist *involvement* in one's workplace, he advises psychological *withdrawal* from work, widening rather than closing the work/leisure dichotomy. He treats identification with one's work solely as a source of psychological stress in times of economic insecurity, rather than as a potential rallying point. While it is true that the reduction of one's sense of self to one's status as a worker is psychologically damaging and has been a part of traditional masculinity the movement is and should be challenging, it is also true that total withdrawal from identification with one's work is equally damaging.

Nichols holds up as models "successful men" who "have dropped out of the system to recapture a more vibrant sense of living."[6] This kind of romanticization of poverty, and the accompanying advocacy of downward mobility as a political strategy, is an affliction of the privileged, not found among the poor, to which the men's movement has been particularly vulnerable. The extremes to which this can be taken are evident in the following passage from the same chapter of Nichols' book:

> "Some Jewish survivors of Nazi concentration camps have detailed their discoveries of themselves after being stripped of all possessions. One writer, who had his doctoral thesis taken away, the gold removed from his teeth, and his clothing stolen, spoke of how he had found himself. . . . What he discovered were the values that stood at his core: those facets of character giving him dignity as a human being."[7]

While many did find in themselves previously undiscovered reservoirs of dignity and strength in the midst of the hell that was the Nazi camps, to offer this as an example of the virtues of lesser attachment to material possessions in the context of an affluent society is a shockingly insensitive trivialization of the experience of the holocaust.

While the moralistic strategy of downward mobility produces feelings of virtue on the part of the downwardly mobile, in reality its principal effects are increased competition for lower level jobs leaving the social structure unchanged. This strategy denies the movement access to positions of power, and alienates men who come from working class backgrounds. The feminist action would be to use the power granted one by the system subversively, against the institutions which grant it, rather than attempting to give up these positions of power.

We need to be clear that there is no such thing as giving up one's privileges to be "outside" the system. One is always *in* the system. The only question is whether one is part of the system in a way which challenges or strengthens the status quo. Privilege is not something I *take*, and which I therefore have the option of *not* taking. It is something that society *gives* me, and unless I change the institutions which give it to me, they will continue to give it, and I will continue to *have* it, however noble and egalitarian my intentions.

For example, counter-culture men who consider themselves ex-middle or upper class cannot divest themselves of the reserve security they gain from having the option of falling back on old family ties and funds, as well as skills learned in earlier times, an option not available to those whose poverty is forced and

not voluntary. And my relative safety in walking the streets, the added authority the timbre of my voice gives what I say, my peace of mind in knowing that
however dismal the economy or my personal finances become I will have an
advantage in seeking a job, are all aspects of male privilege embedded in social
structures, and not subject to my personal renunciation. While men who are
pessimistic about the possibilities of social change often express pride in having
at least surrendered their own privileges, this attitude reflects a fundamental
misunderstanding. To give up male privilege is impossible, to overthrow it is
not.

A POLITICAL PERSPECTIVE

In contrast to the individualistic, psychological orientation of middle class ideology, working class men tend to have a greater appreciation of the need for
organized political solutions. Here is another reason, in addition to simply
broadening our base and gaining political strength, why we need to increase
working class involvement in the movement. Working class culture embodies a
more politicized, rather than moralistic, consciousness. One of the most cherished of middle class illusions is the belief that simply behaving properly and
desiring that others do the same satisfies the demands of morality. This too is
part of the apolitical "life-style" manner in which movement issues are conceptualized. But it is naive to think it sufficient that men support progressive legislation as a matter of personal conviction but not organize other men to demonstrate this support; or that men remain content with not being rapists without
working to make the streets safer for women.

Working class men tend not to view middle class privileges as the fault of the
individual men who possess them. In contrast, middle class men often respond
to their class privilege with guilt and project this feeling onto others. For example, I attended one men's workshop in which participants were asked to identify themselves in part through their work. As the high percentage of academics
became apparent, the academics began introducing themselves apologetically,
with embarrassed attempts at self-effacing humor. Finally, one working class
man stated that he and, he thought, other working class men were pleased with
the success the other men had attained and expected them to use these positions
in progressive ways. But their self-demeaning attitudes made him skeptical
about whether they were using these positions to anyone's benefit, since they
were having such difficulty standing up even for themselves.

This personalized guilt is simply the other side of the coin of the personal
pride middle class men often take in their enlightened feminist consciousness.
The social, historical explanation of the origins of this consciousness presented
earlier should help depersonalize these issues and remove both the unwarranted
guilt and pride. Eliminating the former is necessary and prevents middle class
men from using their power effectively. Eliminating the latter is necessary because it hinders outreach to working class men. When middle class men try to
communicate the ideas of the movement to working class men, the assumption
that one's "higher" consciousness is due to one's own ideas and sensitivities,
rather than to the material conditions of one's life, feeds an intellectual elitism
which, however subtle it may be in the consciousness of those speaking, comes
across loud and clear to the working class men doing the listening.

WORKPLACE ISSUES

To make the movement more relevant to working men's lives, we need to focus more attention on workplace issues in a way which demonstrates their relation to antisexist consciousness. A key opening for the men's movement is to challenge conditions of work for men in the name of feminist ideology. To begin with, as men become more involved in raising children, issues of day care, flexible working hours, and parental leave are less and less seen exclusively as women's issues. Furthermore, feminism fosters more non-authoritarian and humane working environments.

Occupational safety should become a central male feminist issue. Like the issue of sexual harassment for the women's movement, occupational safety may become one of the best examples of a class-based male feminist politics, one where we can stress the connections between class and sex injustices. We face an ideology which says men are supposed to be tough and able to take harsh conditions. To complain is to show unacceptable weakness. A little danger even adds to the masculinity of the job. Here sexist ideology reinforces the mistreatment of male workers. This connection was vividly illustrated during the struggle for ERA ratification. Twelve of the 15 states which failed to ratify also have strong anti-union, so-called "right to work" laws.

It is clearly in men's interests to humanize the workplace at all levels and make it a safer and more hospitable environment, whether the dangers be radioactivity, pollution, machine failure, or psychological stress. The movement should serve as a support network, finding better ways for men to deal with work-related health hazards than the traditional male responses leading to alcoholism, ulcers, tension headaches, heart problems, and, ultimately, early deaths.

Our movement needs to be aware of where this may already be happening, even when it may not fit our pre-conceived notions of what "liberated" men look like. One of the first major demonstrations the Reagan administration faced was by coal miners demonstrating for, among other things, better health care and safety inspections in the mines. These demands go far toward breaking the traditional male mold. The men's movement should have been there.

Addressing working class issues more directly may also be one of the best ways the men's movement can support the women's movement. Feminism suffers from an underrepresentation of working class women in the movement. One of the reasons for this has been that working class women have perceived feminism as a movement designed to gain middle class women access to their husbands' jobs. For working class women, access to *their* husbands' jobs is more clearly seen simply as equal rights to exploitation. By challenging the conditions of work, feminism becomes more attractive to the working class. While middle class activists sometimes bemoan the lack of radicalism of the working class — supposedly evidenced by their lack of participation in the movement — it is rather the case that middle class feminism, in stopping short of calling for major economic change, has not offered enough to the working class. The extent to which feminism has not been embraced by the working class is the extent to which feminism has not been radical enough.

Finally, much male violence, domestic and otherwise, is a recycling of abuse men receive at work but feel powerless to resist there. Aiding that resistance is essential to the crucial anti-violence aspect of our movement. A humanized workplace is the inescapable precondition for a more humane world.

I believe the changes I have recommended in how we conceive of ourselves and what issues we raise are fundamental and necessary to the growth of the men's movement. However, new directions in theory alone will not alleviate the underrepresentation of working class men in the movement. We also need to change our practice, which has often alienated working class men. A movement is more than its ideology, and if middle class backgrounds continue to determine the ethos of the movement, we shall remain an isolated minority. I shall turn now to examine anti-working class bias in our rhetoric and conduct.

IMAGERY, LANGUAGE & OPPRESSION

Much of the imagery of the movement reflects class bias. When the drawbacks of the male role are lamented, the focus is usually on the hardships of men in middle and upper class positions. For example, all the examples from Wetzsteon's article quoted earlier fit this mold, and in the chapter on "work" in *The Male Machine*, Marc Feigen Fasteau devotes 20 pages to the upper levels of corporate and professional life, and 4 pages to "factory workers and clerical staff."[8]

When the oppressive behaviors of sexism are criticized, however, the focus is usually on working class stereotypes: hard hat jeers, pin-ups on the shop floor, the violent jock, etc. This discrepancy perpetuates two myths: that working class men are more sexist than other men, and that the refinements of "upper" class life are a prerequisite for the "higher" consciousness of sexism. Yet many women, when the conversation moves past rhetoric to real feelings, admit that they sometimes prefer the direct sexism of traditional men. They know that it often comes coupled with direct support and action, rather than the condescending, pseudo-tolerance they find in many middle class men, which may not directly offend, but cannot be counted on for solid support.

Much of what the men's movement validates as liberated or scorns as traditional is simply a preference for middle class over working class style. This is manifest in areas like the "mellowspeak" adopted by many movement men. With the laudable intention of avoiding traditional masculine power plays, we have on occasion instituted a new form of power — those who conform to middle class styles are listened to, and others not. Martha Cotera quotes Charlotte Bunch's *Class and Feminism* on what Cotera calls "the most maddening classist behavior":

> "Often middle- and especially upper-middle-class women for whom things have come easily develop a privileged passivity . . . Because she has made it by following nice middle-class rules of life, she doesn't like for people to be pushy, dogmatic, hostile, or intolerant . . . and may resist taking a hard political stand or alienating anyone."[9]

Issues of style are intimately related to issues of language, which also reflects class bias. For example, Warren Farrell's *The Liberated Man*, another popular movement book, contains the following as the first entry in the "Introducing Human Vocabulary" chapter, which recommends liberating changes in our language:

"Attaché: (atɔ•shā'; pronounced like attaché case; spelled the same in masculine or feminine form) *An attaché is a person with whom one has a deep
emotional attachment.*[10]

What kind of alienated class consciousness can find in the emotions associated
with an "attaché case" a model for "deep emotional attachment"? How likely is
it that working class men could adopt this vocabulary?

Another example of falsely generalizing from a middle class perspective is the
pressure often exerted on all gay men to come out publicly. While public identification has important political significance, for many working class men who
fear for their jobs this is a life-style luxury they cannot afford. And their family
relationships are often at greater risk as well. Working class family members are
often too dependent on each other to envisage the aloof tolerance middle class
gay men may at least hope for from their families, and they are too familiar
with the experience of oppression to allow a family member to invite additional
oppression when it seems to them it could be avoided.

There are other falsely generalized men's movement issues relating to forms
of oppression other than class, and these should be discussed in their own right.
To give just one example here, emphasis on men touching and hugging each
other is correctly seen as an important issue in an Anglo-Saxon context, where
there are such strong taboos against it. But for many Third World men, whose
cultures do not carry these inhibitions, continual emphasis on the politics of
hugging leaves them baffled and alienated.

TOUGHEN UP

Sensitivity to class and cultural differences is essential so that middle class sensibilities are not imposed where inappropriate. To take an example with which
many will be familiar, the film *Coal Miner's Daughter* contains a particular scene
subject to conflicting interpretations. Early in the film, the Loretta Lynn character is afraid to perform on stage for the first time, a performance arranged by
her husband without her knowledge. She runs into the bathroom followed by
her husband, who yells at her, acts violently, and threatens further violence by
his tone and stance. When she asks why he's doing all this, he responds that it
makes him feel good to see her perform. She performs, and is a rousing success.

By the usual standards of the men's movement, his behavior is despicable. If
he wished to be supportive in the approved style, he would have "respected her
autonomous choice" not to perform. Indeed, his setting up the engagement in
the first place was a serious violation of her independent initiative. And his
reasons for doing this, emphasizing *his* feelings, are certainly invalid. Now, to
the extent that he unconsciously plays out traditional patterns of male domination, these criticisms are sound. Indeed, it is imperative that men be very
sensitive to the issues of physical and emotional violence in male–female relationships. In fact, later in the film we see how this kind of male pressure leads
her to a nervous breakdown, and we also see how self-destructive his violence
is. However, the movement errs in dismissing a certain kind of assertiveness
out of hand without regard to context. One can also imagine cases where, as a
consciously chosen strategy, this kind of behavior might be the best way to
communicate a supportive attitude to a woman in a way she could receive it. In
such a case, nonintervention under the rhetoric of respect for her autonomy
would really be a euphemism for leaving her stuck where she was, a kind of

"benign neglect." In particular cases, the gains and losses of filtering positive support through an oppressive context must be weighed. If done consciously, this kind of behavior which makes one look more aggressive in another cultural context may be exactly what is required in some situations. One can of course self-righteously condemn his behavior for not fitting the approved model, but I and many other feminists cheered to see such aggressive support for a woman from a man.

We must realize that since working class culture differs from middle class culture, working class feminism will also differ from middle class feminism. Middle class men have a lot to learn from these kinds of interchanges. Much that gets validated as non-aggressivity and sensitivity is really middle class timidity and "niceness," cultural inhibitions against letting the rough edges of life show through. As Marilyn French put it in an interview, "The problem with a lot of men who adopt feminist values is they believe that in order to be decent and good they have to give up all force, all strength, and all assertiveness."[11] Put simply, the men's movement needs to get tougher.

UNITING DIVERSE TRADITIONS

To emphasize this is not to romanticize the working class or to claim that oppression makes the oppressed more virtuous. It doesn't. Oppression damages people's psyches and there is much in typical working class behavior which needs to be changed. But this can be criticized only while appreciating that there are also real examples of strength and brotherhood here which can serve as models for all men. This is true of men in the military, for example, as well as of factory workers.

There are valid reasons why so many men reserve a special affection for the camaraderie shared with their old "army buddies." The tragedy is that it takes the fear of death for the barriers between men to drop enough for these feelings to develop. Support for men forced into militaristic behavior, including support for veterans' programs, is a necessary part of a broad-based men's movement. We must identify and eliminate our attitudes which prevent veterans from identifying themselves at men's movement events. There is no contradiction between being anti-war and supporting men from the military.

There are areas in which a counter-culture orientation of some movement men has posed problems. These men draw nurturance at gatherings from rituals of group meditations, chanting, hugs, faerie circles, and so on. But if traditional men were to come to a men's gathering, they would be put off by such rituals. Ways need to be found to allow these cultural expressions to take place without alienating either those to whom all this is foreign (and possibly offensive) or those who cherish this space to freely enjoy these ceremonies. Perhaps some sort of welcoming explanation should accompany all such rituals (e.g., an opening meditation is like a morning cup of coffee, but chanting has no known negative side effects).

An overly-simplistic egalitarianism and middle class guilt over privileges sometimes fuse to form a destructive anti-intellectualism and anti-leadership tone in the movement. This can result in the suppression of the abilities of analytic thinking, articulateness, leadership, and assertiveness which our sexist society has predominantly encouraged men to develop. But this attitude subverts the potential of the movement, and represents the ultimate victory of an oppressive ideology which splits mind from spirit and gives us negative models of intellect and leadership precisely to discourage us from developing our own.

SUMMARY

To summarize, I would like to recall the four ideas that I claimed at the beginning of this article characterized the ideology of the men's movement, and ask the reader to contrast them with the following theses, based on the analysis I have presented:

1. Middle class men predominate in the movement because their socialization through their role in the economy brings them to oppose traditional concepts of masculinity. While at one level the values the movement espouses are universal, in practice its ideas and issues reflect the concerns and life-styles of these men.
2. Men's movement consciousness grows directly out of the dynamics of our society. Since we are of necessity embedded in the system, we cannot give up our privileges, but we can work at overthrowing the system that grants them.
3. We must broaden our class composition for our own survival. To do this we must raise more work-related issues at all levels of society.
4. Successful outreach to working class men necessitates changes in current practices which exclude or alienate them, and a greater focus on institutional, political change, without which consciousness-raising cannot sustain itself.

CONCLUDING PERSONAL NOTE

I would like to end on a personal note, one I hope will also be educative for my readers. As I was writing this article, I found myself getting angry over the issues I was raising. My first reaction was to be proud of myself for having internalized my politics to such a degree that I was feeling other people's indignation as my own. As I continued to write, however, it became clear to me that this explanation was insufficient to account for the intensity with which I was having these feelings. I was driven to look inward to find what in me was resonating so deeply to these questions. I remembered that the political significance of an action is determined more by context than by content. While working class men will experience the dynamics of language and style discussed here as classist, Third World men will experience the same dynamics as racist. The nature of oppression depends on the experiences of the oppressed, not the perspective or intentions of the oppressor group. I, being white and not from a working class background, however, experience the model of "gentility" I was writing about as anti-Semitism, because I identify with my Jewish heritage those parts of me *I* have to repress in order to "pass" in the WASP ethos of the movement. I decided to include this point because I learned a good deal from these reflections, wanted to pass it on, and thought it an appropriate note on which to end.

NOTES

1. Bob Greene, "Watching a Grown Man Cry," *Los Angeles Times*, January 24, 1980, Part IV, p. 1, col. 1.
2. Herbert Marcuse, *Gespräche mit Herbert Marcuse*, ed. Günther Busch, Suhrkamp, Frankfurt, 1978, p. 153 [my translation].

3. Ross Wetzsteon, "The Feminist Man?," in *The Women Say: The Men Say: Women's Liberation and Men's Consciousness*, ed. Evelyn Shapiro and Barry M. Shapiro, Dell, 1979, p. 28.

4. Jack Nichols, *Men's Liberation: A New Definition of Masculinity*, New York, Penguin, 1975, p. 123.

5. Ibid., p. 133.

6. Ibid., p. 129.

7. Ibid., p. 131.

8. Marc Feigen Fasteau, *The Male Machine*, New York, McGraw-Hill, 1974, pp. 115–143.

9. Martha Cotera, "Among the Feminists: Racist Classist Issues," in Shapiro, p. 236.

10. Warren Farrell, *The Liberated Man*, New York, Bantam, 1975, p. XXIX.

11. Marilyn French, "An Interview with Marilyn French," Duane Allen, *M. Gentle Men for Gender Justice*, No. 2, Spring 1980, p. 25.

◆ ◆ ◆

PART SIX

Men and Health: Body and Mind

Why did the gap between male and female life expectancy increase from two years in 1900 to nearly eight years today? Why do men suffer heart attacks and ulcers at such a consistently higher rate than women do? Why are auto insurance rates so much higher for young males than for females of the same age? Are mentally and emotionally "healthy" males those who conform more closely to traditional cultural prescriptions for masculinity, or is it the other way around?

The articles in this section, though focusing on different specific topics, tend to follow and develop the argument of the men's liberation movement of the mid-1970s: Men do enjoy privileges in patriarchal society, but they often pay a heavy price. Narrow, emotionally inexpressive cultural prescriptions for masculinity are not only "stressful," they are in fact "lethal" for men. Alan Alda's article opens this section with a discussion of the "warning signs of testosterone poisoning" — a humorous code term for a socially learned cumpulsively narrow masculinity. On a more serious note, the article by Harrison, Chin, and Ficarrotto explores the specific causes of men's lower life expectancy — higher rates of heart disease, cancer, and death by accident or suicide. Three-quarters of the reasons for men's earlier deaths, they argue, have to do with "the male sex role": men rarely ask for help at early signs of physical or emotional troubles; men may deal with stresses by internalizing them and/or by turning to alcohol, tobacco, or other drugs; men take more unnecessary risks driving cars, in their work and in recreation; and men are more successful in their attempts at suicide than are women.

In the next article, Barry Glassner demonstrates how dominant conceptions of masculinity are encoded in and symbolized by the development of muscular male bodies. Alongside these dominant cultural conceptions of masculinity, there have always been masculinities that have been marginalized and subordinated. Martin Duberman, in a moving personal account of being gay in the 1950s, shows how his own personal and relational problems — and, by extension, those of hundreds of thousands of closeted gay men — were directly linked to the system of compulsory heterosexuality in which they lived. Only a social movement such as that which flourished in the 1970s could redefine gay sexuality as "healthy," and thus provide a context in which gay individuals, connected with one another rather than isolated, could begin to feel better about themselves and their relationships.

Interestingly as gay men were countering the social disease of homophobia in the 1970s, another disease was making inroads in their communities. The AIDS epidemic, according to Kimmel and Levine, has brought homophobes back out of their closets. Yet they argue compellingly that AIDS *not* be viewed as a "gay disease," but that we analyze the relationship between AIDS and masculinity. Echoing the more general discussions of men and health that preceded them, Kimmel and Levine conclude that "until we change what it means to be a real man, every man will die a little bit every day."

"O.K., let's confront the issues of masculinity!"

Alan Alda

WHAT EVERY WOMAN SHOULD KNOW ABOUT MEN

Everyone knows that testosterone, the so-called male hormone, is found in both men and women. What is not so well known is that men have an overdose.

Until now it has been thought that the level of testosterone in men is normal simply because they have it. But if you consider how abnormal their *behavior* is, then you are led to the hypothesis that almost all men are suffering from *testosterone poisoning.*

The symptoms are easy to spot. Sufferers are reported to show an early preference (while still in the crib) for geometric shapes. Later, they become obsessed with machinery and objects to the exclusion of human values. They have an intense need to rank everything, and are obsessed with size. (At some point in his life, nearly every male measures his penis.)

It is well known that men don't look like other people. They have chicken legs. This is symptomatic of the disease, as is the fact that those men with the most aviary underpinnings will rank women according to the shapeliness of *their* legs.

The pathological violence of most men hardly needs to be mentioned. They are responsible for more wars than any other leading sex.

Testosterone poisoning is particularly cruel because its sufferers usually don't know they have it. In fact, when they are most under its sway they believe that they are at their healthiest and most attractive. They even give each other medals for exhibiting the most advanced symptoms of the illness.

But there is hope.

Sufferers can change (even though it is harder than learning to walk again). They must first realize, however, that they are sick. The fact that this condition is inherited in the same way that dimples are does not make it cute.

Eventually, of course, telethons and articles in the *Reader's Digest* will dramatize the tragedy of testosterone poisoning. In the meantime, it is imperative for your friends and loved ones to become familiar with the danger signs.

Have the men you know take this simple test for —

THE SEVEN WARNING SIGNS OF TESTOSTERONE POISONING

1. *Do you have an intense need to win?* When having sex, do you take pride in always finishing before your partner? Do you always ask if this time was "the best" — and gnaw on the bedpost if you get an ambiguous answer?

2. *Does violence play a big part in your life?* Before you answer, count up how many hours you watched football, ice hockey, and children's cartoons this year on television. When someone crosses you, do you wish you could stuff his face full of your fist? Do you ever poke people in your fantasies or throw them to and fro at all? When someone cuts you off in traffic, do violent, angry curses come bubbling out of your mouth before you know it? If so, you're in big trouble, fella, and this is only question number two.

3. *Are you "thing" oriented?* Do you value the parts of a woman's body more than the

woman herself? Are you turned on by things that even *remind* you of those parts? Have you ever fallen in love with a really great doorknob?

4. *Do you have an intense need to reduce every difficult situation to charts and figures?* If you were present at a riot, would you tend to count the crowd? If your wife is despondent over a deeply felt setback that has left her feeling helpless, do you take her temperature?

5. *Do you tend to measure things that are really qualitative?* Are you more impressed with how high a male ballet dancer can leap than with what he does while he's up there? Are you more concerned with how long you can spend in bed, and with how many orgasms you have have, than you are with how you or your partner feels while you're there?

6. *Are you a little too mechanically minded?* Would you like to watch a sunset with a friend and feel at one with nature and each other, or would you rather take apart a clock?

7. *Are you easily triggered into competition?* When someone tries to pass you on the highway, do you speed up a little? Do you find yourself getting into contests of crushing beer cans — with the beer still in them?

If you've answered yes to three or fewer of the above questions, you may be learning to deal with your condition. A man answering yes to more than three is considered sick and not someone you'd want to have around in a crisis — such as raising children or growing old together. Anyone answering yes to all seven of the questions should seek help immediately before he kills himself in a high-wire act.

WHAT TO DO IF YOU SUFFER FROM TESTOSTERONE POISONING

1. *Don't panic.* Your first reaction may be that you are sicker than anyone else — or that you are the one man in the world able to fight it off — or, knowing that you are a sufferer, that you are the one man ordained to lead others to health (such as by writing articles about it). These are all symptoms of the disease. Just relax. First, sit back and enjoy yourself. Then find out how to enjoy somebody else.

2. *Try to feel something.* (Not with your hands, you oaf.) Look at the baby and see if you can appreciate it (not how *big* it's getting, just how nice she or he is). See if you can get yourself to cry by some means other than getting hit in the eye or losing a lot of money.

3. *See if you can listen while someone is talking.* Were you the one talking? Perhaps you haven't got the idea yet.

4. *Practice this sentence:* "You know, I think you're right and I'm wrong." (Hint: it is useful to know what the other person thinks before you say this.)

FOR WOMEN ONLY: WHAT TO DO IF YOU ARE LIVING WITH A SUFFERER

1. Remember that a little sympathy is a dangerous thing. The sufferer will be inclined to interpret any concern for him as appropriate submissiveness.

2. Let him know that you expect him to fight his way back to health and behave like a normal person — for his own sake, not for yours.

3. Only after he begins to get his condition under control and has actually begun to enjoy life should you let him know that there is no such thing as testosterone poisoning.

James Harrison, James Chin, and
Thomas Ficarrotto

WARNING: MASCULINITY MAY BE DANGEROUS TO YOUR HEALTH

In 1900, life expectancy in the United States was 48.3 years for women and 46.3 years for men. In 1984, it was 78.2 years for women and 71.2 years for men (U. S. Department of Health and Human Services, 1987). During this 84-year period life expectancy for both men and women increased by more than 24 years, whereas the difference increased from 2 years in 1900 to 7 years in 1984, consistently favoring women.

This difference grew consistently larger during the course of this century, reaching a peak difference between sexes of 7.8 years in 1975 and 1979. (Recent data suggest, however, that women's advantage is decreasing.)

The gains in life expectancy for both men and women can be attributed to better nutrition and improved health care. But how can the difference between men's and women's life expectancies and the consistent increase in the size of this difference during this century be explained?

Two general perspectives — a biogenetic and a psychosocial — can be distinguished. The former attributes men's greater mortality to genetic factors (Montague, 1953). The latter attributes men's greater mortality in large part to lethal aspects of the male role (Jourard, 1971). This article will evaluate these two perspectives, and assess what can most reliably be said about the consequence of male role behavior for life expectancy.

In comparison to women, there is for men a higher perinatal and early childhood death rate, a higher rate of congenital birth defects, a greater vulnerability to recessive sex-linked disorders, a higher accident rate during childhood and all subsequent ages, a higher incidence of behavioral and learning disorders, a higher suicide rate, and a higher metabolism rate, which may result in greater energy expenditure and a consequent failure to conserve physical resources. In the biogenetic perspective, this broad range of reported physical, psychological, and social sex differences is interpreted as a direct or mediated consequence of genetic differences. These differences are understood to be causally and cumulatively related, and to result in a higher mortality rate for men. There is a quality of inevitability in this perspective — biology is seen as destiny with a vengeance — but in this case males are understood to be in the less favored position. Taken all together, and without consideration of other factors, this perspective constitutes a plausible explanatory system for an array of apparently correct data.

In contrast, the alternative psychosocial perspective hypothesizes that the greater mortality rate of men is at least partially a consequence of the demands of the male role and emphasizes the ways in which male role expectations have a deleterious effect on men's lives, and possibly contribute to men's higher mortality rate. One of the complexities of this sociocultural hypothesis is the problem of specifying what is meant by "male role expectations." This is no simple task.

DEFINING THE MALE ROLE

Brannon (1976) has provided the most detailed and systematic attempt to delineate the various components of the male role. Although noting its elusive quality and the apparent contradictions within it, he abstracts four themes or dimensions that seem to be valid across all specific manifestations of stereotyped male role behavior. He characterizes these components in four short phrases:

1. No Sissy Stuff: the need to be different from women.
2. The Big Wheel: the need to be superior to others.
3. The Sturdy Oak: the need to be independent and self-reliant.
4. Give 'Em Hell: the need to be more powerful than others, through violence if necessary.

Clearly men express more positive and socially valued characteristics than described by these four themes. The attempt to define a normative role specific for only one sex necessarily results in a distorted model of human potential. The fiction that men and women are opposites is perpetuated. The recognition that men and women are essentially similar in what constitutes their humanity although manifesting a range of individual differences both within and between each sex is ignored. It is consequently possible to understand why the attempt to conform to male role expectations has negative consequences for men.

Jourard (1971) assumed that men's basic psychological needs are essentially the same as women's: all persons need to be known and to know, to be depended upon and to depend, to be loved and to love, and to find purpose and meaning in life. The socially prescribed male role, however, requires men to be noncommunicative, competitive and nongiving, and inexpressive, and to evaluate life success in terms of external achievements rather than personal and interpersonal fulfillment. All men are caught in a double bind. If a man fulfills the prescribed role requirements, his basic human needs go unmet; if these needs are met, he may be considered, or consider himself, unmanly. Jourard contended that if these needs are not met, persons risk emotional disorder, they may ignore somatic signals with a resultant failure to seek health care, possibly develop greater vulnerability to illness, and even lose the will to live.

Going beyond Jourard's general assessment, Rosenfeld (1972) has argued that the growing-up process by which boys become men has been made into an achievement or a task rather than a natural unfolding of human potentiality. By what criteria can a boy ever know that he has fulfilled the requirements of the male role? Adults are of little help in clarifying expectations for children, because they too are confused by apparent uncertainties about and inconsistency within male role expectations. Hartley (1959) long since observed that unclear sex-role expectations for children are a major source of anxiety. If severe enough and persistent, such anxiety may lead to serious emotional difficulty that may cause, or contribute to, behavioral and learning disorders.

One way children cope with anxiety derived from sex-role expectations is the development of compensatory masculinity (Tiller, 1967). Compensatory masculine behaviors range from the innocent to the insidious. Boys naturally imitate the male models available to them and can be observed overemphasizing male gait and verbal patterns. But if the motive is a need to prove the right to male status, more destructive behavioral patterns may result, and persist into adulthood. Boys are often compelled to take risks that result in accidents; older youth often begin smoking and drinking as a symbol of adult male status (Farrell, 1974); automobiles are often utilized as an extension of male power; and some men find confirmation of themselves in violence toward those whom they do not consider in conformity to the male role (Churchill, 1967). A convincing case has been made by both Fasteau (1974) and Komisar (1976) that readiness to settle international conflict by war rather than diplomacy is a function of prevalent male role expectations.

In addition, the requirements of the male work role have also been implicated as a cause of men's greater mortality. It has been suggested that stress and the competition to get ahead may result in greater vulnerability for men (Slobogin, 1977).

DATA RELEVANT TO THE BIOGENETIC AND
PSYCHOSOCIAL HYPOTHESES[1]

Madigan's early study (1957) remains influential in defense of the biogenetic perspective because its claimed empirical basis gave it evidential status that the psychosocial hypothesis has only recently begun to amass. The current debate is rightly focused on data about rates of conception, birth, and death that can be attributed to genetic causes, on the one hand, and data about rates of death that can be correlated with sex-role-related behavior.

Rates of Conception and Prenatal Mortality   In spite of the theoretically equal opportunity for parity in male and female conceptions (the primary sex ratio), the known ratio of male to female births (the secondary sex ratio) consistently favors males. This ratio is reported variously as between 103:100 and 106:100 (Tricomi, Serr, & Solish, 1960; Parkes, 1967; Stoll, 1974). The preponderance of evidence suggests that the sex ratio at conception favors males to an even greater degree, but due to greater loss of males during pregnancy the amount of excess males at birth is reduced. Most studies show a higher ratio of males to females in induced abortions, which indicates a higher conception rate for males, and an even higher ratio of males to females in spontaneous abortions, which suggests that the male fetus is less viable. Accordingly the ratio of male to female conceptions is estimated to be between 108:100 and 120:100. It is therefore assumed that the male fetus is more vulnerable *in utero*.

---

1. Several methodological considerations should be noted: First, the psychosocial hypothesis utilizes a conception of causality involving the complex interaction of biological, psychological, and social factors. When assessing the claims of the psychosocial hypothesis, it is difficult to determine the degree to which illness is a consequence of any one factor, or an interaction among a combination of factors. Second, age must be taken into consideration when accounting for sex differences in mortality. For example, in middle life the incidence of death attributable to heart disease is greater for men than women. In old age the cause of death is frequently heart failure for both sexes. When data for all ages are taken together, the large sex differences at different ages are obscured. Third, sex differences in morbidity may be subject to observational and reporting errors, as well as response bias. In addition, mental illness contributes to physical illness, suicide, and death by accidental cause. Although women are assumed to suffer from mental illness more than men, this notion has been seriously challenged by health professionals (see Harrison, 1975). Finally there are limitations on the use of mortality data. Methods and criteria for collection have changed over time, and adequate data are still unavailable for many nonindustrial societies. Therefore comparisons over time and across cultures are made difficult.

TABLE 1   RATIO OF MALE TO FEMALE DEATHS (1982 DATA)[a]

Age in Years	Male:Female
Under 1	125:100
1–4	123:100
5–14	153:100
15–24	289:100
25–34	257:100
35–44	189:100
45–54	185:100
55–64	190:100
65–74	164:100
75–84	164:100
85 +	123:100

[a]Recalculated from data in *Vital Statistics of the United States*, 1982 (USDHHS, 1986).

Greater male mortality continues during early childhood: utilizing 1982 data, the ratio of male to female deaths due to certain causes in infancy is 140:100; and the ratio of male to female deaths at all ages, but attributable to congenital abnormalities, is 118:100. Due to an excess of male over female deaths from all causes, parity is achieved in the sexes ratio during the 25–34 year decade (Parkes, 1967). The excess of male over female deaths continues (see Table 1), resulting in an increasing ratio of females to males alive as age advances.

In sum, the genetic evidence suggests that the male fetus and the male neonate are more vulnerable prior to the time when sociocultural factors could exert an influence sufficient to account for a significant amount of the variance. These innate factors, however, are not sufficient to reduce the sex ratio to parity, since parity is not reached until early adulthood, the time of expected procreation. Subsequent to childhood the excess of the male over the female death rate cannot be attributed solely to biological differences between the sexes.

The greater *in utero* and perinatal mortality of males, along with the slightly higher mortality of males at later ages due to congenital anomalies, suggests the operation of a biological factor that may contribute to the overall higher mortality rate of men. In the absence of evidence to demonstrate the operation of social factors, a biologically reductionist explanation appears plausible. For this reason it is essential to examine the available data in which the possible effect of social factors can be discerned.

Current Adult Mortality   Mortality data, examined in terms of sex differences in specific causes of death, provide the best evidence for the psychosocial hypothesis. In his early study, Madigan (1957) attempted to determine why men had not benefited from technological advances in health care to the same extent as women. He compared the mortality rates in a sample of cloistered members of religious orders with population rates and he hypothesized that the life expectancy of the male "religious" would approach that of the female "religious" and exceed that of men in the general population, if differential mortality rates were due to male role-induced stress. He found no large departure of his subjects from population norms, and concluded that role strain makes only a small contribution to the differences and that biological factors are the chief source of variance.

Madigan recognized that the men and women subjects did not live under identical conditions — that cloistered men were more likely to drink and to smoke than women, for example. He overlooked completely, however, the consequences of the male subject's socialization into male role patterns prior to entering the religious orders, and the further possibility that a cloistered existence may have contributed to rather than reduced the strain that they experienced.

Enterline (1961) argued that a reductionist biological view could not be sustained when variations over time in specific causes of death in different age groups were examined. He identified several trends in the differential death rate between 1929 and 1958 that could not be simply attributed to biological causes: an increase in deaths due to lung cancer and coronary heart disease among 45- to 64-year-old males. Though he was not able to provide an explanatory hypothesis for these differences, in the absence of a satisfactory biological explanation Enterline concluded that environmental determinants were a more likely explanation.

Conrad (1962) extended the analysis of the determinants of differential mortality rates by specifically considering sociological factors. He identified a variety of means by which male role behaviors may contribute to the higher mortality rates of men: the higher accidental death rate at all ages, the greater physical and emotional strain of the male economic role, and the greater exposure to industrial hazards and contaminants.

Waldron and Johnson (Waldron, 1976, 1983a, 1983b; Waldron & Johnson, 1976) have focused attention on sex differences in causes of death by ranking all causes accounting for more than 1% of all deaths in descending order according to the ratio of male to female deaths. In their presentation the first seven categories and the ratio of male to female deaths in each were as follows:

1. Malignant neoplasm of the respiratory system (5.9:1).
2. Other bronchopulmonic disease (4.9:1).
3. Motor vehicle accidents (2.8:1).
4. Suicide (2.7:1).
5. Other accidents (2.4:1).
6. Cirrhosis of the liver (2.0:1).
7. Arteriosclerotic heart disease, including coronary disease (2.0:1).

All seven categories have sex-role behavior correlates, for example, the greater incidence and frequency of smoking, drinking, and propensity toward risk-taking and violence among men.

The present discussion utilizes Waldron's interpretive framework, but is based on more recent data (Tables 2 and 3). The criteria for inclusion of categories of cause of death in Tables 2 and 3 were (1) the 15 major headings defined in the *Vital Statistics* as leading causes of death, (2) following Waldron, all subcategories that account for more than 1% of deaths, and (3) subcategories that have high sex ratios.

There are several significant points of contrast with Waldron's presentation. The data in Tables 2 and 3 are ranked by percentage of deaths attributed to each cause, rather than by rank of the sex ratio, and it is not possible to know how all Waldron's categories compare with those here. In addition, Waldron omitted entirely the cerebrovascular category that accounts for 10.9% of all deaths in our 1972 data and 8.0% of all deaths in our 1982 data, and which in all subcategories account for more female than male deaths. The male to female

TABLE 2   CAUSES OF DEATH (1972 DATA)[a]

	Male/Female Ratio[b]	Male/Female Ratio	Percentage of Deaths
Diseases of the heart	418.5:310.3	1.35	38.5
Acute myocardial infarction	221.5:124.7	1.78	18.2
Chronic ischemic heart disease	157.9:151.4	1.04	16.3
Other	21.2:15.6	1.36	1.9
Malignant neoplasms	185.7:147.2	1.26	17.6
Bucal cavity and pharynx	5.3:2.0	2.65	0.4
Digestive organs	50.3:41.9	1.20	4.9
Respiratory system	60.3:14.8	4.07	3.9
Breasts	0.3:29.2	0.01	1.6
Genital organs	18.9:21.7	0.87	2.2
Urinary organs	10.5:4.8	2.19	0.8
Other	21.6:18.5	1.17	2.1
Lymphatic and hematopoietic tissue	10.5:8.4	1.25	1.0
Cerebrovascular diseases	94.0:110.5	0.85	10.9
Cerebral hemorrhage	17.1:18.2	0.94	1.9
Cerebral thrombosis	24.9:30.2	0.82	2.9
Other	51.6:61.6	0.84	6.1
Accidents	78.6:33.4	2.35	5.9
Motor vehicle	39.6:15.1	2.62	2.9
Other	39.0:18.4	2.12	3.0
Influenza and pneumonia	34.2:26.1	1.31	3.2
Diabetes mellitus	15.6:21.4	0.73	2.0
Certain causes in infancy	19.5:13.2	1.48	1.7
Cirrhosis of the liver	21.1:10.4	2.03	1.7
Arteriosclerosis	13.5:17.6	0.77	1.7
Bronchitis, emphysema, asthma	23.3:6.7	3.48	1.6
Suicide	17.5:6.8	2.57	1.3
Homicide	15.4:3.7	4.16	1.0
Congenital abnormalities	7.7:6.4	1.20	0.8
Nephritis and nephrosis	4.6:3.6	1.27	0.4
Peptic ulcer	5.1:2.5	2.04	0.4
All other	61.1:45.6	1.34	11.6

[a]Calculated from data in USDHEW (1976).
[b]Rate per 100,000 population.

ratio for homicides accounted for more than 1% of all deaths in 1972 and 1982 with a male to female ratio of 4.16:1 and 3.66:1, respectively, which would have qualified this cause of death for second place had the data been ranked as in Waldron's presentation.

It is also noteworthy that the *Vital Statistics* for the years 1972 through 1982 were analyzed for each of the 1972 major causes of death and it was determined that the 1982 statistics were within the limits of a linear trend model. This analysis was complicated by changes in categorization of major causes of death

TABLE 3   CAUSES OF DEATH (1982 DATA)[a]

	Male/Female Rate[b]	Male/Female Ratio	Percentage of Deaths
Diseases of the heart[c]	353.9:299.6	1.18	38.3
Acute myocardial infarction[c]	151.3:101.3	1.49	14.7
Old myocardial infarction and other chronic ischemic heart disease	113.2:108.7	1.04	13.0
Other forms heart disease	72.4:69.3	1.04	8.3
Hypertensive heart disease	7.9:10.0	0.79	1.1
Malignant neoplasms[c]	207.6:167.8	1.23	22.0
Buccal cavity and pharynx[c]	5.2:2.2	2.50	0.4
Digestive organs[c]	52.3:45.0	1.15	5.7
Respiratory system[c]	73.7:28.0	2.63	5.9
Breasts[c]	0.2:31.4	0.01	1.9
Genital organs[c]	21.9:19.2	1.14	2.4
Urinary organs[c]	10.7:5.3	2.01	0.9
Other[c]	24.8:21.2	1.17	2.7
Lymphatic and hematopoietic tissue[c]	10.5:9.2	1.14	1.2
Cerebrovascular diseases[c]	56.7:78.8	0.72	8.0
Cerebral hemorrhage[c]	8.1:9.1	0.89	1.0
Cerebral thrombosis[c]	10.0:14.3	0.69	1.4
Other[c]	38.6:55.4	0.69	5.5
Accidents[c]	58.4:23.8	2.45	4.8
Motor vehicle[c]	29.5:10.6	2.78	2.3
Other[c]	28.9:13.2	2.18	2.4
Chronic obstructive pulmonary disease and allied conditions	35.2:16.9	2.08	3.0
Bronchitis, emphysema, and asthma[c]	11.1:5.8	1.91	1.0
Pneumonia and influenza[c]	22.5:19.8	1.13	2.5
Diabetes mellitus[c]	12.6:17.1	0.73	1.4
Suicide[c]	19.2:5.6	3.42	1.4
Chronic liver disease and cirrhosis[c]	15.9:8.2	1.93	1.4
Arteriosclerosis[c]	9.4:13.6	0.69	1.4
Homicide and legal intervention[c]	15.4:4.2	3.66	1.1
Certain conditions originating in perinatal period	10.5:7.5	1.40	1.1
Nephritis, nephrotic syndrome, and nephrosis	8.1:7.5	1.08	0.9
Congenital abnormalities[c]	6.4:5.4	1.18	0.7
Septicemia	4.9:5.1	0.96	0.6
All other			11.2

[a]Calculated from data in USDHHS (1986).
[b]Rate per 100,000 population.
[c]Comparable to Table 2 (1972 data) categories.

that began in the 1979 *Vital Statistics* with the implementation of the use of the Ninth Revision of the International Classification of Diseases, 1975. Only those causes of death indicated by footnote *c* in Table 3 are directly comparable to similar categories in Table 2. Given these caveats, it was concluded that the statistics for the major causes of death in 1982 that also appeared within the 15 major causes of death in 1972 were not artifactual but consistent with trends through those years.

Examination of the differential mortality rates alone reveals nothing about the antecedents of specific causes of death. The importance of Waldron's analysis is her discussion of these antecedents in relationship to sex-role-related behaviors. Fulfilling the requirements of the male role is characterized as an achievement, not simply the consequences of natural growth and development; it is often bought at the cost of risk and stress. Anxiety about failure to achieve may result in compensatory behaviors designed to show outward conformity to the role. Compensatory behaviors involve risk-taking of various kinds that may lead to accidents, exhibition of violence, excessive consumption of alcohol, and smoking. Reciprocally, anxiety about failure to achieve male role requisites may result in denial of dimensions of human experience more stereotypical associated with women's role. This denial may result in the suppression of gentleness and emotion. These specific male behaviors seem to be significant antecedents to all the major causes of death in which male death rates exceed those of women by a ratio of 2:1, a convention established by Waldron as a criterion of a large sex difference.

Diseases of the Heart   In contrast to Waldron's 1967 data, the ratio of male to female deaths does not exceed the 2:1 ratio in the 1972 or 1982 data when considering all ages combined. The higher coronary heart disease (CHD) death rates among the elderly, however, obscure large sex differences in mortality ratios for the younger age groups. For instance, for individuals between the ages of 20–44 years old in 1982, the sex-morality ratio exceeds 4:1 for acute myocardial infarction and for old myocardial infarction; in the same year, it exceeds 2:1 for hypertensive heart disease.

A biogenetic explanation posits that the female advantage in CHD mortality can be attributed to the protective effects of endogenous sex hormones. This argument is based on several investigations that have found that postmenopausal and oophorectomized women (women who have had their ovaries removed) are at an increased risk for CHD (Waldron, 1976, 1983a). Research supporting a biogenetic explanation, however, has been criticized on the basis of methodological flaws and inconsistent findings.

Evidence that links men's greater vulnerability to CHD to sex differences in smoking patterns, as well as to sex differences in aggressive, "hard-driving," behavior, appears to be a stronger argument explaining the sex differential in CHD mortality.

Of the three major risk factors for CHD, cigarette smoking is far more prevalent in the American population than either hypertension or elevated serum cholesterol (U. S. Surgeon General, 1983). Generally, in the past a greater percentage of men have smoked cigarettes compared to women. The proportion of smokers, however, has declined steadily between 1960 and 1980 in both men and women. This decline was steeper among men than among women. In 1970, male smokers smoked 4.1 more cigarettes per day than female smokers, but in 1980 men smoked only 2.0 more cigarettes per day than did women. Although a greater percentage of men still smoked cigarettes in 1980, and continued to smoke a greater average number of cigarettes per day, the differences between the sexes in 1980 was less than that observed a decade earlier (U. S. Surgeon General, 1983). Thus, as the smoking patterns of women become more similar to that of men, we might expect differences between men's and women's death rates as a consequence of smoking-related causes to diminish.

Behavioral patterns are also related to differential risks for heart disease. The Coronary Prone Behavior Pattern, Type A behavior (Friedman & Rosenman, 1974) is characterized by competitive achievement, striving, time urgency, and a potential for hostility. Type A behavior has been associated with an increased risk of CHD mortality in both men and women (Cooper, Detre, & Weiss, 1981; Booth-Kewley & Friedman, 1987).

Considering the major components of Type A behavior, such as excessive aggressiveness and competitiveness, one might suggest that Type A behaviors are associated with traditional masculine sex-role characteristics. At least six investigations have found positive correlations between Type A behavior and self-rated masculine sex-role characteristics in both male and female students (Blascovitch, Major, & Katkin, 1981; DeGregorio & Carver, 1980; Grimm & Yarnold, 1985; Nix & Lohr, 1981; Stevens, Pfost, & Ackerman, 1984; Zeldow, Clark, & Daugherty, 1985).

Although Type A behavior has been cited as being more prevalent among men than women (see Chesney, 1983), women are by no means exempt from the development of Type A behavior. Sex differences in Type A behavior are apparently reduced once a comparison is made between men and women engaged in similar vocational activities (Ficarrotto & Weidner, 1987). In addition, employment outside the home appears to be a crucial factor in the expression of Type A behavior in women, and higher status occupations among women appear to be associated with higher Type A scores (Morell & Katkin, 1982). Thus, it appears that "sex differences" in Type A behavior might have less to do with gender and more to do with whether a person's putative societal role can be defined as traditionally male.

It should be noted that several prospective studies have failed to find a link between Type A behavior and CHD mortality (see Chesney, Hecker, & Black, 1987). In fact, Ragland and Brand (1988) found that among men who had already suffered a heart attack, Type A behavior was not associated with subsequent CHD mortality. It appears that certain components of the Type A pattern, such as hostility, might be more directly related to CHD mortality than overall Type A scores (Wright, 1988). Interestingly, men display more hostility than do women (Maccoby & Jacklin, 1974; Pleck, 1981; Waldron, 1976; Weidner, Friend, Ficarrotto, & Polowczyk, 1988). This raises the question of whether sex differences in hostility may contribute to men's higher CHD risk.

Malignant Neoplasms   Taking all types of cancer together, men are slightly more vulnerable than women. Utilizing Waldron's criterion, sex differences greater than 2:1 emerge in only four subcategories of malignant neoplasms. Of these, breast cancer is the only category in which women's risk is greater than men's, which seems largely a consequence of endocrine differences. The incidence of all other loci for cancer is greater for men.

Most relevant for this discussion, however, is the male to female ratio for cancer of the mouth and pharynx, 2.65 in 1972 and 2.50 in 1982, and of the respiratory system, 4.07 in 1972 and 2.63 in 1982. Both types of cancer are related to smoking, for which a higher rate is documented for men. Studies of the prevalence of smoking just prior to the 1982 data show that the amount of daily smoking among women was approaching that of men and that the age of onset for smoking was getting earlier for both sexes (Schuman, 1977).

The ratio of cancer of the urinary organs was 2.19 in 1972 and 2.01 in 1982. There is evidence that a high level of smoking increases the risk of cancer of the ureter, and is related to cancer of the bladder at all levels of smoking (USDHEW, 1973, 1974, 1975).

It is also important to note that due to different work roles men are also exposed more often and at a higher level to industrial carcinogens.

Other Respiratory Diseases   In 1982, men still smoked more than women, according to all the parameters by which smoking could be measured. The relevance of this difference is seen again in the 3.48 ratio (1972) and 1.91 ratio (1982) of male to female deaths attributable to bronchitis, emphysema, and asthma. Research findings are consistent across national and ethnic groups. Smokers have higher death rates from chronic bronchitis and emphysema proportionately to the number of cigarettes smoked. Smokers are also more frequently subject to other respiratory infections than nonsmokers and require a longer convalescence (USDHEW, 1973, 1974, 1975). In addition, exposure to air pollution and/or industrial pollutants potentiates the effect of smoking.

Cirrhosis of the Liver   More men than women drink alcohol and more men than women drink to excess by an approximate ratio of 4:1 (Cahalan, 1970; McClelland et al., 1972). Alcohol serves both as a symbolic manifestation of compensatory masculinity and as an escape mechanism from the pressure to achieve. It is not surprising that males should die from causes of death associated with excessive drinking to a greater degree than women; the ratio of cirrhosis of the liver is 2.03 (1972) and 1.93 (1982).

Deaths due to External Causes   Men die more frequently than women from four external causes of death: motor vehicle accidents, 2.62 in 1972 and 2.78 in 1982; other accidents, 2.12 in 1972 and 2.18 in 1982; suicide, 2.57 in 1972 and 3.42 in 1982; and homicide, 4.16 in 1972 and 3.66 in 1982. Abuse of alcohol is clearly implicated in many automobile fatalities, and is very likely a factor in other deaths due to external causes. The consistent excess of male to female deaths due to accidents of other kinds has led some interpreters to presume an innate accident-prone tendency among males. This interpretation, however, is inconsistent with the emphasis on greater skill development among males in this culture. Consequently the greater accident rate can be accounted for more readily by the different socialization of males to perform high-risk activities, the popular assumption that male children are tougher than females, and the subsequent development of compensatory masculine behavior among men as a means of validating their status as males (Cicone & Ruble, 1978).

The greater vulnerability of males to death by suicide and homicide can be understood as a consequence of the greater socialization of men to aggressive and violent behavior. This is especially notable in contrast to the greater rate of suicide attempts by women, which appear to be requests for help rather than a determination to end life. Women more frequently utilize less violent and less effective means of attempting suicide. In sum, differences in the sex ratio of all external causes of death, which account for more than 1% of all deaths, are plausibly related to sex-role socialization.

CONCLUSIONS

A critical reading of presently available evidence confirms that male role socialization contributes to the higher mortality rate of men. Recognizing the multiplicity of variables within the chain of causality, Waldron (1976) estimates that three-fourths of the difference in life expectancy can be accounted for by sex-role-related behaviors that contribute to the greater mortality of men. She estimates that one-third of the differences can be accounted for by smoking, another one-sixth by coronary prone behavior, and the remainder by a variety of other causes. Using more precise statistical techniques to analyze differences in male/female mortality rates in terms of antecedents to specific causes of death, Retherford (1972) attributes half of the differences to smoking alone.

Waldron's estimate that three-fourths of the current 7.0 year difference in life expectancy is attributable to socialization is plausible and concordant with the difference in life expectancy at the turn of the century of approximately 2 years. The evidence we have reviewed suggests that this portion of the variance may be attributable to biogenetic determinants (1983a). However, any biogenetic factor is exacerbated by male role socialization. Parents assume that male children are tougher, when in fact they may be to some degree more vulnerable than female children. Male children are also more likely to develop a variety of behavioral difficulties such as hyperactivity, stuttering, dyslexia, and learning disorders of various kinds. Maccoby and Jacklin's (1974) review of research on childhood sex differences lends little support to the view that these observed sex differences are genetically determined. Insofar as they may be biogenetically predisposed, certainly the development of more functional behavioral patterns should be the goal of the socialization process. Male socialization into aggressive behavioral patterns seems clearly related to the higher death rate from external causes. Male anxiety about the achievement of masculine status seems to result in a variety of behaviors that can be understood as compensatory.

During the period in which the ratio between men's and women's life expectancy has worsened, social policy in the United States, especially in preparation for war and national defense, has been overwhelmingly directed toward reinforcement and support of the stereotyped male role (Fasteau, 1974; Filene, 1974). Recognition of the lethal aspects of the male role has had to await the emergence of a critical theory of sex-role socialization free of the ideological commitment to the status quo. This has been inspired by a critique of traditional psychological research inspired by the feminist movement (Harrison, 1975) and has been focally articulated for men's roles by Pleck (1976, 1981).

In the psychosocial perspective, sex differences, apart from those specifically associated with reproductive function, are understood to be smaller, less biologically based, and less socially significant. This is demonstrated by the greater range of difference within each sex than the average differences between the sexes. Differences in learned personality traits are understood not to be a necessary function of the development of sexual identity, but rather a consequence of social expectation. Finally, learning only stereotypical sex-typed traits is understood to be a handicap rather than an asset.

Traditional sex-role ideology serves as a rationale for the inevitability of psychological sex differences and the traditional division of family, work, and social responsibilities. The newer role liberation perspective provides not only the basis of reassessment of psychological characteristics and social arrangements, but also a basis for the reinterpretation of many previously observed sex differences (Pleck, 1976, 1981; Miller, 1976). Research suggests that it is not so much biological gender that is potentially hazardous to men's health but rather specific behaviors that are traditionally associated with the male sex role that can be taken on by either gender (Weidner et al., 1988; Wright, 1988). Recent data indicating a slight trend of convergence between sexes in mortality due to specific causes correlated with the convergence of smoking habits between the sexes are supportive of the psychosocial hypothesis. As plausible as this conclusion is, it is nevertheless tentative given the multivariate nature of public health data that need to be thoroughly researched along with prospective health and gender studies (Stillion, 1985).

Contemporary research has failed to demonstrate the existence of important intrinsic psychological differences between men and women. However, research on sex-role stereotypes demonstrates the persistence of the belief in such differences in personality traits (Rosencrantz, Vogel, Bee, Brovermann, & Brovermann, 1968). This continuing belief brings to mind W. I. Thomas's famous dictum: "If men [people] define situations as real, they are real in their consequences" (1928, p. 572). It is time that men especially begin to comprehend that the price paid for belief in the male role is shorter life expectancy. The male sex-role will become less hazardous to our health only insofar as it ceases to be defined as opposite to the female role, and comes to be defined as one genuinely human way to live.

Ironically, Madigan, whose work (1957) continues to have an undeserved credibility in discussions of this issue, supported the best possibility of extending male life expectancy. For him, as for many in our society, a technological solution was more probable than the "profound cultural revolution" that he recognized the psychosocial thesis required. But it is precisely that profound cultural revolution that is our need. The best hope for both men and women is overcoming a view of development that turns maturation into a polarized sex-typed achievement.

REFERENCES

Blascovitch, J., Major, B., & Katkin, E. Sex role orientation and Type-A behavior. *Personality and Social Psychology Bulletin*, 1981, 7, 600–604.

Booth-Kewley, S., & Friedman, H. Psychological predictors of heart disease: A qualitative review. *Psychological Bulletin*, 1987, 10, 343–362.

Brannon, R. C. No "sissy stuff": The stigma of anything vaguely feminine. In D. David & R. Brannon (Eds.), *The Forty-Nine Percent Majority*. Reading, MA: Addison-Wesley, 1976.

Broverman, I., Broverman, D., Clarkson, F., Rosencrantz, P., & Vogel, S. 1970. "Sex Role Stereotypes and Clinical Judgments of Mental Health." *Journal of Consulting Psychology 34*: 1–7.

Cahalan, D. *Problem Drinkers*. San Francisco: Jossey-Bass, 1970.

Chesney, M. Occupational setting and coronary prone behavior in men and women. In T. Dembroski, G. Schmidt, & G. Blumchen (Eds.), *Biobehavioral Bases of Coronary Heart Disease*, pp. 79–90. New York: Karger, 1983.

Chesney, M. A., Hecker, M. H., Black, G. W. 1987. "Coronary-Prone Components of Type-A Behavior in the W.C.G.S.: A New Methodology." In B. K. Houston & C. R. Snyder (eds.) *Type-A Behavior Pattern: Current Trends and Future Directions*. New York: John Wiley, pp. 1–31.

Churchill, W. *Homosexuality in a Cross Cultural Perspective*. Englewood Cliffs, NJ: Prentice-Hall, 1967.

Cicone, M., & Ruble, D. Beliefs about males. *The Journal of Social Issues*, 1978, *34*, 5–16.

Conrad, F. Sex roles as a factor in longevity. *Sociology and Social Research*, 1962, *46*, 195–202.

Cooper, T., Detre, T., & Weiss, S. Coronary prone behavior and coronary heart disease: A critical review. *Circulation*, 1981, *63*, 1199–1215.

✓DeGregorio, E., & Carver, C. Type A behavior, sex role orientation, and psychological adjustment. *Journal of Personality and Social Psychology*, 1980, *39*, 286–293.

Enterline, P. Causes of death responsible for recent increases in sex mortality differentials in the United States. *Milbank Memorial Fund Quarterly*, 1961, *39*, 312–328.

Farrell, W. *The Liberated Man*. New York: Random House, 1974.

Fasteau, M. *The Male Machine*. New York: McGraw-Hill, 1974.

Ficarrotto, T., & Weidner, G. Sex differences in coronary heart disease mortality: A psychosocial perspective. Unpublished manuscript, 1987.

Filene, P. *Him/Her/Self: Sex Roles in Modern America*. New York: Harcourt, Brace, Jovanovich, 1974.

Friedman, M., & Rosenman, R. *Type A behavior and your heart*. Greenwich, CT: Fawcett Publications, 1974.

Grimm, L., & Yarnold, P. Sex typing and the coronary prone behavior pattern. *Sex Roles*, 1985, *12*, 171–177.

Harrison, J. A critical evaluation of research on "masculinity/femininity." Doctoral dissertation, New York University, 1975. *Dissertation Abstracts International*, 1975, *36*, 1903B. (University Microfilms No. 75-22890.)

Hartley, R. Sex role pressures in the socialization of the male child. *Psychological Reports*, 1959, *5*, 457–468.

Jourard, S. *The Transparent Self*. New York: Van Nostrand, 1971.

Komisar, L. Violence and the masculine mystique. In D. David and R. Brannon (Eds.), *The Forty-Nine Percent Majority*. Reading, MA: Addison-Wesley, 1976.

Maccoby, E., & Jacklin, C. *The Psychology of Sex Differences*. Stanford, CA: Stanford University Press, 1974.

Madigan, F. Are sex mortality differentials biologically caused? *Millbank Memorial Fund Quarterly*, 1957, *35*, 202–223.

McClelland, D., et al. *The Drinking Man*. Riverside, NJ: Free Press, 1972.

Miller, J. *Towards a New Psychology of Women*. Boston, MA: Beacon Press, 1976.

Montague, A. *The Natural Superiority of Women*. New York: Macmillan, 1953.

Morell, M., & Katkin, E. Jenkins activity survey scores among women of different occupations. *Journal of Consulting and Clinical Psychology*, 1982, *50*, 588–589.

Nathanson, C. Illness and the feminine role: A theoretical review. *Social Science and Medicine*, 1975, *9*, 57–62.

✓Nix, J., & Lohr, J. Relationship between sex, sex role characteristics, and coronary prone behavior in college students. *Psychological Reports*, 1981, *48*, 739–744.

Parkes, A. The sex-ratio in man. In A. Allison (Ed.), *The Biology of Sex*. Baltimore, MD: Penguin Books, 1967.

Pleck, J. The male sex role: Definitions, problems, and sources of change. *Journal of Social Issues*, 1976, *32*(3), 155–163.

✓Pleck, J. *The Myth of Masculinity*. Cambridge, MA: The MIT Press, 1981.

Ragland, D., & Brand, R. Type A behavior and mortality from coronary heart disease. *New England Journal of Medicine*, 1988, *318*, 65–69.

Retherford, R. Tobacco smoking and the sex mortality differential. *Demography*, 1972, *9*, 203–216.

✓Rosenfield, A. Why men die younger. *Readers Digest*, 1972, 121–124.

Rosenkrantz, P., Vogel, S., Bee, H., Brovermann, I., & Brovermann, D. Sex-role stereotypes and self-concepts in college students. *Journal of Consulting and Clinical Psychology*, 1968, *32*, 287–295.

Schuman, L. Patterns of smoking behavior. In Jarvik, M., Cullen, J., Gritz, E., Vogt, T., & West, L. (Eds.), *Research on Smoking Behavior.* NIDA Research Monograph 17. Washington, DC: U. S. Government Printing Office, 1977.

Slobogin, K. Stress. *The New York Times Magazine*, November 20, 1977, 48–50, 96, 98, 100, 102, 104, 106.

Stevens, M., Pfost, K., & Ackerman,M. The relationship between sex role orientation and the Type A behavior pattern: A test of the main effect hypothesis. *Journal of Clinical Psychology*, 1984, *40*, 1338–1341.

Stillion, J. *Death and the Sexes.* Washington, D.C. Hemisphere Publishing Corp., 1985.

Stoll, C. *Female and Male.* Dubuque, IA: Wm. C. Brown, 1974.

Thomas, W. *The Child in America.* New York: Alfred A. Knopf, 1928.

Tiller, P. Parental role division and the child's personality. In E. Dahlstrom (Ed.), *The Changing Roles of Men and Women.* Boston, MA: Beacon, 1967.

Tricomi, V., Serr, O., & Solish, C. The ratio of male to female embryos as determined by the sex chromatin. *American Journal of Obstetrics and Gynecology*, 1960, *79*, 504–509.

U.S. Department of Health and Human Services. The Health Consequences of Smoking: Chronic Obstructive Lung Disease: A Report of the U.S. Surgeon General, 1984. Rockville, MD: Public Health Service, Office on Smoking and Health; Washington, D.C., 1984. (D.H.H.S. [PHS] 84-50205)

United States Department of Health Education and Welfare. *The Health Consequences of Smoking.* Washington, DC: The U. S. Government Printing Office, 1973, 1974, 1975.

United States Department of Health Education and Welfare. *Vital Statistics of the United States.* 1972 (Vol. 2). Washington, DC: U. S. Government Printing Office, 1976.

United States Department of Health and Human Services. *Vital Statistics of the United States,* 1982 (Vol. 2). Washington, DC: U. S. Government Printing Office, 1987.

United States Department of Health and Human Services. *Vital Statistics of the United States,* 1984 (Pre-Publication Monograph). Washington, DC: U. S. Government Printing Office, 1987.

Verbrugge, L. M. 1980. "Recent Trends in Sex Mortality Differentials in the United States." *Women and Health* 5: 17–37.

Waldron, I. Why do women live longer than men? *Journal of Human Stress*, 1976, *2*, 1–13.

Waldron, I. Sex differences in human mortality: The role of genetic factors. *Social Science and Medicine*, 1983a, *17*, 321–333.

Waldron, I. Sex differences in illness incidence, prognosis and mortality: Issues and evidence. *Social Science and Medicine*, 1983b, *17*, 1107–1123.

Waldron, I., & Johnson, S. Why do women live longer than men? *Journal of Human Stress*, 1976, *2*, 19–29.

Weidner, G., Friend, R., Ficarrotto, T., Mendell, N. R. Hostility and cardiovascular reactivity to stress in women and men. *Psychosomatic Medicine.*

✓Wright, L. The Type A behavior pattern and coronary artery disease: Quest for the active ingredients and the elusive mechanisms. *American Psychologist*, 1988, *43*, 2–14.

✓Zeldow, P., Clark, D., & Daugherty, S. Masculinity, femininity, Type A behavior and psychosocial adjustment in medical students. *Journal of Personality and Social Psychology*, 1985, *45*, 481–492.

Barry Glassner

MEN AND MUSCLES

America was built of male muscle, at least according to our popular lore. The standard version of our early years speaks of rugged pioneers fighting the forces of nature and mastering savages with their bare hands. American industry likewise is understood to have been the product of male brawn. The captains of industry in the late nineteenth and early twentieth centuries were portrayed as almost animalistic in their physical power and drive. Aspiring young men were urged to display their own commitment to the same values. A 1920s manual for salesmen, like some of its counterparts in the 1980s, recommended exercises each morning, because muscular strength "imparts a feeling of enthusiasm, physical vigor and power of decision that no other faculty can give."

Bernarr Macfadden, creator of the physical culture movement early in this century, exhorted men to realize that "it lies with you, whether you shall be a strong virile animal . . . or a miserable little crawling worm."

During the world wars, male strength was equated — in political speeches and posters — with patriotism. And men who grew up just after the World War II remember vividly the Charles Atlas ads in comic books of the period. "I manufacture weaklings into MEN," read the headline on the back page of a 1952 issue of *The Fighting Leathernecks* (ten cents a copy). Beside a huge picture of Atlas, "the world's most perfectly developed man," appeared the famous story of how he used to be a ninety-seven-pound weakling. The choice every man had to face is made explicit in these ads: he could either keep his "skinny, pepless, second-rate body" or turn it over to Atlas (or the high school coach or the trainer at the local gym), who would "cram it so full of handsome, healthy, bulging new muscle that your friends will grow bug eyed."

Generations of boys have received the message loud and clear. Sociologist James Coleman asked high school boys in the early sixties how they would like to be remembered. Nearly half chose "athletic star," far more than opted for "brilliant student" or even "most popular." Neither hippies nor drugs nor the women's movement has changed things very much since. When the same question was asked of high schoolers in the seventies and again in the eighties, the same results were obtained: close to half answered "athletic star." What's more, in contemporary studies of college students, muscular men have been shown to be better liked by others and happier with themselves than their less well-developed classmates.

Boys suffer if they can't or won't accept the obligation to develop manly physiques. Every one of 256 nonmuscular adolescent boys examined in one study suffered mood or behavior problems connected to feelings of physical inadequacy. *Sissy* is, after all, a much more negative term than *tomboy*. While a girl is expected to outgrow her tomboyism, a boy who doesn't act boyish may well be sent to a psychiatrist for help. So a boy must prove decisively his commitment to masculinity, and the primary way to do it is through athletics and muscularity.

Reprinted from *Bodies: Why We Look the Way We Do (And How We Feel About It)*. New York: Putnam, 1988. Copyright © by Barry Glassner.

Muscles are *the* sign of masculinity. Author Nancy Huston has pointed out that women are distinguished from men by their ability to give birth, but men have no parallel "mark" of their gender. To fill in for this lack of a distinctive male trait, Huston says, many cultures have granted physical strength to boys and men as a characteristic uniquely their own. Over the years, innumerable scientific and superstitious explanations have been advanced purporting to prove it was God or Nature that made males stronger than females.

Because of the great meaning attached to muscles, nonathletic boys often grow into insecure men. In an "About Men" column in *The New York Times Magazine*, Mark Goodson, the television producer, wrote humorously about the drawbacks of disliking sports. Soon after arriving in New York in the 1940s, "hungry, anxious, in need of work," he was offered a job hosting a sports quiz. "I felt the blood leave my face," he recalls, but he accepted the assignment. Every Monday night for twenty-six weeks he feigned an interest in the subject, well enough that the radio station offered him a job announcing a baseball game. Never having been to a baseball game, he rushed out to buy a book on the rules of the game. "As I got to the tenth page, I collapsed," he reports. "Much as I needed the money, I knew there was no way that I could manage this bluff."

Goodson built a TV production empire despite such setbacks, and he jokes about them now. But he also recognizes that to be male and nonathletic is serious business. "I approach this subject with a light touch, but in truth," he writes, "it has been a problem that has plagued me for most of my life." From early childhood until late adulthood, he hid his disinterest and inability for fear of seeming homosexual. Yet "even after three marriages, three children, and some in between love affairs, plus the sure knowledge that I adore women, I still feel, from time to time, that, somehow, I must be lacking in the right male genes."

One irony, of course, is that for many years now it has not been much easier for a man to be nonathletic if he's gay than if he's straight. The ideal man within the gay world, as in the heterosexual, is powerfully built. "What a shock I had when I came out," said Jim, a twenty-nine-year-old real estate agent I interviewed at the San Francisco apartment he shares with his lover.

Jim had waited until his junior year in college to become involved in the gay community. One aspect of coming out that he'd eagerly anticipated was the opportunity to dress the way he wanted. As far back as he could remember he'd been careful not to wear flamboyant clothes and to camouflage his thin arms and concave chest with a sports coat or sweater.

"I was basically a sissy as a kid," he told me, "and I had a lot of defenses about it. I would get stomachaches from having to play baseball. The whole idea of having to play games at recess or gym class was too much for me. I made a big distinction between intellect and athletics. I always felt that I was a head person and not a body person. Most of the boys in the little Wisconsin town where I grew up were very jock-y. Since I wasn't that, I kept to myself and read a lot and drew pictures. Fortunately, my family never gave me problems about who I was."

Still, Jim was anxious and unhappy during childhood. He remembers crying in the school bathroom in third grade because some boys had mocked him. After that, he practiced a tougher swagger and spiced up his speech with words like "shit" and "pussy."

Things changed in junior high. For starters, there was no more "recess," so he wasn't forced to play ball games; and for another, he found a new role for himself. The boys and girls started mixing with one another, awkwardly, and Jim served as a go-between. He was handsome, but he didn't go after girls sexually, and thus the girls considered him both appealing and trustworthy. For their part, the boys appreciated having a guy around who was neither a nerd nor a competitor.

Still, the idea that he might appear effeminate was abhorrent to him. Once the other kids started dating, he made sure he always had a girlfriend — Catholic girls who, all the boys knew, would never let anyone past first base.

So it was with great anticipation of ending his long years of inauthenticity that he went public with his homosexuality midway through college. He'd had one affair with a man prior to that time but had kept his feelings secret.

"I'd been active in the ecology movement on campus, so I decided that a good way to come out would be through politics. I joined a gay rights group, and of course those were guys who were immersed in gay culture. Most of them at that time were very hard types, and I didn't know what I was getting into. They told me that it would just be a matter of time before I would become a sophisticated S-and-M'er. In a couple of months I would understand why it was correct to be tough and wear leather all the time.

"I tried to make it happen," he laughed, "but there was no way. It took me a few years and a set of barbells to accept that that wasn't me. It's taken even longer to accept the fact that gay men expect one another to dress in tight shirts and tight pants that emphasize their asses and their chests and their dicks. I mean, I've gotten comfortable dressing like that to be camp at a party, but I wouldn't dress that way to walk around Castro Street or go to work."

Instead, Jim dresses unusually "straight," even preppy. For our meeting he wore a cotton V-neck sweater and loose-fitting slacks, neither of which threw into relief any part of his body. On the other hand, Jim hasn't exactly stayed undeveloped. Partly as a result of the AIDS epidemic, the strong-and-healthy look is very much the order of the day where Jim lives. In addition to the barbells he bought in college, he owns a small trampoline and a sit-up board, and while he doesn't relish the thirty minutes every morning he spends exercising, he admitted it's made him happier with himself and has kept his partner interested.

BICEPS MAKE THE MAN

Gay men are by no means the only ones to have experienced conflicts over a lack of muscles. A national survey of 62,000 readers of *Psychology Today* found that a man's self-esteem correlates directly with having a muscular upper body. And in experiments in which male college students are given weight training, as the men grow stronger they become more outgoing and their degree of satisfaction with themselves increases.

Yet there is great variation in how men cope with the physical ideals placed upon them. Some men devote most of their lives to building up their bodies, while others scarcely exercise at all. Generally, a man's choice of one of these options or the other, or something in between, depends on what other people made of his body earlier in his life.

Those who suffer as adults are men who somehow never got into athletics while growing up but always felt parental and community pressure to do so. "I make a great pretense of being happy with these arms," said Larry, the thirty-six-year-old owner of an advertising agency in Atlanta, as he demonstrated how thin his left arm is by cupping the thumb and middle finger of his right hand almost completely around his upper arm. "I kid my friends who work out. I tell them, 'Biceps are just ugly bulges.' But the truth is, I'm not happy with my body.

"There's an event that sticks in my mind," he continued. "Nineteen seventy-two. We'd just graduated from Oberlin, and about a dozen of us took over the summer house of somebody's parents on a private lake in upstate New York for a week. One afternoon they all decided to go skinny-dipping. I begged off at first. I don't take off my clothes even in front of people I'm totally comfortable with. I make love in the dark when I have a choice in the matter. But those were the days of free sex and do-your-own-thing, and it wasn't considered cool to be hung up about nudity. They hassled me until I finally stripped and jumped in the water.

"It was about the worst experience of my life. First off, the other guys all had better bodies than I did. My stomach stuck out, even then, and I had no shoulders or chest, and of course, no biceps." Larry laughed nervously.

"The thing that really did me in was when an ex-girlfriend of mine swam by with the man she was living with at the time and made a comment about how I won the funniest-shape-of-the-day award. It was as if someone had run me over with a Mack truck. I felt embarrassed and betrayed."

Fifteen years later, and Larry still has a puny body he's ashamed about. Now not only doesn't he go skinny-dipping, he doesn't even go swimming. But he's not unattractive. In fact, he has a pleasant face and a full head of wavy black hair. One could easily imagine that if he stood up straight and added an inch or two of muscle in strategic spots, he'd look great in the stylish clothes he wears.

Why doesn't Larry simply work out a few hours a week so that he can feel decent about himself physically? He was unable to answer that question directly. The answer came out, nonetheless, at another point in our discussion, when he described his parents and the nature of his relationship with them as a child. His mother used to criticize him for not being the son she'd imagined having, but anytime he showed some independence or virility, she was unsatisfied with his performance.

As he described it: "Either you played ball with the other kids or you weren't a Real Man. My mother's brother Don was a Real Man. He'd been a guard for the basketball team. He's very tall and very fast. He ran a marathon this summer to celebrate his sixtieth birthday. My mother was very pretty in high school, very 'popular,' and she wanted me to be the same. If I'd had a sister, or even if there'd been another boy for her to lay it on, maybe I wouldn't have felt so pressured. I think I wimped out of sports just to spite her constant chirping about how I ought to be more like my Uncle Don."

At the same time, Larry's father, a man who was already distant, became even more so on the few occasions when Larry shelved his stamp collection and put on a baseball mitt. And at an early age Larry noticed that his mother was affectionate with his father only when his father was sick, a handy trick Larry came to deploy himself.

It's clear that in the crevices of Larry's adult mind there lives the belief that he cannot be fit without losing the attention of those he depends on. In his experience, to be fit was to yield to the wishes of an overpowering mother, whereas to be weak was to gain attention from the most important man in his world. This is just the opposite of many boys, who seduce Mom and buddy up to Dad by playing sports.

Larry survived high school thanks to an extracurricular activity that allowed him to relate to his father and to other males. He took up photography, a long-standing hobby of his father's. Working for the school yearbook, he was assigned to photograph football and basketball games. He became friends with other staffers, and in his senior year he was appointed editor. "The yearbook room was my safe zone, the camera was my weapon," he said.

At artsy Oberlin College in the late sixties, his camera attracted the attention of desirable women. It wasn't until that episode at the lake that he started to pay a price again for his physique.

He was safe in high school and college in part because the culture had changed. Some decades are better than others for men like Larry; fashions in brawn wax and wane. During certain periods, American body trends reward less muscular men. Historians have documented several such periods, including the years just after the Civil War, and the 1960s. At other times, including the early years of this century and the seventies and eighties, American men have been required to be overtly strong in order to be received as attractive and healthy.

Physical fashions for men reflect national political trends. During the Vietnam War, men's bodies took on special significance. In fact, the war was *over* bodies. Each side claimed victory less on the basis of territory taken than on "body counts." Those who opposed the war actively deployed their bodies in the service of opposition. Some were beaten up in protests in Chicago, and many more recast their bodies into symbols of defiance — wearing long hair, beards, and odd clothes that distinguished them from Marines. Suddenly, men who'd enjoyed athletics in high school were viewed as no sexier than their comrades who'd earlier been teased for throwing a ball like a girl. Muscles didn't necessarily contribute much to an antiwar image.

After the war, the oppositional look largely disappeared. The current ideal American male body stands as a symbol of reunification. *We have the same basic values*, the post-Vietnam body proclaims, and these are manifest in the trim, strong figure we admire in our men (and, to a limited degree, in our women). *Our goals are identical*, the post-Vietnam body reassures: liberal or conservative, black or white, we just want to be secure and prosperous and in charge of our own destiny. The American body politic, once torn asunder, is mended.

"Muscles have come to *mean* something again: an obsession with the beauty of health and a growing impatience with having sand kicked in our face have combined to give back to muscles a national symbolic credibility," Charles Gaines observed in *Esquire*.

But let's return to Larry, who hasn't fared at all well during the age of brawn. Just after college he married a graphic artist, who helped him set up his ad agency until she grew bored and status-hungry and went back to school for an MBA. A few years ago, she left Larry for someone she met at the health club where she has a corporate membership.

According to Larry, it's hard to have much success on the singles scene when you're out of shape. An analysis I conducted of "personals" ads in ten newspapers and magazines from across the U.S. and from London bears him out. Words like "athletic" and "well-built" appear in a majority of the men's descriptions of themselves and women's descriptions of their desired mates.

Women who advertise in these publications are primarily upper-middle-class, well educated, and looking for men of the same stripe. Since they've broken out of traditional roles themselves to some extent, they might be expected to be more receptive to less traditionally masculine men. In fact, they often prefer to have rather macho men around, perhaps to offset their fears that they may not be sufficiently feminine. Christine, for instance, the corporate vice-president, made it very clear she has no interest in "pale hairless guys who make great pasta," whom she calls "newts." She dates tall, well-built, handsome fellows. "I don't need to be taken care of," she said, "and I can forge my own way and make a lot of money. I'd sort of like the feminine side of me reinforced by being with a man who is more male than I am. Dealing with a man who has a real female side is unsettling."

Politically left-leaning women can also be suspicious of men with sunken chests. One woman I interviewed, who has refused to wear makeup her entire adult life on the grounds that the cosmetics industry is a capitalist plot to enslave women, said sternly about men: "The obligation to be beautiful is oppressive, the obligation to be strong is empowering. A woman who refuses to 'fix her face' is simply rejecting patriachal oppression, but a man who refuses to build up his body isn't making any kind of statement at all, except that he's lazy."

FEAR MAKES THE BICEPS

Given their poor reception in the outside world, men who are physically weak understandably experience low self-confidence. What's surprising is that their mirror opposites — the hunks and superjocks — often suffer from the same problem.

Perhaps the single greatest force that keeps men working out is insecurity. This is evident in those who exercise chiefly because they're afraid of heart disease. But almost all avid male exercisers are engaged in a passionate battle with their own sense of vulnerability. Herein lies an important distinction between men and women. For both, the key motivation to exercise is improved self-esteem, but the genders differ on what they believe produces these benefits. When surveyed as to why they exercise, women talk about accomplishment, beauty, affiliation with others; men say they're motivated by the chance to pit themselves against nature or other men and to confront physical danger. In other words, men seek to prove to themselves and others that they can survive, that they're winners.

The harder a man exercises, the more he may be trying to overcome his feelings of inadequacy or helplessness. Most bodybuilders in a study conducted in southern California were found to have been stutterers, dyslexics, thin, fat, short, nearsighted, or otherwise unacceptable to their parents when they were children. The author of the study, sociologist Alan Klein, proposes that bodybuilding serves as a kind of "therapeutic narcissism." Through it, those who feel deeply insecure are offered a way to devote their full attention to making themselves big, strong, and commanding of attention.

I developed a vivid appreciation for the sweat-for-salvation aspect of male fitness when I visited a place where a high concentration of America's best-developed men live — a maximum security prison. There I met a man named Nathan, who is famous in several California prisons as an advocate for strengthening and perfecting the body while in jail.

Attractive and well-groomed, Nathan wore a short-sleeved yellow Lacoste shirt along with his starched gray prison pants and gave off a scent of expensive cologne. His closely cropped beard was cut precisely to complement his square features and his short curly black hair, which had obviously been styled by a talented barber. (He had an arrangement, he explained, with an inmate who had worked in a Hollywood hair salon prior to his conviction on drug charges.) Nathan's huge arms, covered with blue tattoos of eagles and naked women, offered a strange counterpoint to his fastidious grooming.

In a small room off the main visiting area, I asked Nathan to describe the different types of men who build up their bodies in jail.

"You got the superheavyweights, over six feet and massively built," he began, over the constant hum of prisoners yelling from the cell blocks in the adjoining buildings. "Then you got the real short guys. The tall ones are usually pretty smart — they don't have a college education, but they have common sense. They don't want to be overly aggressive, they just want to keep people away and do their time. The short ones usually are abrasive. They're looking for trouble. They've got that Napoleon complex. Then you've got the guys that want to box. They go through a very rigorous boxing discipline. They run, they practice all the boxing techniques, jump rope, hit the heavy bag."

Nathan estimated that two-thirds of the inmates at the prisons he's been in are seriously involved in exercise of some type. "When you come to jail you have a lot of time on your hands," he said at first. But as he talked on about prison life, and his own biography, a more complex picture emerged.

"When you're in the streets," he said, "you have a lot of time, but it's not structured into roll calls and meals, so it seems to go very fast. In here you're really conscious of time, and one of the pastimes that you can see some results from is lifting weights. You see people around you and you say, 'Wow, that looks nice, that guy has a nice build.' The way he carries himself, the way he walks, the way people respect him. And when you get big it gives you an artificial sense of security."

In what way is it artificial? I asked, feeling oddly comfortable after only ten or fifteen minutes with this Herculean man whom I knew to have been convicted of murder.

"It's artificial because you have to defeat the fear within your heart," he answered. "How big or small you are doesn't have anything to do with it. I had nineteen-and-a-half-inch arms at one point, but I couldn't pacify the fear in my heart, and people could see that."

His personal fear, he went on to explain, is that he'll spend his entire life in jail. He was first locked up, in a mental hospital, when he was five and a half years old. On that occasion he'd been playing with matches; he set fire to a sheet and his family's apartment went up in flames. His father, who was confined to bed for a back injury, died in the blaze. "My mother wanted to love me," he said with practiced dispassion, having relayed the story many times, "but she couldn't because she blamed me for the death of my father."

Nathan was cast out by his mother and didn't fare much better in his neighborhood. His light-brown skin and his ethnic background marked him for trouble from the time he was a young child. His father had come from the Cape

Verde Islands and his mother from Brazil. In the barrio where Nathan grew up, "people had names like Carlos and José, and here I was Nathan. Kids used to think I was white because I'm so light, and there I was being acculturated into the Chicano culture, yet I couldn't identify with them physically. Everywhere I went it was understood I wasn't one of them."

Most of his formative years were spent in juvenile detention facilities. He was angry and confused, and he struck out with acts of violence ranging from schoolyard fights to armed robbery.

During one of his longer stays on the outside, at age twelve, Nathan shot heroin. He continued off and on until he hit forty, when he took up yoga and physical fitness in prison. The inmate who taught the yoga course espoused the view that drugs are poison and drug users pathetic creatures.

After his release on parole, Nathan became a community crusader against drugs, combing the streets for strung-out kids he could Pied Piper into his martial arts classes, which he conducted free at a recreation center in Watts. The more respect Nathan got in the neighborhood from his physical abilities, the more grandiose he grew, and within a few months he was preaching about "eradicating drugs from the face of the earth."

One afternoon, when an adolescent follower arrived with the news that another was in a coma from an overdose, Nathan went looking for the drug dealer who had sold him the stuff. He beat the man up badly and left him bleeding in an alley. The man died a few hours later, and Nathan was sentenced to twenty-five years to life for murder.

"Once I was back in the joint," Nathan remembered, "I borrowed some law books. I knew I'd spend the rest of my life in the joint unless I could find a way to get around this sentence. But it was hard to concentrate because I was on an open block. You have TVs and radios on full-blast and people yelling twenty-four hours a day, seven days a week. I had to be able to pull myself inward and digest this material, to think of an approach to use at my defense."

Nathan initiated a daily regimen of physical development and purification which he still continues. He says it gave him the willpower to study the law and to argue successfully before the parole board in 1985 that his sentence should be reduced to six to twelve years.

Today, Nathan's routine goes something like this. He rises at 5:00 A.M., when the cell block is still reasonably quiet. Without making enough noise to wake anyone, he repeats twelve times each a series of special exercises that combine calisthenics and yoga. In describing these to me, he left his chair and demonstrated. Assuming a squatting position, he took a very deep breath that expanded his chest muscles to their fullest; he held this for a few seconds, then gracefully raised himself upward to a full standing position, from which he bent forward while slowly exhaling, until his palms touched the floor.

On his way back up, Nathan caught a glimpse of the concerned expression on the face of the guard outside our cubicle and sat down again. He continued his description: "As you see, I don't look anything like yogis. If you see them in a book, they look like they're malnourished, whereas my body is well-developed everywhere. Yet I can put my elbows on the ground from a standing position with my knees locked. I'm superflexible. In America you want to have a good, healthy, rich image, not malnourished. My concept is that you can maintain that look and at the same time have flexibility."

After his predawn exercises, which take an hour, Nathan eats breakfast in his cell. He refuses to eat in the mess hall he said, because the food isn't healthy. Instead, with money or cigarettes earned from advising other inmates on legal matters, he orders health foods through the prison commissary. Friends who work in the mess hall also bring him milk, fish, and vegetables a few times a week.

After lineup, he attends a class offered in the prison by a local university. At the juvenile detention facilities where Nathan grew up, schooling was provided only a few hours a day; the rest of the time Nathan hauled coal and cut grass. His formal education was poor at best, and so it's no minor accomplishment that at the time I met him, he was about to graduate from college as valedictorian of his prison class of twenty-eight.

He credited his educational achievement to his bodily discipline. "It really opened my mind and gave me a sense of direction and a focus for my energies," he said. Classes in the prison are offered in the mornings and early evenings. In between, nonstop from 1:00 until 5:00 P.M., Nathan can be found in the jailyard working out with a group of inmates who have taken up his fitness system. They run a few laps to limber up, then move into the same sorts of exercises Nathan performs alone in his cell.

Life in a hot, violent, noisy prison is hell for anyone. Still, Nathan has a busy and secure life behind bars. "This has become like a womb for me, where I can function and be successful," he let drop at one point in the interview. Each time he's been released, he's come unhinged within a few months. As an adolescent, "just having been in prison was a status symbol. When I went home they had a party and everybody said, 'There goes a sure-enough bad dude.' I felt great. Then, two days later, I had to prove myself all over, and I'd get into trouble again." As an adult who has spent so much time behind bars, he says he can't maintain routines when he's on the outside. "I overindulge. I stay out every night dancing and having sex, trying to make up for lost time. I become totally fatigued, and then I feel bad because I'm not keeping my mind and body as sharp as I know I'm supposed to. I get paranoid and confused on the street."

It may be ironic, and it's surely unfortunate, but Nathan feels more at home in jail than he does on the outside. Behind bars he can maintain some measure of self-respect and control, thanks to his fitness regimen. His exercise program has given his life order and predictability and is a source of personal pride.

CALMING THE STORM

Among the law-abiding men I interviewed who exercise obsessively for periods of weeks or months, the same basic motivations apply. They discipline themselves through fitness in order to stave off the impending chaos they confront in their daily lives.

A case in point is Roger, a forty-two-year-old Chicago lawyer. While growing up, he played softball in the neighborhood; in college he did nothing beyond a morning wakeup routine of push-ups and sit-ups; and in law school he "hardly had time to eat." Although Roger was in the top quarter of his University of Chicago Law School class, he was terrified he'd fail the bar exam, as his older brother had. He countered his fears by bingeing on exercise. "I've played racquetball exactly twenty-two times in my life, and they were all within the space of the last three weeks before my bar exam," he reported. "Racquetball made me feel better. When I couldn't study, it loosened me up. I didn't play particularly *well*, but nobody played *harder*. I broke several racquets and messed up my arm pretty badly a couple of times."

That was the first of three times in the past fifteen years that Roger has gone on and off the exercise wagon. From the day he received notification that he'd passed the bar, about the only exercise Roger got was lifting heavy law books in the back offices of a large firm — until, that is, his second exercise blitz, which began a couple of years out of law school when he found himself unable to sleep the nights before he was to do battle with another lawyer in court. He'd awaken at four in the morning, his jaws clenched and his stomach knotted. In the middle of an argument in the courtroom the next day, his mouth would go dry and he'd lose his train of thought. Once a judge asked him to approach the bench and in a peevish voice advised Roger to request that his firm send him to a public speaking course.

Instead, Roger took up running. On his way back from court, he bought an expensive pair of Etonics, and each morning thereafter he ran three or four miles around Grant Park before going to his office in the Loop. "My father had had a heart attack at a young age," he said. "With all the reports coming out at that time about the benefits of running, I decided to join in." Before long he was doing eight miles a day, then ten and twelve. Some days he didn't feel like running but would run anyway: "A mile into the run I would get that feeling of relaxation, of going on forever, a real kind of power." And he was able to sleep at night and to present a strong case in court.

By the end of his third year out of law school Roger was, in his own words, "a damned good trial attorney." Within a year, his confidence firmly in place, the running fell off to a few miles every other day, then diminished to nothing. He blames the long hours at work required to make partner.

Except for a taste of golf, which he found boring, Roger again went without exercise until a year before our interview. The event that precipitated this, his third exercise spree, was sudden rejection by a long-term girlfriend. As an antidote to the pain and vulnerability he felt, Roger hired a private exercise trainer known in Chicago executive circles to be unsparing, even sadistic, in his drive to get his clients back in shape. For ten months prior to our meeting, the trainer had greeted Roger every Monday, Wednesday, and Thursday at 6:00 P.M. upon Roger's arrival home from work, and Saturdays at 4:00 P.M. For a grueling hour he orchestrated Roger's workout in the gym they set up in the spare bedroom of Roger's Lake Shore Drive apartment. "I never would have thought it possible that I could be in such great physical condition," Roger claimed. "I feel great and I look great."

Nevertheless, when I met him he was already showing signs that the end of this current exercise cycle was in sight. He told me of plans to decrease the number of training sessions each week; and although he "swore off women" after his disappointment the year before, a few weeks prior to our interview he began sleeping regularly with a thirty-two-year-old physician.

Men who exercise for purposes of deliverance (like Roger and Nathan), as well as those who abstain from exercise (like Larry), differ in an important regard from men who are at neither of those extremes. Exercise is not a highly charged activity for those who pursue it in a more moderate way. They don't attach magical significance to lifting heavy objects or hitting balls.

A hallmark of a sane exercise program is that it is integrated into a person's daily life. It's just something a man does, like eating lunch or getting a haircut. He goes to the Y or health club regularly to play basketball or handball or pump a little iron with his buddies. And although his sports activities may take up a fair amount of leisure time, he foregoes them if a family or business emergency takes precedence.

At times — when he's angry with someone at work, for instance — he may play rough and injure himself, but the displacement of frustration is not what his athleticism is about. The role of athletics in his life is much more basic than that. Typically he has been involved with sports since childhood. He loves to reminisce about a particular game from his youth, or the day his dad installed a hoop on the garage at the end of the driveway when he was five or six. He has a vivid memory of his father placing the massive basketball in his arms and lifting him up so he could sink it through the basket. In the twenty or thirty or forty years since, there's never been a period when he hasn't played some kind of sport; in high school he may even have made it onto a team. And he devotedly follows college and pro teams on TV.

Lifelong jocks are living evidence for a current view of human development called, appropriately enough, "continuity theory." It holds that our interests during adulthood are usually extensions of what we enjoyed as children. Continuity theory disputes the myth perpetrated by sports magazines and health clubs — that a devoted couch potato can, with a bit of willpower, transform himself at age forty into a championship marathon runner or ball player. Men who try athletics for the first time during adulthood seldom succeed; like Roger, they don't stick with any activity very long.

Several studies show that men who engage in exercise on a regular basis as adults also did so during their childhood or adolescence. One of the best predictors of whether a man will be athletic in midlife (and later) is whether his father participated in sports and brought him up to do so as well.

Men who've grown up athletic are the great beneficiaries of the American male role. When social scientists track down high school athletes ten or more years after graduation, they find them holding better-paying, higher-status jobs than their classmates from similar socioeconomic backgrounds. Their body image and self-esteem are greater too.

Who can say whether these positive outcomes are the result of their athleticism or are coincidental with it? Whichever it may be, other men envy these men their comfort with their masculinity and their physiques, and women wish it were as easy for them to stay pretty as it is for these men to stay handsome. How unfair, I've heard women complain, that such men need merely continue to play the games of their youth, while to maintain their beauty women must spend hours in beauty salons having perms, facials, manicures, and pedicures; must starve themselves on diets; must wear uncomfortable shoes . . . and on top of all that, exercise whether they enjoy it or not.

Although some men do fit that picture, they're a small minority. Most men, even if they've kept themselves reasonably fit, are privately insecure about their looks and more vain than others imagine them to be.

Martin Duberman

GAY IN THE FIFTIES

My first sexual experience with a man? About age 20. Well, a few earlier ones. At summer camp in the forties we did something we called "fussing." We had a mattress at the bottom of the closet in our bunk. (The closet no less!) We were pretty well organized. Don't know how old I was — about 12, I think. The code question we'd ask each other was, "You feel like 'fussing'?" If "yes," we'd go into the closet, two at a time. Body-rubbing, essentially. There was a definite hierarchy, too. You know: who got to go into the closet with whom — who did the choosing. Just like a gay bar.

On one level, I knew early on I was gay. At seventeen, for instance, I went on a bike trip — old fashioned "bike" — across the country. Camped out every night, went through the Rockies: all that. At one point we stopped in Calgary, Canada for the big rodeo. I remember going to see a fortune teller. She told me to write on a piece of paper "the question closest to my heart" and to put it under the (literal) crystal ball sitting on the table between us. "Put it under the crystal, close your eyes, concentrate very hard and I will then be able to answer your question". What I wrote on the piece of paper was, "Will I always be a homosexual?"

Fortunately — being rebellious by nature — I didn't follow her instructions to the letter. I peeked. I saw her take the piece of paper out through some opening in the bottom of the table, read it, then put it back. "Open your eyes now," she said. "You're a very troubled young man. I'm getting that very strongly. But your particular trouble can be cured. What you must do is leave your old life and join our gypsy caravan." Even the gypsies were into "cures"!

I was tempted — though I'd seen her trick with the piece of paper. A measure, I guess, of my desperation. "Maybe she can cure you," I thought, "maybe you should go with her." I felt terribly torn up, couldn't decide. In the end, I did not show up at dawn with all my worldly goods.

The "sickness" model of homosexuality had been drummed into me. That's why I waited so long before I had sex. It wasn't until my first year in graduate school at Harvard in 1953 that I finally got up the courage to go into my first gay bar. Soon after, I met a man — I'll call him "Larry" — and was with him for five years. Our relationship wasn't entirely monogamous, but nearly so for the first few years. I was very close to him. He was different from me in many ways — I'm usually attracted to opposites; not always, but usually. Larry was 19 or 20 when we met (I was 22) working class Irish Catholic, from a small town near Boston. Very attractive physically — to me anyway. He was my romantic ideal, I was his intellectual one. That's one way to put it, I suppose. I was living in the graduate dorm and later, from 1954–57 in Adams House as a resident tutor, Larry lived with his family, but he'd often stay with me. There was no way we could afford to live together on a regular basis. Neither of us had any money. He had a lousy job in a department store, I was trying to get by on my tutor's salary . . .

You know, sometimes when I think about the Fifties, I think everything has changed — the culture, me, the community. Other times I think very little has changed. A student

From "Interview: Martin Duberman," *Gay Sunshine*, Spring 1977.
Reprinted from *Salmagundi*, Fall 1982–Winter 1983.

of mine from when I taught at Princeton (1962–1971) recently came to see me (1977).
He's 26 now, but has been "out" only a year. His big breakthrough to date has been meeting
a guy in one of the johns at the porno movies he frequents who "actually talked to me!"
This is a bright, politically sophisticated guy — active in SDS as an undergraduate. Yet
here he is at age 26 not knowing where to go to meet other gay men, except for bathrooms.
It made me think things are no easier for gay people now than they ever were. In other
moods I know — or hope — that's wrong. But I'm not sure.

Like take my relationship with Larry. We had a damn good thing. And a support
group, a circle of friends. There were bars, too. The life was circumscribed and secretive,
of course. And our self-image wasn't so hot. I remember long talks with my gay friends
at Harvard about whether we could achieve any sort of satisfying life, "stunted" as we
were. We accepted as given that as homosexuals we could never reach "full adult matur-
ity" — whatever the fuck that means. Then it meant what everybody said it did:
marrying, settling down, having a family. We knew we'd never qualify, and despised
ourselves for it. But it's too simple to reduce "growing up gay in the Fifties" to a one-
dimensional horror story . . .

EXCERPTS FROM MY DIARY OF 1956–7 — PLUS MY FEELINGS ON
RE-READING THEM IN 1981

August 28, 1956   Told Weintraupt today [*the therapist I'd been seeing for about a*
year] that I was going to quit. By the time the hour was up, I had, as usual,
changed my mind. Mostly because I got him to qualify the ban on homosexual
contacts. He now says it's *Larry* I must stay away from [*following Weintraupt's*
dictate, I'd broken off with Larry a month previously], not necessarily all contacts —
though the greater the abstemiousness, the better. All I needed was an opening:
I spent three hours tonight touring the bars, river, common, etc. . . .

August 29   1:00 a.m.: Just back from the bars. Roger asked me home. He and
Paul, it seems, are all finished. Three months ago he was quoted as saying: "I
don't think I could live without him." At least not for three months. And so it
always seems to go. Is any genuine commitment between homosexuals possible? God knows I miss Larry. How I wish he were here tonight waiting for me
in bed, sweet, affectionate . . . and yet I can't really settle down with him. I
have no confidence in our building any sort of a life . . .

September 2   . . . went to the bars. I was in one of my exuberantly vain
moods — I looked well, Larry was safely on the Cape [*vacationing*] and couldn't
directly prick my conscience ("You supposedly gave me up for the analysis, and
here you are a month later cruising in the bars") — I had a luxurious three hours
to exert my charms on the multitude.

Got quite drunk and came home with a youngish guy who I thought would
be a good fuck. But he was lousy in bed — inexperienced physically, inane in
every other way: "You're different from any of the others I've met"; "What
nationality are you? — part Russian? — they must be a passionate race"; "You're
a hairy pest from Budapest."

After two hours of non-erect activity, we finally managed an orgasm. I was
afterwards completely repulsed by what I'd done; this absurd compulsive inti-

macy with an anonymous body — and a disappointing one at that (which is perhaps why I'm so righteously repulsed).

He left early this morning. I've been moping around ever since. Came very close to rushing off to see Larry on the Cape. It's extraordinary how "right" seeing him would make everything. But I've yielded to this too many times before, and always without lasting satisfaction. It's been a full month now since we've seen each other — I've *got* to hold off — I *cannot* form any lasting relationship with him — why, I'm not sure — but this I do know, that it won't work, and I must give him a chance to free himself.

September 3   The great drought is over — with the usual awful results. Last night Larry called. I was so glad to hear from him, and under almost no pressure, agreed to meet him . . . eventually I was talking drunkenly — meaning it all — about giving up the analysis, about missing him terribly, etc. And finally, sex. As miraculous as ever, and followed, as ever, by panic over what I had done and remorse over what I had said.

Will it ever be resolved? When I see him I'm lost; and I can't seem to stop myself from seeing him. Yet it's never enough. Could I really give up the analysis and accept my life as it now stands? Also impossible . . .

September 4   Nervous about having to tell Weintraupt what happened last night. Half hoping, like a renegade schoolboy, to be "dismissed." But I was unable to goad either him or myself into it.

The confessional did me good. And now, I suppose, the usual drifting till the next crisis. What of all the promises I made to Larry last night? Today I consummate the immorality by not even calling him. What else can I do? If I call, I merely re-establish a lifeline that consists of half-promises that always remain unfulfilled, and yet always remain. If only I could know that after my physical and neurotic needs are spent, there's still something left for us to live on. I sometimes think there is — but Weintraupt has thrown so many of my feelings into doubt and confusion, I can't even be sure of "sometimes." And so I'll continue to drift; trying not to call — hoping he'll call me; continuing to go to Weintraupt — planning imminently to quit.

(1981): Weintraupt was not my first therapist. I had previously gone (been sent, *by my parents) at age 15 to find out why I was so monosyllabic and moody. It was enlightened in 1945 to send your kid for therapy. It would have been more so if everyone in the family had gone: I wouldn't have felt that tensions at home were exclusively of my making. The therapist helped further to convince me that they were. I saw him for several months, at the end of which time he announced his "solution": I should embrace my mother and tell her how much I loved her. Yup — swear to God! I paced my bedroom for hours trying to get up the courage; I had trouble talking to my mother, let alone touching her. "Do it!" I yelled at myself, "Do it!!" I went downstairs, grabbed the startled woman, hugged her like a robot out of* R.U.R., *and said a loud, metallic, "I love you!" — and was promptly showered with tears of joy. "I knew it was going to be all right," she kept repeating, "I knew it would be." Idiot therapist! The thaw at home lasted a couple of days or weeks. Then* status quo ante pace.

I never told that therapist about my homosexual feelings — though I was already aware of them. I think I came closest when relating a dream. I was in a glass house masturbating (or was it having sex with a man?), terrified that people were watching from every adjacent apartment house. "What were you terrified of," asked Sigmund Pangloss. "Dunno," I mumbled.

September 7. 1:30 a.m. Just back from the bars. Larry was there and we mooned around each other — with intermittent snarls — all night. Curse Weintraupt and my bloody fine powers of resistance! I'm so sick of considering consequences, "looking ahead" — to what? To a question mark, to the bare possibility that I may someday be able to marry and have children.

1:45: Larry called a few minutes ago. "Can I borrow your car to get home?" "Sure, I'll meet you at the gate [*of Adams House*] in 2 minutes." And at the gate he looked so beautiful. Then he cried and said he loved me and swore he'd never "bother" me again. How the hell can I resist? I asked him to come upstairs. He hesitated and said he was tired of "taking the blame." We went through this 3 or 4 times. Finally, in a pique at his stubbornness, I walked away — half expecting and more than half hoping to be called back. But no, he let the gate close. So now I'm back in my room. Chastity intact, but virtue assuredly not. So much for self-congratulation — celibacy by necessity this time, not choice.

September 8. 2:00 a.m. I'm like a stupid child who can't profit from experience. Larry returned the car during the afternoon and I invited him up, although I was playing cards. He slept while we played and then when the others left, I woke him, crawled into bed, caressed him — and that was that. I simply made no effort to resist. Why invite him up in the first place? Why not wake him hurriedly? — "late for dinner"; "let's catch the early show," etc. No, none of those sensible things. Attraction, tenderness, wonderfully passionate sex — and then the usual regret over the destructiveness of my lust, both to Larry and to my analysis.

September 10. I quit the analysis this morning. After months of indecision, the final action was almost unexpected. I told Weintraupt about Saturday night with Larry — and about a dream in which my "auditing" a course evolved into a symbolic reenactment of my attitude towards the analysis — i.e., an onlooker, an auditor, rather than a participator. From there it was only a step to being told my attitude made the analysis circular and endless; and since in honesty I couldn't swear that I would be able to change it, it was mutually agreed that it would be best to stop. Yet having made the decision, I can't accept it. Accepting it means accepting my life, being satisfied with it. And I can't . . .

Larry arrived unexpectedly in my room immediately after I got back from Weintraupt. He's just had word that he may have Hodgkin's disease — brought on by his lung ailment.

(1981): Larry had had mysterious growths on his lungs ever since I'd known him. One winter the doctors performed an exploratory operation which did nothing to lessen the mystery but left his torso criss-crossed with ugly scars. His doctors kept shifting their diagnosis — and kept Larry shuttling in and out of hospitals.

I spent the evening with him — the Brockton Fair — and tried to take his mind off the news [*soon after, the diagnosis was retracted*]. His reaction under pressure is (as always) remarkable — his deep upset obvious, but uncomplaining and free of self-pity. He's an extraordinary stoic; I never admire and love him more than when I see his quiet acceptance of unhappiness. I couldn't get myself to tell him about quitting the analysis, because he would expect me now to be propelled into his arms — permanently . . . What to do? I need more time to think. My first impulse is to resume analysis — but this time making the greatest possible effort to resist all homosexual contact. Have I ever *really* tried before? Or have I assumed incapability and infirmity and comforted myself with the thought that although I continued to act out, I was nevertheless "improving" simply by sticking to the mechanics of treatment. If I go back this time, I must *truly* commit myself to it . . .

September 11. 1:30 a.m.   Didn't call Weintraupt. I think I've passed beyond the initial stage of feeling lost and helpless. I'm going to try it this way for a while . . . saw Larry for dinner. We had sex later — how great not to follow it with panic and guilt: I told him I'd quit the analysis but that I wouldn't be able to commit myself to a monogamous relationship, that I remain incapable (don't all homosexuals?) of finding satisfaction permanently with one person. He didn't press for further explanation or commitment, since he sensed I wasn't ready or willing. He's extraordinarily perceptive in gauging my moods. And extraordinarily tolerant of them.

(1981): To spell out the obvious: I'd wholly internalized the then standard view of the "homosexual condition" — namely, to be homosexual was to be incapable of commitment to another human being. I'd internalized, too, the sex negativism of the culture: not to be monogamous, to enjoy sex with more than one person was to be "irresponsible." Homosexuality equalled promiscuity, and promiscuity equalled irresponsibility. Put another way, "health" could be recognized by the absence of desire — or at least the need to act on the desire — for more than one person.

Though I now take issue with the perjorative label "promiscuous" being automatically applied to all non-monogamous sexual activity, I do still feel (a residue from the earlier years of psychoanalytic indoctrination?) that some distinction exists and needs to be maintained between compulsive promiscuity and enjoying a variety of sexual experiences. The degree of compulsiveness involved — the driven quality — may be central to that distinction; it's the difference between being open to the pleasures of variety and obsessively needing a multiplicity of sexual experiences (to reinforce a sense of self-worth, or whatever).

As for Larry and me, after being together for three years, I had discovered — as do most people — that after obsession eases, resistance lessens, mutuality increases, the rest of the world comes back into focus — and some of it in shapely form. Again like most people (in the Fifties) I took this deviation from the monogamous ideal as a symptom of in-capacity — for commitment, intimacy — even though I deviated more in the realm of fantasy than action.

September 13. New York   1:00 a.m. Drove down from Boston today for the rehearsal for Don's [*a boyhood friend*] wedding . . . so *much* contentment . . . wives bearing, husbands beaming . . . perhaps I mistake it — and am merely romanticizing . . .

September 15. New York   . . . dinner with Kenny [*an old friend; in 1975 he was murdered in New York City by a hustler*] at "East 55." Good meal, but expensive, and my! so elegant. The place filled with babbling queens who, because they can afford to spend $5 on a dinner, feel they are also entitled to talk at the top of their lungs. Oh why criticize — I suppose the sick should stick together!

(1981): Since my homophobia's already well established, the only real surprise in this entry is $5 for dinner being thought "expensive."

  Then down to Lennie's [*a gay bar*] in the Village for a night of drinking. Spent most of it talking to a redhead from Toronto named Rick: simple, unassuming, good-natured — and I *thought*, very attractive. As per usual, it took going to bed with him to prove I was wrong. Pudgy, hairy, slight cock, less technique. These disappointments seem to be my stock in trade. Perhaps I purposely single out those to whom I'm only marginally attracted — thus ensuring disappointment. A way of punishing myself? Of preventing any further involvement? Anyway, I swear it — no more nights like tonight. Wholehearted desire or *nothing.*

(1981): A luxurious oath, a function of youth; this demanding American Adam, entitled to uncompromising fulfillment as a birthright. In time, oaths turn to pleas — for that very marginal sex we foreswore as beneath us. The young are marvelously arrogant. Age is grateful for the occasional mercy fuck. Or, if cursed with unrelenting standards of "beauty," learns the importance of money.

September 18   Adams House — and Cambridge — full of sound again. It's exciting watching everyone return and bustle about. And being busy. I love squeezing in my research [*I was working on my doctoral thesis in history*] between appointments, meetings, errands, etc. It exhilarates me to have a crowded daily schedule. Am I afraid of too much free time — empty, unplanned, threatening of the unexpected? Oh in part, yes — but surely not *all* my responses are sick! Being on the threshold of new experiences — buying new books, thinking of a new teaching schedule, directing a new play in the House — it's *fun*, damn it, and I refuse to reduce all my experiences and motives to psychological (neurotic) explanations . . .

(1981): In these years I was rarely in touch with my anger at being categorized as "sick" — after all, I believed it — and still less often did I let it surface (as in the above entry). Yet a subterranean defiance, however suppressed and deprecated, helped (I now see in retrospect) to sustain and, ultimately to extricate me from reductive psychosocial "explanations" of my being. Yet the rebellion against self-castigation which therapy (society) instilled in me would take a long, long time to consolidate and assert itself with any consistency. Before that could happen, I needed to recognize the importance of culture — of the role social moralizing about same gender love and lust plays in producing disabling self-recrimination. I also needed to understand (and this awaited the gay liberation movement of the late sixties/early seventies) that it isn't individual variations on the norm that require "amelioration" (through "treatment" punishment, guilt) but rather a cultural climate that equates variance with "disturbance."

September 21   Peculiarly depressed today. No apparent reason. I think I begin to regret leaving the analysis. Every *thing* is in order; all goes well — I am "free," busy, have enough money again, etc. No overt problems — nothing, in other words, on which to focus my anxiety. Nothing is wrong. And yet nothing is right.

September 22   Big scene with Larry. I told him the plain truth — I don't want to lose him but can't be completely faithful. What a goddamn mess I am. Simply not capable of love. Can anything be worse than a life of promiscuity, of objects not people? That's what I'm faced with and have to accept. Larry put a ban on our having sex. "We've got to try to form a new kind of relationship — friends, since lovers hasn't worked; and occasional sex with each other is merely postponing the adjustment." Sensible, logical. But the unfortunate fact remains that we *want* to continue going to bed with each other. If exclusive, Larry would consider it ideal; if occasional, I would. But the thought of *never*, frightens me more than Larry. *I* want everything.

(1981): Part of the trouble, probably most of it, was the going social definition of what constituted being a "mess." Homosexuality was sign enough, as the current consensus saw it, but to want to sleep with more than one man during a lifetime was considered the equivalent of being unable to "love." The One-Person-Now-And-Forever model of "health" was applied in the Fifties almost as rigorously to heterosexuals. That is, officially. As Kinsey had already shown in his books, a large percentage of married men paid greater fealty to the ideal of monogamy in their rhetoric than in their behavior. Like most American women, I had been trained to believe that interest in anyone other than the Beloved was all at once a definition of emotional immaturity and the equivalent of emotional treachery.

September 26   A call from George L. tonight. His trial's been postponed and he needs bail money [*George had been arrested by the state police in Ogunquit, Maine, where our crowd often vacationed. The beach at night was a well-known cruising spot. Police spotlights had caught George just as he was going down on somebody.*] I sent him $50, promising more next week when my salary check arrives . . . I suppose my motive was largely egotistical — "you're a great chap"; "most people wouldn't be bothered," etc. In fact, I feel some but not much sympathy for him; word has long since been out that the beach is dangerous. I sent him money not out of active sympathy but out of the *decision* to be helpful. Maybe that's not so bad. Maybe we could all use more artificiality — the conscious cultivation of our feeble impulses to generosity. Anyway, I did the right act — in which case can the motive ever be wrong?

October 1   Burning after urination . . . of course I can think of all kinds of reasons for penis pains — guilt over my resumed homosexuality, guilt over my ambivalent treatment of Larry, the desire, by pleading invalidism to *escape* homosexual contact . . .
    And so what? Can I *know* which if any of these "causes" is the true one? Is it so impossible for me to have an actual physical symptom — a nice, *healthy* disease? Probably. Weintraupt made me so aware of my hypochondria that I

have become a double prisoner of it — as both an unconscious drive, and a conscious explanation.

October 3   Starting writing today [*doctoral thesis on Charles Francis Adams*]. Very excited in spots. Thought everything put with inexpressible beauty and incisiveness. Then this evening I read the few pages to Larry and it seemed mostly flat and wordy. Now I feel it's all dreadful and I can't possibly continue. I won't try to correct — but will just keep going, otherwise I'll be endlessly polishing. I become absorbed in the writing itself, rather than the content. The *sound* of the sentences and the word patterns interest me more than the material I'm supposedly conveying . . . hardly an "historical" approach.

October 4   Spend the evening with Frank D. He's just failed his Generals [*Ph.D. Orals*] and is badly affected . . . a horrible blow to those as self-centered as most homosexuals are. With their intellectual self-respect destroyed, there's nothing much to fall back on, since the "academic queens" at least have been long using it as a compensation — a mask — for what they consider to be their other defects and inadequacies. With the "binder" gone, Frank has quite literally fallen apart.

(1981): Apparently I'd never seen a straight person "fall apart" after failing Generals. Which means I either couldn't see or had a remarkably limited circle of friends.

October 8   . . . good luck at the bars. Instead of posing — and waiting — made a move for once, and directly approached someone. Got a pleasant response and left with him but wasn't sure until he actually asked "if I'd like to come up" whether I was going to have to be content with a "nice conversation" . . . Probably the best-looking person I've ever been to bed with . . . Just graduated from Ohio State — in Boston for a visit — name of Bob E. A marvelous combination of youthfulness (superb skin, lovely body) and yet masculinity. He was shy of certain "practices" [*meaning, if my memory serves, he wouldn't let me fuck him*], yet wonderfully affectionate — even passionate. And I did him without a qualm — in fact with regret when it was over. [*Ordinarily I had such qualms, except with Larry.*].
    . . . I spent the night with him at his hotel and was rebuffed when I tried to have sex with him this morning. Nor could I pin him down to another meeting before he goes back to Ohio.
    I already have an awful incapacity to remember him in any tangible way . . . deep pleasure briefly and then intensified frustration in attempting to re-create it . . . anguish at having realized the ideal and having lost it again so soon. I almost wish I hadn't met him. I feel as if I've sleep-walked through the experience . . .

October 12   . . . continuing discomfort on urinating. Occasionally, seeing a pus-like emission. Called Dr. P. [*urologist*], but he can't see me until Tuesday. In the meantime I sit and fret, imagining — when I do specify the anxiety — cancer of the prostate, the end of sexual activity, etc. Of course P. checked all this last week (but not the prostate) and said I had torn the skin, or some such and there was no disease. Still, this was before I noticed the mucous-like substance and since I've seen him there's been no change whatsoever. What I want,

I suppose, is for him to check the prostate, tell me it's fine — reassure me, in other words, as to my "intactness." If I had to bet on it, I would place all odds on the trouble being either a minor one, or wholly imaginary. And yet realizing this does nothing towards relieving my anxiety.

October 14   Went to a most enjoyable party at Margaret R's — charmed by a cameo-like Radcliffe girl named Ann. But promptly at 10:00 — fearing I would turn into a man! — I deserted the party on some pretext and rushed to the bars for a little more self-torture. And I got it. Larry was there, faithfully watching and waiting — compounding thereby my unhappiness. Out of default I left with him and talked "straight" — I hate tormenting him and yet I am incapable now of changing my insane pace of promiscuity. [*As I look back over the diary, I had had sex once in two weeks.*] I said I'm useless to both of us. We agreed not to see each other any more.

October 15   Went to Dr. P. and this time he *did* find an infection in the urinary tract. I'm relieved that the cause of the pain was such a relatively minor one — and especially that there *was* a cause! . . .
    Spent a pleasant evening at Ray's [*my closest friend, also a graduate student*] . . . lots of drink, talk. Nice people — like them all . . . especially David E., who I haven't known before . . . warm, sensitive . . . not at all an intrusive, "look-at-me" personality. Rare anywhere, but especially in a homosexual. I must stop this business of judging homosexuals as a separate breed (but aren't they?) and being so persistently amazed at the occasional nice ones — there are few enough anywhere and should be admired as such apart from categories —

October 16–17   . . . sick the last few days from the acromycin Dr. P. prescribed. It upset me badly — without helping the urinary infection, so today he has switched me to sulphur. No matter how minor the disorder I seem able to cling to it with amazing tenacity! . . .

October 18   . . . Larry called unexpectedly . . . The usual happened — talk leading to desire leading to sex . . . The desire returns, but not sufficiently to make me want to give up my roaming.

October 19   3:00 a.m. . . . told Larry he could stay over at my place — since he has to go to work in the morning. But passing the river [*Harvard's chief cruising ground*] on our way home, he saw that it was crowded and decided to stop off. That was an hour ago and he hasn't appeared. Obviously he's met someone, and . . . I'm upset. But when I dropped him at the river I was actually *relieved*. I didn't want to have sex with him and rushed home to get to "sleep" before he returned . . . He just arrived. Has only been talking to someone he previously met. He's all affection. What an imbecile I am — I disgust myself at times . . .

October 20   . . . Stayed in tonight . . . I feel so much better when I do . . . Really a bourgeois at heart — early to bed, etc. Feel cleaner and more satisfied with myself.

(1981): Maybe Descartes is where it all went wrong — all the splits and separations, the moralistic dichotomies (staying at home versus the "neurotic" drive to look for sex/com-

panionship, etc.) The hideous overlay of metaphysical categories on garden variety shifts in moods and needs!

October 23   Larry was here tonight and we had sex . . . we simply wanted to and we did. I sometimes think all our "scenes" — eternal farewells, etc. — are indulged in part for pleasure: the stimulation of love forsaken and found again; of playing on the subtler threads of the relationship to test how far we can or cannot drive the other and then how easily we can or cannot recapture him. If we were legally tied to each other — as in marriage — it might soon degenerate into mutual disinterest.

October 24   . . . to see O'Neill's "Long Day's Journey Into Night" . . . O'Neill reminds me of Dreiser — formless, heavy-handed, crudely powerful. Really a mediocre epic poet . . . The best lines in the play were Baudelaire's.

November 4   1:00 a.m. The news from Hungary is shattering. How unimportant our election seems in light of it. Discount political exaggeration, and how much difference does it really make whether Eisenhower or Stevenson wins? A difference between complacent efficiency and at least the possibility of imaginative leadership — but agreement is already established on major questions . . .

November 5   1:00 a.m. Heard Stevenson's final campaign speech on TV this evening. It was magnificent. He has extraordinary eloquence . . . an imagination equal to the possibilities of our country . . . a great man — and one who will never be President.

November 19   I feel towards this delinquent Diary the way I used to towards Weintraupt — guilt at not keeping it up! . . . My routine, in truth, is so busily monotonous, that I'm lulled into a dull sort of contentment . . . I feel repugnance at merely recording the trivial and the obvious, partly because the thesis writing is proving some sort of catharsis for my energies.
   But, we'll try again —

November 20   One of my tutees, Alex S., a sophomore, came to see me today — appealingly confused, boyishly upset at his sudden lack of interest in history . . . He wants to "justify" his work, to find value beyond mere enjoyment (he doesn't seem to realize how rare *that* is among the "professionals") . . . I tried to keep my own disillusionment out of it, so as not to confuse him still further . . . I think I did well by him and this pleased me; helped him to see his *own* problems and aims without (miracolo!) obtruding mine. Of course, his extraordinary attractiveness accounted for my special effort . . . we are not indiscriminate in our attentions — no one treats all the world alike. . .

(1981): I do still feel that eroticism is often a component of good teaching. I can be attracted to (care about) qualities of character or mind enough to make a special effort. But if I care about a body too, that much more of myself goes into the contact. And if the body is spectacular enough, the effort will match it — even without qualities of character or mind. I want to matter (become part of?) my somatic ideal. I think the Greeks understood this — even to sanctioning physical contact between older men (teachers, guides) and

younger. In our society, the mere recognition that an erotic element is present in teaching — and of course not only male/male — would constitute an enormous advance. Finding a way to acknowledge that element would constitute utopia.

November 26 . . . Isabel [*she and I had met at Ogunquit the previous summer*] was here for the weekend — mainly because Don, Joan, *et al* were due from New York for the Yale-Harvard festivities and I felt compelled to produce a date. Isabel means more to me than a convenience . . . yet I was relieved to see her leave early Sunday . . .

(1981): I'm almost sure it was on this visit that Isabel came into my bed one morning (she was sleeping on the sofa bed, in the living room). Sweetly, warmly, she cuddled with me. Tensely, mechanically, I cuddled back, frightened that she wanted to have sex. Either she didn't or she got my message; we never did more than cuddle. And I felt guilty and wretched over my "inadequacy."

All of which reminds me of my debate at Fordham in April, 1973 with Dr. Irving Bieber. Three out of four male homosexuals he's studied show "fear of female genitalia." Pathology, he says. And the source? A detached, minimizing father. But has anyone studied the degree of fear in male hetero-sexuals? I suspect it might match or exceed that of homosexuals — especially if the sample studied was as skewed (102 patients in treatment) as Bieber's. Besides, Bieber ignores the contribution of social pressure in producing "fear" (whether in gay or straight men). If society didn't insist that the definition of male adultness was an omnipresent desire to fuck females, there wouldn't be the built-in sense of inadequacy when that desire isn't present, nor the avoidance of closeness with women as a device for avoiding the feeling of inadequacy . . . I wonder what it might have been like for Isabel and me if I hadn't gotten into that bed with a destructive set of expectations in my head. I would have enjoyed the cuddle. And maybe more.

. . . Jim came over . . . a new contact [*we met the previous week*], someone I was attracted to and eager to impress. We spent about four hours drinking — and five in bed — which has left me feeling empty and disgusted . . . I was interested in Jim — beyond the physical . . . the sex partly cooled my ardor (for what? conquest?) and the conversation completed the job. There was something hard about him which came out only by degrees, occasionally blatant egoism, sometimes just (just indeed!) a lack of concern, of tenderness for his partner — in conversation or sex. I suppose I'll see him again, but the disappointment adds to this morning's depression. I keep telling myself I'm looking for something permanent — someone to grow with, to do things for, to bring meaning into routine. Yet when I go to the bars, I consistently look for the most physically appealing person. These pick-up bars don't allow for any other form of contact. Sex is the basis of meeting, and sex is the first, rather than the final expression of the relationship. I tell myself how meaningless this anonymous cycle of body and body is, but I continue to repeat it; partly, no doubt, because of the necessity to keep proving myself, but also because the means of forming a healthier, more complete relationship are slight. With Jim, I thought there was some hope; I really don't now. But my disappointment is real, which makes me hope that my desire for permanence is also real.

(1981): The standard social values and therapeutic vocabulary of the day: sexual pleasure can only be justified in the context of a "meaningful" (i.e. "caring," "permanent") rela-

tionship; disconnected lust leads to emptiness and disgust. The self-recriminations that followed my failing to measure up to stereotypic norms were more than a strategy of atonement, expiation for having experienced pleasure not officially sanctioned. They affected the experience itself, diluting and distorting it. As the entry makes clear, what one expects in advance from an encounter is usually what one ends up taking away from it.

December 15   Up late last night — Adams House Xmas party. Most of today on the bed, reading; due to virus and bad throat. Didn't go to either Margy or Ina's party — not "up to it." Yet miraculously, I found the strength at 10:30 to find my way to the bars. Uneventful. Home with a worse throat.

December 17   Still feeling sick . . . Was going to the bars, but decided to be sensible — that is, to cater to my hypochondriacal rather than my homosexual neurosis!

February 16, 1957   For some reason I feel like writing an entry today — the first in many weeks. Some impressions I want to get down after a surfeit night of drink and sex. I successfully maneuvered Thom H., one of my heros — at a distance — to bed. Good sex. Though my fantasy of 6'3" of rock-like masculinity progressively flattened as the usual nice, ineffectual mama's boy came out. But still, good, if not ideal. And yet today my guilt, or at least revulsion, is working overtime. All sorts of resolutions, too. Eager for work — never going to waste time barhopping again, etc. No satisfaction there anyway. All set for a return to analysis; must have a wife and family, only possible things that matter, etc. These illuminations, of course, are easy to produce after the appetite has been depressed by booze and sex.

(1981): I can't help but smile as I type the above. At the unerring self-dramatization. At the sorrowings of young Werther. At the conviction that everyone else (but especially all heterosexuals) were and would be happier than I. At the effort — age 26 — to strike a world-weary elegiac note. And — the smile disappears here — at the air-tight formulas into which I kept squeezing my experience; formulas which accurately parrotted social norms of the day, but almost entirely failed to help me understand what in fact I was living through.

I wish to change . . . but parallel with this desire runs the stronger current of neurotic drive and compulsion, thwarting most of my efforts to change. I can neither give up my homosexual activities, nor devote myself guiltlessly to them. Paralyzed on the one side by desire and on the other by knowledge. Is this merely the neurotic or the human condition?

If I could only maintain the strong sense of disgust and renunciation which I felt all day — perhaps then I could make the necessary effort to change the pattern of my life. But I can already feel the resolution draining out of me, and the old empty compulsion taking its place —

(1981): I should have read more anthropology. A Siwan version of the above: When Arab offered me his son last night for anal intercourse — as any thoughtful host would — my pleasure in the boy was compromised by my neurotic equation of sexual satisfaction with heterosexuality. As a result, intercourse seemed little more than mutual

masturbation. If I could maintain the strong sense of disgust that I felt all day, perhaps then I could make the necessary effort to change the pattern of my life.

I've sought advice from the Elders. They feel I hold on to my deviance out of defiance — a stubborn refusal to let nature take its bisexual course. Their words make entire sense to me. Yet I can already feel the resolution draining away, and the empty compulsion to sleep only with women taking its place.

June 13   So much has happened since my last entry [*4 months earlier*] Grandma's death, Lucile's [*sister*] divorce, my Yale appointment, my ulcer, my completed doctorate. Today was graduation. I'm left this evening with nothing much to do and a sense of slight depression, so thought I would start the Diary again. A little something to keep me busy, I suppose — a new project. I can't yet relax from the rush and tension of the last few months. But the sense of incompletion goes deeper. I need work to focus on; these brief pauses, though much anticipated during the preceding months of hard work, are more distressing than the strain of a heavy schedule. I'm already planning ahead for my courses at Yale next year . . . I seem to enjoy myself most when I take occasional hours from a "productive" day rather than indulging in long periods of unplanned, unfilled leisure. Free time — in any large dose — becomes flabby and suffocating.

September 16   Now that I'm settled in at Yale [*my first full-time teaching job*] I thought I'd try keeping the Diary again . . .

I just got back last night from a quick run up to Boston. Classes begin on Wednesday and after that the chances of my getting away will be less. Spent most of the time alone with Larry . . . Why is it that only on the point of severance do I become most keenly aware of the deep affection . . . as if I allow myself the full emotion only when I safely know that it can be indulged in only infrequently.

September 18   A tough few minutes at the beginning of my first class today. I was literally choked up with nervousness. Arrived ten minutes early, sat in the chair at the front of the room and buried myself in the *N.Y. Times*. As the students poured in (31!) I occasionally mustered enough courage to glance up from the paper. Eventually — after I started to talk (what else?!) — I settled down into mild terror. I must have given a lousy impression — stuffy and stern.

September 20   Dr. Igen [*therapist*] accepted me as a patient today — 3 times a week at $20 per hour — I don't really want to start the pain and upset of analysis all over again. But I must, if I'm ever to have an identity . . .

(1981): Meaning, its perhaps redundant to add, an "acceptable" identity, some placation of my passionate craving to fit in, to "belong."

September 21   Much depressed — woke up feeling this way. Stomach kicking up, which both helped cause the "pits" and was the result of them. Spent the day reading and doing odds and ends around the apartment [*I was living off campus*] . . . evening went to the gay bars, which I had sworn pre-arrival at New Haven, that I would stay out of. Once having started, I'll probably continue; I can't really stay away from it. So I risk my job — but I'm sufficiently depressed not to care. If I could stand still and *understand* the depression (something about teaching and the insecurities it arouses, plus being unsettled and lonesome — but this doesn't get below the surface), I'd no doubt be better off. But homosexuality has been a channel — *the* channel — for so long — that it's easier to keep running.

(1981): Poor bastard. You wanted some companionship and sex, but had "learned" to cover over those human enough needs with a shit-load of self-castigation.

September 24   Had a good session with Dr. Igen today, but my stomach trouble and depression continue apace. Called Larry this evening for a little long-distance solace. Can't wait till he arrives on Friday. Despite the wild fluctuations in my feeling for him over the last few years, my genuine attachment to him has never been more apparent.

September 29   Larry just left. We had an awfully good weekend together — didn't really do very much — saw the Yale-Conn. football game yesterday (boring as always) and had dinner at Mory's. Except for that — none of it exactly new and exciting for me — we stayed near the apartment, ran errands, took rides, etc. It all went too fast. If I don't love him, why did I cry so painfully when it came time for him to leave? If I do love him, why has our relationship fluctuated so wildly the last few years. A riddle I long since gave up on. Anyway, it's awful being alone again . . .

(1981): The riddle's a little less dense these days: it's hard to sustain intimacy if you can't sustain a sense of self-worth. And to have grown up gay in America in the Fifties was to view oneself as emotionally shallow, stunted.

October 2   Went to the Taft, George and Harry's and Pierelli's [*New Haven's semi-gay bars — that is, bars where gay men were known to appear*] tonight — the works! Nothing happened, but aside from that, I've all but given up the idea of restricting my activity to outside of N. Haven. The hell with it — N.Y. and Boston are too far away and I'm too horny. Anyway I now tell myself that nothing really dire could happen . . . if a student reports me to a Dean or some such, what can he really say except that he saw me in a homosexual bar. It's unlikely the Administration would take action on what is only a suspicion.

(1981): My concern was realistic, not paranoid. These were the years when a half dozen male faculty members were hounded from their jobs at Smith when discovered to be in possession of "pornographic" (gay) materials. As I was soon to discover, attitudes at Yale were comparable. In 1958 ('59?) a faculty member and friend of mine — I'll call him "Eli" — was fired, though under somewhat different circumstances than having been seen in a compromising bar. At a drunken student/faculty party, Eli followed up on a student's verbal pass — groped him in a corner? whispered sweet scatalogical nothings in his ear? I don't know. Whatever, the student freaked, ran shouting (literally) into the night — and ultimately into the Dean's office. The Administration (humanely, some might argue, given the fierce homophobia of the day) hinted that if Eli would deny the incident, it would be overlooked. Eli wouldn't. The Administration then asked for his resignation, offering to help him find work in an administrative capacity (not as a teacher) in some other school. Eli refused that, too.

October 13   Saturday night, bar-hopping in New York. Met a Bill N. in the Annex [*a gay bar*]. Despite my attraction, shouldn't have gone with him mainly because (a) he had a lover — no future and (b) he was of limited interest to me as a person — also no future. Yet my six weeks in New Haven made me feel as if I "had" to have sex, so off we went and on the whole, it came off rather better than most of my experiences of this nature do. He was sufficiently attractive physically, and technically proficient, to make bearable, even to a degree unnecessary, the lack of emotional attachment.

October 14   Feeling lonely most of the day, though a full evening's work has helped dissipate it. The prospect of spending my life alone has become more alive and painful — living off-campus and inaccessible to casual "droppers-in" and having to cook and eat by myself. The prospects of a lasting homosexual relationship are too slim for me to get much comfort from the possibility; and a satisfying heterosexual relationship is still so remote that I can barely even wish for it. But perhaps either luck in the first area or Dr. Igen in the latter will make one or the other come true. In the meantime, I remain skeptical and unhappy.

October 21   The weekend in Boston started badly, with Larry failing to meet me according to arrangement, or waiting for dinner as I'd asked him to — all the result, though he won't admit it, of my having gone to New York last weekend instead of to Boston. Understandable enough; since we have no "official" ties, his resentment has to come out indirectly. On my side, I was more angered at his studied disinterest than I had a "legal" right to be, clinging as I do to the double standard of my freedom and his devotion . . . By Saturday, we had more or less patched things up . . . I think.

October 29   Staying busy, which I need to avoid the very real anguish of loneliness I've been feeling. I've never been so fully conscious of being quite literally "apart," "unconnected." My impulse at times like this is to run — to give up teaching, friends, the future — and devote myself to find *the* one — that never-never "right" person who'll make everything sweet and meaningful. Yet when I do search, I invariably end up in frantic pursuit not of a person but of a mere physical fantasy.

   Dr. I. feels that at this point I would be foolish to try to resolve basic difficulties by any rash decisions — e.g. giving up teaching, moving to New York, etc. I have to sit tight and try to work the problems out slowly and deliberately through the analysis. So sit we will.

(1981): I still think it makes sense to take time with important decisions — and to try to avoid making them under the pressure of momentary panic or impulse. But impulses should be attended to, not dismissed out of hand; a valuable insight can come swiftly — and prolonged brooding can dissipate rather than clarify its force. Besides, some complaints deserve to be taken at face value; they aren't always a cover, a technique of avoidance. A worker in an automobile factory who complains about the boredom of the assembly line isn't necessarily displacing his "status anxiety." The "surface" problems I brought to therapy — about loneliness, teaching, the life of scholarship, living in New Haven — deserved more serious consideration as valid issues in themselves; I was never encouraged to regard them as other than a "blind."

November 5   To New York. Ended up going to Everard's two nights in a row.

(1981): Everard's was a gay bathhouse. It still is, though it closed briefly a few years back after a disastrous fire — caused by the criminal negligence of the management in failing, as specified by law, to install a proper sprinkling system — killed and maimed a dozen men.

   Everard's was one of the places I frequented during the late Fifties/early Sixties on my weekend trips to New York. My usual pattern at the baths was to meet one man and go to a room with him. I avoided orgiastic scenes, especially the steamroom. If I was going to be gay, I was going to be gay in a way that was "seemly." In a way that approximated how straight people — sensible, adult, healthy straight people — behaved. You find one person and stick with him (her). My sexual repertoire was comparably limited in those days. With Larry I played the stereotypical male (dominant) role; out of bed, made the decisions, in bed did the fucking.

Much reasonably enjoyable sex with moderately attractive people — sufficient to black out any upsetting hesitations and doubts. But lack of sleep (I spent the weekend on Henry's [*a New York friend*] living room floor) soon produced the ripe conditions for reaction. Driving back up here last night filled with thoughts of renunciation, of an acute sense of the "disarray" such wantonness produces in my life. But resolution, like the guilt which prompts it, soon disappears. I can hardly lose sight of the fact that such behavior is destructive, but the compulsion to such activity (the bars being only a lesser version) remains even stronger . . .

November 7   Beginning to pick up the pieces after the upset of my weekend "frolic" in New York; though the degree of upset varies with the type of experience, I'm less prone than in the past to lay my sense of frustration or dissatisfaction at the door of "inadequate" sex (i.e. not the "right" person) . . . I begin to see that it's the homosexual act itself which disturbs me — despite the physical pleasure and neurotic gain involved.

(1981): The new therapist — a decent, likeable man — had been helping me to this "clarification." Dr. Igen was less given to ideology than most psychiatrists of the day. Still, he had no doubt that homosexuality was symptomatic of a character disorder. But he never scrutinized — apparently never dreamed there might be a need to scrutinize — any of the assumptions that underlay his diagnoses and prescriptions. He merely accepted (as did most people in the Fifties, therapists and otherwise) the dictum that homosexuality by its nature was destructive to individual growth; biological law — unspecified, unexamined — not oppressive social norms, produced the disturbing bi-products of same gender love or lust.

November 10   Went to New York last night to meet Tom F., who was in from Texas . . . We spent the night together at Henry's (who was away for the weekend). If we could have stopped short of actual sex, the evening would have been far pleasanter. The preliminaries were deeply satisfying — I felt close and complete — but proceeding beyond, we seemed to draw further apart. I wanted his affection, not his body; being pushed into contact with his body, I gradually lost whatever affection I had felt. Ended up feeling distant and antagonistic and said good bye this morning with feelings of real relief . . .

Dr. Igen left today for his eye operation. Surprised myself by the depth of my upset — surprised and yet pleased at such a sign of significant involvement. He won't be back for at least a month. Rather than "hold the fort," I'll more likely destroy it. Don't see how I can curtail my activity without at least the security and profit of my visits to him. At any rate, a comfortable excuse for future promiscuity.

(1981): Igen, like Dr. Weintraupt before him, had recently made it clear that if I hoped to make further progress in analysis, I had to make a greater effort to control my impulses and show more willingness to face rather than run from my anxiety. I can still hear his litany: "Homosexuality is the channel through which you act out your anxieties. We must close the escape hatch. Only in that way can the anxieties surface, be analyzed and treated." I had explained (implored) that I'd tried that before, with Dr. Weintraupt, and the strain had proved intolerable. He persuaded me that I'd changed since then, that I was now older and wiser, better able to withstand the neurotic pressure to "act out." Besides, as he put it, "the injunction from above now coincides more exactly with what you feel within." Flattered, encouraged, I once more swore to take the veil.

November 22   Picked the wrong weekend to stay in New Haven. Everything is crawling with Yalies and their dates — the big Yale/Harvard weekend. Stayed here to catch up on work and especially to prepare my next two lectures. Hoped to take in the New Haven bars in the process, but a quick reconnaissance to-night convinced me of the folly of that — too many students wandering into too many strange places. Just not worth the chance. Yet I wish so much that someone was here with me tonight.

(1981): For a moment I thought this might have been the football weekend of my drunken tangle in the small park that fronted fraternity row. But now I remember that was much earlier — when I was an undergraduate at Yale (in 1951 or '52): I followed some stocky, equally drunk 20 year old out-of-towner into the park and (I think he encouraged me), groped him. He reacted in a rage, swung at me drunkenly, got hold of the collar of my jacket and ripped it down my back as I struggled out of reach and raced down the street. I told my roommates I'd gotten into a fight with "some townie." With my torn jacket as proof, I was treated as a hero. I trembled inside for days.

This was, if my sense of chronology holds, my very first homosexual "contact" — give or take those rubbing sessions as a boy in summer camp; plus one experiment in mutual fellatio with a high school friend (not to orgasm).

But soon after my fraternity row fracas Don, an undergraduate friend, casually mentioned that I should stay away at night from the "Green" (the large park in front of the Old Campus) — "it's a hangout for fairies." I was shocked — and overjoyed; at last a place to meet someone (I was 20 years old). That same night I got drunk, reeled down to the Green and sat on a bench opposite the only other person I could see in the area — a very fat, middle-aged black man. He whistled tantalizingly in my direction. I got up, reeled over and stood boldly in front of him. He started playing with my cock, then took it out of my pants. Wildly excited, I started to fondle him.

"Do you have any place we can go?" I whispered.

"Nope. No place."

Suddenly I heard laughter and noise coming in our direction. I was sure it was some undergraduates — and equally sure we'd been seen. Zipping up my fly, I ran out of the park — ran without stopping, panicked, hysterical, ran for my life back to my dorm room. I stayed in the shower for hours, cleaning, cleaning. I actually washed my mouth out with soap, though I hadn't used my mouth — other than to make a prayerful pact with the Divinity that if He let me off this time, I'd never, never go near the Green again. The panic lasted for days. By the end of the week I was back on the Green, drunk again. I met a dancer. We had sex in his car — that is, I let him blow me.

I can remember only one other experience while an undergraduate: being picked up by an older man cruising the area in his car. I got in, then changed my mind. He begged me to stay, said he'd "do anything I wanted to do." I got out, not unmindful (I now suspect) of the special pleasure fellow victims can derive from tormenting each other. Those are the only undergraduate encounters I can recall, the sum of my "sex life" until age 21. With men, I mean.

I had been through most of the heterosexual rituals. At age 15 (16?), staying with two high school friends at one of their parent's homes in Palm Beach, we went to a whore house one night. (A version of this, with some — and I don't know for certain which — details re-imagined, is my one-act play, "The Recorder"). I hadn't been able to get an erection. The prostitute kindly put some ointment in the urethral opening of my cock, wrapped it in gauze and snapped on a rubberband. (Can this really have been standard preventive treatment for v.d. in the Forties?). With the outward credentials of having fucked, I could brag about "how great it had been" to my friends (one of whom had no gauze bandage; suspicion deflected to him). I remember the prostitute's effort to comfort me with off-handed remarks: "married men often come into the house and can't get it up either — it's nothing to worry about, kid." I made her promise not to tell my friends that I'd "failed." She agreed; I remember her warm, sympathetic smile.

Still more vivid is the night of the senior prom in high school. I was 17 and had been dating a "wild" girl, Rachel, for a long time. We had promised ourselves — and announced to our friends — that we would "consummate our love" that night. (Some of this is also in "The Recorder"). After the prom our crowd went to Al's family apartment: very fancy, fit setting for the Big Event. Everyone lay around on the living room floor drinking and making out — and waiting for the moment when Rachel and I would go into the back bedroom; the whole group was vicariously losing its virginity through us. In the bedroom, Rachel and I got undressed and lay together on the huge bed. Again, I was impotent — but this time desperate, crazed:

"The doctor warned me that I've been making out too much. He said this would happen if I didn't cut down."

Rachel neither questioned nor accused. "I love you. I love you even if you can't get it up."

Again I lied to my friends. This time the excuse (agreed to by Rachel — I was lucky in my choice of women) was that we hadn't been able to do it because she was having a period. I was celibate till aged 20, when I had those few furtive experiences on the New Haven Green.

During my first year of graduate school at Harvard (1952–3), I made my first timid foray into a gay bar, the Napoleon. I met Ray. We went home that same night and had sex in my dormitory room. For weeks afterwards I avoided him, rushing in the opposite direction whenever I caught sight of him on campus. He finally cornered me one day: "Look — can't we be friends at least?" Caught somewhere between hysteria and relief, I managed to mumble "yes."

It was the beginning of a friendship that's lasted to the present day. The beginning, too, of allowing myself to know other gay people socially, of gradually developing a circle of friends and entering a subculture that brought me from individual isolation to collective secrecy — a considerable advance, if one can understand (in a day when all furtiveness is decried) the quantum jump in happiness from private to shared anguish.

Soon after, I had my first affair — with "Rob" (at the time, as with most affairs, it seemed a good deal more profound; but then I was measuring it against the few desperate, anonymous forays of my undergraduate years, not against the intensity of the relationship with Larry that was soon to begin). I met Rob on one of my first visits to the Napoleon. He had been a classmate at Yale, but we had barely known each other there. Rob had long been "out" sexually, adored and pursued me, glamorized me with his family estates and connections. He came from a rich WASP family, long on lineage, proud of its service in the diplomatic corps.

One evening Rob took me to meet his grandmother; something of a formal presentation. She received us in the library of her Manhattan triplex (not, I presume, as the prospective in-law her grandson had in mind — but one can never be sure about the sophisticated insights of the upper class in these matters). The butler ushered us into the presence of a seemingly ancient and unquestionably formidable woman. Sitting unmoving in an arm-chair, dressed in a full length black gown, a mass of snow-white hair framing a still beautiful face, she allowed the exchange of a few rigorous pleasantries. Dazed and inti-mated, I neither heard them fully then nor can recall any part of them now. But I do remember it was that same night, as Rob and I changed clothes in an upstairs bedroom, that I told him I probably loved him. For the first time. Tit for tat, he let me fuck him. I resisted his badgering insistence that I pronounce it the "best fuck" I had ever had, though I had had precious few. It may have been my father's peasant stubbornness asserting itself, bristling at the hint of droit de seigneur.

Though we called ourselves "lovers," our lovemaking was sharply circumscribed. Most of the time I was "trade" for Rob — I would let him blow me. The boundaries suited us both; they assuaged my guilt, fed his preferred image as guide to the uninitiated. Within a few months, our affair ended traumatically. I had to drop out of graduate school for a series of operations on my back, and while recuperating at home, wrote a "compromising" letter that my mother intercepted. She demanded an explanation, tapped a ready reservoir of self-loathing. I explained that Rob was queer, but I, of course, was not; I had let him blow me now and then because "my back problem prevented me from seeking the usual sexual outlets"; he had been a convenience. My mother "accepted" the explanation. In gratitude, I broke off with Rob. I've never seen him since. My memories of him are ungenerous, ironic. Even now — my head ostensibly transformed — resentment against the man who tried to take me a step beyond furtive anonymity in sex, lies like a stone in my gut, an immutable pleistocene fossil.

December 1   Disappointing holiday in Boston. Larry and I got along only spo-radically. My feelings toward him, as always, fluctuated between deep affection and sudden antagonism. I don't excuse him completely. He did two or three overtly nasty things (suggesting, for example, that we go to the Turkish baths together Saturday night). The weekend ended in a burst of mutual recrimina-tion and sullenness . . . Time, I suppose, finally to put an end to the whole torturous business . . . But I still feel so tied to him — in some deeply neurotic way — that I can't seriously envision cutting off all contact.

(1981): Why "neurotic"? Because of the fluctuations in feelings? But that's true of all deep attachments. Maybe our arc swung wider and more often than most, but I auto-matically ascribed that to personal deficiencies, never to the self-distrust engendered in us

by a culture insistent that it was wrong ("sinful," "neurotic" — depending on whether the rhetoric was based on the religious of psychiatric model) for two men to be physical lovers, to care "too" much about each other.

December 5 A lengthy, elegant meal at Jack's [*a gay faculty member I'd recently come to know*] for a group of bachelor fellows. Superb food, beautifully prepared and served; all very "upper-class homosexual." Mozart on the victrola, white Wedgewood plates, much clever banter. Pleasant enough people, I don't deny, but my points of meaningful contact with them are limited and I don't wish to join with an artificial band of "solidarity" what genuine interest and affection cannot cement.

I intend to try to stay put this weekend — not so much because of my work-load, but more for the analysis. "Sitting still and suffering for science." (No — I must keep remembering it's for *me*) . . . I hope I last through tomorrow night!

December 8 Depressing weekend. Stayed in New Haven . . . ulcer kicking up and generally unhappy.

December 10 Harry D. [*a graduate student I'd met at a party; we'd been immediately attracted to each other, but he'd let me know his lover was visiting*] called last night at 2:00 a.m. — a surprise to say the least, after 6 weeks of silence. He came over tonight and like last time, I found him very attractive. Still, we went to bed too fast, before he had a chance to become a person to me.

(1981): More of the current cant. Yes, getting to know a person can enhance sex with them. It can also complicate and inhibit sex. No one formula can cover all moods, impulses, needs — and consequences. But an entity called lust does exist, often is evoked and heightened by anonymity and can — quite independent of "emotional commitment" — produce very *satisfying sex. All of which is hardly news, but if known in 1957 was rarely acknowledged; and by me, apparently not known.*

I didn't really get excited in bed, though physically he didn't disappoint me in the slightest. Too impersonal, I suppose; too routine.

(1981): Nuts. I remember the evening well. Harry had an enormous cock; in these, my reticent years, that got translated — even in the privacy of my own diary — as "physically he didn't disappoint in the slightest." He got instantly and stayed unyieldingly hard — and aggressively insisted his cock belonged up my ass. I demurred (that's the word) secretly thrilled, eager to please yet not in the way he wanted and therefore without confidence I could in any way. The kind of insecurity often present, initially, with someone I'm deeply attracted to. Though "insecurity" may itself be too standard a circumlocution. Realistic fear may be more accurate. Realistic because of the accurate recognition that a stranger is unexpectedly in control of my sense of well-being. Frightened because the transfer of power makes me aware of the fragility of that well-being, aware that primitive urges, a confluence of accidents, can at any moment disrupt my illusion of being in control.

December 17 Getting lax with this . . . nothing vivid enough to make me want to record it. Stayed in New Haven again over the weekend and went to a gay party . . . had a long chat with my first two real live "dikes" [*sic*] — both very feminine and talkative. Hope to see them in New York; a safe way of enjoying female company.

(1981): I cringe at this, but have resisted — barely — the temptation to delete it. With the possible exception of the last clause, it could have been written by John Wayne. Which is why I've included it: it serves as a measure of the gulf between gay men and lesbian women (now as well as then, though less so now — I think), as well as graphically demonstrating the usually unacknowledged bond between gay men and straight men. In their behavior and values, gay men are often males first and gays second. The priority has recently begun to shift — at least within limited circles. But many gay men continue to patronize lesbians, dismissing them with the same stereotypic contempt employed by the society at large. And this is the chief (though not the only) reason gay men and lesbians have had so much trouble working together harmoniously in the "movement." On the other hand, I don't think sexism is as strong among gay men as among straight; some gay men — and in increasing number, I believe — are more than rhetorically committed to feminism. But many feminists would dispute that, and others would go no further than wary optimism.

December 17   I'm writing this to exorcise John D . . . At my request, he came to see me about his failing grades . . . he told me his whole life revolved around a girl back home; that to him this emotional involvement was far more important than the trivia he was told to absorb in his classes . . . I agreed, but argued that love sometimes served as an excuse for blocking off other aspects of available experience that might prove satisfying; that he had in college the opportunity to become interested in those aspects; that it was *natural* for human beings to be curious, alert and involved; that to the degree that he was refusing to be, he was denying part of his nature. But in the process of saying all this, I wondered, and wonder even more now, whether *anything* I said made sense . . . I do believe in the function of a University as something above and beyond servicing the social order. I believe education *does* make better human beings, because it raises doubts, instills humility, encourages flexibility. I said all this to John and I think I believe it; but I'm left with a gnawing sense of inadequacy — as if I said all the "right" things without having said any of the true ones . . . I'm so aware of the inadequacy of the "intellectual life" that I always feel a little absurd in extolling its virtues — especially to one who already possesses what to me seems infinitely more important and infinitely more unattainable.

December 20   Ever since the bad time with Larry three weeks ago, I've been rushing around filling the void with the usual pointless activities. The last two weekends I've had bad experiences. First with a set of lovers from Jersey — almost panic-stricken with regret after going home with them.

(1981): I remember it well. They picked me up in a bar in New York City, then drove me out to their place in the country. The older of the two was tall and angular — marginally attractive. The younger was devastating: a short, powerfully-built farm boy from Maine, with an enormous cock. We started out to have a threesome, but the older man soon withdrew and went upstairs to bed. I was surprised and confused. Did he find me unattractive (as I did him), or had it been pre-arranged between them — had I been picked up to keep the younger one happy? I remember how lonesome I felt, after sex, when

Maine withdrew upstairs to sleep with his lover, not inviting me to join them. I dozed for a few hours on the living room couch, then woke them early morning and asked to be taken to the bus. Why the panic? That model in my head again. The contrast between my aloneness, my "inability to make it with someone on a sustained basis," and their togetherness.

The other bad experience was last weekend in New York . . . met a guy named Lou in the Big Dollar [*a gay bar*] and went home with him. Rugged Italian type . . . one track mind sexually — wanted, deliriously, to fuck me. His persistence excited me. It brought out all my passive desires — to be used, possessed, overpowered; which only occasionally come to the surface and which I act on rarely. I was tempted to give in this time, but controlled the impulse by telling myself what I knew was true — that the fantasy of being "taken" was more exciting than the actuality and that the subsequent psychological upset, plus the worry over disease, would far overbalance the slight pleasure. I wonder what lies behind the fantasy in the first place. I present an exterior of manliness, and in much of my actual sex life, play the dominant role, but there is a parallel and conflicting desire in me — sometimes very strong — to be passive sexually. In some complicated way I think all my homosexual activity is an attempt (among other things) to identify with a masculinity I was never sure I had. Being entered by a man is perhaps the most direct way of incorporating and absorbing that masculinity. And yet when I do allow myself to be "browned" [*the going genteel gay euphemism for "fucked"*] I almost never receive physical pleasure from it; that comes instead from assuming the opposite role — from browning others. But the fantasy remains strong: to be possessed by — and thereby to possess — a real man and his qualities.

(1981): A "real man" penetrated, dominated, fucked. This kind of sexual stereotyping — still so prevalent — was an integral aspect of the medical model of sexuality with which I identified. It managed all at once to be homophobic and patriarchal: a "real man" was heterosexual and unyieldingly dominant. All sexual acts intrinsically denoted "active" or "passive" attributes. There seemed to be no understanding — certainly none that was transmitted to patients wavering "dangerously" in their proclivities — that the muscular contractions of the anus, say, or the vagina, could, by several definitions, be considered an "active" agent in producing any cohabitation worthy of the name. The strict division of all sexual behavior into active or passive categories did serve as a convenient guide for those terrified of being confused (especially in their own minds) about the proper role to assume, which acts to perform (or not) in order to win certification as Male.

Though I now get angry at these one-dimensional models — being "entered" connotes "passivity," connotes "femininity" — that did so much to shape and constrict my understanding, I have to resist the urge to be just as categorical in rejecting them, for the latest theories and vocabularies have no conclusive validation either and will themselves doubtless be subjected in time to yet further reformulations.

Besides, the derision with which I view my former values, the contempt with which I regard my former self, may be designed in part to keep me from owning (which is harder than owning up to) the person I was. Yes, I was often callow, fatuous (especially in my tenacious "self-scrutiny"), grandiose. Yet not taking possession of the earlier me, amounts to not accepting myself now; for despite my efforts at disassociation, the two are one, the past is present, has left some mark; denying it raises the suspicion that the mark may be more pronounced than I like to admit. Memory is one powerful ingredient in forming identity. If I cut off my own legs, that leaves me floating in space. A neat trick, but not one in my non-Eastern bag. It's important to stop talking about "him" and "me" — to accept the totality. "He" may have been simplistic and self-pitying, but so would any mocking disavowal of him be (tempted though I am to indulge it). Not to forgive my earlier self is not to do several things that need doing: to implicate society for the self-sabotage it generated in gay people; to refuse myself an anterior history which, however, painful, is an integral part of my being; to deny that I had a place from which I needed to grow . . .

January 5, 1958   Back from spending vacation in New York with Larry. Looks like the final split between us. Larry announced it was time to recognize that what was left of our relationship is only a "bad joke," that he felt unwelcome, that I should please not write or contact him at all from now on. I agreed with little reluctance — though I've since had occasional pangs. The simple and absurd truth is that we're basically incompatible and nothing either of us can do will ever change that. Unfortunately, incompatibility is no guarantee against strong attraction and real feeling . . . I'm fired up again with the determination to resist all homosexual contact, to change . . .

(1981): I wish, at this juncture of my life, I'd been encouraged to ask a different set of questions about what did indeed prove to be the final break-up with Larry. They might have produced a different attitude about myself and a different set of expectations for the future. I wish I'd looked more closely at what our "incompatibility" consisted of. I only knew our obvious differences — in background, education, temperament. I doubt if these constituted a significant, let alone sufficient explanation for the problems we had. Our differences often made for some of our happiest times — we knew about different things and saw some things in different ways, and by that much added to each other's lives.

More basic to the split, in retrospect, was our shared assumption (much stronger on my part, though Larry's Catholic upbringing induced guilt enough) that two men could never make it together, that to be homosexual was, by definition, to be incapable of sustained commitment to another human being. Plus the conviction, bred into us by the culture (into heterosexuals, too) that sexual fidelity and an unwavering level of caring were the two crucial indices for evaluating the "success" of a relationship. Any erosion of erotic zest for one's partner was suspect, suggestive of incompatibility as well as immaturity. But the reigning standard of sexual fidelity was applied more stringently to gay men than to straight ones, "adventuring" automatically seen in them as a symptom of character disorder.

Such formulas squeezed my experience into dry moulds that caricatured it. What I needed were terms — ways of thinking — that would have helped me to question those formulas. That's precisely where psychiatry failed me.

I wish I'd been encouraged to ask why I wanted a lifetime companion, and then — if convinced I did — to recognize that if my choice was to settle down into "matehood," I had better stop thinking of the relationship in the adolescent/romantic terms of perfect accord, unconditional caring, eternal bliss.

Beyond my relationship with Larry, the standard psychoanalytic formulas (the moral norms of the country, or my corner of it) on which I was weaned in the Fifties, kept me from myself — encouraged me to distrust my feelings, to malign "mere" sexual pleasure, to avoid risk, to associate legitimate social discontent with private neurosis, to doubt my capacity for closeness and to misread and denigrate any evidence to the contrary.

I wish I had spent my time analyzing the tyrannical formulas then current for recog-

nizing a "real" relationship, instead of repetitively exploring the presumed neuroses which I was told (and believed) would forever obstruct its realization. But I learned what was taught. I learned to regard any hope of a loving relationship with another man as the essence of fantasy and to set the goal of monogamous heterosexuality as the essence of reality. What I needed to change during my years with Larry — and for many years thereafter — was my self-centered, perfectionist view of what relationships are — not who they're with.

EPILOGUE

I remained in therapy — with brief time out for bad behavior — for nearly a dozen years, becoming still more intensively involved after I moved to New York City in 1964. At that point I added group therapy to my individual sessions. During those many years I continued to hear the familiar litany about my "sickness," about the need to renounce my ways and devote myself to "getting well." Spasmodically I tried to follow instructions, the effort alternating with intervals of furious rebellion — a cycle already gruesomely familiar from the Fifties. In retrospect, I'm astonished at the tenacity with which I continued to buy into imposed, arbitrary definitions of "normalcy" and self-worth — into a state of self-abdication. Suffice it to say that no one will ever have to explain to me the "mystery" of Jonestown.

By the late Sixties, my entangled cocoon did finally begin to unravel, a process greatly aided by the advent of the modern homophile movement, with its liberating new perspectives and options.

Dispiriting residues remain, sometimes propelling back into my head with those once-favorite lines from Matthew Arnold:

> *"Wandering between two worlds, one dead,*
> *the other powerless to be born . . ."*

Sometimes; but less and less and less.

Michael S. Kimmel and Martin P. Levine

MEN AND AIDS

Over 93% of all adult Americans with AIDS are men (as of December 1987), and 73% of all adult AIDS cases occur among gay men (and all cases among homosexuals are male). Eight out of every 10 cases linked to intravenous drug use are men (AIDS Surveillance Report, Center for Disease Control, December 1987). In New York City, AIDS is the leading cause of death among men aged 30 to 44.[1] Most instances of the other AIDS-related diseases are also among men. These conditions mark earlier stages of infection with the virus causing AIDS, the Human Immune Deficiency virus (HIV). They include AIDS-related complex (ARC) and AIDS virus antibody positivity (HIV seropositivity).

Note: This essay is dedicated to the memory of José A. Vigo, 1950–1988.

Although the prevalence of these conditions is presently unknown, they appear to be concentrated among male intravenous drug users and homosexual men (Institute of Medicine, 1986).

And yet no one talks about AIDS as a men's disease. No one talks about why men are so overwhelmingly at greater risk for AIDS, ARC, and HIV seropositivity. No one talks about the relationship between AIDS and masculinity. In fact, the rhetoric is more often about AIDS as a moral disease. Christian Voice leader Bob Grant says that people with AIDS are simply "reaping the results" of their "unsafe and immoral behavior" (Kropp, 1987). Evangelist Jerry Falwell calls AIDS "the wrath of God among homosexuals" (cited in Altman, 1986: 67).[2] These pronouncements enjoy some popular acceptance. Almost one-third of the respondents in one survey believed that "AIDS is a punishment that God has given homosexuals for the way they live." (Although, echoing Falwell, these respondents seem to be unaware that lesbians who are not intravenous drug users are virtually risk free.) And one-fourth of those same respondents believed that AIDS victims are "getting what they deserve" (*Los Angeles Times*, 12 December 1985). "The poor homosexuals," explained Patrick Buchanan, a conservative columnist and aid to President Reagan, sarcastically, "they have declared war upon Nature, and now Nature is exacting an awful retribution" (*The New York Post*, 24 May 1983). And almost two-fifths of the respondents (37%) to another survey said that AIDS had made them less favorably disposed toward homosexuals than they had been before (*The New York Times*, 15 December 1985).

Such beliefs confuse the cause of the disease with transmission. Sin does not cause AIDS, a virus does. Homosexual intercourse and sharing intravenous needles are but two of the ways in which this virus is transmitted. Other forms include heterosexual relations, blood transfusions, and the exchange of blood during pregnancy. In fact, in Africa, most people infected are heterosexual non-intravenous drug users (Quinn, Mann, Curran, and Prot, 1986).

But in the United States, AIDS is a disease of men. The seriousness of the disease demands that we pose the question: what is it about masculinity that puts men at greater risk for AIDS-related illness? To answer that question, we will explore the links between manliness and practices associated with risks for HIV infection; that is, we will examine the relationship between masculinity and risk-taking. To do this, we will first outline the norms of masculinity, the defining features of what it means to be a "real" man in our society. Then we will look at how these norms predispose men to engage in behaviors that place them at greater risk for AIDS. And finally, we will discuss how this perspective may shed new light on strategies of AIDS prevention.

I. MASCULINITY AS SOCIAL CONSTRUCTION

What does it mean to be a man in contemporary American society? Most experts believe that the answer to this question lies in the prevailing cultural construction of masculinity.[3] This perspective maintains that our understanding of masculinity and femininity derives less from biological imperatives or psychological predispositions than from the social definitions of what is appropriate behavior for each gender. Men acquire the scripts that define gender-appropriate behavior through socialization; the family, educational and religious institutions, and the media all contribute to this cultural definition. Such a perspective insists that the cultural definitions of masculinity and femininity are not

universal, but culturally and historically specific; what it means to be a man or
a woman varies from culture to culture, within any one culture over time, and
over the course of one's life.[4]

What, then, are the expectations of gender behavior that men in the United
States learn? What are the norms of manliness? Social scientists Deborah David
and Robert Brannon (Brannon, 1976) group these rules into four basic themes:
(1) *No Sissy Stuff*: anything that even remotely hints of femininity is prohibited.
A real man must avoid any behavior or characteristic associated with women;
(2) *Be a Big Wheel*: masculinity is measured by success, power, and the admiration of others. One must possess wealth, fame, and status to be considered
manly; (3) *Be a Sturdy Oak:* manliness requires rationality, toughness, and self-
reliance. A man must remain calm in any situation, show no emotion, and admit
no weakness; (4) *Give 'em Hell:* men must exude an aura of daring and aggression,
and must be willing to take risks, to "go for it" even when reason and fear
suggest otherwise.

This cultural construction of masculinity indicates that men organize their
conceptions of themselves as masculine by their willingness to take risks, their
ability to experience pain or discomfort and not submit to it, their drive to
accumulate constantly (money, power, sex partners, experiences), and their res-
olute avoidance of any behavior that might be construed as feminine. The pressures accompanying these efforts cause higher rates of stress-related illnesses
(heart disease, ulcers) and venereal diseases among men. The norms encouraging risk-taking behaviors lead men to smoke, drink too much, and drive reck-
lessly, resulting in disproportionate incidences of respiratory illness, alcoholism,
and vehicular accidents and fatalities. And the rules urging aggressiveness induce higher rates of violence-related injury and death among men. Over a century ago, Dr. Peter Bryce, director of a mental institution in Alabama, underscored the relationship between masculinity and mental health. "The causes of
general paresis," Dr. Bryce wrote (cited in Hughes, 1988: 15):

> are found to prevail most among men, and at the most active time of life,
> from 35 to 40, in the majority of cases. Habitual, intemperance, sexual
> excesses, overstrain in business, in fact, all those habits which tend to keep
> up too rapid cerebral action, are supposed to induce this form of disease.
> It is especially a disease of *fast life*, and fast business in large cities.

"Warning," writes one modern psychologist, "the male sex role may be dangerous to your health!" (Harrison, 1978).

MASCULINITY AND MALE SEXUALITY

These norms also shape male sexuality, organizing the scripts that men follow
in their sexual behaviors. Men are taught to be rational, successful, and daring
in sex: Real men divorce emotions from sexual expression, have sex without
love and are concerned solely with gratification. Real men "score" by having
lots of sex with many partners, and they are adventurous and take risks.

The norms defining masculinity also significantly increase men's vulnerability to AIDS. The virus causing AIDS is spread through bodily fluids such as
blood, semen, and vaginal secretions. To become infected with this virus, men
(and women) must engage in practices that allow these fluids to enter the blood-

stream. Such practices are known as "risk behaviors" (see Frumkin and Leonard, 1987: Ch. 4).

The most common risk behaviors among adults are unprotected sexual intercourse, oral sex, and sharing needles. Heterosexual or homosexual intercourse can cause tiny breaks in the surface linings of these organs, through which infected bodily fluids can enter the bloodstream directly. In oral sex, the fluids enter through breaks in the lining of the mouth.[5] Sharing needles allows these infected fluids to enter the bloodstream directly on needles containing contaminated blood.

Fortunately, there are ways one can avoid contact with the AIDS virus. Authorities recommend avoiding risk behaviors. This can be accomplished in several ways: (1) abstinence: the avoidance of sexual contacts and use of intravenous drugs; (2) safer sex: the avoidance of all sexual behaviors in which semen or blood are passed between partners (usually accomplished by the use of condoms); and (3) safer drug use: avoidance of all unsterilized needles. Safer drug use means not sharing needles if possible; if needles must be shared, they must be cleaned (with bleach or rubbing alcohol) before each use.

Unfortunately, these types of risk-reduction behavior are in direct contradiction with the norms of masculinity. The norms of masculinity propel men to take risks, score, and focus sexual pleasure on the penis. Real men ignore precautions for AIDS risk reduction, seek many sexual partners, and reject depleasuring the penis. Abstinence, safer sex, and safer drug use compromise manhood. The behaviors required for the confirmation of masculinity and those required to reduce risk are antithetical.

STRATEGIES OF AIDS PREVENTION

Given this perspective, how might we evaluate the various strategies that have been developed to combat the AIDS epidemic? To what extent do they reproduce or encourage precisely the behaviors that they are designed to discourage? The procedures developed to combat the AIDS epidemic ignore the links between masculinity and risk behaviors. The battle against AIDS relies heavily upon the public health strategies of testing and education (Gostin, in Dalton and Burris, 1987). But each of these is limited by the traditional norms of masculinity, as well as other factors.

Testing   Testing involves the use of the HIV antibody test to screen the blood for antibodies to the AIDS virus, and posttest counseling. People who test positive for the HIV antibodies are regarded as infected, that is, as carrying the virus and capable of transmitting it to others. These individuals are counseled to avoid risk behaviors.

AIDS antibody testing, however, even when coupled with counseling, is not a sufficient method to deal with the AIDS epidemic. The rationale for testing has been that it will encourage safer-sex behavior among those already infected but not yet ill, and thus curtail the epidemic. Yet this rationale remains unproven. Although this procedure may have been successful in the past with other infectious diseases, Dr. William Curran of the Harvard School of Public Health argues that it does not apply to AIDS (Curran, 1986). One study found that a positive result on the AIDS antibody test does not necessarily promote safe-sex behaviors. "It is not the test that promotes safe sex," the authors write, "but education and social support for safe sex" (Beeson, Zones, and Nye, 1986: 14).

AIDS antibody testing also has negative side effects, such as psychological distress, the possibility of social sanctions such as losing one's job, loss of medical care or life insurance, or the possibility of forced quarantine, if specific public policy recommendations are adopted by voters. Thus, antibody testing is opposed by nearly all medical and epidemiological experts. The Institute of Medicine of the National Academy of Sciences recently summarized their findings that testing was

> impossible to justify now either on ethical or practical grounds . . . [raising] serious problems of ethics and feasibility. People whose private behavior is illegal are not likely to comply with a mandatory screening program, even one backed by assurances of confidentiality. Mandatory screening based on sexual orientation would appear to discriminate against or to coerce entire groups without justification. (Institute of Medicine, 1986: 14)

From our perspective, as well, we must examine the ways in which the norms of masculinity impede the effectiveness of AIDS antibody testing. These rules compel men to shun stereotypical "feminine" concerns about health. "Real" men do not worry about the dangers associated with smoking, drinking, and stress — why should they worry about the risks associated with intravenous drug use and sex? Manly nonchalance will keep men from getting tested. Early reports from New York City indicate that more women than men are being tested for AIDS (Sullivan, 1987).

These norms of masculinity also impede the effectiveness of counseling. During counseling, men are warned against spreading the virus. Such warnings, however, contradict the dictates of manliness. "Real" men score, and their sexuality is organized phallocentrically, so counseling, which would encourage men to deemphasize the penis and emphasize sexual responsibility, may fall on deaf ears. To demonstrate manliness, seropositive men may actually give the virus to someone else.

Public Health Education   Public health authorities have also utilized education as an AIDS prevention strategy. The Institute of Medicine of the National Academy of Sciences recommends "a major educational campaign to reduce the spread of HIV" and that "substantially increased educational and public awareness activities be supported not only by the government, but also by the information media, and by other private sector organizations that can effectively campaign for health." For intravenous drug users, the Institute recommends "trials to provide easier access to sterile, disposable needles and syringes" (Institute of Medicine, 1986: 10, 12, 13).

Educational efforts have been developed by both public sector agencies, such as federal, state, and local health departments, and private organizations, such as local AIDS groups, and groups of mental health practitioners. These public and private efforts are each faced with a different set of problems, and each confronts different components of the norms of masculinity.

Public health education campaigns, funded by taxpayer dollars, have utilized mass transit advertisements, billboards, brochures, and hotlines to explain the medical facts about AIDS, its causes, how it affects the body, how it is transmitted, and who is at risk. Such campaigns deemphasize information about safe sex behaviors, because such information might be seen as condoning or even encouraging behaviors that are morally or legally proscribed. As Dr. James Mason, undersecretary for health in the Department of Health and Human Services said, "[w]e don't think that citizens care to be funding material that encourages gay lifestyles" (cited in Anderson, 1985). Editor and writer Norman Podhoretz criticized any efforts to stop AIDS because to do so would encourage homosexuality so that "in the name of compassion they are giving social sanction to what can only be described as brutish degradation" (cited in *New York Times*, 18 March 1986). And North Carolina Senator Jesse Helms, one of the nation's most vocal critics of education programs, sponsored an amendment that stipulated that no federal funds be used to promote or encourage homosexual activity, and emphasized that AIDS education emphasize abstinence outside a sexually monogamous marriage as the only preventive behaviors that the government would fund. The choice that Helms offers, he claims, is "Reject sodomy and practice morality. If they are unwilling to do that, they should understand the consequences" (Helms, 1987).

The content of these educational campaigns reflects the political ideology embedded within them. The pamphlet issued by the U.S. Public Health Service's Center for Disease Control, "What You Should Know About AIDS," counsels that the "safest way to avoid being infected by the AIDS virus is to avoid promiscuous sex and illegal drugs." Teenagers, especially, "should be encouraged to say 'no' to sex and illegal drugs" (Center for Disease Control, 1987).

The effectiveness of such strategies is extremely limited by the myopic moralizing that is embedded within them. "It is too late to be prudish in discussing the crisis with youngsters," warns an editorial in *The Washington Post*, urging explicit safe-sex education in the schools ("AIDS Education," 1987). But more than this, they are limited because they violate the traditional norms of masculinity. Just saying "no" contradicts the norms that inform men that "real" men score in sex, by having many sexual partners and by taking risks, or, more accurately, by ignoring potential risks in their pursuit of sex. Because of the norms of masculinity, which are especially salient for teenagers and younger men, the burden of just saying "no" will undoubtedly fall upon the shoulders of women. Efforts to halt the spread of a sexually transmitted disease by encouraging men to abstain have never been successful in American history, although such strategies have been attempted before, during the syphillis epidemic following World War I (see Brandt, 1986).

Private-Agency Educational Campaigns   Educational campaigns sponsored by privately funded agencies have developed various mechanisms that are far less negative about sexuality, and may, therefore, have far greater chances of reaching male populations. These campaigns vary in tone and effect. Some organizations that have emerged from within the gay community in major cities across the nation have given explicit information about safer sex practices. "Plain Talk about Safe Sex and AIDS" (published by Baltimore Health Education Resource Organization and also distributed in Boston) uses scare tactics:

> You must be aware that AIDS will almost certainly kill you if you get it. No fooling. It's that deadly. And at this moment it's incurable. This is no

wishy washy Public Health "warning" from the Surgeon General, determining that cigarette smoking is dangerous to your health. The medical
breakthrough hasn't happened yet. In other words, if you contract AIDS,
the chances are that you'll be dead within a year, probably. Got it? Let's
put it in plain language. If you develop AIDS, kiss your ass goodbye.

The San Francisco AIDS Foundation condemns past practices among gay men,
such as anonymous sex, bathhouses, backrooms, bookstores, and parks, while
giving this advice:

> We do know that the long standing health problems caused by sexually
> transmitted diseases in the gay community could be reduced if everyone
> were to heed the suggestions outlined here. If, as many believe, repeated
> infections also weaken the immune system, these suggestions can help you
> lead a healthier and safer life. If our comments sound rather judgmental
> or directive, understand that we, too, have and are experiencing these
> diseases and are trying to follow our own recommendations. . . . [W]e
> believe that intimacy, both sexual and emotional, is necessary as we move
> toward a more healthy regard for our own bodies and those we love.

Other educational efforts attempt to remain sex-positive, such as Houston's
"AIDS Play Safe" campaign, whose slogan is "Adapt, Enjoy, Survive." Their
pamphlet states:

> You don't have to give up good times, being social, having fun, going out,
> or even having sex, but you can change to safe sex, accept the experience
> and enjoy it. The results are lower risk of AIDS, less fear and anxiety,
> your health, and possibly your life. Come on, let's party. Don't be left
> behind, don't sit at home fretting. You can still have a good time, you can
> still enjoy your sexuality, you can still enjoy your lifestyle, you can still
> party, dance, play, have sex, and get the most out of life. You don't have
> to deny it to yourself. Adapt, enjoy and survive. And we'll see you around
> next year.

This position is echoed in the "Healthy Sex Is Great Sex" pamphlet published
by the Gay Men's Health Crisis in New York City. Other efforts to educate gay
men about safe sex practices include safe sex videos, house parties where information and free condoms are distributed on a model of Tupperware parties, and
workshops run by professionals on eroticizing safe sex encounters.

In general, these campaigns developed by local gay organizations have had
remarkable success. By a variety of measures — impressionistic, comparative,
and surveys — unsafe sex practices have declined sharply among those groups
who have access to explicit information about safe sex behaviors. Impressionistic journalistic reports indicate that gay baths and bars are less crowded and
monogamous coupling is on the rise. The rates of other venereal disease, a certain marker of promiscuity and unsafe sex practices, have plummeted among
gay men across the country.

The results of survey data reveal a significant decrease in unsafe sex practices
among gay men. The San Francisco AIDS Foundation found in 1984 that almost all respondents were aware that certain erotic behavior could result in
AIDS, and two-thirds had stopped engaging in high risk behavior (*Advocate*,
428, 3 September 1985). Another San Francisco survey found widespread

awareness about safe sex guidelines, and a continued decline in high risk behaviors among subjects between 1984 and 1985 (Research and Decisions Corporation, 1985).

Some Lingering Problems   But we are concerned not with the significant numbers of men who have altered their behavior in the face of serious health risk, but with the residual numbers who have not changed. How can we explain that one-third of those men surveyed in 1984 and one-fifth of the men surveyed in 1985 continued to engage in unsafe sex? How do we explain the conclusion of the 1985 study, which reported that the "men in these groups were uniformly well informed for AIDS risk reduction. Despite their knowledge of health directives, the men in this sample displayed discrepancies between what they believed about AIDS and their sexual behavior" (McKusik, et. al. 1985:495). It appears that a significant number of men continue to engage in high risk behavior, even though they know better.

Such continued high risk behavior cannot be attributed to homophobia, since the information provided is by local gay groups. And it is not attributable to sex-negativism, since much of the material is also sexually explicit about safe sex practices and gay-affirmative in tone. We believe that the cultural norms of masculinity compose one of the hidden impediments to safe sex education. That men's sexuality is organized around scoring, associates danger with sexual excitement, and is phallocentric limits the effectiveness of safer sex educational campaigns. In one study, 35% of the gay men who agreed that reducing the number of sexual partners would reduce risks had sex with more than five different men during the previous month (McKusik, et. al. 1985). Over four-fifths of the men who agreed with the statement "I use hot anonymous sex to relieve tension" had three or more sexual partners the previous month. And almost 70% of the men having three or more sexual partners the previous month agreed with the statement "It's hard to change my sexual behavior because being gay means doing what I want sexually."

CHALLENGING TRADITIONAL MASCULINITY AS RISK REDUCTION

Here we see the question in its boldest form: gay male sex is, above all, male sex, and male sex, above all, is risky business. Here, we believe, the social scientist can inform public health campaigns and epidemiological research. We need to recapitulate our understanding of how masculinity informs sexual behavior, and how masculinity might serve as an impediment to safer sex behaviors among men. Since there is no anticipatory socialization for homosexuality, boys in our culture all learn norms for heterosexual masculinity. This means that gay or straight, men in our culture are cognitively oriented to think and behave sexually through the prism of gender. Gay male sexuality and straight male sexuality are both enactments of scripts appropriate to gender; both have, in their cognitive orientations, "male" sex.

What this means concretely includes the meanings that become attached to our sexual scripts in early adolescence. Through masturbation and early sexual experiences, boys learn that sex is privatized, that emotions and sexuality are detached, that the penis is the center of the sexual universe, that fantasy allows heightened sexual experience, that pleasure and guilt are intimately linked, and that what brings sexual pleasure is also something that needs to be hidden from one's family. Masculinity is enacted in sexual scripts by the emphasis on scoring, by its recreational dimension (the ability to have sex without love), and by the pursuit of sexual gratification for its own sake, and by the association of danger and excitement (enacted through the link of pleasure and guilt). The male sexual script makes it normative to take risks, to engage in anonymous sex, and to have difficulty sustaining emotional intimacy, and it validates promiscuous sexual behavior.

In such a script, "safe sex" is an oxymoron. How can sex be safe? How can safety be sexy? Sex is about danger, excitement, risk; safety is about comfort, security, softness. And if safe sex isn't sexy, many men, enacting gender scripts about masculinity, will continue to practice unsafe sex. Or they may decide not to engage in sex at all. "I find so-called safe sex comparable to putting my nose up against a window in a candy store when I'm on a diet. I'd rather not go near the window at all, because seeing the candy makes me want to eat at least three or four pieces," said one man explaining his two-year voluntary celibacy as a response to AIDS ("Sex in the Age of AIDS," 1986). To educate men about safe sex, then, means to confront the issues of masculinity.

In spite of the efforts of some policy makers, whose misplaced moralism is likely to cost thousands of lives, we know that "health education is the only tool that can stem this epidemic," as the executive director of the Gay Men's Health Crisis put it. "AIDS education should have started the moment it was realized that this disease is sexually transmitted," wrote one medical correspondent (cited in Watney, 1987: 135). It would appear that a public health policy that was truly interested in reducing the spread of AIDS (instead of punishing those who are already stigmatized and at risk) would need to add two more considerations to the impressive educational efforts already underway. First, we will need to make safer sex sexy. Second, we will need to enlarge the male sexual script to include a wider variety of behaviors, to allow men a wide range of sexual and sensual pleasures.

Safer sex can be sexy sex. Many organizations are developing a safer sex pornography. GMHC in New York City offers safe sex videos as a form of "pornographic healing." In his important new book, *Policing Desire: Pornography, AIDS, and the Media*, English author Simon Watney argues that gay men "need to organize huge regular Safe Sex parties in our clubs and gay centers . . . with workshops and expert counseling available. We need to produce hot, sexy visual materials to take home, telephone sex-talk facilities, and safe sex porno cinemas" (Watney, 1987: 133).

And while we make safer sex into sexy sex, we also need to transform the meaning of masculinity, to enlarge our definition of what it means to be a man, so that sexuality will embrace a wider range of behaviors and experiences. As Watney argues, we "need to develop a culture which will support the transition to safer sex by establishing the model of an erotics of protection, succour and support within the framework of our pre-AIDS sex lives" (Watney, 1987: 132).

CONCLUSION

The process of transforming masculinity is long and difficult, and AIDS can spread so easily and rapidly. Sometimes it feels as if there isn't enough time. And there isn't. While we are eroticizing safer sex practices and enlarging the range of erotic behaviors available to men, we must also, as a concerned public, increase our compassion and support for AIDS patients. We must stand with them because they are our brothers. We are linked to them not through sexual orientation (although we may be) or by drug-related behavior (although we may be), but by gender, by our masculinity. They are not "perverts" or "deviants" who have strayed from the norms of masculinity, and therefore brought this terrible retribution upon themselves. They are, if anything, overconformists to destructive norms of male behavior. They are men who, like all real men, have taken risks. And risk taking has always implied danger. Men have always known this and have always chosen to take risks. Until daring has been eliminated from the rhetoric of masculinity, men will die as a result of their risk taking. In war. In sex. In driving fast and drunk. In shooting drugs and sharing needles. Men with AIDS are real men, and when one dies, a bit of all men dies as well. Until we change what it means to be a real man, every man will die a little bit every day.

NOTES

1. New York City Department of Health, personal communication, January 11, 1988.

2. For an overview of moralistic interpretations of AIDS, see Fitzpatrick (1988).

3. Our work here draws upon the "social constructionist" model of gender and sexuality. The pioneering work of John Gagnon and William Simon, *Sexual Conduct* (1973), has been followed up by our recent work. See, for example, Michael Kimmel and Jeffrey Fracher (1987), "Hard Issues and Soft Spots: Counseling Men About Sexuality," John Gagnon and Michael Kimmel (1988), *Gender and Desire*, and Martin P. Levine (1986), *Gay Macho: The Ethnography of the Homosexual Clone*.

4. Gender norms also vary within any culture by class, race, ethnicity, and region. Although there are many masculinities or femininities in the contemporary United States, however, we will elaborate the standard for white middle-class men in major metropolitan areas, because this is the model that is the hegemonic form that is defined as generalizable and normative. It is essential to understand its universality as a power relation and not as a moral ideal (see Connell, 1987).

5. The evidence for oral sex as a mode of transmission is only speculative. To date, there are no reported instances of transmission in this way (Green, 1987).

REFERENCES

"AIDS Education." Editorial in *Washington Post*, 28 February 1987.

"AIDS: The Public Reacts." *Public Opinion*, 8, December 1986.

Altman, Dennis. 1986. *AIDS in the Mind of America*. New York: Doubleday.

Anderson, Jack. 1985. "Fear consigns AIDS material to the shelf." *Newark Star Ledger*, 11 November 1985.

Beeson, Diane R., Jane S. Zones and John Nye. 1986. "The social consequences of AIDS antibody testing: Coping with stigma." Paper presented at annual meetings of the Society for the Study of Social Problems, New York.

Brandt, Alan. 1986. *No Magic Bullet*. New York: Oxford University Press.

Brannon, Robert. 1976. "Introduction." In Robert Brannon and Deborah David, eds. *The Forty-Nine Percent Majority*. Reading, MA: Addison-Wesley.

Center for Disease Control. "AIDS Surveillance Report," December 1987.

Curran, William. 1986. AIDS. Cambridge: Harvard School of Public Health.

Dalton, Harlon and Scott Burris, eds. 1987. *AIDS and the Law: A Guide for the Public*. New Haven: Yale University Press.

Fitzpatrick, James K. "AIDS is a Moral Issue" in Lynn Hall and Thomas Mode, (eds.). *AIDS: Opposing Viewponts*. St. Paul: Greenhaven Press. pp. 32–37.

Frumkin, Lyn and John Leonard. 1987. *Questions and Answers on AIDS*. New York: Avon.

Gagnon, John and William Simon. 1973. *Sexual Conduct*. Chicago: Aldine.

Gagnon, John and Michael Kimmel. 1989. *Gender and Desire*. New York: Basic Books, in progress.

Gostin, Larry. 1987. "Traditional public health strategies." In Harlon Dalton and Scott Burris, eds. *AIDS and the Law: A Guide for the Public*. New Haven: Yale University Press.

Green, Richard. 1987. "The transmission of AIDS." In Harlon Dalton and Scott Burris, eds. *AIDS and the Law: A Guide for the Public*. New Haven: Yale University Press.

Hall, Lynn and Thomas Modl, eds. 1988. *AIDS: Opposing Viewpoints*. St. Paul: Greenhaven Press.

Harrison, James. 1978. "Caution: Masculinity may be hazardous to your health." *Journal of Social Issues*, 34(1), pp. 65–86.

Helms, Jesse. 1987. "Only morality will effectively prevent AIDS from spreading." Letter to *The New York Times*, November 12, 1987.

Hughes, John. 1988. "The madness of separate spheres: Insanity and masculinity in late 19th century Alabama." Paper presented at Conference on Masculinity in Victorian America, Barnard College, 9 January 1988.

Institute for Advanced Study of Human Sexuality. 1986. *Safe Sex in the Age of AIDS*. Secaucus, NJ: Citadel Press.

Institute of Medicine, National Academy of Sciences. 1986. *Confronting AIDS: Directions for Public Health, Health Care and Research*. Washington, D.C.: National Academy Press.

Kimmel, Michael and Jeffrey Fracher. 1987. "Hard issues and soft spots: Counseling men about sexuality." In Murray Scher et al., eds. *Handbook of Counseling and Psychotherapy with Men*. Newbury Park, CA: Sage Publications.

Kropp, Arthur. 1987. "Religious right cashing in on AIDS epidemic." *Houston Texas Post*, July 20, 1987.

Levine, Martin P. *Gay Macho: The Ethnography of the Homosexual Clone*. Ph.D. dissertation, New York University, 1986.

Los Angeles Times, 12 December 1985.

McKusik, Leon, William Hortsman and Thomas J. Coates. 1985. "AIDS and sexual behavior reported by gay men in San Francisco." *American Journal of Public Health*, 75(5). May.

New York Post, 24 May 1983.

The New York Times, 15 December 1985.

The New York Times, 18 March 1986.

Quinn, Thomas C., Jonathan M. Mann, James W. Curran and Peter Prot. 1986. "AIDS in Africa: An epidemiological paradigm." *Science*, 234, November 21.

"Sex in the Age of AIDS," a symposium. 1986. *The Advocate*, July 8.

Sullivan, Ronald. 1987. "More women are seeking test for AIDS." *The New York Times*, 23 May 1987.

Watney, Simon. 1987. *Policing Desire: Pornography, AIDS and the Media*. Minneapolis: University of Minnesota Press.

◆ ◆ ◆

PART SEVEN

Men with Women: Intimacy and Power

Why do many men have problems establishing and maintaining intimate relationships with women? What different forms do male–female relational problems take within different socioeconomic groups? How do men's problems with intimacy and emotional expressivity relate to power inequities between the sexes? Are rape and domestic violence best conceptualized as isolated deviant acts by "sick" individuals, or are they the illogical consequences of male socialization? This complex web of male–female relationships, intimacy, and power is the topic of this section.

Lillian Rubin begins this section with a psychoanalytic interpretation of male–female relational problems. Early-developmental differences, rooted in the social organization of the nuclear family (especially the fact that it is women who care for infants), have set up fundamental emotional and sexual differences between men and women that create problems and conflicts for heterosexual couples. Clyde W. Franklin, in examining conflicts between black males and females, focuses more on how the larger socioeconomic structure of society places strains on black family life, and especially on black males' work and family roles. Whereas Rubin's and Franklin's articles tend to portray both males and females as being victimized by socially structured gender differences and problems with intimacy and communication, Jack W. Sattel asks some different questions. Male emotional and verbal inexpressivity, rather than being a "tragedy," might better be conceptualized as a situational strategy that males utilize to retain control in their relationships with women. Intimacy and power are closely intertwined.

Some men, we learn from John Krich's article, remain intent on retaining very traditional forms of power and control over women in the face of the social empowerment of women spearheaded by the women's movement. These men have resorted to becoming consumers in "the blossoming business of imported love." Krich gives us a fascinating glimpse of gender relations within an international context: men from advantaged societies who are insecure and angry in the face of the empowerment of women in their own society; young women from Third World nations who, because of economic necessity, marry these men and find themselves in an extremely subordinate role in their new families. But, as we find out, the "imported brides" often do not remain as submissive as we might expect. Gender expectations and relations become strained and contested in the new context.

Men's anger and insecurities toward women surface in other ways too. Wayne Ewing's article stresses that male violence against women is best conceptualized as resulting from a "civic advocacy" of male violence. The man who batters women and/or children should not be viewed as a "deviant" from some healthy "norm," but rather as an "overconformist" to mainstream male norms. Similarly, Beneke's article suggests that rape is the illogical consequence of male insecurity, anger, and need for control, expressed within a social context that condones sexual violence. As sociologist Diana Russell has written,

> Rape is not so much a deviant act as an over-conforming act. Rape may be understood as an extreme acting-out of qualities that are regarded as super masculine in this and many other societies: aggression, force, power, strength, toughness, dominance, competitiveness. To win, to be superior, to be successful, to conquer — all demonstrate masculinity to those who subscribe to common cultural notions of masculinity, i.e., the *masculine mystique*. And it would be surprising if these notions of masculinity did not find expression in men's sexual behavior. Indeed, sex may be the arena where these notions of masculinity are most intensely played out, particularly by men who feel powerless in the rest of their lives, and hence, whose masculinity is threatened by this sense of powerlessness. (P. 1)

(Diana Russell, "Rape and the Masculine Mystique," paper presented to the American Sociological Association, New York, 1973.)

What links all the articles in this section is *not* a sense that males are inherently incapable of authentic emotional connections with women, or that men are "naturally" batterers or rapists. The problems that men and women have relating to each other are rooted in the socially structured system of gender difference and inequality. As feminists have long since argued, the humanization of men is directly linked to the social empowerment of women. As long as men feel a need to control and subordinate women, either overtly or subtly, their relationships with women will be impoverished.

Lillian B. Rubin

THE APPROACH–AVOIDANCE DANCE:
MEN, WOMEN, AND INTIMACY

> For one human being to love another, that is perhaps the most difficult of
> all our tasks, the ultimate, the last test and proof, the work for which all
> other work is but preparation.
>
> RAINER MARIA RILKE

Intimacy. We hunger for it, but we also fear it. We come close to a loved one,
then we back off. A teacher I had once described this as the "go away a little
closer" message. I call it the approach–avoidance dance.

The conventional wisdom says that women want intimacy, men resist it. And
I have plenty of material that would *seem* to support that view. Whether in my
research interviews, in my clinical hours, or in the ordinary course of my life,
I hear the same story told repeatedly. "He doesn't talk to me," says a woman.
"I don't know what she wants me to talk about," says a man. "I want to know
what he's feeling," she tells me. "I'm not feeling anything," he insists. "Who can
feel nothing?" she cries. "I can," he shouts. As the heat rises, so does the wall
between them. Defensive and angry, they retreat — stalemated by their inability to understand each other.

Women complain to each other all the time about not being able to talk to
their men about the things that matter most to them — about what they themselves are thinking and feeling, about what goes on in the hearts and minds of
the men they're relating to. And men, less able to expose themselves and their
conflicts — those within themselves or those with the women in their lives —
either turn silent or take cover by holding women up to derision. It's one of the
norms of male camaraderie to poke fun at women, to complain laughingly about
the mystery of their minds, wonderingly about their ways. Even Freud did it
when, in exasperation, he asked mockingly, "What do women want? Dear God,
what do they want?"

But it's not a joke — not for the women, not for the men who like to pretend
it is.

> The whole goddamn business of what you're calling intimacy bugs the
> hell out of me. I never know what you women mean when you talk about
> it. Karen complains that I don't talk to her, but it's not talk she wants, it's
> some other damn thing, only I don't know what the hell it is. Feelings,
> she keeps asking for. So what am I supposed to do if I don't have any to
> give her or to talk about just because she decides it's time to talk about
> feelings? Tell me, will you; maybe we can get some peace around here.

The expression of such conflicts would seem to validate the common understandings that suggest that women want and need intimacy more than men
do — that the issue belongs to women alone; that, if left to themselves, men
would not suffer it. But things are not always what they seem. And I wonder:

"If men would renounce intimacy, what is their stake in relationships with women?"

Some would say that men need women to tend to their daily needs — to prepare their meals, clean their houses, wash their clothes, rear their children — so that they can be free to attend to life's larger problems. And, given the traditional structure of roles in the family, it has certainly worked that way most of the time. But, if that were all men seek, why is it that, even when they're not relating to women, so much of their lives is spent in search of a relationship with another, so much agony experienced when it's not available?

These are difficult issues to talk about — even to think about — because the subject of intimacy isn't just complicated, it's slippery as well. Ask yourself: What is intimacy? What words come to mind, what thoughts?

It's an idea that excites our imagination, a word that seems larger than life to most of us. It lures us, beckoning us with a power we're unable to resist. And, just because it's so seductive, it frightens us as well — seeming sometimes to be some mysterious force from outside ourselves that, if we let it, could sweep us away.

But what is it we fear?

Asked what intimacy is, most of us — men and women — struggle to say something sensible, something that we can connect with the real experience of our lives. "Intimacy is knowing there's someone who cares about the children as much as you do." "Intimacy is a history of shared experience." "It's sitting there having a cup of coffee together and watching the eleven o'clock news." "It's knowing you care about the same things." "It's knowing she'll always understand." "It's him sitting in the hospital for hours at a time when I was sick." "It's knowing he cares when I'm hurting." "It's standing by me when I was out of work." "It's seeing each other at our worst." "It's sitting across the breakfast table." "It's talking when you're in the bathroom." "It's knowing we'll begin and end each day together."

These seem the obvious things — the things we expect when we commit our lives to one another in a marriage, when we decide to have children together. And they're not to be dismissed as inconsequential. They make up the daily experience of our lives together, setting the tone for a relationship in important and powerful ways. It's sharing such commonplace, everyday events that determines the temper and the texture of life, that keeps us living together even when other aspects of the relationship seem less than perfect. Knowing someone is there, is constant, and can be counted on in just the ways these thoughts express provides the background of emotional security and stability we look for when we enter a marriage. Certainly a marriage and the people in it will be tested and judged quite differently in an unusual situation or in a crisis. But how often does life present us with circumstances and events that are so out of the range of ordinary experience?

These ways in which a relationship feels intimate on a daily basis are only one part of what we mean by intimacy, however — the part that's most obvious, the part that doesn't awaken our fears. At a lecture where I spoke of these issues recently, one man commented also, "Intimacy is putting aside the masks we wear in the rest of our lives." A murmur of assent ran through the audience of a hundred or so. Intuitively we say "yes." Yet this is the very issue that also complicates our intimate relationships.

On the one hand, it's reassuring to be able to put away the public persona —

to believe we can be loved for who we *really* are, that we can show our shadow side without fear, that our vulnerabilities will not be counted against us. "The most important thing is to feel I'm accepted just the way I am," people will say.

But there's another side. For, when we show ourselves thus without the masks, we also become anxious and fearful. "Is it possible that someone could love the *real* me?" we're likely to ask. Not the most promising question for the further development of intimacy, since it suggests that, whatever else another might do or feel, it's we who have trouble loving ourselves. Unfortunately, such misgivings are not usually experienced consciously. We're aware only that our discomfort has risen, that we feel a need to get away. For the person who has seen the "real me" is also the one who reflects back to us an image that's usually not wholly to our liking. We get angry at that, first at ourselves for not living up to our own expectations, then at the other, who becomes for us the mirror of our self-doubts — a displacement of hostility that serves intimacy poorly.

There's yet another level — one that's further below the surface of consciousness, therefore, one that's much more difficult for us to grasp, let alone to talk about. I'm referring to the differences in the ways in which women and men deal with their inner emotional lives — differences that create barriers between us that can be high indeed. It's here that we see how those early childhood experiences of separation and individuation — the psychological tasks that were required of us in order to separate from mother, to distinguish ourselves as autonomous persons, to internalize a firm sense of gender identity — take their toll on our intimate relationships.

Stop a woman in mid-sentence with the question, "What are you feeling right now?" and you might have to wait a bit while she reruns the mental tape to capture the moment just passed. But, more than likely, she'll be able to do it successfully. More than likely, she'll think for a while and come up with an answer.

The same is not true of a man. For him, a similar question usually will bring a sense of wonderment that one would even ask it, followed quickly by an uncomprehending and puzzled response. "What do you mean?" he'll ask. "I was just talking," he'll say.

I've seen it most clearly in the clinical setting where the task is to get to the feeling level — or, as one of my male patients said when he came into therapy, to "hook up the head and the gut." Repeatedly when therapy begins, I find myself having to teach a man how to monitor his internal states — how to attend to his thoughts and feelings, how to bring them into consciousness. In the early stages of our work, it's a common experience to say to a man, "How does that feel?," and to see a blank look come over his face. Over and over, I find myself listening as a man speaks with calm reason about a situation which I know must be fraught with pain. "How do you feel about that?" I'll ask. "I've just been telling you," he's likely to reply. "No," I'll say, "you've told me what happened, not how you *feel* about it." Frustrated, he might well respond, "You sound just like my wife."

It would be easy to write off such dialogues as the problems of men in therapy, of those who happen to be having some particular emotional difficulties. But it's not so, as any woman who has lived with a man will attest. Time and again women complain: "I can't get him to verbalize his feelings." "He talks, but it's always intellectualizing." "He's so closed off from what he's feeling, I don't know how he lives that way." "If there's one thing that will eventually ruin this marriage, it's the fact that he can't talk about what's going on inside him." "I have to work like hell to get anything out of him that resembles a feeling that's something besides anger. That I get plenty of — me and the kids, we all get his anger. Anything else is damn hard to come by with him." One woman talked eloquently about her husband's anguish over his inability to get problems in his work life resolved. When I asked how she knew about his pain, she answered:

> I pull for it, I pull hard, and sometimes I can get something from him. But it'll be late at night in the dark — you know, when we're in bed and I can't look at him while he's talking and he doesn't have to look at me. Otherwise, he's just defensive and puts on what I call his bear act, where he makes his warning, go-away faces, and he can't be reached or penetrated at all.

To a woman, the world men live in seems a lonely one — a world in which their fears of exposing their sadness and pain, their anxiety about allowing their vulnerability to show, even to a woman they love, is so deeply rooted inside them that, most often, they can only allow it to happen "late at night in the dark."

Yet, if we listen to what men say, we will hear their insistence that they *do* speak of what's inside them, *do* share their thoughts and feelings with the women they love. "I tell her, but she's never satisfied," they complain. "No matter how much I say, it's never enough," they grumble.

From both sides, the complaints have merit. The problem lies not in what men don't say, however, but in what's not there — in what, quite simply, happens so far out of consciousness that it's not within their reach. For men have integrated all too well the lessons of their childhood — the experiences that taught them to repress and deny their inner thoughts, wishes, needs, and fears; indeed, not even to notice them. It's real, therefore, that the kind of inner thoughts and feelings that are readily accessible to a woman generally are unavailable to a man. When he says, "I don't know what I'm feeling," he isn't necessarily being intransigent and withholding. More than likely, he speaks the truth.

Partly that's a result of the ways in which boys are trained to camouflage their feelings under cover of an exterior of calm, strength, and rationality. Fears are not manly. Fantasies are not rational. Emotions, above all, are not for the strong, the sane, the adult. Women suffer them, not men — women, who are more like children with what seems like their never-ending preoccupation with their emotional life. But the training takes so well because of their early childhood experience when, as very young boys, they had to shift their identification from mother to father and sever themselves from their earliest emotional connection. Put the two together and it does seem like suffering to men to have to experience that emotional side of themselves, to have to give it voice.

This is the single most dispiriting dilemma of relations between women and men. He complains, "She's so emotional, there's no point in talking to her." She protests, "It's him you can't talk to, he's always so darned rational." He says, "Even when I tell her nothing's the matter, she won't quit." She says, "How can I believe him when I can see with my own eyes that something's wrong?" He says, "Okay, so something's wrong! What good will it do to tell her?" She cries, "What are we married for? What do you need me for, just to wash your socks?"

These differences in the psychology of women and men are born of a complex interaction between society and the individual. At the broadest social level is the rending of thought and feeling that is such a fundamental part of Western thought. Thought, defined as the ultimate good, has been assigned to men; feeling, considered at best a problem, has fallen to women.

So firmly fixed have these ideas been that, until recently, few thought to question them. For they were built into the structure of psychological thought as if they spoke to an eternal, natural, and scientific truth. Thus, even such a great and innovative thinker as Carl Jung wrote, "The woman is increasingly aware that love alone can give her her full stature, just as the man begins to discern that spirit alone can endow his life with its highest meaning. Fundamentally, therefore, both seek a psychic relation one to the other, because love needs the spirit, and the spirit love, for their fulfillment."*

For a woman, "love"; for a man, "spirit" — each expected to complete the other by bringing to the relationship the missing half. In German, the word that is translated here as spirit is *Geist*. But *The New Cassell's German Dictionary* shows that another primary meaning of *Geist* is "mind, intellect, intelligence, wit, imagination, sense of reason." And, given the context of these words, it seems reasonable that *Geist* for Jung referred to a man's highest essence — his mind. There's no ambiguity about a woman's calling, however. It's love.

Intuitively, women try to heal the split that these definitions of male and female have foisted upon us.

> I can't stand that he's so damned unemotional and expects me to be the same. He lives in his head all the time, and he acts like anything that's emotional isn't worth dealing with.

Cognitively, even women often share the belief that the rational side, which seems to come so naturally to men, is the more mature, the more desirable.

> I know I'm too emotional, and it causes problems between us. He can't stand it when I get emotional like that. It turns him right off.

Her husband agrees that she's "too emotional" and complains:

> Sometimes she's like a child who's out to test her parents. I have to be careful when she's like that not to let her rile me up because otherwise all hell would break loose. You just can't reason with her when she gets like that.

It's the rational-man–hysterical-woman script, played out again and again by two people whose emotional repertoire is so limited that they have few real options. As the interaction between them continues, she reaches for the strongest tools she has, the mode she's most comfortable and familiar with: She becomes progressively more emotional and expressive. He falls back on his best weapons: He becomes more rational, more determinedly reasonable. She cries for him to attend to her feelings, whatever they may be. He tells her coolly, with a kind of clenched-teeth reasonableness, that it's silly for her to feel that way, that she's just being emotional. And of course she is. But that dismissive word "just" is the last straw. She gets so upset that she does, in fact, seem hysterical. He gets so bewildered by the whole interaction that his only recourse

---

*Carl Gustav Jung, *Contributions to Analytical Psychology* (New York: Harcourt, Brace & Co., 1928), p. 185.

is to build the wall of reason even higher. All of which makes things measurably worse for both of them.

> The more I try to be cool and calm her the worse it gets. I swear, I can't figure her out. I'll keep trying to tell her not to get so excited, but there's nothing I can do. Anything I say just makes it worse. So then I try to keep quiet, but . . . wow, the explosion is like crazy, just nuts.

And by then it *is* a wild exchange that any outsider would agree was "just nuts." But it's not just her response that's off, it's his as well — their conflict resting in the fact that we equate the emotional with the nonrational.

This notion, shared by both women and men, is a product of the fact that they were born and reared in this culture. But there's also a difference between them in their capacity to apprehend the *logic* of emotions — a difference born in their early childhood experiences in the family, when boys had to repress so much of their emotional side and girls could permit theirs to flower.

. . . It should be understood: Commitment itself is not a problem for a man; he's good at that. He can spend a lifetime living in the same family, working at the same job — even one he hates. And he's not without an inner emotional life. But when a relationship requires the sustained verbal expression of that inner life and the full range of feelings that accompany it, then it becomes burdensome for him. He can act out anger and frustration inside the family, it's true. But ask him to express his sadness, his fear, his dependency — all those feelings that would expose his vulnerability to himself or to another — and he's likely to close down as if under some compulsion to protect himself.

All requests for such intimacy are difficult for a man, but they become especially complex and troublesome in relations with women. It's another of those paradoxes. For, to the degree that it's possible for him to be emotionally open with anyone, it is with a woman — a tribute to the power of the childhood experience with mother. Yet it's that same early experience and his need to repress it that raises his ambivalence and generates his resistance.

He moves close, wanting to share some part of himself with her, trying to do so, perhaps even yearning to experience again the bliss of the infant's connection with a woman. She responds, woman style — wanting to touch him just a little more deeply, to know what he's thinking, feeling, fearing, wanting. And the fear closes in — the fear of finding himself again in the grip of a powerful woman, of allowing her admittance only to be betrayed and abandoned once again, of being overwhelmed by denied desires.

So he withdraws.

It's not in consciousness that all this goes on. He knows, of course, that he's distinctly uncomfortable when pressed by a woman for more intimacy in the relationship, but he doesn't know why. And, every often, his behavior doesn't please him any more than it pleases her. But he can't seem to help it.

Clyde W. Franklin II

BLACK MALE–BLACK FEMALE CONFLICT:
INDIVIDUALLY CAUSED AND CULTURALLY NURTURED

Who is to blame? Currently, there is no dearth of attention directed to Black male–Black female relationships. Books, magazine articles, academic journal articles, public forums, radio programs, television shows, and everyday conversations have been devoted to Black male–Black female relationships for several years. Despite the fact that the topic has been discussed over the past several decades by some authors (e.g., Frazier, 1939; Drake and Cayton, 1945; Grier and Cobb, 1968), Wallace's *Black Macho and the Myth of the Superwoman* has been the point of departure for many contemporary discussions of the topic since its publication in 1979.

Actually, Wallace's analysis was not so different in content from other analyses of Black male–Black female relationships (e.g., Drake and Cayton's analysis of "lower-class life" in *Black Metropolis*). But Wallace's analysis was "timely." Coming so soon on the heels of the Black movement in the late 1960s and early 1970s, and, at a time when many Black male-inspired gains for Blacks were disappearing rapidly, the book was explosive. Its theme, too, was provocative. Instead of repeating the rhetoric of the late 1960s and early 1970s that blamed conflictual relationships between Black men and Black women on White society, Wallace implied that the blame lay with Black males. In other words, the blame lay with those Black warriors who only recently had been perceived as the "saviors" of Black people in America. Wallace's lamenting theme is captured in a quote from her book: "While she stood by silently as he became a man, she assumed that he would finally glorify and dignify Black womanhood just as the White man has done for White women." Wallace goes on to say that this has not happened for Black women.

Wallace updates her attack on Black men in a later article entitled "A Black Feminist's Search for Sisterhood" (1982:9). Her theme, as before, is that Black men are just as oppressive of Black women as White men. She states:

> Whenever I raised the question of a Black woman's humanity in conversations with a Black man, I got a similar reaction. Black men, at least the ones I knew, seemed totally confounded when it came to treating Black women like people. . . . I discovered my voice and when brothers talked to me, I talked back. This had its hazards. Almost got my eye blackened several times. My social life was like guerilla warfare. Here was the logic behind our grandmother's old saying, "A nigga man ain't shit."

Wallace, however, is not alone in placing the blame on Black men for deteriorating relations between Black men and Black women. Allen (1983:62), in a recent edition of *Essence* magazine, states:

From *Journal of Black Studies* 15 (2, December 1984): 139–154. © 1984 Sage Publications, Inc. Reprinted by permission of Sage Publications, Inc.

Black women have a tendency to be male-defined, subjugating their own needs for the good of that fragile male ego. . . . The major contradiction is that we Black women, in our hearts, have a tendency to believe Black men need more support and understanding than we do. We bought the Black Revolutionary line that a woman's place was three paces behind the man. We didn't stomp Stokeley when he made the statement that the only position for a woman in the movement was prone.

Such attacks on Black men have been met with equally ferocious counterattacks by some Black authors (both Black men and Black women). A few months following the publication of Wallace's book, an entire issue of the *Black Scholar* was devoted to Black male–Black female relationships. Of the responses to Wallace by such scholars as Jones (1979), Karenga (1979), Staples (1979), and numerous others, Karenga's response is perhaps the most controversial and maybe the most volatile. Karenga launches a personal attack on Wallace suggesting that she is misguided and perhaps responding from personal hurt. Recognizing the complexity of Black male–Black female relationships, Karenga contends that much of it is due not to Black men but to the White power structure. Along similar lines, Moore (1980) has exhorted Black women to stop criticizing Black men and blame themselves for the disintegrating bonds between Black men and Black women.

Staples, in his response to Wallace and others who would place the blame on Black men for disruptive relationships between Black men and Black women, points out that while sexism within the Black culture may be an emerging problem, most Black men do not have the institutionalized power to oppress Black women. He believes that the Black male's "condition" in society is what bothers Black males. Staples devotes much attention to the institutional decimation of Black men and suggests that this is the reason for Black male–Black female conflict. Noting the high mortality and suicide rates of Black men, the fact that a half a million Black men are in prison, one-third of urban Black men are saddled with drug problems and that 25% to 30% do not have steady employment, Staples implied that Black male–Black female conflict may be related to *choice.* This means that a shortage of Black men may limit the choices that Black women have in selecting partners. As Braithwaite (1981) puts it, the insufficient supply of Black men places Black women at a disadvantage by giving Black men the upper hand. In a specific relationship, for example, if a Black woman fails to comply with the Black man's wishes, the Black man has numerous other options, including not only other Black women but also women of other races.

In a more recent discussion of Black male–Black female relationships, Alvin Poussaint (1982:40) suggests that Black women "adopt a patient and creative approach in exploring and creating new dimensions of the Black male–Black female bond." Others, like Ronald Braithwaite, imply in their analyses of relationships between Black men and Black women that Black women's aggressiveness, thought to be a carryover from slavery, may be partly responsible for Black male–Black female conflict.

Succinctly, by and large, most Black male and Black female authors writing on the subject seem to agree that many Black male–Black female relationships today are destructive and potentially explosive. What they do not agree on, however, are the causes of the problems existing between Black men and Black women. As we have seen, some believe that Black men are the cause. Others contend that Black women contribute disproportionately to Black male–Black female conflict. Still others blame White racism solely, using basic assumptions that may be logically inadequate (see Franklin, 1980). Many specific reasons for the conflict often postulated include the notions that Black men are abusive toward Black women, that Black men are irresistibly attracted to White women (despite the fact that only approximately 120,000 Black men were married to White women in 1980), that too many Black men are homosexual, that Black women are too aggressive, that Black women don't support Black men — the list goes on. Few of these reasons, however, really explore the underlying cause of the conflict. Instead, they are descriptions of the conflict-behaviors that are indicators of the tension between Black men and Black women. But what is the cause of the behavior — the cause of the tension that so often disrupts harmony in Black male–Black female relationships?

Given the various approaches many Black authors have taken in analyzing Black male–Black female relationships, it is submitted that two major sources of Black male–Black female conflict can be identified: (1) the noncomplementarity of sex-role definitions internalized by Black males and Black females; and (2) structural barriers in the environments of Black males and Black females. Each source is explored separately below.

SOURCES OF CONFLICT BETWEEN BLACK MEN AND BLACK WOMEN

Sex-Role Noncomplementarity among Black Males and Black Females   Much Black male–Black female conflict stems directly from incompatible role enactments by Black males and Black females. Incompatible role enactments by Black men and Black women occur because they internalize sex-role definitions that are noncomplementary. For example, a Black woman in a particular conflictual relationship with a Black male may feel that her Black man is supposed to assume a dominant role, but she also may be inclined to exhibit behaviors that are opposed to his dominance and her subordinance. In the same relationship, the Black man may pay lip service to assuming a dominant role but may behave "passively" with respect to some aspects of masculinity and in a dominant manner with respect to other aspects.

One reason for role conflict between Black men and Black women is that many contemporary Black women internalize two conflicting definitions of femininity, whereas many contemporary Black men internalize only a portion of the traditional definition of masculinity. Put simply, numerous Black women hold attitudes that are both highly masculine and highly feminine. On the other hand, their male counterparts develop traits that are highly consistent with certain aspects of society's definition of masculinity, but that are basically unrelated to other aspects of the definition. Thus, in a given relationship, one may find a Black woman who feels and behaves in ways that are both assertive and passive, dominant and subordinate, decisive and indecisive, and so on. Within that same relationship, a Black man may exhibit highly masculine behaviors, such as physical aggressiveness, sexual dominance, and even violence, but behave indifferently with respect to the masculine work ethic — assuming responsibility for family-related activities external to the home, being aggressive in the work place and the like.

The reason these incongruent attitudes and behaviors exist among Black men and Black women is that they have received contradictory messages during early socialization. It is common for Black women to have received two messages. One message states, "Because you will be a Black woman, it is imperative that you learn to take care of yourself because it is hard to find a Black man who will take care of you." A second message frequently received by young Black females that conflicts with the first message is "your ultimate achievement will occur when you have snared a Black man who will take care of you." In discussing early socialization experiences with countless young Black women in recent years, I have found that most of them agree that these two messages were given them by socialization agents and agencies such as child caretakers, relatives, peer group members, the Black church, and the media.

When internalized, these two messages often produce a Black woman who seems to reject aspects of the traditional female sex role in America such as passivity, emotional and economic dependence, and female subordinance while accepting other aspects of the role such as expressiveness, warmth, and nurturance. This is precisely why Black women seem to be more androgynous than White women. Black women's androgyny, though, may be more a function of necessity than anything else. It may be related to the scarcity of Black men who assume traditional masculine roles in male–female relationships.

Whatever the reason for Black women's androgynous orientations, because of such orientations Black women often find themselves in conflictual relationships with Black men or in no stable relationships at all. The scenario generally can be described as follows. Many Black women in early adulthood usually begin a search for a Black Prince Charming. However, because of the dearth of Black men who can be or are willing to be Prince Charmings for Black women, Black women frequently soon give up the search for such a Black man. They give up the search, settle for less, and "like" what they settle for even less. This statement is important because many Black women's eventual choices are destined to become constant reminders that the "female independence"message received during the early socialization process is the correct message. But, because Black women also have to deal with the second socialization message, many come to feel that they have failed in their roles as women. In an effort to correct their mistakes, Black women often choose to enact the aspect of their androgynous role that is decidedly aggressive and/or independent. They may decide either to "go it alone" or to prod their Black men into becoming Prince Charmings. The first alternative for Black women often results in self-doubt, lowered self-esteem, and, generally, unhappiness and dissatisfaction. After all, society nurtures the "find a man" message far beyond early socialization. The second message, unfortunately, produces little more than the first message because Black women in such situations usually end up in conflictual relationships with Black men, who also have undergone a rather complicated socialization process. Let us explore briefly the conflicting messages numerous Black men receive during early socialization.

One can find generally that Black men, too, have received two conflicting messages during early socialization. One message received by young Black males is "to become a man means that you must become dominant, aggressive, decisive, responsible, and, in some instances, violent in social encounters with others." A second message received by young Black males that conflicts with the first is, "You are Black and you must not be too aggressive, too dominant, and so on, because the *man* will cut you down." Internalization of these two messages by some Black men (a substantial number) produces Black men who enact a portion of the traditional definition of masculinity but remain inactive with respect to other parts of traditional masculinity. Usually those aspects of traditional masculinity that can be enacted within the Black culture are the ones exhibited by these Black men. Other aspects of the sex role that require enactment external to the Black culture (e.g., aggressiveness in the work place) may be related to impassively by Black men. Unfortunately, these are aspects of the male sex role that must be enacted if a male is to be "productive" in American society.

Too many Black men fail to enact the more "productive" aspects of the male sex role. Instead, "being a man," for many Black males who internalize the mixed messages, becomes simply enacting sexual aggression, violence, sexism, and the like — all of which promote Black male–Black female conflict. In addition, contributing to the low visibility and low salience of "productive" masculine traits among Black men is the second socialization message, which provides a rationale for nonenactment of the role traits. Moreover, the "man will get you" message serves to attenuate Black men's motivations to enact more "positive" aspects of the traditional male sex role. We must keep in mind, however, that not all of the sources of Black male–Black female conflict are social-psychological. Some of the sources are structural, and in the next section these sources are discussed.

Structural Barriers Contributing to Black Male–Black Female Conflict   It is easy to place the blame for Black male–Black female conflict on "White society." Several Black authors have used this explanatory approach in recent years (e.g., Anderson and Mealy, 1979). They have suggested that Black male–Black female conflict is a function of America's capitalistic orientation and White society's long-time subjugation of Black people. Certainly historical conditions are important to understand when discussing the status of Black people today. Often, however, too much emphasis is placed on the historical subjugation of Black people as the source of Black male–Black female conflict today. Implicit in such an emphasis is the notion that independent variables existing at some point in the distant past cause a multiplicity of negative behaviors between Black males and Black females that can be capsulized as Black male–Black female conflict. A careful analysis of the contemporary environments of Black men and women today will show, instead, that factors responsible, in part, for Black male–Black female conflict are inextricably interwoven in those environments. In other words, an approach to the analysis of conflict between Black men and Black women today must be ahistorical. Past conditions influence Black male–Black female relationships only in the sense that vestiges of these conditions exist currently and are identifiable.

Our society today undoubtedly remains structured in such a manner that the vast majority of Black men encounter insurmountable barriers to the attainment of a "masculine" status as defined by most Americans (Black and White Americans). Black men still largely are locked within the Black culture (which has relatively limited resources), unable to compete successfully for societal rewards — the attainment of which defines American males as "men." Unquestionably, Black men's powerlessness in society's basic institutions such as the government and the economy contributes greatly to the pathological states of many Black men. The high mortality and suicide rates of young Black men, the high incarceration rates of Black men, the high incidence of drug addiction among Black men, and the high unemployment rate of Black men are all functions of societal barriers to Black male upward mobility. These barriers render millions of Black males socially impotent and/or socially dysfunctional. Moreover, as Staples has pointed out, such barriers also result in a scarcity of functional Black men, thereby limiting Black women's alternatives for mates.

While some may be tempted to argue for a psychological explanation of Black male social impotence, it is suggested here that any such argument is misguided unless accompanied by a recognition of the role of cultural nurturance factors. Cultural nurturance factors such as the rigid castelike social stratum of Blacks in America foster and maintain Black men's social impotence. The result is powerless Black men primed for conflictual relationships with Black women. If Black men in our society were not "American," perhaps cultural nurturance of Black people's status in our society could not be translated into cultural nurturance of Black male–Black female conflict. That Black men are Americanized, however, is seen in the outcome of the Black movement of the last decade.

The Black movement of the late 1960s and early 1970s produced little structural change in America. To be sure, a few Black men (and even fewer Black women) achieved a measure of upward mobility; however, the vast majority did not reap gains from the Black movement. What did happen, though, was that Black people did get a glimpse of the rewards that can be achieved in America through violence and/or aggression. White society did bend when confronted by the Black movement, but it did not break. In addition, the few upward mobility doors that were ajar during the height of the movement were quickly slammed shut when the movement began to wane in the middle and late 1970s. Black men today find themselves in a position similar to the one Black men were in prior to the movement. The only difference this time around is that Black men are equipped with the psychological armor of aggression and violence as well as with a distorted perception of a target — Black women, the ones who "stood silently by."

Wallace's statement that Black women "stood silently by" must not be taken lightly. Black women did this; in addition, they further internalized American definitions of masculinity and femininity. Previously, Black women held modified definitions of masculinity and femininity because the society's definition did not fit their everyday experiences. During the Black movement they were exhorted by Black men to assume a sex role that was more in line with the traditional "feminine" role White women assumed in male–female relationships. Although this may have been a noble (verbal) effort on the part of Black men to place Black women on pedestals, it was shortsighted and doomed to fail. Failure was imminent because even during the peak of the Black movement, societal resistance to structural changes that would benefit Black people was strong. The strength of this resistance dictated that change in Black people's status in America could come about only through the united efforts of both Black men and Black women.

Unfortunately, the seeds of division between Black men and Black women were sown during the Black movement. Black men bought the Moynihan report (1965) that indirectly blamed Black women for Black people's underclass status in America. In doing so, Black men convinced themselves that they could be "men" only if they adopted the White male's sex role. An examination of this role reveals that it is characterized by numerous contradictions. The traditional White masculine role requires men to assume protective, condescending, and generally patriarchal stances with respect to women. It also requires, ironically, that men display dominant, aggressive, and often violent behaviors toward women. Just as important, though, is that White masculine role enactment can occur only when there is full participation in masculinist American culture. Because Black men continue to face barriers to full participation in American society, the latter requirement for White male sex-role assumption continues to be met by only a few Black men. The result has been that many Black men have adopted only a part of the culture's definition of masculinity because they are thwarted in their efforts to participate fully in society. Structural barriers to Black male sex-role adoption, then, have produced a Black male who is primed for a conflictual relationship with Black women. In the next section, an exploration is presented of some possible solutions to Black male–Black female conflict that arise from the interactive relationship between the noncomplementarity of sex-role internalization by Black men and Black women and structural barriers to Black men's advancement in American society.

TOWARD SOLVING BLACK MALE–BLACK FEMALE CONFLICT

Given that societal conditions are extremely resistant to rapid changes, the key to attenuating conflict between Black men and Black women lies in altering three social psychological phenomena: (1) Black male and Black female socialization experiences; (2) Black male and Black female role-playing strategies; and (3) Black male and Black female personal communication mechanisms. I first propose some alterations in Black male and Black female socialization experiences. . . .

Black female socialization must undergo change if Black men and Black women are to enjoy harmonious relationships. Those agents and agencies responsible for socializing young Black females must return to emphasizing a monolithic message in young Black female socialization. This message can stress warmth, caring, and nurturance, but it must stress simultaneously self-sufficiency, assertiveness, and responsibility. The latter portion of this message requires that young Black females must be cautioned against sexual freedom at relatively early ages — not necessarily for moral reasons, but because sexual freedom for Black women seems to operate against Black women's self-sufficiency, assertiveness, and responsibility. It is important to point out here, however, that this type of socialization message must be imparted without the accompanying castigation of Black men. To say "a nigger man ain't shit" informs any young Black female that at least one-half of herself "ain't shit." Without a doubt, this strategy teaches self-hate and sets the stage for future Black male–Black female conflict.

Young Black males, on the other hand, must be instructed in self-sufficiency, assertiveness, and responsibility without the accompanying warning opposed to these traits in Black males. Such warnings serve only to provide rationales for future failures. To be sure, Black men do (and will) encounter barriers to upward mobility because they are Black. But, as many Black men have shown, such barriers do not have to be insurmountable. Of course it is recognized that innumerable Black men have been victims of American racist policies, but some, too, have been victims because they perceived only that external factors hindered their upward mobility and did not focus on some internal barriers that may have thwarted their mobility. The former factors are emphasized much too often in the contradictory socialization messages received by most young Black males.

Along with the above messages, young Black males must learn that the strong bonds that they establish with their mothers can be extended to their relationships with other Black women. If Black men perceive their mothers to be symbols of strength and perseverance, they must also be taught that most other Black women acquire these same qualities and have done so for generations. It must become just as "cool," in places like urban Black barbershops, to speak of Black women's strength and dignity as it is now to hear of Black women's thighs, breasts, and hips.

On an issue closely related to the above, few persons reading this article can deny that Black men's attempts to enact the White male sex role in America are laughable. Black men are relatively powerless in this country, and their attempts at domination, aggression, and the like, while sacrificing humanity, are ludicrous. This becomes apparent when it is understood that usually the only people being dominated and aggressed against by Black men are Black women (and other Black men). Moreover, unlike White males, Black males receive no societal rewards for their efforts; instead, the result is Black male–Black female disharmony. Black men must avoid the tendency to emulate the nauseatingly traditional male sex role because their experiences clearly show that such a role is counterproductive for Black people. Because the Black man's experiences are different, his role-playing strategies must be different and made to be more complementary with Black females' altered role-playing strategies. The Black females' role-playing strategies, as we have seen, are androgynous, emphasizing neither the inferiority nor the superiority of male or female sex roles.

On a final note, it is important for Black people in our society to alter their personal communication mechanisms. Black men and Black women interact with each other in diverse ways and in diverse situations, ranging from intimate to impersonal. Perhaps the most important element of this diverse communication pattern is empathy. For Black people in recent years, this is precisely the element that has undergone unnecessary transformation. As Blacks in America have accepted increasingly White society's definition of male–female relationships. Black men and Black women have begun to interact with each other less in terms of empathy. While Black women have retained empathy in their male–female relationships to a greater degree than Black men have, Black men have become increasingly nonexpressive and nonempathic in their male–female relationships. Nearly 60% of Black women (approximately 25,000) in a recent *Essence* survey cited nonexpressiveness as a problem in male–female relationships; 56% also pointed out that Black male nonempathy was a problem (Edwards, 1982). It seems, then, that as Black males have attempted to become "men" in America they have shed some of the important qualities of humanity. Some Black women, too, who have embraced the feminist perspective also have discarded altruism. The result of both phenomena, for Black people as a whole, has been to divide Black men and Black women further. Further movement away from empathic understanding in Black male–Black female relationships by both Black men and Black women undoubtedly will be disastrous for Black people in America.

REFERENCES

Allen, B.
   1983 "The Price for Giving It Up." *Essence* (February):60–62, 118.
Anderson, S. E., and R. Mealy
   1979 "Who Originated the Crisis: A Historical Perspective." *Black Scholar* (May/June):40–44.
Braithwaite, R. L.
   1981 "Interpersonal Relations between Black Males and Black Females." In *Black Men*, L. E. Gary, ed., pp. 83–97. Beverly Hills, Calif.: Sage.
Drake, S. C., and H. R. Cayton
   1945 *Black Metropolis*. New York: Harcourt.
Edwards, A.
   1982 "Survey Results: How You're Feeling." *Essence* (December):73–76.
Franklin, C. W., II
   1980 "White Racism As a Cause of Black Male–Black Female Conflict: A Critique." *Western Journal of Black Studies* 4 (1):42–49.
Frazier, E. F.
   1939 *The Negro Family in the United States*. Chicago: University of Chicago Press.
Grier, W. H., and P. M. Cobb
   1968 *Black Rage*. New York: Basic Books.
Jones, T.
   1979 "The Need to Go beyond Stereotypes." *Black Scholar* (May/June):48–49.
Karenga, M. R.
   1979 "On Wallace's Myth: Wading through Troubled Waters." *Black Scholar* (May/June):36–39.
Moore, W. E.
   1980 "Black Women, Stop Criticizing Black Men — Blame Yourselves." *Ebony* (December):128–130.
Moynihan, D. P.
   1965 *The Negro Family: The Case for National Action*. Washington, D.C.: U.S. Department of Labor, Office of Planning and Research.
Poussaint, A. F.
   1982 "What Every Black Woman Should Know about Black Men." *Ebony* (August):36–40.
Staples, R.
   1979 "The Myth of Black Macho: A Response to Angry Black Feminists." *Black Scholar* (March/April):24–32.
Wallace, M.
   1979 *Black Macho and the Myth of the Superwoman*. New York: Dial.
   1982 "A Black Feminist's Search for Sisterhood." In *All the Blacks Are Men, All the Women Are White, but Some of Us Are Brave*, G. T. Hull et al., eds., pp. 5–8. Old Westbury, N.Y.: Feminist Press.

Jack W. Sattel

THE INEXPRESSIVE MALE:
TRAGEDY OR SEXUAL POLITICS?

In this brief essay, I am concerned with the phenomenon of "male inexpressive-ness" as it has been conceptualized by Balswick and Peek (1971). In their con-ceptualization, male inexpressiveness is seen as a culturally produced tempera-ment trait which is learned by boys as the major characteristic of their forthcoming adult masculinity. Such inexpressiveness is evidenced in two ways. First, adult male behavior which does not indicate affection, tenderness, or emotion is inexpressive behavior. Second, and somewhat differently, behavior which is not supportive of the affective expectations of one's wife is inexpressive behavior. It is the latter variety of inexpressiveness which occupies the major concern of Balswick and Peek. They suggest that the inability of the American male to unlearn inexpressiveness in order to relate effectively to a woman is highly dysfunctional to the emerging standards of the companionate, intimate American marriage. Ironically, Balswick and Peek see inexpressiveness in con-texts outside the marriage relationship as functional insofar as in nonmarital situations the inexpressiveness of the male to females other than one's spouse works to prevent threats to the primacy of the marital bond, that is, it presum-ably functions to ward off infidelity. The authors further suggest two styles of adult inexpressiveness: the "cowboy — John Wayne" style of almost total inar-ticulateness and the more cool, detached style of the "playboy," who commu-nicates only to exploit women sexually.

The article has proved to be an important one in forcing sociologists to re-think old conceptual stereotypes of masculinity and femininity. In part, it has helped to contribute to efforts to rescue for both sexes qualities and potentials that previously were thought to belong to only one sex. On the other hand, it would be unfortunate if Balswick and Peek's conceptualization would enter the sociological literature as the last word on the dilemma of male inexpressive-ness — unfortunate because, despite their real insight, I think they fundamen-tally misconstrue both the origin and the playing out of male inexpressiveness in our society.

In the note which follows, I would like to reconsider the phenomenon of male inexpressiveness, drawing upon my own and other men's experiences in con-sciousness-raising groups (especially as recounted in *Unbecoming Men: A Men's Consciousness-Raising Group Writes on Oppression and Themselves* (Bradley et al., 1971), as well as some of the literature which has appeared since Balswick and Peek first published their article.

I.
BECOMING INEXPRESSIVE: SOCIALIZATION

The process of becoming inexpressive is cast by Balswick and Peek in the tra-ditional vocabulary of the literature of socialization:

> Children, from the time they are born both explicitly and implicitly are taught how to be a man or how to be a woman. While the girl is taught to act "feminine," . . . the boy is taught to be a man. In learning to be a man, the boy in American society comes to value expressions of masculinity . . . [such as] physical courage, toughness, competitiveness, and aggressiveness. (1971: 363–364)

Balswick and Peek's discussion of this socialization process is marred in two ways. Theoretically, their discussion ignores the critique of the socialization literature initially suggested by Wrong (1961) in his analysis of sociology's "oversocialized concept of man [sic]." Wrong, using a largely Freudian vocabulary, argued that it is incorrect to see the individual as something "hollowed out" into which norms are simply poured. Rather, "conformity" and "internalization" should always be conceptualized as problematic. For example, if we consider inexpressiveness to be a character trait, as do Balswick and Peek, we should also be aware that the normative control of that trait is never complete — being threatened constantly by both the presumably more expressive demands of the id and the excessive ("perfectionist") demands of the "internalized norms" of the superego. Wrong's point is well taken. While the norms of our society may well call for all little boys to to grow up to be inexpressive, the inexpressiveness of the adult male should never be regarded as complete or total, as Balswick and Peek would have it.

For them to have ignored this point is particularly crucial given their concern to rescue some capacity of authentic expressiveness for the male. Their suggestion that men simply "unlearn" their inexpressiveness through contact with a woman (spouse) is unsatisfactory for two reasons. First, it forfeits the possibility that men can rescue themselves through enhanced self-knowledge or contact with other men. Second, *it would seem to make the task of rescuing men just one more task of women.* That is, the wife is expected to restore to her husband that which was initially taken from him in socialization.

A second problem with Balswick and Peek's discussion of socialization and inexpressiveness is that they ignore the peculiarly asymmetrical patterns of socialization in our society which make it much more dangerous for a boy to be incompletely socialized than a girl. For example, much of the literature suggests that parents and other adults exert greater social control to insure that boys "grow up male" than that girls "grow up female" (Parsons, 1951) — as can be seen in the fact that greater stigma is attached to the boy who is labeled a sissy than to the girl who is known as a tomboy. Failure to even consider this asymmetry reveals, I think, the major weakness of Balswick and Peek's conceptualization of male inexpressiveness. They have no explanation of *why* male inexpressiveness exists or *how* it came into being and is maintained other than to say that "our culture demands it." Thus, while we can agree that male inexpressiveness is a tragedy, their analysis does not help us to change the social conditions which produce that tragedy.

INEXPRESSIVENESS AND POWER

To break this chain of reasoning, I would like to postulate that, in itself, male inexpressiveness is of no particular value in our culture. Rather, it is an instrumental requisite for assuming adult male roles of power.

Consider the following. To effectively wield power, one must be able both to convince others of the rightness of the decisions one makes and to guard against one's own emotional involvement in the consequences of that decision; that is, one has to show that decisions are reached rationally and efficiently. One must also be able to close one's eyes to the potential pain one's decisions have for others and for oneself. The general who sends troops into battle must show that his decision is calculated and certain; to effectively implement that decision — hence, to maintain his position of power to make future decisions — the general must put on a face of impassive conviction.

I would argue, in a similar vein, that a little boy must become inexpressive not simply because our culture expects boys to be inexpressive *but because our culture expects little boys to grow up to become decision makers and wielders of power.*

From this example, I am suggesting that inexpressiveness is not just learned as an end in itself. Rather, it is learned as a means to be implemented later in men assuming and maintaining positions of power. More generally:

(A) INEXPRESSIVENESS in a role is determined by the corresponding *power* (actual or potential) of that role.

In light of this generalization, we might consider why so many sociologists tend to merge the universalistic–particularistic (rational) and the affective neutrality–affectivity (expressive) distinction in any discussion of real social behavior. In the case of the general, it would seem that the ability to give an inexpressive — that is, an affectively neutral — coloring to his decisions or positions contributes to the apparent rationality of those decisions or positions. Inexpressiveness validates the rightness of one's position. In fact, the social positions of highest power — not incidentally always occupied by men — demand veneers of both universalism and inexpressiveness of their incumbents, suggesting that at these levels *both* characteristics merge into a style of control. (Consider both Kennedy in the missile crisis and Nixon at Watergate. While otherwise quite dissimilar, in a crisis and challenge to their position, both men felt that "stonewalling" was the solution to the situation.)

From the above, it also follows logically that inexpressiveness might be more a characteristic of upper-class, powerful males than of men in the working classes. Many people — sociologists included — would probably object to such a deduction, saying the evidence is in the other direction, pointing at the Stanley Kowalski or Marty of literary fiction. I am not so sure. To continue with examples from fiction for a moment, the early autobiographical novels of, say, James Baldwin and Paul Goodman, dealing with lower- and working-class youth, consistently depicted "making it" as a not unusual tradeoff for one's sensitivity and expressiveness. More empirically, the recent work of Sennett and Cobb in their study of working-class life, *The Hidden Injuries of Class* (1972), suggests that upward mobility by working-class men was seen by them as entailing a certain phoniness or inauthentic relationship with one's *male* peers as well as a sacrifice of a meaningful expressive relationship with children and wife. The result of this for the men interviewed by Sennett and Cobb was often a choice to forego upward mobility and power because it involved becoming something one was not. It involved learning to dissemble inauthentic displays of expressiveness toward higher-ups as well as involving the sacrifice of already close relationships with one's friends and family.

INEXPRESSIVENESS AND POWER AS SITUATIONAL VARIABLES

In their article, Balswick and Peek include a notion of inexpressiveness not just as a socially acquired temperament trait but also as a situational variable. Thus, while they argue that all males are socialized into inexpressiveness, they also argue that "for many males . . . through progressively more serious involvements with women (such as going steady, being pinned, engagement, and the honeymoon period of marriage), [these males] begin to make some exceptions. That is, they may learn to be *situationally rather than totally inexpressive*" (1971: 365–366). As noted above, this is seen by Balswick and Peek as functional for men and for the marriage relation in two ways. It meets the wife's expectations of affective support for herself while usually being accompanied by continued inexpression toward women who are not one's spouse. Thus, in this sense, the situational unlearning of inexpressiveness enhances the marital relationship while guarding against extramarital relationships which would threaten the basic pairing of husband–wife.

There is, on the surface, a certain descriptive validity to Balswick and Peek's depiction, although, interestingly, they do not consider a latent function of such unlearning. To the extent that an ability to be expressive *in situ* with a woman leads to satisfactory and gratifying consequences in one case, it probably doesn't take long for the male to learn to be expressive with *any* woman — not just his spouse — as a mode of approaching that woman. Some men, for example, admit to this in my consciousness-raising group. This, in fact, is a way of "coming on" with a woman — a relaxation of the usual standards of inexpressiveness as a calculated move to establish a sexual relationship. Skill at dissembling in this situation may have less to do with handing a woman a "line" than with showing one's weaknesses and frailties as clues intended to be read by her as signs of authentic male interest. In many Latin cultures, which might be considered to epitomize traditional male supremist modes, the style of *machismo*, in fact, calls for the male to be dependent, nominally open, and very expressive to whichever woman he is currently trying to "make." The point of both these examples is to suggest that the *situational unlearning* of inexpressiveness need not lead to strengthening the marriage bond and, in fact, may be detrimental to it, since what works in one situation will probably be tried in others.

Following the argument developed in the previous section concerning the interplay between power and inexpressiveness, I would suggest a different conceptualization of the situational relevance of inexpressiveness:

 (B) EXPRESSIVENESS in a sexist culture empirically emerges as an effort on the part of the male to *control* a situation (once again, on his terms) and to maintain his position.

What I am suggesting is that in a society such as ours, which so permeates all social relationships with notions of power and exchange, even what may appear on the surface to be authentic can be an extension rather than a negation of (sexual) politics.

This is even more true of male inexpressive behavior in intimate male–female relationships. The following dialogue is drawn from Erica Jong's novel of upper-middle-class sexual etiquette, *Fear of Flying*. Consider the political use of male inexpressiveness:

SHE: "Why do you always have to do this to me? You make me feel so lonely."
HE: "That comes from you."
"What do you mean it comes from me? Tonight I wanted to be happy. It's Christmas Eve. Why do you turn on me? What did I do?"
Silence
"What did I do?"
He looks at her as if her not knowing were another injury. "Look, let's just go to sleep now. Let's just forget it."
"Forget what?"
He says nothing.
"Forget the fact that you turned on me? Forget the fact that you're punishing me for nothing? Forget the fact that I'm lonely and cold, that it's Christmas Eve and again you've ruined it for me? Is that what you want me to forget?"
"I won't discuss it."
"Discuss what?" "What won't you discuss?"
"Shut up! I won't have you screaming in the hotel."
"I don't give a fuck what you won't have me do. I'd like to be treated civilly. I'd like you to at least do me the courtesy of telling me why you're in such a funk. And don't look at me that way . . ."
"What way?"
"As if my not being able to read your mind were my greatest sin. I *can't* read your mind. I *don't* know why you're so mad. I can't intuit your wish. If that's what you want in a wife you don't have it in me."
"I certainly don't."
"Then what is it? Please tell me."
"I shouldn't have to."
"Good God! Do you mean to tell me I'm expected to be a mind reader?
"Is that the kind of mothering you want?"
"If you had any empathy for me . . ."
"But I *do*. My God, you just don't give me a chance."
"You tune out. You don't listen."
"It was something in the movie wasn't it?"
"What in the movie?"
"The quiz again. Do you have to quiz me like some kind of criminal. Do you have to cross-examine me? . . . It was the funeral scene . . . The little boy looking at his dead mother. Something got you there. That was when you got depressed."
Silence
"Oh, come on, Bennett, you're making me *furious*. Please tell me. Please."

(He gives the words singly like little gifts. Like hard little turds.) "What was it about the scene that got me?"

"Don't quiz me. Tell me!" (She puts her arms around him. He pulls away. She falls to the floor holding onto his pajama leg. It looks less like an embrace than a rescue scene, she sinking, he reluctantly allowing her to cling to his leg for support.)

"Get up!"

(Crying) "Only if you tell me."

(He jerks his leg away.) "I'm going to bed." (Jong, 1973: 108–109)

One wonders if this is what Balswick and Peek mean by a man "unlearning" his inexpressiveness. Less facetiously, this is clearly an example which indicates that inexpression on the part of the male is not just a matter of inarticulateness or even a deeply socialized inability to respond to the needs of others. The male here is *using* inexpression to guard his own position. To *not* say anything in this situation is to say something very important indeed: that the battle we are engaged in is to be fought by my rules and when I choose to fight. In general:

(C) Male INEXPRESSIVENESS empirically emerges as an intentional manipulation of a situation when threats to the male position occur.

INEXPRESSIVENESS AND MALE CULTURE

Balswick and Peek see inexpressiveness as a major quality of male–female interaction. I have tried to indicate about where they might be right in making such an attribution as well as some of the inadequacies of their conceptualization of the origins of that inexpressiveness. A clear gap in their conceptualization, however, is their lack of any consideration of the inexpressive male in interaction with other men. In fact, their conceptualization leads to two contradictory deductions. First, given the depth and thoroughness of socialization, we might deduce that the male is inexpressive with other men, as well as with women. Second, the male, who is only situationally inexpressive, can interact and express himself truly in situations with other men. This latter position finds support in the notions of male bonding developed by Lionel Tiger (1969). The former position is validated by some of the contributors to Pleck and Sawyer's recent reader on *Men and Masculinity* (1974; esp. Candell, Jourard, and Fasteau). In this section, I would like to raise some of the questions that bear on the problem of male-to-male inexpressiveness. (1) Is there a male subculture? Subcultural differences are usually identified as having ethnic, religious, occupational, etc., boundaries; gender is not usually considered to define subcultural differences. This is so even though gender repeatedly proves to be among the most statistically significant variables in most empirical research. Yet, if we think of a subculture as consisting of unique patterns of belief, value, technique, and language use, there would be a *prima facie* case for considering "male" and "female" definitive of true subcultures in almost all societies. (2) What is the origin of male and female subcultures? This question is probably the most inclusive of all the questions one can ask about gender and sex-role differences. It thrusts us into the very murky swamp of the origin of the family, patriarchy, sexism, etc. Sidestepping questions of the ultimate origin of male and female

*Laurier
AM
PM*

cultural differences, I would only suggest that a good case might be made for considering the persistence — if not the origin — of male and female subcultural differences as due to male efforts to maintain privilege and position *vis-à-vis* women. This is the point anthropologists have been quick to make about primitive societies. The ritual and magic of the males is a secret to be guarded against the women's eyes. Such magic is privy only to the men, and access to it in rites of passage finally determines who is man and who is only *other*. Similar processes are at work in our own society. Chodorow's distinction between "being" and "doing" (1971) is a way of talking about male and female subcultural differences that makes it clear that what men "do" defines not only their own activity but the activity ("being") of women as well. Benston's (1969) distinction between male production of exchange-value in the public sphere and female creation of use-value in the private sphere captures the same fundamental differential of power underlying what appears to be merely cultural. (3) Is male culture necessarily inexpressive? Many observers would say it is flatly wrong to assert that men are inexpressive when interacting with other men. Tiger (1969), for example, talks of the games (sport) men share as moments of intense and authentic communication and expression. In fact, for Tiger, sport derives from the even more intense solidarity of the prehistoric hunt — a solidarity that seems, in his scheme, to be almost genetic in origin. I think Tiger, and others who would call our attention to this capacity for male expressiveness, are saying something important but partial. Perhaps the following example drawn from adult reminiscences of one's fourteenth year can make this clearer:

> I take off at full speed not knowing whether I would reach it but knowing very clearly that this is *my* chance. My cap flies off my head . . . and a second later I one-hand it as cool as can be. . . . I hear the applause. . . . I hear voices congratulating my mother for having such a good athlete for a son. . . . Everybody on the team pounds my back as they come in from the field, letting me know that I've *made it*. (Candell in Pleck and Sawyer, 1974: 16)

This is a good picture of boys being drawn together in sport, of sharing almost total experience.

But is it? The same person continues in the next paragraph:

> But I know enough not to blow my cool so all I do is mumble thanks under a slightly trembling upper lip which is fighting the rest of my face, the rest of being, from exploding with laughter and tears of joy. (Candell in Pleck and Sawyer, 1974: 19)

Why this silence? Again, I don't think it is just because our culture demands inexpression. I think here, as above, silence and inexpression are the ways men learn to *consolidate* power, to make the effort appear as effortless, to guard against showing the real limits of one' potential and power by making it *all* appear easy. Even among males alone, one maintains control over a situation by revealing only strategic proportions of oneself.

Further, in Marc Fasteau's very perceptive article "Why Men Aren't Talking"

(Pleck and Sawyer, 1974), the observation is made that when men do talk, they talk of "large" problems — war, politics, art — but never of anything really personal. Even when men have equal credentials in achieved success, they tend not to make themselves vulnerable to each other, for to do so may be interpreted as a sign of weakness and an opportunity for the other to secure advantage. As Fasteau puts it, men talk, but they always do so for a *reason* — getting together for its own sake would be too frightening — and that reason often amounts to just another effort at establishing who *really* is best, stronger, smarter, or ultimately, more powerful.

INEXPRESSIVENESS AND THE SOCIOLOGY OF SEX ROLES

In the preceding sections, I have tried to change the grounds of an explanation of male inexpressiveness from one which holds that it is simply a cultural variable to one which sees it as a consequence of the political (power) position of the sexes in our society. I have not tried to deny that male inexpressiveness exists but only that it does so in different forms and for different reasons than Balswick and Peek suggest. I am making no claims for the analytic completeness of the ideas presented here.

A direct result of the feminist movement has been the effort on the part of sociologists concerned with family and sex-role-related behavior to discard or recast old concepts in the face of the feminist critique. One tendency of this "new sociology" has been an attempt to rescue attributes of positive human potential from the exclusive domain of one sex and, thus, to validate those potentials for all people. Although they do not say this explicitly, some such concern certainly underlies Balswick and Peek's effort. I think that this is social science at its best.

On the other hand, I am not convinced, as Balswick and Peek seem to be, that significant change in the male sex role will be made if we conceptualize the problem as one that involves individual males gradually unlearning their inexpressiveness with individual females. Balswick (1974) wrote an article based on the analysis developed with Peek entitled "Why Husbands Can't Say 'I Love You'" and printed it in a mass distribution women's magazine. Predictably, the article suggests *to the wife* some techniques she might develop for drawing her husband out of his inexpressive shell. I think that kind of article — at this point in the struggle of women to define themselves — is facile and wrongheaded. Such advice burdens the wife with additional "emotional work" while simultaneously creating a new arena in which she can — and most likely will — fail.

Similarly, articles that speak to men about their need to become more expressive also miss the point if we are concerned about fundamental social change. Such arguments come fairly cheap. Witness the essentially honest but fatally narrow and class-bound analyses of Korda (1973) and Farrell (1974). Their arguments develop little more than strategies capable of salvaging a limited number of upper-class male heterosexual egos. The need I see and feel at this point is for arguments and strategies capable of moving the majority of men who are not privileged in that fashion. What such arguments would say — much less to whom they would be addressed — is a question I cannot now answer. But I know where my work lies. For if my argument is correct — and

Dreikurs, Rudolf. Social Equality: The challenge of our time.

I believe it is — that male inexpressiveness is instrumental in maintaining positions of power and privilege for men, then male sociologists might well begin to search through their own experiences and the accumulated knowledge of the sociological literature for <u>sensitizing models which might indicate how, and if, it would be possible to relinquish the power which has historically been ours.</u>

REFERENCES

Balswick, Jack. 1974. "Why husband's can't say 'I love you.'" *Woman's Day*, April.

Balswick, Jack and Charles Peek. 1971. "The inexpressive male: a tragedy of American society." *The Family Coordinator*, 20:363–368.

Benston, Margaret. 1969. "The political economy of women's liberation." *Month Review*, 21:13–27.

Bradley, Mike. 1971. *Unbecoming Men: A Men's Consciousness-Raising Group Writes on Oppression and Themselves.* New York: Changing Times Press.

Chodorow, Nancy. 1971. "Being and doing: a cross-cultural examination of the socialization of males and females." Pp. 259–291 in Gornick and Moran (ed.), *Woman in Sexist Society.* New York: New American Library.

Farrell, Warren. 1974. *The Liberated Man.* New York: Random House.

Jong, Erica. 1973. *Fear of Flying.* New York: New American Library.

Korda, Michael. 1973. *Male Chauvinism:* How It Works. New York: Random House.

Parsons, Talcott. 1951. *The Social System* (Chapter VI and VII). Glencoe, Illinois: Free Press.

Pleck, Joseph and Jack Sawyer. 1974. *Men and Masculinity.* Englewood Cliffs, New Jersey: Prentice-Hall.

Sennett, Richard and Jonathan Cobb. 1973. *The Hidden Injuries of Class.* New York: Random House.

Tiger, Lionel. 1971. *Men in Groups.* London: Granada Publishing.

Wrong, Dennis. 1961. "The oversocialized conception of man in modern sociology." *American Sociological Review*, 26:183–193.

John Krich

HERE COME THE BRIDES
THE BLOSSOMING BUSINESS OF IMPORTED LOVE

The condominiums come in mirror images, but not the occupants. On the front door of one stucco chalet hangs a Chinese character made of brass. Call it cross-cultural mistletoe for the couple living inside, another product of a growing American phenomenon. The husband turns out to be a small-town white kid come to the big city, prematurely middle-aged, middlebrow in his conspicuous collections of carvings and trophies, middle management, though never quite as managerial as he'd like, flashing a salesman's charm that readily gives way to anger. The wife is young, comely, and Asian; wearing house sandals but groomed for a party, a good listener whose skills have been severely taxed, uncomfortable with her new language but comforted by her new surroundings, covering her suspicion with drowsiness, a bit sunken along with the living room. As she offers tea and the homemade egg rolls called *lumpia*, nurses her newborn, and beams at the wedding album, it is hard to imagine that she was plucked from a row of snapshots in a mail-order catalog. Or that this marriage wasn't arranged in heaven, but in Hawaii — by an introduction service called Cherry Blossoms.

Then come the corrections in one another's version of events, made most gingerly; the nervous jokes about age difference; the curious blanks drawn when trying to remember the names of close in-laws; the references to unspecified conflicts and secret diaries where "he write that he travel looking for other girls to marry after me"; the questions that the wife pretends she can't grasp until she retreats into the "no comment" of a nap, causing the whispered confessions — which come whenever she "lets me out of her sight" — about how "it's been no picnic," about the bitching, the sulking, the misunderstandings.

And there's that troublesome word *love*, which is either actively disdained — in favor of talk about "trade-offs" or "liabilities and assets" — or flashed continually, like an expensive Javanese mask. Love is blind, as they say — especially in this context, where there's so much to be blind about. The longer they tell their story, the more this couple reveals the forces rending them apart, and the fears that made them cleave together. Cozy as it all seems, the world beyond keeps swirling through this condo. Settled on their white ottoman, they remain a man and a woman in flight — like so many who have chosen the path of these postal courtships.

The men: *"The woman I yearn to spend my life with does not seem to reside in North America."*

The women: *"I believe the god will let us to be together one day. Is that a dream? I love only American music."*

That world is not only getting smaller; it's getting lonelier. Never has it been easier for nations to mingle, and never have expectations been greater for one culture to provide what the other lacks. Economic interdependencies give way to psychic ones: those with power seek those with beauty, those with money seek those with heart. It's not surprising then that the delivery of Asian brides to mostly white American grooms has, within the last five years, become a multimillion-dollar-a-year industry. Since there's a perceived shortage of U.S. homemakers willing to shoulder traditional matrimonial tasks, some entrepreneurs are going abroad — where the labor can be bought cheaper and the quality control kept more rigid. Imperialists of the heart, these men strike out for poorer lands in search of the raw materials necessary to the manufacture of their fantasies. If emotional fulfillment is as vital to U.S. national security as South African chrome, then it must be secured in regular shipments. Love itself has become the ultimate consumer good, and, as with so many others, an increasing number of shoppers are no longer buying American.

The catalogs: *"Congratulations! You have taken the first step towards discovering an eternal treasure! For many discerning men, there can be no other choice than a Lady of the Orient. These women possess wit, charm and grace unmatched anywhere in the world.*

[They] are faithful and devoted to their husbands. . . . When it comes to sex, they are not demonstrative; however, they are uninhibited [and] believe sex is healthy. She wakes up in the morning with a smile on her face and she does *wake up in the morning! You have heard the phrase 'A Woman of the 80s.' We recommend a Woman for all time.* An Asian Woman!"

There are now over a thousand organizations in the United States, Canada, Western Europe, and Australia peddling introductions to those women. They can be found in the classifieds of upstanding journals, innocently offering "international friendship" and "pen pals." Once their brochures arrive, the pitch is hard sell and carefully aimed — emphasizing the "soft, feminine, and cooperative" over the "crude, rude, and overbearing." Despite ostentatious logos like "Jewels of the Orient," "Asian Sweethearts," and "East Meets West Club," most are struggling, small-time operations, run out of a post office box. Many have been started by couples who met through some other agency and decided to put their own coupling to work: "My adorable little Asian princess . . . and I are so deliriously happy with one another," bubbles one typical operator, "that we wish to share our experience with others like yourself." Nowhere in this sharing is there any guarantee of sexual favors, or marriage, or even that the men's letters will be answered. So long as there's no actual or implied promise of specific services, these businesses remain legally invulnerable.

Although no one has kept exact figures, it's a safe bet that 10,000 marriages have resulted from these air-mail relationships over the past 12 years. Most of the pen pal businesses are crude copies of the formula established by Cherry Blossoms, which, under the direction of Harvard Ph.D. and ex-hippie John Broussard, has become the highest-volume matchmaking shop. Begun at the whimsical request of a single male in 1974, Cherry Blossoms has now expanded to publishing three separate, bimonthly directories, running up to 48 pages, featuring Philippine "Island Blossoms," Asian women in general, and miscellaneous hopefuls from Peru to Yugoslavia. The services' fees run from $5 to $10 dollars for an introductory batch of a few sample addresses to $300 for all current and back issues — depending upon a variety of plans in which the subscriber may be offered "first crack" at a designated number of women. The clients also get their predilections listed in the services' register and their names placed in newspaper ads throughout the Far East.

Cherry Blossoms sends along a chatty newsletter describing women deemed less photogenic, offered at discount rates. This mimeographed sheet also alerts the men to "rotten apples": women who use their letters to solicit "samples of foreign currency" for their private collection or ask for donations to "typhoon relief."

The subscribers' package is bulked out with a handbook, *How to Write to Oriental Ladies.* Rewritten elsewhere as *From "Dear Lady" to "I Do,"* the booklet includes rudimentary tips on how to get the correspondence ball rolling, advice on travel and immigration procedures, and a glossary of handy phrases in Thai or Tagalog. While these outfits insist at every turn that Asian women aren't fussy about trivial matters like age or race, their booklets feature lengthy advice on how to soften or conceal potential blemishes — such as being black, disabled, or divorced. Dedicated "to gentle people and faithful lovers everywhere," the Cherry Blossoms guide nonetheless advances the basic rule: "When in doubt, leave it out." This genteel discretion is not extended to potential brides: they are typically subjected to questionnaires urging them to reveal everything from stints of prostitution to membership in communist organizations, their attitudes on premarital sex to abortion. The inequity of power is heightened by an inequity of knowledge.

The men: "*There are a lot of desperate men out there. Attractive men, successful men, microbiologists. They're not losers. They're just not attracted to American women anymore — because these women have become impossible.*"

The women: "*Due to a hurting experience before, I want to meet someone who's total stranger to me.*" "*I look a man even he's above 70 years old or he's driver or welder or any.*"

There is no mystery to commerce — even when it deals in bodies. The credits and debits are balanced like yin and yang. On one side of the Pacific, there's a limitless supply of desperately poor females who'll do anything to become U.S. citizens. On the other, there's an increasing demand for their services from men who'll do anything to retain their power advantage within family life. At first glance, the moral to this story seems obvious, the vicious villains and helpless heroines easily identifiable. Unfortunately, as in the world's larger geopolitical drama, the rich often need more from the poor than the other way around. Too bad the world, in getting smaller, is not getting simpler. There are subplots galore in this tale of two continents — and two sexes.

The men: "*It's a great relationship — her life's me and that's it.*"

The women: "*I'm OK now. I'm great, with someone who takes care and is so understanding to me.*"

The tale begins with the men doing most of the telling — and all of the buying. As one of the mail-order operators jokes, in a retort aimed at the feminist critics ever at his heels, "It's not helpless Asian ladies we exploit for money. It's horny Western men." There's been a surplus of distressed females throughout the ages, but there would be no trade in Asian brides without the frustrations created by this particular age. It doesn't matter whether he's a cocky Texas lawyer, a fastidious high school teacher, a former All-American athlete, or a chipper electronic whiz; each husband prefaces his remarks with a portrait of the women he's lost, rather than the ones he's found. Our narrators do not so much share some fetish for the exotic, as a disillusionment — bordering on revulsion — with what is around the corner.

The men: "*American girls left me really disappointed. They look like tubs of lard stuffed into Levi's. They're pushy, spoiled rotten, and they talk like sailors. They're not cooperative, but combative — and they never appreciate what you do for them. In the morning, you wonder how many guys before me? Was it the football team? Maybe it's our fault, the fault of men for repressing them for so long. But they're not psychologically together. They just don't seem to know what they want.*"

Haven't we heard this somewhere before? In a curious role reversal, these last of the supermachos offer the classic complaints women have long made about men: they're confused, immature, promiscuous; they're also opinionated and materialistic. They fear commitments and neglect personal satisfactions in favor of careers. They let themselves go to seed: one disgruntled husband even suggested that all women want is "to watch TV and booze it up." Worst of all, they tend to be smarter or more successful than the men, who are left exhausted by the jostling for position entailed by the recent redefining of sexual roles.

The men: "*It's not easy when everything is up for discussion. Why don't you do this? Why don't you do that? Even my mother gives me a hard time. She wants to know why*

I don't cook once in a while. Now I just smile and tell her, 'I'm retired from all that.'
My wife smiles too."

Few of these men are trailer park misfits or the sort of gents who paper their bedrooms in aluminum foil. In one of the many surveys that the introduction services trot out as proof of their mainstream appeal, the statistics indicate that those who seek Asian brides are above average in education, income, and status.

These same samplings tell us that the average age at marriage for the husbands is 52; for the wives, 32. The Asian bride trade is tailor-made for those men driven to sustain youth beyond its normal bounds. For divorced men and elderly widowers with more modest goals, it can simply be a quick means of re-acquiring a sock-sorter or a live-in nurse.

But the surveys cannot test the would-be husbands for insecurity. The more the men rail against the women's movement, the more they show themselves to be its unwanted offspring. They want a refuge from chaos: all of them speak of wanting someone "who'll be there every night," as one put it, "who won't cheat, and who I can trust to do right by me — even down to how she takes care of the dog." Responding to the lure of far-off places, these men seek the girl-next-door. Through no fault of their own, she's become the girl-next-continent.

The men: "*All this mail-order jazz is a lot of bull. If you meet someone at a dance, you wouldn't call her a dancehall girl. It's not like the Wild West where brides came out in a stagecoach. After the introduction's made, it's up to you.*"

For now, most couples find out all they want to know through old-fashioned letter writing — and they seem to like it that way. As a holdover from less hurried, more reasoned times, the slow pace of the mail befits those who wish to be holdovers too. Some men prove to be inveterate correspondents — with alphabetized file cabinets of pen pals from Anabella to Zhou Ying. Oh, the thrills of romance from across the Pacific! The exotic East delivered to the doorstep, in harmless half-ounce packets! The men emphasize that their moves toward matrimony are considered, often agonizing. But why hurry to reduce their postal harem? Suddenly, each of them's the most popular guy on the block. And they've done it without having to splash on cologne, haunt cocktail lounges, dust off dubious charms, reveal a bald spot or a paunch. Shopping by mail can even be justified as a money-saving measure. Think of how much it costs to date in this country! Or to hang out in bars! The silk route turns out to be a path of least resistance — where procedures are clear, risks minimal.

The men: "*It's very safe. There are no messy endings. And it's slow enough that you really get to know someone — not like dating here, when suddenly you get in way over your head.*"

Once they get to know someone, the men venture out to meet their pen pal — or pals. For some of them, their travels in search of Miss Right constitute their sole and fleeting opportunity to feel like swashbucklers. They recount their "shopping trips," as they call them, in a tone usually reserved for discoverers of the North Pole: "We didn't know each other. We're from two different cultures; and here, in the middle of Taipei, we were gonna meet up for a blind date, which was, when you think about it, unbelievable." Lo and behold, the sales clerks from Peoria cross the international date line to become the emperors of Quezon City! Their pen pals serve as a parade of willing tour guides, and the two-week vacation takes on the power of a hallucination. In such heady moments, they may forget that they came for a mate and instead use a variety of appetites — especially since, as one pointed out, "a lot of the girls, even if they're virgins, will spend the night with you if they think that will do the trick." Others concentrate dutifully on their chosen lady — presuming her charms match up to her penmanship — savoring a courtship whose Victorian pace is enforced by watchful relatives.

The men: "*I couldn't believe it once I got over there. The choices were mindboggling. All the girls called me 'Superman.' It was like I was a white god. You walk around here, you're just another schmuck. In Cebu City, the heads were turning. You'd think Robert Redford or Paul Newman hit town.*"

The women: "*I tell him, if you make love to me, you must marry me. I thought him sincere because he travel to see my mother. Thirty hours to Mindanao. Even after he propose, he keeps looking. He go to Hong Kong, Malaysia, traveling around for long time to see pen pals there. He had other girlfriend in Philippines. I go up to his hotel room instead of waiting in the lobby. I find them together. Then the game was up.*"

The men: "*They got this system of chaperones in the Philippines. In my case, it seems like the whole family tagged along. We always had 15 people on our dates because everyone wanted a meal. When I asked permission from her father, I said, 'Sir, I'd like to marry your daughter.' He answered, 'Can I have another sandwich?'*"

The choice made, the blessed event follows apace. It is usually staged in the bride's home country, because a U.S. visa is far easier to obtain for a spouse than for a fiancée and because the women tend to place more value on the ceremony itself. Often there are two consecrations: one civic, the other Buddhist or Shinto or Catholic or Moslem. The Kodachrome record shows one pale, nervous face surrounded in the warm circle of a hundred new relatives. It is the first perk of the traditional family life he's been seeking.

The men: "*She is spoiling me, though, with all the attention I get, all of my nails manicured, gives me a shower daily, body massage nightly, shines my shoes and no sooner take a garment off till she has hung it up. She is well worth the price of your catalog.*"

But why do these men journey eastward in the first place? Similar mail-order agencies now tout the semi-Asian virtues of Latin American "*chiquitas,*" who would seem to share the same "traditional" values and financial need.

Alas, when it comes to being stereotyped, Asian women have a 5,000-year head start. From yesterday's geishas to today's Singapore Girl, the pampered courtesans of the mandarins to the pick-by-number masseuses of Bangkok, the world's largest pool of females has long been tagged with a single occupation and preoccupation. The dependent, man-pleasing image remains easy to put over — even though Asian women have long labored in the rice paddies or on the looms, just as they are now filling the ranks of the most modern occupations in some of the most urbanized spots on the planet.

Since the Second World War, this myth of the Kama Sutra goddess has taken on the weight of historic inevitability. Because of the widespread American military presence in the Far East, jet-age prostitution has developed as a major component in the financial stability of such puppet states as the Philippines, Thailand, and Taiwan. Catering first to the needs of U.S. servicemen, and now aimed at the wholesale, assembly line satisfaction of Japanese and European executives, "sex tourism" is not merely condoned throughout Asia; it is encouraged as an important source of foreign currency. Without a ready supply of poor and uneducated peasant girls, most Asian governments would be in debt up to their epaulets. Without the mystique that casts Asian women as sexual toys, such a massive industry could not exist — and neither could its legally sanctioned adjunct, the mail-order trade.

The men: *"Of course, lots of them have to become prostitutes, because the only thing that they have to negotiate with is their body. But I'd rather marry a Philippine prostitute than an American woman any day. They're good girls looking for one man."*

The women: *"My husband, he always say that I am foxy. I don't know what he means by that."*

The mystique works so well because it is two sided. While the sinful reputation of her fallen sisters attests to considerable bedroom skills, the Asian woman is all the more desirable when viewed as the world's last unsullied creature, one whose spiritual and moral purity has been safeguarded by tradition. The potential whore is reconstituted as the uncorrupted virgin; the destitute waif bears her lot with the dignity of a princess. It makes for powerful rescue fantasies.

The men: *"My wife was a simple, barefoot girl. She lived in a house with no electricity and no TV. She was 21 years old and she'd never been on a date. Never. She wouldn't even hold my hand. She was very, very pure. With her, what I saw was what I got. I wasn't going to pay for someone else's mistakes. They come out of these hovels — these shacks you or I wouldn't put a pig or a chicken in — and they're wearing these perfectly clean, white, starched dresses. Everyone of them comes out looking like Miss Universe."*

There are certainly enough Asian misses willing to enter this ultimate of beauty contests. That's because the prize is no mere tiara, but includes among other dividends the more highly valued green card offered to permanent residents by the U.S. Immigration and Naturalization Service. Marriage to an American, unless determined to be a sham by the INS, not only guarantees that green card; it also makes a woman's relatives eligible to immigrate and reduces her wait for full citizenship from five years to three. A few small ads placed in Asian newspapers combine with word of mouth to lure a torrent of interest — especially since the women are listed in the catalogs for free. So the aspirants come forward, in most cases from the Philippines — that perfect hothouse for pro-American, anti-divorce wives — but also from tranquil Javanese villages, Malaysian rubber plantations, palm-fringed Thai atolls, the everenlarging industrial smudges along the coasts of Taiwan, and even the work brigades of Beijing. They apply in a wobbly hand.

The women: *"With this short letter, I will lay my hands to your staff for the personal assistance and possible success in the near future! I have sincere wish you join your club. I only have honest and good intention. I am, after all, a human being and not an android or something, and I have feelings, compassion, and sorrow just like you."*

Human beings, after all, they become anonymous merchandise stacked in neat catalog rows. The snapshots are often blurred, but the women's terrifying innocence is sharply in focus. Clutching Snoopy dolls or their kids, they lounge in tiny bedchambers inundated with American trash and American hopes, cluttered with cheap souvenirs of lives waiting to be led, the journey yet to be undertaken. With their Calvin Klein jeans and Robby Benson T-shirts, most look up-to-date, but the catalog layouts display the cultural leaps being attempted: Javanese dancers in embroidered sarongs are juxtaposed with miniskirted secretaries. The women's fractured English — left purposefully uncorrected, as if to further emphasize their vulnerability — attests to distinctly unAmerican outlooks.

The women: *"Interests: the tandem bicycle, sweet potato, Chinese sit crosslegged. Hobbies: badminton, reading the books, hearing the songs, and clean a house compound.*

Favorite actor: Clint Eastwood. Favorite actress: Brooke Shields. Favorite dish: Chinese dish."

In this lineup of spouses where everything seems out in the open, nothing really is. The dutiful lists of hobbies and interests never include job hunting or making ends meet. From these catalogs, you get the impression that these women while away their time "strumming guitar," dancing, waterskiing. "He [my husband] must have great courage, for I am a poor singer, interested in singing loudly." There is not a hint anywhere about financial hardship. Only yearning, motiveless hearts! They work hard to create the impression of looking solely for intellectual companions from afar: "I'm quite confident that the differences between our two countries would make an extremely captivating topic." The approved look is virginal, the talk calculated coy: "My name mean yellow fruit, which tastes very sweet. It's hard to explain; you got to try for yourself."

That fruit grows best in the Philippines. Take horrendous underemployment, add a working familiarity of American culture, widespread schooling in English, a dash of the colonial mentality, just enough prosperity to elicit a craving for more, Catholicism, family oriented mores breaking down in the face of economic chaos — and *voilà! Mabuhay!* "On every corner, in every candy store," one husband remembers, "the girls want to know, 'You married, mister?'" The urgency of the question is further fueled by the impending threat of civil war. "Some of the Filipinas are writing to 60, 70 guys — in Norway, Switzerland, Japan," one husband says. "Answering letters becomes their job for the day." And enough of a full-time obsession for many that a member of the Philippine opposition recently introduced a bill in parliament making it a crime punishable by up to eight years imprisonment "to publish or broadcast any advertisement recruiting or selling Filipino women as wives to foreigners." Yet where prostitution and underemployment loom, marriage to some febrile foreign gent can be a means of remaining relatively unbought.

The men: *"Hey, some of them would marry the most obnoxious slobs, 20-karat assholes — when they're starving and there's a steak dinner on the other side of the plate. On the other hand, a lot of girls are choosing amongst hundreds of letters. They wouldn't sell themselves off for anything that wasn't good value in return."*

While they're aware of the women's economic distress, the husbands manage to find ways to exempt their choices from such motivation. The brides have ways too. They cling to a discretion whose origins may be tactical and cultural. Many won't even admit that they were looking to escape their countries in the first place. "A friend, she get my picture and send it without asking," went one standard refrain. "After I get so many letters . . . , I think maybe this is a chance to improve my English." Surely, there's an easier way to learn another language. And are these women really willing to yield up their lifetime's fealty just to have a roof over their heads? Such an assumption shows more disregard for the dignity of these women than even the worst sexist could muster — and the women's letters and ads suggest that those who take the leap have other motives as well.

The women: *"The men I have known in my country are not gentlemen. Philippine men, they beat their wives. American men treat their wives better."*

Green cards aside, interest in Western men may be prompted by the search for a more sensitive, less autocratic mate. The irony here is that their search must be conducted amid the group of American men least likely to fit that description. Many of the women are victims of "our old traditions. I got married without love between us. I must obey my parents." Irony upon irony: the mail-order trade that appears the highest expression expression of coercion can be the first opportunity for some Asian women to use their own feelings in choosing a mate.

Many of the women seeking foreign husbands are unwed or abandoned mothers, unacceptable to the men of their own countries because they carry the stigma of failure or bring with them the financial burden of another man's offspring. For them, a foreigner may represent their last chance. Others are simply "still looking for the right guy that make my heart beat quickly." That search, never easy, has been made more problematic by the vast social displacements that have come with economic development in Asia. With the influx into the cities, the old family networks that eased matchmaking are breaking down. With American-style progress has come American-style atomization.

"The funny thing about men these days," writes one woman from Kuala Lumpur, "is that they want to do everything with women except to have commitment."

The men: *"I don't think the transition was too rough on her. She cried every day for two years."*

The women: *"I don't cry anymore. I used to write every day. Now I write only at Christmas. A neighbor teach me to play bingo. Now I have bingo; I don't miss my family so much."*

For the mail-order bride, commitment is the easy part. Once married and ensconced in the United States, the women find that persistent homesickness is only the first hurdle. The standard refugee traumas are bad enough, but these imported brides have to grapple in isolation with two equally challenging adjustments. They must learn the customs of a new country and a new husband all at once. Often, they become acquainted with the hindrances of the latter before they've been exposed to the opportunities of the former. If becoming an American is their main aim, they are at the complete mercy of their spouse for the three years until citizenship is granted — and the husband holds the power to deport her if she doesn't play by his rules. It is in this sense that every mail-order bride, no matter how willing, is a captive.

The women: *"That first year, I cannot go out by myself. I would get lost. I know how to drive. I got my license. I just don't know the area too well, and I'm afraid to talk to other people. . . . I rather stay in Taiwan. Speak my own language. I feel more useful there."*

The men: *"Most girls think they know what to expect, but they don't. Most of the guys lie and bullshit to them. They make them think this is the land of milk and honey. They assume that as soon as you get off the boat, there's a job waiting for you."*

A surprising number of these "traditionalist" couples want, or need, the women to seek employment. But lacking the language skills, or finding that their education counts for little, those who expect to work for a living quickly learn that those vaunted opportunities are not quite open at all.

And strangely enough, the common complaint that the husbands seem to voice is that they have gotten too much "loyal wife" for the money. These men who claim to abhor the assertiveness of their own countrywomen report that they can't communicate with their new partners until they've become a bit more like themselves. To a man, they speak of having to teach their wives to express their feelings, even anger. Americanization begins at home.

The women: "*It's true. I don't want to write check without his permission. I take a long time to learn to say it is not his money, but* our *money."*

The men: "*She won't go anywhere without me or do anything without me — not even go to sleep. She practically asks for permission to go to the toilet. She always says it's the Filipino way. And finally, sometimes, I have to just say, honey, this is not the goddamn Philippines. And this is my way."*

"My way" can be enforced with fists, although actual instances of wife battering among mail-order couples are difficult to trace. Many of the women are not aware of shelters and social services or are reluctant to use them for fear of deportation. For every rare one who does come forward, there are surely many more who must cope by themselves with some gradient of coercion. Challenged with evidence of abuse cases, the mail-order husbands like to cite the rumors they've heard of brides who take their American men for all the money they're worth, then disappear once they've got their citizenship papers. To the husband, one crime is no more justifiable than the other. In this bargain, the terror cuts both ways — and the keeper is often as fearful and watchful as the captive.

The men: "*My wife keeps saying she's going to walk out one of these days — I can't tell if she's kidding or not."*

The women: "*Here, I got more freedom. But mostly I don't look out window. My husband not like me talking. He's not bad man, just a nasty guy, with temper."*

Just as the situation breeds betrayal, sudden or gradual, so it provides incentives for success. It will take many years before we know whether these marriages prove any more durable than those of American marriages in general — although, statistically speaking, that wouldn't take much. Yet unlike their American counterparts, these newlyweds show an uncommon determination to bridge their differences. Few of the wives are going to casually give up on their effort: most have been schooled in making the best of it on the home front and do not accept divorce as an alternative. These women have cast too much aside — and the men have invested an equal amount in effort, cash, and the idealization of their quest.

The men: "*The first year was very tough. With the conflicts we had, if we hadn't already been married, we probably never would have gotten married."*

The women: "*Your mate is picked by God. You have only to be patient and get along."*

If Asian women seem more willing than their American sisters to make compromises, that is because some bring with them a different model of what marriage is supposed to provide. Where wedlock is seen primarily as a pragmatic partnership, it ceases to carry the burden as an emotional cure-all. This view of marriage, based in its most idealized form on mutual aid and on the slow unearthing of feeling, has certainly proven useful to the continuation of the species throughout the centuries — and it is one these 20th-century husbands strain to emulate.

The men: "*When I married her, I didn't love her. I admired her and I respected her, and I decided to take a chance. In the Asian tradition, one learns to love someone. And I feel it's growing every day. It's not the same thing as in the States. It comes slowly; it's healthier this way."*

The replacement of American homemakers with Asian stand-ins confirms the old axiom that "none are free until all are free." Still, taken as a whole, the phenomenon hardly represents a serious inroad into the gains made by women. These are gains that appear irreversible worldwide, and it will take a great deal more than a few thousand rather fragile "old-fashioned" marriages to reverse the tide. The march toward a workable equality of the sexes is not what's threatened by the growing attraction of white American males to Asian women and the ideal they are imagined to embody; the only thing threatened is the relatively new concept of marrying for passion and separating for lack of same. It is one more joust — this time from the male side — over our contemporary prescriptions for happiness.

The men: "*We believe in traditional roles — like the man washes the car, the woman sweeps. It's so easy to get along that way, where everything's clear.*"

The women: "*It's not true that Asian men and American men different. Men are men everywhere — some help the women out, and some don't.*"

Some American feminists and Asian American organizations have condemned the mail-order trade as legalized prostitution and pen pal marriage as inherently abusive, but such rhetoric serves to obscure reality rather than transform it. If the Asian trade leads to a kind of slavery, then it is a volunteered servitude that is but a single link of chain apart from the unwritten contract that binds any man to any woman. Judging these brides by Western standards often means trying to convince the oppressed of just how unhappy they would feel if they could only see their true condition. Unfortunately, the path of human want is rarely politically correct, and history does not move by morally approved acts. Listening to the voices rising from these catalogs of need, what emerges is that those needs are not there to be labeled false or backward. They are there to be met.

The women: "*I am here in this stranger place, with no one can share my loneliness.*" "*Do you think you can maybe like me, love me? Need someone for loving. Isn't a joke.*"

There are bound to be more and more stories of intercultural courtship — where happy endings are unlikely, but surprise endings can do the same job. For often as not, the reprieve that's granted is that neither party ends up getting anything that resembles the order they've placed. "If it was really mail order," one husband joked, "I'd have made my wife a bit younger. And a lot richer!" Where a human heart is the cargo, the customer can never be sure of exactly what he's ordering or whether he ever gets it delivered intact. The no-fault bride turns out to know very well how to point a finger. The bullying husband ends up in an arm wrestle with his own stereotypes.

The men: "*Asian women are not the subservient types that the media make us believe.*" "*They can be very strong willed. I'll tell you, my wife won't take no shit off nobody.*"

The women: "*In America, it's not easy like I think. You can't pick money off the streets. It's hard work, enjoying my life.*"

In the Posturepedic nuptial bed, over morning bowls of Raisin Bran, on proverbial weekend outings, it turns out that, most of the time, there's no Suzy Wong present, no Simon Legree. He is no John Wayne and she is no geisha. Instead of "inborn submissiveness," she demonstrates, with exposure to new possibilities, a pesky tendency toward human enlargement. Confronted with the silence that comes with slavish assent, reinforcing his solitude, he discovers rather enlightened cravings for a loud and living mate. Behind the triple locks of matrimony, the sprinkler systems and the electric eyes, they are not master and servant, but two people grappling with the long odds against durable understanding. Trapped in the most daunting circumstances, impelled by the most muddled intentions, all they can do is carry on the grim work of making the world one — with an ancient talisman hung outside for good luck.

Wayne Ewing

THE CIVIC ADVOCACY OF VIOLENCE

The ruling paradigm for male supremacy remains, to this hour, physical violence. This paradigm remains unchecked and untouched by change. Critically, the permissive environment for male violence against women is supported by a civic advocacy of violence as socially acceptable, appropriate and necessary. Physically abusive men, particularly men who batter their spouses, continue for the most part to be a protected population. And the sources which provide us with what we know of the batterer — largely clinical and treatment models — have themselves remained too isolated from sexual politics and from a social analysis of male cultures. Until the code of male violence is read, translated and undone, male batterers will not be largely affected by what we are coming to know about them.

PROFILING THE MALE BATTERER

I sometimes think that none of the literature will ever move our knowledge dramatically further than Erin Pizzey's observation that all batterers are either alcoholics or psychotics or psychopaths or just plain bullies. That is good common sense applied to the all too ordinary affair of men beating up women. I also think that the following observation, more often than not made rhetorically and politically, has a measure of significance that we can draw on. When the question is raised, "Who is the male batterer?" the answer is sometimes given, "Every man!" Without pushing too quickly let me simply point out here that this observation is accurate. It is not simply an attention-getter. Attempts to profile the male batterer always wind up with a significant body of information which points to . . . every man.

I believe the most striking example of this is found in those studies which support the — in my estimation, accurate — view of male violence as a learned behavior. Depending on the study, 81% to 63% of the population of batterers researched have either experienced abuse as victims in the home of their childhood or have witnessed their fathers beat their mothers. While that is significant enough to support our forming knowledge that socialization into violence in the home perpetuates violence, and that individual men can be conditioned to domestic violence as normal, I do not believe we have spent enough time looking at the chilling fact that remains: from 19% to 37% of these populations have literally invented violence in an intimate relationship. It is clear that the experience as victim or observer of physical violence is not necessary to "produce" a violent, abusive man.

And so it is with any of the many categories of inquiry applied to populations of male batterers. I will tick some of these off here, and in each case refer to the batterers with whom I work in Denver. *Ethnic backgrounds*, for example, will closely parallel the ethnic makeup of the community in which the study is

Reprinted from *M.*, Spring 1982.

Adapted from a paper delivered in the Women's Studies Division of the Western Social Science Association annual meeting, 1981, and part of a book-length manuscript in progress, *Violence Works/Stop Violence*.

made. In intake interviews of men either volunteering or ordered by the Courts into the men's groups of our project in Denver, the statistics generated on ethnicity are the statistics available about our community in general. *Age* is not a major factor. While most physically abusive men are in their 20s or early 30s, batterers are also under 20 and over 50. The fact that slightly more than half the men we deal with in Denver are in their 20s is attributable to so many other possibilities, that the fact itself recedes in significance. *Education* is not a major determinant. While a majority of batterers may have a high school education, the ones we know are equally balanced on either side by men with undergraduate, graduate and professional degrees and men with less than a high school education. *Income* studies do not support the popular idea that battering men are low income earners. Over a third of the men studied in Denver have incomes of $15,000 and above; and regular employment is as much a feature of the batterer as is infrequent employment. The *onset and frequency of violence* within a relationship are not consistent indicators of the behavior profile of the male batterer. The only conclusion safely drawn from these inquiries is that the probability of maiming and permanently crippling injury for the victim rises with the increase of frequency, and that the period of contrition on the part of the batterer becomes briefer between episodes as frequency increases. *Substance abuse* may as easily accompany battering episodes as not. In Denver, it is involved in a little over a third, while in other populations studied, substance abuse may figure in as much as 80% of battering episodes. And of course the self-reported *"causes"* of violence from both victims and abusers runs from sex to in-laws to money to housework to children to employment and around and around and around. There is no real clue to the profile of the abusive male in these reported occasions for battering episodes. With respect to the *psychological makeup* of the abusive male, there is considerable consensus that these men evidence low self-esteem, dependency needs, unfamiliarity with their emotions, fear of intimacy, poor communication skills and performance orientation. But what is intriguing about these observations is that they span all of these other indicators.

And so I end this brief review where I started. The abusive male — that is, the violent man of low self-esteem, high dependency need, slow on affect, fearful of intimacy, poor in communicating emotions, and oriented to performance — the abusive male is every man.

THE CYCLE OF VIOLENCE

How is it we know so little, then, about the male batterer? In part this is due to the fact that the movement begun by the female victims of male violence has not spawned a fervent desire to look at the abuser. The simple fact is that as massive as male domestic violence is, we know more about the victims than we do about the abusers. There are some very obvious realities at work here. If we are to serve, counsel, protect, renurture and heal victims, we must come to know them, to understand the cycle of violence in which they are terrorized and victimized. We need to elicit from them the motivation to break the cycle of violence. But if we are to intervene in the cycle of violence in society at large — which is after all, the sustainer of violence from men toward women — the batterer must be known as well. For every female victim who is freed from the cycle of violence without intervening in the actual behavior of the male abuser, we still have a battering male-at-large.

We do know that a particular characteristic of the cycle of male violence — the period of contrition — is critical to how the cycle repeats itself in relationships: the building up of tension and conflict; the episode of battering; the time of remorse; the idyllic time of reconciliation. And then the cycle begins again. What is going on in the time of remorse? How is it that this apparent recognition of violent behavior is insufficient to provoke change and to begin a cycle of non-violent behaviors? It seems to me that remorse is a time-honored device, within male-dominant, sexist cultures, for "making things right" again. I refer of course to the Judeo-Christian model of "making things right" — as it was always stated until very recently in the texts of theology and of devotion — between "God and man." This whole pattern of remorse, guilt, repentance, newly invigorated belief, and forgiveness has had one of the most profound symbolic impacts on Western male consciousness.

When a man physically abuses a woman, it is a matter of course for him to fall back on this model. Things can be "made right," not by actual change, but by feeling awful, by confessing it, and by *believing* that the renewal of the relationship is then effected. That this is more hocus-pocus than authentically religious hardly matters. A crippling consequence of this major model for renewal and change — remorse followed by forgiveness-taken-for-granted — is an almost guaranteed start up of the previous behavior once again. The *non* resolution which we violent men rehearse by remorse and "resolve" is vacuous. It is the exercise of a mere accompaniment to violence. And particularly where our dependency on the female victim of our abuse is so strong, the simple telling of the "resolve" not to be violent again is seen as establishing how good we are in fact.

Actually, the interweaving of the violence and the remorse is so tight that the expression of remorse to the victim establishes how good we have been, and how good we are. The remorse is not even a future-oriented "resolve"; it is more an internalized benediction we give to the immediately preceding episode of battery. There is no shock of recognition here in the cycle of violence. It is not a matter of "Oh my god, did I do that?" It is a matter of *stating* "Oh my god, I couldn't have done that," implying that *I in fact did not do it.* The confession of remorse then only reinforces the self-perception that I did not do it. Remorse, in this model of "making things right" again, literally wipes the slate clean. Over and over again we violent men are puzzled as to how it is our victims come to a place where they will not tolerate our violence and so report us or walk out on us. Can't they see that the violence no longer counts as real, because I said I was sorry?

Whatever clinical research reveals to us about the population of batterers, the fact of denial built into the cycle of violence itself veils from both us and the batterer the reality of the violence. Over and over again, abusive men will ask what the fuss is all about. They hold as a right and privilege the behavior of assault and battery against "their" women. Our groups in Denver are filled with men from all walks and circumstances of life to whom it has never occurred that battering is wrong. In other words, one reason we know so little about male batterers is that they only reluctantly come to *speak* of battering at all.

Another factor further veils this population from us. Male batterers continue to be deliberately protected: in the careful construction of familial silence; in the denial of neighbors, friends, clergy, teachers and the like that battering can be "true" for John and Mary; in the failure of law enforcement to "preserve and protect" the victims of domestic violence; in the unwillingness of local and state governments to provide shelter for victims; or in the editorializing of the Eagle Forum that the safe house movement is an anti-male, lesbian conspiracy. Male violence has become the ordinary, the expected, the usual.

THE CIVIC ADVOCACY OF VIOLENCE

What remains is for us to deal with what very few of us want to confront: American life remains sexist and male supremacist in spite of the strides of the second wave of American feminism. Whether it be snide — "You've come a long way, baby" — or whether it be sophisticated — George Gilder's *Sexual Suicide* — the put down of women's quest for equality, dignity and freedom from male oppression is damn near total in the America of the 1980s. I contend that the ultimate put down is the continuing advocacy of violence against women, and that until we confront that advocacy with integrity and resolve, the revolution in men's consciousness and behavior cannot get underway.

I used to think that we simply tolerated and permitted male abusiveness in our society. I have now come to understand rather, that we *advocate* physical violence. Violence is presented as effective. Violence is taught as the normal, appropriate and necessary behavior of power and control.

We apparently have no meaningful response to violence. I am convinced that until the voices that say "No!" to male violence are more numerous than those that say "Yes!," we will not see change. Nor will we men who want to change our violent behaviors find the support necessary to change. And silence in the face of violence is heard as "Yes!"

Under the governing paradigm of violence as effective and normal, every man can find a place. The individual male who has not beaten a woman is still surrounded by a civic environment which claims that it *would* and *could* be appropriate for him to beat a woman. He is immersed in a civic advocacy of violence which therefore contends that should he have committed battery, it is normal; and should he have not committed battery, it is only that he has not *yet* committed battery, given the ordinary course of affairs. In sexual political terms, we men can simply be divided into pre-battery and post-battery phases of life.

The teaching of violence is so pervasive, so totally a part of male experience, that I think it best to acknowledge this teaching as a *civic*, rather than as a cultural or as a social phenomenon. Certainly there are social institutions which form pieces of the total advocacy of violence: marriage and family; ecclesiastical institutions; schools; economic and corporate institutions; government and political institutions. And there are cultural and sub-cultural variations on the theme and reality of violence, of course. I believe, however, that if we are to crack the code of violent male behavior, we must begin where the environment of advocacy is total. Total civic advocacy is the setting for all the varieties of cultural adaptations from which violent men come.

For this total, pervasive advocacy of violence, I can find no better word than *civic*. The word has a noble ring to it, and calls up the manner in which the people of a nation, a society, a culture are schooled in basic citizenship. That's precisely what I want to call up. Civic responsibilities and civil affairs are what we come to expect as normal, proper and necessary. Violence, in male experience, *is* just such an expectation. Violence is *learned* within the environment of civic advocacy.

Demonstrating this is perhaps belaboring the obvious. But when we fail to belabor the obvious, the obvious continues to escape us and becomes even in its pervasiveness, part of an apparently innocent environment or backdrop. "Oh, say can you see. . . ." Our National Anthem can perhaps be thought of as simply romanticizing war, mayhem, bloodshed and violence. But more than that, reflection on the content of the song shows that we pride ourselves, civically, on the fortress mentality of siege, endurance and battle. The headier virtues of civic responsibility — freedom and justice — are come to only in the context of violence. "The rockets' red glare, the bombs bursting in air," are as ordinary to us as the school event, the sporting event, the civic sanction in which we conjure up hailing America "o'er the ramparts."

"I pledge allegiance. . . ." The flag of violence becomes the object of fidelity and devotion for American children even before they know the meaning of "allegiance." Yet feudal-like obeisance — the hand over the heart and devotional hush to the recitation — to the liege lords of violence is sanctioned as appropriate behavior quite calmly with this ritual.

We might assume of course that because this is ritual no one takes it seriously. That's precisely my point. We don't take it seriously at all. We just take it, live it, breathe it, feel awkward when we don't participate in the ritual, feel condemnatory when others around us don't participate in the ritual, and so on. The environment of civic advocacy of violence *is* ordinary, and not extraordinary.

THE EVERYDAY LANGUAGE OF VIOLENCE

Language is not innocent of meaning, intent and passion. Otherwise, there would be no communication between us at all. Yet words fall from our mouths — even in the civil illustrations above — as if there were no meaning, intent and passion involved. What I make of this is that the advocacy of violence is so pervasive, that the human spirit somehow, someway, mercifully inures itself to the environment. We are numbed and paralyzed by violence, and so continue to speak the language of violence as automatons.

I am not referring to the overt, up front renditions of violence we men use in describing battery and battering. "Giving it to the old woman" and "kicking the shit out of her" however, are phenomenologically on the same level of meaning, intention and passion as: assaulting a problem; conquering fear, nature, a woman; shooting down opinions; striking out at injustices; beating you to the punch; beating an idea to death; striking a blow for free enterprise, democracy; whomping up a meal; pounding home an idea; being under the gun to perform; "It strikes me that. . . ." You can make your own list of violent language. Listen to yourself. Listen to those around you. The meaning, intent and passion of violence are everywhere to be found in the ordinary language of ordinary experience.

Analyses which interweave the advocacy of male violence with "Super-Bowl Culture" have never been refuted. It is too obvious. Civic expectations — translated into professionalism, financial commitments, city planning for recreational space, the raising of male children for competitive sport, the corporate ethics of business ownership of athletic teams, profiteering on entertainment — all result in the monument of the National Football League, symbol and reality at once of the advocacy of violence. How piously the network television cameras turn away from out-and-out riots on the fields and in the stands. But how expertly the technologies of the television medium replay, stop action, and replay and replay and replay "a clean hit." Like the feelies of George Orwell's 1984, giant screens in bar and home can go over and over the bone-crunching tackle, the quarterback sack, the mid-air hit — compared in slow motion to dance and ballet, sophisticating violence in aesthetic terms. We love it. We want it. We pay for it. And I don't mean the black market price of a Bronco season ticket or the inflated prices of the beer, automobile accessories and tires, shaving equipment and the like which put the violence on the screen. I mean the human toll, the broken women and children of our land, and we frightened men who beat them. And even if I were to claim that neither you nor I is affected by the civic advocacy of violence in commercialism and free enterprise, we would still have to note that the powers and scions of industry *believe* — to the tune of billions of dollars a year — that we are so affected.

Pornography is no more a needed release for prurient sexual energies than would be the continuation of temple prostitutes. But it is sanctioned, and the civic advocacy of violence through pornography is real. It is not on the decrease. Soft porn is no longer *Charlie's Angels* or the double entendres of a Johnny Carson-starlet interview; that's simply a matter of course. Soft porn is now *Playboy*, *Penthouse*, and *Oui*, where every month, right next to the chewing gum and razor blades at the corner grocery, air-sprayed photographs play into male masturbatory fantasies. Hard porn itself is becoming more "ordinary" every day; child porn and snuff films lead the race in capturing the male market for sex and violence. We love it. We want it. And we pay for it. Violence works.

Insofar as violence works, the male batterer is finally, and somewhat definitively, hidden from us. I would not denigrate or halt for a moment our struggle to know the male batterer through clinical research models. But I would call all who are interested in knowing him and in intervening in and ending the cycle of the violence of men against women, to the larger context of the civic advocacy of violence. There, I believe, is the complement of the analysis generated by profiling the male batterer.

Until the code of male violence is undone, male dominance and sexism will prevail. Until the commerce in violence against women ceases, and we finally create an environment in which violence is no longer acceptable or conceivable, male supremacy will remain a fact of life for all of us.

Tim Beneke

MEN ON RAPE

Rape may be America's fastest growing violent crime; no one can be certain because it is not clear whether more rapes are being committed or reported. It *is* clear that violence against women is widespread and fundamentally alters the meaning of life for women; that sexual violence is encouraged in a variety of ways in American culture; and that women are often blamed for rape.
  Consider some statistics:

- In a random sample of 930 women, sociologist Diana Russell found that 44 percent had survived either rape or attempted rape. Rape was defined as sexual intercourse physically forced upon the woman, or coerced by threat of bodily harm, or forced upon the woman when she was helpless (asleep, for example). The survey included rape and attempted rape in marriage in its calculations. (Personal communication)

- In a September 1980 survey conducted by *Cosmopolitan* magazine to which over 106,000 women anonymously responded, 24 percent had been raped at least once. Of those, 51 percent had been raped by friends, 37 percent by strangers, 18 percent by relatives, and 3 percent by husbands. 10 percent of the women in the survey had been victims of incest. 75 percent of the women had been "bullied into making love." Writer Linda Wolfe, who reported on the survey, wrote in reference to such bullying: "Though such harassment stops short of rape, readers reported that it was nearly as distressing."

- An estimated 2–3 percent of all men who rape outside of marriage go to prison for their crimes.[1]

- The F.B.I. estimates that if current trends continue, one woman in four will be sexually assaulted in her lifetime.[2]

- An estimated 1.8 million women are battered by their spouses each year.[3] In extensive interviews with 430 battered women, clinical psychologist Lenore Walker, author of *The Battered Woman*, found that 59.9 percent had also been raped (defined as above) by their spouses. Given the difficulties many women had in admitting they had been raped, Walker estimates the figure may well be as high as 80 or 85 percent. (Personal communication.) If 59.9 percent of the 1.8 million women battered each year are also raped, then a million women may be raped in marriage each year. And a significant number are raped in marriage without being battered.

- Between one in two and one in ten of all rapes are reported to the police.[4]

- Between 300,000 and 500,000 women are raped each year outside of marriage.[5]

What is often missed when people contemplate statistics on rape is the effect of the *threat* of sexual violence on women. I have asked women repeatedly, "How

Reprinted from *Men on Rape* by Tim Beneke. New York: St. Martin's Press, 1982.

would your life be different if rape were suddenly to end?" (Men may learn a lot by asking this question of women to whom they are close.) The threat of rape is an assault upon the meaning of the world; it alters the feel of the human condition. Surely any attempt to comprehend the lives of women that fails to take issues of violence against women into account is misguided.

Through talking to women, I learned: *The threat of rape alters the meaning and feel of the night.* Observe how your body feels, how the night feels, when you're in fear. The constriction in your chest, the vigilance in your eyes, the rubber in your legs. What do the stars look like? How does the moon present itself? What is the difference between walking late at night in the dangerous part of a city and walking late at night in the country, or safe suburbs? When I try to imagine what the threat of rape must do to the night, I think of the stalked, adrenalated feeling I get walking late at night in parts of certain American cities. Only, I remind myself, it is a fear different from any I have known, a fear of being raped.

It is night half the time. If the threat of rape alters the meaning of the night, it must alter the meaning and pace of the day, one's relation to the passing and organization of time itself. For some women, the threat of rape at night turns their cars into armored tanks, their solitude into isolation. And what must the space inside a car or an apartment feel like if the space outside is menacing?

I was running late one night with a close woman friend through a path in the woods on the outskirts of a small university town. We had run several miles and were feeling a warm, energized serenity.

"How would you feel if you were alone?" I asked.

"Terrified!" she said instantly.

"Terrified that there might be a man out there?" I asked, pointing to the surrounding moonlit forest, which had suddenly been transformed into a source of terror.

"Yes."

Another woman said, "I know what I can't do and I've completely internalized what I can't do. I've built a viable life that basically involves never leaving my apartment at night unless I'm directly going some place to meet somebody. It's unconsciously built into what it occurs to women to do." When one is raised without freedom, one may not recognize its absence.

The threat of rape alters the meaning and feel of nature. Everyone has felt the psychic nurturance of nature. Many women are being deprived of that nurturance, especially in wooded areas near cities. They are deprived either because they cannot experience nature in solitude because of threat, or because, when they do choose solitude in nature, they must cope with a certain subtle but nettlesome fear.

Women need more money because of rape and the threat of rape makes it harder for women to earn money. It's simple: if you don't feel safe walking at night, or riding public transportation, you need a car. And it is less practicable to live in cheaper, less secure, and thus more dangerous neighborhoods if the ordinary threat of violence that men experience, being mugged, say, is compounded by the threat of rape. By limiting mobility at night, the threat of rape limits where and when one is able to work, thus making it more difficult to earn money. An obvious bind: women need more money because of rape, and have fewer job opportunities because of it.

The threat of rape makes women more dependent on men (or other women). One woman said: "If there were no rape I wouldn't have to play games with men for their protection." The threat of rape falsifies, mystifies, and confuses relations between men and women. If there were no rape, women would simply not need men as much, wouldn't need them to go places with at night, to feel safe in their homes, for protection in nature.

The threat of rape makes solitude less possible for women. Solitude, drawing strength from being alone, is difficult if being alone means being afraid. To be afraid is to be in need, to experience a lack; the threat of rape creates a lack. Solitude requires relaxation; if you're afraid, you can't relax.

The threat of rape inhibits a woman's expressiveness. "If there were no rape," said one woman, "I could dress the way I wanted and walk the way I wanted and not feel self-conscious about the responses of men. I could be friendly to people. I wouldn't have to wish I was ugly. I wouldn't have to make myself small when I got on the bus. I wouldn't have to respond to verbal abuse from men by remaining silent. I could respond in kind."

If a woman's basic expressiveness is inhibited, her sexuality, creativity, and delight in life must surely be diminished.

The threat of rape inhibits the freedom of the eye. I know a married couple who live in Manhattan. They are both artists, both acutely sensitive and responsive to the visual world. When they walk separately in the city, he has more freedom to look than she does. She must control her eye movements lest they inadvertently meet the glare of some importunate man. What, who, and how she sees are restricted by the threat of rape.

The following exercise is recommended for men.

> Walk down a city street. Pay a lot of attention to your clothing; make sure your pants are zipped, shirt tucked in, buttons done. Look straight ahead. Every time a man walks past you, avert your eyes and make your face expressionless. Most women learn to go through this act each time we leave our houses. It's a way to avoid at least some of the encounters we've all had with strange men who decided we looked available.[6]

To relate aesthetically to the visual world involves a certain playfulness, a spirit of spontaneous exploration. The tense vigilance that accompanies fear inhibits that spontaneity. The world is no longer yours to look at when you're afraid.

I am aware that all culture is, in part, restriction, that there are places in America where hardly anyone is safe (though men are safer than women virtually everywhere), that there are many ways to enjoy life, that some women may not be so restricted, that there exist havens, whether psychic, geographical, economic, or class. But they are *havens*, and as such, defined by threat.

Above all, I trust my experience: no woman could have lived the life I've lived the last few years. If suddenly I were restricted by the threat of rape, I would feel a deep, inexorable depression. And it's not just rape; it's harassment, battery, Peeping Toms, anonymous phone calls, exhibitionism, intrusive stares, fondlings — all contributing to an atmosphere of intimidation in women's lives. And I have only scratched the surface; it would take many carefully crafted short stories to begin to express what I have only hinted at in the last few pages.

I have not even touched upon what it might mean for a woman to be sexually assaulted. Only women can speak to that. Nor have I suggested how the threat of rape affects marriage.

Rape and the threat of rape pervade the lives of women, as reflected in some popular images of our culture.

"SHE ASKED FOR IT" — BLAMING THE VICTIM

Many things may be happening when a man blames a woman for rape.

First, in all cases where a woman is said to have asked for it, her appearance and behavior are taken as a form of speech. "Actions speak louder than words" is a widely held belief; the woman's actions — her appearance may be taken as action — are given greater emphasis than her words; an interpretation alien to the woman's intentions is given to her actions. A logical extension of "she asked for it" is the idea that she wanted what happened to happen; if she wanted it to happen, she *deserved* for it to happen. Therefore, the man is not to be blamed. "She asked for it" can mean either that she was consenting to have sex and was not really raped, or that she was in fact raped but somehow she really deserved it. "If you ask for it, you deserve it," is a widely held notion. If I ask you to beat me up and you beat me up, I still don't deserve to be beaten up. So even if the notion that women asked to be raped had some basis in reality, which it doesn't, on its own terms it makes no sense.

Second, a mentality exists that says: a woman who assumes freedoms normally restricted to a man (like going out alone at night) and is raped is doing the same thing as a woman who goes out in the rain without an umbrella and catches a cold. Both are considered responsible for what happens to them. That men will rape is taken to be a legitimized given, part of nature, like rain or snow. The view reflects a massive abdication of responsibility for rape on the part of men. It is so much easier to think of rape as natural than to acknowledge one's part in it. So long as rape is regarded as natural, women will be blamed for rape.

A third point. The view that it is natural for men to rape is closely connected to the view of women as commodities. If a woman's body is regarded as a valued commodity by men, then of course, if you leave a valued commodity where it can be taken, it's just human nature for men to take it. If you left your stereo out on the sidewalk, you'd be asking for it to get stolen. Someone will just take it. (And how often mean speak of rape as "going out and *taking it*.") If a woman walks the streets at night, she's leaving a valued commodity, her body, where it can be taken. So long as women are regarded as commodities, they will be blamed for rape.

Which brings us to a fourth point. "She asked for it" is inseparable from a more general "psychology of the dupe." If I use bad judgment and fail to read the small print in a contract and later get taken advantage of ("screwed" or "fucked over") then I deserve what I get; bad judgment makes me liable. Analogously, if a woman trusts a man and goes to his apartment, or accepts a ride hitchhiking, or goes out on a date and is raped, she's a dupe and deserves what she gets. "He didn't *really* rape her" goes the mentality — "he merely took advantage of her." And in America it's okay for people to take advantage of each other, even expected and praised. In fact, you're considered dumb and foolish if you don't take advantage of other people's bad judgment. And so, again, by treating them as dupes, rape will be blamed on women.

Fifth, if a woman who is raped is judged attractive by men, and particularly if she dresses to look attractive, then the mentality exists that she attacked him with her weapon so, of course, he counter-attacked with his. The preview to a popular movie states: "She was the victim of her own *provocative beauty.*" "Provocation: "There is a line which, if crossed, will *set me off* and I will lose control and no longer be responsible for my behavior. If you punch me in the nose then, of course, I will not be responsible for what happens: you will have provoked a fight. If you dress, talk, move, or act a certain way, you will have provoked me to rape. If your appearance *stuns* me, *strikes* me, *ravishes* me, *knocks me out*, etc., then I will not be held responsible for what happens; you will have asked for it." The notion that sexual feeling makes one helpless is part of a cultural abdication of responsibility for sexuality. So long as a woman's appearance is viewed as a weapon and sexual feeling is believed to make one helpless, women will be blamed for rape.

Sixth, I have suggested that men sometimes become obsessed with images of women, that images become a substitute for sexual feeling, that sexual feeling becomes externalized and out of control and is given an undifferentiated identity in the appearance of women's bodies. It is a process of projection in which one blurs one's own desire with her imagined, projected desire. If a woman's attractiveness is taken to signify one's own lust and a woman's lust, then when an "attractive" woman is raped, some men may think she wanted sex. Since they perceive their own lust in part projected onto the woman, they disbelieve women who've been raped. So long as men project their own sexual desires onto women, they will blame women for rape.

And seventh, what are we to make of the contention that women in dating situations say "no" initially to sexual overtures from men as a kind of pose, only to give in later, thus revealing their true intentions? And that men are thus confused and incredulous when women are raped because in their sexual experience women can't be believed? I doubt that this has much to do with men's perceptions of rape. I don't know to what extent women actually "say no and mean yes"; certainly it is a common theme in male folklore. I have spoken to a couple of women who went through periods when they wanted to be sexual but were afraid to be, and often rebuffed initial sexual advances only to give in later. One point is clear: the ambivalence women may feel about having sex is closely tied to the inability of men to fully accept them as sexual beings. Women have been traditionally punished for being openly and freely sexual; men are praised for it. And if many men think of sex as achievement of possession of a valued commodity, or aggressive degradation, then women have every reason to feel and act ambivalent.

These themes are illustrated in an interview I conducted with a 23 year old man who grew up in Pittsburgh and works as a file clerk in the financial district of San Francisco. Here's what he said:

"Where I work it's probably no different from any other major city in the U.S. The women dress up in high heels, and they wear a lot of makeup, and they just look really *hot* and really sexy, and how can somebody who has a healthy sex drive not feel lust for them when you see them? I feel lust for them, but I don't think I could find it in me to overpower someone and rape them.

But I definitely get the feeling that I'd like to rape a girl. I don't know if the actual act of rape would be satisfying, but the *feeling* is satisfying.

"These women look so good, and they kiss ass of the men in the three-piece suits who are *big* in the corporation, and most of them relate to me like "Who are *you*? Who are *you* to even *look* at?" They're snobby and they condescend to me, and I resent it. It would take me a lot longer to get to first base than it would somebody with a three-piece suit who had money. And to me a lot of the men they go out with are superficial assholes who have no real feelings or substance, and are just trying to get ahead and make a lot of money. Another thing that makes me resent these women is thinking, "How could she want to hang out with somebody like that? What does that make her?"

"I'm a file clerk, which makes me feel like a nebbish, a nurd, like I'm not making it, I'm a failure. But I don't really believe I'm a failure because I know it's just a phase, and I'm just doing it for the money, just to make it through this phase. I catch myself feeling like a failure, but I realize that's ridiculous.

What exactly do you go through when you see these sexy, unavailable women?

"Let's say I see a woman and she looks really pretty and really clean and sexy, and she's giving off very feminine, sexy vibes. I think, "Wow, I would love to make love to her," but I know she's not really interested. It's a tease. A lot of times a woman knows that she's looking really good and she'll use that and flaunt it, and it makes me feel like she's laughing at me and I feel *degraded*.

"I also feel dehumanized, because when I'm being teased I just turn off, I cease to be human. Because if I go with my human emotions I'm going to want to put my arms around her and kiss her, and to do that would be unacceptable. I don't like the feeling that I'm supposed to stand there and take it, and not be able to hug her or kiss her; so I just turn off my emotions. It's a feeling of humiliation, because the woman has forced me to turn off my feelings and react in a way that I really don't want to.

"If I were actually desperate enough to rape somebody, it would be from wanting the person, but also it would be a very spiteful thing, just being able to say, "I have power over you and I can do anything I want with you," because really I feel that *they* have power over *me* just by their presence. Just the fact that they can come up to me and just melt me and make me feel like a dummy makes me want revenge. They have power over me so I want power over them. . . .

"Society says that you have to have a lot of sex with a lot of different women to be a real man. Well, what happens if you don't? Then what are you? Are you half a man? Are you still a boy? It's ridiculous. You see a whiskey ad with a guy and two women on his arm. The implication is that real men don't have any trouble getting women.

How does it make you feel toward women to see all these sexy women in media and advertising using their looks to try to get you to buy something?

"It makes me hate them. As a man you're taught that men are more powerful than women, and that men always have the upper hand, and that it's a man's society; but then you see all these women and it makes you think, "Jesus Christ, if we have all the power how come all the beautiful women are telling us what to buy?" And to be honest, it just makes me hate beautiful women because they're using their power over me. I realize they're being used themselves, and they're doing it for the money. In *Playboy* you see all these beautiful women who look so sexy and they'll be giving you all these looks like they want to have sex so bad; but then in reality you know that except for a few nymphomaniacs, they're doing it for the money; so I hate them for being used and for using their bodies in that way.

"In this society, if you ever sit down and realize how manipulated you really are it makes you pissed off — it makes you want to take control. And you've been manipulated by women, and they're a very easy target because they're out walking along the streets, so you can just grab one and say, "Listen, you're going to do what I want you to do," and it's an act of revenge against the way you've been manipulated.

"I know a girl who was walking down the street by her house, when this guy jumped her and beat her up and raped her, and she was black and blue and had to go to the hospital. That's beyond me. I can't understand how somebody could do that. If I were going to rape a girl, I wouldn't hurt her. I might *restrain* her, but I wouldn't *hurt* her. . . .

"The whole dating game between men and women also makes me feel degraded. I hate being put in the position of having to initiate a relationship. I've been taught that if you're not aggressive with a woman, then you've blown it. She's not going to jump on *you*, so *you've* got to jump on *her*. I've heard all kinds of stories where the woman says, "No! No! No!" and they end up making great love. I get confused as hell if a woman pushes me away. Does it mean she's trying to be a nice girl and wants to put up a good appearance, or does it mean she doesn't want anything to do with you? You don't know. Probably a lot of men think that women don't feel like real women unless a man tries to force himself on her, unless she brings out the "real man," so to speak, and probably too much of it goes on. It goes on in my head that you're complimenting a woman by actually staring at her or by trying to get into her pants. Lately, I'm realizing that when I stare at women lustfully, they often feel more threatened than flattered."

NOTES

1. Such estimates recur in the rape literature. See *Sexual Assault* by Nancy Gager and Cathleen Schurr, Grosset & Dunlap, 1976, or *The Price of Coercive Sexuality* by Clark and Lewis, The Woman's Press, 1977.

2. *Uniform Crime Reports*, 1980.

3. See *Behind Closed Doors* by Murray J. Strauss and Richard Gelles, Doubleday, 1979.

4. See Gager and Schurr (above) or virtually any book on the subject.

5. Again, see Gager and Schurr, or Carol V. Horos, *Rape*, Banbury Books, 1981.

6. From "Willamette Bridge" in *Body Politics* by Nancy Henley, Prentice-Hall, 1977, p. 144.

7. I would like to thank George Lakoff for this insight.

◆ ◆ ◆

PART EIGHT

Men with Men: Friendships and Fears

What is the nature of men's relationships with other men? Do most men have close, intimate male friends, or do they simply bond together around shared activities and interests? How do competition, homophobia, and violence enter into men's relationships with each other?

Traditionally, in literature and in popular mythology, the Truly Great Friendships are those among men. In the late 1960s and early 1970s, the concept of civilization being a "fraternity of men" was criticized by feminists, who saw women as isolated and excluded from public life. In the mid-1970s, though, the men's liberation literature began to focus on the *quality* of men's relationships, and found them wanting. Men, we discovered, have "acquaintances," "activities buddies," but rarely true friends with whom they can intimately share their inner lives. Lillian Rubin and others argued that it is not that men do not want or need closeness with other men, it is just that they are so very threatened by the actuality of intimacy. Thus, when men organize their time together around work, watching a game, or playing cards, the structure of the activity mediates their time together, thus maintaining a "safe" level of emotional distance.

But why do men need emotional distance from each other? And what are the costs of maintaining emotionally shallow relationships with other men? What kinds of pressure does this place on women to be the primary "emotion workers" in men's lives? In this section, Garfinkel points out that most men, when asked who their best friend is, will name a woman, often their wife. (Few women, by the way, will name their husband — most will name another woman.) Men, he points out, rarely feel comfortable with intimate self-disclosure with other men. Certainly an overemphasis on competition among males, from a very early age, is one factor that places a damper on intimate self-disclosure among men. Why would a man give away information that would make him vulnerable among his competitors in games, education, or the workplace? Another important barrier to male–male intimacy, as the article by Lehne and the song by Morgan point out, is homophobia. The fear of homosexuality — or of being thought to be homosexual by others — places severe limitations on the emotional, verbal, and physical interactions among men.

Violence among men — particularly "queerbashing" — is one logical result of the need to prove one's heterosexual masculinity by separating one's self from the "other" men. Prison rape, as Brownmiller describes it in her article, is an act that is usually performed by otherwise "straight" men as a means solidifying positions of power and control in the inter-male dominancy hierarchy. Here competition among men, homophobia, and the devaluation of the "feminine" all come together. The same distorted need for power and control that leads some men to rape women, we learn, forms the basis for male rape of other men.

White sounds an optimistic note with his discussion of how many gay men have discovered that there is friendship after sex. He argues that the combination of passion and comraderie often seen in gay men's relationships can be seen as a positive model for relationships among other groups in society. Yet Luna warns that relationships among gay men are not immune from other forms of social prejudice. Gay men may be aware of how they are oppressed by compulsory heterosexuality, but many still have not begun to confront the ways in which racism still infects their relationships.

Perry Garfinkel

MALE FRIENDSHIP:
NO MAN'S LAND

If one would have a friend, one must be willing to wage war for him: and in order to wage war, one must be capable of being an enemy. . . . In one's friend, one shall find one's best enemy.

— The Philosophy of Nietzsche

Every single one of my male friendships is tainted with some kind of competition: "Where do I stand in terms of that guy."

— Tim, thirty-one

MY DINNER WITH DENNIS

I had not seen Dennis for seven years. We had grown up in the same neighborhood, played basketball, baseball, or football every day after school, played music together, gone to countless parties, movies, sports events. We were what you call friends. We hung out a lot. We "rapped," as I recall, but I could not tell you how he really felt about things — about his bossy father, about the pressure of "being a man," about anything of emotional significance. After high school we went our separate ways. Since I had last seen him he had been through a tumultuous marriage and a vindictive divorce, moved from the suburbs to the city, transferred from a small firm to a major corporation. Ostensibly, we were getting together to talk about our friendship as part of my research.

Our first two hours together were awkward. We talked about our work, about the upcoming election, our travels. Had he seen so-and-so? Had I heard from whats-his-face? Dead end. In the cab on the way to dinner we said almost nothing. I wondered: Is the evening going to be a total loss? Do we have anything in common anymore? In traffic I mumbled about the atrocities one must put up with to live in the city. He told me his parents had moved from our old neighborhood. An elegant dinner consumed and distracted our attention. We ordered, admired the decor, and discussed the food and the clientele around us. It was not until we were sipping our coffee that we got to talking about anything that resembled how *we felt* about ourselves, our lives, and what we had gone through in the last couple of years.

"So how goes the battle?" I tried.

"It goes."

"It goes how?"

"It goes hard. Up and down. Now that the divorce is final I feel like I'm finally recovered from a long case of the grippe."

"You mind me asking?"

"No, it's o.k."

"So . . . what happened with you and her?"

"I don't know. Things just. . . ." His voice trailed off. I waited.

"What? Things just what?"

"Things just . . ." he started and looked up from his empty coffee cup, searching my eyes for a sign of betrayal. Was I still his trusted friend? "Things just broke down. She was too demanding, too selfish. She wanted me to be available for her when she wanted me, but she wanted her space too. I started to feel like a yo-yo. And then. . . ." He stopped, looked away, looked back at me. I could almost hear his interior thought: *Can I trust him?*

"I was having sexual problems."

So he told me about his sexual problems and then I told him about my sexual problems and then our sexual problems did not seem like such a problem anymore. It was a moment of disarmament; the barriers dropped. We went back to his apartment, now talking about everything. He played a couple of songs he had written. It was like old times again.

That encounter — replete with its disappointments and its fulfillments — is a pretty good example of the cautious approach two men take toward each other in establishing contact. Step-freeze, step-freeze seems to sum it up and generally at each freeze point men are sizing each other up. *How will I compare to him? Can I trust him?*

Behind the bear hugs of camaraderie, men seem to be holding each other at arm's length. They keep a safe distance — a buffer zone — between themselves and other men. This safe space is quite literally a *no man's land*, an emotional twilight zone few men appear to be willing to navigate.

And who can blame us for assuming an avoidance stance after an initiation into man-to-man relationships such as we have had? After all, what had come of trusting fathers, mentors, brothers? Betrayal. Disappointment. Distrust. Unrequited love. Men enter into friendships with men well-trained in the disciplines of masculinity. We should not be surprised, then, that the issues of power and competition, one-upmanship, and a failure to communicate feelings verbally for each other permeate men's interrelationships.

Nor should we be surprised, therefore, that so many men report so few "best friends."

"Who's your best male friend?" I asked in interviews. Repeatedly I'd get unfulfilling answers:

"I have none; I'm a loner."

"I had a close friend from my old neighborhood but we haven't talked in a long time."

"I have a number of acquaintances but none who I'd call a best friend."

"That's not in my context."

"I see it as a continuum. My best friend last year is not my best friend this year, and will not be my best friend next year."

So unconditioned were many men to the arena of male friendship that they would answer as though they had not heard the question:

"My wife."

"My girlfriend."

The replies seemed contorted and evasive until I was confronted with the complexity of the issue when the tables were turned on me. Who was *my* best friend? I was hard put to name the single man in whom I truly confided. There were several, spread over time and place. Or there were none at the moment. And too, I could not be sure that my current "best friend" also considered me his best friend, and that seemed important if not relevant.

Daniel Levinson in *The Seasons of a Man's Life*, wrote: "In our interviews, friendship was largely noticeable by its absence. . . . Most men do not have an intimate male friend of the kind that they recall fondly from boyhood or youth."

Still, men do establish friendly relationships with other men. The desire for male contact is a pull men cannot ignore. We are each other's mirrors, each other's source of energy, each other's touchstones to an elusive and evolving male reality.

But how *do* men relate to each other? And why do women ask me that question more frequently than men — and why are they always too quick with their own answer: "They don't." And why are men, presumably closer to the truth of it, much slower with and less sure about their responses?

At least part of the quality of — and appeal of — men's friendships includes, I have learned, their enigmatic nature. Men grope for descriptions of what makes a particular friendship unique or special.

"We just click."

"He's a nice guy."

"Whenever we see each other — no matter how much time has gone by — there's this sort of golden chord that we strike together."

None of it seemed to satisfy. All of it indicated men's ambiguity, ambivalence, and lack of clarity about their relationships with all men.

Part of the dilemma of men's friendships — as in other male–male dyads — is the discrepancy between real and ideal. Men have high expectations of men friends. They expect loyalty, someone who will stand behind them to the bitter end. A friend who would lend any amount of money, provide a place to stay for any length of time, drive any distance in an emergency. A friend who would lend an ear, listen to one's problems when no one else will.

In reality, that mythical friend more than likely did not and does not exist — or he may have at one point but, as I heard so often, time passed and so did the friendship.

But through the interviews there emerged some answers to questions such as:

How and by what criteria do men choose friends?
When do men go to each other?
How do they communicate? What do they talk about?
What types of friendships are there?
How do the issues of power and competition effect men's friendships?

Social science studies tell us that male friendships are formed in the playgrounds and continue down the corporate corridors, from nursery school to nursing home. From the start, research shows, the relationships that boys develop with other boys differ substantially from those girls have with girls. When asked to represent "best friends" of one's own sex in a play construction task, boys put greater spatial distance between figures standing for themselves and their best friends than do girls. Also, boys show less stability in their best friendships than girls. Psychologists Elizabeth Douvan and Joseph Adelson found male–male friendships among adolescents less intimate than those among young women. Parental expectations also play into the picture: One study found that parents expected young boys to be less involved in personal relationships than girls.

As adults, Sidney Jourard pointed out in *The Transparent Self*, males generally disclose less about themselves to other men than women do to women. Sociologist Alan Booth compared men's and women's friendship patterns and observed that while men report a greater number of friendships than do women, men's friendships are described as less close and spontaneous. Constraints imposed on men's friendships by society and the family inhibit intimacy. Thus, men's friendships tend more toward sociability than intimacy. There is even evidence that men see simply *wanting* relationships with men as a negative quality. Men rated high in the motivational syndrome known as "need for affiliation" are judged by other men as being dependent and needing approval — qualities they consider unappealing.

To put it in context, psychologists Douvan and Adelson had this to say about adult friendship in general:

> To a disquieting degree, the adult friendship is no more than a mutual flight from boredom — a pact against isolation, with an amendment

against intimacy. Those things which are crucial to personal integration, such as a person's history, values or work are studiously excluded from the interaction.

This description accurately portrays the male–male interaction. In my own case, I was embarrassed at how little personal history I knew of interviewees whom I already considered close personal friends. "What was your father like? What was your relationship with him like?" These seem now like such basic questions to ask a man if you want to get to know him or understand him better. But I asked it so infrequently. Did I not care enough to probe that deeply? Or did I understand that the question had the power to let loose a flood of deep, dark emotional undercurrents? When we do ask personal history — "Where'd you grow up?" "Where'd you go to school?" "How do you like your job?" — it is with the unspoken agreement that we will not break the code against intimacy. We will not show too much of ourselves.

Gregory K. Lehne

HOMOPHOBIA AMONG MEN:
SUPPORTING AND DEFINING THE MALE ROLE

Homophobia is the irrational fear or intolerance of homosexuality. Although both men and women can be homophobic, homophobia is most often associated with the fear of male homosexuality. Homophobia is not currently classified as a "mental illness" (neither is homosexuality), although psychiatrists such as Dr. George Weinberg (1972) have stated, "I would never consider a patient healthy unless he had overcome his prejudice against homosexuality." Homophobia is the threat implicit in *"What are you, a fag?"* If male homosexuality were no more threatening than being left-handed, for example, homophobia would not exist. In many ways, and in all but extreme cases, homophobia is a socially deter- mined prejudice much like sexism or racism, rather than a medically recognized phobia.

Homophobia, as I will show, does not exist in most cases as an isolated trait or prejudice; it is characteristic of individuals who are generally rigid and sexist. Homophobia, with its associated dynamic of fear of being labeled a homosex- ual, is an underlying *motivation* in maintaining the male sex role. I believe that it must be eliminated for fundamental changes to occur in male and female roles. To support this thesis, I will discuss first whether homophobia reflects an ac- curate perception and understanding of homosexuality or whether it is an irra- tional fear. Then I will examine the social aspects of homophobia and personal characteristics of people who are highly homophobic. Finally, I will explore the social functions of homophobia in maintaining the male sex role, and its effects on society and the individual.

IS HOMOPHOBIA IRRATIONAL?

Homophobia is irrational because it generally embodies misconceptions and false stereotypes of male homosexuality. These belief systems, or prejudices, are rationalizations supporting homophobia, not causes of homophobia. Levitt and Klassen's 1973 Kinsey Institute study of 3,000 American adults found the following beliefs about homosexuality to be widespread: homosexuals are afraid of the opposite sex (56% of the sample believed this), homosexuals act like the opposite sex (69%), only certain occupations are appropriate for homosexuals, homosexuals molest children (71%), and homosexuality was unnatural.

First, let us consider the mistaken belief that homosexual men do not like women. Since relations with women (especially sexual) are considered one of the proving grounds of masculinity, homosexual men who do not treat women as sex objects are regarded as suspect and unmanly in our male-oriented culture. Research does not support the belief, however, that homosexual males are afraid of women. About 20% of men who consider themselves homosexuals have been married, or currently are married; about half of these gay men are fathers (Bell and Weinberg, 1978). Around 75% of homosexual males have engaged in heterosexual kissing and necking, and about 50% have participated in heterosexual intercourse in their youth, with a frequency and success rate highly similar to that of heterosexual males (Saghir and Robins, 1973). About 50% of the homosexual men in this comprehensive study reported to have at some time established a relationship with a woman, lasting more than one year and including sexual relations.

Although homosexual males were not adequately satisfied with their heterosexual experiences, they generally did not have negative reactions toward women or heterosexual activities. In studies measuring the change in the penis to various stimuli, it was found that homosexual men gave neutral (not negative) responses to pictures of female nudes (McConaghy, 1967; Freund, Langevin, Gibiri, and Zajac, 1973), pictures of mature vulva or breasts (Freund, Langevin, and Zajac, 1974), or auditory or written descriptions of heterosexual intercourse (Freund, Langevin, Chamberlayne, Deosoran, and Zajac, 1974). Heterosexual men, in comparison, were turned on by the pictures of female nudes, but revealed their homophobia through decreased penile volume in response to pictures of male nudes, or male homosexual activities (McConaghy, 1967; Turnbull and Brown, 1977). Thus, the evidence shows that homosexual males have no particular aversion to women or heterosexual intercourse, although heterosexual males often do have aversions to male nudes and homosexual activity.

Another popular stereotype is that homosexual men are similar to women, in appearance and/or psychological functioning. For example, Tavris (1977) reports that 70% of the *Psychology Today* readership believes that "homosexual men are not fully masculine." Studies reported by Freedman (1971) as well as Saghir and Robins (1973) suggest that only about 15% of male homosexuals appear effeminate. Effeminacy itself is highly stigmatized in the homosexual subculture. Weinberg and Williams (1974) estimate that not more than 20% of male homosexuals are suspected of being gay by the people they come in contact with, although Levitt and Klassen (1973) report that 37% of the American public believes that "it is easy to tell homosexuals by how they look."

Appearances aside, some studies indicate that homosexual men are psychologically sex typed similar to heterosexual men (e.g., Heilbrun and Thompson, 1977), whereas others find they are more androgynous or sex-role undifferentiated than heterosexuals (Spence and Helmreich, 1978). Homosexual men have not been found to be similar to women in their psychological functioning. Androgynous sex-role behavior, expressing a wider variety of interests and sensitivity than stereotypic male or female roles, is believed by many to represent a better level of psychological adjustment than more rigid sex-role-defined personalities (for example, see Kaplan and Bean, 1976). Several studies report that the psychological adjustment of homosexuals who have accepted their sexual orientation is superior in many cases to most heterosexual males in terms of openness and self-disclosure, self-actualization, lack of neurotic tendencies, and happiness or exuberance (Bell and Weinberg, 1978; Freedman, 1975; Weinberg and Williams, 1974).

Levitt and Klassen (1973) found that many people (the percentages given in parentheses below) stereotyped some professions as appropriate for homosexuals and others as inappropriate. For example, the "unmasculine" careers of artist (83%), beautician (70%), florist (86%), and musician (84%) were believed appropriate for homosexual men. But the "masculine" careers of medical doctors

(66%), government officials (66%), judges (76%), teachers (76%), and ministers (75%) were considered inappropriate for homosexuals.

Gallup in 1977 found a decrease since 1970 in public opinion seeking to deny homosexuals the right to be doctors (44%), teachers (65%), or ministers (54%). Notice that the professions that people would close to homosexuals are those characteristic bastions of either male power or social influence. In the real world of work, however, there is no evidence that homosexual men tend to avoid characteristically "masculine" or professional occupations. Ironically it may be true that heterosexual men avoid certain stereotyped "homosexual" occupations, resulting in a higher proportion of homosexuals in those fields.

Many studies of homosexual males have found that they tend to be disproportionately concentrated in higher status occupations, especially those requiring professional training (Saghir and Robins, 1973; Weinberg and Williams, 1974). A study in Germany suggests that homosexual males tend to be more upwardly mobile than comparable heterosexuals (Dannecker and Reiche, 1974). This carefully conducted study of a large group of homosexuals found that the social class of the families of homosexual men was representative of the general population, whereas the social status of the homosexual men themselves was higher than would be predicted from their family backgrounds, even when the mobility trends of the entire population were taken into account. This suggests that in spite of the prejudice that homosexuals encounter in work, they are still highly successful in fields outside the low-status occupations that the general public seems to feel are appropriate for homosexuals.

Although the belief that homosexuals often molest children is widespread, I have been unable to locate any scientific research supporting it. A pedophile, an adult who seeks sex with young children, generally does not have sexual relationships with other adults and thus could not appropriately be considered either heterosexual or homosexual. Many of these individuals have sex with children of either gender. Pedophilia is a rare disturbance. Heterosexual rape, involving adolescents or adults, is much more common than homosexual rape, according to court records and sexual experience surveys. The fear that homosexuals molest children (or rape adolescents) is grossly exaggerated, and ultimately is based on the confusion of pedophilia with homosexuality.

There is evidence supporting the effectiveness of gay people in positively dealing with children. Gay parents tend to provide a psychologically healthy environment for their own children, who are actually no more predisposed than the children of heterosexuals to become homosexuals themselves, or to exhibit signs of psychological disturbance (Bell, 1973; Kirkpatrick, Roy, and Smith, 1976). Dorothy Riddle (1978) has done a sensitive analysis of the positive ways in which gay people relate to children, and their effectiveness as role models fostering healthy psychological development in children. Public fears of the negative effects of gay people on children tend to be totally unfounded.

A final misconception relevant to homophobia is the idea that homosexuality is "unnatural." Evidence reviewed by Ford and Beach (1951) indicates that homosexual activities occur in the majority of species of animals. Some porpoises form lifelong, monogamous, homosexual relationships. Homosexual relations are common, and are important in establishing dominance, among monkeys and various canines. Lorenz (1974) has discussed homosexual coupling among geese and other birds, concluding that it is often very adaptive.

Homosexual activities are as common or "natural" in human society as in the animal world. In 49 of the 77 societies for which we have adequate anthropological data, homosexual activities are socially sanctioned; in some situations they are virtually compulsory (Churchill, 1967). In most of Europe and many other parts of the world, homosexual relations are legal. The "unnatural" rationalization supporting homophobia receives further disconfirmation from the experiences of the 37% of the American male population who Kinsey, Pomeroy, and Martin (1948) reported had homosexual experiences to orgasm after adolescence.

Robert Brannon characterizes contemporary scientific thinking about the "naturalness" of homosexuality in this way:

> Every human society in the world today, from vast industrial nations to the smallest and simplest tribes in remote parts of the world, has some degree of homosexuality. Every society in the history of the Earth for which we have records, going back to the beginnings of recorded history, had some degree of homosexuality.
>
> Some of these societies accepted homosexuality readily while others severely condemned it, but *all* human societies have been aware of it because homosexuality has always existed wherever human beings have existed.
>
> The closest scientific analogy to homosexuality is probably the phenomenon of left-handedness, the origins and causes of which also remain unknown to science. Like homosexuality, left-handedness exists for a minority of people in every human society on record. There is no more objective reason to consider homosexuality unnatural than there is to consider left-handedness unnatural.

These facts about homosexuality suggest an interesting dilemma. Even if the stereotypes about homosexuality were accurate (I have tried to show that they are not), then why should homosexuality be threatening to males who presumably do not fit these stereotypes? If these stereotypes are not valid, then how and why are the rationalizations of homophobia maintained?

Since sexual orientation, unlike race or sex, is rarely known for certain in everyday interactions, it is relatively easy to maintain false stereotypes of the invisible minority of homosexuals. Men who appear to exhibit parts of the stereotypes are labeled homosexual, and the rest are presumed to be heterosexual. Thus, as long as most homosexuals conceal their sexual preference, homophobia is easily maintained, because heterosexuals are rarely aware of homosexuals who do not reflect their stereotypes of homosexuality.

Since stereotypes of homosexuals are not characteristic of most homosexuals, it is clear that these stereotypes are not learned from direct experiences with homosexuals. Homophobia is socially learned and transmitted. It precedes and encourages the development of stereotypes of homosexuals, in a world in which most homosexuals are not known. The presence of homophobia even among some homosexuals, whose experiences disconfirm stereotypes of homosexuality, suggests that homophobia must be derived from other sources. For homophobia to exist as a threat, it is necessary that the associated stereotypes of homosexuality be false; otherwise the taunt, *"What are you, a fag?,"* would be so patently untrue that it would not be threatening.

HOMOPHOBIA AND SOCIAL BELIEFS

Although there is no rational basis for the negative stereotypes of homosexuals, and thus for homophobia, nevertheless homophobia is widespread. It is characteristic of entire societies as well as individuals. The bases for homophobic social attitudes are generally related to (1) religious beliefs that homosexuality is morally wrong, (2) scientific theories of homosexuality as an illness or deviance, and (3) social beliefs that homosexuality is damaging to society.

Religious prohibitions have sometimes been considered to be the source of homophobia (Symonds, 1896; Churchill, 1967; Weinberg, 1972; Weinberg and Williams, 1974). The United States, as a result of its puritan heritage, is generally considered one of the most homophobic (and erotophobic) cultures in the world. Although some researchers (such as Irwin and Thompson, 1977) have shown a strong relationship between church attendance, religious beliefs, and antihomosexual attitudes, religion seems unlikely to be a causal factor in homophobia for most Americans.

Science seems to have replaced religion as a source of justification of homophobia for many people. However, there is no scientific evidence that homosexuality is a mental illness. In 1973 the American Psychiatric Association removed the classification of homosexuality from its official list of mental illnesses. The belief among many psychiatrists that homosexuality is a mental illness, in spite of the lack of scientific evidence, is probably a result of their uncritical acceptance of common stereotypes of homosexuals (see Fort, Steiner, and Conrad, 1971; Davidson and Wilson, 1973), and the important fact that they frequently overgeneralize from homosexuals who were possibly mentally ill, and sought treatment, to the entire homosexual population. Nevertheless, the psychologically untenable conceptualization of homosexuality per se as a mental illness, which can be "cured," is still believed by 62% of the American adult population, according to Levitt and Klassen (1973).

Certain psychological theories, such as Freud's, posit that although homosexuality is not an illness, it is nevertheless also not "normal." Freud viewed it as a form of arrested psychosexual development, related to aspects of the parent/child relationship. Psychoanalysts such as Bieber (Bieber *et al.*, 1962) have selectively analyzed cases of homosexuals from their clinical practice that they interpret as supporting Freud's theory. Bieber's conclusions have not been supported in other studies sampling a cross section of homosexuals (Saghir and Robins, 1973).

Freud further believed that homophobia, and also paranoia, is related to "latent homosexuality," which he thought to be present in nearly everyone, since he conceived of people being born ambisexual and later developing heterosexuality. Freud's belief in latent homosexuality has received general acceptance in our culture, both among heterosexuals and homosexuals. Latency, by definition, implies the existence of no behavioral evidence. Therefore if it is possible for anyone to be a latent homosexual, in spite of the absence of sexual activity, it becomes extremely difficult for a person to prove beyond a doubt that he is not a homosexual. Thus, the concept of latent homosexuality contributes in a major way to homophobia, for it allows the possibility that anyone might be a secret homosexual even though the person does not exhibit any of the stereo-types, or behaviors, of homosexuals.

Sociological studies of homosexuality provide another popular scientific jus-tification of homophobia, as they tend to label homosexuality as deviant since it is practiced by only a small proportion of society. However, the term deviant has taken on moral connotations not in keeping with its scientific meaning of "not majority." (See Scarpitti and McFarlane, 1975, for further discussion of this point.) When Simmons (1965) asked a cross section of Americans to list the people who they considered deviant, the most common response was homosex-uals (49%). The equation of deviance with bad or immoral, although it may be indicative of popular thinking, is not inherent in sound sociological research.

Another possible source of homophobia is the belief that homosexuality is damaging to society. An Opinion Research Center poll in 1966 showed that more than 67% of the people contacted viewed homosexuality as "detrimental to society." The Harris Survey has been asking large cross sections of American households whether they feel homosexuals (and other groups) do more harm than good for the country. In 1965 homosexuals were placed third (behind Com-munists and atheists), with 82% of the males and 58% of the females thinking they were primarily a danger to the country. In 1973 about 50% of the respond-ents still felt that homosexuals did more harm than good. Levitt and Klassen (1973) similarly found that 49% of their sample agreed that "homosexuality is a social corruption which can cause the downfall of a civilization." These studies do not make it clear, however, why homosexuality is perceived as a social menace, especially by men. Legislatures in 24 states have decriminalized sexual activities commonly engaged in by consenting homosexual adults, as recom-mended in the model penal code of the American Bar Association. Homosex-uality is also legal in most other countries, including Canada, England, Ger-many, and France. Thus, there is not general official support or evidence, either here or abroad, for the misconception that homosexuality is damaging to society.

Two arguments have been frequently advanced against legalization of ho-mosexuality, in states considering legal reform. Groups such as firemen and policemen have argued that if homosexuality is legalized, homosexuals will "sex-ually corrupt" their fellow workers. (This is also a belief of 38% of Americans, according to Levitt and Klassen, 1973.) In reality, homosexual men have little interest in sexual relationships with unwilling heterosexual colleagues.

The most influential argument advanced against decriminalizing homosexu-ality is that it would allow homosexuals to "convert" or to molest children. We have discussed the distinction between pedophiles and homosexuals and the mistaken stereotype that homosexuals molest children. The children's issue is a red herring because in no state has legalization of sex acts between adults and children ever been proposed. Homosexuals are not seduced or converted into homosexuality. In a study by Lehne (1978) only 4% of the male homosexuals reported that they were somewhat seduced into their first homosexual act, and in not one case was force involved. By comparison, Sorensen (1973) reports that the first sexual experience of 6% of adolescent girls was heterosexual rape. Lehne's study also found that most of the homosexual men reported that they were aware of their sexual orientation (because of their sexual fantasies) about four to five years before their first homosexual experience. The notion that homosexuals, legally or illegally, will seduce, rape, or convert others into homosexuality is not supported by any substantial data. There seems to be no reason to believe that homosexuals act any less morally than most Americans of different sexual orientations, or that they in fact pose a threat to society.

HOMOPHOBIA AND THE INDIVIDUAL

Although homophobia is still widespread in American society, it is increasingly a fear of only a minority of people. Studies of homophobia in individuals suggest that it is not an isolated prejudice or fear; it is consistently related to traditional attitudes about sex roles and other social phenomena. This supports the conceptualization that homophobia functions as a motivation or threat in defining and maintaining the male role.

In an early study of homophobic attitudes, Smith (1971) found that college students who held negative attitudes toward homosexuals were significantly more status conscious, more authoritarian, and more sexually inflexible than individuals scoring low on homophobia. Later research refined Smith's methodology and analysis to show that homophobia is most closely related to traditional sex-role beliefs, and to general lack of support for equality between the sexes (see Morin and Garfinkle, 1978).

MacDonald (MacDonald, 1974, 1976; MacDonald, Huggins, Young, and Swanson, 1973; MacDonald and Games, 1974) developed effective scales of Attitudes toward Homosexuality and a Sex Role Survey. In research with several different adult populations, he demonstrated clear relationships between negative attitudes toward homosexuality and support for the double standard in sex-role behavior and conservative standards of sexual morality. Through the analysis of the semantic differential, he showed that homosexual males are devalued and viewed as less powerful due to their association with femininity, whereas lesbians are seen to be more powerful than heterosexual women because they are believed to be more masculine. Similar analyses were also reported by Storms (1978) and Shively, Rudolph, and DeCecco (1978). The public confusion between sexual orientation and sex role contributes to the devaluation of homosexuals, since they are believed to violate sex-role norms.

MacDonald's findings have been confirmed by numerous other researchers. Weinberger and Millham (1979) concluded that "homophobia is associated with valuing traditional gender distinctions," whereas Minnigerode (1976) found that nonfeminist and conservative sex attitudes were closely related to homophobia. These and other researchers found that people reacted more negatively to same-sex homosexuals, and in particular men were more negative toward male homosexuals than they were toward lesbians, and men overall were more negative in their homophobic attitudes than were women (Nutt and Sedlacek, 1974; Steffensmeier and Steffensmeier, 1974; Turnbull and Brown, 1977). Some researchers, including MacDonald, did not find such clear sex differences; Morin and Garfinkle (1978) have reviewed these studies and related the lack of findings of sex differences to the different methodologies that were used.

A constellation of traditional or sex-negative beliefs was found to be characteristic of homophobic individuals in several other studies. Morin and Wallace (1975, 1976) found that belief in a traditional family ideology was a slightly better predictor of homophobia than traditional beliefs about women; traditional religious beliefs and general sexual rigidity were also related. Negative beliefs about premarital and extramarital affairs were closely associated with homophobia in Nyberg and Alston's (1976–77) analysis of a representative sample of the American population. With a similar sample, Irwin and Thompson (1977) found traditional sex-role standards to be closely related to homophobia. Individuals with nontraditional sex-role behavior were less likely to hold negative attitudes toward homosexuality (Montgomery and Burgoon, 1977), whereas personal anxiety and guilt about sexual impulses were also characteristic of homophobic individuals (Berry and Marks, 1969; Millham, San Miguel, and Kellogg, 1976).

The general picture that emerges from this research is that individuals who are not comfortable with changes in sex roles and sexual behavior are most likely to be homophobic. Cross-cultural research has confirmed the relationship between high levels of sex-role stereotyping and antihomosexual attitudes among West Indians, Brazilians, and Canadians (Dunbar, Brown, and Amoroso, 1973a; Dunbar, Brown, and Vourinen, 1973b; Brown and Amoroso, 1975). Research with homosexuals has also shown that although they are not generally as homophobic as heterosexuals, those holding negative attitudes toward homosexuality are also likely to have traditional beliefs of sex-role stereotyping. Those homosexuals with positive attitudes and self-concepts are more likely to support equality between the sexes and have positive views on feminism (May, 1974; Lumby, 1976; McDonald and Moore, 1978; Glenn, 1978). Thus, homophobia seems to be a dynamic in maintaining traditional sex-role distinctions, rather than an isolated belief or attitude.

The negative influence of homophobic attitudes on social behavior has been demonstrated in several clever research studies. Morin, Taylor, and Kielman (1975) showed that in an interview situation, men and women sit further away from an interviewer wearing a "Gay and Proud" button than they do from the same nonidentified interviewer; this effect is strongest for men, who sit three times as far away from a male homosexual than a lesbian. On a task arranging stick figures, Wolfgang and Wolfgang (1971) found that homosexuals were placed further away than were marijuana users, drug addicts, and the obese, and past homosexuals were viewed as even less desirable and less trustworthy than present homosexuals. Subjects, particularly men, in another experiment were found to be significantly less willing to personally interact with homosexuals than heterosexuals (Millham and Weinberger, 1977). San Miguel and Millham (1976) found that people with homophobic attitudes were significantly more aggressive toward homosexuals than heterosexuals, even when they lost money in a cooperation experiment as a result of their aggression. They were highly aggressive regardless of whether their interaction with the individual prior to labeling as a homosexual was positive, and they were most aggressive toward homosexuals perceived as otherwise similar to themselves. Clearly homophobia is not only reflected in attitudes, but influences social behavior, and thus can have a potent influence in maintaining conformity to conventional sex-role behavior.

The process of homosexual labeling also has strong influences on behavior. Men labeled as homosexuals were perceived as more feminine, emotional, submissive, unconventional, and weaker than when the same men were not labeled (Weissbach and Zagon, 1975). Karr (1978) found also that the male who identified another man as a homosexual was perceived as more masculine, sociable, and desirable, and that highly homophobic individuals would sit further away from the labeled homosexual. Karr effectively demonstrates that one's status as a man can be improved in social situations merely by the act of labeling someone else as gay. Another study found that men who were (incorrectly) labeled as a homosexual became increasingly more stereotypically masculine in their behavior (Farina, 1972); thus, the stigmitization of homosexuals can be a powerful molder of social behavior and conformity to traditional sex roles.

This growing body of research clearly supports the conceptualization that homophobia among individuals is closely related to traditional beliefs about sex roles, rather than individual prejudices against homosexuals. Furthermore, it demonstrates that these homophobic attitudes devalue in thought and action anyone who deviates from traditional sex-role stereotypes, and that this devaluation is reflected in social behavior. Homophobia reduces the willingness of others to interact with a suspected or labeled homosexual, and it may support direct aggression against the labeled deviant. Clearly homophobia is a powerful motivation for maintaining traditional sex-role behavior. MacDonald's assertions (1974, 1976) that sex-role issues are crucial for gay liberation, and that people seeking changes in traditional sex roles must be prepared to also challenge homophobia, are strongly supported by these data.

HOMOPHOBIA AND THE MALE ROLE

The male role is predominantly maintained by men themselves. Men devalue homosexuality, then use this norm of homophobia to control other men in their male roles. Since any male could potentially (latently) be a homosexual, and since there are certain social sanctions that can be directed against homosexuals, the fear of being labeled a homosexual can be used to ensure that males maintain appropriate male behavior. Homophobia is only incidentally directed against actual homosexuals — its more common use is against the heterosexual male. This explains why homophobia is closely related to beliefs about sex-role rigidity, but not to personal experience with homosexuals or to any realistic assessment of homosexuality itself. Homophobia is a threat used by societies and individuals to enforce social conformity in the male role, and maintain social control. The taunt *"What are you, a fag?"* is used in many ways to encourage certain types of male behavior and to define the limits of "acceptable" masculinity.

Since homosexuals in general constitute an invisible minority that is indistinguishable from the 49% male majority in most ways except for sexual preference, any male can be accused of being a homosexual, or "latent" homosexual. Homosexuality, therefore, can be "the crime of those to whom no crime could be imputed." There is ample historical evidence for this use of homophobia from Roman times to the present. For example, even homosexual fantasies were made illegal in Germany in 1935, and Hitler sent more than 220,000 "homosexuals" to concentration camps (Lauritsen and Thorstad, 1974). It is probable that many of these men actually were not homosexuals. But since there was no satisfactory way for individuals to prove that they were not homosexuals (and for this offense in Germany, accusation was equivalent to conviction), imputed homosexuality was the easiest way to deal with undesirable individuals. Homosexuality was likewise an accusation during the American McCarthy hearings in the 1950s when evidence of Communism was lacking. The strong association of homophobia with authoritarianism means that the potential for this exploitation of homophobia is very real during times of stress and strong-arm governments. This is no accident, but is in fact an explanation for the maintenance of homophobia. When homosexuality is stigmatized, homophobia exists as a device of social control, directed specifically against men to maintain male behavior appropriate to the social situation.

Homophobia may also be used to enforce social stereotypes of appropriate sex-role behavior for women. In general men define and enforce women's roles, and men who do not participate in this process may be suspected of being homosexuals. The direct use of homophobia to maintain female roles is necessary only in extreme cases, since male power is pervasive. But it is sometimes alleged that women who do not defer to men, or who do not marry, or who advocate changes in women's roles, are lesbians. There are, of course, other factors besides homophobia that maintain sex roles in society. I am arguing not that the elimination of homophobia will bring about a change in sex roles, but that homophobia must be eliminated before a change in sex roles can be brought about.

THE PERSONAL PAIN OF HOMOPHOBIA

The pain that *heterosexual* males bear as a consequence of homophobia is so chronic and pervasive that they probably do not notice that they are in pain, or the possible source of their discomfort. Homophobia is especially damaging to their personal relationships. Homophobia encourages men to compete. Since competition is not a drive easily turned on and off at will, there is probably a tendency for homophobic men to compete with others in their personal lives as well as at work. Only certain types of relationships are possible between competitors. Love and close friendship are difficult to maintain in a competitive environment because to expose your weaknesses and admit your problems is to be less than a man, and gives your competitor an advantage.

When men realize the intensity of their bonds with other men, homosexuality can be very threatening, and might lead to a limiting of otherwise fulfilling relationships. On the basis of a suggestion from Lester Kirkendall, I've asked men to describe their relationships with their best male friends. Many offer descriptions that are so filled with positive emotion and satisfaction that you might think they were talking about their spouses (and some will admit that they value their close male friendships more than their relationship with their wife, "although they're really different, not the same at all"). However, if I suggest that it sounds as if they are describing a person whom they love, these men become flustered. They hem and haw, and finally say, "Well, I don't think I would like to call it love, we're just best friends. I can relate to him in ways I can't with anyone else. But, I mean, we're not homosexuals or anything like that." Homosexual love, like heterosexual love, does not imply participation in sex, although many people associate love with sex. The social stigma of homosexual love denies these close relationships the validity of love in our society. This potential loss of love is a pain of homophobia that many men suffer because it delimits their relationships with other men.

Because men are unwilling to admit the presence of love in their male friendships, these relationships may be limited or kept in careful check. If male love is recognized, these men may be threatened because they may mistakenly believe this indicates they are homosexuals. Male friendships offer an excellent opportunity to explore ways in which individuals can relate as equals, the type of relationship that is increasingly demanded by liberated women. Most men have learned to relate to some other men as equals, but because they deny themselves the validity of these relationships they respond to equality with women out of fear, or frustration that they don't know how to deal with this "new" type of relationship. Loving male relationships are part of the experiences of many men that are rarely thought about or discussed because of homophobia. As a consequence, many men are unable to transfer what they have learned in these male relationships to their relationships with women. They may also deny to themselves the real importance of their relationships with other men. Male love is so pervasive that it is virtually invisible.

Homophobia also circumscribes and limits areas of male interest. Homophobic men do not participate in sissy, womanly, "homosexual" activities or interests. Maintenance of the male sex role as a result of homophobia is as limiting for men as female sex roles are for women. An appreciation of many aspects of life, although felt by most men at different times in their lives, cannot be genuinely and openly enjoyed by men who must defend their masculinity through compulsively male-stereotyped pursuits. Fear of being thought a homosexual thus keeps some men from pursuing areas of interest, or occupations, considered more appropriate for women or homosexuals.

The open expression of emotion and affection by men is limited by homophobia. Only athletes and women are allowed to touch and hug each other in our culture; athletes are allowed this only because presumably their masculinity is beyond doubt. But in growing up to become men in our culture, we learned that such contact with men was no longer permissible, that only homosexuals enjoy touching other men, or that touching is only a prelude to sex. In a similar way men learn to curb many of their emotions. They learn not to react emotionally to situations in which, although they may feel the emotion, it would be unmasculine to express it. Once men have learned not to express some of their emotions, they may find it difficult to react any other way, and may even stop feeling these emotions. Men are openly allowed to express anger and hostility, but not sensitivity and sympathy. The expression of more tender emotions among men is thought to be characteristic only of homosexuals.

Is a society without homophobia a fairy tale, or will it become a reality? Only when men begin to make a serious attempt to deal with their prejudice against homosexuality can we look forward to living in a world that is not stratified by rigid sex-role distinctions.

REFERENCES

Alston, J. P. "Attitudes toward extramarital and homosexual relations." *Journal of the Scientific Study of Religion*, 1974, *13*, 479–481.

Bell, A. P. "Homosexualities: Their range and character." In J. K. Cole & R. Dienstbier (Eds.), *Nebraska Symposium on Motivation*, Vol. 21. Lincoln: University of Nebraska Press, 1973.

Bell, A. P., & M. Weinberg. *Homosexualities: A Study of Human Diversity.* New York: Simon & Schuster, 1978.

Berry, D. F., & F. Marks. "Antihomosexual prejudice as a function of attitudes toward own sexuality." *Proceedings of the 77th Annual Convention of the American Psychological Association*, 1969, *4*, 573–574.

Bieber, I. *et al. Homosexuality: A Psychoanalytic Study of Male Homosexuals.* New York: Basic Books, 1962.

Brown, M., & D. Amoroso. "Attitudes toward homosexuality among West Indian male and female college students." *Journal of Social Psychology,* 1975, *97,* 163–168.

Churchill, W. *Homosexual Behavior Among Males: A Cross-Cultural and Cross Species Investigation.* Englewood Cliffs, N.J.: Prentice-Hall, 1967.

Dannecker, M., & R. Reiche. *Ger gewoehnliche Homosexuelle.* Frankfurt am Main, Germany: S. Fischer, 1974.

Davidson, G., & T. Wilson. "Attitudes of behavior therapists toward homosexuality." *Behavior Therapy,* 1973, *4*(5), 686–696.

Dunbar, J., M. Brown, & D. Amoroso. "Some correlates of attitudes toward homosexuality." *Journal of Social Psychology,* 1973, *89,* 271–279. (a)

Dunbar, J., M. Brown, & S. Vourinen. "Attitudes toward homosexuality among Brazilian and Canadian college students." *Journal of Social Psychology,* 1973, *90,* 173–183. (b)

Farina, A. "Stigmas potent behavior molders." *Behavior Today,* 1972, *2,* 25.

Ford, C., & F. Beach. *Patterns of Sexual Behavior.* New York: Harper & Row, 1951.

Fort, J., C. Steiner, & F. Conrad. "Attitudes of mental health professionals toward homosexuality and its treatment." *Psychological Reports,* 1971, *29,* 347–350.

Freedman, M. *Homosexuality and Psychological Functioning.* Belmont, Ca.: Brooks/Cole, 1971.

Freedman, M. "Homosexuals may be healthier than straights." *Psychology Today,* 1975, *1*(10), 28–32.

Freund, K., R. Langevin, R. Chamberlayne, A. Deosoran, & Y. Zajac. "The phobic theory of male homosexuality." *Archives of General Psychiatry,* 1974, *31,* 495–499.

Freund, K., R. Langevin, S. Gibiri, & Y. Zajac. "Heterosexual aversion in homosexual males." *British Journal of Psychiatry,* 1973, *122,* 163–169.

Freund, K., R. Langevin, & Y. Zajac. "Heterosexual aversion in homosexual males: A second experiment." *British Journal of Psychiatry,* 1974, *125,* 177–180.

Gallup, G. "Gallup poll on gay rights: Approval with reservations." *San Francisco Chronicle,* July 18, 1977, 1, 18.

Gallup, G. "Gallup poll on the attitudes homosexuals face today." *San Francisco Chronicle,* July 20, 1977, 4.

Glenn, G. L. "Attitudes toward homosexuality and sex roles among homosexual men." Unpublished M.A. Thesis: Antioch University/Maryland, 1978.

Heilbrun, A. B., & N. L. Thompson. "Sex-role identity and male and female homosexuality." *Sex Roles,* 1977, *3,* 65–79.

Irwin, P., & N. L. Thompson. "Acceptance of the rights of homosexuals: A social profile." *Journal of Homosexuality,* 1977, *3,* 107–121.

Kaplan, A. G., & J. P. Bean (Eds.). *Beyond Sex-Role Stereotypes: Readings toward a Psychology of Androgyny.* Boston: Little, Brown, 1976.

Karr, R. "Homosexual labeling and the male role." *Journal of Social Issues,* 1978, *34*(3), 73–84.

Kinsey, A., W. Pomeroy, & C. Martin. *Sexual Behavior in the Human Male.* Philadelphia: Saunders, 1948.

Kirkpatrick, M., R. Roy, & K. Smith. "A new look at lesbian mothers." *Human Behavior,* August 1976, 60–61.

Langevin, R., A. Stanford, & R. Block. "The effect of relaxation instructions on erotic arousal in homosexual and heterosexual males." *Behavior Therapy,* 1975, *6,* 453–458.

Lauritsen, J., & D. Thorstad. *The Early Homosexual Rights Movement (1864–1935).* New York: Times Change Press, 1974.

Lehne, G. "Gay male fantasies and realities." *Journal of Social Issues,* 1978, *34*(3), 28–37.

Levitt, E., & A. Klassen. "Public attitudes toward sexual behavior: The latest investigation of the Institute for Sex Research." Paper presented at the annual convention of the American Orthopsychiatric Association, 1973.

Levitt, E., & A. Klassen. "Public attitudes toward homosexuality: Part of the 1970 National Survey by the Institute for Sex Research." *Journal of Homosexuality,* 1974, *1,* 29–43.

Lorenz, K. Interviewed by R. Evans in *Psychology Today*, November 1974, 82–93.

Lumby, M. E. "Homophobia: The quest for a valid scale." *Journal of Homosexuality*, 1976, *2*, 39–47.

MacDonald, A. "The importance of sex role to gay liberation." *Homosexual Counselling Journal*, 1974, *1*, 169–180.

MacDonald, A. "Homophobia: Its roots and meanings." *Homosexual Counselling Journal*, 1976, *3*, 23–33.

MacDonald, A., & R. Games. "Some characteristics of those who hold positive and negative attitudes toward homosexuals." *Journal of Homosexuality*, 1974, *1*, 9–27.

MacDonald, A., J. Huggins, S. Young, & R. Swanson. "Attitudes toward homosexuality: Preservation of sex morality or the double standard?" *Journal of Counselling and Clinical Psychology*, 1973, *40*, 161. Extended report available from the author (1972).

May, E. P. "Counselors', psychologists', and homosexuals' philosophies of human nature and attitudes toward homosexual behavior." *Homosexual Counselling Journal*, 1974, *1*, 3–25.

McConaghy, N. "Penile volume changes to moving pictures of male and female nudes in heterosexual and homosexual males." *Behavior Research and Therapy*, 1967, *5*, 43–48.

McDonald, G., & R. Moore. "Sex-role self-concepts of homosexual men and their attitudes toward both women and male homosexuality." *Journal of Homosexuality*, 1978, *4*, 3–14.

Millham, J., C. San Miguel, & R. Kellogg. "A factor analytic conceptualization of attitudes toward male and female homosexuals." *Journal of Homosexuality*, 1976, *2*, 3–10.

Millham, J., & L. Weinberger. "Sexual preference, sex role appropriateness and restriction of social access." *Journal of Homosexuality*, 1977, *2*, 343–357.

Minnigerode, F. "Attitudes toward homosexuality: Feminist attitudes and social conservation." *Sex Roles*, 1976, *2*, 347–352.

Montgomery, C., & M. Burgoon. "An experimental study of the interactive effects of sex and androgyny on attitude change." *Communication Monographs*, 1977, *44*, 130–135.

Morin, S., & E. Garfinkle. "Male homophobia." *Journal of Social Issues*, 1978, *34*, 29–47.

Morin, S., K. Taylor, & S. Kielman. "Gay is beautiful at a distance." Paper presented at the meeting of the American Psychological Association, Chicago, August 1975.

Morin, S., & S. Wallace. "Religiosity, sexism, and attitudes toward homosexuality." Paper presented at the meeting of the California State Psychological Association, March 1975.

Morin, S., & S. Wallace. "Traditional values, sex-role stereotyping, and attitudes toward homosexuality." Paper presented at the meeting of the Western Psychological Association, Los Angeles, April 1976.

Nutt, R., & W. Sedlacek. "Freshman sexual attitudes and behaviors." *Journal of College Student Personnel*, 1974, *15*, 346–351.

Nyberg, K., & J. Alston. "Analysis of public attitudes toward homosexual behavior." *Journal of Homosexuality*, 1976–77, *2*, 99–107.

Riddle, D. "Relating to children: Gays as role models." *Journal of Social Issues*, 1978, *34*, 38–58.

Rooney, E., & D. Gibbons. "Social reactions to crimes without victims." *Social Problems*, 1966, *13*, 400–410.

Saghir, M., & E. Robins. *Male and Female Homosexuality: A Comprehensive Investigation*. Baltimore: Williams & Wilkins, 1973.

San Miguel, C., & J. Millham. "The role of cognitive and situational variables in aggression toward homosexuals." *Journal of Homosexuality*, 1976, *2*, 11–27.

Scarpitti, F., & P. McFarlane (Eds.). *Deviance: Action, Reaction, Interaction*. Reading, Mass.: Addison-Wesley, 1975.

Shively, M., J. Rudolph, & J. DeCecco. "The identification of the social sex-role stereotypes." *Journal of Homosexuality*, 1978, *3*, 225–234.

Simmons, J. "Public stereotypes of deviants." *Social Problems*, 1965, *13*, 223–232.

Smith, K. "Homophobia: A tentative personality profile." *Psychological Reports*, 1971, *29*, 1091–1094.

Sorensen, R. *Adolescent Sexuality in Contemporary America*. New York: World, 1973.

Spence, J., & R. Helmreich. *Masculinity & Feminity.* Austin, Tx.: University of Texas Press, 1978.

Steffensmeier, D., & R. Steffensmeier. "Sex differences in reactions to homosexuals: Research continuities and further developments." *The Journal of Sex Research,* 1974, *10,* 52–67.

Storms, M. "Attitudes toward homosexuality and feminity in men." *Journal of Homosexuality,* 1978, *3,* 257–263.

Symonds, J. *A Problem in Modern Ethics.* London: 1896.

Tavris, C. "Men and women report their views on masculinity." *Psychology Today,* January, 1977, 35.

Turnbull, D., & M. Brown. "Attitudes toward homosexuality and male and female reactions to homosexual slides." *Canadian Journal of Behavioural Science,* 1977, *9,* 68–80.

Weinberg, G. *Society and the Healthy Homosexual.* New York: Doubleday, 1972.

Weinberg, M., & C. Williams. *Male Homosexuals.* New York: Oxford University Press, 1974.

Weinberger, L., & J. Millham. "Attitudinal homophobia and support of traditional sex roles." *Journal of Homosexuality,* 1979, *4,* 237–246.

Weissbach, T., & G. Zagon. "The effect of deviant group membership upon impressions of personality." *Journal of Social Psychology,* 1975, *95,* 263–266.

Wolfgang, A., & J. Wolfgang. "Exploration of attitudes via physical interpersonal distance toward the obese, drug users, homosexuals, police and other marginal figures." *Journal of Clinical Psychology,* 1971, *27,* 510–512.

Geof Morgan

HOMOPHOBIA

Back when I was very young
I was a curious boy
One day my daddy came to me and said
Son, you know that ain't no toy.
You keep playing with yourself
You'll never learn the social rules
My son's gonna be a football hero
Not one of those sissy fools.

CHORUS: Now it's homophobia
               in the locker room when I took gym
               Homophobia
               it keeps me from touching my friends.

I don't remember who told me exactly
or when I first heard
But I could tell by the tone in their voice

the meaning of the words.
The women teachers who lived alone
Everybody knew were weird.
And some strange man giving me a ride
was something my mother always feared.

CHORUS

First I learned it was evil
Then I got liberated and learned it was sick
And now I see things differently
But that early training won't quit.
Sometimes it feels just like a wall,
or a river in me that froze
But though I can't really touch it
it keeps me from getting too close.

CHORUS

Susan Brownmiller

WHEN MEN ARE THE VICTIMS OF RAPE

It is finally being acknowledged that one of the main problems of prison life is the assault and rape of other inmates by their fellow men. Shrouded in secrecy and misinformation, so-called homosexual "abuse" in prison was formerly thought to be symptomatic of the deranged brutality of a few prison guards or an "infection" spread throughout a cellbock by a certain number of avowed homosexuals within the prison population. More information and a relatively enlightened modern perspective have drastically altered this old-fashioned view. Prison rape is generally seen today for what it is: an acting out of power roles within an all-male, authoritarian environment in which the younger, weaker inmate, usually a first offender, is forced to play the role that in the outside world is assigned to women. . . .

In the summer of 1973 a 28-year-old Quaker pacifist named Robert A. Martin, a former seaman with a background in journalism, held a stunning press conference in Washington, D.C. Arrested during a peace demonstration in front of the White House, Martin had chosen to go to prison rather than post a $10 bond. . . .

During his first evening recreation period . . . the boyish-looking pacifist was invited into a cell on the pretext that some of the men wanted to talk with him. Once inside, he said, "My exit was blocked and my pants were forcibly taken off me, and I was raped. Then I was dragged from cell to cell all evening." Martin was promised protection from further assaults by two of his violators. The next night his "protectors" initiated a second general round of oral and rectal rape. The pair stood outside his cell and collected packs of cigarettes from other prisoners wanting a turn. When his attackers gave him a brief rest period to overcome his gagging and nausea, Martin made his escape and alerted a guard. He was taken to D.C. General Hospital where he underwent VD tests and a rectal examination. The following morning a Quaker friend posted his bond. . . .

Public recognition of rape in prison is increasing. From a pile of newsclips I can pull the following items:

- Nine inmates at Sumter Correctional Institute in Florida are charged with raping other prisoners during a prison riot.
- Two inmates at Florida's Raiford Prison are charged with raping other inmates at knife point.
- A county judge in upstate New York refuses to send a young offender, who is homosexual, to Attica. His stated reason: "I just couldn't see throwing him into that situation. He'd become an object of barter there, completely dehumanized if he wasn't killed. This is a heck of a thing, and the public ought to know about it."
- Two bright young Nixon aides who plead guilty to Watergate offenses and know they face a jail sentence admit they are apprehensive about the possibility of a sexual assault. . . .

A comprehensive study of rape within the Philadelphia prison system was jointly conducted in 1968 by the district attorney's office and the Philadelphia police department after two embarrassing incidents came to light. One was a gang rape by detainees in a sheriff's van upon a youth who was being transported to court for his trial; the second incident concerned a youth who was sexually assaulted "within minutes of his admission" to the Philadelphia Detention Center for a presentencing evaluation. (In both cases the youth's lawyer reported his rape to the court.)

Alan J. Davis, the chief assistant district attorney who was put in charge of the resulting investigation, was forced to conclude that sexual assault in Philadelphia prisons was "epidemic." Meticulously documenting 156 cases of rape during a two-year period through task-force interviews with more than 3,000 reluctant inmates and guards, the use of lie-detector tests and examination of prison records, Davis believed he had merely touched "the top of the iceberg," and that the true number of rapes during this period was probably closer to 2,000 in a shifting inmate population of 60,000 men. However, a total of only 96 rapes had actually been reported by victimized inmates to prison authorities, and of this number only 64 had been written up in prison records. Prison officials had imposed some form of internal discipline on 40 of the offenders and 26 of the cases had been passed on to the police for legal prosecution.

Davis disclosed that "virtually every slightly built young man committed by the courts is sexually approached within a day or two after his admission to prison. Many of these young men are repeatedly raped by gangs of inmates. . . .

Homosexual rape in the Philadelphia prisons turned out to be a microcosm of the female experience with heterosexual rape. Davis discovered that prison guards put pressure on inmates not to report their rapes by using the argument that the victim wouldn't want his parents and friends to find out about his humiliation. But not telling did not cause the humiliation to "go away": "After a young man has been raped," Davis learned, "he is marked as a victim for the duration of his confinement. This mark follows him from institution to institution. Many of these young men return to their communities ashamed and full of hatred."

Matching the woman's experience with rape in the outside world, Davis found that in a closed society without women, men who raped other men in prison as a group were on the average three years older, one inch taller and fifteen pounds heavier than their prison victims. Also in parallel to the outside world, prison rape appeared to be a function of youthful aggression. Although the average age of an inmate within the Philadelphia prison system was 29, the average prison rapist was found to be 23 years old and the average age of his victim was slightly under 21. Men who raped in prison had usually been put there for crimes of violence: robbery, assault, and heterosexual rape. Men *who were raped* in prison looked young for their years, appeared unathletic and were noticeably better looking than their predators. Their crimes, as might be expected, were usually on the nonassaultive end of the spectrum: auto theft, going AWOL, or violating parole. . . .

Homosexual rape in prison could not be primarily motivated by the need for sexual release, Davis observed, since autoerotic masturbation to orgasm is "much easier and more normal." But conquest and degradation did appear to be a primary goal: "We repeatedly found that aggressors used such language as 'Fight or fuck,' 'We're going to take your manhood,' 'You'll have to give up some face,' and 'We're gonna make a girl out of you.'" Significantly, in the penal institution, economic clout proved as persuasive as physical force: "Typically, an experienced inmate will give cigarettes, candy, sedatives, stainless-steel blades, or extra food pilfered from the kitchen to an inexperienced inmate, and after a few days the veteran will demand sexual repayment." In the fear-charged atmosphere of prison society, the "threat of rape, expressed or implied, would prompt an already fearful young man to submit" for a guarantee of future protection from gang assault or for an easier time of it. "Prison officials," Davis concluded, "were too quick to label such activities 'consensual.'"

In sum, Davis found that prison rape was a product of the violent subculture's definition of masculinity through physical triumph, and those who emerged as "women" were those who were subjugated by real or threatened force.

Edmund White

PARADISE FOUND:
GAY MEN HAVE DISCOVERED THAT THERE IS FRIENDSHIP AFTER SEX

My mother, after years now of getting used to the idea of a "liberated gay" who happens to be her son, nevertheless will say from time to time, "Why don't you get married? To a nice career girl, someone not too interested in sex. A good companion who will take care of you when you're old and feeble. A nice, sexless marriage, the sort we used to call a *marriage blanc* but that now, I suppose, you call a 'New York Marriage.'"

Her sophisticated nomenclature and equally up-to-date way of thinking about marriage scarcely conceal the conservatism of being a parent: we expect for our children the ideal bourgeois lives of the past (lives no one perhaps ever led). Similarly, we fear our children will be crushed by fates we've already embraced. My mother, for example, divorced my father 35 years ago, has lived on her own ever since, runs a clinic for mentally retarded children, had one long affair and is now about to turn 80 as unmarried as the day she was born and a good deal happier. Although she has never been conventional, she has found her freedom privately exhilarating but theoretically regrettable; the regret is applied to the next generation, as though it were a debt that had to be paid.

The truth is that American gay men today (I won't presume to speak for lesbians) are like banyan trees, which, with their elaborate root systems, can draw sustenance from an acre of ground, as opposed to the simple taproots of marriage, deep but narrow. Of the two kinds of arrangement, the marital seems to be the more easily uprooted, the less tenacious. In the past, before people moved around so much, the married couple naturally ramified into the extended family, the neighborhood and the whole tangled undergrowth of friendships that had lasted since childhood. But now the mobile home is a sadly self-contained unit, shunted from Boston to Kalamazoo to Denver (where one popular service does nothing but instantly integrate the arriving corporate wife into the community before she's whisked off somewhere else). In traditional China, literary training was a prerequisite to entering the bureaucracy, and officials were not permitted to serve in their native district; that is why so much Chinese poetry is about parting — a theme that would surely dominate our verse as well if execs were bards.

Gay men, of course, move around quite a bit, too; but since there are relatively few gays in corporate life, they are seldom moved anywhere against their will, and the places they migrate to are usually predictable. For instance, it's almost a rite of passage for a gay New Yorker in his early 30s to feel he must enjoy the twilight of his youth in San Francisco or Los Angeles. But this transplantation seldom sticks, and even during the three or four years he's out west, he's scarcely out of touch with his old friends (many of whom have also made the move). Bicoastals are far more frequently encountered these days than bisexuals, and city-hopping for holidays — even for one great party — is common among affluent gays. A week after the Hawaiian Shirt Party on Fire Island, gays in Laguna Beach are conspicuously displaying their snapshots of the event — the bronzed bodies in the pool or on the deck and there, in their midst, like the ghost of Banquo, a pale Andy Warhol in black with his shock of white hair and his camera poised for attack. It's a bit like a Noel Coward play, in which the same four or five faces keep regrouping all over the world.

In Andrew Holleran's novel about the smart gay set, *Dancer from the Dance*, there are many references to "circuit queens," those men who not only live in a milieu of bars, baths and discos in their own town, but also relentlessly fly from one gay watering place to another — New York to Atlanta to Key West to New Orleans to Los Angeles to San Francisco to Denver and home again. In each of these cities, despite local differences, a uniform gay culture is being created: a standard look, with its emphasis on macho work clothes and the heavily muscled body; and a uniform set of values, cheerfully hedonistic though recently being imbued with a sense of responsibility to less fortunate members of the gay community. This new social consciousness is evidenced by such organizations as the Gay Men's Health Crisis, which raises money to underwrite research into such diseases as AIDS (Acquired Immune Deficiency Syndrome), the mysterious and usually fatal affliction that has been spreading at an alarming rate throughout the gay community. As a result of AIDS, more and more gays are either entering monogamous affairs or forging circles of partners.

Camaraderie has always been a feature of American gay life. When I was a gay teen-ager in the 1950s I first discovered the democracy of the bars, the instant intimacy of the one-night stand; but in those good bad old days before gay pride, there was always a trace of contempt in the air ("You're sick, Miss Thing, and you're an evil bitch") or of bathetic self-pity ("Oh, God, why can't I push a button and just be *normal*?"). That was the era of outcasts clustering for comfort, pariahs seeking a sullen consolation in one another. But don't let me paint too bleak a picture — there really was a speakeasy excitement about those gay bars of the past, where not only gays congregated but also every other misfit in town: the drunk old lady who belted out show tunes as she accompanied herself on a rinky-tink piano; the unshaved little guy who was some sort of a preacher and would start sermonizing late at night; and the quiet, middle-aged black insurance salesman and his fat white ladyfriend, the waitress, the two of them contentedly holding hands in the obscurity of a back booth and murmuring words of love.

Today, 14 years after the Stonewall uprising and the beginning of gay liberation, there is a great deal more self-acceptance among gays, even a welcome show of arrogance. Moreover, in the 1970s the Clone emerged, that overexercised, monosyllabic, aggressively masculine monument to machismo, and he had a good deal less tolerance for weirdoes than did the old-fashioned Queen of the past. But in truth, the Clone look is more a look than an essence: it's a convenient, easily acquired and highly efficient set of appearances rather than an indelible identity.

The Clone may not be a troubling phenomenon, but conformism in gay life certainly is. Gay liberation grew out of the progressive spirit of the 1960s — a strange and exhilarating blend of socialism, feminism and the human potential movement. Accordingly, what gay leaders in the late 1960s were anticipating

was the emergence of the androgyne, but what they got was the superbutch
stud; what they expected was a communal hippie freedom from possessions,
but what has developed is the acme of capitalist consumerism. Gays not only
consume expensive vacations, memberships in gyms and discos, cars, elegant
furnishings, clothes, haircuts, theater tickets and records, they also consume
each other. From the perspective of the present, we can now look back at the
beginning of gay liberation and observe that it flowered exactly at the moment
when gays became identified, by themselves and by the market, as a distinct
group of affluent and avid consumers. There had been earlier gay uprisings
against straight oppression long before Stonewall, but none of them com-
manded the attention of the media nor had the far-ranging consequences of
Stonewall. The success of gay liberation in the 1970s, of course, was largely
political, but it was also, I'd contend, strongly related to the rise of the
gay market. Unfortunately, today this rampant and ubiquitous consumerism not only characterizes gay spending habits but also infects attitudes
toward sexuality: gays rate each other quantitatively according to age, physical dimensions and income; and all too many gays consume and dispose
of each other, as though the very act of possession brought about instant
obsolescence.

I don't want to overstate this point or suggest that to the degree it exists it's
exclusively a gay problem. Moreover, if anonymous sex in the gay world can
be consumerist, friendship is warm, wry, sustaining. The women's movement
is permitting a whole new generation of women to enjoy each other's company,
whereas in the past they were all to often ashamed to be seen together in public
"unescorted," as though belonging to a "hen party" were the ultimate admission
of failure in the mating sweepstakes; in the same way, gay liberation has en-
franchised gay society, making it sufficient unto itself. Militancy has led to a
sense of authenticity, surely the prerequisite of any genuine society. Gay men
no longer look longingly over their shoulders at straight life, and they take each
other seriously as mentors, buddies, sidekicks, brothers, lovers. When I was a
boy, gay men were always mooning over straight GIs; now we lust after each
other. Perhaps that's the origin of the Clone: we've become what we always
wanted.

The singles scene among straights is quickly taking on the fluidity of the gay
mainstream; but even so, the flow of straight society is always impeded or diverted by the pull of its institutions: Marriage, Childbirth, Divorce, Property
Settlements. What I'm suggesting is that the economic, social and religious *consequences* of straight life — the subliminal historic sense that the second date can
lead to holy matrimony and a station wagon full of toys and groceries — lend
a certain gravity, even stiffness, to straight courtship. What's more, there is a
mathematical difference as well, since during any country weekend spent together by four strictly heterosexual couples, there are only 16 possibilities for
coupling whereas four gay couples can link up into 28 possible pairs. Obviously,
French farce writers of the 19th century should have made gay life their subject,
since the two gay rivals who duck under the bed can easily emerge as the newest
pair of lovers. I remember that in my own case, when I was in my early 20s, I
tricked out with a famous playwright — my first infidelity to my lover of two
years. After I had sex with the playwright, he told me that I made love exactly
like this kid he'd met a week before — and he named my lover, whom I

promptly telephoned from the playwright's apartment. We all dissolved into peals of laughter.

Because gay life is not institutionalized and because, at least potentially, anyone can become anyone else's partner, romantic arrangements are a good deal more casual than they are among straights. This casualness is still further enhanced by the fact that one is dealing with members of the same sex, i.e., people programmed with the same expectations and values. In this easygoing fraternity of sex and sociability, which is presided over by the male spirit of the hunt, dramatic breakups have a way of quickly settling down into cozy friendships. Again and again I've seen two men who have stopped being lovers continue to live together; as for myself, I can count on several ex-lovers as close friends. Movies and pop songs are, after all, about heterosexual love, and parents and priests weep over straight marriages and straight divorces. Gays have been largely ignored by the shamans — a silence that may sometimes make us feel strangely invisible, though the mercy of obscurity is that our unions and severings are less public, less mythic, altogether less resonant. As marginal beings we are able to invent ourselves.

For instance, my next-door neighbor is a six-foot-four blond muscleman with a love of books and a flair for business, a cultivated and soon-to-be-rich 33-year-old who can get himself up on Saturday nights to look like a Hell's angel, but whose heart is truly angelic, scholarly and wise. Five years ago I dated "Tom" for six months. At the time the affair was intense. We were together constantly and he stayed over with me almost every night. From time to time I'd see Tom's roommate, "Bill," a Southern man who's close to 40 but looks 25 and who's a bit of a loner, a whiz at every kind of computer game and electronic folly, but who never speaks at a party, though he follows the conversation avidly with eyes so big and glossy they seem to have been buttoned on. Bill was always wonderfully cordial to me. Not until a year after Tom and I drifted out of our affair did I learn that Bill was not just Tom's roommate but also his lover — that in fact they've been together almost a decade in nearly perfect tranquility. Bill stays home with his gadgets or goes to dance class, counsels Tom in his extramarital sprees, keeps books for Tom's expanding empire, while Tom has affairs that are more short-lived than his adventures in business.

But this kind of attachment is more common than rare in contemporary big-city gay life. I know many gay couples, and in every case the marriage is open; the only question is how that given is to be legislated. Most couples discuss their "contract" frankly and set their own rules for their "infidelities." Pointless to go into all these arrangements here; suffice it to say that open marriages can turn into disasters or into complex networks of friends and lovers. Even the word *lover* is too crude for all the gradations of commitment and intimacy; one friend uses an ascending scale of Trick, Number, Fuck Buddy, Lover and Husband. My point is: gays, in their efforts to invent themselves, have become equally ingenious in devising complex erotic molecules.

Of course promiscuity, no matter how institutionalized and hedged round by rules it might be, can threaten and even end a relationship. If one permits one's lover to sleep around or, especially, to date other men, he may well fall in love with someone else. That's the danger of giving too long a leash, though the resentment that crops up from keeping someone on too short a leash is likely to doom a relationship even more rapidly. This double-edged problem is very similar in straight and gay life, with a few differences. It seems that gays are more capable than straights of distinguishing between sex and love. I know two gay guys who have met for lunch once a week for several years, though each man has a lover whom he's not about to give up. The luncheons (or "nooners," as we used to call them) are strictly for pleasure, a joy that is completely self-contained, that leads nowhere.

The other odd feature about gay promiscuity is that the jealousy (I don't want you to sleep with that guy) can actually be a disguised form of lust or envy (I wish I were sleeping with that guy). Many years ago I was hopelessly in love with someone who didn't want to sleep with me but who was wildly infatuated with a third guy. I never did seduce my love, but at least I had the rather wan and philosophical consolation of sleeping with my rival. In fact, that rival came to prefer me to the man I loved; I became my own love's rival — surely a peculiar twist possible only in gay life.

A year ago I was without a lover but I felt elated in a wonderful square dance of partners and friends, an allemande-left of amorous intrigue in which no one got hurt and everyone was amused, stimulated, appreciated. For the past five years I have been friends with "Hank," a tall, dark hunk from Colorado with a mixture of Spanish and Irish blood, a boxer's body and the soul of a saint. He's someone who will go to bed with anyone; as he says, he practices the "generosity of the body." His way of dealing with the clawing, scratching and conniving that others resort to in order to trick him into bed is to surrender at once. For that reason I call him "the Bodhisattva of Sex," in honor of those Buddhas who forestall personal salvation out of compassion for needy humanity.

Despite his philosophy, I had somehow assumed his beauty put him out of my league — until, after four years of knowing him, we stumbled into each other's arms. Since he was a writer as well, we had always had plenty to talk about, and sex merely confirmed a longstanding intimacy.

Hank's generosity inspired me to emulate him by introducing him to all of my friends. One of these friends was "Kevin," a slender blond Norwegian and at that time my roommate. Kevin was someone I had fallen for so hard that I had tried to dissuade him from moving in with me, since I realized he reciprocated my love but not my passion. But Kevin had convinced me everything would work out — and two months later I knew it was working out splendidly. We seldom had sex but we slept with our arms around each other every night he was in town (he was often away on business). When he was around he had a way of making me calm down — he seemed to generate alpha waves. On the night of his 28th birthday, I invited Hank over to help us celebrate. After a lot of champagne and a few joints, the three of us went to bed — but it wasn't five feverish minutes in the dark; rather, an emotional and sensual ceremony, that frankly physical and physically frank kind of lovemaking men like.

Hank and Kevin went out with each other for a while. I wasn't jealous, but I don't know whether to ascribe my equanimity to age, wisdom, indifference or, simply, self-discipline. Had I at last learned not to expect devotion from much younger and more attractive men-about-town (and in Kevin's case, an especially hot man new-to-town)? Or were we trading in romance for something less exclusive, more nourishing, less futile and feudal?

Perhaps we were all just finding safety in numbers, for soon a young student of French politics had joined the circle, someone who read two books a day (the book read before noon had to have been written before 1900; the afternoon book, after), who worked out two hours a day at the gymnasium yet still found time for us. He slept with Hank, he slept with Kevin, he slept with me — and we all still laugh about that delirious month, that ecologically sound recycling of affection and (as the mad general in *Dr. Strangelove* put it) "precious bodily fluids."

I'm certainly not denying that gays are as capable as anyone else of turning their romances into soap operas. The ways people behave in love are determined probably not so much by sexual orientation as by experience, ethnic background and one's momentary expectations. If Kevin, Hank, the French scholar and I were all civilized as we danced *la ronde*, we could afford to be: no one was in love, and now, a year later, though we're still all very close, we sleep with each other rarely. Yet I'm proud to have been a member of that erotic little society, to have heard Hank's novel and to have watched Kevin take New York by storm (in his lowkey, alpha-wave assault), to have witnessed the French scholar's adventures in reading — and to have experienced them and myself bodily as well as socially. In his late books, the French critic Roland Barthes speaks again and again about a utopian entity, "the body," something sacred and separate from the corruptions of social codes: for that brief moment I felt our bodies expressed both our public sense of forming a society as well as our more private emotions. In conventional, straight America, people honor only the permanent and dismiss, even forget (or at least forget to mention) the transitory. Only what lasts is good. This prejudice in favor of what endures is unfortunate, I'd say, a concession to social institutions rather than a recognition of human experiences — of *lived beauty* in particular.

Friendship need not be transitory, of course: my point is precisely that friendships outlast passion. Nor need friendships originate in or pass through a sexual stage. It's a luxurious pleasure to be able to sleep with our friends — a privilege and a resource — yet sex is by no means a prerequisite for intimacy (sex can, of course, be a way of avoiding intimacy). Rather than rehearse that truism, however, I would like to dwell a moment longer on the unexpected consequences of the primacy of sexuality in gay life. Whereas a straight man may even nowadays choose his wife not mainly for sexual compatibility but for her social connections, her religious affiliation, her likelihood to be a good mother, her maturity and constancy, her chances of helping him rise in the world, her aura or glamour, a gay man, by contrast, has nothing concrete to gain from the status of his partner. His choice, uncensored by society and based solely on desire, can be rather eccentric; when a whole social set is pieced together out of one's friends and the men they've made into lovers, the result is richly improbable. The 40-year-old professor of German and his lover, the 20-year-old windsurfer, sit down to dinner with the exiled Argentine rancher and his lover, the Harvard University MBA. It's no wonder that gays always seem to know such funds of recherché information; they've listened to the most heterogeneous table talk imaginable.

The only society of the past that approximated the conditions of the current gay world was ancient Japanese court life as pictured in Sei Shōnagon's tenth-century diary, *The Pillow Book*. As a wit celebrated for her tart tongue and dandiacal whims, Sei Shōnagon gives us in her fascinating jottings a cleanly etched representation of the values of her world, that of imperial court functionaries and ladies in waiting. The women are free to bestow their favors on whomever they please, and the rule is the one-night stand, conducted with a measure of decorum and a nod toward sentiment (the gentleman sends the lady a morning-after poem comparing the dawn dew on his sleeve to his tears at parting). But despite the decorum, sexual interest flares up suddenly, even ferociously; sex seems incompletely assimilated into society, not quite housebroken. Friendship — and Sei Shōnagon has several long-lasting friendships with men who admire her taste and her knowledge of the classics — intertwines with sexual adventure and almost always outlasts it; a casual encounter can lead to a lifelong, romantic but sexless friendship. (Marriage, arranged by older relatives strictly for dynastic purposes, is never confused with love or sexual attraction.)

I cite Heian court life simply as a precedent for a society in which sex, love and friendship may overlap but are by no means wholly congruent. In this society, moreover, it is friendship that provides the emotional and social continuity, whereas sexuality is no more and no less than an occasion for gallantry (the game, the thrill, the poetic pretext). Love in the Proustian sense — a grand, consuming, one-sided passion based on jealousy and thwarted possessiveness that evaporates the instant it is reciprocated — this sort of love is unknown, just as is the domestic bliss of bourgeois marriage.

To be sure, Sei Shōnagon belonged to a tiny, privileged elite whose functions were almost entirely ceremonial — a special case if there ever was one. But her book can be read at least as a hypothesis about a world in which sex is not required to bear the emotional and mythic burden it carries for many. I'm suggesting that among gay men today, as among the Japanese of *The Pillow Book*, sex serves many purposes — as a form of curiosity, of symbolic conquest and submission, as an exercise in the serious business of fantasy — but the one purpose it does not serve is the promotion of continuity and fidelity. I have no doubt many gays are reading me now and mumbling indignantly, "How dare he speak for us?" but I'm not attempting to describe those homosexuals whose lives follow straight conventions. Indeed, by saying *gay* instead of *homosexual* I'm attempting to describe a lifestyle rather than a sexual orientation.

The one part of straight life I may seem to be describing is adolescence. That's always the insult tossed ever so casually at gays by modern moralists, those artful dodgers who have learned they dare not tell us we're bad but who don't hesitate to tell us we're "immature." I should mention right away that the charge may or may not be accurate, but it never sounds to me as condescending as intended; I have no contempt for that time of life when our friendships are most passionate and our passions incorrigible and none of our sentiments yet compromised by greed or cowardice or disappointment. The volatility and intensity of adolescence are qualities we should aspire to preserve; interestingly, those societies in which the participants can afford to behave as they please (Versailles under Louis XIV or Hollywood now) always choose to preserve their "adolescent" character — the rapid succession of affairs, the scheming and intrigue, the scrambling after popularity, the dismissal of the solid future in favor of the shimmering present.

If gay men seem attractively adolescent (steamy with emotion, available to romantic, imaginative discovery), they should not be credited with superior wisdom or staying power. It occurs to me throughout this essay that I might seem to be ascribing unusual virtues to gay men, but in fact I know that no group is innately superior to another. Nevertheless, the conditions of one's ex-

istence — even the seemingly unfortunate conditions — can promote new understandings and new modes of behavior. In the case of gays, our childlessness,
our minimal responsibilities, the fact that our unions are not consecrated, even
our very retreat into gay ghettos for protection and freedom: all of these objective conditions have fostered a style in which we may be exploring, even in
spite of our conscious intentions, things as they will someday be for the heterosexual majority. In that world (as in the gay world already), love will be built
on esteem rather than passion or convention, sex will be more playful or fan-
tastic or artistic than marital — and friendship will be elevated into the supreme
consolation for this continuing tragedy, human existence.

Albert Luna

GAY RACISM

"There is a situation that's happened to me every time I've gone out. White men
will approach me. They assume I don't know anything. They assume I'm uneducated and stupid," remarks Jimmy J. "They don't expect me to be able to
carry on a conversation. But, when they find that I can converse and I do know
something, then they're not interested. They walk away. They want *their*
images."

Jimmy is 27, well-educated, a salesperson, and a Black man. He is a victim
of the vicious stereotypes which all Black people must confront every day.

Negative assumptions, images and stereotypes are at the heart of the matter;
they are what racism is built upon and continues to feed on. Such negative
beliefs are what people use to bludgeon each other in quiet and simple ways,
but the violence inherent in this type of racism is every bit as real as the lynch-
ing, burning and maiming that went on in the post-Civil War South. People are
scarred psychologically by racism and, because we all participate in this, we are
all ruined.

The Philadelphia gay male community has never really come to grips with
the problem of racism in its midst. This article attempts to uncover the problem, long buried by uncaring, uniformed and unrealistic attitudes. "They don't
want to deal with racism because they don't think it affects them. They don't
really dislike Blacks; they just don't think about Black people," comments
Charles B., a 32-year-old artist. Charles' observation touches on another facet
of racism: what writer Ralph Ellison called the invisibility of Blacks. People
disregard what does not immediately concern them. In this way, many problems lose visibility until they impinge upon the world of the non-thinker.

This two-edged, racist sword is evident in the gay male community as well
as in America at large. On the one hand, Black gays are largely an invisible

Reprinted from *Black Men/White Men*, Michael J. Smith, ed. San Francisco: Gay Sunshine
Press, 1983. Reprinted by permission.

minority. They are invisible, that is, until they attempt to mix with the White gay community. Then, all the negative stereotypes leap to the minds of the people involved.

Surprise is not uncommon among black gay men when they find White gays to be racist. "I was surprised. Yes, in a way I was. I thought, 'Here's this group of people, a subculture sharing common interests, looking out for each other.' But it wasn't the case at all," remembers Van, a 33-year-old office worker. His experience is similar to Charles'. As Charles says, "I originally saw gays as a breed unto themselves. I assumed there would be a bond among all gay people. I was naive. Then I realized that the prejudices of society bled into the gay world."

Many Black gays did not have this preconceived notion about gays being more open. Ricardo D., 24, an office manager, declares, "I knew they were racist. People are people, whether they're gay or straight. They will have the same feelings and idiosyncracies." Far more of the men I interviewed echoed Ricardo's thoughts. Racism was no surprise, but it did hurt.

HOW DOES GAY RACISM WORK?

Racism is put into practice through a variety of discriminatory techniques aimed at keeping minority group members from participating fully in society. The most visible form of discrimination in the gay community is at the bars — our most public and popular gathering places.

Carding is the practice of demanding a Liquor Control Board (LCB) card at the door of a bar before entrance is permitted.

This routine is meant to keep those people under the age of 21 out of the bars. But, as it is most frequently used, the LCB card is a means of keeping Black gays out of White gay bars — because only Black patrons are asked to produce their cards. It has gone on (or is going on) at almost every major gay bar in the city of Philadelphia.

Just going out becomes a real ordeal. "Your heart is in your throat. A block before you come to the bar, you get this awful feeling in your stomach. You wonder what will happen at the door. It makes you feel like trash. You can't even feel like an equal," remembers Stan A., a 27-year-old music student. In reliving the experience he seems almost out of breath.

"It happened to me early this summer at Odyssey II," relates Herb J., a hospital administrator. "We went to the door and were asked for IDs. We are not young looking. I showed my driver's license. The doorman said it was unacceptable." Herb takes a long deep breath — he's obviously trying to control his emotions. "Then, right in front of me, young, White gays were let into the bar. So I asked again if we could go in. We were refused. I would have called the police, but my friends didn't want to press charges."

Almost every bar in town was mentioned by one interviewee or another. There is no set policy — none set down so that you could see it, that is. The only real guide is money. Money talks. Bar owners listen to their patrons and their White patrons do not want to rub elbows with Black customers.

Two bars in town, the Smart Place and the now-defunct Letters, opened with the express purpose of being places where discrimination would not happen. In a short time, both bars became all-Black establishments, due to the refusal of most White gay men to patronize the bars on equal terms with Black gays. As Ed, the White former owner of Letters said some time before his bar closed, "White customers came to me several times and told me, 'It's getting too dark in here. If it doesn't stop, we're not coming back.' I told them that Letters was a bar for everyone."

Robin S., a graduate student in American culture and a Black activist as well as a gay activist, has his own ideas about Black acceptance in White gay bars. "One of the problems that Whites have with Blacks in bars is that they (the Whites) feel overwhelmed by the Blacks. Black men tend to be more social than middle-class, non-ethnic Whites. Also, the music in bars is music derived from Black music. It's okay to listen to Black women singing, but when it comes to having Black folk near you, they can't have it. It's a ripoff of Black culture. They take only what they like from it."

Getting past the door is only the beginning of a racist journey for some Black gays. Once inside, they are subjected to an array of racist emotions and reactions.

THE RACIST ORDEAL

"Just to walk across the floor of the bar can be an ordeal. The expressions on some people's faces. The questioning looks, the 'why are you here?' expressions are all frightening. It can be mentally challenging, sometimes even physically challenging depending on the people and how hostile they are," according to Alan C., a 24-year old development researcher. Alan shifts uncomfortably in his seat as he talks about his experiences. With a sense of indignation he adds, "It's a very natural part of being a Black person. People have preconceptions. In a gay bar the preconception is: 'You shouldn't be here.' The response I must have is: 'I have every right to be here.' Dealing with this takes a lot of energy."

Like Alan, everyone has developed his own way of dealing with being in a White gay bar. Charles "will not go into a White gay bar alone." He feels strongly that "there are more important places to fight for civil rights."

But David, 32, a government worker, girds himself with feelings of self-worth and plunges ahead. "I don't go into any bar with the feeling that I may encounter discrimination. I've learned that racism is a White problem, not mine. So I go into bars and clubs with that attitude. If they don't respond to me that's their problem. I don't care how they feel or what they think. I can't let that affect my life to the point where I will become withdrawn."

Once over the initial hostile feelings, Black gay men are usually in for a variety of other experiences, all rooted in racist assumptions.

Like Jimmy, Alan has had men walk away because he did not fit their images. "I've had people talk to me, but when they find out you have some brains, they're not interested."

Herb remembers an acquaintance coming up to him in a bar and telling him, "You're too preppy. Where's your ski cap and blue jeans?" He uneasily recalls the incident and the hurt it caused him. "I thought that maybe I wasn't dressing right. I didn't know what to think. But then I decided that I'd dress the way I wanted."

Stan walked into Equus one evening and saw a person he thought was a friend. This "friend," a well-known gay activist, did not notice who Stan was from across the room. The activist did notice, however, that Stan was wearing a Lacoste shirt. Then in a loud voice the activist told the people he was with, "Well, those clothes are sure popular, even the *niggers* (emphasis added) are wearing them." Stan was shocked. "I couldn't believe it. He wasn't joking either. I've never spoken to him since. I thought he was a friend."

Another common occurrence for Black men in bars is described by John. "I'll be standing there and some White man will come up to me and, without saying a word, not even one word, he'll grab me in the crotch and look me in the eye. In front of everyone. I guess I'm expected to follow immediately. I usually tell them what will happen to their arms if they don't move." Wayne A., a college freshman with a similar experience, says, "They assume that Black men have big dicks, and that's all they're interested in. They're size queens, that's all."

SEXUAL STEREOTYPES

Sexual stereotypes are common and burdensome to Black men, who feel that they are expected to behave in certain ways or meet other arbitrarily imposed standards. Charles thinks for a moment before dealing with the question: "Basically Black people are pictured as being sexually uninhibited and passionate. White men may want to receive this passion and fervor without having to give anything in return."

"They just want their fantasies," Dean interjects bluntly. "They want to be dominated by this dark man with this humongous dick and wonderfully passionate nature."

Surprisingly, with all the resentment this treatment can cause, Jimmy has room to be introspective and philosophical. He tries to cast a positive light on the matter. "I think a lot of White men are attracted to Black men because of the strength we have — not physical strength, but a spiritual strength which comes from putting up with a lot of bullshit." He is aware that this, too, is an image in some men's minds. "We ingest images that allow us to sexually objectify people, consume them, and discard them. It naturally follows that it can be done to Black men."

Sexual stereotyping is rampant, and again, the only reality is the imagery existing in the minds of those possessed of these stereotypes. Alan's anger flashes through his words: "If you don't fit their stereotypes, they become very cold. They don't bother to contact you or to communicate in any way."

Novelist James Baldwin sums up the matter in *A Rap on Race:* "They come to you for the most part, as though you're some extraordinary phallic symbol . . . As if you're nothing but a walking phallus . . . no head, no arms, no nothing . . . actually the act of love becomes an act of murder in which you are also committing suicide."

Donald has experienced another typical approach that some White men have toward Black men. "I will see White men in bars who want nothing to do with me. They're with their White friends and don't want to show their true feelings. They don't even seem to notice me. But, later in the evening, our paths will cross again at the baths. Now they're alone. Their friends are not around to see what they do and who they do it with. They try like hell to get me into bed when no one is around to see. I remind them that they were not interested in me at the bar, and now, I'm not interested in them. If you won't deal with me in the light, you won't get me at night." He smiles as he says this.

Bathhouses also present situations for racism to occur on a variety of levels. The most obvious, of course, is discrimination at the door.

Several years ago, it was rumored that a popular bathhouse would not permit Black men in. A weekly gay newspaper no longer published in Philadelphia, *The Weekly Gayzette*, decided to test the case. Two people were sent, one White, one Black. The White person had a membership, the Black man was seeking one. At the door, the White man said he wanted to sponsor his Black friend. The clerk on duty announced, "I'm sorry, but our membership is full right now. We aren't accepting any more people. But take this card, fill it out and we'll contact you in two weeks." The bathhouse never made contact.

Just this year, a bathhouse which published an ad featuring one-night passes was said to have gone back on its advertised offer. Kenneth C. said, "I was with a friend. It was after we had been in the bars and we decided to go to the baths. We went there and since neither of us had a membership, we asked for their one-night card. The guy at the desk said, 'There isn't any such thing.' I told him it was in their ad. I pointed out the offer to him. Then he told me, 'We don't do that anymore.' I guess it was because we're both Black."

Inside the baths there are areas which are poorly lit or not lighted at all, places where the most anonymous sex happens. But even here racism finds a way. White patrons will be in these areas when someone comes along — someone they attempt to initiate sexual contact with. They reach out trying to connect. The two men will then come together for sexual contact, but on many occasions Victor B. says the following has happened: "The guy will feel me all over, then he'll reach up and feel my hair. As soon as he does that he figures out that I'm Black and loses all interest. He pushes me away." Victor was not alone in mentioning this phenomenon.

NEGATIVE ASSUMPTIONS

The negative assumptions do not stop at the bars and the baths, but follow people into the confines of the bedroom, where one's inhibitions are supposed to be much lower. Jimmy bristles with sexual memories: "I've gone home with White men who are always certain I'm going to steal something. If I say I have to go to the bathroom, I get escorted from the bed to the bathroom and then back again." Herb agrees: "If you meet someone, they're usually afraid to go home with you because they think it won't be safe in your neighborhood. They are also frightened to take you home because they think you'll steal half the house. They walk around the house with you and they check if you're clean."

Others, like John, have experienced relationships in which they are only sex objects. "Once I got to his apartment, I was treated like a toy. I had to do this or that. He wanted to do whatever he wanted, without considering my feelings at all."

Some see racist patterns in the interracial couples they know or observe. Charles says he has noticed "a plantation mentality in the interracial couples I've seen. The Black man is expected to be docile, timid, and often financially dependent on the White man. I maintain that when one man has to degrade himself in order to keep another, I can't see how either will benefit."

Donald sees many of the same features among the interracial couples he knows. "The White man is usually more financially well-to-do than the Black man. This perpetuates many of the stereotypes."

But Alan, who has a White lover, disagrees. "Despite the fact that one may appear dominant, this doesn't mean that this is in fact true. It is easier for them to act this way when the couple is out. A Black man gets a lot more negative attention when he chauffeurs a White man around, buys a drink for a White man, or buys clothes for a White man. You don't always want to deal with that attention. It's a defense."

Dean is quick to point out that interracial couples are subjected to another subtle form of racism built on the assumption that the White man is in control. "In restaurants, the maitre d' will talk to the White man. The waiters always give the check to the White man. Or they assume that the credit card belongs to the White man."

The instances pile up over and over again. The sense of outrage and resentment grows geometrically. Solutions seem unavailable and hope for better relations has never been more elusive. What can be done to change things? If not the world at large, what can be done to make the gay community less racist?

Almost everyone interviewed feels the same way about solving the problem of racism. "Since racism and discrimination are functions of White attitudes and White actions," concludes Robin, "it is White people who have to deal with it." Dale agrees wholeheartedly: "Blacks should stop taking the responsibility for solving the problem of racism. After all, it's not really *our* problem. We, unfortunately, reap the effects of it, though."

From this starting point — White responsibility — people had all manner of suggestions for solving the problem. They ranged from Dale's exhortation for people to "be willing to be wrong because that's where learning starts," to Jimmy who says that White gay men should try to understand what it means to be Black. "It's not fully possible, but there's a way. I ask White gay men to completely 'own' their own gayness and display it constantly, every day as I do my Blackness. This way they can see how pervasive the oppression is out there."

"They've got to acknowledge there is a problem," Robin insists, "and then acknowledge that it should be changed. This doesn't go on. Racism and discrimination exist in bars because they exist on a personal basis. It's not just the carding: it's the White people who see the carding and do nothing about it. They do *nothing*. That perpetuates it. White gays allow it to continue. That's the only way it *can* continue. Racism exists because the majority of White male gays support it."

CAN BLACK GAYS HELP?

Not everyone felt that Whites should have to go the distance on their own. Charles, along with others, feels that, although Whites must do the majority of the work in battling racism, Blacks can help.

"There are three ways Black people can react to White racism: (a) they can accept the programming and feel inferior; (b) they can resent it and respond with hatred; (c) they can feel compassion for Whites and work with them and help them. The last way is obviously the most constructive way."

"It's everybody's problem," declares Van animatedly. "If there's a White person who recognizes discrimination or a racist attitude, he or she should say something about it. By the same token, if the incident happens to a Black person, they should say something. It's very difficult for a person to take action if he thinks he's all alone. That's part of the problem. Part of the solution is to let people know that if they feel or think that racism is wrong, then they're not alone."

Alone or not, the problem must be dealt with. The question is: How? Charles Silberman in *Crisis in Black and White*, writes ". . . it is up to Whites to lead the way; the guilt and responsibility are theirs." Again the question is: How?

Unquestionably, a sensible, careful program is needed to begin dealing with racism in the gay male community. The following is a proposal, based on discussion with others, for a program to start with. It must be remembered that these are only suggestions and that these suggestions are merely a starting point. If every facet of this program is followed, racism will still exist and will still present a problem. This program only suggests a starting place. The only certainty is that a start must be made.

One crucial element must be worked at on all levels. Brian, a city planner, hit on this point: "You cannot turn people around unless you first convince them that the change is in their own best interest." The task is ours to work out.

Step One: Recognition and Discussion of the Problem

To deal with the problems of the gay male community they must be recognized and fully explored. Gay men have never really explored themselves or their feelings as have our lesbian sisters. In order to accomplish this, a series of all-male town meetings are required.

Because racism is the foremost problem in our community this should be the topic of, at least, the first of these meetings. Such meetings could consist of:

a. a panel of Black and White men openly and truthfully discussing the problem of racism and methods for ending it;
b. a psychodrama concerning racism (perhaps provided by Plays for Living) and a discussion following;
c. subsequent meetings to deal with racism through role playing, expert lecturers, and problem-solving sessions

Step Two: Action to End Discrimination and Racism

Led by various community groups (the gay religious groups, the Philadelphia Lesbian and Gay Task Force, Black and White Men Together, Philadelphia Black Gays) a plan of action should be formulated to put a stop to discrimination at all public gathering places for gays:

a. open access to bars and baths should be insisted upon. The use of LCB cards to discriminate against Blacks should be stopped;
b. a meeting of bar owners/managers with the leaders of this anti-racist coalition of community groups should be held to discuss the problem of racism and the role bars play in it;
c. a vigilance committee should be set up to ensure that such discrimination does not continue.

This same coalition of groups should set up another vigilance committee to watch gay publications. Robin points out that "positive images of Blacks are

necessary to ending racism. The truth must be told about the part that Blacks
have played in history. For example, the Black people that were involved in the
Stonewall Riots of 1969 which started the modern gay movement."

Step Three: Continuing Communication
In order for racism to be eradicated, anti-racist activity must be continual.
Our community must also begin to cooperate with the Black community and
support its causes and concerns. As Charles said, "When people show up on
picket lines set up by Black people for Black causes, then I'll know they're
concerned." To this end, various courses of action can be taken:

a. the anti-racist coalition of groups can meet with groups from the Black community
   and offer help;
b. a series of rap groups can be set up and run by PBG or BWMT or some other
   outside agency so that the rap group will have a program and a set procedure;
c. consciousness-raising sessions on the topic of racism should be held at the Gay and
   Lesbian Community Center and perhaps even in some bars;
d. support groups for those interested in continuing the fight against racism should be
   set up and managed;
e. cultural sharing sessions to be held at the Community Center could explore Black
   and White cultures in a positive way, with an emphasis on sharing.

Step Four: Strengthening the Bonds
Gay men have not begun to explore the concept and the comfort of Brotherhood. Our lesbian sisters have long known the joys of Sisterhood. They have,
for a long time, drawn on the strengths and supports inherent in Sisterhood.

Gay men have yet to begin the journey on the long road to Brotherhood. Our
common bonds as men as well as our strengths, weaknesses, and concerns are
still to be explored and exploited.

To this end, a series of Brotherhood meetings should be tried, utilizing the
Community Center and all of our community groups. Our community can only
gain from such exploration.

◆◆◆

PART NINE

Male Sexualities

How do many men learn to desire women? What are men thinking about when they are sexual with women? Are gay men more sexually promiscuous than straight men? Are gay men more obsessed with demonstrating their masculinity than straight men, or are they likely to be more "effeminate?" Recent research indicates that there are no simple answers to these questions. What is increasingly clear though is that men's sexuality, whether homosexual, bisexual, or heterosexual, is experienced as an experience of their gender.

Since there is no anticipatory socialization for homosexuality and bisexuality, future straight and gay men receive the same socialization as boys. As a result, sexuality as a gender enactment is often a similar internal experience for all men. Early socialization teaches us — through masturbation, locker-room conversations, sex-ed classes and conversations with parents, and the tidbits that boys will pick up from various media — that sex is private, pleasurable, guilt provoking, exciting, and phallocentric, and that orgasm is the goal toward which sexual experience is oriented.

The articles in this section explore how male sexualities express issues of masculinity. Alan E. Gross and John Lippert each describes the ways in which male heterosexuality is related to masculinity. Robert Staples explains how the norms of masculinity are expressed in somewhat different ways among black heterosexual males. Fracher and Kimmel argue that men discuss their sexual experiences — both their "successes" and their "failures" — in terms of gender, not pleasure. A man experiencing, for instance, premature ejaculation would be more likely to complain that he wasn't "enough of a man" than that he was unable to feel enough pleasure.

Articles by Stoltenberg, Donnerstein and Linz, and Chris Clark explore some of the controversial political implications of pornography as a source of both straight and gay men's sexual information. Next, Rochlin's questionnaire challenges us to question the normative elements of heterosexuality. In a similar vein, Kinsman argues that we can begin to understand the present lives of gay men only by constructing a "history of heterosexuality." In the past, what we call "homosexual behavior" has always existed, but social definitions and meanings surrounding sexual expression have shifted dramatically — most recently in response to the gay liberation movement.

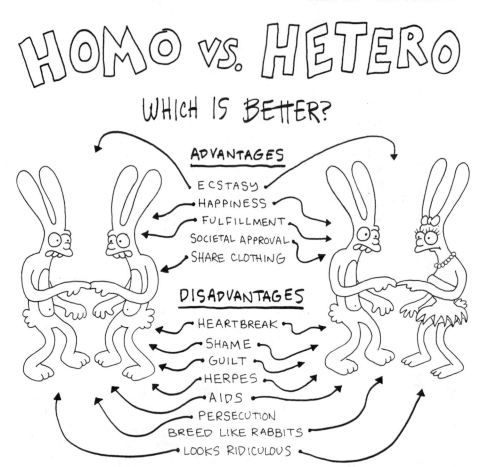

HOMO vs. HETERO
WHICH IS BETTER?

ADVANTAGES
- ECSTASY
- HAPPINESS
- FULFILLMENT
- SOCIETAL APPROVAL
- SHARE CLOTHING

DISADVANTAGES
- HEARTBREAK
- SHAME
- GUILT
- HERPES
- AIDS
- PERSECUTION
- BREED LIKE RABBITS
- LOOKS RIDICULOUS

Cartoon by Matt Groening.

Alan E. Gross

THE MALE ROLE AND HETEROSEXUAL BEHAVIOR

Whether myth or biological fact, men and women generally believe and act as if sex is more central, enjoyable, and necessary for males. For example, responses to an extensive series of interviews with married couples (Rainwater, 1965) indicate that husbands, especially those in the lower economic classes, are much more likely than their wives to find sex enjoyable. A typical husband in Rainwater's sample asserts, "Sex is the most important thing, say 95% of mar-

Revised version of article from *Journal of Social Issues* 34(1), 1978. © 1988 by Alan Gross. Reprinted by permission of the author.

riage" (p. 83). In contrast, many wives in the same sample simply tolerate sex: "He thinks sex is very important . . . He couldn't live without it, I guess. . . . Me, I could do without it; our feelings are completely opposite" (p. 113).

Some men have escaped or resisted socialization forces which encourage them to sexualize relationships, but even these men are usually aware that they must meet the general sexual expectations of others to be considered truly manly. A particularly poignant example of a boy attempting to fulfill sexual role expectations was related in a letter to Ann Landers (1976). The 16-year-old letter writer, responding to a previous letter in which a 15-year-old girl lamented that she had to either "put out or sit home," revealed why the boys in his crowd were sexually aggressive with girls: "Most of us try because we think it's expected. But it's a relief when the answer is no. Then we don't have to prove anything."

Men tend to isolate sex from other social aspects of life. A major consequence of early genital focus, reinforced in adolescence by heavy peer pressure to seek sex in order to validate masculinity (Kanin, 1967), is that men tend to experience sex as separate from other social and psychological aspects of living. At the extreme this tendency may manifest itself as an overwhelming or even exclusive emphasis on sexuality in a relationship. It is probably true that in recent years the purely sexual male image has assumed more subtle forms, but these new low-key seduction styles seem more surface adaptations than evidence that men have relinquished the basic belief that it is necessary to be "on the make" to be masculine.

Fasteau (1974) hypothesizes that isolated sex is a defense against male vulnerability. He believes that when men allow themselves to combine sexual attraction and intimacy, they become dependent on their partner, and that this kind of dependency, especially on a woman, is not compatible with the internalized masculine ideal. A more general explanation for the reluctance of some males to establish deep intimate bonds with women is that women are generally viewed unfavorably (Broverman et al., 1972; McKee & Sherriffs, 1957), and that men, especially men concerned about their masculinity, feel hesitant to relate closely to women because the association is potentially stigmatizing (Brannon, 1976).

Certainly a picture of the male as interested only in isolated sex is overdrawn, but there are recent data which indicate that men more than women are likely to view any heterosexual relationship in a sexual-romance framework (Rytting, 1975). College males in Rytting's study less often made distinctions between friendly and sexual relationships, and were more likely to expect sex as part of the relationship. Additional support for the view of men as evaluating heterosexual relationships along a central sexual-romantic dimension comes from Guinsburg's (1973) study of platonic and romantic relationships. Males in this study had difficulty distinguishing the two kinds of relationships.

From the sex differences which emerge in his study, Rytting proposes that definitions of intimacy from masculine and feminine perspectives differ: Men view "sex as being ubiquitous and therefore a focal point for all relationships with woman," while women distinguish sexual from nonsexual intimacy. Drawing on additional data, especially a negative correlation between perceived sexual behavior and verbal intimacy for males, Rytting concludes that the male perspective leads to indiscriminate sexual decision making and, even worse, tends to inhibit intimacy.

Sexual problems between men and women often develop because genital focus and subsequent sexual isolation in the male are out of phase with female
development. Gagnon and Henderson (1975) have outlined some of the problems that emerge when boys and girls first meet each other sexually in
adolescence:

> The young male, pressed on by his male peers and his prior masculinity
> training . . . pushes for more sexual activity when dating. Conversely,
> many young females . . . spend a good deal of time preventing sexual
> intimacy. Therefore, because of earlier differences in learning how to be
> sexual, males committed to sexuality but less trained in affection and love,
> may interact with females who are committed to love but relatively un-
> trained in sexuality. (p. 38)

These difficulties are not limited to youth. Many adult men find it difficult
or impossible to integrate heterosexual sex with friendship. In the worst cases,
sex becomes so incompatible with emotional closeness that it actually seems to
preempt intimacy.

This sex difference is both reflected and maintained by numerous features of
Western culture. Purely pornographic materials as well as slick sexually-ori-
ented magazines of the *Playboy* genre are aimed at the male market, while emotional love stories are typically found in women's publications. Even the language used by boys and men to denote sexual intercourse is more explicitly
sexual and frequently aggressive, e.g., "screw," "fuck," "bang," as contrasted
with favored female phrases for coitus, such as "make love with," "go to bed
with," which extend the context and diminish sexual/genital connotations
(Sanders, Note 3).

GOALS AND SUCCESS

One of the dominant themes that a boy learns as he approaches manhood is that
success in his work is important, and that success is operationalized in terms of
specific goals. The American male has been characterized as having his eye so
firmly fixed on objectives as he attempts to climb the status ladder that he is
unconcerned with the present quality of his life. This achievement theme has
some obvious implications when it is transferred from the work place to the
sexual arena.

The most direct parallel to goal orientation at work is orgasm orientation in
bed. Preoccupation with orgasm as an indicator of sexual accomplishment not
only applies to the traditional male's selfish attempts to satisfy himself, but it
extends to the modern male-lover's preoccupation with bringing his partner to
climax. As Fasteau (1974) puts it, "Since orgasm is thought to be the only real
point of making love, physically competent performance, delivering the goods,
easily becomes the sole basis for men's sexual self-esteem" (p. 27).

It is not surprising that traditional adult men still count mental notches for
each sexual partner or even for each sexual act, while more sophisticated modern men count the number of orgasms they "produce" for their partners. And
in some subcultures, this quantitative approach to sexuality expresses itself as a
positive association between degree of masculinity and number of children.

While the orgasm itself is a specific goal, many men consider the entire sexual encounter as a goal. Fasteau (1974) observes that "For most men, courting and seduction are nuisances. The focus is almost exclusively on reaching the goal of conquest with all possible speed" (p. 32). Whether the goal is general — "conquest" — or more specific — orgasm — men's concerns with ends often cheat them of process pleasures.

When sex is perceived as goal rather than process, a man may come to value sexual activities not according to his own feelings, but contingent on the feedback he receives from his partner. And women, not insensitive to the frailty of the male sexual ego, often collude by providing the positive responses the man seems to need, ranging from mild verbal praise to passionate histrionics; in one survey (Tavris, 1973) more than two-thirds of women reported faking orgasm.

Perhaps the most deleterious consequence of the male obsession with goals and success is that honest communication is often inhibited between men and their sexual partners. Success or the appearance of success becomes so important to the man that he cannot — and his partner knows he cannot — tolerate critical comments or even friendly suggestions related to his sexual functioning.

CONTROL AND POWER

Not surprisingly, characteristic male behaviors and attitudes associated with maintaining control and power at work and home are commonly found in sexual relationships as well. One means by which a man maintains sexual control is to play the role of initiator.

Carlson concludes that the "initiation of sexual activity is (still) viewed by both spouses as being a husband-oriented activity" (p. 105). A very recent study of college-educated young marrieds yielded data which corroborate Carlson's results that husbands are the primary initiators (Crain and Roth, Note 1). And Peplau et al. (1977) note that virtually all of the men in their sample of college couples exert positive control by playing the role of initiator.

The initiation norm that prescribes that the man must make the first sexual move is usually extended to prescribe male control during the sexual interaction itself.

Safilios-Rothschild (1977) believes that even contemporary women feel uncomfortable taking the sexual lead and that their discomfort may be related to their empathy with the male's fear of losing control: "[Men are] ambivalent in their reactions toward sexually active and skilled women" (p. 112). And some of Komarovsky's (1976) intensive interviews with college males support the notion that men have difficulty accepting sexual invitations from women.

The male role of sexual expert is closely related to a general male caveat against help-seeking. Rugged independence, even when inappropriate or harmful, has become an integral part of traditional masculinity. This is illustrated in a modern fable dealing with the socialization of a young boy (Allen, 1972). The boy is instructed, "You must never ask anyone for help, or even let anyone know that you are confused or frightened. That's part of learning to be a man." In sexual matters, so central to the male ego, admitting ignorance, asking for information, or seeking help are especially difficult. In a recent survey, Skovholt, Nagy, and Epting (Note 4) found that college men were significantly less able than college women to ask sexual questions of a friend.

This male attitude toward admitting ignorance publicly may explain the tremendous burgeoning of sex manuals in the past few years. Although some of these manuals do provide helpful information, many of them tend to promote sex as a purely technical and therefore less human activity. This technical approach to sex has the advantage of allowing private learning, but it permits men to remain in control by appearing to solve difficult human problems within a typical masculine framework which values logic and concrete results (Farrell, 1974).

Like some other aspects of the traditional male role, needs for power and control have important negative effects of heterosexual relationships. When men occupy the role of expert, teacher, initiator, leader, pleasure-giver, etc., women are deprived of experiencing the positive aspects of these roles; moreover men deprive themselves of positively experiencing complementary roles which involve relaxing and receiving pleasure.

AGGRESSION AND VIOLENCE

Probably the most extreme sexual manifestation of male aggression is rape. A number of writers (Brownmiller, 1975; Medea & Thompson, 1974; Russell, 1975) view rape as less an aberrant criminal act than a natural outgrowth of traditional male socialization. Russell, whose analysis is based on accounts of rape by rapists and their victims, suggests:

> [Rape] may be understood as an extreme acting out of the qualities that are regarded as supermasculine in this and many other societies: aggression, force, power, strength, toughness, dominance, competitiveness . . . sex may be the arena where those notions of masculinity are most intensely acted out, particularly by men who feel powerless in the rest of their lives. (p. 260)

Because only a small percentage of men actually commit rape, and even fewer are brought to trial and convicted, there has been a tendency to view sexual aggression as a relatively limited phenomenon applying only to rapists and their victims. A series of interview studies by Eugene Kanin provides a sobering counterpoint to the comforting belief that heterosexual sex offenses are perpetuated only by a small population of deviant criminals. Offenses committed even by males of above average education are so pervasive that in one study (Kanin, 1965) more than 25% of the male undergraduate respondents admitted at least one incident of "sex aggression" since entering college. Sex aggression in this study was defined as a self-reported forceful attempt at coitus that resulted in the victim reacting by "crying, fighting, screaming, pleading, etc." (p. 221).

Both Kanin (1957) and Russell (1975) point out that heterosexual aggression may be encouraged by male fantasies that are commonly portrayed in the media. A dangerous prototype of this sort occurs in Peckinpaugh's violent film, *Straw Dogs*, in which a female rape victim valiantly resists for a few moments before acquiescing and ultimately responding ardently to her attacker. Selkin (1975) provides some evidence that these fantasies are sometimes translated into violent action. He reports that some convicted rapists insist that their victims enjoy sexual assault. Along these lines, Russell (1975), relates this account of a rape: "Her date finally succeeded in raping her after a two-hour struggle, but he could not understand why she was so upset. . . . He considered himself a lover in the tradition of forceful males and expected to have a continuing relationship with her" (p. 258). In milder form, many women can attest to the sometimes unconscious confusion of sex and aggression that emerges in the many forms of "normal" male heterosexual activity.

Although peers probably reward men more for charming and manipulating women into bed than for coercing sex from female victims, it is likely that the overwhelming pressure on men to prove their masculinity via sexual performance indirectly leads to aggression and rape. Kanin (1970) reports that college peer groups, especially fraternities, "stress the erotic goal to such a degree that, in the face of sexual failure, there is a resorting to physical aggression" (p. 35).

TRADITIONAL AND MODERN MALE SEX ROLES

In the popular literature there presently exist at least two popularly held but contradictory characterizations of heterosexual man:

1. Man as exploitative sexual animal, an insensitive user of women, constantly on the prowl, grasping at any sexual opportunity, and gratifying himself quickly with little if any real caring or feeling for his partner.
2. Man as technically competent lover who strives to create multiple orgasmic pleasure for his partner; he asks, or better even senses, what she wants and then endeavors to provide it in his undaunting efforts to satisfy her.

The second, apparently more sensitive characterization has gained prominence in the past few years. Although the evolution from animal to technician (reflected and influenced by the proliferation of modern sex manuals, and perhaps best chronicled in the *Playboy* Advisor column) may at first appear egalitarian and progressive, it can be argued that this shift is basically a superficial one, and in any event largely restricted to the middle class (Rainwater, 1965; Rubin, 1976; Pleck, 1976).

In making a general distinction between modern and traditional sex roles, Pleck (1976) argues that the modern role has not served as a panacea for heterosexual ills; in fact it has brought with it a host of new problems. Using a sexual example, Pleck (Note 6) discusses the shift from the traditional male goal of numerous sexual acts with many women to the more modern goal of sexually satisfying at least one woman. Both goals are quantitative: number of conquests in the former case, number of orgasms in the latter.

Rubin (1976) captures the essence of a related modern problem in an interview with one of several wives in her sample who were preoccupied with their own orgasms "primarily because their husbands' sense of manhood rested on it":

> It's really important for him that I reach a climax and I try to every time. He says it just doesn't make him feel good if I don't. But it's hard enough to do it once! What'll happen if he finds out about those women who have lots of climaxes? (p. 92)

While few contemporary couples retain nostalgia for the days when men could efficiently "exercise marital rights" rather than "make love," it is apparent that the modern male role with its focus on sexual competence has created a whole set of new problems for heterosexual relationships.

NOTES

1. Crain, S., & Roth, S. "Interactional and interpretive processes in sexual initiation in married couples." Paper presented at the meeting of the American Psychological Association, San Francisco, August 1977.

2. Rytting, M. B. "Sex or intimacy: Male and female versions of heterosexual relationships." Paper presented at the meeting of the Midwestern Psychological Association, Chicago, May 1976.

3. Sanders, J. S. *Female and male language in communication with sexual partners.* Paper presented at the meeting of the Association for Women in Psychology, St. Louis, February 1977.

4. Skovholt, T. M., Nagy, F., & Epting, F. "Teaching sexuality to college males." Paper presented at the meeting of the American Psychological Association, Washington, D.C., August 1976.

REFERENCES

Allen, B. Liberating the manchild. *Transactional Analysis Journal*, 1972, *2*, 68–71.

Allen, J. G., & Haccoun, D. M. Sex differences in emotionality: A multidimensional approach. *Human Relations*, 1976, *29*, 711–722.

Balswick, J., & Avertt, C. P. Differences in expressiveness: Gender, interpersonal orientation, and perceived parental expressiveness as contributing factors. *Journal of Marriage and the Family*, February 1977, pp. 121–127.

Balswick, J., & Peek, C. The inexpressive male: A tragedy of American society. *The Family Coordinator*, 1971, *20*, 363–368.

Bardwick, J. M. Psychological conflict and the reproductive system. In J. M. Bardwick, E. Douvan, M. S. Horner, & D. Gutmann (Eds.), *Feminine personality and conflict.* Monterey, CA: Brooks/Cole, 1970.

Bardwick, J. M. *Psychology of women.* New York: Harper & Row, 1971.

Bem, S. L. The measurement of psychological androgyny. *Journal of Consulting and Clinical Psychology*, 1974, *72*, 155–162.

Bengis, I. *Combat in the erogenous zone.* New York: A. A. Knopf, 1972.

Berkowitz, L. *A survey of social psychology.* Hinsdale, IL: Dryden Press, 1975.

Brannon, R. The male sex role: Our culture's blueprint of manhood, and what it's done for us lately. In D. S. David & R. Brannon (Eds.), *The forty-nine percent majority: The male sex role.* Reading, MA: Addison-Wesley, 1976.

Broverman, I. K., Broverman, D. M., Clarkson, F. E., Rosenkrantz, P.S., & Vogel, S. R. Sex-role stereotypes and clinical judgments of mental health. *Journal of Consulting Psychology*, 1972, *34*, 1–7.

Brownmiller, S. *Against our will.* New York: Simon & Schuster, 1975.

Byrne, D. Social psychology and the study of sexual behavior. *Personality and Social Psychology Bulletin*, 1977, *3*, 3–30.

Carlson, J. E. The sexual role. In F. I. Nye (Ed.), *Role structure and analysis of the family.* Beverly Hills, CA: Sage Publications, 1976.

Davies, N. H., & Fisher, A. Liberated sex: The rise and fall of male potency. *Marriage and Divorce*, March/April 1974, pp. 66–69.

Deaux, K. *The behavior of women and men.* Monterey, CA: Brooks/Cole, 1976.

Farrell, W. *The liberated man: Beyond masculinity.* New York: Random House, 1974.

Fasteau, M. F. *The male machine.* New York: McGraw-Hill, 1974.

Freud, S. *Sexuality and the psychology of love.* New York: Macmillan (Collier Books), 1963. (Originally published, 1905.)

Gagnon, J. *Human sexualities.* Glenview, IL: Scott, Foresman and Company, 1977.

Gagnon, J., & Henderson, B. *Human sexuality: An age of ambiguity.* Boston: Educational Associates, 1975.

Gagnon, J., & Simon, W. *Sexual conduct: The social sources of sexuality.* Chicago: Aldine, 1973.

Gingold, J. One of these days — Pow! Right in the kisser: The truth about battered wives. *Ms.*, August 1976, p. 51.

Ginsberg, G. L., Frosch, W. A., & Shapiro, T. The new impotence. *Archives of General Psychiatry*, 1972, *26*, 218–220.

Griffin, S. Rape: The all-American crime. *Ramparts Magazine*, September 1971, pp. 26–35.

Guinsburg, P. F. An investigation of the components of platonic and romantic heterosexual relationships. (Doctoral dissertation, University of North Dakota, 1973). (University Microfilms No. 73-39, 623)

Hunt, M. Today's man. *Redbook*, October 1976, pp. 112–113; 163–170.

Julty, S. A case of "sexual dysfunction." *Ms.*, November 1972, pp. 18–21.

Kaats, G. R., & Davis, K. E. The social psychology of sexual behavior. In L. S. Wrightsman (Ed.), *Social psychology in the seventies*. Monterey, CA: Brooks/ Cole, 1972.

Kanin, E. J. Male aggression in dating-courtship relations. *American Journal of Sociology*, 1957, *63*, 197–204.

Kanin, E. J. Male sex aggression and three psychiatric hypotheses. *Journal of Sex Research*, 1965, *1*, 221–231.

Kanin, E. J. Reference groups and sex conduct norm violations. *The Sociological Quarterly*, 1967, *8*, 495–504.

Kanin, E. J. Selected dyadic aspects of male sex aggression. *Journal of Sex Research*, 1969, *5*.

Kanin, E. J. Sex aggression by college men. *Medical Aspects of Human Sexuality*, September 1970, pp. 28–40.

Kinsey, A., Pomeroy, W. B., & Martin, C. E. *Sexual behavior in the human male*. Philadelphia: W. B. Saunders, 1948.

Kirkpatrick, C., & Kanin, E. Male sex aggression on a university campus. *American Sociological Review*, 1957, *22*, 52–58.

Koedt, A. *The myth of the vaginal orgasm*. Somerville, MA: New England Free Press, 1970.

Komarovsky, M. Cultural contradictions and sex roles. *American Journal of Sociology*, 1946, *52*, 182–89.

Komarovsky, M. *Dilemmas of masculinity: A study of college youth*. New York: W. W. Norton & Company, 1976.

Korda, M. *Male chauvinism: How it works*. New York: Random House, 1973.

Landers, A. One boy's view of sex. The *St. Louis Post-Dispatch*, May 29, 1976.

Maccoby, E. E., & Jacklin, C. N. *The psychology of sex differences*. Stanford, CA: Stanford University Press, 1974.

Masters, W. H., & Johnson, V. E. *Human sexual response*. Boston: Little, Brown & Company, 1966.

Masters, W. H., & Johnson, V. E. *Human sexual inadequacy*. Boston: Little, Brown & Company, 1970.

McKee, J. P., & Sherriffs, A. C. The differential evaluation of males and females. *Journal of Personality*, 1957, *25*, 356–371.

Medea, A., & Thompson, K. *Against rape*. New York: Farrar, Straus, and Giroux, 1974.

Nichols, J. *Men's liberation: A new definition of masculinity*. New York: Penguin Books, 1975.

Nobile, P. What is the new impotence, and who's got it? *Esquire*, 1972, pp. 95–98.

Peplau, L. A., Rubin, Z., & Hill, C. T. Sexual intimacy in dating relationships. *Journal of Social Issues*, 1977, *33* (2), 86–109.

Pietropinto, A., & Simenauer, J. *Beyond the male myth: What women want to know about men's sexuality*. New York: Times Books, 1977.

Pleck, J. H. The male sex role: Definitions, problems, and sources of change. *Journal of Social Issues*, 1976, *32*(3), 155–164.

Rainwater, L. Sexual and marital relations. In *Family Design*. Chicago: Aldine, 1965.

Reik, T. *Sex in men and women: Its emotional variations*. New York: Noonday Press, 1960.

Rook, K. S., & Hammen, C. L. A cognitive perspective on the experience of sexual arousal. *Journal of Social Issues*, 1977, *33*(2).

Rubin, L. *Worlds of pain: Life in the working class family*. New York: Basic Books, 1976.

Russell, D. E. H. *The politics of rape: The victim's perspective*. New York: Stein & Day, 1975.

Rytting, M. B. *Self-disclosure in the development of a heterosexual relationship*. Unpublished doctoral dissertation, Purdue University, 1975.

Safilios-Rothschild, C. *Love, sex and sex roles*. Englewood Cliffs, NJ: Prentice-Hall, 1977.

Sawyer, J. On male liberation. *Liberation*, 1970, *15*, 32–33.

Selkin, J. Rape. *Psychology Today*, August 1975, pp. 70–76.

Sheehy, G. *Passages: Predictable crises of adult life*. New York: E. P. Dutton & Co., 1976.

Singer, M. Sexism and male sexuality. *Issues in Radical Therapy*, 1976, *3*, 11–13.

Stein, M. L. *Lovers, friends, slaves*. New York: Berkeley Publishing Company, 1974.

Tavris, C. Woman & man. In C. Tavris (Ed.), *The female experience*. Del Mar, CA: CRM Publishing Company, 1973.

Tavris, C., & Pope, D. Masculinity: What does it mean to be a man? *Psychology Today*, October 1976, pp. 59–63.

Tavris, C. Men and women report their views on masculinity. *Psychology Today*, August 1977, pp. 34–42; 82.

Tharp, R. G. Dimensions of marriage roles. *Marriage and Family Living*, November 1963, pp. 389–404.

Weis, K., & Borges, S. S. Victimology and rape: The case of the legitimate victim. *Issues in Criminology*, 1973, *8*, 71–115.

John Lippert

SEXUALITY AS CONSUMPTION

I work at a Fisher Body plant over in Elyria, Ohio. And so I spend about sixty hours each week stacking bucket seats onto carts. I used to spend all my time here in Oberlin as a student. But I had to give up that life of comfort as it became financially impossible and as it became psychologically and politically a less and less satisfactory alternative. I still try to remain rigorous about my intellectual growth, though, and so I still take a few courses here at the College. Such a schizophrenic role is at times hard to bear psychologically, and the work load is often staggering. But such a dual life-style also gives me something of a unique perspective on both Oberlin and Fisher Body. I feel this perspective is a useful contribution to this conference on men's sexuality.

One of the things that really surprised me when I went to work for Fisher Body is that it really is hard to go to work every day. I don't know why that surprised me. At first I thought that everyone around me was pretty well adjusted and that I was still an irresponsible hippie at heart. But then I found that just about everyone I know at the plant has to literally struggle to go back to work every day. Again I was surprised, but this time also encouraged, because I made the very casual assumption that I could look to the people around me

Reprinted by permission of Times Change Press, Box 1380, Ojai CA 93023 from *For Men Against Sexism: A Book of Readings*, edited by Jon Snodgrass. Copyright © 1977 by Jon Snodgrass.

for help in facing the strain of that factory. But I soon found that there is nothing "casual" about this kind of support: it is incredibly difficult to find. I have lots of friends now, from all over Northern Ohio and from all different kinds of cultural backgrounds. But most of these relationships seem based on a certain distance, on an assumption that we really do face that factory alone. At first I had to look to see if it was my fault, to see if there was something in me that made it hard to have nurturing relationships with the people I work with. I soon found out that it is my fault, but that it is part of more general phenomena. I began to explore these "phenomena" as completely as I could: this exploration became an essential part of my struggle to go to work every day.

In trying to look at these barriers between me and the people around me, I was struck immediately with the kind of role sexuality plays in mediating the relationships of people in the factory. I spend much time working with men in almost complete isolation from women. I soon found that instead of getting or giving nurture to these men that I was under intense pressure to compete with them. We don't seem to have any specific goal in this competition (such as promotions or status, etc.). Each member of the group seems concerned mainly with exhibiting sexual experience and competency through the competition. Past sexual history is described and compared in some detail: as a newcomer, I was asked to defend my sexual "know-how" within a week of joining the group. Also, we try to degrade each other's sexual competency verbally, through comments like, "Well, why don't you introduce your wife to a *real* man," or "Well, I was at your house last night and taught your wife a few things she didn't know." But it is important to note that none of what happens between men in the plant is considered "sexuality." That remains as what we do with (or to) our women when we get home. And so even though homosexuality is generally considered to be some kind of disease, most men are free to engage in what seems to be a pretty basic need for physical intimacy or reassurance. This can be expressed very simply, through putting arms around shoulders or squeezing knees, but it can also become much more intense and explicit, through stabbing between ass cheeks or pulling at nipples. But all of this physical interaction occurs within this atmosphere of competition. It takes the form of banter, horseplay, thrust and parry seemingly intended to make the need for such physical interaction seem as absurd as possible. But even through this competition, it is easy to see that many, many men enjoy this physical interaction and that they receive a kind of physical satisfaction from it that they just don't get when they go home.

My relationships with women seem somehow equally distorted. Entry of women into the factory is still a relatively recent event, at least recent enough so that contact between men and women is still unique and very noticeable. Much occurs before words are even spoken. Like every other man there, I discuss and evaluate the physical appearance of the women around men. This analysis is at times lengthy and involved, as in "She's pretty nice but her legs are too long in proportion to the rest of her body." Of course this evaluation goes on in places other than the factory, but here it seems particularly universal and intense. Perhaps a reason for this intensity is that the factory is an ugly place to spend eight or ten hours a day, and attractive people are much nicer to look at.

I guess I really do get some sort of satisfaction from engaging in this analysis. But there is an incredible gap between the kind of pleasure I get when I sleep with someone and the kind of pleasure I get when I see someone attractive in the shop. And yet I behave as if there is some connection. Many men are completely unabashed about letting the women know they are being watched and discussed, and some men are quite open about the results of their analysis. Really attractive women have to put up with incredible harassment, from constant propositions to mindless and obscene grunts as they walk by. Men who call out these obscenities can't actually be trying to sleep with the women they are yelling at; they are simply making the women suffer for their beauty.

In this attack they are joined by some older men who just don't like the thought of working with women. Many women have been told they ought to leave the factory and get a husband, and then they are told in some detail what they have to do to get a husband! It is really difficult for women to work in that factory. In many cases women have merely added eight hours a day of boredom and frustration in the factory to eight or more hours a day of housework and childcare at home. And they have to contend with this harassment on top of all that.

But women are getting more secure in the factory. More and more now, men who are particularly offensive in this harassment are responded to in kind, with a flippant, "Up your ass, buddy!" In any case, by the time I get close enough to a woman to actually talk to her, I feel like a real entrepreneur. By that time I've already completed my analysis of the woman's physical appearance, and in the beginning of the conversation we are both trying to find out the results of the analysis. And to reinforce this feeling of entrepreneurship, when I get back to the men I'm working with, I get all kinds of comments like "Did you tap it?" or "Are you going to?"

But one thing that really amazes me about my sexuality at the factory is that it has a large effect on my sexuality at home. I first began to notice this when, in the first week, I began to feel an incredible amount of amorphous and ill-defined sexual energy at the moment I left the plant. This energy makes the drive home pretty exciting and it influences my behavior the rest of the day. I often think something like, "Well, I have two hours before I go back to work, and it would really be nice if I could get my rocks off before then." I found that dissipating this sexual energy really does make it easier to go back. Also, I began to notice that my sexuality was becoming less physically oriented (as in just being close to someone for a while) and more genitally oriented (as in making love and going to sleep). Also, as household chores were becoming more formidable while working, I began to ask people who came to my house — and for some reason, especially my sexual partners — to take more responsibility in keeping the place fixed up.

In trying to understand how my sexuality was being influenced by the factory, this relationship between sexuality at home and at work became an important clue. Working is much more than an eight-hour-a-day diversion; it influences everything I do. If I'm not actually working I'm either recuperating or getting ready to go back. Because I confront this fact every day, it's not hard for me to imagine the changes in my sexuality as essentially in response to the fact that I have to go to work every day.

Now there is an important contradiction in this "I go to work." When I'm at work, I'm not really "me" any more, at least in some very large ways. I don't work *when* I want to; I don't work *because* I want to; I don't work *at* something I'd like to be doing. I don't enjoy my job; I feel no sense of commitment to it;

and I feel no satisfaction when it's completed. I'm a producer; my only significant role is that I make money for Fisher Body. Now Fisher Body values me
highly for this, and at the end of each week they reward me with a paycheck
which is mine to consume as I like. But notice: I have to spend a large part of
that check and much of my time off in preparation for my return to my role as
producer. To a large extent, I don't consume so that I can feel some satisfaction
or something like that. Now In consume so that I can go back to work and
produce. And that part of my consumption which I actually do enjoy is influenced by my work in that what I enjoy has to be as completely removed from
my work as possible. I build elaborate and often expensive systems (such as
families, stereos, or hot rods) into which I can escape from my work each day.
And this is as true of my sexuality as it is true of the music I consume for escape
each day, the car I consume to get back and forth, or the soap I consume to
wash the factory's dirt off me when I get home.

There is an important adjunct to this: the specifically asexual or even anti-
sexual nature of the work I do. For the last three months my role as producer
has consisted of stacking bucket seats on carts. That's it; nothing more and nothing less. Many parts of me are stifled by this type of work; we've all read about
the monotony and so on. What is relevant here is that whatever dynamic and
creative sexual energy I have is ignored for eight hours each day and at the end,
is lost.

I hope that by now a picture is beginning to emerge which explains much of
what is happening to me sexually as a function of this split between my role as
producer and my role as consumer. What is the nature of this picture? The
essential conflict is that in my role as producer, much of what is organic and
natural about my sexuality is ignored for eight hours each day and at the end
lost. I have to spend much of the rest of the day looking for it.

But notice: already I have lost much of what seems such a basic part of me.
My sexuality is something which is no longer mine simply because I am alive.
It is something which I have to look for and, tragically, something which someone else must give to me. And because my need to be sexually revitalized each
day is so great, it becomes the first and most basic part of a contract I need to
make in order to ensure it. The goal of this contract is stability, and it includes
whatever I need to consume: sex, food, clothes, a house, perhaps children. My
partner in this contract is in most cases a woman; by now she is as much a slave
to my need to consume as I am a slave to Fisher Body's need to consume me.
What does she produce? Again: sex, food, clothes, a house, babies. What does
she consume for all this effort? — all the material wealth I can offer plus a life
outside of a brutal and uncompromising labor market. Within this picture, it's
easy to see why many women get bored with sex. They get bored for the same
reason I get bored with stacking bucket seats on carts.

But where did this production/consumption split originate and how does it
exert such a powerful influence over our lives? The essential conflict is that we
really do have to go to work and we really do have to let our employers tell us
what to do. There's nothing mysterious about this. People who will not or can
not make a bargain similar to the one that I have made with Fisher Body are
left to starve. If we are unable to convince ourselves of this by looking around
this room or this College, we need only expand our observation slightly. Furthermore, Fisher Body and other employers have spent decades accumulating
bureaucracies and technologies which are marvelous at producing wealth but

which leave us with some awfully absurd jobs to perform. We have no say in deciding the nature of these jobs; they are designed only from the point of view of profit maximization.

But to question the economic power of Fisher Body is to question most of what is to our lives essential and leads us to an intellectual tradition which most of us find repugnant. But if we are to have an adequate look at our sexuality we must begin with these observations: that our society is largely influenced by two relationships which are universal in our society: *that as producers we are forced into roles which we cannot design and which ignore our sexuality precisely because it is an unprofitable consideration, and that as consumers our sexuality becomes a pawn in our need to escape from the work we do and our need to return to work each day refreshed and ready to begin anew.*

Now what is the power of the conclusion we have just made? It is a conclusion which was reached through the exploration of day-to-day experience, but at this point it is an intellectual abstraction which leaves much out. For instance, it doesn't consider important influences of family and school on sexuality. At this point, the conclusion is general enough to apply equally well to blue and white collar workers (the main conflict is that we really do have to go to work). The conclusion doesn't attempt to explain every detail of the life of every worker. It does, however, attempt to describe a certain dynamic to which those lives respond and certain boundaries within which those lives occur. This conclusion is necessary for us in this conference if only from the point of view of intellectual clarity; we can hardly proceed unless we are aware that we as men and the College as an institution play a particular kind of economic role in society. Enough self-awareness to include the discussion of sexuality is a form of consumption that is simply not available to the mass of the people in our society. And it is to their time spent as producers that we owe our own extravagant consumption.

But what is the political significance of the conclusions we have reached? That is, can our discussion of sexuality affect the evolution of Fisher Body's power over us? For today, the answer seems no, that for today Fisher Body is incredibly strong because, like myself, the majority of people who work for it are basically committed to their jobs. But we need only consider individual survival for a moment to see that it can only be sought in the long run in a collective consciousness which is capable of challenging the power Fisher Body has over our lives. And this is why we need to confront our sexuality; because our sexuality is based on competition among men and at best distorted communication between men and women, it will make building that collective consciousness an incredibly difficult task.

In a short time we in the United States will feel the need for that collective consciousness much more sorely than we feel it today. The Third World is in revolt and the U.S. economy is in the midst of an economic collapse which rivals the collapse of the Thirties in proportions. As a result, we face massive unemployment in this country and the awesome prospect of battles between different groups of people fighting for the "privilege" of working for Fisher Body. If people see that it is only Fisher Body that can gain from such a battle, they may decide not to fight it. And if people see that a victory for Fisher Body means inevitably a return to a lifetime of alienation and oppression inside offices and factories, they may decide to fight instead for the right to control their own lives.

Robert Staples

STEREOTYPES OF BLACK MALE SEXUALITY:
THE FACTS BEHIND THE MYTHS

It is difficult to think of a more controversial role in American society than that of the black male. He is a visible figure on the American scene, yet the least understood and studied of all sex-race groups in the United States. His cultural image is typically one of several types: the sexual superstud, the athlete, and the rapacious criminal. That is how he is perceived in the public consciousness, interpreted in the media and ultimately how he comes to see and internalize his own role. Rarely are we exposed to his more prosaic role as worker, husband, father and American citizen.

The following essay focuses on the stereotypical roles of black male heterosexuality, not to reinforce them, but to penetrate the superficial images of black men as macho, hypersexual, violent and exploitative. Obviuously, there must be some explanation for the dominance of black men in the nation's negative statistics on rape, out-of-wedlock births, and premarital sexual activity. This is an effort to explore the reality behind the image.

BLACK MANHOOD

As a starting point, I see the black male as being in conflict with the normative definition of masculinity. This is a status which few, if any, black males have been able to achieve. Masculinity, as defined in this culture, has always implied a certain autonomy and mastery of one's environment. It can be said that not many white American males have attained this ideal either. Yet, white males did achieve a dominance in the nuclear family. Even that semblance of control was largely to be denied black men. During slavery he could receive the respect and esteem of his wife, children and kinsmen, but he had no formal legal authority over his wife or filial rights from his children. There are numerous and documented instances of the slave-owning class's attempts to undermine his respect and esteem in the eyes of his family.[1]

Beginning with the fact that slave men and women were equally subjugated to the capricious authority of the slaveholder, the African male saw his masculinity challenged by the rape of his woman, sale of his children, the rations issued in the name of the woman and children bearing her name. While those practices may have presaged the beginning of a healteir sexual egalitarianism than was possible for whites, they also provoked contradictions and dilemmas for black men in American society. It led to the black male's self-devaluation as a man and set the stage for internecine conflict within the black community.

A person's sex role identity is crucial to their values, life-style and personality. The black man has always had to confront the contradiction between the normative expectations attached to being male in this society and the proscriptions on his behavior and achievement of goals. He is subjected to societal opprobrium for failing to live up to the standards of manhood on the one hand and for being super macho on the other. It is a classical case of "damned if you do and damned if you don't." In the past there was the assertion that black men were effeminate because they were raised in households with only a female parent or one with a weak father figure. Presently, they are being attacked in literature, in plays, and at conferences as having succumbed to the male chauvinist ideal.

Although the sexual stereotypes apply equally to black men and women, it is the black male who has suffered the worst because of white notions of his hypersexuality. Between 1884 and 1900 more than 2,500 black men were lynched, the majority of whom were accused of sexual interest in white women. Black men, it was said, had a larger penis, a greater sexual capacity and an insatiable sexual appetite. These stereotypes depicted black men as primitive sexual beasts, without the white male's love for home and family.[2] These stereotypes persist in the American consciousness.

It is in the area of black sexual behavior, and black male sexuality in particular, that folk beliefs are abundant but empirical facts few. Yet public policy, sex education and therapeutic programs to deal with the sex-related problems of black people cannot be developed to fit their peculiar needs until we know the nature and dynamics of black sexual behavior. Thus, it is incumbent upon researchers to throw some light on an area enmeshed in undocumented myths and stereotypes.

SEXUALITY OF THE MALE ADOLESCENT

The Kinsey data, cited by Bell,[3] reveal that black males acquire their knowledge about condoms at a later age than white males. The white male learns about sexual intercourse at a later age than black males. Because of poorer nutrition, the black male reaches puberty at a later age than his white male counterpart. A critical distinction between black and white males was the tendency of the more sexually repressed white male to substitute masturbation, fellatio and fantasy for direct sexual intercourse. Masturbation, for instance, was more likely to be the occasion of the first ejaculation for the white male while intercourse was for the black male. A larger percentage of white males reported being sexually aroused by being bitten during sexual activity, seeing a member of the opposite sex in a social situation, seeing themselves nude in the mirror or looking at another man's erect penis, hearing dirty jokes, reading sadomasochistic literature and viewing sexy pictures. Conversely, black males tended to engage in premarital intercourse at earlier ages, to have intercourse and to reach orgasm more frequently. As Bell notes in his analysis of these data, the black male's overabundance of sexuality is a myth. The sexuality of black and white men just tends to take different forms and neither group has any more self-control or moral heroism than the other.

Among young black American males, sexual activity begins at an earlier age, is more frequent and involves more partners. Apparently white males are more likely to confine their associations in the adolescent years with other men. Larson and his associates found that black male adolescents were twice as likely to be romantically involved with women than white males.[4] The kind of rigid gender segregation found in white culture is largely absent from black society. For example, blacks are less likely to be associated with all male clubs, organizations or colleges.

The sexual code of young black males is a permissive one. They do not, for example, divide black women into "good" (suitable for marriage) and "bad" (ineligible for marriage) categories. In the lower income groups, sexual activity is often a measure of masculinity. Thus, there is a greater orientation toward premarital sexual experimentation. In a study of premarital sexual standards among blacks and whites in the 1960's, Ira Reiss found that the sexual permissiveness of white males could be affected by a number of social forces (e.g., religion), but the black male was influenced by none of them.[5] Leanor Johnson and this author found that few black male adolescents were aware of the increased risk of teenage pregnancy, but there was an almost unanimous wish not to impregnate their sexual partner. Another survey of black male high school students reported their group believed that a male respects his partner when he uses a condom.[6]

POVERTY AND THE BLACK FATHER

The period of adolescence, with its social, psychological and physical changes (particularly sex-role identity and sexuality), is the most problematic of the life cycle stages. The prolongation of adolescence in complex technological society and the earlier onset of puberty have served to compound the problem. While adolescents receive various messages to abandon childlike behavior, they are systematically excluded from adult activity such as family planning. This exclusion is justified not only by their incomplete social and emotional maturity, but by their lack of marketable skills which are necessary to command meaningful status-granting jobs. Unskilled adolescents are further disadvantaged if they are members of a minority racial group in a racially stratified society.

Parenthood at this stage of the life cycle is most undesirable. Yet, recent upsurges in teenage pregnancy and parenthood have occurred, specifically among females younger than 14. Approximately 52% of all children born to black women in 1982 were conceived out-of-wedlock. Among black women under age 20, about 75% of all births were out-of-wedlock compared with only 25% of births to young white women.[7] Although the rate of white out-of-wedlock pregnancy is increasing and that of non-whites decreasing, black unwed parenthood remains higher than that of whites.

Because life and family support systems of black males are severely handicapped by the effects of poverty and discrimination, the consequences of becoming a father in adolescence are more serious for the minority parent. Many family planning agencies offer counseling to the unwed mother, while the father is usually involved only superficially or punitively — as when efforts are made to establish legal paternity as a means for assessing financial responsibility. This omission, however, is not unique to black males. It is, perhaps, the single fact of inadequate economic provision which has resulted in the social agencies' premature conclusion that unwed fathers are unwilling to contribute to the future of their child and the support of the mother. Furthermore, sociological theory purports that slavery broke the black man's sense of family responsibility. Thus, it is assumed that black women do not expect nor demand that black men support them in raising their children.

FAMILY PLANNING

Recent evidence, however, suggests that the matrifocality of present theory and social services is myopic. Studies have demonstrated that most unwed fathers are willing to face their feelings and responsibilities.[8] The findings suggest that unmarried black males do not consider family planning a domain of the female, but rather a joint responsibility to be shared by both parents.[9]

Throughout the world one of the most important variables affecting birth rates is the male attitude toward family planning and the genesis of this attitude. Too often we are accustomed to thinking of reproduction as primarily a female responsibility. Since women are the main bearers and main rearers of children in our society, we tend to believe that they should be primarily concerned with planning the size of a family and developing those techniques of contraception consistent with family's earning power, their own health and happiness and the psychological well-being of their children.

However, in a male-dominated world it is women who are given the burden of having and raising children, while it is often men who determine what the magnitude of that burden should be. Unfortunately, the male's wishes in regard to the size of his family are not contingent on the effect of childbearing on the female partner, but are often shaped by his own psychological and status concerns.

Within many societies there is an inseparable link between men's self-image and their ability to have sexual relations with women and the subsequent birth of children from those sexual acts. For example, in Spanish-speaking cultures this masculine norm is embedded in the concept of "machismo." "Machismo," derived from the Latin word "masculus," literally means the ability to produce sperm and thus sire — abilities which define the status of a man in society. In male-dominated society other issues involved in reproduction are subordinated to the male's desire to affirm his virility, which in turn confirms his fulfillment of the masculine role. The research literature tells us that the male virility cult is strongest in countries and among groups where the need for family planning is greatest.

Thus, we find that in underdevloped countries — and among low-income ethnic groups in industrialized societies, including much of the black population in the U.S. — men are resistant to anything but natural controls on the number of children they have. Studies show that males who strongly believe that their masculine status is associated with their virility do not communicate very well with their wives on the subject of family planning. As a result the wives are less effective in limiting their families to the number of children they desire.

SEXUAL AGGRESSION

Sexual attacks against women are pervasive and sharply increasing in this country. The typical rapist is a black male and his victim is most often a black female. However, the most severe penalties for rape are reserved for black males accused of raping white women. Although 50% of those convicted for rape in the South were white males, over 90% of those executed for this crime in that region were black. Most of their alleged victims were white. No white male has ever been executed for raping a black woman.[10]

As is probably true of white females, the incidence of rape of black women is underreported. Ladner reported that an eight-year-old girl has a good chance of being exposed to rape and violence if she is a member of the black under-class.[11] While widespread incidents of this kind are rooted in the sexist sociali-zation of all men in society, it is pronounced among black men who have other symbols of traditional masculinity blocked to them. Various explanations have been put forth to explain why black men seem to adopt the attitudes of the majority group toward black women. Poussaint believes that because white men have historically raped black women with impunity, many black males believe they can do the same.[12]

Sexual violence is also rooted in the dynamics of the black dating game. The majority of black rape victims know their attacker — a friend, relative, or neighbor. Many of the rapes occur after a date and are what Amir describes as misfired attempts at seduction.[13] A typical pattern is for the black male to seek sexual compliance from his date, encounter resistance which he thinks is feigned, and proceed to forcibly obtain his sexual gratification from her. Large numbers of black men believe sexual relations to be their "right" after a certain amount of dating.

Rape, however, is not regarded as the act of a sexually starved male but rather as an aggressive act toward females. Students of the subject suggest that it is a long-delayed reaction against authority and powerlessness. In the case of black men, it is asserted that they grow up feeling emasculated and powerless before reaching manhood. They often encounter women as authority figures and teachers or as the head of their household. These men consequently act out their feelings of powerlessness against black women in the form of sexual aggression. Hence, rape by black men should be viewed as both an aggressive and political act because it occurs in the context of racial discrimination which denies most black men a satisfying manhood.

Manhood in American society is closely tied to the acquisition of wealth. Men of wealth are rarely required to rape women because they can gain sexual access through other means. A female employee who submits to the sexual demands of a male employer in order to advance in her job is as much an unwilling partner in this situation as is the rape victim. The rewards for her sexual compliance are normatively sanctioned, whereas the rapist does not often have the resources to induce such sexual compliance. Moreover, the concept of women as sexual property is at the root of rape. This concept is peculiar to capitalistic, western societies rather than African nations (where the incidence of rape is much lower). For black men, rape is often an act of aggression against women because the kinds of status men can acquire through success in a job is not available to them.

RECOMMENDATIONS

To address the salient issues in black male sexuality, I offer the following recommendations:

1. An educational program for black men must be designed to sensitize them to the need for their responsibility for, and participation in, family planning. This program will best be conducted by other men who can convey the fact that virility is not in and of itself the measure of masculinity. Also, it should be emphasized that the use of contraception — or obtaining a vasectomy — does not diminish a male's virility.
2. An over-all sex education program for both sexes should begin as early as kindergarten, before the male peer group can begin to reinforce attitudes of male dominance. Sex education courses should stress more than the physiological aspects in its course

content. Males should be taught about the responsibility of men in sex relations and procreation. Forms of male contraception should be taught along with female measures of birth control.

3. The lack of alternative forms of role fulfillment available to many men, especially in industrialized societies, must be addressed. In cases of unemployment and underemployment, the male often resorts to the virility cult because it is the only outlet he has for a positive self-image and prestige within his peer group. Thus, we must provide those conditions whereby men can find meaningful employment.

4. Lines of communication must be opened between men and women. A supplement to the educational program for men should be seminars and workshops involving both men and women. Hopefully, this will lead to the kind of dialog between men and women that will sensitize each of them to the feelings of the other.

NOTES

1. Robert Staples, *The Black Family: Essays and Studies.* (Belmont, CA: Wadsworth, 1978.)

2. Robert Staples, *Black Masculinity.* (San Francisco: The Black Scholar Press, 1982.)

3. Alan P. Bell, "Black Sexuality: Fact and Fancy" in R. Staples, ed., *The Black Family: Essays and Studies*, pp. 77–80.

4. David Larson, et al., "Social Factors in the Frequency of Romantic Involvement Among Adolescents." *Adolescence* 11: 7–12, 1976.

5. Ira Reiss, *The Social Context of Premarital Sexual Permissiveness.* (New York: Holt, Rinehart and Winston, 1968.)

6. Leanor Johnson and Robert Staples, "Minority Youth and Family Planning: A Pilot Project." *The Family Coordinator* 28: 534–543, 1978.

7. U.S. Bureau of the Census, *Fertility of American Women.* (Washington, D.C. U.S. Government Printing Office, 1984.)

8. Lisa Connolly, "Boy Fathers." *Human Behavior* 45: 40–43, 1978.

9. B. D. Misra, "Correlates of Males' Attitudes Toward Family Planning" in D. Bogue, ed., *Sociological Contributions to Family Planning Research.* (Chicago: Univ. of Chicago Press, 1967), pp. 161–167.

10. William J. Bowers, *Executions in America.* (Lexington Books, 1974).

11. Joyce Lander, *Tomorrow's Tomorrow: The Black Woman.* (Garden City, New York: Doubleday, 1971.)

12. Alvin Poussaint, *Why Blacks Kill Blacks.* (New York: Emerson-Hall, 1972.)

13. Menachim Amir, "Sociocultural Factors in Forcible Rape" in L. Gross, ed., *Sexual Behavior.* (New York: Spectrum Publications, 1974), pp. 1–12.

Jeffrey Fracher and Michael S. Kimmel[1]

HARD ISSUES AND SOFT SPOTS: COUNSELING MEN ABOUT SEXUALITY

Nothing shows more clearly the extent to which modern society has atomized itself than the isolation in sexual ignorance which exists among us. . . . Many cultures, the most primitive and the most complex, have entertained sexual fears of an irrational sort, but probably our culture is unique in strictly isolating the individual in the fears that society has devised.

— Lionel Trilling[2]

Sam[3] is a 28-year-old white, single factory worker. He lives alone in a two-family home which he owns, and attends night school at a community college. The third of six sons in a blue-collar, Eastern European Catholic family, Sam is a conscientious, hardworking, and responsible man with very traditional values. He describes himself as a sexual late-bloomer, having begun dating only after graduation from an all-male Catholic high school. Although strong and handsome, he has always lacked confidence with women, and describes himself as male peer oriented, actively involved in sports, and spending much of his leisure time with "the boys."

Prior to his first sexual intercourse, two years ago at age 26, Sam had fabricated stories to tell his friends so as not to appear inadequate. He felt a great deal of shame and embarrassment that his public presentation of his sexual exploits had no basis in reality. His limited sexual knowledge caused him great anxiety and difficulty, especially since the woman with whom he was involved had had previous sexual encounters. Upon completion of intercourse, she reported that "he came too fast" (i.e., less than one minute, or after several thrusts), a statement that, he reported, "hit me between the eyes." His second attempt at intercourse was no more successful, inspite of his use of a condom to reduce sensation, and he subsequently broke off this relationship because of the shame and embarrassment about his sexual incompetence, and the fear that word would leak out to his friends. He subsequently developed a secondary pattern of sexual avoidance, and when he first came to treatment, indicating that he was "not a real man because I can't satisfy a woman," he had not had sex for two years, and was reluctant to resume dating until his premature ejaculation was vastly improved.

Joe is a 34-year-old C.P.A. who has been married for three years. The youngest of five children and the only male in a middle class Irish-American family, Joe feels his father had high expectations for him, and exhibited only neutrality or criticism. Joe was without a male role model who conveyed that it was OK to fail. In fact, he portrayed men as strong, competent, without feelings, and without problems or failings, and believes he can never live up to the image his

Reprinted from *Handbook of Counseling and Psychotherapy with Men* (edited by Murray Scher, Mark Stevens, Glenn Good, and Gregg Eichenfield). Newbury Park, CA: Sage Publications, 1987. © 1987 by Sage Publications. Reprinted by permission.

father had for him. Consequently, Joe is terrified that failure to please a woman sexually may result in criticism that will challenge his masculinity; he will not be a "real man." Anticipating this criticism from his wife, his sexual interest is reduced.

When first seen in therapy, Joe evidenced a total lack of sexual interest in his wife, but a high degree of sexual interest involving sexual fantasies, pornography, and masturbation. He said "lust is an obsession with me," indicating a high sex drive when sex is anonymous and though he felt sexually inadequate with his wife, he felt sexually potent with women he devalues, such as prostitutes. He could not understand his almost total lack of sexual interest in his wife.

Bill is a 52-year-old engineer, who has been married for 25 years. From a white, middle-class Protestant background, he has one grown child, and initially came to treatment upon referral from a urologist. He had seen numerous physicians after experiencing erectile dysfunction three years ago, and has actively sought a physical explanation for it.

Bill's wife, Ann, was quite vocal about her disappointment in his failure to perform sexually. Bill had always been the sexual initiator, and Ann had come to expect that he should be in charge. Both believed that the only "real sex" is intercourse with an erect penis. Ann frequently commented that she felt "emotionally empty" without intercourse, thereby adding to his sense of inadequacy. The loss of his capacity for erection, Bill told the therapist, meant that he had lost his masculinity, and he worried openly about displeasing Ann and her possibly leaving him.

His fear of lost masculinity spilled over into his job performance, and he became depressed and withdrew from social activities. Bill was unaware that as an older man, he required more direct penile stimulation for an erection, since he had never required it in the past, and was unable to ask for it from Ann. He felt that a "real man never has to ask his wife for anything sexually," and should be able to perform without her help. The pattern of erectile dysfunction was part of a broader pattern of inability to tolerate failure, and he had begun to lose self-confidence since his masculinity was almost entirely predicated upon erectile functioning. "Nothing else matters," he confided, if his masculinity (evidenced by a functional erection) was not present. Everything was suddenly on the line — his self-worth, his marriage, and his career — if he proved unable to correct his problem.

Sam, Joe, and Bill manifest the three most common sexual complaints of men seeking therapy. But underlying premature ejaculation, inhibited sexual desire, and erectile dysfunction is a common thread, binding these and other sexual problems together. Each fears that his sexual problem damages his sense of masculinity, making him less of a "real man." In a sense, we might say that all three men "suffer" from masculinity.

This chapter will explore how gender becomes one of the key organizing principles of male sexuality, informing and structuring men's sexual experiences. It will discuss how both gender and sexuality are socially constructed, and how therapeutic strategies to help men deal with sexual problems can raise issues of gender identity. This is especially important, of course, since so many therapeutic interventions rely on a diagnostic model that is simultaneously overly individualistic (in that it locates the source of the problem entirely within the individual) and transhistorical (in that it assumes that all cultures exhibit similar patterns at all times). The chapter combines a comparative and historical understanding of how both gender and sexuality are socially constructed with a psychoanalytic understanding of the transformative possibilities contained within the therapeutic relationship. This combination will lead us to discuss both social and therapeutic interventions that might facilitate healthier sexual expression for men.

THE SOCIAL CONSTRUCTION OF SEXUALITY AND MASCULINITY

Sexuality is socially constructed, a learned set of both behaviors and cognitive interpretations of those behaviors. Sexuality is less the product of biological drives than of a socialization process, and this socialization process is specific to any culture at any particular time. This means that "social roles are not vehicles for the expression of sexual impulse but that sexuality becomes a vehicle for expressing the needs of social roles" (Gagnon and Simon, 1973: 45). *That* we are sexual is determined by a biological imperative toward reproduction, but *how* we are sexual — where, when, how often, with whom, and why — has to do with cultural learning, with meanings transmitted in a cultural setting. Sexuality varies from culture to culture; it changes in any one culture over time; it changes over the course of each of our lives. Sexual beings are made and not born; we make ourselves into sexual beings within a cultural framework. Although it may appear counterintuitive, this perspective suggests that the elusive quality commonly called "desire" is actually a relatively unimportant part of sexual conduct. As Gagnon and Simon argue (1973: 103), "the availability of sexual partners, their ages, their incomes, their point in the economic process, their time commitments . . . shape their sexual careers far more than the minor influence of sexual desire." Sexuality is learned in roughly the same way as anything else is learned in our culture. As Gagnon writes (1977: 2):

> In any given society, at any given moment, people become sexual in the same way as they become everything else. Without much reflection, they pick up directions from their social environment. They acquire and assemble meanings, skills and values from the people around them. Their critical choices are often made by going along and drifting. People learn when they are quite young a few of the things that they are expected to be, and continue slowly to accumulate a belief in who they are and ought to be through the rest of childhood, adolescence, and adulthood. Sexual conduct is learned in the same ways and through the same processes; it is acquired and assembled in human interaction, judged and performed in specific cultural and historical worlds.

If sexuality is socially constructed, perhaps the most significant element of the construction, the foundation on which we construct our sexuality, is gender. For men, the notion of masculinity, the cultural definition of manhood, serves as the primary building block of sexuality. It is through our understanding of masculinity that we construct a sexuality, and it is through our sexualities that we confirm the successful construction of our gender identity. Gender informs sexuality; sexuality confirms gender. Thus, men have a lot at stake when they confront a sexual problem: they risk their self-image as men.

Like sexuality, gender in general, and masculinity in particular is socially constructed; that is, what we understand to be masculine varies from culture to culture, over historical time within any one culture, and over the course of any one person's life within any culture. What we consider masculine or feminine in our culture is the result of neither some biological imperative nor some religious requirement, but a socially organized mode of behavior. What is masculine is not set in stone, but historically fluid. The pioneering research on gender by anthropologist Margaret Mead (1935) and others has specified how widely the cultural requirements of masculinity — what it takes to be a "real man" in any particular culture — vary. And these gender categories also shift in any one culture over time. Who would suggest, for example, that what was prescribed among upper class Frenchmen in the eighteenth century — rare silk stockings and red patent leather high heels, prolific amounts of perfume and facial powder, powdered wigs and very long hair, and a rather precious preoccupation with love poems, dainty furniture, and roses — resembles our contemporary version of masculinity?

The assertion of the social construction of sexuality and gender leads naturally to two related questions. First, we need to specify precisely the dimensions of masculinity within contemporary American culture. How is masculinity organized as a normative set of behaviors and attitudes? Second, we need to specify precisely the ways in which this socially constructed gender identity informs male sexual development. How is masculinity expressed through sexuality?

Brannon's (Brannon and David, 1976: 12) summary of the normative structure of contemporary American masculinity is relevant here. Masculinity requires the avoidance and repudiation of all behaviors that are even remotely associated with femininity ("No Sissy Stuff"); this requires a ceaseless patrolling of one's boundaries and an incessant surveillance of one's performances to ensure that one is sufficiently male. Men must be "Big Wheels," since success and status are key determinants of masculinity, and be "Sturdy Oaks," exhuding a manly air of self-confidence, toughness, and self-reliance, as well as reliability. Men must "Give 'em Hell," presenting an aura of aggression and daring, an attitude of constantly "going for it."

The normative organization of masculinity has been verified empirically (cf. Thompson and Pleck, 1986) and has obviously important implications for male sexuality. In a sense, sexuality is the location of the enactment of masculinity; sexuality allows the expression of masculinity. Male sexual socialization informs men that sexuality is the proving ground of adequate gender identity, and provides the script that men will adopt, with individual modification, as the foundation for sexual activity.

In a sense, when we examine the normative sexuality that is constructed from the typical organization of masculinity, it is not so much sexual problems that are of interest, but the problematization of "normal" sexuality, understanding perhaps the pathological elements within normal sexual functioning. This allows us to bridge the chasm between men who experience sexual dysfunction and those who, ostensibly, do not, and explore how men array themselves along a continuum of sexual expressions. Because masculinity provides the basic framework of sexual organization, and because masculinity requires adherence to certain rules that may retard or constrain emotional expression, we might fruitfully explore how even "normal" male sexuality evidences specific pathological symptoms, so that men who present exaggerated versions of these symptoms in therapy may better perceive their problems in a larger, sociological context of gender relations in contemporary society.[4]

The social construction of male sexuality raises a crucial theoretical issue. In the past, both social science research and clinical practice were informed by a model of discrete dichotomies. Categories for analysis implied a dualistic world view in which a phenomenon was classified as either X or Y. Thus, one was either male or female, heterosexual or homosexual, normal or pathological. Since the pioneering studies of Alfred Kinsey and his associates (cf. Kinsey et al., 1948, 1953), however, this traditional model of mutually exclusive dichotomous variables has given way to a model of a continuum of behaviors along which individuals array themselves. The continuum model allows individuals to reposition themselves at different moments in the life course, and it allows the researcher or clinician a point of entry into a relationship with the behaviors being discussed. The people we study and the people we counsel are less some curious "other" and more a variation on a set of behaviors that we, ourselves, embody as well. The articulation of the continuum model also requires that the level of analysis of any behavior include a social analysis of the context for behavior and the social construction of definitions of normality. It thus permits a truly *social* psychology.

THE MALE SEXUAL SCRIPT

Male sexual socialization teaches young men that sex is secret, morally wrong, and pleasurable. The association of sexual pleasure with feelings of guilt and shame is articulated early in the young boy's development, and reinforced throughout the life course by family, school, religion, and media images of sexuality. Young males are instructed, in locker rooms and playgrounds, to detach their emotions from sexual expression. In early masturbatory experience, the logic of detachment accommodates the twin demands of sexual pleasuring and guilt and shame. Later, detachment serves the "healthy" heterosexual male by permitting delay of orgasm in order to please his sexual partner, and serves the "healthy" homosexual male by permitting numerous sexual partners without cluttering up the scene with unpleasant emotional connection. (We will return to an exploration of the similarities between heterosexual and homosexual male sexuality below.)

Detachment requires a self-objectification, a distancing from one's self, and the development of a "secret sexual self" that performs sexual acts according to culturally derived scripts (Gagnon and Simon, 1973: 64). That men use the language of work as metaphors for sexual conduct — "getting the job done," "performing well," "achieving orgasm" — illustrates more than a passing interest in turning everything into a job whose performance can be evaluated; it reinforces detachment so that the body becomes a sexual machine, a performer instead of an authentic actor. The penis is transformed from an organ of sexual pleasure into a "tool," an instrument by which the performance is carried out, a thing, separate from the self. Many men report that they have conversations with their penises, and often cajole, plead with, or demand that they become and remain erect without orgasmic release. The penis can become the man's enemy, ready to engage in the most shameful conspiracy possible: performance failure. Is it any wonder that "performance anxiety" is a normative experience for male sexual behavior?

Men's earliest forays into sexuality, especially masturbation, are the first location of sexual anxiety. Masturbation teaches young men that sexuality is about the detachment of emotions from sex, that sex is important in itself. Second, men learn that sex is something covert, to be hidden; that is, men learn to privatize sexual experience, without skills to share the experience. And masturbation also teaches men that sexuality is phallocentric, that the penis is the center of the sexual universe. Finally, the tools of masturbation, especially sexual fantasy, teach men to objectify the self, to separate the self from the body, to focus on parts of bodies and not whole beings, often to speak of ones self in the third person.

Adolescent sexual socialization reinforces these behavioral demands that govern male sexuality. Passivity is absolutely forbidden, and the young male must attempt to escalate the sexual element at all times. To do otherwise is to avoid "giving 'em hell" and expose potential feminine behaviors. This constant pressure for escalation derives from the phallocentric component to male sexuality — "it only counts if I put it in," a student told one of the authors. Since normative heterosexuality assigns to men the role of "doer" and to women the role of "gatekeeper," determining the level of sexual experience appropriate to any specific situation, this relentless pressure to escalate prevents either the male or the female from experiencing the sexual pleasure of any point along the continuum. No sooner does he "arrive" at a particular sexual experience — touching her breast, for example, than he begins strategizing the ways in which he can escalate, go further. To do less would expose him as less than manly. The female instantly must determine the limits of the encounter and devise the logistics that will prevent escalation if those limits have been reached. Since both male and female maintain a persistent orientation to the future (how to escalate and how to prevent escalation) neither can experience the pleasure of the points en route to full sexual intercourse. In fact, what men learn is that intercourse is the appropriate end-point of any sexual encounter, and that only intercourse "counts" in the tabulation of sexual encounters.

Since the focus is entirely phallocentric and intercourse is the goal to be achieved in adolescent sexual encounters, the stakes regarding sexual performance are extremely high, and consequently so is the anxiety about performance failure. Big wheels and sturdy oaks do not experience sexual dysfunction.

This continuum of male sexual dysfunction — ranging from what we might call the "normatively operative dysfunctional" to the cases of extreme distress of men who present themselves for therapeutic intervention — is reinforced in adult heterosexual relations as well. How do men maintain the sexual distancing and objectification that they perceive are required for healthy functioning? American comedian Woody Allen described, in his nightclub routines, a rather typical male strategy. After describing himself as "a stud," Allen comments:

> While making love, in an effort [pause] to prolong [pause] the moment of ecstasy, I think of baseball players. All right, now you know. So the two of us are making love violently, and she's digging it, so I figure I better start thinking of baseball players pretty quickly. So I figure it's one out, and the Giants are up. Mays lines a single to right. He takes second on a wild pitch. Now she's digging her nails into my neck. I decide to pinch-hint for McCovey. [pause for laughter] Alou pops out. Haller singles,

Mays takes third. Now I've got a first and third situation. Two outs and the Giants are behind by one run. I don't know whether to squeeze or to steal. [pause for laughter] She's been in the shower for ten minutes already. [pause] I can't tell you anymore, this is too personal. [pause] The Giants won.[5]

Readers may be struck by several themes — the imputation of violence, how her pleasure leads to his decision to think of baseball players, the requirement of victory in the baseball game, and the sexual innuendo contained within the baseball language — but the text provides a startlingly honest revelation of male sexual distancing. Here is a device that is so successful at delaying ejaculation that the narrator is rendered utterly unaware of his partner. "She's been in the shower for ten minutes already," Allen remarks, as if he's just noticed.

Much of peer sexual socialization consists of the conveying of these strategic actions that the male can perform to make himself a more adequate sexual partner. Men are often told to think of sports, work, or some other nonsexual event, or to repeat multiplication tables or mathematical formulas in order to keep themselves from premature ejaculation. It's as if sexual adequacy could be measured by time elapsed between penetration and orgasm, and the sexual experience itself is transformed into an endurance test in which pleasure, if present at all, is almost accidental.

The contemporary male sexual script — the normative construction of sexuality — provides a continuum along which men array themselves for the script's enactment. The script contains dicta for sexual distancing, objectification, phallocentrism, and a pressure to become and remain erect without ejaculation for as long as possible, all of which serve as indicators of masculinity as well as sexual potency. Adequate sexual functioning is seen as the proof of masculinity, so sexual problems will inevitably damage male gender identity. This is what makes treatment of sexual disorders a treatment of gender-identity issues.

Although this chapter has concentrated on sexual disorders for heterosexual men, this is neither for analytic reasons nor from a sense of how these problems might manifest differently for gay men. Quite the contrary, in fact. Since gender identity is the key variable in understanding sexual behaviors, we would argue that heterosexual and homosexual men have more in common in regard to their sexuality than they evidence differences. This is especially true since 1969, when the Stonewall riots in New York, and the subsequent emergence of the Gay Liberation Movement, led to the possibility for gay men to recover and repair their "damaged" sense of masculinity. Earlier gay men had been seen as "failed men," but the emergence of the gay male "clone" particularly has dispelled that notion. In the nation's gay ghettos, gay men often enact a hypermasculine ethic, complete with its attendant sexual scripting of distancing, phallocentrism, objectification, and separation of emotion from physical sensation. Another reason that heterosexual and homosexual men exhibit similar genderbased sexual behaviors is that all boys are subject to an anticipatory socialization toward heterosexuality, regardless of their eventual sexual preference. There is no anticipatory socialization toward homosexuality in this culture, so male gender socialization will be enacted with both male and female sexual partners. Finally, we have not focused on gay men as a specific group because to do so would require the marginalization of gay men as a group separate from the normative script of male sexuality. Both gay and straight men are men first, and both have "male sex."

THERAPEUTIC INTERVENTIONS

Our analysis of the social context of men's sexual problems makes it essential that therapeutic strategies remain aware of a context larger than simple symptom remission. Treatment must also challenge the myths, assumptions, and expectations that create the dysfunctional context for male sexual behavior (cf. Kaplan, 1974, 1983; LoPiccolo and LoPiccolo 1978; Tollison and Adams, 1979).

Men seeking treatment for sexual difficulties will most often present with a symptom such as erectile failure, premature ejaculation, or inhibited desire. However, the *response* to this symptom, such as anxiety, depression, or low self-esteem, is usually what brings the man into treatment, and this response derives from the man's relationship to an ideal vision of masculinity. The construction of this masculine ideal, therefore, needs to be addressed, since it often creates the imperative command — to be in a constant state of potential sexual arousal, to achieve and maintain perfectly potent erections on command, and to delay ejaculation for a long time — which results in the performance anxiety that creates the symptom in the first place.

Sex therapy exercises, such as those developed by William Masters and Virginia Johnson and others, are usually effective only when the social context of gender ideals has also been addressed. This is accomplished by exploring and challenging the myths of male sexuality, modeling by the therapist of a different version of masculinity, giving permission to the patient to fail, and self-disclosure by the therapist of the doubts, fears of inadequacy, and other anxieties that all men experience. These will significantly reduce the isolation that the patient may experience, the fear that he is the only man who experiences such sexually linked problems. These methods may be used to reorient men's assumptions about what constitutes masculinity, even though the therapist will be unable to change the entire social edifice that has been constructed on these gender assumptions. Both the cognitive as well as the physical script must be addressed in treating sexual dysfunction; the cognitive script is perhaps the more important.

Recall these specific examples we drew from case materials. Sam's sexual performance was charged with anxiety and shame regarding both female partners and male peers. He was adamant that no one know he was seeking therapy, and went to great lengths to assure that confidentiality be preserved. He revealed significant embarrassment and shame with the therapist in early session, which subsided once the condition was normalized by the therapist.

Sam had grown up with exaggerated expectations of male sexual performance — that men must perform sexually on cue and never experience any sexual difficulty — that were consistent with the social milieu in which he was raised. He held women on a pedestal, and he believed that a man must please a woman or risk losing her. The stakes were thus quite high. Sam was also terrified of appearing "unmanly" with women, which resulted in a high degree of performance anxiety, which, in turn, prompted the premature ejaculation. The cycle of anxiety and failure finally brought Sam to treatment. Finally, Sam was detached from his own sexuality, his own body both sexually and emotionally. His objectification of his penis made it impossible for him to monitor impending ejaculation, and he was therefore unable to moderate the intensity of sensation prior to the point of ejaculatory inevitability. This common pattern among men who experience premature ejaculation suggests that such a response comes not from hypersensitivity but rather an atrophied sensitivity, based on objectification of the phallus.

Sam's treatment consisted of permission to experience this problem from another man, and the attempt by the therapist to normalize the situation and reframe it as a problem any man might encounter. The problem was redefined as a sign of virility rather than an indication of its absence; Sam came to understand his sexual drive as quite high, which led to high levels of excitement that he had not yet learned to control. The therapist presented suggestions to control ejaculation that helped him moderate the intensity of arousal in order to better control his ejaculation. The important work, however, challenged the myths and cognitive script that Sam maintained regarding his sexuality. The attention given to his sexual performance, what he demanded of himself and what he believed women demanded of him, helped him reorient his sexuality into a less performance-oriented style.

Joe, the 34-year-old C.P.A. experienced low sexual desire with his wife though he masturbated regularly. Masturbatory fantasies involving images of women wanting him, finding him highly desirable, populated his fantasy world. When his self-esteem was low, as when he lost his job, for example, his sexual fantasies increased markedly. These fantasies of prowess with devalued women restored, he felt, his worth as a man. Interest in pornography included a script in which women were passive and men in control, very unlike the situation he perceives with his wife. He complained that he is caught in a vicious cycle, since without sexual interest in his wife he's not a "real man," and if he's not a "real man" then he has no sexual desire for her. He suggested that if he could only master a masculine challenge that was not sexual, such as finding another job or another competitive situation, he believed his sexual interest in his wife would increase. He felt he needed the mastery of a masculine challenge to confirm his sense of self as a man, which would then find further conformation in the sexual arena. This adds an empirical confirmation of Gagnon and Simon's argument (1973) that genital sexuality contains many nonsexual motives, including the desire for achievement, power, and peer approval. Joe came to therapy with a great deal of shame at having to be there, and was especially ashamed at having to tell another man about his failures as a man. He was greatly relieved by the therapist's understanding, self-disclosure, and nonjudgmental stance, which enhanced the therapist's credibility and Joe's commitment to treatment.

One cognitive script that Joe challenged in counseling was his embrace of the "madonna/whore" ideology. In this formulation, any woman worth having (the madonna — mother or wife) was perceived as both asexual and as sexually rejecting of him, since his failures rendered him less of a real man. A "whore," on the other hand, would be both sexually available and interested in him, so she is consequently devalued and avoided. He could be sexual with her because the stakes are so low. This reinforces the cultural equation between sexual pleasure and cultural guilt and shame, since Joe would want to be sexual only with those who would not want to be sexual with him. This common motif in male sexual socialization frequently emerges in descriptions of "good girls" and "bad girls" in high school.

Joe's therapy included individual short-term counseling with the goal of helping him see the relationship between his self-esteem and his inhibited sexual desire. Traditional masculine definitions of success were the sole basis for Joe's self-esteem, and these were challenged in the context of a supportive therapeutic environment. The failure of childhood male role models was contrasted with new role models that provide permission to fail and helped Joe view sexuality as noncompetitive and nonachievement-oriented activity. Joe began to experience a return of sexual desire for his wife, as he became less phallocentric and more able to see sex as a vehicle for expressing intimacy and caring rather than a performance for an objectified self and other.

Bill, the 52-year-old married engineer presented with erectile failure, which is part of a larger pattern of intolerance of failure in himself. The failure of his penis to function properly symbolized to him the ultimate collapse of his manhood. Not surprisingly, he had searched for physiological etiologies before seeking psychological counseling, having been referred by a urologist. It is estimated that less than 50% of all men who present themselves for penile implant surgery have a physiological basis for their problem; if so, the percentage of all men who experience erectile disorders whose etiology is physiological is less than 5%. Yet the pressure to salvage a sense of masculinity that might be damaged by a psychological problem leads thousands of men to request surgical prosthesis every year (cf. for example, Tiefer, 1986).

Bill and his wife, Ann, confronted in therapy the myths of male sexuality that they embraced, including such dicta as "a real man always wants sex," "the only real sex is intercourse," and "the man must always be in charge of sex" (cf. Zilbergeld, 1978). The therapist gave Bill permission to fail by telling him that all men at some time experience erectile dysfunction. Further, Bill was counseled that the real problem is not the erectile failure, but his reaction to this event. Exercises were assigned in which Bill obtained an erection through manual stimulation and then purposely lost the erection to desensitize himself to his terrible fear of failure. This helped him overcome the "what if" fear of losing the erection. Bill was counseled to "slow down" his sexual activity, and to focus on the sensations rather than the physical response, both of which were designed to further remove the performance aspects from his sexual activity. Finally, the therapist helped Bill and Ann redefine the notion of masculinity by stating that "a real man is strong enough to take risks, eschew stereotypes, to ask for what he needs sexually from a partner, and, most of all, to tolerate failure."

As Bill and Ann's cognitive script changed, his ability to function sexually improved. Though Bill still does not get full erections on a consistent basis, this fact is no longer catastrophic for him. He and Ann now have a broader script both physically and cognitively, which allows them to have other sexual play and the shared intimacy that it provides.

As one can see from these case studies, several themes run consistently through therapeutic strategies in counseling men about sexual problems, and many of these themes also relate directly to issues of social analysis as well as clinical practice. For example, the therapeutic environment must be experienced as supportive, and care must be taken so that the therapist not appear too threatening or too "successful" to the patient. The gender of the therapist with the male patient will raise different issues at this point. A male therapist can empathize with the patient, and greatly reduce his sense of isolation, whereas a female therapist can provide positive experience with a woman that may translate to nontherapeutic situations.

Second, the presenting symptom should be "normalized," that is it should be cast within the wider frame of male socialization to sexuality. It is not so much that the patient is "bad," "wrong," or "abnormal," but that he has experienced some of the contradictory demands of masculinity in ways that have become dysfunctional for his sexual experiences. It is often crucial to help the patient realize that he is not the only man who experiences these problems, and that these problems are only problems seen from within a certain construct of masculinity.

In this way, the therapist can help the patient to dissociate sexuality from his sense of masculinity, to break the facile identification between sexual performance and masculinity. Masculinity can be confirmed by more than erectile capacity, constant sexual interest, and a long duration of intercourse; in fact, as we have argued, normal male sexuality often requires the dissociation of emotional intimacy and connectedness for adequate sexual functioning. Raising the level of analysis from the treatment of individual symptoms to a social construction of gender and sexuality does not mean abandoning the treatment of the presenting symptoms, but rather retaining their embeddedness in the social context from which they emerge. Counseling men about sexuality involves, along with individualized treatment, the redefinition of what it means to be a man in contemporary American society. Therapeutic treatments pitched at both the social and the individual levels can help men become more expressive lovers and friends and fathers, as well as more "functional" sexual partners. That a man's most important sexual organ is his mind is as true today as ever.

NOTES

1. This paper represents a full collaboration, and our names appear in alphabetical order for convenience. Critical reactions from John Gagnon, Murray Scher, and Mark Stevens have been very helpful.

2. Lionel Trilling, *The Liberal Imagination*. New York: Alfred Knopf, 1954.

3. The names of the individual patients have been changed.

4. To assert a pathological element to what is culturally defined as "normal" is a contentious argument. But such an argument derives logically from assertions about the social construction of gender and sexuality. Perhaps an analogy would prove helpful. One might also argue that given the cultural definition of femininity in our culture, especially the normative prescriptions for how women are supposed to look to be most attractive, *all* women manifest a problematic relationship to food. Even the most "normal" woman, having been socialized in a culture stressing unnatural thinness, will experience some pathological symptoms around eating. This assertion will surely shed a very different light on the treatment of women presenting eating disorders, such as bulemia or anorexia nervosa. Instead of treating them in their *difference* from other women, by contextualizing their symptoms within the larger frame of the construction of femininity in American culture, they can be seen as *exaggerating* an already culturally prescribed problematic relationship to eating. This position has the additional benefit, as it would in the treatment of male sexual disorders, of resisting the temptation to "blame the victim" for her/his acting out an exaggerated version of a traditional script.

5. Woody Allen, *The Nightclub Years*, United Artists Records, 1971. Permission requested.

REFERENCES

Brannon, Robert and Deborah David (1976). *The Forty-Nine Percent Majority.* Reading, MA: Addison-Wesley.

Gagnon, John (1977). *Human Sexualities.* Chicago: Scott, Foresman.

Gagnon, John and William Simon (1973). *Sexual Conduct.* Chicago: Aldine.

Kaplan, Helen Singer (1974). *The New Sex Therapy.* New York: Brunner-Mazel.

Kaplan, Helen Singer (1983). *The Evaluation of Sexual Disorders.* New York: Brunner-Mazel.

Kimmel, Michael, ed. (1987). *Changing Men; New Directions in Research on Men and Masculinity.* Beverly Hills, CA: Sage Publications.

Kinsey, Alfred C., Wardell Pomeroy, and C. Martin (1948). *Sexual Behavior in the Human Male.* Chicago: Saunders.

Kinsey, Alfred C. and Paul Gebhard (1953). *Sexual Behavior in the Human Female.* Chicago: Saunders.

LoPiccolo, J. and L. LoPiccolo (1978). *Handbook of Sex Therapy.* New York: Plenum Press.

Mead, Margaret (1935). *Sex and Temperament in Three Primitive Societies.* New York: William Morrow.

Thompson, Edward and Joseph Pleck (1986). "The Structure of Male Role Norms." *American Behavioral Scientist* 29(5), May–June.

Tiefer, Leonore (1986). "In Pursuit of the Perfect Penis: The Medicalization of Male Sexuality." *American Behavioral Scientist* 29(5).

Tollison, C.D. and H. Adams (1979). *Sexual Disorders: Treatment, Theory, and Research.* New York: Gardner Press.

Wagner, Gorm and Richard Green (1984). *Impotence: Physiological, Psychological, Surgical Diagnosis and Treatment.* New York: Plenum.

Zilbergeld, Bernard (1978). *Male Sexuality.* New York: Simon and Schuster.

John Stoltenberg

PORNOGRAPHY AND FREEDOM

There is a widespread belief today that sexual freedom is an idea whose time has come. But if you look closely at what is supposed to be sexual freedom, you can become very confused.

Let's say, for instance, you understand that a basic principle of sexual freedom is that people should be free to be sexual and that one way to guarantee that freedom is to make sure that sex be free from imposed restraint. That's not a bad idea. But if you happen to look at a magazine photograph in which a woman is bound and gagged and lashed down on a plank with her genital area open to the camera, you might well wonder: where is the freedom from restraint? where's the sexual freedom?

Reprinted from *Changing Men*, Fall 1985.

Adapted from a speech delivered in Washington, D.C., July 1, 1984, at the Ninth National Conference on Men and Masculinity. Copyright © 1985 by John Stoltenberg.

Let's say you understand that people should be free to be sexual and that one way to guarantee that freedom is to make sure that people can feel good about themselves and each other sexually. That's not a bad idea. But if you happen to read random passages from books such as the following, you could become quite perplexed:

> "Baby, you're gonna get fucked tonight like you ain't never been fucked before," he hissed evilly down at her as she struggled fruitlessly against her bonds.

> The man wanted only to abuse and ravish her till she was totally broken and subservient to him. He knelt between her widespread legs and gloated over the cringing little pussy he was about to ram his cock into.

A passage such as that might well make you wonder: where are the good feelings about each other's body? where's the sexual freedom?

Let's say you understand that people should be free to be sexual and that one way to guarantee that freedom is to make sure that people are free from sexualized hate and degradation. But let's say you come upon a passage such as this:

> Reaching into his pocket for the knife again, Ike stepped just inches away from Burl's outstretched body. He slid the knife under Burl's cock and balls, letting the sharp edge of the blade lightly scrape the underside of Burl's nutsac. As if to reassert his power over Burl, Ike grabbed one of the bound man's tautly stretched pecs, clamping down hard over Burl's tit and muscle, latching on as tight as he could. He pushed on the knife, pressing the blade into Burl's skin as hard as possible without cutting him. "Now, you just let us inside that tight black asshole of yours, boy, or else we're gonna cut this off and feed it to the cattle!"

After reading that, you might well ask: where's the freedom from hatred? where's the freedom from degradation? where's the sexual freedom?

Let's say you understand people should be free to be sexual and that one way to guarantee that freedom is to make sure people are not punished for the individuality of their sexuality. And then you find a magazine showing page after page of bodies with their genitals garroted in baling wire and leather thongs, with their genitals tied up and tortured, with heavy weights suspended from rings that pierce their genitals, and the surrounding text makes clear that this mutilation and punishment are experienced as sex acts. And you might wonder in your mind: why must this person suffer punishment in order to experience sexual feelings? why must this person be humiliated and disciplined and whipped and beaten until he bleeds in order to have access to his homoerotic passion? why have the Grand Inquisitor's most repressive and sadistic torture techniques become what people do to each other and call sex? where's the sexual freedom?

FREEDOM AND JUSTICE

If you look back at the books and magazines and movies that have been produced in this country in the name of sexual freedom over the past decade, you've got to wonder: *Why has sexual freedom come to look so much like sexual repres-*

sion? Why has sexual freedom come to look so much like unfreedom? The answer, I believe, has to do with the relationship between freedom and justice, and specifically the relationship between *sexual* freedom and *sexual* justice. When we think of freedom in any other sense, we think of freedom as *the result* of justice. We know that there can't truly *be* any freedom until justice has happened, until justice exists. For any people in history who have struggled for freedom, those people have understood that their freedom exists on the future side of justice. If you told them they should try to have their freedom without there being justice, they would laugh in your face. Freedom *always* exists on the far side of justice. That's perfectly understood — except when it comes to sex.

So-called sexual freedom in this country has never really meant that individuals should have sexual self-determination, that individuals should be free to experience the integrity of their own bodies and be free to act out of that integrity in a way that is totally within their own right to choose. Sexual freedom has never really meant that people should have absolute sovereignty over their own erotic being. And the reason for this is simple: Sexual freedom has never really been about sexual *justice* — between men and women. Instead, it's been about maintaining men's superior status, men's power over women; and it's been about sexualizing women's inferior status, men's subordination of women. Essentially, sexual freedom has been about preserving a sexuality that preserves male supremacy.

What makes male supremacy so insidious, so pervasive, such a seemingly permanent component of all our precious lives, is the fact that erection can be conditioned to it. And orgasm can be habituated to it. There's a cartoon: A man and woman are in bed. He's on top, fucking her. The caption reads: "I can't come unless you pretend to be unconscious." The joke could as well have taken any number of variations: "I can't get hard unless . . . I can't fuck unless . . . I can't get turned on unless . . . I can't feel anything sexual unless. . . ." Then fill in the blanks: "Unless I am possessing you. Unless I am forcing you. Unless I am in control of you. Unless I am humiliating you. Unless I am hurting you. Unless I have broken your will. . . ."

Once sexuality is stuck in male supremacy, all the forms of unjust power at the heart of it become almost physically addictive. All the stuff of our primitive fight-or-flight reflexes — a pounding heart, a hard sweat, heaving lungs — these are all things the body does when it is in terror, when it is lashing out in rage, and these are all things it is perfectly capable of doing during sex acts that are terrifying and sex acts that are vengeful. Domination and subordination — the very essence of injustice and unfreedom — have become culturally eroticized, and we are supposed to believe that giving eroticized domination and subordination free expression is the fullest flowering of sexual freedom.

Some of us know how male-supremacist sexuality feels better than do others. Some of us know how that sexuality feels inside because we do it, or we have done it, or we would like to do it, or we would like to do it more than we get a chance to. It's the sexuality that makes us feel powerful, virile, in control — then utterly empty. Some of us have known how that sexuality feels when it is happening inside someone else, someone who is having sex with us, someone whose body is inhabited by it, someone who is experiencing its particular imperative and having male-supremacist sex against our flesh. And some of us don't really know this sexuality directly; in fact our bodies haven't adapted to male supremacy very successfully at all — it is not the sexuality that moves us, that touches us, that comes anywhere near feeling as good as we imagine we want our sexual feelings to feel. We don't recognize a longing for anything like it in our own bodies, and we've been lucky so far — very lucky — not to have experienced it *against* our bodies. Nonetheless, we know that it exists; and the more we know about pornography, the more we know what it looks like.

PORNOGRAPHY AND MALE SUPREMACY

Male-supremacist sexuality is important to pornography, and pornography is important to male supremacy. Pornography *institutionalizes* the sexuality that both embodies and enacts male supremacy. Pornography says about that sexuality, "Here's how." Here's how to act out male supremacy in sex. Here's how the action should go. Here are the acts that impose power over and against another body. And pornography says about that sexuality, "Here's who." Here's who you should do it to and here's who she is: your whore, your piece of ass, yours. Your penis is a weapon, her body is your target. And pornography says about that sexuality, "Here's why": Because men are masters, women are slaves; men are superior, women are subordinate; men are real, women are objects; men are sex machines, women are sluts.

Pornography institutionalizes male supremacy the way segregation institutionalizes white supremacy. It is a practice embodying an ideology of biological superiority; it is an institution that both expresses that ideology and enacts that ideology — makes it the reality that people believe is true, keeps it that way, keeps people from knowing any other possibility, keeps certain people powerful by keeping certain people *down*.

Pornography also *eroticizes* male supremacy. It makes dominance and subordination feel like sex; it makes hierarchy feel like sex; it makes force and violence feel like sex; it makes hate and terrorism feel like sex; it makes inequality feel like sex. Pornography keeps sexism sexy. It keeps sexism *necessary* for some people to have sexual feelings. It makes reciprocity make you go limp. It makes mutuality leave you cold. It makes tenderness and intimacy and caring make you feel like you're going to disappear into a void. It makes justice the opposite of erotic; it makes injustice a sexual thrill.

Pornography exploits every experience in people's lives that *imprisons* sexual feelings — pain, terrorism, punishment, dread, shame, powerlessness, self-hate — and would have you believe that it *frees* sexual feelings. In fact the sexual freedom represented by pornography is the freedom of men to act sexually in ways that keep sex a basis for inequality.

You can't have authentic sexual freedom without sexual justice. It is only freedom for those in power; the powerless cannot be free. Their experience of sexual freedom becomes only a delusion borne of complying with the demands of the powerful. Increased sexual freedom under male supremacy has had to mean an increased tolerance for sexual practices that are predicated on eroticized injustice between men and women: treating women's bodies or body parts as merely sexual objects or things; treating women as utterly submissive masochists who enjoy pain and humiliation and who, if they are raped, enjoy it; treating women's bodies to sexualized beating, mutilation, bondage, dismemberment. . . . Once you have sexualized inequality, once it is a learned and internalized prerequisite for sexual arousal and sexual gratification, then anything goes. And that's what sexual freedom means on this side of sexual justice.

PORNOGRAPHY AND HOMOPHOBIA

Homophobia is absolutely integral to the system of sexualized male supremacy. Cultural homophobia expresses a whole range of antifemale revulsion: It expresses contempt for men who are sexual with men because they are believed to be "treated like a woman" in sex. It expresses contempt for women who are sexual with women just *because* they are women and also because they are perceived to be a rebuke to the primacy of the penis. Notwithstanding all the macho, hypermasculine posturing by some of our gay male contemporaries and notwithstanding recent lesbian emulations of male sexual sadism, the fact remains that cultural homophobia is a byproduct of cultural misogyny: The faggot is stigmatized because he is perceived to participate in the degraded status of the female; the dyke is held in contempt already as a woman and even more so for having the gall not to flatter the phallic ego. The notion that you can erode homophobia while leaving male supremacy and misogyny in place has got to be one of the most ill-conceived bases for a political movement in recent history. Gay liberation without women's liberation can't possibly happen. Gay rights without women's rights is a male-supremacist reform.

Cultural homophobia is not merely an expression of woman hating; it also functions to protect men from the sexual aggression of other men. Homophobia keeps men doing to women what they would not want done to themselves. Cultural homophobia acts as a check on male sexual aggression, keeps it directed toward women. Homophobia keeps men acting in concert as male supremacists so that they won't be perceived as an appropriate target for male-supremacist sexual treatment. Male supremacy *requires* homophobia in order to keep men safe from the sexual aggression of men. Imagine this country without homophobia: There would be a woman raped every three minutes and a man raped every three minutes. Homophobia keeps that statistic at a manageable level. The system is not fool-proof, of course. It breaks down, for instance, in prison and in childhood — when men and boys are often subject to the same sexual terrorism that women live with almost all the time. But for the most part homophobia serves male supremacy by keeping males who act like real men safe from sexual assault. So if you think that within the social structure of male supremacy you can carve out a little personal space free of homophobia, you're wrong; if you think male supremacy is going to yield on systematized homophobia, you're out of your mind.

Pornography is one of the major enforcers of cultural homophobia. Pornography is rife with gay-baiting and effemiphobia. Portrayals of allegedly lesbian "scenes" are a staple of heterosexual pornography: The women with each other are there for the male viewer, the male voyeur; there is not the scantest evidence that they are there for each other. So-called men's sophisticate magazines — the "skin" magazines — outdo one another in their insults against feminists, who are typically derided as "sapphic" at best, "lezzies" at worst. The inuendo that a man is a fairy or a faggot is, in pornography, a kind of dare or a challenge to prove his cocksmanship. And throughout pornography, the male who is perceived to be the passive orifice in sex is tainted with the disdain that "normally" belongs to women.

Meanwhile gay male pornography, which often appears to present an ideal-ized, all-male, superbutch world, also contains frequent derogatory references to women, or to feminized males. In order to give vent to male sexual aggression and sadism in homosexual pornography and to also circumvent the cultural stigma that ordinarily attaches to men who are "treated like a woman" in sex, gay male pornography has developed several specific "codes." One such code is that a man who is "capable" of withstanding "discipline" — extremely punishing bondage, humiliation and fist-fucking, for instance — is deemed to have achieved a kind of supermasculinity, almost as if the sexual violence his body ingests from another man enhances his own sexual identity as a man. (This is quite the reverse in heterosexual pornography, where sexual sadism against a woman simply confirms her in her subordinate status.) Another code common in gay male pornography, one found frequently in films, is that if a man is shown being ass-fucked, he will generally be shown ass-fucking someone else in turn — this to avoid the connotation that he is at all feminized by being fucked. Still another code in gay male pornography is that depictions of mu-tuality are not sustained for very long without an intimation or explicit scene of force or coercion — so you don't go limp out of boredom or anxiety that you've been suckered into a scene where there's no raw male power present.

There is, not surprisingly, an intimate connection between the male suprem-acy in both heterosexual and homosexual pornography and the woman hating and femiphobia in them both as well. That connection is male-supremacist sex — the social power of men over women acted out as eroticized domination and subordination. The difference is that gay male pornography invents a way for men to be the *objects* of male-supremacist sex without seeming to be its *vic-tims*. In its own peculiar fashion, gay male pornography keeps men safe from male-supremacist sex — by holding out the promise that you'll come away from it more a man. Needless to say, for homosexual men who buy into this, it can become a really important part of one's sexual identity as a gay man. Because if you think the problem facing you is that your masculinity is in doubt because you're queer, then the promise of gay male pornography looks like forgiveness and redemption. Not to mention what it feels like: communion with true virility.

Now this is the situation of men within male supremacy: Whether we are straight or gay, we have been looking for a sexual freedom that is utterly spe-cious, and we have been looking for it through pornography, which perpetuates the very domination and subordination that stand in the way of sexual justice. Whether we are straight or gay, we have been looking for a notion of freedom that leaves out women; we have been looking for a sexuality that preserves men's power over women. So long as that is what we strive for, we cannot possibly feel freely, and no one can be free. Whatever sexual freedom might be, it must be after justice.

FREEDOM AND EQUALITY

Historically, when people have not had justice and when people have not had freedom, they have had only the material reality of injustice and unfreedom. When freedom and justice don't exist, they're but a dream and a vision, an abstract idea longed for. You can't really know what justice would be like or what freedom would feel like. You can only know how it feels *not* to have them, and what it feels like to hope, to imagine, to desire them with a passion. Sexual freedom is an idea whose time has *not* come. It can't possibly be truly experienced until there is sexual justice. And sexual justice is incompatible with a definition of freedom that is based on the subordination of women.

Equality is still a radical idea. It makes some people very angry. It also gives some people hope.

When equality is an idea whose time has come, we will perhaps know sex with justice, we will perhaps know passion with compassion, we will perhaps know affection and ardor with honor. In that time, when the integrity within everyone's body and the whole personhood of each person is celebrated whenever two people touch, we will perhaps truly know the freedom to be sexual in a world of real equality.

According to pornography, you can't get there from here. According to male supremacy, you should not even want to try.

Edward Donnerstein and Daniel Linz

MASS MEDIA SEXUAL VIOLENCE AND MALE VIEWERS:
CURRENT THEORY AND RESEARCH

The influence of pornography on male viewers has been a topic of concern for behavioral scientists for many years, as well as a recent volatile political and legal question. Often research on pornography and its effects on behavior or attitudes are concerned with sexual explicitness. But it is not an issue of sexual explicitness; rather, it is an issue of violence against women and the role of women in "pornography" that is of concern to us here. Research over the last decade has demonstrated that sexual images per se do not facilitate aggressive behavior, change rape-related attitudes, or influence other forms of antisocial behaviors or perceptions. It is the violent images in pornography that account for the various research effects. This will become clearer as the research on the effects of sexual violence in the media is discussed. It is for these and other reasons that the terms *aggressive pornography* and *sexually violent mass media images* are preferred. We will occasionally use the term *pornography* in this article for communication and convenience.

In this chapter we will examine both the research on aggressive pornography and the research that examines nonpornographic media images of violence against women — the major focus of recent research and the material that provokes negative reactions. Our final section will examine the research on nonviolent pornography. We will also refer to various ways in which this research has

Reprinted from *American Behavioral Scientist*, 29(5), May/June 1986. © 1986 by Sage Publications. Reprinted by permission.

AUTHORS' NOTE: This research was partially funded by National Science Foundation Grant BNS-8216772 to the first author and Steven Penrod.

been applied to the current political debate on pornography and offer suggestions to mitigate the negative effects from exposure to certain forms of pornography and sexually violent mass media.

RESEARCH ON THE EFFECTS OF AGGRESSIVE PORNOGRAPHY

Aggressive pornography, as used here, refers to X-rated images of sexual coercion in which force is used or implied against a woman in order to obtain certain sexual acts, as in scenes of rape and other forms of sexual assault. One unique feature of these images is their reliance upon "positive victim outcomes," in which rape and other sexual assaults are depicted as pleasurable, sexually arousing, and beneficial to the female victim. In contrast to other forms of media violence in which victims suffer, die, and do not enjoy their victimization, aggressive pornography paints a rosy picture of aggression. The myths regarding violence against women are central to the various influences this material has upon the viewer. This does not imply that there are not images of suffering, mutilation, and death — there are. The large majority of images, however, show violence against women as justified, positive, and sexually liberating. Even these more "realistic" images, however, can influence certain viewers under specific conditions. We will address this research later.

There is some evidence that these images increased through the 1970s (Malamuth & Spinner, 1980). However, more recent content analysis suggests that the increase has abated in the 1980s (Scott, 1985). The Presidential Commission on Obscenity and Pornography of 1970 did not examine the influence of aggressive pornography, mainly because of its low frequency. This is important to note, as it highlights differences between the commission and the position outlined in this chapter. The major difference is not in the findings but in the type of material being examined. (The Commission on Obscenity and Pornography was interested only in sexually explicit media images.)

In many aggressive pornographic depictions, as noted, the victim is portrayed as secretly desiring the assault and as eventually deriving sexual pleasure from it (Donnerstein & Berkowitz, 1982; Malamuth, Heim, & Feshbach, 1980). From a cognitive perspective, such information may suggest to the viewer that even if a woman seems repelled by a pursuer, eventually she will respond favorably to forceful advances, aggression, and overpowering by a male assailant (Brownmiller, 1975). The victim's pleasure could further heighten the aggressor's. Viewers might then come to think, at least for a short while, that their own sexual aggression would also be profitable, thus reducing restraints or inhibitions against aggression (Bandura, 1977). These views diminish the moral reprehensibility of any witnessed assault on a woman and, indeed, suggest that the sexual attack may have a highly desirable outcome for both victim and aggressor. Men having such beliefs might therefore be more likely to attack a woman after they see a supposedly "pleasurable" rape. Furthermore, as there is a substantial aggressive component in the sexual assault, it could be argued that the favorable outcome lowers the observers' restraints against aggression toward women. Empirical research in the last few years, which is examined below, as well as such cases as the New Bedford rape, in which onlookers are reported to have cheered the rape of a woman by several men, suggests that the above concerns may be warranted.

AGGRESSIVE PORNOGRAPHY AND SEXUAL AROUSAL

Although it was once believed that only rapists show sexual arousal to depictions of rape and other forms of aggression against women (Abel, Barlow, Blanchard, & Guild, 1977), research by Malamuth and his colleagues (Malamuth, 1981b, 1984; Malamuth & Check, 1983; Malamuth & Donnerstein, 1982; Malamuth, Haber, & Feshbach, 1980; Malamuth, Heim, & Feshbach, 1980) indicates that a nonrapist population will show evidence of increased sexual arousal to media-presented images of rape. This increased arousal primarily occurs when the female victim shows signs of pleasure and arousal, the theme most commonly presented in aggressive pornography. In addition, male subjects who indicate that there is some likelihood that they themselves would rape display increased sexual arousal to all forms of rape depictions, similar to the reactions of known rapists (Malamuth, 1981a, 1981b; Malamuth & Donnerstein, 1982). Researchers have suggested that this sexual arousal measure serves as an objective index of a proclivity to rape. Using this index, an individual whose sexual arousal to rape themes was found to be similar to or greater than his arousal to nonaggressive depictions would be considered to have an inclination to rape (Abel et al., 1977; Malamuth, 1981a; Malamuth & Donnerstein, 1982).

AGGRESSIVE PORNOGRAPHY AND ATTITUDES TOWARD RAPE

There are now considerable data indicating that exposure to aggressive pornography may alter the observer's perception of rape and the rape victim. For example, exposure to a sexually explicit rape scene in which the victim shows a "positive" reaction tends to produce a lessened sensitivity to rape (Malamuth & Check, 1983), increased acceptance of rape myths and interpersonal violence against women (Malamuth & Check, 1981), and increases in the self-reported possibility of raping (Malamuth, 1981a). This self-reported possibility of committing rape is highly correlated with (a) sexual arousal to rape stimuli, (b) aggressive behavior and a desire to hurt women, and (c) a belief that rape would be a sexually arousing experience for the rapist (see Malamuth, 1981a; Malamuth & Donnerstein, 1982). Exposure to aggressive pornography may also lead to self-generated rape fantasies (Malamuth, 1981b).

AGGRESSIVE PORNOGRAPHY AND
AGGRESSION AGAINST WOMEN

Recent research (Donnerstein, 1980a, 1980b, 1983, 1984; Donnerstein & Berkowitz, 1982) has found that exposure to aggressive pornography increases aggression against women in a laboratory context. The same exposure does not seem to influence aggression against other men. This increased aggression is most pronounced when the aggression is seen as positive for the victim and occurs for both angered and nonangered individuals.

Although this research suggests that aggressive pornography can influence the male viewer, the relative contribution of the sexual and the aggressive components of the material remains unclear. Is it the sexual nature of the material or the messages about violence that are crucial? This is an extremely important question. In many discussions of this research the fact that the material is aggressive is forgotten and it is assumed that the effects occur owing to the sexual nature of the material. As we noted earlier, the sexual nature of the material is not the major issue. Recent empirical studies shed some light on this issue.

THE INFLUENCE OF NONPORNOGRAPHIC DEPICTIONS OF VIOLENCE AGAINST WOMEN

It has been alleged that images of violence against women have increased not only in pornographic materials but also in more readily accessible mass media materials ("War Against Pornography," 1985). Scenes of rape and violence have appeared in daytime TV soap operas and R-rated movies shown on cable television. These images are sometimes accompanied by the theme, common in aggressive pornography, that women enjoy or benefit from sexual violence. For example, several episodes of the daytime drama *General Hospital* were devoted to a rape of one of the well known female characters by an equally popular male character. At first the victim was humiliated; later the two characters were married. A similar theme was expressed in the popular film, *The Getaway*. In this film, described by Malamuth and Check (1981):

> Violence against women is carried out both by the hero and the antagonist. The hero, played by Steve McQueen, is portrayed in a very "macho" image. At one point, he slaps his wife several times causing her to cry from the pain. The wife, played by Ali McGraw, is portrayed as deserving this beating. As well, the antagonist in the movie kidnaps a woman (Sally Struthers) and her husband. He rapes the woman but the assault is portrayed in a manner such that the woman is depicted as a willing participant. She becomes the antagonist's girlfriend and they both taunt her husband until he commits suicide. The woman then willingly continues with the assailant and at one point frantically searches for him. (p. 439)

In a field experiment, Malamuth and Check (1981a) attempted to determine whether or not the depiction of sexual violence contained in *The Getaway* and in another film with similar content influenced the viewers' perceptions of attitudes toward women. A total of 271 male and female students participated in a study that they were led to believe focused on movie ratings. One group watched, on two different evenings, *The Getaway* and *Swept Away* (which also shows women as victims of aggression within erotic contexts). A group of control subjects watched neutral, feature-length movies. These movies were viewed in campus theaters as part of the Campus Film Program. The results of a "Sexual Attitudes Survey," conducted several days after the screenings, indicated that viewing the sexually aggressive films significantly increased male but not female acceptance of interpersonal violence and tended to increase rape myth acceptance. These effects occurred not with X-rated materials but with more "prime-time" materials.

A recent study by Donnerstein and Berkowitz (1985) sought to examine more systematically the relative contributions of aggressive and sexual components of aggressive pornography. In a series of studies, male subjects were shown one of four different films: (1) the standard aggressive pornography used in studies discussed earlier, (2) an X-rated film that contained no forms of aggression or coercion and was rated by subjects to be as sexual as the first; (3) a film that contained scenes of aggression against a woman but without any sexual content and was considered less sexual and also less arousing (physiologically) than were the previous two films; and (4) a neutral film. Although the aggressive pornographic film led to the highest aggression against women, the aggression-only film produced more aggressive behavior than did the sex-only film. In fact, the sex-only film produced no different results than did the neutral film. Subjects were also examined for their attitudes about rape and their willingness to say they might commit a rape. The most callous attitudes and the highest percentage indicating some likelihood to rape were found in the aggression-only conditions; the X-rated sex-only film was the lowest.

This research suggests that violence against women need not occur in pornographic or sexually explicit context in order for the depictions to have an impact on both attitudes and behavior. Angered individuals became more aggressive toward a female target after exposure to films judged not to be sexually arousing but that depict a woman as a victim of aggression. This supports the claim by Malamuth and Check (1983) that sexual violence against women need not be portrayed in a pornographic fashion for greater acceptance of interpersonal violence and rape myths.

In the Malamuth and Check study the victim's reaction to sexual violence was always, in the end, a positive one. Presumably the individual viewer of nonsexually explicit rape depictions with a positive outcome comes to accept the view that aggression against women is permissible because women enjoy sexual violence. In the studies by Donnerstein and Berkowitz, however, several other processes may have been at work. Exposure to nonpornographic aggression against women resulted in the highest levels of aggressive behavior when subjects were first angered by a female confederate of the experimenter or when the victim of aggression in the film and the female confederate were linked by the same name. Presumably, subjects did not come to perceive violence as acceptable because victims enjoy violence from this material. Instead, the cue value or association of women with the characters in the film (Berkowitz, 1974) and the possibility that the pain cues stimulated aggression in angry individuals might better account for the findings. When the individual is placed in a situation in which cues associated with aggressive responses are salient (for example, a situation involving a female victim) or one in which he is predisposed to aggression because he is angered, he will be more likely to respond aggressively both because of the stimulus–response connection previously built up through exposure to the films and/or because the pain and suffering of the victim reinforce already established aggressive tendencies.

An important element in the effects of exposure to aggressive pornography is violence against women. Because much commercially available media contain such images, researchers have begun to examine the impact of more popular film depictions of violence against women. Of particular interest have been R-rated "slasher" films, which combine graphic and brutal violence against women within a sexual context. These types of materials do not fit the general definition of pornography, but we believe their impact is stronger.

THE EFFECTS OF EXPOSURE TO
R-RATED SEXUALIZED VIOLENCE

In a recent address before the International Conference on Film Classification and Regulation, Lord Harlech of the British Film Board noted the increase in

R-rated sexually violent films and their "eroticizing" and "glorification" of rape and other forms of sexual violence. According to Harlech:

> Everyone knows that murder is wrong, but a strange myth has grown up, and been seized on by filmmakers, that rape is really not so bad, that it may even be a form of liberation for the victim, who may be acting out what she secretly desires — and perhaps needs — with no harm done. . . . Filmmakers in recent years have used rape as an exciting and titillating spectacle in pornographic films, which are always designed to appeal to men.

As depictions of sex and violence become increasingly graphic, especially in feature-length movies shown in theaters, officials at the National Institute of Mental Health are becoming concerned:

> Films had to be made more and more powerful in their arousal effects. Initially, strong excitatory reactions [may grow] weak or vanish entirely with repeated exposure to stimuli of a certain kind. This is known as "habituation." The possibility of habituation to sex and violence has significant social consequences. For one, it makes pointless the search for stronger and stronger arousers. But more important is its potential impact on real life behavior. If people become inured to violence from seeing much of it, they may be less likely to respond to real violence.

This loss of sensitivity to real violence after repeated exposure to films with sex and violence, or "the dilemma of the detached bystander in the presence of violence," is currently a concern of our research program. Although initial exposure to a violent rape scene may act to create anxiety and inhibitions about such behavior, researchers have suggested that repeated exposure to such material could counter these effects. The effects of long-term exposure to R-rated sexually violent mass media portrayals are the major focus of our ongoing research program investigating how massive exposure to commercially released violent and sexually violent films influence (1) viewer perceptions of violence, (2) judgments about rape and rape victims, (3) general physiological desensitization to violence, and (4) aggressive behavior.

This research presents a new approach to the study of mass media violence. First, unlike many previous studies in which individuals may have seen only 10–30 minutes of material, the current studies examine 10 hours of exposure. Second, we are able to monitor the process of subject's desensitization over a longer period of time than in previous experiments. Third, we examine perceptual and judgmental changes regarding violence, particularly violence against women.

In the program's first study, Linz, Donnerstein, and Penrod (1984) monitored desensitization of males to filmed violence against women to determine whether this desensitization "spilled over" into other kinds of decision making about victims. Male subjects watched nearly 10 hours (five commercially released feature-length films, one a day for five days) of R-rated or X-rated fare — either R-rated sexually violent films such as *Tool Box Murders, Vice Squad, I Spit on Your Grave, Texas Chainsaw Massacre;* X-rated movies that depicted sexual assault; or X-rated movies that depicted only consensual sex (nonviolent). The R-rated films were much more explicit with regard to violence than they were with

regard to sexual content. After each movie the men completed a mood questionnaire and evaluated the films on several dimensions. The films were coun-
terbalanced so that comparisons could be made of the same films being shown
on the first and last day of viewing. Before participation in the study subjects
were screened for levels of hostility, and only those with low hostility scores
were included to help guard against the possibility of an overly hostile individual imitating the filmed violence during the week of the films. This is also
theoretically important because it suggests that any effects we found would
occur with a normal population. (It has been suggested by critics of media violence research that only those who are already predisposed toward violence are
influenced by exposure to media violence. In this study, those individuals have
been eliminated.) After the week of viewing the men watched yet another film.
This time, however, they saw a videotaped reenactment of an actual rape trial.
After the trial they were asked to render judgments about how responsible the
victim was for her own rape and how much injury she had suffered.

Most interesting were the results from the men who had watched the R-rated
films such as *Texas Chainsaw Massacre* or *Maniac*. Initially, after the first day of
viewing, the men rated themselves significantly above the norm for depression,
anxiety, and annoyance on a mood adjective checklist. After each subsequent
day of viewing, these scores dropped until, on the fourth day of viewing, the
males' levels of anxiety, depression, and annoyance were indistinguishable from
baseline norms.

What happened to the viewers as they watched more and more violence? We
believe they were becoming desensitized to violence, particularly against
women, which entailed more than a simple lowering of arousal to the movie
violence. The men actually began to perceive the films differently as time went
on. On Day 1, for example, on the average, the men estimated that they had
seen four "offensive scenes." By the fifth day, however, subjects reported only
half as many offensive scenes (even though exactly the same movies, but in
reverse order, were shown). Likewise, their ratings of the violence within the
films receded from Day 1 to Day 5. By the last day the men rated the movies
less graphic and less gory and estimated fewer violent scenes than they did on
the first day of viewing. Most startling, by the last day of viewing graphic
violence against women the men were rating the material as significantly less
debasing and degrading to women, more humorous, and more enjoyable, and
they claimed a greater willingness to see this type of film again. This change in
perception due to repeated exposure was particularly evident in comparisons of
reactions to two specific films — *I Spit on Your Grave* and *Vice Squad*. Both films
contain sexual assault; however, rape is portrayed more graphically in *I Spit on
Your Grave* and more ambiguously in *Vice Squad*. Men who were exposed first to
Vice Squad and then to *I Spit on Your Grave* gave nearly identical ratings of sexual
violence. However, subjects who had seen the more graphic movie first saw
much less sexual violence (rape) in the more ambiguous film.

The subjects' evaluations of a rape victim after viewing a reenacted rape trial
were also affected by the constant exposure to brutality against women. The
victim of rape was rated as more worthless and her injury as significantly less
severe by those exposed to filmed violence when compared to a control group
of men who saw only the rape trial and did not view films. Desensitization to
filmed violence on the last day was also significantly correlated with assignment

of greater blame to the victim for her own rape. (These types of effects were not observed for subjects who were exposed to sexually explicit but nonviolent films.)

MITIGATING THE EFFECTS OF EXPOSURE TO SEXUAL VIOLENCE

This research strongly suggests a potential harmful effect from exposure to certain forms of aggressive pornography and other forms of sexualized violence. There is now, however, some evidence that these negative changes in attitudes and perceptions regarding rape and violence against women not only can be eliminated but can be positively changed. Malamuth and Check (1983) found that if male subjects who had participated in such an experiment were later administered a carefully constructed debriefing, they actually would be less accepting of certain rape myths than were control subjects exposed to depictions of intercourse (without a debriefing). Donnerstein and Berkowitz (1981) showed that not only are the negative effects of previous exposure eliminated, but even up to four months later, debriefed subjects have more "sensitive" attitudes toward rape than do control subjects. These debriefings consisted of (1) cautioning subjects that the portrayal of the rape they had been exposed to is completely fictitious in nature, (2) educating subjects about the violent nature of rape, (3) pointing out to subjects that rape is illegal and punishable by imprisonment, and (4) dispelling the many rape myths that are perpetrated in the portrayal (e.g., in the majority of rapes, the victim is promiscuous or has a bad reputation, or that many women have an unconscious desire to be raped).

Surveys of the effectiveness of debriefings for male subjects with R-rated sexual violence have yielded similar positive results. Subjects who participated in the week-long film exposure study that was followed by a certain type of debriefing changed their attitudes in a positive direction. The debriefings emphasized the fallacious nature of movie portrayals that suggests that women deserve to be physically violated and emphasized that processes of desensitization may have occurred because of long-term exposure to violence. The results indicated an immediate effect for debriefing, with subjects scoring lower on rape myth acceptance after participation than they scored before participation in the film viewing sessions. These effects remained, for the most part, six weeks later. The effectiveness of the debriefing for the subjects who participated in two later experiments (one involving two weeks of exposure to R-rated violent films) indicated that even after seven months, subjects' attitudes about sexual violence showed significant positive change compared to the preparticipation levels.

This research suggests that if the callous attitudes about rape and violence presented in aggressive pornography and other media representations of violence against women are learned, they can likewise be "unlearned." Furthermore, if effective debriefings eliminate these negative effects, it would seem possible to develop effective "prebriefings" that would also counter the impact of such materials. Such programs could become part of sex education curricula for young males. Given the easy access and availability of many forms of sexual violence to young males today, such programs would go a long way toward countering the impact of such images.

THE IMPACT OF NONAGGRESSIVE PORNOGRAPHY

An examination of early research and reports in the area of nonaggressive pornography would have suggested that effects of exposure to erotica were, if anything, nonharmful. For instance:

> It is concluded that pornography is an innocuous stimulus which leads
> quickly to satiation and that the public concern over it is misplaced.
> (Howard, Liptzin, and Reifler, 1973, p. 133)

> Results . . . fail to support the position that viewing erotic films produces
> harmful social consequences. (Mann, Sidman, & Starr, 1971, p. 113)

> If a case is to be made against "pornography" in 1970, it will have to be
> made on grounds other than demonstrated effects of a damaging personal
> or social nature. (President's Commission on Obscenity and Pornography,
> 1970, p. 139)

A number of criticisms of these findings, however (such as Cline, 1974;
Dienstbier, 1977; Wills, 1977), led to a reexamination of the issue of exposure
to pornography and subsequent aggressive behavior. Some — for example,
Cline (1974) — saw major methodological and interpretive problems with the
Pornography Commission report; others (for example, Liebert & Schwartzberg,
1977) believed that the observations were premature. Certainly the relationship
between exposure to pornography and subsequent aggressive behavior was
more complex than first believed. For the most part, recent research has shown
that exposure to nonaggressive pornography can have one of two effects.

A number of studies in which individuals have been predisposed to aggression and were later exposed to nonaggressive pornography have revealed increases in aggressive behavior (such as Baron & Bell, 1977; Donnerstein, Donnerstein, & Evans, 1975; Malamuth, Feshbach, & Jaffe, 1977; Meyer, 1972;
Zillmann, 1971, 1979). Such findings have been interpreted in terms of a general arousal model, which states that under conditions in which aggression is a
dominant response, any source of emotional arousal will tend to increase aggressive behavior in disinhibited subjects (for example, Bandura, 1977; Donnerstein, 1983). A second group of studies (Baron, 1977; Baron & Bell, 1973;
Donnerstein et al., 1975; Frodi, 1977; Zillmann & Sapolsky, 1977) reports the
opposite — that exposure to pornography of a nonaggressive nature can actually
reduce subsequent aggressive behavior.

These results appear contradictory, but recent research (Baron, 1977; Donnerstein, 1983; Donnerstein et al., 1975; Zillmann, 1979) has begun to reconcile
seeming inconsistencies. It is now believed that as pornographic stimuli become
more arousing, they give rise to increases in aggression. At a low level of
arousal, however, the stimuli distract individuals, and attention is directed away
from previous anger. Acting in an aggressive manner toward a target is incompatible with the pleasant feelings associated with low-level arousal (see Baron,
1977; Donnerstein, 1983). There is also evidence that individuals who find the
materials "displeasing" or "pornographic" will also increase their aggression
after exposure, whereas those who have more positive reactions to the material

will not increase their aggression even to highly arousing materials (Zillmann, 1979).

The research noted above was primarily concerned with same-sex aggression. The influence of nonaggressive pornography on aggression against women tends to produce mixed effects. Donnerstein and Barrett (1978) and Donnerstein and Hallam (1978) found that nonaggressive pornography had no effect on subsequent aggression unless constraints against aggressing were reduced. This was accomplished by both angering male subjects by women and giving subjects multiple chances to aggress. Donnerstein (1983) tried to reduce aggressive inhibitions through the use of an aggressive model but found no increase in aggression after exposure to an X-rated nonviolent film. It seems, therefore, that nonaggressive sexual material does not lead to aggression against women except under specific conditions (for example when inhibitions against aggression are lowered deliberately by the experimenter).

Almost without exception, studies reporting the effects on nonviolent pornography have relied on short-term exposure; most subjects have been exposed to only a few minutes of pornographic material. More recently, Zillman and Bryant (1982, 1984) demonstrated that long-term exposure (4 hours and 48 minutes over a six-week period) to pornography that does not contain overt aggressiveness may cause male and female subjects to (1) become more tolerant of bizarre and violent forms of pornography, (2) become less supportive of statements about sexual equality, and (3) become more lenient in assigning punishment to a rapist whose crime is described in a newspaper account. Furthermore, extensive exposure to the nonaggressive pornography significantly increased males' sexual callousness toward women. This latter finding was evidenced by increased acceptance of statements such as, "A man should find them, fool them, fuck them, and forget them," "A woman doesn't mean 'no' until she slaps you," and "If they are old enough to bleed, they are old enough to butcher." Zillman and others (such as Berkowitz, 1984) have offered several possible explanations for this effect, suggesting that certain viewer attitudes are strengthened through long-term exposure to nonviolent pornographic material.

A common scenario of the material used in the Zillman research is that women are sexually insatiable by nature. Even though the films shown do not feature the infliction of pain or suffering, women are portrayed as extremely permissive and promiscuous, willing to accommodate any male sexual urge. Short-term exposure to this view of women (characteristic of early studies of nonviolent pornography) may not be sufficient to engender changes in viewers' attitudes congruent with these portrayals. However, attitudinal changes might be expected under conditions of long-term exposure. Continued exposure to the idea that women will do practically anything sexually may prime or encourage other thoughts regarding female promiscuity (Berkowitz, 1984). This increase in the availability of thoughts about female promiscuity or the ease with which viewers can imagine instances in which a female has been sexually insatiable may lead viewers to inflate their estimates of how willingly and frequently women engage in sexual behavior. The availability of thoughts about female insatiability may also affect judgments about sexual behavior such as rape, bestiality, and sadomasochistic sex. Further, these ideas may endure. Zillman and Bryant (1982), for example, found that male subjects still had a propensity to trivialize rape three weeks after exposure to nonviolent pornography. It is important to point out, however, that in these studies long-term exposure did not increase aggressive behavior but in fact decreased subsequent aggression.

Unfortunately, the role that images of female promiscuity and insatiability play in fostering callous perceptions of women can only be speculated upon at this point because no research has systematically manipulated film content in an experiment designed to facilitate or inhibit viewer cognitions. One cannot rule out the possibility, for example, that simple exposure to many sexually explicit depictions (regardless of their "insatiability" theme) accounts for the attitudinal changes found in their study. Sexual explicitness and themes of insatiability are experimentally confounded in this work.

Another emerging concern among political activists about pornography is its alleged tendency to degrade women (Dworkin, 1985; MacKinnon, 1985). This concern has been expressed recently in the form of municipal ordinances against pornography originally drafted by Catherine MacKinnon and Andrea Dworkin that have been introduced in a variety of communities, including Minneapolis and Indianapolis. One central feature of these ordinances is that pornography is the graphic "sexually explicit subordination of women" that also includes "women presented in scenarios of degradation, injury, abasement, torture, shown as filthy or inferior, bleeding, bruised, or hurt in a context that makes these conditions sexual" (City County general ordinance No. 35, City of Indianapolis, 1984). These ordinances have engendered a great deal of controversy, as some individuals have maintained that they are a broad form of censorship. A critique of these ordinances can be found in a number of publications (for example, Burstyn, 1985; Russ, 1985).

The framers of the ordinance suggest that after viewing such material, "a general pattern of discriminatory attitudes and behavior, both violent and non-violent, that has the capacity to stimulate various negative reactions against women will be found" (Defendants' memorandum, U.S. District Court for the Southern District of Indiana, Indianapolis Division, 1984, p. 8). Experimental evidence is clear with respect to the effects of pornography showing injury, torture, bleeding, bruised, or hurt women in sexual contexts. What has not been investigated is the effect of material showing women in scenarios of degradation, as inferior and abased.

No research has separated the effect of sexual explicitness from degradation, as was done with aggressive pornography, to determine whether the two interact to foster negative evaluations of women. Nearly all experiments conducted to date have confounded sexual explicitness with the presentation of women as a subordinate, objectified class. Only one investigation (Donnerstein, 1984) has attempted to disentangle sexual explicitness and violence. The results of this short-term exposure investigation, discussed above, revealed that although the combination of sexual explicitness and violence against a woman (the violent pornographic condition) resulted in the highest levels of subsequent aggression against a female target, the nonexplicit depiction that showed only violence resulted in aggression levels nearly as high and attitudes that were more callous than those that resulted from the combined exposure. The implication of this research is that long-term exposure to material that may not be explicitly sexual but that depicts women in scenes of degradation and subordination may have a negative impact on viewer attitudes. This is one area in which research is still needed.

CONCLUSION

Does pornography influence behaviors and attitudes toward women? The answer is difficult and centers on the definition of pornography. There is no evidence for any "harm"-related effects from sexually explicit materials. But research may support potential harmful effects from aggressive materials. Aggressive images are the issue, not sexual images. The message about violence and the sexualized nature of violence is crucial. Although these messages may be part of some forms of pornography, they are also pervasive media messages in general, from prime-time TV to popular films. Males in our society have callous attitudes about rape. But where do these attitudes come from? Are the media, and in particular pornography, the cause? We would be reluctant to place the blame on the media. If anything, the media act to reinforce already existing attitudes and values regarding women and violence. They do contribute, but are only part of the problem.

As social scientists we have devoted a great deal of time to searching for causes of violence against women. Perhaps it is time to look for ways to reduce this violence. This chapter has noted several studies that report techniques to mitigate the influence of exposure to sexual violence in the media, which involves changing attitudes about violence. The issue of pornography and its relationship to violence will continue for years, perhaps without any definitive answers. We may never know if there is any real causal influence. We do know, however, that rape and other forms of violence against women are pervasive. How we change this situation is of crucial importance, and our efforts need to be directed to this end.

REFERENCES

Abel, G., Barlow, D., Blanchard, E., & Guild, D. (1977). The components of rapists' sexual arousal. *Archives of General Psychiatry, 34,* 395–403, 895–903.

Bandura, A. (1977). *Social learning theory.* Englewood Cliffs, NJ: Prentice-Hall.

Baron, R. A. (1977). *Human aggression.* New York: Plenum.

Baron, R. A. (1984). The control of human aggression: A strategy based on incompatible responses. In R. Green & E. Donnerstein (Eds.), *Aggression: Theoretical and empirical reviews* (Vol. 2). New York: Academic Press.

Baron, R. A., & Bell, P. A. (1977). Sexual arousal and aggression by males: Effects of type of erotic, stimuli and prior provocation. *Journal of Personality and Social Psychology, 35,* 79–87.

Berkowitz, L. (1974). Some determinants of impulsive aggression: Role of mediated associations with reinforcements for aggression. *Psychological Review, 81,* 165–179.

Berkowitz, L. (1984). Some effects of thoughts on anti- and prosocial influences of media events: A cognitive-neoassociation analysis. *Psychological Bulletin, 95,* 410–427.

Brownmiller, S. (1975). *Against our will: Men, women and rape.* New York: Simon & Schuster.

Burstyn, V. (1985). *Women against censorship.* Manchester, NH: Salem House.

Burt, M. R. (1980). Cultural myths and supports for rape. *Journal of Personality and Social Psychology, 38,* 217–230.

Check, J. V. P., & Malamuth, N. (1983). Violent pornography, feminism, and social learning theory. *Aggressive Behavior, 9,* 106–107.

Check, J. V. P., & Malamuth, N. (in press). Can participation in pornography experiments have positive effects? *Journal of Sex Research.*

Cline, V. B. (Ed.). (1974). *Where do you draw the line?* Salt Lake City: Brigham Young University Press.

Dienstbier, R. A. (1977). Sex and violence: Can research have it both ways? *Journal of Communication, 27,* 176–188.

Donnerstein, E., & Berkowitz, L. (1985). *Role of aggressive and sexual images in violent pornography.* Manuscript submitted for publication.

Donnerstein, E. (1980a). Pornography and violence against women. *Annals of the New York Academy of Sciences, 347,* 277–288.

Donnerstein, E. (1980b). Aggressive-erotica and violence against women. *Journal of Personality and Social Psychology, 39,* 269–277.

Donnerstein, E. (1983). Erotica and human aggression. In R. Geen & E. Donnerstein (Eds.). *Aggression: Theoretical and empirical reviews.* New York: Academic Press.

Donnerstein, E. (1984). Pornography: Its effect on violence against women. In N. Malamuth & E. Donnerstein (Eds.). *Pornography and sexual aggression.* Orlando, FL: Academic Press.

Donnerstein, E., & Barrett, G. (1978). The effects of erotic stimuli on male aggression toward females. *Journal of Personality and Social Psychology, 36,* 180–188.

Donnerstein, E., & Berkowitz, L. (1982). Victim reactions in aggressive-erotic films as a factor in violence against women. *Journal of Personality and Social Psychology, 41,* 710–724.

Donnerstein, E., & Hallam, J. (1978). Facilitating effects of erotica on aggression against women. *Journal of Personality and Social Psychology, 36,* 1270–1277.

Donnerstein, E., & Linz, D. (1984, January). Sexual violence in the media, a warning. *Psychology Today,* pp. 14–15.

Donnerstein, E., Donnerstein, M., & Evans, R. (1975). Erotic stimuli and aggression: Facilitation or inhibition. *Journal of Personality and Social Psychology, 32,* 237–244.

Dworkin, A. (1985). Against the male flood: Censorship, pornography, and equality. *Harvard Women's Law Journal,* 8.

Frodi, A. (1977). Sexual arousal, situational restrictiveness, and aggressive behavior. *Journal of Research in Personality, 11,* 48–58.

Howard, J. L., Liptzin, M. B., & Reifler, C. B. (1973). Is pornography a problem? *Journal of Social Issues, 29,* 133–145.

Liebert, R. M. & Schwartzberg, N. S. (1977). Effects of mass media. *Annual Review of Psychology, 28,* 141–173.

Liuz, D., Donnerstein, E., & Penrod, S. (1984). The effects of long-term exposure to filmed violence against women. *Journal of Communication, 34,* 130–147.

MacKinnon, C. A. (1985). Pornography, civil rights, and speech. *Harvard Civil Rights-Civil Liberty Law Review, 20* (1).

Malamuth, N. (1981a). Rape proclivity among males. *Journal of Social Issues, 37,* 138–157.

Malamuth, N. (1981b). Rape fantasies as a function of exposure to violent-sexual stimuli. *Archives of Sexual Behavior, 10,* 33–47.

Malamuth, N. (1984). Aggression against women: Cultural and individual causes. In N. Malamuth & F. Donnerstein (Eds.) *Pornography and sexual aggression.* Orlando, FL: Academic Press.

Malamuth N., Feshbach, S., & Jaffe, Y. (1977). Sexual arousal and aggression: Recent experiments and theoretical issues. *Journal of Social Issues, 33,* 110–133.

Malamuth, N. M., & Spinner, B. (1980). A longitudinal content analysis of sexual violence in the best-selling erotic magazines. *Journal of Sex Research, 16*(3), 116–237.

Malamuth, N., & Check, J. V. P. (1981). The effects of mass media exposure on acceptance of violence against women: A field experiment. *Journal of Research in Personality, 15,* 436–446.

Malamuth, N., & Check, J. V. P. (1983). Sexual arousal to rape depictions: Individual differences. *Journal of Abnormal Psychology, 92,* 55–67.

Malamuth, N., & Donnerstein, E. (1982). The effects of aggressive pornographic mass media stimuli. In L. Berkowitz (Ed.), *Advances in experimental social psychology (vol. 15).* New York: Academic Press.

Malamuth, N., & Donnerstein, E. (Eds.), 1983). *Pornography and sexual aggression.* New York: Academic Press.

Malamuth, N., Haber, S., & Feshbach, S. (1980). The sexual responsiveness of college students to rape depictions: Inhibitory and disinhibitory effects. *Journal of Research in Personality,* 14, 399–408.

Mann, J., Sidman, J., & Starr, S. (1971). Effects of erotic films on sexual behavior of married couples. In *Technical Report of the Commission on Obscenity and Pornography (vol. 8).* Washington, DC: Government Printing Office.

Meyer, T. (1972). The effects of viewing justified and unjustified real film violence on aggressive behavior. *Journal of Personality and Social Psychology,* 23, 21–29.

President's Commission on Obscenity and Pornography (vol. 8). Washington, DC: Government Printing Office.

Russ, J. (1985). *Magic mommas, trembling sisters, puritans and perverts.* New York: Crossing.

Scott, J. (1985). *Sexual violence in* Playboy *magazine: Longitudinal analysis.* Paper presented at the meeting of the American Society of Criminology.

The war against pornography. (1985, March 18). *Newsweek,* pp. 58–62, 65–67.

Wills, G. (1977, November). Measuring the impact of erotica. *Psychology Today,* pp. 30–34.

Zillman, D. (1971). Excitation transfer in communication-mediated aggressive behavior. *Journal of Experimental Social Psychology,* 7, 419–433.

Zillman, D. (1979). *Hostility and aggression.* Hillsdale, NJ: Erlbaum.

Zillman, D. (1984). *Victimization of women through pornography.* Proposal to the National Science Foundation.

Zillman, D., & Bryant, J. (1982). Pornography, sexual callousness, and the trivialization of rape. *Journal of Communication,* 32, 10–21.

Zillman, D., & Bryant, J. (1984). Effects of massive exposure to pornography. In N. Malamuth & E. Donnerstein (Eds.), *Pornography and sexual aggression.* New York: Academic Press.

Zillman, D., & Sapolsky, B. S. (1977). What mediates the effect of mild erotica on annoyance and hostile behavior in males? *Journal of Personality and Social Psychology,* 35, 587–596.

Chris Clark

PORNOGRAPHY WITHOUT POWER?

I like to look at naked men. I admit it. I have for a long time now. I liked it as a child when I'd play "I'll show you mine/You show me yours" with other boys. I liked it growing up seeing older men in locker rooms. I liked it in puberty, discovering my father's collection of *Playboy* and being fascinated with pictures of naked men in the "Sex in Cinema" features; or going to the library and looking through sex books or any book — art, theater, photography — that had a picture of a naked man. I liked it in my late teens, having girlfriends who knew I was gay buy *Playgirl* for us to look at. I like to look at naked men.

As a product of this desire to see naked men, I discovered pornography, specifically gay male pornography. This brought to light a whole new dimension to my pleasure, seeing naked men together, holding, touching, naked men being sexual together. I think I remember that first picture: two men embracing on a dock, no genitals visible, one man with one eye partially open, looking at the

Reprinted from *Changing Men,* Fall 1985.

viewer. There were stories and real-life fantasies and occurrences, all for my pleasure. It and my masturbation viewing it, was an *affirmation* of my sexuality.

Yet, my pleasure was private! It had to be hidden. I had to sneak the porn into my house — not only was it pornography, "dirty" in itself, but it was *gay* porn! It became somewhat of an obsession. I would sneak it in with other magazines, with other packages, any way I could. When I widened my freedom by moving out on my own, I also removed the bars on my obsession — I became a collector.

At first, I collected whole magazines, and when that grew too bulky, I started cutting pictures out and putting them in collections — "My Favorite Porn" — then simply collecting the pictures in large plain envelopes. They were "my men," my sexuality.

Not coincidentally, my entrance into "gay culture" was through porn. Growing up in a small city, the only openly advertised public sex venue was a gay male porn movie house — complete with live nude dancers. (Until I went, I was never really sure whether it was for men or women — that's how "openly gay" it was.) Here I saw films of men having sex (doing things I didn't know existed or had only read about), and I saw men dancing naked, again for my pleasure. I felt my sexuality affirmed. How could I now take any position other than *for* that which first affirmed and then later confirmed my deviant sexuality?

> To gay men, the fear of sexuality, especially in the form of internalized self-hatred and self-disgust, is the most pernicious expression of sexism in our society. The first step towards personal communal liberation is unlearning those lessons of socialization which make our cocks and asses dirty. The acceptance of our bodies, the unhindered celebration of our sexuality and the act of loving other men spiritually, romantically and physically is the necessary first step toward liberation. Anything that helps to free our repressed selves — including pornography — has a positive value.

This is a radical statement. (It's from "Gay Porn — a discussion" in *Achilles Heel*, a British anti-sexist men's magazine.) Pornography, like other expressions of sexuality must be put into context, viewed through cultural, social, political and economic filters.

Many in the argument over porn seek to clarify the distinction between pornography and erotica. Though noble in purpose, such distinctions are themselves reflective of sexual preferences and social norms and biases. As Ellen Willis argues, it may simply become: "What turns me on is erotica, what turns you on is pornographic." To maintain a broad perspective, I use Ellen Willis' definition of pornography as "any image or description intended or used to arouse sexual desire," and follow her generalization that

> pornography is the return of the repressed, of feelings and fantasies driven underground by a culture that atomizes sexuality, defining love as a noble affair of the heart and mind, lust as a base animal urge centered in unmentionable organs. Prurience — the state of mind I associate with pornography — implies a sense of sex as forbidden, secretive pleasure, isolated from any emotional or social context.

It is here that gay male pornography and straight pornography overlap — a union rarely seen or addressed.

We are all affected by the social construction of gender and sexuality. Women, gay men and other sexual "minorities" and sub-cultures are oppressed. Straight men are forced, some with an unwillingness in spite of the many rewards, into the role of oppressor. This polarization of gender identity into female and male is what produces pornography. Three issues converge here: power, violence, and objectification. The three issues together form the basis of the anti-porn argument, and are also why I have some reservations about taking a pro-porn position.

Power is linked to socially defined sexuality in exactly the same way that aggression is linked to "maleness." Pornography as a product of male sexuality is thus a reflection of power issues. Power *can* be sexual and yet sexuality *can* be portrayed without power. Sex without power is often portrayed in gay porn where the relation between two partners has the possibility of gender equality. Sexual power is evident in most straight porn because of the imbalance of power implicit in the relations between men and women. To refute this distinction between gay and straight porn is itself homophobic; since gay men begin as gender-equals, the only way to conflate gay and straight porn is to label one participant as the passive-feminine role.

Power and violence are linked to sexuality in our culture and porn simply reflects this situation. As Gloria Steinem argues,

> It takes violence or the threat of it to maintain the unearned dominance of any group of human beings over another. Moreover, the threat must be the most persuasive wherever men and women come together intimately and are most in danger of recognizing each other's humanity.

However, though violence maintains dominance, and porn often depicts violence, attacking porn is not the answer. This is trying to cure the symptoms — pornography — and leaving the disease — our socialization into strictly dichotomous roles — to express itself elsewhere. Those opposing pornography are venting their rage at sexual oppression and violence on a by-product of the oppression.

My other reservation in taking a proporn position is also common to both straight and gay pornography: objectification. It is an implicit function of any representation of reality, a function of focus. Pornography is a representation of sexuality; it focuses intently on it, and thus objectifies it. I am victimized by this objectification because I want a link between my sexuality and my emotions. Pornography obscured that link even while affirming my sexuality. In my case, objectification manifested itself in promiscuity. Realizing this, I began to examine my objectification of sexual partners. I began to control the objectification and restore the link between sex and emotion. I see now how porn aided the construction of my sexuality; I also see, and can now control, the side-effects.

Arguments over pornography produce, from many positions, many solutions. The most visible, advocated by those against porn, is censorship or restriction of visibility of porn, such as legal ordinances against pornography. But Steinem reminds us that

. . . any societal definition of pornography in a male-dominated society . . . probably would punish the wrong people. Freely chosen homosexual expression might be considered more "pornographic" than snuff movies, or contraceptive courses for teenagers more "obscene" than bondage. Furthermore, censorship in itself . . ., would drive pornography into more underground activity . . .

This moralisitc solution, in a patriarchal society would reify the good girl/bad girl split for women, the repression of any "unacceptable" sexuality — i.e., that which is not heterosexual or male defined. Instead, I would suggest, with Deirdre English, that we "need, even more than women against pornography . . ., women pornographers — or eroticists, if that sounds better." The gay porn I've seen has been moving in this direction. Movies are focusing more on coming out and love relationships. Magazines are shifting toward more self-affirming stories and photo images. We need *more* porn addressing our oppression and affirming our sexuality. Let's join forces — those of us who are repressed by current norms — and create a new porn, a pornography without power, that glorifies the freedom to choose our own form of sexual expression.

REFERENCES

"Gay Porn — a Discussion," *Achilles Heel*, 1983.

Gloria Steinem, "Erotica vs. Pornography" in *Outrageous Acts and Everyday Rebellions* (NY: Holt, Rinehart, 1983).

Ellen Willis, "Feminism, Moralism and Pornography," *Village Voice*, 1979.

M. Rochlin

THE HETEROSEXUAL QUESTIONNAIRE

1. What do you think caused your heterosexuality?
2. When and how did you decide you were a heterosexual?
3. Is it possible that your heterosexuality is just a phase you may grow out of?
4. Is it possible that your heterosexuality stems from a neurotic fear of others of the same sex?
5. If you have never slept with a person of the same sex, is it possible that all you need is a good Gay lover?
6. Do your parents know that you are straight? Do your friends and/or roommate(s) know? How did they react?
7. Why do you insist on flaunting your heterosexuality? Can't you just be who you are and keep it quiet?
8. Why do heterosexuals place so much emphasis on sex?
9. Why do heterosexuals feel compelled to seduce others into their lifestyle?

Reprinted by permission from *Changing Men*, Spring 1982. © 1982 *Changing Men*.

10. A disproportionate majority of child molesters are heterosexual. Do you consider it safe to expose children to heterosexual teachers?

11. Just what do men and women *do* in bed together? How can they truly know how to please each other, being so anatomically different?

12. With all the societal support marriage receives, the divorce rate is spiraling. Why are there so few stable relationships among heterosexuals?

13. Statistics show that lesbians have the lowest incidence of sexually transmitted diseases. Is it really safe for a woman to maintain a heterosexual lifestyle and run the risk of disease and pregnancy?

14. How can you become a whole person if you limit yourself to compulsive, exclusive heterosexuality?

15. Considering the menace of overpopulation, how could the human race survive if everyone were heterosexual?

16. Could you trust a heterosexual therapist to be objective? Don't you feel s/he might be inclined to influence you in the direction of her/his own leanings?

17. There seem to be very few happy heterosexuals. Techniques have been developed that might enable you to change if you really want to. Have you considered trying aversion therapy?

18. Would you want your child to be heterosexual, knowing the problems that s/he would face?

Gary Kinsman

MEN LOVING MEN:
THE CHALLENGE OF GAY LIBERATION

The limits of "acceptable" masculinity are in part defined by comments like "What are you, a fag?"[1] As boys and men we have heard such expressions and the words "queer," "faggot," and "sissy" all our lives. These words encourage certain types of male behavior and serve to define, regulate, and limit our lives, whether we consider ourselves straight or gay. Depending on who is speaking and who is listening, they incite fear or hatred.

Even among many heterosexual men who have been influenced by feminism, the taboo against loving the same sex remains unchallenged. Lines like "I may be anti-sexist, but I am certainly not gay" can still be heard. These men may be questioning some aspects of male privilege, but in attempting to remake masculinity they have not questioned the institution of heterosexuality.[2] As a result their challenge to male privilege is partial and inadequate.

Gay men have often found much support in the "men's movement" or in groups of men against sexism. At the same time we have also seen our concerns

Reprinted from *Beyond Patriarchy: Essays by Men on Pleasure, Power and Change*, Michael Kaufman, ed. Toronto: Oxford University Press, 1987.

as gay men marginalized and pushed aside and have often felt like outsiders, Joe Interrante expresses some of the reservations of gay men about the "men's movement" and its literature:

> As a gay man . . . I had suspicions about the heterocentrist bias of this work. It told me that my gayness existed "in addition to" my masculinity, whereas I found that it colored my entire experience of manhood. I distrusted a literature which claimed that gay men were just like heterosexual men except for what they did in bed.[3]

The literature of the men's movement has tended to produce an image of men that is white, middle-class, and heterosexual. As Ned Lyttleton has pointed out, "an analysis of masculinity that does not deal with the contradictions of power imbalances that exist between men themselves will be limited and biased, and its limits and biases will be concealed under the blanket of shared male privilege."[4] A series of masculinities becomes subsumed under one form of masculinity that becomes "masculinity." As a result, socially organized power relations among and between men based on sexuality, race, class, or age have been neglected. These power relations are major dividing lines between men that have to be addressed if progressive organizing among men is to encompass the needs and experiences of all men. The men's movement has reached a turning point.[5] It has to choose whether it is simply a movement for men's rights — defending men's rights to be human too — or whether it will deepen the challenge to an interlocked web of oppression: sexism, heterosexism, racism, and class exploitation. We have to choose between a vision of a world in which men are more sensitive and human but are still "real" men at the top of the social order, and a radically new vision that entails the transformation of masculinity and sexuality and the challenging of other forms of domination.

In developing this radical vision — radical in the sense of getting to the roots of the problem — the politics of gay liberation and the politics of lesbian feminism are important. So too are the experiences of those of us who have been made into outsiders, people labelled "faggot," "queer," or "dyke" who have reclaimed these stigmatized labels as ways of naming experiences of the world and as weapons of resistance to heterosexual hegemony. The struggle against the institutionalized social norm of heterosexuality opens up the door to other kinds of social and personal change.

GAY LIBERATION VERSUS HETEROSEXUAL PRIVILEGE

In our society heterosexuality as an institutionalized norm has become an important means of social regulation, enforced by laws, police practices, family and social policies, schools, and the mass media. In its historical development heterosexuality is tied up with the institution of masculinity, which gives social and cultural meaning to biological male anatomy, associating it with masculinity, aggressiveness, and an "active" sexuality. "Real" men are intrinsically heterosexual; gay men, therefore, are not real men.

While gay men share with straight men the privilege of being in a dominant position in relation to women, we are at the same time in a subordinate position in the institution of heterosexuality. As a result, gay men's lives and experiences are not the same as those of heterosexual men. For instance, while we share with straight men the economic benefits of being men in a patriarchal society, we do not participate as regularly in the everyday interpersonal subordination of women in the realms of sexuality and violence. Although, like other men, we have more social opportunities, we are not accepted as open gays in corporate boardrooms or in many jobs, sports, and professions. We can still be labeled "national security risks" and sick, deviant, or abnormal. Consequently, gay men experience a rupture between the presumably universal categories of heterosexual experience and their own particular experience of the world, a rupture that denies many of our experiences; for gay men exist in social situations that allow us to see aspects of life, desire, sexuality, and love that cannot be seen by heterosexual men.[6]

Gay men have had to question the institution of masculinity — which associates masculinity with heterosexuality — in our daily lives. We have experimented with and developed new ways of organizing our sexual lives and our love and support relations, of receiving and giving pleasure. Heterosexual men interested in seriously transforming the fabric of their lives have to stop seeing gay liberation as simply a separate issue for some men that has nothing to say to them. They should begin to ask what the experience of gay men can bring into view for them. As we break the silence and move beyond liberal tolerance toward gays and lesbians, we can begin to see how "queer baiting" and the social taboo against pleasure, sex, and love between men serves to keep all men in line, defining what proper masculinity is for us. Gay liberation suggests that heterosexuality is not the only natural form of sexuality but has instead been socially and culturally made the "normal" sexual practice and identity. As the Kinsey Institute studies suggested, the actual flux of human desire cannot be easily captured in rigid sexual categories. Many men who define themselves as straight have had sexual experiences with other men.[7] This has demonstrated the contradictions that can exist between our actual experiences and desires and the rigid social categories that are used to divide normal from deviant and that imply that any participation in homosexual activity automatically defines one as a homosexual.

Breaking the silence surrounding homosexuality requires challenging heterosexism and heterosexual privilege. Lesbian-feminist Charlotte Bunch once explained to heterosexual women that the best way to find out what heterosexual privilege is all about is to go about for a few days as an open lesbian:

> What makes heterosexuality work is heterosexual privilege — and if you don't have a sense of what privilege is, I suggest that you go home and announce to everybody that you know — a roommate, your family, the people you work with — everywhere that you go — that you're a queer. Try being a queer for a week.[8]

This statement could also be applied to the situation of straight men, and any heterosexual man can easily imagine the discomfort, ridicule, and fear he might experience, how his "coming out" would disrupt "normal" relations at work and with his family. Such experiences are the substance of gay oppression that make our lives different from those of straight men. Gay men in this heterosexist society are labeled with many terms of abuse. Young boys hurl the labels "queer," "fag," or "cocksucker" at each other before they know what the words mean. As we grow up we are denied images of men loving men and any models for our lives outside heterosexuality. In the United States, the age of consent varies from state to state, usually from sixteen to eighteen, although in some states all homosexual acts remain technically illegal. Under Canadian and British law males under twenty-one are denied the right to have sexual relations with other boys and men. Many members of the medical and psychiatric professions still practice psychological and social terrorism against us by trying to adjust us to fit the norm. We are excluded as open lesbians and gay men from most activities and institutions. When the mass media does cover us they use stereotypes or other means to show us to be sick, immoral, indecent, as some sort of social problem or social menace, or they trivialize us as silly and frivolous.[9] The police continue to raid our bookstores and seize our magazines. In 1983–6, the media fostered fear and hatred against gay men by associating all gay men with AIDS. Such media stories shift and mold public opinion against us. On city streets we are often violently attacked by gangs of "queerbashers." Most countries deny lesbians and gay men the basic civil and human rights, leaving us open to arbitrary firings and evictions.

A variety of sexual laws are used to regulate and control gay men's sexual and community lives. Police in many cities have a policy of systematically entrapping and harassing gays. In recent years hundreds of men across North America have been arrested and often entrapped by the police in washrooms and parks. These campaigns — especially in small towns and cities — and the associated media attention have torn apart the lives of these men, many of whom define themselves as heterosexual and are married with families.

In fact, the society in which we have all grown up is so profoundly heterosexist that even many gays have internalized the social hatred against us in forms of "self-oppression."[10] This fear keeps many of us isolated and silent, hiding our sexuality. One of the first steps in combating this self-oppression is to reject this denial of our love and sexuality by affirming our existence and pride publicly. Assertions that "gay is good" and affirmations of gay pride are the beginning of our resistance to heterosexual hegemony on the individual and social levels.

THE HISTORY OF SEXUALITY

In addressing the matter of gay and lesbian oppression, we have to ask where this oppression has come from. How did heterosexuality come to be the dominant social relation? How did homosexuality come to be seen as a perverse outcast form of sexuality? If we can answer those questions, we can begin to see how we could break down the institution of heterosexuality and its control over our lives.

As a result of numerous cross-cultural and historical studies that have demonstrated that there is no natural or normal sexuality, we can no longer see sex as simply natural or biologically given. Our biological, erotic, and sexual capabilities are only the precondition for the organization of the social and cultural forms of meaning and activity that compose human sexuality. Our biological capabilities are transformed and mediated culturally, producing sexuality as a social need and relation. As Gayle Rubin explained, each social system has its own "sex/gender system" which

> is the set of arrangements by which a society transforms biological sexuality into products of human activity, and in which these transformed sexual needs are satisfied.[11]

Recent historical studies have challenged the assumed natural categories of heterosexuality and homosexuality themselves.[12] Gay, lesbian, and feminist historians have expanded our understanding of sexual meaning and identity, contesting the dominant ways in which sexuality has been discussed and viewed in our society.[13] The dominant perspective for looking at sexuality is what has been called the "repression hypothesis," which assumes that there is a natural sexuality that is repressed to maintain social and moral order. Many leftists argue that sexuality is repressed by the ruling class — to maintain class society because of capitalism's need for the family and a docile work force. This interpretation was popularized in the writings and activities of Wilhelm Reich,[14] who called for the end of sexual repression through the liberation of natural sexuality, which was for him completely heterosexual. Variations of this repression theory, and its corresponding call for the liberation of natural sexuality, have inspired sexual liberationist politics, including much of the gay liberation movement, which sees homosexuality as a natural sexuality that simply needs to be released from social repression.

The experience by women of the male sexual (i.e., heterosexual) revolution of the sixties and seventies has led much of the feminist movement to a more complex understanding of sexuality than simple theories of sexual repression. Feminism has exposed the contradictions in a sexual revolution that increased women's ability to seek sexual satisfaction but only within male-dominated heterosexual relations. Feminism has also begun to explore how sexuality and social power are bound together and how sexuality has been socially organized in male-dominated forms in this society.[15] This view of sex opens up new possibilities for sexual politics — our sexual lives are no longer seen as divorced from human and social activity but as the results of human praxis (the unity of thought and activity). Sexual relations are therefore changeable and are themselves the site of personal and social struggles. We can then begin to question the natural appearance of such sexual categories as heterosexual and homosexual and to make visible the human activity that is involved in the making of sexuality. This opens up a struggle, not for the liberation of some inherent sexuality that just has to be freed from the bonds of capitalism or repressive laws, but for a much broader challenge to the ways our sexual lives are defined, regulated, and controlled. It opens up questions about the very making and remaking of sex, desire, and pleasure.

Enter the Homosexual   The historical emergence of the "homosexual" required a number of social preconditions, which can be summarized as three interrelated social processes: first, the rise of capitalist social relations, which created the necessary social spaces for the emergence of homosexual cultures;[16] second, the regime of sexuality that categorized and labeled homosexuality and sexual "deviations"; and third, the activities, cultural production, and resistance to the oppression of men in these same-sex desire-based cultures.

The rise of capitalism in Europe between the fifteenth and nineteenth centuries separated the rural household economy from the new industrial economy and undermined the interdependent different-sex household economy. The working class was made, and made itself, in the context of this industrialization, urbanization, and commercialization. This separation of "work" from the household and the development of wage labor meant that it became possible for more

men in the cities to live outside the family, earning a wage and living as board-
ers. Later they would be able to eat at restaurants or taverns and rent their own
accommodation. This created the opportunities for some men to start organizing what would become, through a process of development and struggle, the
beginnings of a homosexual culture, from the eighteenth century on.[17]

A regime of sexuality has emerged as part of a series of social struggles over
the last two centuries. The transition from feudalism to capitalism in the western countries meant a transition in the way kinship and sexual and class relations
were organized. The new ruling class was no longer able to understand itself or
organize its social life simply through the old feudal ties of blood or lineage.[18]
New forms of family and state formation led to new forms of self-understanding, class consciousness, and notions of moral and social order. Sexuality
emerged as an autonomous sphere separate from household production. A
proper, respectable sexual and gender identity became an essential feature of
the class unity of the bourgeoisie. This process is linked to the emergence of
the ideology of individual identity. The regime of sexual definitions was first
applied to the bodies of the bourgeoisie itself through its educational and medical systems and through the sexological knowledge that was generated by the
new professional groups of doctors and psychiatrists and that served to draw a
boundary between bourgeois respectability and the "bestial" sexual practices of
the outcast poor and "lower orders." These norms of sex and gender definition
helped organize the relations of the bourgeois family and its sexual morality.

Later these same norms of sexual identity and morality were used against the
urban working class and poor, who were considered a threat to social order by
middle-class and state agencies. The working class both resisted this enforcement of social norms and at the same time adopted them as its own. The male-
dominated "respectable" sections of the working class developed their own
norms of family and sexual life that incorporated the socially dominant norms
of masculinity, femininity, and reproductive heterosexuality. The uneven and
at times contradictory development of sexual identity in different classes, genders, races, and nationalities is a subject that remains to be more fully explored.

In the big cities sexuality becomes an object to be studied and a terrain for
the expanding male-dominated fields of medicine, psychiatry, and sexology.
Various forms of sexual behavior were categorized, classified, and ranked, with
heterosexuality on the top and homosexuality and lesbianism near the bottom.
The norm and the perversions were defined, separating normal and abnormal
behavior. In this context sex in the ruling discourses became the truth of our
being.[19]

The heterosexual man was no longer simply carrying out the types of activities he had to carry out in the sexual divisions of labor, or the activities that
would lead to the reproduction of the species; rather he had become someone
with a particular erotic, sexual, and gender identity that linked his masculinity
to an exclusively heterosexual way of life. The heterosexual and the homosexual
emerged in relation to each other as part of the same historical and social process
of struggle and negotiation.

Men who engaged in sexual relations with other men in this emerging regime
of sexuality (and who were affected by the ideology of individualism) began to
organize their lives around their sexuality and to see themselves as separate and
different from other men. They fought against campaigns by religious fundamentalists and the police who wished to curtail their activities.[20] In the last

century, the emergence of sexology, increased police regulation of sexual behavior, and the passing of laws against sexual offenses combined with the development of these same-sex desire-based cultures to make the new social experience and social category of homosexuality.

The term homosexual itself was not devised until 1869, when Károly Mária Benkert, a Hungarian, coined the term in an appeal to the government to keep its laws out of peoples lives.[21] The category of homosexuality was originally elaborated by some homosexuals themselves, mostly professional men it seems, in order to name their "difference" and in order to protect themselves from police and legal prohibitions. The word was taken up by the various agencies of social regulation from the medical profession to the police and courts. Homosexuality was defined as an abnormality, a sickness, and a symptom of degeneracy. The efforts of medical and legal experts

> were chiefly concerned with whether the disgusting breed of perverts could be physically identified for courts and whether they should be held legally responsible for their acts.[22]

An early Canadian reference — in 1898 — to same-sex "perversion" among men by a Dr. Ezra Stafford (which refers to the work of Krafft-Ebing, one of the grandfathers of sexology) linked sex between men with prostitution in a theory of degeneracy. Stafford wrote that these things "may lead to the tragedy of our species."[23] This connection between homosexuality and prostitution as stigmatized social and sexual practices continued even to England's Wolfenden report of 1957, which linked these topics, and it continues to this day, in, for example, the use by the Canadian police of bawdy-house legislation, originally intended to deal with houses of female prostitutes, against gay men.

Simultaneously the needs of capitalism for a skilled labor force and a continuing supply of wage-laborers led to an emphasis on the heterosexual nuclear family. The rise of modern militarism and the scramble for colonies by the western powers led to demands for a larger and healthier supply of cannon fodder at the beginning of the twentieth century. An intensification of military discipline resulted in stiff prohibitions against homosexuality, which was seen as subversive of discipline and hierarchy in the armed forces. As a result, reproductive heterosexuality was reinforced for men, and motherhood further institutionalized for women.[24]

The category of the male homosexual emerged in sexology as an "invert" and was associated with some form of effeminacy and "gender inversion." A relation between gender dysfunction and abnormal sexuality was established:

> As defined by the ancient civil or canonical codes, sodomy was a category of forbidden acts. . . . The nineteenth century homosexual became a personage, a past, a case history, and a childhood, in addition to being a type of life, a life form, and a morphology, with an indiscreet anatomy and possibly a mysterious physiology. Nothing that went into his total composition was unaffected by his sexuality. . . . Homosexuality appeared as one of the forms of sexuality when it was transposed from the practice of sodomy onto a kind of interior androgyny, a hermaphrodism of the soul. The sodomite had been a temporary aberration; the homosexual was now a species.[25]

The categorization of "perverse" sexual types also provided a basis for resistance. Sexual categorization, as Foucault puts it,

> also made possible the formation of a "reverse" discourse: homosexuality began to speak on its own behalf, to demand that its legitimacy or "naturality" be acknowledged, often in the same vocabulary, using the same categories by which it was radically disqualified.[26]

Homosexuals themselves used this category to name their experiences, to articulate their differences and cultures, moving this category in a more progressive direction. There has been a century-long struggle over the meaning of homosexuality that has involved sexologists, the police, lawyers, psychiatrists, and homosexuals, a struggle that continues today. The regime of sexuality and the specification of different sexual categories in an attempt to buttress the emerging norm of heterosexuality have unwittingly also provided the basis for homosexual experiences, identities, and cultures. Through these experiences a series of new social and sexual needs, human capacities, and pleasures have been created among a group of men. This homosexual experience, along with the slightly later emergence of a distinct lesbian experience,[27] and the feminist movement have created the basis for contemporary challenges to the hegemony of heterosexuality.

Enter Gay Liberation and the Gay Community   Recent social changes in the western capitalist countries have put in question the patriarchal, gender, and sexual relations established during the last century. A prolonged crisis in sexual and gender relations and in the meaning of sexuality has occurred. The feminist and gay liberation movements, for example, have challenged the relegation of sexual relations and particularly "deviant" forms of sexuality to the socially defined private realm, subverting the public/private categories that have been used to regulate our sexual lives. The development of contraceptive and reproductive technologies has made it more and more possible to separate heterosexual pleasure and procreation, although the struggle continues about who will have access to, and control over, this technology. The expansion of consumer markets and advertising in the post-war period has led to an increasing drawing of sexuality and sexual images into the marketplace and the public realm.[28] This increasing public visibility of sexual images and sexual cultures has led to objections from those who would wish to reprivatize sexuality, in particular its "deviant" strains. And feminists have challenged the patriarchal values that are visible in much advertising and heterosexual male pornography.

The social ferment of the sixties — particularly the civil rights, black power, and feminist movements — combined with earlier forms of homosexual activism and the expansion of the gay commercial scene and culture to produce the gay liberation movement, which erupted in 1969 in the Stonewall Riot in New York City.[29] The movement developed a new, positive identity that has served as a basis for our resistance to heterosexual hegemony. The movement's most significant achievements were its contesting of the psychiatric definition of homosexuality as a mental illness and its creation of a culture and community that have transformed the lives of hundreds of thousands of men and women. As usual in a patriarchal society, many more opportunities have opened up for men than for women.

In a challenge to the "universality" of heterosexuality, gays have affirmed that gay is just as good as straight, calling on lesbians and gay men to affirm themselves and their sexualities. This has challenged the gender and social policies of the state, suggesting that sexual activity does not have to be solely for reproduction, but can also be for play, pleasure, love, and support, and questioning the very right of the state to regulate people's sexual lives. We have affirmed our right to sexual self-determination and control over our own bodies and sexuality and have affirmed this right for others as well.

The growth of a visible gay community and the emergence of gay streets and commercial areas in many big cities have led to a reaction from the police, conservative political parties, and the new right. These groups fear the breakdown of "traditional" sexual and family relations, which they associate with social and moral order, and see the challenge that gay liberation presents to heterosexual hegemony as a threat to the ways in which their lives and institutions are organized. They want lesbians and gay men out of public view and back in the closets, threatening our very existence as a public community.

In a sense the gay ghetto is both a playground and a potential concentration camp. While it provides people a place to meet and to explore and develop aspects of their lives and sexuality, it can also separate people from the rest of the population in a much larger closet that can be isolated and contained. The ghetto can tend to obscure the experiences gay men share with other men in their society. Locking people into the new categorization of gays as minority group or community may weaken the critique of sex and gender relations in society as a whole. As Altman explains, the "ethnic homosexual" has emerged, "the widespread recognition of a distinct cultural category which appears to be pressing for the same sort of 'equality,' in Western society as do ethnic minorities."[30] However, lesbians and gay men are not born into a minority group, but like heterosexuals assume a sexual identity through social and psychological processes.[31] Gays and lesbians are not only a minority group but also an oppressed and denied sexuality. The position that gays are simply a new minority group can deflect our challenges to the dominant way of life.

In challenging heterosexuality as the social norm gays have brought into question aspects of the institutions of masculinity and male privilege. Over the last decade images of gay men have shifted from the effeminacy of the "gender invert" to the new macho and clone looks that have dominated the gay men's community. This imagery challenges the previous stereotypes of homosexuals that associated our sexuality with gender nonconformity and has asserted that we can be both homosexual and "masculine" at the same time.[32] In defining ourselves as masculine we have had to make use of and transform the existing images of straight masculinity we find around us. These new images challenge heterosexual norms that associate "deviant" gender stereotypes with sexual "deviancy," for instance effeminacy with male homosexuality, but at the same time also tend to create new standards and stereotypes of what gay men are supposed to be like. These images and styles themselves continue to be imprisoned within the polarities of gender dichotomy. While gay men often believe we have freed ourselves from the social organization of gender, what we have actually done is exchange "gender inversion" for a situation where homosexuality can be organized through "normal" gender identifications. This assertion of masculinized imagery can to some extent lead us away from the critique of the institution of masculinity and its effects in our lives and persuade us that gender is no longer a problem for gay men.

It is ironic that some forms of resistance to past ways in which we were stigmatized can serve to accommodate us to aspects of the existing order of things. It is in this context that some of the challenges to masculinity and gender norms by straight men fighting against sexism will also be valuable to gay men. To be successful, gay liberation must challenge not only the institutionalization of heterosexuality as a social norm but also the institution of masculinity.

GAY LIBERATION AND THE RULING REGIME OF SEX

Gay liberation has emerged from the contradictions within the ruling system of sexual regulation and definition. It is fundamentally a struggle to transform the norms and definitions of sexual regulation. Gay liberation strives for the recognition of homosexuality as socially equal to the dominant social institution of heterosexuality. Yet as Weeks suggests,

> the strategic aim of the gay liberation movement must be not simply the validation of the rights of a minority within a heterosexual majority but the challenge to all the rigid categorizations of sexuality. . . . The struggle for sexual self-determination is a struggle in the end for control over our bodies. To establish this control we must escape from those ideologies and categorizations which imprison us within the existing order.[33]

The struggle to transform our sexual norms and to end the control of the institution of heterosexuality over our lives holds out the possibility of beginning to disengage us from the ruling regime of sex and gender. As Foucault suggested, movements that have been called sexual liberation movements, including gay liberation, are

> movements that start with sexuality, with the apparatus of sexuality in the midst of which they are caught and which make it function to the limit; but, at the same time, they are in motion relative to it, disengaging themselves and surmounting them.[34]

The struggle for gay liberation can be seen as a process of transformation. The assertion that gay is just as good as straight — which lies at the heart of gay liberation — is formally within the present regime of sexual categorization, for it still separates gay from straight as rigid categories and assigns value to sexuality, thus mirroring the limitations of the current sexual regime. However, the gay liberation movement operates both within *and* against this regime of sexual regulation. In asserting equal value for homosexuality and lesbianism, it begins to turn the ruling practices of sexual hierarchy on their head. Resistance begins within the present regime of sexual definitions, but it begins to shift the sexual boundaries that they have defined, opening up the possibility of transcending their limitations. By naming our specific experiences of the world, gay liberation provides the basis for a social and political struggle that can transform, defy, cut across, and break down the ruling regime of sex and gender.

The gay and lesbian communities, like other oppressed social groups, oscillate between resistance and accommodation to oppression. This is a struggle on two closely interrelated fronts. First, the gay community itself needs to strengthen cultures of resistance by building on sexual and cultural traditions that question gender norms and the relegation of erotic life to the state-defined private sphere. This will involve challenging the internalization and reproduction of sexism, racism, ageism, and class divisions within the gay community, as well as building alliances with other social groups fighting these forms of domination. Secondly, it requires a struggle outside the gay and lesbian communities for the defense of a community under attack by the police, government, and media. A key part of this strategy would be campaigning for new social policies that uproot heterosexuality as *the* social norm.

OPENING UP EROTIC CHOICES FOR EVERYONE

In developing a radical perspective we need to draw on the insights of lesbian feminism about the social power of heterosexuality and also on the historical perspectives provided by the new critical gay history, which reveals the social and historical process of the organization of heterosexual hegemony and the present system of sexual regulation more generally. These understandings create the basis for alliances between feminists, lesbians, gay liberationists, anti-sexist men, and other groups against the institution of heterosexuality, which lies at the root of the social oppression of women, lesbians, and gays. This alliance would contest the hegemony of heterosexuality in the legal system, state policies, in forms of family organization, and in the churches, unions, and other social bodies. The struggle would be for women, gays, and others to gain control over our bodies and sexuality and to begin to define our own eroticism and sexuality. A fundamental aspect of such an approach would be the elaboration and exploration of the experiences and visions of those of us living outside institutionalized heterosexuality.

Proposals for new and different ways of living (including collective and non-sexist ways of rearing children) are particularly vital since the new right and moral conservatives in their various incarnations are taking advantage of people's fears about changes in family organization and sexual mores to campaign in support of patriarchal and heterosexist social norms. The defense of a male-dominated heterosexuality is not only central to the policies of the new right and moral conservatives regarding feminism and gay liberation, but is a central theme of their racial and class politics as well.[35] The progressive movement's failure to deal with people's real fears, concerns, and hopes regarding sexual and gender politics is an important reason why right-wing groups are able to gain support. Feminism, gay liberation, and all progressive movements will have to articulate a vision that will allow us to move forward beyond the confines of institutionalized heterosexuality.

Gay liberation enables heterosexual men who question heterosexism to contribute to this new social vision. The issues raised by gay liberation must be addressed by all men interested in fundamental change because heterosexism limits and restricts the lives of all men. This challenge will only be effective, however, if heterosexual privilege is challenged in daily life and in social institutions. This could help begin the long struggle to disentangle heterosexual desire from the confines of institutionalized masculinity and heterosexuality. Together we could begin to redefine and remake masculinity and sexuality. If sexuality is socially produced, then heterosexuality itself can be transformed and redefined and its pleasures and desires separated from the social relations of power and domination. Gay liberation can allow all men to challenge gender and sexual norms and redefine gender and sex for ourselves in alliance with feminism; it can allow all men to explore and create different forms of sexual pleasures in our lives. This redefining of masculinity and sexuality will also help destroy the anxieties and insecurities of many straight men who try so hard to be "real men." But the success of this undertaking depends on the ability to develop alternative visions and experiences that will help all people understand how their lives could be organized without heterosexuality as the institutionalized social norm. Such a goal is a radically transformed society in which everyone will be able to gain control of his or her own body, desires, and life.

ACKNOWLEDGMENTS

Special thanks to Ned Lyttleton, Brian Conway, and Bob Gardner for comments on this paper. For more general comments on matters that pertain to topics addressed in this paper I am indebted to Varda Burstyn, Philip Corrigan, Bert Hansen, Michael Kaufman, Ian Lumsden, Dorothy E. Smith, George Smith, Mariana Valverde, and Lorna Weir.

NOTES

1. See G. K. Lehne, "Homophobia Among Men," in Deborah David and Robert Brannon, *The Forty-Nine Percent Majority* (Reading, Mass.: Addison-Wesley, 1976), 78.

2. On the notion of institutionalized heterosexuality see Charlotte Bunch, "Not For Lesbians Only," *Quest* 11, no. 2 (Fall 1975). Also see Adrienne Rich, "Compulsory Heterosexuality And Lesbian Existence," in Snitow, Stansell and Thompson, eds., *Powers of Desire: The Politics of Sexuality* (New York: Monthly Review Press, 1983): 177–205.

3. Joe Interrante, "Dancing Along the Precipice: The Men's Movement in the '80s," *Radical America* 15, no. 5 (September–October 1981): 54.

4. Ned Lyttleton, "Men's Liberation, Men Against Sexism and Major Dividing Lines," *Resources for Feminist Research* 12, no. 4 (December/January 1983/1984): 33. Several discussions with Ned Lyttleton were very useful in clarifying my ideas in this section and throughout this paper.

5. Interrante, *op. cit.*, 54.

6. For further elaboration see my *The Regulation of Desire* (Montreal: Black Rose, 1986).

7. See Kinsey, Pomeroy, and Martin, *Sexual Behavior in the Human Male* (Philadelphia: W.B. Saunders, 1948) and Mary McIntosh, "The Homosexual Role," in Plummer, ed., *The Making Of The Modern Homosexual* (London: Hutchinson, 1981), 38–43.

8. Bunch, "Not For Lesbians Only."

9. See Frank Pearce, "How to be Immoral and Ill, Pathetic and Dangerous all at the same time: Mass Media and the Homosexual," in Cohen and Young, eds., *The Manufacture of News: Deviance, Social Problems and the Mass Media* (London: Constable, 1973), 284–301.

10. See Andrew Hodges and David Hutter. *With Downcast Gays, Aspects of Homosexual Self-Oppression* (Toronto: Pink Triangle Press, 1977).

11. Gayle Rubin, "The Traffic In Women: Notes on the Political Economy of Sex," in Reiter, eds., *Towards An Anthropology Of Women* (New York: Monthly Review Press, 1975), 159. I prefer the use of sex and gender relations to sex/gender system since the notion of system tends to conflate questions of sexuality and gender and suggests that sex/gender relations are a separate system from other social relations rather than an integral aspect of them.

12. See Joe Interrante, "From Homosexual to Gay to?: Recent Work in Gay History," in *Radical America* 15, no. 6 (November–December 1981): Martha Vicinus, "Sexuality and Power: A Review of Current Work in the History of Sexuality," *Feminist Studies* 8, no. 1 (Spring 1982): 133–56; and Robert A. Padgug, "Sexual Matters: On Conceptualizing Sexuality In History," *Radical History Review*, "Sexuality in History" Issue, no. 20 (Spring/Summer 1979): 3–23.

13. See for instance Michel Foucault, *The History Of Sexuality* (New York: Vintage, 1980), vol. 1, *An Introduction;* Jeffrey Weeks, *Sex, Politics and Society: The Regulation of Sexuality since 1800* (London: Hutchinson, 1981); and Jonathan Ned Katz, *Gay/Lesbian Almanac* (New York:

Harper and Row, 1983). For recent feminist explorations of sexuality see Snitow, Stansell and Thompson, *Powers of Desire* (New York: Monthly Review, 1983); Carol Vance, ed., *Pleasure and Danger, Exploring Female Sexuality* (Boston: Routledge and Kegan Paul, 1984); Rosalind Coward, *Female Desire, Women's Sexuality Today* (London: Routledge and Kegan Paul, 1984); and Mariana Valverde, *Sex, Power and Pleasure* (Toronto: Women's Press, 1985).

14. See Wilhelm Reich, *The Sexual Revolution* (New York: Straus and Giroux, 1974) and Baxandall, ed., *Sex-Pol. Essays, 1929–1934, Wilhelm Reich* (New York: Vintage, 1972).

15. Unfortunately, over the last few years some anti-pornography feminists have suggested that sexuality is only a realm of danger for women, obscuring how it can also be a realm of pleasure. Some anti-porn feminists have been used by state agencies in attempts to clamp down on sexually explicit material including sexual material for gay men and lesbians. See Vance, *Pleasure and Danger;* Varda Burstyn, ed., *Women Against Censorship* (Vancouver and Toronto: Douglas and McIntyre, 1985); and Varda Burstyn, "Anatomy of a Moral Panic" and Gary Kinsman, "The Porn Debate," *Fuse* 3, no. 1 (Summer 1984).

16. On this see the work of John D'Emilio, for instances his "Capitalism and Gay Identity," in Snitow, Stansell and Thompson, eds., *Powers of Desire*, 100–13, and his *Sexual Politics, Sexual Communities* (Chicago: University of Chicago Press, 1983).

17. See Randolph Trumbach, "London's Sodomites: Homosexual Behaviour and Western Culture in the 18th Century," *Journal of Social History*, Fall 1977, 1–33; Mary McIntosh, "The Homosexual Role," in Plummer, ed., *The Making of The Modern Homosexual;* Alan Bray, *Homosexuality in Renaissance England* (London: Gay Men's Press, 1982); and Jeffrey Weeks, *Sex, Politics and Society.*

18. See Foucault, *The History of Sexuality*, vol. 1 and Kinsman, *The Regulation of Desire.*

19. This idea comes from the work of Foucault.

20. See Bray, *Homosexuality in Renaissance England* for the activities of the Society for the Reformation of Morals, which campaigned against same-sex desire-based networks in the early eighteenth century.

21. John Lauritsen and David Thorstad, *The Early Homosexual Rights Movement* (New York: Times Change Press, 1974), 6.

22. Arno Karlen, *Sexuality and Homosexuality* (New York: W. W. Norton, 1971), 185.

23. Ezra Hurlburt Stafford, "Perversion," the *Canadian Journal of Medicine and Surgery* 3, no. 4 (April 1898).

24. On this see Anna Davin. "Imperialism and Motherhood," *History Workshop*, no. 5 (Spring 1978).

25. Foucault, *op. cit.*, 43.

26. *Ibid.*, 101.

27. See Lillian Faderman, *Surpassing The Love Of Men* (New York: William Morrow, 1981); Christina Simmons, "Companionate Marriage and the Lesbian Threat," in *Frontiers* 4, no. 3 (Fall 1979); Martha Vicinus, "Sexuality and Power"; and Ann Ferguson, "Patriarchy, Sexual Identity, and the Sexual Revolution," *Signs* 7, no. 1 (Fall 1981): 158–72.

28. See Gary Kinsman, "Porn/Censor Wars And The Battlefields of Sex," in *Issues of Censorship* (Toronto: A Space, 1985), 31–9.

29. See John D'Emilio, *Sexual Politics, Sexual Communities.*

30. Dennis Altman, "What Changed in the Seventies?," in Gay Left Collective, eds., *Homosexuality, Power and Politics* (London: Allison and Busby, 1980), 61.

31. One prejudice that is embodied in sexual legislation and social policies is the myth that lesbians and gay men are a special threat to young people and that gay men are "child molesters." Most studies show, on the contrary, that more than 90 percent of sexual assaults on young people are committed by heterosexual men and often within the family or home. Breines and Gordon state that, "approximately 92 percent of the victims are female and 97 percent of the assailants are males." See Wini Breines and Linda Gordon, "The New Scholarship on Family Violence," *Signs* 8, no. 3 (Spring 1983); 522. Also see Elizabeth Wilson, *What Is To Be Done About Violence Against Women* (London: Penguin, 1983), particularly 117–34. We have to eliminate special age restrictions on the right to participate in consensual lesbian and gay sex so that lesbian and gay young people can express their desires and instead challenge the principal source of violence

against children and young people — the patriarchal family and straight-identified men. We have to propose changes in family relations and schooling and alternative social policies that would allow young people to take more control over their own lives, to get support in fighting unwanted sexual attention *and* to be able to participate in consensual sexual activity.

32. See John Marshall, "Pansies, Perverts and Macho Men: Changing Conceptions of Male Homosexuality" and Greg Blachford, "Male Dominance In The Gay World," in Plummer, ed., *The Making of The Modern Homosexual;* and also Seymour Kleinberg's article elsewhere in this volume for a different approach.

33. Jeffrey Weeks, "Capitalism and the Organization of Sex," Gay Left Collective, eds., *Homosexuality, Power and Politics* 19–20.

34. Michel Foucault, "Power and Sex," *Telos,* no. 32 (Summer 1977): 152–61.

35. See Allen Hunter, "In the Wings, New Right Ideology and Organization," *Radical America* 15, no. 1–2 (Spring 1981): 127–38.

Rex Reece

COPING WITH COUPLEHOOD

Lloyd and Eric came into my office, sat on the sofa, looked questioningly at each other and then at me.

"Where do we start?" Lloyd broke the ice. He was the older of the couple; I guessed thirty-five, based on his thinning blond hair and the increasing dimension of his waist.

"Sometimes it's hard to start talking about very personal things with a complete stranger, but often it helps just to jump right in and say what's on your mind. Then later we can fill in the background and feelings," I urged.

Eric followed my suggestion. "Well, we've been together for a year and it's been good, but now we're fighting so much that we're afraid it's not going to last. We want it to, and we were hoping you could help." Eric was taller, younger, darker. He looked like he'd win scholarships if he answered ads about male modeling schools.

"Yeah," Lloyd seconded, "I think we've tried everything and it doesn't seem to work. We're at a standstill, a block. It feels hopeless sometimes."

Both men were dressed in gay summer fashion. Lloyd had appeared in the basics — Adidas, jeans, and Lacoste; Eric presented a more extraordinary impression with his earth-colored earth sandals and bright canary jumpsuit. The yellow was reflected in the sparkle of his dark eyes and was almost jarring in contrast to his glossy black curls and carefully trimmed mustache.

After a few moments more of general introductory interaction, I suggested that one of them wait in another room while I spoke privately with the other. Eric chose to leave, and I continued the interview alone with Lloyd.

Lloyd's gestures quickened, his voice edged upwards, and his hesitance seemed to fade somewhat with Eric out of the room.

The Advocate, October 19, 1977, pp. 31–32. Reprinted by permission of the author.

"I know you're not supposed to find a lover at the baths," he reasoned as his body strained forward in the direction of his outstretched hand. "Believe me, I've been around long enough to know that. At least, none of my friends ever met each other there." He paused momentarily, then added quickly, "But *we* did." He spoke emphatically, almost defensively, as if he felt that having met at the baths was one strike against the survival of their relationship.

"It was one of those slow times, you know, during the day. I used to go a lot in the daytime," he continued parenthetically. "I never did like those hot, crowded nights when the air is heavy with the smell of sex and poppers." His palm caressed his cheek. "I had gone there out of being sort of down — I had made a goof at work that day. So I came home to take a shower and forget. After the shower I realized I had the crabs. I thought it was just the summer heat, you know?

"So I went to the baths, to forget, to relax. Part of me didn't want to make it with anybody, because I had just washed with A-200, I wasn't sure how well it worked or how long it took, and I didn't want to chance giving the crabs to anyone. They're a real pest, you know, the little buggers." He could chuckle momentarily. "But I decided to take the risk.

"To tell you the truth, I guess I was, as usual, hoping that 'he,' you know, the 'right one' would be there and would fall madly in love with me." He punctuated this last sentence with a cynical guffaw; its unexpected loudness startled us both.

Fond recollections took command of his body movements. He slumped against the sofa, grinned, let his shoulders fall; his gaze fell toward his left hand as its fingers parted the sunbleached thick blond softness on his other wrist.

"I know you're not going to believe this — it sounds as corny as 'Kansas in August' — but we saw each other and that was it. We, or I at least, never saw another person the rest of the evening."

He sat quietly for a couple of minutes, then connected with my eyes again. "It was really great those first few days, even for weeks, I guess. We saw a lot of each other for a couple of months, and after talking about it a lot, we decided Eric should move into my apartment. I had a lot of furniture and stuff; I was close to work and Eric had to drive around a lot to different parts of town anyway. So he moved in with me."

"And sex?" I asked. His face lit up again with a broad smile of spontaneous warmth. I could understand Eric's loving this man. "Well, I've never felt better, more free, more able to be myself in bed than when I'm with Eric. That's how I felt with him — free. You know, we didn't do anything really trippy, but I felt *good* with him. Most times I just liked being close to him, touching him, holding him. We didn't always have to be doing anything."

His face hardened, and his eyes left mine. "But it didn't last. After a couple of months' living together, we started nagging each other and drifting apart. Eric started going to bed with other guys; I was jealous, and we started fighting about that and most everything else." Here he stopped, breathed deeply, and tried to reverse the downward spiral of his words. He wasn't successful. "Why didn't it last? Why doesn't the feeling ever last?"

During this first session, Lloyd told me how things started going wrong. At first he had been very turned on by Eric's classic good looks and felt a real ego boost when he went out with Eric. He was proud to be seen with such a "hot number." But he found himself increasingly threatened by this same beauty; he felt a nagging insecurity because of the attention Eric received from other men. He wondered if he was good enough to hold onto Eric.

Lloyd felt competitive with Eric on several other levels. The kitchen belonged to Eric. Their friends gave Eric many strokes for performing so well with the soups and spoons. And Eric was much more the star when other people were around. He was comfortable with many different kinds of people and was often the center of attention, with his quick humor and tales of past adventures. Lloyd frequently felt ignored and jealous.

His arms unfolded in an expansive gesture of incomprehension. "We fight over the stupidest things," he continued, "like how the furniture should be arranged, the capital city of Nigeria, who should empty the garbage, and who should supervise the guy who comes in to clean the apartment on Mondays. They're trivial issues, but they seem terribly important when we fight about them."

Before the end of this first session, Lloyd had given a familiar and despairing recital. "I've been in many relationships that don't last very long. I've done enough of the bar, bath, and park trip. I'm tired of that; it doesn't give me what I want. I'm tired of the superficial one-night stands or quickies here and there. They all just leave me guilty and empty until the hornies strike again." Here he was fairly spitting out the words, almost out of breath. He paused, and I felt an expectation that's become familiar in my counseling experience — a feeling that the next point is the key issue for the speaker.

"Besides, the body's going, and I don't want to be alone when I'm up there in years."

He didn't stop there but continued with disparaging and self-accusatory questions. "Are gay men really so confused, insincere, and tacky that we can't make a relationship last? Do you think I have it in me to be able to love someone? Did I miss out on something? *What's wrong with me?*"

As Lloyd left the office, he sighed and asked — this time with a note of both hope and hopelessness in his voice — "Can we keep it together? Do you think you can help?"

"I want to. Together we'll work on it, we'll see what we can do." I did want to help; I hoped I would be able, but I hesitated to offer any guarantees.

Eric had a somewhat different perspective on their relationship, past and present. "I was doubtful from the first. I've been in and out of numerous affairs and short-lived relationships. I guess I'm just one of those people who find it hard to make a commitment." There was a sense of resignation and defeat in his tone. His hand grasped the arm of my sofa so hard that the whiteness stood out sharply against his tanned skin. The stiff fingers of his other hand pushed rhythmically up and down his left thigh. His voice was deep, his left leg bent and crossed over the right knee at the ankle. His posture, position, manner, and movements presented a comfortable picture of masculinity. He was a "natural man," with no pretense, no studied, self-conscious attempt at proper role-playing.

Eric listed his complaints. "Lloyd continues to ignore my feelings and desires — about everything from what movie to see to when and how to have sex. He's really selfish, but he won't listen when I try to talk with him about it. He just accuses me of the same fault. For example, he knows I like to eat out a lot, but he never suggests it, even on special occasions. I also like to cuddle a lot, but he never seems to initiate that. I should think that if he really cared for me, he would do some of the things I like sometimes. *He knows how I feel.*"

Here Eric changed his position, relaxed more, and took a deep breath before continuing his recital of grievances. "And he never listens to me. I try to talk about how I feel about things sometimes — I guess I'm the sensitive one — but he never really seems interested. All he wants to talk about is the bank. So I go see my friend Tony sometimes and we talk about things we have in common, things that Lloyd doesn't seem to care about. Then he gets jealous because I spend so much time away or because he's afraid I'm out having sex with other people. And sometimes I do. Not with Tony — he's too good a friend — but sometimes I make it with other guys."

His momentum continued to build; it was as if he'd been waiting to unburden himself. "And I feel guilty as hell about that. You can't just go hopping from person to person all the time if you're in love with one guy, can you? And it makes Lloyd so scared and mad and jealous. I try to tell him that those people don't matter, but he can't believe it.

"What do other people do? Can I learn to limit my sexual interest only to Lloyd?" He didn't wait for a response, but continued. "It's kind of depressing to think that I may be stuck forever with some sexual routine that's not very exciting."

He had turned sideways and was looking out the window during this release. Now he turned to me. His body was facing me directly, open to what I had to offer. "But I want to work it out." He repeated, "I want to work it out; I don't want to go out to the sex market again."

There was fear in his voice now. For a moment he was lost in thought, as if he were examining his reflected profile; then he startled himself back to the interaction with me. "But perhaps the worst feeling I have with him is that I am inferior." This confession he made with conviction. "Look, he's got a good job, managing a whole department, and still on the way up. And me, I'm still struggling, trying to find out if I can write. I get so depressed sometimes, wondering if I'll ever make it, frustrated because of the repeated rejections and angry because I have to smile and pretend to be enjoying myself as I talk to all those people who are judging my material. Lloyd is sane, secure, and smart. I feel like a neurotic scatterbrain sometimes by comparison. I know that I criticize and yell at him sometimes, but I do it partially because I feel so inadequate."

By now the hand that had been caressing his thigh was clasped tightly into a fist and was lightly pounding the pillow. There was a slight yet perceptible quiver in his chin, and his eyes seemed more moist and sparkly then before. He punched the cushion once again, swallowed, and his facial expression changed to grim determination. "I want to make this one last. Tell me what to do."

The frustrations and confusion expressed in this first counseling session with Lloyd and Eric represent only a few of what I believe are often serious barriers to the development of committed gay male relationships. Our culture has taught us much about being men and being gay. We've been conditioned in many ways that create conflicts in our love relationships. Recognizing these conventional problems — the existence of competition, the withholding of feelings of need and the conflicting expectations about sexual behavior — can help couples like Lloyd and Eric maintain satisfying relationships. Let's look more closely at these three barriers.

Men are supposed to win. Eric sometimes yelled at Lloyd because he felt inferior; he couldn't win. Lloyd was too "sane, secure, and smart." Lloyd reported that they "fought over the stupidest things." It seems that some of us must win, no matter how insignificant the issue. Our bodies were male when we were born, and as children we could not avoid the demands that we act like men. "Go out there and show them how it's done"; "Losers are sissies"; "It's a dog-eat-dog world"; "Don't let him take your toy away"; and "Don't settle for anything less than being number one." All these and many similar messages told us how to behave if we wanted to be loved, worthwhile, and appropriate — men. Remember for a moment the praise that came as a result of winning, from being the strongest, the first, the fastest, the brightest, the biggest, the best.

As a corollary to the exhortations to compete, to win, not to give in, we were taught to believe that softness, tenderness, acknowledgment of weaknesses and needs, and asking rather than demanding would make us lose, especially when we were in competition with other men. Sometimes we intensified these competitive values and fears of vulnerability. We couldn't accept early realizations that our feelings were somehow different from the feelings men around us seemed to express. Some of us didn't want to compete with other boys, but wanted to hold them, to be tender with them, so we overreacted to this unacceptable feeling by becoming even more competitive and distant. That indoctrination is not easy to forget, even when we later accept that it's good to love another man, physically and with feeling.

Eric *assumed* that Lloyd knew how he felt and was angry that Lloyd did not respond to these hidden feelings. He also feared letting Lloyd know he felt inadequate, afraid that Lloyd would then assert his supposed superiority or would reject Eric for his unmanly weaknesses. After all, we are attracted to *men*, and men are supposedly strong. Eric was trapped — he couldn't expose himself because he would feel awful about himself if he was not somehow stronger than Lloyd — he needed to win. How can two men who both need to be on top ever work it out?

A third broad area that creates barriers between men who want to stay together is sex. Again, as boys, many of us were taught that men are supposed to be sexually active, experienced, ready, and able. Can you remember exaggerating about your sexual experiences, especially during the teenage years or early twenties? There's also a myth that men are always horny, that men are all bubbling cauldrons of hot passion ready to explode any time in almost any circumstance. Unfortunately, many of us have bought this misconception.

The barriers to loving relationships become greater when you add some of the stereotypes and expectations about being gay. Everyone knows that all gay men do is have sex, right? If we don't, can't, or aren't interested, we begin to wonder what's wrong. Even if we accept that we can get by without so much sex, we still struggle to present what we think other men expect. In other words, "If I want him to like me, I have to be good in bed, I have to do what he wants sexually — I have to prove I'm a man in bed."

Lloyd feared that his relatively undramatic sexual needs and performances had become boring; Eric, in turn, had come to believe that sex must be continually new and innovative. He'd confused the need for closeness and acceptance with the need for sex. He was afraid to ask for the closeness, but because of an unfulfilled need, he demanded sexual attention from Lloyd. Lloyd felt the pressure and came to feel inadequate in satisfying Eric's desires. When Eric felt frustrated at Lloyd's lack of interest and attention, he sought the fulfillment of these needs in exciting sex with new people. He had great difficulty in expressing these needs directly and resented Lloyd's not responding without a request. But then he felt guilty about making it with other people because he knew Lloyd wanted a monogamous sexual relationship.

Because of the training many of us received as we grew up as well as the continuing values that surround us, we are often confronted with a sort of no-win situation when we attempt to become involved in loving relationships. Lloyd and Eric are two people who were taught that we should always win, we should never let anyone better us, we should take control and always be strong. But one of the ingredients of ongoing love and intimacy seems to be an ability to be vulnerable, to let one's weaknesses show and let the potential lover see the real thing. Many of us have a difficult time taking the risk. We've been taught well that if we let down our guard, another man will take advantage of our openness.

This catch-22, no win, Scylla and Charybdis situation also applies to the conventional wisdom many of us accept about the relationship between love and sex and marriage. Many of us assumed we would grow up, fall in love, and get married. After all, that's what adults seemed to do, or want to do at least. Since many of us were told that sex, marriage, and love go together, many gay men learned to value a committed, monogamous relationship.

But we also got a contradictory message. Remember: Men are supposed to be sexually experienced and active. Add to that expectation the stereotype that gay men are supposed to have lots of sex with lots of different people, and we have a man being pulled in two different directions. On the one hand, to be happy and continue a relationship, a man must be sexually and lovingly monogamous. To fill the *gay male* role expectation, however, he must be sexually involved with different people, often, and good at it.

Many assumptions must be questioned by couples like Lloyd and Eric. This process can begin the realization that they each have choices about how their relationship can fit their unique needs. After watching them interact for several sessions, learning more of their history, and nourishing the relationship among the three of us, I approached some of these questions with both of them.

"Eric, what's the terrible thing that's likely to happen if Lloyd really becomes aware of how inferior you feel?" I asked this question during our eighth session together.

Lloyd smiled nervously while his index finger rapidly massaged his lower lip. Eric hesitated; he was at the edge of something, ready to see a familiar situation with new eyes. "I'm afraid." He spoke quietly, hesitated again, and allowed his glance to catch Lloyd's eyes, seeking reassurance and encouragement to go on.

"Sometimes it helps, Eric, if you can say what you're feeling right now." I gave additional encouragement.

"I want to know that Lloyd . . ." He looked from me to Lloyd and took one of Lloyd's hands between his two, squeezing gently as he spoke. "I'm afraid you won't respect me if you see my need for you. Compared to you I feel young and dumb and incompetent and I'm afraid that if you knew that, you'll go look for somebody stronger." After this rush of words, Eric dropped his head, waiting, not able to look at Lloyd's face.

Lloyd pulled his hand from between Eric's and tenderly placed it on one of Eric's cheeks. Then he tilted his face upwards so they could look directly and closely at each other. A tear on Eric's cheek quickly tumbled to his chin. Lloyd's voice was suddenly broken and unsure.

"Do you know how many times I've wanted to say the same to you? How many times I've felt unable to please you sexually? How much I feel I've let you down?" The questions continued as their arms enclosed each other.

In counseling couples like Eric and Lloyd, one of the things I try to do is help them become aware of the "role expectation messages" they've received about masculinity, sex, and relationship. I try to emphasize the messages that surround all of us as gay men, both in our larger culture and our own gay culture today. In understanding that these roles are arbitrary, many gay men can begin to move beyond attitudes, behaviors, and feelings that are limiting to the formation and continuation of loving relationships. We try to discover through an examination of values, expectations, and anxieties what kind of working relationship will be most suitable for the particular individuals in a couple. In other words, we work to get beyond the old messages as much as possible and discover what it is that these particular people need, want, or expect from each other in terms of sex, power, control, dependency, and roles.

After a few more sessions, we were ready to work at redefining the relationship according to Lloyd's and Eric's specific and individual needs.

"Lloyd, now that you accept that Eric's sexual activities with others aren't a reflection of your inadequacies, can you describe your feelings about his going out?"

By now, they had both learned that they were to talk with each other rather than through me. Lloyd looked at Eric; Eric turned toward Lloyd.

"I'm willing to allow your sexual contact with others," he vowed. "I'll probably continue to feel jealous sometimes, and I guess you'll just have to live with how that makes me behave." He paused and seemed to search in his thoughts and feelings for anything else he wanted to say. "I want to continue to tell you how I feel, but I know I won't be able. Sometimes I'll need your help, your reassurance, your encouragement."

With such couples, I work on actively integrating new ways of relating that will increase the likelihood of their individual interdependency needs being met. We achieve some of this changed behavior through role-playing and various skill-training exercises directed at opening up communication. We rehearse statements that begin "I want . . .," "or I feel . . .," or "When you do that, I feel . . ." Couples go home with instructions for experiences that are directed toward developing the ability to express tenderness and vulnerability, for making requests, for losing, but losing gracefully.

Acknowledging that we sometimes interact in unsatisfactory ways because of our early conditioning helps take away feelings of inadequacy and supplies energy for more self-direction. No longer do we hear: "What's wrong with me?" Instead, it's: "I do have some control, some choice over how I will relate with this person." Practicing new ways to express ourselves, awkward though it may be, gives us the tools for getting more of what we want with each other and sometimes, of course, without each other.

There are conditions in our culture that make it difficult for gay men to "get it together." Many of them have to do with sex-role expectations or with self-fulfilling prophecies resulting from stereotypes about being a gay man. But be-

cause we are gay, there are also more opportunities for self-direction and definition in the way we interrelate. We *can* find our way out of the locked-in,
expected patterns of interaction and discover new and more individually satisfying ways of relating to each other. We *can* develop our own definitions of
relationship, through struggle and caring. And for some of us, this may evolve
into a choice not to be in a committed one-to-one relationship at all, now or in
the future.

PART TEN

◆ ◆ ◆

Men in Families

Are men still taking their responsibilities as family breadwinners seriously? Are today's men sharing more of the family housework and childcare than those in previous generations? The answers to these questions are complex, and often depend on which men we are talking about and what we mean when we say "family."

Many male workers long ago won a "family wage," and with it made an unwritten pact to share that wage with a wife and children. But today, as Barbara Ehrenreich argues in her influential book, *The Hearts of Men*, increasing numbers of men are revolting against this traditional responsibility to share their wages, thus contributing to the rapidly growing impoverishment of women and children. Ehrenreich may be correct, at least with respect to the specific category of men who were labeled "yuppies" in the 1980s. But as Sidel points out in her article, if we are looking at the growing impoverishment of women and children among poor, working class, and minority families, the causes have more to do with dramatic shifts in the structure of the economy — including skyrocketing unemployment among young black males — than they do with male irresponsibility. Increasing numbers of men, she argue, have no wage to share with a family.

But how about the New Dual-Career Family? Can we look to this emerging family type as a model of egalitarianism? Weiss's research indicates that the growth of dual-career families has not totally undermined the traditional sexual division of labor in the home. Men may "help out" more today, but most still maintain "traditional conceptions of marital responsibility," thus leaving women with the "double workday" so often remarked on by feminist sociologists. On a more positive note, Kimball's article outlines the characteristics of a still small, but growing number of men who are developing more egalitarian arrangements with their mates.

As the high divorce rate indicates, many married couples are finding it increasingly difficult to maintain lasting and meaningful intimate relationships over time. And if it is difficult for heterosexual couples to stay together — even in a culture that celebrates and institutionally supports the marital bond — imagine how difficult it must be for gay men to create and maintain meaningful and lasting relationships within a homophobic culture. The narrow social definition of "The Family" as being a heterosexual nuclear family with 2.2 children places severe constraints and pressures on gay couples, as Rex Reece points out in his article, and on gay fathers, as Miller illustrates. Finally, this part concludes with Garfinkel exploring a largely ignored topic: the important role of grandfathers in families.

Ruth Sidel

BUT WHERE ARE THE MEN?

somebody almost run off wit alla my stuff/& I was standin there/lookin at
myself/the whole time & it waznt a spirit took my stuff/waz a man whose
ego walked round like Rodan's shadow/was a man faster in my innocence/
waz a lover/i made too much room for/almost run off wit alla my stuff/&
I didnt know i'd give it up so quik/& the one running wit it/dont know he
got it/& i'm shoutin this is mine/& he dont know he got it/my stuff is the
anonymous ripped off treasure of the year.[1]

— *Ntozake Shange*

Over and over as I interviewed women in different parts of the country I heard
stories of men walking out on women. Sometimes the couple was young and
had been together a short time, other times they were middle-aged and had
been together for many years; but almost always, the man was the one who
walked out — often with little or no warning — and the woman and children
were left to cope as best they could. From the women of Maine to the Native
American families of New Mexico, I met mothers and children trying to make
it on their own and trying to deal with their pain and anger.

Men are not always the ones who walk out, of course. Sometimes the women
leave; sometimes the split is mutual; and sometimes the man was never really
there. But whether because of divorce, separation, or not marrying at all, the
grouping that remains is mothers with their children, children with their mothers. And where are the men? Some have simply vanished, gone on to other
things. Others have started new families. Some feel that they cannot live up to
their roles as fathers because they cannot live up to their roles as breadwinners.

Barbara Ehrenreich, in her recent book *The Hearts of Men*, claims that over
the past thirty years American men have been fleeing from commitment to the
family. She points out that in the 1950s "adult masculinity was indistinguishable
from the breadwinner role. . . ."[2] Gradually, according to Ehrenreich, the prod-
ding of cultural forces such as *Playboy* — which encouraged, as one sociologist
has described it, the "fun morality" — and the health profession's warning that
the stress that came from the role as breadwinner could well lead to coronary
heart disease encouraged men to drift more and more toward a commitment to
self, toward "doing one's own thing," and away from the confines and conflicts
of wife, children, mortgage, and the pressures of new shoes for the first day of
school. As Ehrenreich states, "The result of divorce, in an overwhelming number of cases, is that men become singles and women become single mothers."[3]

While there is little doubt that much of Ehrenreich's analysis is valid, it is not
the whole story. In the first place, her analysis is valid not just for men but for
much of American society as a whole. The shift toward concern with self, with
individual needs and desires, with personal growth, toward narcissism, has been
widespread and is a result, I believe, of fundamental societal developments over

the course of the twentieth century — urbanization, the changing nature of work, and the development of a consumer society.

Urbanization has, as is well known, been a major factor in the fragmentation of primary groups. The pressures, variety, and opportunities of the city, together with the anonymity it provides, have made it increasingly possible for individuals to shake off their obligations to others, to walk away without fear of censure from the "group," for there is hardly any group left. If family members are scattered, if there is no defined community, if there are no elders to censure, why not simply walk away from upsetting and restrictive commitments?

While urbanization was disrupting networks of community and kin, specialization was becoming the primary mode of work in twentieth-century America. As French sociologist Emile Durkheim pointed out nearly a hundred years ago, when societies are small and everyone does much the same kind of work, a "collective consciousness" develops based on similar socialization and shared experiences and values. When, however, each person does just one small piece of an overall task, and this task has little relationship to what others are doing, individualism is fostered. Durkheim predicted that such a division of labor and the resulting growth of individualism would lead to a breakdown in commitment to social norms, the situation Ehrenreich seems to be describing.[4] Add to urbanization and an extreme division of labor the pressures of a consumer society — in which we are systematically taught to believe that we are what we wear, what we own, what we buy; an unrelenting pressure to acquire new goods in order to redefine ourselves continually — and a social milieu develops in which individualism and self-gratification are rewarded, and commitment to others is devalued. That commitment is particularly constraining if it seems to diminish one's own options, one's own pleasures, one's own "personal growth."

And, of course, men are not the only ones who have been affected by these profound changes in American society. Women, and specifically those in the women's movement, have been affected by the emphasis on individualism, by the increasing legitimacy of individual needs and aspirations, of individual happiness. If "We Shall Overcome" was the anthem of the 1960s, perhaps Madonna sings the anthem of the 1980s in her song "Material Girl."[5]

It is striking, however, that while many women are concerned with the quality of their lives, with their own development and careers, with their "material world," they remain, as Ehrenreich correctly points out, the primary caregivers for their children. While many men have abdicated their parental responsibilities, women for the most part have not.

Part of the explanation of women's special relationship to their children lies, clearly, in the special nature of the mothering role, with the bonding that takes place in utero and then during the first few weeks and months of an infant's life, and the ongoing intimate relationship women continue to have with children. But another part of the explanation of the male ability to avoid the responsibilities of fatherhood may well lie in the nature of the fathering role in our society. Is the role of father such that it produces a lack of genuine involvement with children, a lack of real connectedness? Are the majority of fathers simply expected to bring home a paycheck and occasionally to throw a baseball around — and is this kind of relationship just too tenuous to bind men to their children? With the increasing erosion of the patriarchal role, we must develop an equally meaningful way for men to relate to their children.

Profound class differences exist in the ways men relate to their families today. The models written up on the women's pages of leading newspapers — of men trying to take paternity leave, of "househusbands," of a recent best-seller in which a father lyrically describes the first year of his daughter's life — are those of relatively few, usually highly educated, upper-middle-class men. While a fair number of men near Columbia University or in Harvard Square or in Berkeley may lovingly carry their babies in Snugglies, it is hardly a common sight at the entrance to auto plants, in accounting firms, or among men who hang out on the streetcorners of urban ghettos. Clearly behavior that is encouraged and rewarded in one segment of the upper middle class is considered unacceptable in much of the rest of the country; until the perceptions and values and norms of the larger society change, we cannot rationally expect individual behavior to alter significantly.

The bottom line of the male flight from commitment, of many fathers' lack of involvement with their children and, above all, of economic factors usually beyond the individual's control, is that the majority of men who are not living with their wives and children are also not supporting them. The issue of child support has received considerable attention over the past few years because of the unprecedented increase in the number of female-headed families during the 1970s. The importance of child support to the economic well-being of mothers and children is underscored by women's low earning ability. According to a Working Paper published by the Wellesley College Center for Research on Women, women "with the sole custody of children experience the most severe decline in family income."[6] A spring 1982 Census Bureau survey found that over 8 million women are raising at least one child whose father is absent from the home. Of these 8 million women, only 5 million had been awarded child support by the courts. Of the women who were supposed to be receiving payments in 1981, 47 percent received the full amount, 37 percent received less than half of what they were supposed to receive, and 28 percent received no payments at all.[7] Ironically, the women most likely to receive court-ordered child support are "educated, employed, divorced women" rather than separated, never married, minority women.[8] The average annual child-support payment in 1981 was $2,180 for white women, $2,070 for Hispanic women, and $1,640 for black women.[9]

Why don't men pay child support more regularly? Some men withhold payment in reaction to the bitterness of a divorce, some as a way of protesting what they feel is an unfair financial settlement, and some because they want to use their money to recapture the sense of being single, of being free.

Betty Levinson, a New York lawyer who devotes approximately one-third of her practice to matrimonial law, feels that in most divorce cases she sees there is simply not enough money to support two households. These families, mostly middle and upper middle class, are "premised on plastic." Often these couples cannot afford to separate; both husbands and wives must learn to "trim their expectations in planning for their lives after divorce."

On the issue of nonsupport Levinson feels that many men would rather pay for a lawyer than support their children. She suggests that one scenario is: "Now that it's over I can't deal with you anymore. You represent a failure for me and therefore I don't want to deal with the kids either because I associate the kids with the failed marriage and with you." Another scenario is that the man has remarried and is supporting his new wife and her children, who, in turn, are not being supported by their father. Part of the message such a man gives to his former wife is, "When you took custody you took responsibility." The fathers who say this, according to Levinson, are frequently men who do not see their kids very often, because they live in another state or for some other reason.

The third scenario involves the father who sees his kids, but mainly for Sunday visits. According to Betty Levinson, "It's incredible the kind of money these fathers will spend on these weekly visits — theater, ski trips, and so forth — but they resist giving more in the way of child support. Often the father's feeling is, 'Yes, I understand that the child needs this now, but I have to think of my future.' The ultimate responsibility for the children," she states flatly, "is with the mother. No matter what happens, the mother takes care of the children."

Researchers and activists, both those who work for more stringent child-support legislation and spokespersons on behalf of men's groups, agree that the payment of child support is often tied to the altered parent–child relationship. Researchers have found that after divorce fathers often experience a loss of identity, a loss of status within the family, and a "particularly poignant sense of loss associated with the altered father–child relationship. The divorced father is no longer part of the day-to-day life of the child, but is abruptly relegated to a visitor status. . . . Many fathers cope by distancing themselves from the parent–child relationship."[10] What better way to do this than by withholding financial support?

James A. Cook, president of the National Congress for Men, a four-year-old coordinating group of 125 men's rights organizations with ten thousand members, also ties the problem of economic support to fathers' lack of access to their children. He asks, "Can we levy responsibility on these fathers without an equivalent right, the right of access to the child?"[11] John A. Rossler of the Equal Rights for Fathers of New York State agrees: "Many men have had to beg for access to their children. The system of divorce in America often results in the removing of all fathering functions save for one, the monetary obligation. A man is more than a wallet to his kids."[12] Rossler and other representatives of men's groups, strongly endorse custody reform: "Whether you call it joint custody, shared custody, liberal visitation or co-parenting, we are talking about actively involving the noncustodial parent in all areas of his child's upbringing."[13]

Betty Levinson, on the other hand, feels that joint custody is a very "trendy" issue; it is thought to be "the thing to do." She claims that men are made to feel that if they do not demand joint custody that they are not the fathers they should be. But it is, she points out, a very difficult arrangement. The husband and wife must cooperate extremely well for it to work. She goes on to state emphatically:

> Joint custody becomes an economic bludgeon on the wife by the husband. Asking for joint custody or trying to take custody away from the mother is a surefire way to freak out the mother. And after they have freaked her out, the father and his lawyer will often say, "Okay, you take 75 percent of our financial agreement instead of 100 percent and I'll give you full custody." It has become a way of negotiating the money.

On August 16, 1984, a comprehensive bill to enforce payment of child support became federal law. Approved by unanimous roll call votes in both houses of Congress, the new law requires child-support orders issued or modified after October 1, 1985, to permit the withholding of wages if a parent becomes delinquent in payments and enables states to "'require that an absent parent give security, post a bond, or give some other guarantee'" to ensure final payment of child support in cases where there has been a pattern of delinquency.[14] This law is a significant victory for those groups that have been advocating more stringent regulations and collection methods to improve the rate of payment of child support.

But voluntary nonpayment of child support is clearly only one facet of the problem of the absent father. Many fathers provide little or no support — either in economic or emotional terms — to their children and to the children's mothers because they are unable to play the traditional fathering role, that of breadwinner. In January 1983 approximately 12 million people, over 10 percent of the American work force, were actively looking for jobs and were the officially designated unemployed. While that number has since fallen to 7.2 percent, this stark figure, the highest rate since the Great Depression, has stimulated additional studies on the physiological, psychological, and sociological aspects of unemployment.

First, it must be pointed out that federal unemployment statistics significantly minimize the problem of unemployment. Figures released by the Bureau of Labor Statistics do not include those who reluctantly move from full-time to part-time employment; those who take jobs well below their skill level; those who must move from one temporary, low-paying job to the next; and those who become "permanently discouraged" and stop looking for work altogether. Nor do the statistics, as one researcher has movingly written, "reflect the anxiety, depression, deprivation, lost opportunities, violence, insecurity, and anger people feel when their source of livelihood is severed and they lose control of a significant aspect of their environment."[15] As Paula Rayman, sociologist and director of the New England Unemployment Project, has written, "When an adult has work taken away, the focus of life's daily pattern is removed. Time and space, the sense of self, are radically altered, and what is left is a sense of impotency."[16]

The work of Johns Hopkins sociologist and epidemiologist Harvey Brenner demonstrates the dramatic effect unemployment has on the entire family's health and well-being. Brenner has found, for example, that admissions to psychiatric hospitals, deaths from cardiovascular and alcohol-related illnesses, homicide and suicide rates increase significantly during periods of economic decline.[17] Other researchers have found that male unemployment is associated with high blood pressure, alcoholism, increased smoking, insomnia, anxiety, and higher levels of psychiatric symptoms among men. In addition, "The wives in unemployed families were significantly more depressed, anxious, phobic, and sensitive about their interpersonal relationships" than spouses in families in which there is no unemployment.[18] The longer the period of unemployment, the greater the stress on the family and on family cohesion. In a study of the unemployed in Hartford, Rayman and Ramsey Liem found three times as much marital separation among the unemployed group as among the control group.[19]

Clinical observations of unemployed people who go to social agencies for counseling indicate that they are coping with feelings of loss, anger, and guilt — a "sense of losing a part of the self." Observers have likened these feelings to feelings of bereavement. Studies find that people anticipating or experiencing unemployment "suffer loss of self-esteem, loss of personal identity, worry and uncertainty about the future, loss of a sense of purpose, and depression."[20] With these reactions to unemployment, is it any wonder that family stability is being undermined?

While there has been a limited economic recovery since the height of the 1982–1983 recession, many workers' incomes have declined sharply since the late 1970s. For example, the average income of workers laid off by the United States Steel Corporation's South Works in Chicago has fallen in the last five years by 50 percent. Over two thousand workers were laid off from 1979 to 1981, and another thirty-three hundred were laid off from 1981 to 1983. Many of these workers have had long periods of unemployment; 46 percent remained unemployed as of October 1984. The laid-off workers, whose annual household income averaged $22,000 in 1979, had a median household income in 1983 of approximately $12,500. According to one worker, "To go from earning $20,000-plus to being at an employer's mercy for $3.35 an hour is devastating."[21] Moreover, unskilled workers and black and Hispanic male workers have extremely limited opportunities for work and suffer from the highest unemployment rates. In a 1983 study of the New York City job market, it was found that the decline in manufacturing and the expansion of the service sector have led to a decrease in job opportunities in the city for workers with few skills and limited education. Of all adults, black and Hispanic men twenty-five to thirty-four years old "generally do the worst in the job market": They experience extended periods of unemployment, withdraw from the labor force because they become "discouraged," and have a high rate of involuntary part-time work. Moreover, among blacks and Hispanics, the length of unemployment for men is twice what it is for women: for black men, twenty-seven weeks; for black women, twelve weeks; for Hispanic men, twenty-two weeks; for Hispanic women, nine weeks.[22]

Nationally, unemployment among blacks is officially twice the rate for whites, but the statistics tell only part of the story. Researchers at the Center for the Study of Social Policy claim that the true figure is that 4 million out of 9 million working-age black men — 46 percent — are jobless. For white men the comparable figure is 22 percent.[23] Unemployment of this magnitude must have a dramatic impact on family stability and therefore be a major cause of the feminization of poverty. In 1960, according to this method of calculation, approximately three-quarters of all black men were employed; today only 54 percent are employed. Since 1960 the number of black families headed by women has more than tripled.[24] There is little question that the unemployment of black men has had a direct impact on the rise of black female-headed families.

Furthermore, unemployment is only one of many severe problems black men must face. The National Urban League recently released a report stating that black men must deal with a "singular series of pressures from birth through adulthood." The report stated, "The gantlet that black men run takes its toll at every age." In addition to the problems of educational and employment discrimination, Dr. James McGhee, the league's research director, cited higher mortality rates, greater likelihood of being arrested, and the rising incidence of self-destructive behavior such as drug and alcohol abuse. Black men have the highest death rates from accidents and violence of all groups, and their suicide rate has risen far more sharply in recent years than that of white men.[25] In addition, homicide is the leading cause of death for black males ages fifteen to forty-four.

Black men represent only 5 percent of the U.S. population but represent 44 percent of its homicide victims.[26] Many studies suggest that there is a direct correlation between feelings of frustration, powerlessness, and hopelessness and high rates of violence. According to sociologist and researcher on black families Andrew Billingsley, because of racial discrimination, many black men are distant from "any meaningful engagement with the economy, education and social system."[27]

Elliot Liebow, in what has become a classic study of streetcorner black men in Washington, DC, points out the close connection between a man's work and his relationships with family and friends: "The way in which the man makes a living and the kind of living he makes have important consequences for how the man sees himself and is seen by others; and these, in turn, importantly shape his relationships with family members, lovers, friends and neighbors."[28] Liebow points out that the unskilled black man has little chance of obtaining a permanent job that would pay enough to support a family. He eventually becomes resigned to being unable to play the traditional father role, and rather than being faced with his own failure day after day, year after year, he often walks away.

Ironically, the children with whom these men are closest are not those they have fathered and therefore have an obligation to support; but rather the children of the women they are currently seeing, who have been fathered by someone else. With someone else's children, whatever the men can give in the way of financial or emotional support is more than they need to give, and it therefore represents a positive gesture rather than yet another failure.[29]

What is saddest about these dismal facts is how American ideology, which is apparently accepted by the majority of Americans and has been legitimized by the Reagan administration, blames the poor, rather than racism and the economic system, for their plight. While some of these issues were briefly addressed during the 1960s, the War on Poverty was woefully inadequate to reverse the damage done, particularly to blacks, in our society; and no sooner did it get started than Vietnam, inflation, and the Nixon administration had begun to subvert it. As Michael Harrington has so aptly stated, "The savior that never was became the scapegoat that is."[30]

American policymakers have an uncanny ability to obfuscate and compartmentalize social problems — to recognize on the one hand that the United States has an unacceptably high level of unemployment, particularly among specific groups, and to recognize that we also have an incredibly high number of female-headed families, particularly within the same groups; but to avoid the cause-and-effect relationship between the two phenomena. This unwillingness to recognize the obvious correlation between the lack of economic opportunities for millions of American men — a lack of opportunity that will consign them, in all likelihood, for their entire lifetimes to the bottom of the class structure — and their lack of commitment to and steady participation in family life, is a shocking denial of the obvious impact of social and economic factors on the well-being of the family group.

As Eleanor Holmes Norton, former chairperson of the Equal Employment Opportunity Commission and currently a professor at the Georgetown University Law Center, has stated:

> This permanent, generational joblessness is at the core of the meaning of the American ghetto. The resulting, powerful aberration transforms life

in poor black communities and forces everything else to adapt to it. The female-headed household is only one consequence. The underground economy, the drug culture, epidemic crimes and even a highly unusual disparity between the actual number of men and women — all owe their existence to the cumulative effect of chronic joblessness among men.[31]

This avoidance has several advantages for those who seek to maintain the status quo in the United States: It discourages those at the bottom from developing a viable political and economic analysis of the American system, instead promoting a blame-the-victim mentality; a false consciousness of individual unworthiness, of self-blame; a belief that if only the individual worked harder, tried harder, he would "make it" and be the success every American thinks he should be. Not only does the unemployed male blame himself for not getting and keeping a decent job, thereby being unable to provide for his family in the way he would like, but the woman may also blame him. As one woman in *Tally's Corner* says with a bitter smile, "I used to lean on Richard. Like when I was having the baby, I leaned on him but he wasn't there and I fell down. . . . Now, I don't lean on him anymore. I pretend I lean, but I'm not leaning."[32] Or the woman blames herself for not choosing her man more wisely, for not holding the family together despite the odds, for being either too assertive or not assertive enough. And yet virtually no one blames an economic system that deprives millions of workers of jobs and then somehow indicates it is their fault.

Sandra Wittaker, a black woman from California who is raising her two children alone puts it this way:

> Black men are able to cope far less than black women. They are feared more by society and therefore have far fewer opportunities. All the men I have known, my brothers, my father, my male friends, my husband, have not made it in society. Many of them take to drinking and dope — some kind of escape. Black males are suffering far more than females.
>
> My son has had three role models and none of them were any good. He has not had a mature man to model himself on. . . . He has nightmares. He's afraid of being a failure and he's already opted out. By the time he was four, my son did not even want to be black. It is terrible to watch your child and know that he is going to be hurt constantly.

If there is a group that has been hit even harder than blacks, it is Native Americans. Unemployment among the 1 million American Indians is said to range between 45 and 55 percent, but it reaches 80 percent in some areas and in some seasons.[33]

Among the Pueblo Indians who live approximately sixty miles southwest of Albuquerque, New Mexico, for example, the unemployment rate is 70 percent. After the nearby uranium mines were closed in 1981–1982, there were no other jobs available. According to Jean Eller, a young physician who worked at the Acoma Canoncita Laguna Indian Health Hospital in Acoma, New Mexico, people now just "hang around." There is nothing for them to do. And the young people are torn between their desire to find a job in a nearby town or city and pressure from their elders to return to the reservation. The elders are afraid the young people will lose touch with their culture if they move off the reservation, but there are few opportunities there, either.

Tied to the unemployment rate, Dr. Eller believes, is an enormous problem with alcohol and suicide rate that is the highest of any ethnic group in the country. Alcohol is mainly a male problem; some of the younger women drink, but the older women usually do not. According to Dr. Eller, there are three bars, run by non-Indians, near the reservation. One bar half a mile from the reservation serves "all the beer you can drink" free on Monday nights. These bars serve thirteen-year-olds, fourteen-year-olds and never check their ID's. "Many people hate these places and would like to blow them up!" Dr. Eller states quietly but angrily. She feels the significant amount of wife abuse that exists on these reservations is directly related to the amount of drinking, particularly on the weekends.

According to other medical personnel who work in the area, women are the backbone of the Indian family. Many feel that men have fallen apart more than women and are in a "cycle of destruction." The rates of alcoholism, wife abuse, child neglect, homicide, and suicide are at least three to four times the national rate.

There is also a high rate of teenage pregnancy, particularly among girls fifteen and under. The men rarely support their children, and some women move up and out of the reservation; many are, in fact, ostracized by their communities for doing so. The infant is then often cared for by the grandmother and brought up with the grandmother's own children as siblings. Indian women are clearly not first-class citizens even within Indian culture but they have very little recourse since the tribal councils are largely run by men.

The reservation in Acoma is in the middle of incredibly beautiful terrain. As you approach Acoma, the earth varies from beige to darker shades of brown, sometimes flat, sometimes hilly, with stark red clay rock formations that look almost like amphitheaters. Acoma is famous for handsome pottery, much of it black, white, and clay-reddish brown; several of the potters from this reservation sell to private collectors, some to museums. Mt. Taylor, snowcapped even in late spring, can be seen in the distance. Amid this truly splendid scenery, the reservation seems unbearably barren and depressed. During the day there is hardly a man to be seen. There are only women, children, and dogs — scrawny, hungry-looking dogs who roam near the houses.

Lena Ross is a heavyset woman with a weathered face and dark hair pulled back at the nape of her neck. She has moved within the past few days to a modern adobe-colored house in a settlement of new homes, most of which are still empty. The house has several bedrooms furnished with beds and colorful quilts and blankets, a kitchen with the latest in modern appliances, and a large, empty living room.

Ten of Lena Ross's thirteen children and her two grandchildren live with her. She has no husband. "I take care of the children myself," she tells me. She receives AFDC for the children who are still in school, and social security for the grandchildren. While we talk, her one-and-a-half-year-old grandson sits on his grandmother's lap. He is a lively boy with long, dark hair and beautiful dark eyes. He is wearing a good-looking blue-and-white-striped shirt and is playing with a small car. Through the living room window is a picture-postcard view of Mt. Taylor.

While some of these families' material needs are being met, there is an overriding sense of hopelessness, of being caught in a net not of their own making, and from which they cannot get free. For they know, as a CBS news report stated succinctly, "Their destiny is in the hands of strangers."[34] The juxtaposition of the new, modern house and this immovable hopelessness is profoundly disturbing.

Mary Sanchez is a thirty-six-year-old mother of five. Her oldest child is seventeen, her youngest ten. Her seventeen-year-old sister is also living with her; she finished only the eighth grade and has two children, one four and one ten months old. In addition, Mary's oldest daughter has a ten-month-old who also lives there, and one of her brothers lives with her as well. In all, eleven people live in a small wooden house off of a small dirt road; Mary's parents live next door.

Mary and most of the children are on welfare and receive food stamps. The two youngest, the ten-month-old babies, are not on welfare because the welfare worker said she wanted to force the fathers to pay for their upkeep. Mary told the worker to forget it.

Both of the men who fathered her children are dead. The first died of natural causes, but the second, the father of four of her children, died while hitchhiking with another man and two women. "They all must have been drunk," she says simply, "and weaving down the street. A gas truck was coming along and swerved to avoid hitting them. The truck turned over and exploded and all four were burned to death. When relatives went to claim the body, they couldn't tell who it was."

The entire time we talked, a soap opera was on in the background, an intricate melodrama of well-dressed upper-middle-class Anglos lulling these women and their children through the day. The women do not seem despairing but rather fatalistic. When I asked if it was hard for them to manage, they said they managed. When I asked what could be done to make things better, they couldn't think of a thing. It feels as though it takes everything they've got just to get from day to day.

NOTES

1. Ntozake Shange, *For Colored Girls Who Have Considered Suicide When the Rainbow Is Enuf* (New York: Bantam, 1980), 53–54.

2. Barbara Ehrenreich, *The Hearts of Men: American Dreams and the Flight from Commitment* (Garden City, N.Y.: Anchor Press, 1983), 20.

3. Ibid., 121.

4. Emile Durkheim, *The Division of Labor in Society* (Glencoe, Ill.: Free Press, 1964; originally published in 1893).

5. Peter Brown and Robert Rans, "Material Girl," on Madonna, *Like a Virgin*. Sire Records, 1984.

6. Joyce Everett, "Patterns and Implications of Child Support and Enforcement Practices for Children's Well-being." Working Paper No. 128 (Wellesley, Mass.: Wellesley College Center for Research on Women, 1984).

7. Ibid.

8. Ibid.

9. "Child Support Frequently Not Paid," *New York Times* (8 July 1983).

10. Everett, "Patterns and Implications of Child Support."

11. Glenn Collins, "Why Fathers Don't Pay Child Support," *New York Times* (1 September 1983).

12. Ibid.

13. Ibid.

14. Robert Pear, "Reagan Signs Bill Forcing Payments for Child Support," *New York Times* (17 August 1984).

15. Thomas Keefe, "The Stresses of Unemployment," *Social Work* 29 (May–June 1984): 264–268.

16. Paula M. Rayman, "The Private Tragedy Behind the Unemployment Statistics," *Brandeis Quarterly* 2 (July 1982): 2–4.

17. M. Harvey Brenner, "Estimating the Effects of Economic Change on National Health and Social Well-Being," study prepared for the use of the Subcommittee on Economic Goals and Intergovernmental Policy of the Joint Economic Committee (Washington, D.C.: U.S. Government Printing Office, 1984): 3.

18. Ramsay Liem and Paula Rayman, "Health and Social Costs of Unemployment," *American Psychologist* 37 (October 1982): 1116–1123.

19. Ibid.

20. Keefe, "The Stresses of Unemployment."

21. Steven Greenhouse, "Former Steelworkers' Income Falls by Half," *New York Times* (31 October 1984).

22. Damon Stetson, "City Survey Finds Unskilled in Bind," *New York Times* (4 September 1983).

23. Tom Joe and Peter Yu, "Black Men, Welfare and Jobs," *New York Times* (11 May 1984).

24. Ibid.

25. James Barron, "Urban League Cites Pressures on Black Men," *New York Times* (1 August 1984).

26. "Curbing the High Rate of Black Homicide," *NASW* (National Association of Social Workers) *NEWS* (September 1984): 3–4.

27. Ronald Smothers, "Concern for the Black Family: Attention Now Turns to Men," *New York Times* (31 December 1983).

28. Elliot Liebow, *Tally's Corner: A Study of Negro Streetcorner Men* (Boston: Little, Brown, 1967), 210.

29. Ibid., 84.

30. Michael Harrington, *The New American Poverty* (New York: Holt, Rinehart & Winston: 1984), 20.

31. Eleanor Holmes Norton, "Restoring the Traditional Black Family," *New York Times Magazine* (2 June 1985): 43, 79, 93, 96, 98.

32. Liebow, *Tally's Corner*, 132.

33. Ian Robertson, *Sociology* (New York: Worth, 1981), 304.

34. Segment on CBS Sunday morning news, February 10, 1985.

Robert S. Weiss

MEN AND THEIR WIVES' WORK

There is much research to attest to the emotional importance to women of employment outside their homes — to the value of "multiple roles" (Baruch, Bar-

Copyright © 1987 by Robert S. Weiss. Reprinted from *Spouse, Parent, Worker: On Gender and Multiple Roles*, Faye Crosby, ed. New Haven: Yale University Press, 1987. Published by permission. I would like to acknowledge the helpful comments on an earlier draft of this paper provided by Carolyn Bruse and Sharon Spector. Support for the work reported here provided by NIMH, Grant Nos. MH 36708 and MH 39353.

nett, and Rivers, 1983). But what is the meaning to their husbands of such employment? Are husbands happy to have their wives work outside their homes, grudging in their acceptance, or indifferent? Do they view their wives' paid employment as an activity no different in its essentials or its implications from their own or as some other, lesser, thing?

Joseph H. Pleck (1983), on the basis of an exhaustive review of research, reports that men whose wives are employed do not appreciably increase the time they give to home maintenance, childcare, and other familial activities. They perform a larger proportion of familial tasks than is performed by men whose wives are not employed; but this is because their wives do less, not because the men do more. This suggests that men do not revise their assumptions regarding the distribution of marital responsibilities when their wives become employed. How, then, do they understand their wives working?

This chapter is based on information from a study of occupationally successful men. My colleagues and I conducted six to twelve hours of interviews with each of seventy men chosen randomly from the street lists of four upper-income Boston suburbs. The only restrictions placed on eligibility for our sample were that respondents be aged between thirty-five and fifty-five and that they occupy what seemed to be prestigious positions in business or administration. About 75 percent of those contacted agreed to participate in the study.

We also conducted six to twelve hours of interviews with the wives of twelve of the men in the sample and interviewed both partners of an additional eight couples who lived in an upper-income neighborhood of central Boston. The husbands in these couples were in the same age group and occupational category as the men in our suburban sample. In these inner city families, more than in the suburban families, the wives tended to have careers, not just jobs. (See also Weiss, 1985.)

In all but one or two instances, including the dual-career inner-city couples, the men seemed to maintain traditional assumptions of marital responsibilities. These included the following:

- The husband is responsible for the provision of income.
- The wife is responsible for childcare and home maintenance, except that certain home-centered chores may be the husband's, including those that require mechanical skills or skills associated with the building trades, those that are performed on the outside of the home, or those that require physical strength.
- Husband and wife are each obligated to foster the other's well-being and the well-being of the children.
- The husband is the partner ultimately responsible for the protection of the family from external threat.
- Each partner will help in the other's domain of responsibility. The actual amount of help provided will be decided by weighing the need of the one to be helped against the time and energy of the helper. Helping out can be offered freely or can be a matter of negotiation.

This understanding of the partnership agreement of marriage is very close to English common-law expectations of marital partners (Weitzman, 1981:2–3), in which the husband is head of the household and responsible for support and the wife is responsible for domestic services and childcare. The men's understandings differ from common-law expectations in only two ways: first, they believe that the husbands' and wives' obligations also include a responsibility to

542 PART X Men in Families

help each other, subject to negotiation; and second, most of the men subscribe to a less hierarchical view than that implied by the common law. While the common law states that "the husband is head of the household," these men appear to believe that marriage is more nearly a partnership of equals, albeit one in which the man is the partner ultimately responsible for the provision of income and for the family's protection.

Whether the understandings brought to their marriages by their wives were the same as those of the husbands, we cannot say with confidence. Interviews with wives suggested that in many respects they were. However, one basis for marital quarrels could be a husband's refusal to accept a home maintenance chore as a responsibility, even though he was willing to help out by performing it. In these cases, the husband's stand might be "I'm happy to help out if she'll tell me what to do"; the wife's might be, "I don't want to have the responsibility of having to tell him what to do."

The clearest expression of traditional understandings occurs in households in which the wife does not work. Mr. Orcutt is in middle management in a public utility. He and his wife have two children of school age and one not yet of school age. His wife is not employed outside the home. Mr. Orcutt explained how they had arrived at their division of labor.

> I rely on Myra to make sure I've got plenty of clean shirts. I would say Myra relies on me to fix things, keep the cars going, keep the house going. Bring the paycheck home, I guess, would be the biggest thing.
>
> I don't think we ever sat down to say, you'll do this and I'll do that. Right off the bat, Myra was the cook. I never tried my hand at it. If I had to depend on myself to feed myself I'd probably starve. The week that Myra was in the hospital with a leg fracture it was Burger King, pizza, and sub sandwiches.
>
> When Myra was in the hospital I learned how to run the washing machine and dryer. And then for three or four weeks she was home immobile with a cast on her leg, so I sort of had to take over.
>
> Almost anything, whatever the need is, I'm there. The shade just fell off the roller; put it back on the roller. The other night Myra turned the garbage disposal on and it stopped. Well, it blew a fuse.
>
> We do things within our limits of capability. I put the new heating system in. I don't think Myra could have done that.

In the Orcutts' implementation of the rule of helping out, Mr. Orcutt does a good deal around the house. But it is important to note that so long as the tasks are in his wife's domain, it is up to her to give him assignments.

> As far as washing dishes, vacuuming floors, washing floors, we both do that. We both wash windows, we both rake leaves. Not always at the same time. Like this dinner that we had for twelve people, it's a lot of preparation work ahead of time, and as Myra is getting the food ready I may be waxing the kitchen floor or vacuuming.
>
> Myra might say, "Gee, if you have a minute, could you. . .?" or I might say, "All right, what else can I do?" There's no clear-cut division of you do this and I do this. There are certain jobs within our limits of capability that we each do individually. But these other jobs, I'll do it. And the kids will pitch in.

There are many jobs where she is very helpful to me. I'm putting up a ceiling. There are certain jobs that require another pair of hands. I'll be in the middle of something and I can't do it with only two hands, so she is around. Or if one of the kids is around, well, the older one is pretty helpful.

Men do not modify their understandings of marital responsibilities when their wives are employed outside their homes. They may well accept a lower standard of housekeeping or, with less good grace, less attention to the children. They may also accept that they must help out more (although Pleck [1983] found that, while men believe they help out more, diary records show that they do not). In any event, they continue to believe that housekeeping and childcare are their wives' responsibilities. Another of our respondents, Mr. Brewer, has a highly successful catering service. His wife works with him about twenty hours a week taking orders and doing bookkeeping.

Along with working, she keeps the house up and does the shopping and keeps everything rolling inside. I try to get everything outside, the repairs, things like that, paying the bills. She takes care of the household end — the food and the wash and whatever needs to be cleaned. Even though I try to help her out once in a while, I haven't been successful lately.

There are many variations on this basic model, to be sure. One respondent, whose wife has a full-time job, notes that he participates in fetching things for the dinner table. He also says that he is the one who makes coffee.

My wife does the meal preparation, but it's as likely as not that I'll get up from the table to add something or do something for myself rather than ask for it. Since I am probably the greater coffee drinker, I'll almost always do it.

A few men say they are more concerned than are their wives with neatness and so will take it on themselves to clean a room or to straighten up the house when guests are expected. But these instances of husbands doing household chores seemed, at most, minor modifications of basic understandings. In at least one instance, in which a husband did laundry, it was a way of behaviorally criticizing his wife for not having done it sooner — and his wife reacted with defensiveness and anger.

The traditional understandings seem to hold even when the wife has a career and not just a job. Mr. Foster is a highly successful lawyer; his wife earns a small but still substantial salary as a C.P.A. in a large accounting firm.

We have separate bank accounts. Paula can sign on mine; I can't sign on hers. We've always had separate bank accounts. I used to give her money before she went to work.

Paula buys the groceries. There's a guy who comes once a week with the groceries — that's a pretty good bill. And she pays for the housekeeping. And I pay for essentially everything else. I pay for the telephone and the light and tuitions and insurance. She buys a lot of stuff for the house that she wants to buy. Large furniture, that gets in a gray area. If we go to dinner, I pay. Generally. If I have money.

Certainly Paula's working has made a very big different in what we could do. But I have become the court of last resort. I mean, I'm the backstop.

Before Mrs. Foster returned to work, Mr. Foster's income supported the family. Now, although Mr. Foster is no longer his family's sole source of support, he remains ultimately responsible. Mrs. Foster pays bills in her domain of home maintenance, but he is, as he puts it, "the court of last resort." Mr. Foster makes his checking account available to his wife; he does not have access to hers.

The set of traditional understandings I have listed seem entirely acceptable to male respondents. They take pride in their responsibility for their family's support. Rarely do they object to their wives' being responsible for housework, although they do at times regret not having more influence over their children's care. When they disagree with their wives' approach to childraising, as they sometimes do, they can feel frustrated by their impotence to change things or sadly resigned to its inevitability. One respondent, at work an effective manager, exemplified the way men acceded to their wives' childraising styles.

> I tend to go along with the wife's beliefs and desires in terms of what those kids should have and what would be good for them. I'm a peacemaker. If I don't think that things are extremely wrong — and I don't find too many that are — or if I don't really feel all that strongly about them one way or the other, it's more comfortable for me to go along with it. I figure that life is too short to fight everything.

Given their persistent view that providing the family income is a male responsibility, how do the men in our study understand their wives' working? In general they assimilate their wives' employment to their assumptions about how the marital partnership should work. Insofar as the income from their wives' work is helpful to the family, they see it as a matter of their wives helping out — analogous to their own contributions to home maintenance. But they also may view their wives' working as important for their wives' development or mental health. In this case they understand their own support of their wives' working as a contribution to their wives' well-being. And fostering their wives' well-being is one of their marital responsibilities.

We asked the head of a growing high-tech firm how he would react if his wife wanted to go to work. He and his wife have small children and his wife is currently full-time at home. He believes that if she did go to work, he would have to share more of the responsibility for childcare and this would be a burden for him. But, if she really wanted to work and if this would make her happier, then it would be his responsibility as a husband to support her.

> If my wife went to work, it would mean that she would not have the time to do all the things she currently does, and so she would obviously try to move some of those things to me, at some level. Right now we have one daughter in grade school and one daughter in preschool. I suspect that we'd have to bring in some additional people to help raise the children when she's not there and I'm not there. And that probably would be a joint responsibility. And we'd probably have to have other people do some things she normally was doing. It's not consistent with my traditional values, where I think it's nice when the children come home from school that they have a mother there. And that's what I would, philosophically, pre-

fer. But if that wasn't best for my wife and I realized it wasn't going to work, then I would let her do what she wants to do.

Mr. Foster took just this position when actually faced by his wife's need to work. Mr. Foster's wife, at home full-time with their three children, began to display depressive symptoms. After a while he decided that his wife's malaise resulted from her lack of an occupation she could herself value. He strongly supported her desire to return to school to do advanced work in accounting, even though it would mean more work for himself.

> That time she was at home trying to deal with kids, I think that was probably the hardest part of our marriage. She was just restless, very restless and not feeling very accomplished. She was having a difficult time coping with being married and having kids and not having a career and being away from her family and just generally moving on into life. At least that was my analysis.
>
> We never got to the point of having any help, or anything along those lines. But it sure was difficult. And we weren't able to talk very much about it, because it wasn't very well defined. But these were problems that were festering in there. She wasn't very happy, and that's about it. She just wasn't very happy.
>
> Looking back on it, I think that I would really say she was pretty disturbed. I remember now, the way she woke up crying a couple of times, like in bed, talking about her life. I used to get bored with it all. I'd say, "Just relax and go to sleep," that kind of thing. It was just sort of unarticulated anxiety on her part, a lot of self-doubt. And I remember it was very repetitive and it kept going around in circles. And she didn't quite know what was bugging her, but something sure as hell was bugging her. I was trying to be supportive. Trying to make it work.
>
> And what we did, she went back to school. I was absolutely supportive of her going back to school. Absolutely! More than supportive. I pushed it. Because, why the hell shouldn't she? Why should she stay home? It's ridiculous. Her working, I don't think, has affected me very much at all. I've done just about what I would have done before. I did the dishes before. I'll do whatever has to be done around here. I always have. My kids do. I don't want to get waited on. Not that she would!
>
> I think what's been harder for me than it's been for her is when she was a housewife it was the natural thing to do entertaining. But as soon as she started to go to school, the aspect of our lives kind of passed away. And I'm a very gregarious person. I've got lots of friends and I do like to entertain and like to see people. It's not easy. But that's not a big deal.

It should be noted that Mr. Foster and his wife have a good deal of household help — he is not taking over as much housekeeping as his comments may suggest. Still, there are sacrifices for him in his wife's working, especially in her lessened availability as someone to facilitate his social life. Nevertheless, he believes it would have been wrong had he not supported his wife's desire to be out of the house, working in a field she cares about.

Mr. Foster thus views his wife's employment as something he has done for her rather than something she is doing for him and the family. His employment, in contrast, is important not only for him but also for the family. His income permits him to guarantee that the family will have the money it needs. But his wife's work is important for her along — although, to be sure, her extra income is a help. By supporting his wife's work, Mr. Foster sees himself as unselfishly fulfilling his responsibility to support her well-being.

> I think men who aren't accepting of their wives' working are probably pretty selfish. I know there are a lot of people like that. We spent Saturday night with a couple like that. He wants his wife *there*. Why the hell should she be *there* at his beck and call? Women are people too! And they have a right to life. Even wives are people.

One respondent, Mr. Williams, whose children were in high school and college, was pressing his wife to go to work because he thought it would be good for her, although she was herself uncertain. For him, as for Mr. Foster, the money his wife might earn was not important. He thought she would achieve greater self-realization if she worked.

For respondents who are not quite as affluent as Mr. Foster or Mr. Williams, the money their wives bring home makes a difference in what they can afford. If the children no longer require their wives' full attention, these men may want their wives to work to "help out" with bills — just as their wives might ask them to do dishes or put the kids to bed as a way of helping out. Mr. Ryder, a manager of a design department, is in this situation:

> When we got married, twenty-two years ago, it was the wife's role to stay home and take care of the kids. Which Elizabeth did. She made herself available when the kids wanted her. She was around. And she had a very nice relationship with both our children. She devoted time to it. She never got bored or anything like that. A lot of women go out to work because they get bored or they might think they are making a contribution to the world, but she didn't look at things that way. She was happy, essentially, with what she was doing. And I was comfortable with that. That was the way it was supposed to be. The man would go out and make a living and the wife would stay at home and take care of the house and spend most of the time with the kids.
>
> Then two things came together. In the first place, we no longer have any children at home. And in the second place, we will need money, at least for a couple of years, to pay two tuition bills. Those two things kind of came together at the same time. And she is going to be working and getting some money to help us over the hump with the tuition bills. After the tuition bills stop or maybe after we have only one child in school, if she wants to work, fine. If she doesn't it is really up to her.
>
> I don't have the kind of pride that thinks my wife shouldn't work. Especially to raise the kind of money you need for college, it seems a reasonable thing to do. I don't really see any reason why I should be out working and she should stay home, just enjoying herself.

Just as men insist that they be directed when they are in their wives' domain of home maintenance, they also insist that they be the dominant figure when their wives enter their own domain of income production. Men who have their own businesses sometimes want their wives to fill in for an absent employee or to take on temporary responsibility at a time of high demand. Almost invariably, in our materials, they put their wives in positions in which the wives' subordination is emphasized. One man, for example, had his wife's desk in a corridor outside his office. (His wife accepted this for over a year, then blew up.) A single exception in our materials is a wife who became the bookkeeper in her husband's business and was defined as a junior partner. While at work, she maintained some distance from her husband.

Mr. Stavros, president and chief executive officer of a manufacturing firm, is typical of the men who brought their wives into their offices to help out.

> When Connie is an employee at the company she has a different relationship with my secretary than when she is the president's wife. When Connie is at the company, if I want something done, I give it to my secretary and she might give it to Connie. She goes to Connie representing the President of the company and says, "You do it."

This arrangement seems rarely without tension. When men "help out" at home, they may bridle if their wives are peremptory about asking them to repair an appliance or run an errand. Although they view the home and the children as their wives' domains of responsibility, they want to be treated with respect when given assignments in those domains. The men are less aware of their wives' desire for respect when helping out in the husbands' domains. One respondent's wife, a skilled accountant, refused to continue to help her husband with his business because of the way he treated her there.

On the other hand, men feel themselves pledged to protect their wives from misuse by others. This protectiveness displays itself in relation to their wives' experiences at work. Mr. Foster's wife had done much of the work of making her department successful but was then refused promotion. One of the reasons given her was that she didn't need the additional income because her husband's income was so large. Mr. Foster was outraged on his wife's behalf.

> This is a textbook case, what went on there. People who don't have daughters or wives, men who don't have daughters or wives who have gone through this, don't believe it goes on! This was so blatant it ought to be written up. I can't stand those people anymore. I just absolutely see red! Just the hypocrisy of it! That's what it is, it's hypocrisy! A liberal firm, that's what it prides itself on being.
>
> They said to her, "You handle things and run things." And it was all going very well. And then she walked into this meeting and they say, "We don't think you have enough experience." And then they said, "You know, she doesn't need the money anyway"!
>
> She doesn't need the money anyway! It's unbelievable! But you have a situation where you've got this group of people that, what they really care about is their own jobs and their own staffs. And they don't really care about any common goal for the department.

At this point the interviewer asked Mr. Foster how he had reacted to the mistreatment of his wife. His first concern was to help his wife recover from her hurt. But then, thinking about what had been done to her, Mr. Foster said his reaction became one of outrage. This was his *wife* who had been hurt, and he wanted to do battle for her.

Another respondent, Mr. Layton, a manager in an insurance company, said that his protective impulses had made his wife anxious. Mr. Layton's wife is a vice president of a home sales firm and reports to a man who can be hot-tempered.

> She would tell me things about the things her boss did. Well, I knew her
> boss and "That is my *wife*!" I was ready to say, "I'm going to call him
> tomorrow and tell him off." It caused some conflicts there. She said, "Hey,
> don't you dare. Don't you dare. It means my career."

This is quite a different reaction from the one the men themselves receive when they come home to say that they have been misused at work. Then their wives ordinarily act to support the men's self-esteem, often by reassurance that the men can count on their continued respect. Men tend to be less supportive of their wives' self-esteem and more ready to do battle for them.

An extreme instance of husbandly protectiveness was reported by a respondent whose wife had been fired by the music school in which she was a department head, apparently because someone had decided that the school would present a better image if her position were filled by a man. Our respondent's wife, whom we talked with, said that although she was deeply hurt, she would not herself have fought the school's action. She disliked the administrators for their treatment of her and would have been pleased to be away from them. Our respondent, however, would not permit the administrators to get away with misusing his wife. He insisted that she take the school to court for illegal discriminatory behavior. She did, won, and was reinstated. Working in the school has continued to be unpleasant for her.

Somehow, in the midst of all this turmoil, our respondent's wife was able to continue composing music. One of her pieces won an important competition. Our respondent is proud of her.

Pride in their wives' achievements is common among our respondents. One, whose wife is a visiting nurse, after first complaining that her work took her away from their home, described with pride her management of a potentially suicidal adolescent. An accomplished and occupationally successful wife is, in a way, an ornament. The husbands could feel that by supporting their wives' employment they had helped to produce their wives' successes. It should be noted that our respondents were themselves sufficiently successful so that they were not threatened by their wives' successes.

Together with pride in their wives' achievements at work, however, some men resented having to help out more in their wives' domains of responsibility. There was great variation in feelings of this sort — much seemed to depend on the extent to which men felt that they had the time and energy to take on more at home while still meeting their first responsibilities to their own work. One man said:

> How I feel about her working, I am really glad about the job. I think that
> she's got an interesting job and she is making it more interesting and chal-
> lenging than it might otherwise have been. And I can see it reawakening
> feelings of competence and mastery. I think it is wonderful for her to have
> that interest, to be enjoying the job. And in the long run if she does well
> and makes money, that is good for the whole family.
>   She would be frustrated if I gave her a hard time about putting extra
> time into the job. But it never bothers her that *I'm* frustrated. Still, along
> with being frustrated, I want her to be happy.

It was putting some strains on the family situation. She got tired. She wasn't used to working and the mental and physical energy that she was putting into it. So she would be on the couch when I got home, watching the news and not physically unable but maybe psychologically too tired to get up and make dinner or play with our son or anything. So I would walk in the door and, bang, I would have to take care of all these things.

But we talked about it a couple of times, about how we would divide up the chores and that seems to be working out pretty well. I took on more of the shopping and cooking one night a week in addition to helping her out other nights on cooking. And on a whole host of little things.

Other respondents, too, display the same mix of feelings. They want to support their wives; they are happy for their wives if their wives enjoy their work and proud of them if they do well at it. On the other hand, they feel they are making do with a lesser contribution by their wives to the household. The men feel that supporting their wives' employment is one of the ways they discharge their responsibility to support their wives' well-being, albeit at some cost to themselves.

We have found that men's traditional understandings of marriage are in no way modified by wives working, even if the wives have significant careers. Men whose wives do not work and men whose wives do work share traditional understandings of the nature of marital responsibilities. Instead of changing these understandings, men whose wives work — and the great majority of our respondents' wives do — assimilate their wives' work to the traditional understandings.

This means that men view their wives' work as quite different in familial meaning from their own. Their own work is a way of meeting their responsibilities to their families. Their wives' work, while it may help pay bills, is in their view primarily a way in which their wives achieve a better life. Therefore the men feel themselves to be unselfish as they support their wives' employment. It is easy for them to feel misused when in addition to forgoing their wives' presence in the household, they are expected to contribute more to the household division of labor.

Yet, if men's understandings of how their marriages should function have not changed, the behaviors to which these understandings lead have changed greatly. Thus, men continue to understand themselves as responsible for helping out in their wives' domains — one of the principles of traditional marriage. Today, however, this is likely to mean helping with housework rather than simply taking care of the children for a while; in some instances, it can mean sharing of meal production or other tasks that were formerly reserved for wives. In general, the tasks men perform are much more accessible to change than are men's understandings of who is genuinely responsible for the tasks. Marriages that may at first appear to be highly symmetric (Young and Willmot, 1973) thus may on closer scrutiny turn out not to be symmetric at all — at least as far as the husbands are concerned.

REFERENCES

Baruch, G., Barnett, R., and Rivers, C. (1983). *Lifeprints: new patterns of love and work for today's women.* New York: McGraw-Hill.

Pleck, J. H. (1983). Husband's paid work and family roles: Current research issues. In H. Lopata and J. H. Pleck (eds.) *Research in the interweave of social roles: Families and jobs*, vol. 3. Greenwich, Conn.: JAI Press.

Weiss, R. S. (1985). Men and the family. *Family Process*, 24 (March), 49–58.

Weitzman, L. J. (1981). *The marriage contract*. New York: Free Press.

Young, M., and Willmot, P. (1973). *The symmetrical family*. New York: Pantheon.

Gayle Kimball

EGALITARIAN HUSBANDS

"What strikes me is how few men are in any way prepared to share fully in a relationship and in the running of a household and the raising of children. I'm struck by how difficult it is for them, unless they are extremely motivated to get those skills and do it."

— *A Connecticut husband*

> *He and his wife have two young children. Although they are college graduates, they have chosen to share a bus-driving job in order to have time with their family and to engage in work for peace through the Catholic Worker movement. They share a large old house with two single women. His political commitment is a major influence in his dedication to shared family roles.*

If it is difficult for men to be equal partners in family work, the backgrounds of men who have equal marriages are worth examining. One husband feels thousands of women could step into his wife's shoes but very few men could replace him.[1] His wife, a teacher, agrees, "They key is not me; it's Don." Other men ask him how he manages to do most of the cooking, share in the care of their daughter, and attend law school. It is difficult to replicate what he does, he believes, since other men "need to see it on TV or read about it and there is nowhere to do that." Another wife agrees that men are less willing than women to be in an egalitarian marriage. Because we live in a society where men have more power, they have more to give up; men have to be willing to put their privilege on the line. She feels it is a rare man who will try equality for a while and not quit when it "gets hard."

PARENTS: POSITIVE OR NEGATIVE EXAMPLES

Many egalitarian men are not threatened by strong women because they have an achieving mother whom they respect. The isolation and small size of the family mandate that the parents shape the child's views about the gender to which he or she belongs. A man with a manipulative mother is often suspicious of women, while a mother who helps her son establish self-esteem produces the expectation that women are pleasant people. It is not surprising, as studies found, that husbands of achievement-oriented wives often have close relationships with capable mothers who work outside the home.[2]

Probably the single most crucial factor contributing to an egalitarian man is his mother. A lawyer in Maine, Cathy, observes about her husband, Paul, also a lawyer:

> I really do believe that when you look at a man's mother you see a lot how he relates to women. I was struck by the fact that his mom is a very feminine woman and very competent and intelligent. I really like her a lot. She is no wimp at all. She is very confident, although she has no career.

As a result, Cathy's husband is comfortable with her being a "racehorse," ambitious in her job. In contrast, a man whose mother catered to him reports he had difficulty recognizing his share of responsibility during the first several years of his marriage.

AVOIDING TRAINING INTO A MACHO MOLD

Some husbands feel they escaped the traditional socialization into rigid male roles. "I was left to my own devices. I sort of grew up and they provided a place for me to be," notes a California businessman who was the youngest child. Clinton, the youngest child of sixteen children in a poor North Carolina family, also felt distant from his parents. A restaurant owner, he later encouraged his wife to run for local office because he always wished everyone could have the opportunity to achieve his or her goals, perhaps because his parents did not spend enough time with him to teach him their prejudices.

A youngest son, born when his mother was forty, views his birth order as significant:

> You know how the first child is always the image that the parents want and the second child is a little farther, and the third child is . . . Well, I was the third child and last child. I grew up so free. I was kind of an afterthought. The family didn't put much pressure on me to do anything.

As a result, his wife characterizes him as having a lot of tolerance and sympathy for the underdog.

Most men are deeply influenced by the cultural expectations for proper male behavior and find it hard to free themselves from their conditioning. It is a difficult process, according to a Pennsylvania psychologist:

> As a man it has been really difficult for me to let go of my male conditioning even though I was coming from a place of wanting to and at the beginning thinking it would be easy. I didn't expect that I would have leftover feelings that would get in the way of my doing what I wanted to do, which was take care of my children half of the time and be a nurturing father and share in the housework. I found that a lot of my male socialization got in my way and I really had to deal with that. I talked to other men about it and examined myself.

A characteristic of many egalitarian husbands is their view of themselves as nonconformists. "I challenge traditional thinking. I tend not to accept the given. I don't assume that everything should be the way it is," states a physician. As a hospital administrator, he has appointed a majority of women administrators; he likes and respects women. Another husband described himself as naturally rebellious although he is now mayor of a large city. Several men considered themselves hippies during the 1960s. One of them, operating an air-conditioning business in Massachusetts, says he consciously worked against everything he was brought up to accept, including sex roles. A lawyer states, "I never grew up being very much of a cultural stereotype. I have always been somewhat aloof from the prevailing culture."

Living Alone   Most of the role-sharing husbands lived alone for some period during their twenties and learned to take care of their domestic lives by themselves. They believe that being on their own was vital and that it is foolish to go from mother to wife without space in between to learn independence. Some men learned home economics in a class, in Boy Scouts, in military school, or in the Army. Survival necessitated their learning how to cook, mend, and clean, and they do not let their skills grow rusty even in marriage. Delaying marriage and children is also beneficial in that as men get older they have less pressure to prove their masculinity through completion and career achievement. Many men in their thirties make a transition to more emotional expressiveness.[3]

A Previous Marriage   One remarried husband suggested that he needed a first marriage for practice in how to have an equal second one. Other couples suggested the importance of living together before marriage, although research has indicated that it makes no difference to marital success or to more egalitarian roles.[4] Men who had previous marriages with traditional wives reacted against the distance created by separate roles. They found it boring not to be able to have lively conversations with stay-at-home wives. One husband said he was lonely in his first marriage because he and his wife had little to say to each other. His wife was unfulfilled and, as a result, he did not respect her. In contrast, his second wife reports that she is very different from his first wife and that it changed his self-image to marry a lawyer.

A California man, Philip, describes the distance he felt from his attractive first wife. He married her when he was a college student. When they became parents of a son, she did not work outside the home.

> I was married for seven years in a very traditional relationship and was divorced and swore I would never do it again. It was a no-growth situation and I felt like I was in a rut. It was unfulfilling and too lonely. We didn't get a chance to share anything real. She didn't really want to be part of my world and I didn't want to be part of hers. So we got to be like two strangers and just drifted apart. It was a pretty traditional American disaster.

He also felt victimized by being the sole wage earner.

> The roles were so defined that if I had a job and the job terminated, it was necessary for me to be the number-one breadwinner. I would have to

go out right away and find almost any job. I have taken some really awful and humiliating jobs.

His second wife, Susan, taught the same subject he did in a community college. She shares many of his interests in poetry and folklore, as well as their children.

It gets tiresome trying to play ball with yourself, explains another remarried husband. He's thrilled his second wife, a feminist, catches the ball. He got tired of being solely responsible in his first marriage and enjoys being able to share. His wife has four adolescent children from her first marriage and is putting herself through college by working as a secretary. She learned independence as a single parent and applies it to her second marriage.

THE WIFE WHO INSISTS ON EQUALITY

Some husbands in egalitarian marriages had no particular personal history that directed them toward sharing tasks. Rather, they went along with the strong feelings of their wives, as one Colorado husband, Ted, explains:

> I think there are a lot of men, like myself, who don't feel that they're doing anything out of the ordinary. It just happens that the woman he falls in love with decides to assert herself, and that's fine. I've met a lot of women who think they're liberated but can't really carry it through. Maybe there are more men who are receptive to this than there are women who are willing to assert themselves. By the same token, there are women who know what they want and go out and get it. If Judi would have been a Suzie Cream Cheese, we probably would have had a different relationship.

Judi is an actress, whose first marriage taught her not to be submissive. In contrast, wives in some traditional dual-career families "crowd out their husbands from family work, such as child care. One study found that husbands spend less time with their children when their wives work outside the home, as the woman monopolizes child care when she is at home.[5]

A Michigan husband, Michael, states simply that his wife is a very strong woman and that is the reason they share roles. It is easy to be lazy and let someone else take care of the work, observes Tom, a Montana wildlife biologist. He adds, though, that he could not live with his conscience if he behaved like men he knows who don't life a finger around the house or are ignorant about how to take care of their children. Tom has never lived with a woman "who would put up with that b.s.," so he has not had a chance to try it.

Some couples started sharing after their marriage was well established. In those cases, the wife underwent a major change, often encouraged by participation in a feminist group or by reading feminist books. The husband, who thought he fulfilled his main duty to be a good provider, usually was bewildered by the change. One such husband explained that "I had to grit my teeth and try new things. She felt very strongly about it. It really wasn't as bad as I had suspected." He is a Washington, D.C., physician who did not have any models for equality: It took his father two weeks to learn how to operate a washing machine after his wife was in an accident.

Since role-sharing means the man must give up some leisure, it naturally provokes resistance. Many arguments about sharing housework occurred before some men changed. "We had some real discussions about the whole thing," says Will, a president of a New Jersey company. It took a while, for example, for him to get over the belief that he was helping with his wife Cleo's job when he did the dishes or laundry, although she shares management of their company with him as well as the care of their son. It is a slow process to undo a lifetime of separation of men's and women's duties and responsibilities.

LOGIC AND FAIRNESS

Numerous role-sharing husbands state that the reason for their lifestyle is its logic and fairness. They define themselves as rational, a stereotyped male attribute that can be put to good use in breaking out of rigid roles.

Applying the golden rule is part of the fairness applied by husbands who want a companion rather than a maid or a mother. Steve, a California attorney, states that he could not stay home and take care of four kids, so it is not fair to expect his wife to stay home. He refrains from sitting down with the "boob tube" after she works all day as a data processor. A psychologist has his version of empathy for his spouse: He could probably live with an arrangement where his wife did all the housework, but

> I'm also objective enough to know that if I was in that situation I certainly wouldn't put up with it. I look at it pretty logically. I believe in sharing. I didn't want to marry a mother, I already had one and I had no intentions of being a daddy to a wife. I wanted a companion and friend. I feel a big part of friendship requires sharing. To have an equal partner you treat your partner the way you want to be treated.

Appealing to a man's sense of logic and fairness is one of the best tactics a woman can use to point out the rationale for shared roles, since men are usually trained to rely on their reason rather than their emotions.

POLITICAL ORIENTATION

Working in the civil rights or peace movement sharpened some husbands' sense of equity, and they resolved to practice at home what they preached to others. A few husbands are socialists or had socialist parents. Men who were politically active in the anti-war and racial integration movements of the sixties sensed that justice for minorities carried over to women's issues. The decade of the sixties had a major impact, sometimes indirectly through the influence of older brothers and sisters. Many couples became more liberal and more antiestablishment because of their rebellion against cruelties perpetrated by the U.S. government during the Vietnam war.

A couple who were in college in that period explains that while they were not campus leaders or activists for peace, just being students then was enough to make them critical of authority. He contrasts his political sense with that of younger teachers recently out of college who seem unaware politically and uninterested in issues such as the Equal Rights Amendment. In contrast, the husbands (and wives) in my survey of traditional couples were more likely to describe their political orientation as conservative or moderate. (Current polls of

bright teenage students find them increasingly conservative, socially and politically, which raises the question of the probability of equal marriage among
young people not influenced by the sixties.)

The women's movement made many men think about sex roles, fair division
of labor, and role models for their children. They read feminist books and a few
joined men's groups. A Louisiana husband, David, describes his conversion to
feminism: "Like Paul on the road to Damascus, the intuition swept over me
with enormous power of understanding the problems of women in this society."
As a result, he spoke on talk shows, convinced a woman sitting next to him on
an airplane to buy a dishwasher to save her time, aided his wife in her candidacy
for political office, and shared equally in child care.

Some husbands view sharing roles as a political act, as does Art, a Pennsylvania psychologist:

> The movements of the sixties and the seventies had a profound influence
> on me. I was really influenced by feminism. I went through a revolution-
> ary personal change in the early seventies and got in touch with my nur-
> turing side. In getting together with Cathleen I wanted to explore that
> further and being a half-time parent was a way to do that. To be really
> close to my children felt wonderful. I want to acknowledge that there's a
> political decision involved. I think the nuclear family is a real disaster and
> that the ideal human condition would be some sort of tribal existence. In
> spending so much time with my children and in home tasks, I think I'm
> making a political statement about that.

Older husbands who started out traditionally were afraid they would be labeled henpecked if a neighbor saw them changing diapers or doing dishes. They
have recently found more support for sharing. The women's movement has
made domestic involvement less threatening for men.

Not being white, Anglo-Saxon, and Protestant was a factor in some men's
egalitarian attitudes: "I'm probably more sensitive to fairness and shafting" because of identification with the oppression of Jews, explains a Delaware market
researcher. A wife traces her husband's attitude to "a lot of sympathy for the
underdog that comes from being Jewish and the Jewish leftist position." A Jewish heritage was also an important influence for a Washington psychologist because of its humanitarian and intellectual orientation: He describes his male
relatives as temperate and reflective. One man whose father is Chicano felt that
he was taught a sense of duty to family and a gentle manliness emphasizing
involvement, respect, and obligation to women and family, contrary to prevailing views about machismo. An Asian-American and a black husband also emphasized that family was central to them, partly as a protection against the
dominant culture. Even though there is an emphasis in black families on the
male as the head of the family, in reaction to the myth of the black matriarchy,
in practice studies show that roles are shared more than in white families.

Additional influences on men's awareness of equality are their education in a
liberal college environment,[6] their practicing a helping profession, or their belief
in a religion whose members are involved in social action. Although one man's
family was conservative, his exposure to radicals at Oberlin College changed
his political orientation, which carried over to his attitudes toward sex roles.
Being a history major and reading about social reform movements in the United

States had a liberalizing impact on an Ohio business president. One man traces his openness to new ideas to his work as a newspaper reporter, while some therapists feel their training in sensitivity to others has made them more egalitarian husbands. Men in Unitarian, Quaker, Catholic Worker movement, or Protestant denominations, which deal openly with sexism, learn awareness of equality issues.

BEING SECURE

"I have a fundamental premise that people who are bigots and people who want to keep women in their place at home are afraid of their own inadequacy." This statement is perhaps the most revealing of the nature of egalitarian men; they have strong self-images and do not need to control their wives.[7] A woman seeking a role-sharing husband should avoid men who are constantly proving their manhood to an invisible jury that never lets them relax except when they are numbed by television or drinking. Role-sharers do not have an image to defend because they are content with who they are. Several men spoke of the social pressure to maintain a masculine image and recalled how they rejected it; a man who is insecure about his image will likely stay away from cooking, sewing, and changing diapers, according to a New York television engineer.

Being secure allows flexibility; it doesn't restrict activity to traditionally masculine or feminine behavior. Several husbands sew for their families because they like the technical challenges of sewing, while traditional men would be afraid to be seen operating a sewing machine. Other men enjoy cooking or are fascinated by learning about birth. A California geologist, Steve, relates why he likes to get involved in all aspects of daily life:

> My hunger is to understand as much as I can, which means experiencing it myself. And for that reason I find it important and very satisfying to go through all the steps in making something happen; understand it, get a feel for it, and get my hands dirty with it. We planned the wedding and the birth much the same way: We had the birth of the kid in our bedroom.

Being a middle-class, well-educated professional is different from being a blue-collar worker. Betty, who works in a Texas factory, describes her male fellow workers as seeing their wives' main function as taking care of them, so they forbid their wives to work outside the home except for minor employment such as selling cosmetics in their spare time. The men would never dream of doing housework and they give Betty "a lot of slack" for working. Social class is a strong determinant in attitudes toward sex roles, but the desire to keep women as nurturers crosses class lines. A hard-hat worker who admits helping his wife with family work is frowned upon at work as a scab. Blue-collar men do not have a monopoly on that tactic, however: A business executive on vacation with other couples reported the other men razzed him when he did his share of domestic chores.

Egalitarian husbands' definitions of masculinity include being nurturing and open about emotions. Since they accept themselves, they can also accept a woman for her honest self and not expect her to fit a stereotyped feminine image. Their wives frequently describe them as easygoing. Maddy, a Wisconsin teacher, relates that her husband, Don,

> is totally non-threatened. He's absolutely not a macho man. He's not the type that carries his ego on his shoulder and waits for somebody to knock it off. He's calm, easygoing, gentle, and sensitive. Don bakes bread for ERA fund raisers and his masculinity isn't at stake. His brothers consider him a pariah in the family because of his support for women; but due to his strong sense of self, he doesn't bend to their pressure.

Another woman, an attorney, describes her husband's confidence:

> I think it's easier right now for a woman to assume nontraditional roles than for a man. Chuck is extremely strong in his ability to say, "I do not need traditional trappings or role models to feel good about myself."

Men who are continually anxious about their masculinity clearly are going to find it difficult to be in a 50/50 marriage. (Yet masculinity is so tied to performance that uncertainty in young men is almost inevitable; a student who read this manuscript pointed out, "I'm continually anxious about my masculinity but I'm not 'macho.'")

Growing up in America makes most men fearful about proving their maleness, as Herb Goldberg spells out in *The Hazards of Being Male* and *The New Male*, which describe how the traditional male role emphasizes performance, competition, and denial of emotions, causing stress-related illness.[8] Male fears that get in the way of equal relationships are explained by Clay, a New York computer scientist:

> I don't feel I'm a faggot if I live with a woman who does some tasks that men are supposed to do. I have a very strong sense of having worked through things that men are normally worried about because of our culture. Men are secretly afraid that they are gay or can't perform and are going to be lesser human beings. As boys we grow up admiring maleness and set yardsticks for proving that. Many men are threatened by women who want to be self-directed. I think they are threatened because they consciously or unconsciously worry about themselves.

If a man does not need his wife to make him feel superior, he can appreciate a partner who will challenge him. "One of the worst things in the world is to spend your life with a half person, a woman who will only reflect you without any aspirations of her own and be dependent," states David, a Louisiana writer. His wife is an administrator and a feminist, and she is active in politics. A man who is comfortable with himself will not need his wife to diminish herself to make him feel important.

NOTES

1. Jeff Bryson and Rebecca Bryson, *Dual-Career Couples* (New York: Human Sciences Press, 1978), pp. 37, 64. Linda Holmstrom, *The Two-Career Family* (Cambridge, Mass.: Schenkman, 1972), p. 111. Ronald Burke and Tamara Weir, "Some Personality Differences between Members of One-Career and Two-Career Families," *Journal of Marriage and Family*, vol. 38, no. 3, August 1976, p. 457.

2. Rhona and Robert Rapoport, "Three Generations of Dual-Career Family Research," in Fran Pepiton-Rockwell, ed., *Dual-Career Couples* (Beverly Hills, Calif.: Sage, 1980), p. 30.

3. Aida Tomeh and Catherine Vasko, "Analysis of Reversed Sex Roles," *Journal of Comparative Family Studies*, vol. 11, no. 2, Spring 1980, p. 167.

4. John Moreland, "Age and Change in Adult Sex Roles," *Journal of Sex Roles*, vol. 6, no. 6, 1980, p. 815.

5. Jeffrey Jacques and Karen Chason, "Cohabitation: Its Impact on Marital Success," *Family Coordinator*, vol. 28, no. 1, January 1979, p. 35. Rebecca Stafford, Elaine Backman, and Pamela Dibona, "The Division of Labor among Cohabiting and Married Couples," *Journal of Marriage and Family*, vol. 39, no. 1, January 1977, p. 54.

6. Michael Lamb, ed., *The Role of the Father in Child Development* (New York: Wiley, 1981), p. 303.

7. Donald St. Johns-Parsons, "Continuous Dual-Career Families," in Bryson and Bryson, p. 37.

8. George Farkas, "Education, Wage Rates and the Division of Labor between Husband and Wife." *Journal of Marriage and Family*, vol. 38, no. 3, August 1976, p. 452.

Franz Kafka

LETTER TO HIS FATHER

For me you took on the enigmatic quality that all tyrants have whose rights are based on their person and not on reason. I was, after all, weighed down by your mere physical presence. There I was, skinny, weakly, slight; you, strong, tall, broad. I felt a miserable specimen, and what's more, not only in your eyes but in the eyes of the whole world, for you were for me the measure of all things. You were . . . completely tied to the business, scarcely able to be with me once a day, and therefore made all the more profound an impression on me, never really leveling out into the flatness of habit. What was always incomprehensible to me was your total lack of feeling for the suffering and shame you could inflict on me with your words and judgments. It was as though you had no notion of your power. How terrible for me was, for instance, that: "I'll tear you apart like a fish." It was also terrible when you ran around the table, shouting, grabbing at one, obviously not really trying to grab, yet pretending to, and Mother (in the end) had to rescue one, as it seemed. Once again one had, so it seemed to the child, remained alive through your mercy and bore one's life hence forth as an undeserved gift from you.

Brian Miller

LIFE-STYLES OF GAY HUSBANDS
AND FATHERS

The words "gay husband" and "gay father" are often regarded as contradictions in terms. This notion is hinted at in Anita Bryant's widely quoted non sequitur, "Homosexuals recruit because they cannot reproduce." Researchers estimate, however, that in America there are six million gay husbands and fathers (Bozett, 1987; Schulenberg, 1985). Why do these men marry and have children? How do they organize their lives? What are their difficulties and joys as a consequence of their behavior?

To address these questions, 50 gay husbands and fathers were contacted in 1976 by means of multiple-source chain-referral samples. At first interview, 24 of the men were living with their wives; three years later at the second interview, only three had intact marriages. Approximately two-third of the respondents have been followed to the present and all of them are now separated (Humphreys and Miller, 1980a). To show the modal developments in gay husbands' and fathers' life-styles, the data are organized along a four-point continuum: Covert Behavior, Marginal Involvement, Transformed Participation, and Open Endorsement.

COVERT BEHAVIOR

Early in adult life, gay husbands and fathers tend to regard their homosexual feelings as nothing more than genital urges. They are reluctant to refer to either themselves or their behavior as gay: "I hate labels" is a common response to questions about sexual orientation. These men have unstable self-concepts — one day thinking they are homosexual and another day thinking they are not. Their reluctance to label their same-sex activity as homosexual is not because they hate labels per se; indeed they strive to present themselves to others under a heterosexual label. Rather, they dislike a label that calls attention to behaviors they would prefer to forget.

Premarital homosexual experiences are often explained away with "It's only a phase" or "God, was I drunk last night!" These men report such activities prior to marriage as arranging heterosexual double-date situations in which they would perform coitus in the back seat of the car, for example, while fantasizing about the male in the front seat. Others report collaborating with a buddy to share a female prostitute. These ostensibly heterosexual acts allowed the men to buttress their sense of heterosexuality while gratifying homosexual urges. During the premarital period, respondents discounted gay life-styles and romanticized heterosexual family living as the only way to achieve the stable home life, loyal companionship, and fatherhood they desired.

These men married in good faith, thinking they could overcome their gay desires; they did not believe they were deceiving their spouses. In fact, most men broached the issue of their homosexual feelings to their wives before marriage, but the information was usually conveyed in an oblique manner and downplayed as inconsequential. This kept their future wives from thinking that they might be marrying homosexuals. Wives' denials of their husbands' homosexuality were further facilitated by the fact that half the women, at their nuptials, were pregnant by the men they were marrying.

In the early years of marriage, high libido provided husbands with easy erections for coitus. Respondents report, however, that this situation tended to deteriorate shortly after the birth of the first child. Increasingly, they found themselves fantasizing about gay erotica during coitus.

Marriage engulfs the men in a heterosexual role, making them marginal to the gay world. Their social isolation from others who share their sexual interests burdens them with "I'm-the-only-one-in-the-world" feelings. These men, realizing their behavior is inconsistent with their heterosexual reputation, try to reduce their anxiety and guilt by compartmentalizing gay and nongay worlds. One respondent said: "I never walk in the door without an airtight excuse of where I've been." Some men avoid the strain of remembering stories by intimidating the wife into silence: "She knows better than to question my whereabouts. I tell her, 'I get home when I get home; no questions asked.'" In these respects, respondents have parallels to their adulterous heterosexual counterparts (Libby and Whitehurst, 1977).

Extramarital sex for respondents usually consists of clandestine, impersonal encounters in parks, tearooms, or highway rest stops, with hitchhikers or male hustlers. (Regarding this, single gays sometimes comment, "Married gays give the rest of us a bad name.") Occasionally, furtiveness itself becomes eroticized, making the men sexually dysfunctional in calmer contexts. Recreational gay scenes such as dances, parties, and gay organizations are not used by respondents, primarily because they dread discovery and subsequent marital dissolution. Many are further limited by fears that their jobs would be threatened, by lack of geographical access to gay institutions, or by religious scruples. In fact, these men are largely unaware of gay social events in their communities and have little idea of how to participate in them. They tend to be ideologically ambivalent about the gay world, sometimes thinking of it as exotic, and other times condemning it as "superficial, unstable, full of blackmail and violence." Given their exposure to only the impersonal homosexual underground, and not to loving gay relationships, their negative perception is somewhat justified. As long as they remain marginal to the gay world, the likelihood of their participation in safe, fulfilling gay relationships remains minimal (Miller and Humphreys, 1980).

Some men regard their homosexual desires not as an orientation, but as a compulsion: "I don't want to do these things, but I'm driven to do them." Other accounts that explain away their homosexual behavior, emphasize its nonseriousness, and minimize its consequences include (1) "I might be okay if my wife learned to give good blow jobs." (2) "I only go out for it when I'm drunk or depressed." (3) "I go to the truckstop and meet someone. We're just a couple of horny married guys relieving ourselves. That's not sex. [It] doesn't threaten my marriage like adultery would." (4) "Sex with men is a minor aspect of my life that I refuse to let outweigh more important things."

The respondent who gave this last account also presented conflicting evidence. He spent time, effort, and anxiety in rearranging his schedule to accommodate sex, spending money on his car and fuel to search for willing men, constructing intricate stories to fool work associates and family, and buying his wife penance gifts. He also experienced near misses with police and gay bashers. Still, he viewed all this as only a "minor aspect" of his life.

Another rationalization is "I'm not really homosexual since I don't care if it's a man, woman or dog that's licking my cock. All I want is a hole." Further questioning, however, made clear that this respondent was not looking for just any available orifice. He stated that it was equally important that he persuade the most attractive man available to fellate him.

Another account is the "Eichmann dodge." Men may claim, like Eichmann, that they are the victims of other men's desire, inadvertently caught up and swept along by the events, thereby absolving themselves of responsibility. Men stating this rationalization, however, are often skilled at seducing others into making the first move. Some gay husbands and fathers claim that they limit themselves to one special "friendship" and that no one else of their sex could excite them. If they think of homosexuality at all, they conceive it as promiscuous behavior done by degenerates, not by people like themselves who are loyal and who look conventional.

These accounts help respondents deny homosexuality while practicing it. They find it difficult to simultaneously see themselves as worthwhile persons and as homosexuals, and to reconcile their masculine self-image with the popular image of gays as effeminate. The most they can acknowledge is that they get together with other men to ejaculate and that they fantasize about men during sex with their wives. In spite of their rationalizations, however, these men report considerable anxiety and guilt about maintaining their compartmentalized double lives.

Respondents are reluctant to rate their marriages as "happy," typically referring to them as "duties." The ambivalence is expressed by one who said: "My wife is a good person, but it's funny, I can't live with this marriage and I can't live without it." Respondents report conflict with wives who object to the disproportionate time these men spend away from home, neglecting parental responsibilities. The men view alternatives to marriage as limited, not seeing life in the gay world as a viable option. They find it difficult to talk about their children and express guilt that their work and sex schedules do not allow them to spend as much time with their children as they would like. Nevertheless, most of the men report that their children are the main reason for remaining married: "In this horrible marriage, [the children] are the consolation prize."

MARGINAL INVOLVEMENT

Respondents at this point on the continuum engage in homosexual behavior and have a gay self-identity. However, these men are marginal to the gay community since they have heterosexual public identities, and are often living with their wives. Still, they are much more comfortable with their homoerotic desires than are those in the Covert Behavior group and are more disclosing about their sexual orientation to other gays.

Compared with men in the previous group, Marginally Involved respondents have an expanded repertoire of sexual outlets. They sometimes compile telephone-number lists of sex partners and have limited involvement with small networks of gay friends. The men maintain secrecy by using post office boxes or separate office phones for gay-related business. Fake identities and names may be constructed to prevent identification by sexual partners. Employing male "masseurs" or maintaining a separate apartment for gay sex provide other relatively safe outlets. Consequently, these men are less likely to encounter police entrapment or gay bashers. Gay bars are somewhat inaccessible since they often start too late, and the men cannot regularly find excuses for extended absences from home. Some men resort to lunch-hour or presupper "quickies" at the baths.

In spite of these measures, respondents report many facade-shattering incidents with heterosexuals. Such difficulties include being caught on the street with a gay friend whose presence cannot be explained, blurting out praise about an event, then remembering it was attended with a gay friend, not one's wife, and transferring body lice or a veneral disease from a hustler to the wife, an especially dangerous occurrence in this time of AIDS (Pearson, 1986). Many respondents, however, continue to deny wives' knowledge about their homosexuality: "I don't think my wife really knows. She's only mentioned it a couple of times, and only when she was too drunk to know what she was saying."

Men who travel as part of their business or who have loosely structured working hours enjoy relative freedom. For them, absences and sexual incidents may be more easily covered. A minority of men, specifically those in artistic and academic fields, are able to mix their heterosexual and homosexual worlds. Their circle is that of the relatively wealthy and tolerant in which the epithet "perversion" is replaced by the more neutral "eccentricity," and variant behavior is accepted as long as the man is discreet and does not "rub the wife's nose in it." Several respondents socialize openly with similarly situated men or with gay sex partners whom wives and others ostensibly know as merely work assistants or friends of the family.

Because Marginally Involved respondents are "out" to some audiences and not to others, they sometimes resemble, as one man said, "a crazy quilt of contradictions." This is emphasized by playing word games with questioners or with those who try to penetrate their defenses. Playing the role of the eccentric and giving mixed messages provide a smokescreen for their emotional whereabouts from both gays and nongays.

This adjustment, however, is tenuous and respondents are often ambivalent about maintaining their marriages. They fantasize about life as a gay single, and entertain ideas of divorce. The guilt these respondents experience is sometimes reflected in what might be called Santa Claus behavior. They shower their children — and sometimes their wives — with expensive gifts to counteract feelings that they have done a terrible thing to their family by being homosexual: "It's the least I can do for having ruined their chance to grow up in a normal home." Using credit cards to manage guilt has many of these men in serious debt and laboring as workaholics.

Like men in the first category, these men regret that performing their breadwinner, husband, and homosexual roles leaves little time for the father role. Nevertheless, they are reluctant to leave their marriages, fearing permanent separation from their children. They also fear community stigma, ambivalently regard the gay world, and are unwilling to endure the decreased standard of living necessitated by divorce.

Over time, it becomes increasingly difficult for these men to reconcile their discordant identities as husband and as homosexual. Although some are able to routinize compartmentalization, others find sustaining the necessary maneuvers for secrecy to be not worth it. Conspiracies of silence and denial within the families become strained, if not transparent. Respondents tend to seek closure by communicating, directly and indirectly, their orientational needs to wives and by becoming more explicit in their methods of making gay contacts. Others are exposed by vice arrests or by being victimized by men they solicit. Most wives are surprised by the direct confrontation. Respondents are surprised that their wives are surprised since respondents may have thought their wives already knew, and tacitly accepted it. Initially wives often react with disbelief, revulsion, and anger: "I feel betrayed." This frequently gives way to a feeling of couple solidarity, that "we can conquer the problem together." When this is the adaptation, respondents do not come out of the closet so much as take their wives into the closet with them.

Couples try a variety of techniques to shore up the marriages. Respondents may seek therapy to "cure" their homosexuality. Some men generously offer wives the freedom to experience extramarital affairs too, although it appears this is done mostly to relieve respondents' guilt since they know that wives are unlikely to take them up on the offer. When wives do not put the offer to the test, respondents further console their guilt by interpreting this as evidence that the wives are "frigid" or low in "sex drive," although data from the wives dispute this characterization (Hays and Samuels, 1988).

Some couples try instituting new sexual arrangements: a *menage à trois*, or the husband is allowed out one night a week with gay friends. In the former interaction, wives tend to report feeling "used" and, in the latter, men tend to report feeling they are on a "leash."

Sexual conflicts spill into other domestic areas. Tardiness or missed appointments lead to wives' suspicions and accusations and general marital discord. One man calls this compromise period "white-knuckle heterosexuality." By negotiating groundrules that reinstate partial denial and by intellectualizing the situation, some couples maintain for years the compromise period. This uneasy truce ends if groundrules are repeatedly violated and when the wife realizes (1) that her husband finds men sexier than herself, (2) that he is unalterably gay, (3) that her primary place as object of permanent affection is challenged, and (4) that she has alternatives and can cope without the marriage. Wives gradually come to resent romanceless marriages with men who would rather make love to another man, and the homosexual husbands come to resent, as one man said, being "stifled in a nuptial closet."

Couples who remain married after disclosure tend not to have rejected divorce, but rather have an indefinite postponement of it: "After the children leave home," "After the finances are in order." Other considerations that keep the couples together include religious beliefs, family pressure, wives dependence, and the perceived nonviability of the gay world.

In most cases, the immediate impetus for ending the marriage is the husband's establishment of a love relationship with another man. As such relationships intensify, men begin to reconstruct the gay world as favorable for effecting companionship and social stability. It is usually wives, however, who take action to terminate the marriages. Painful as this experience is, it somewhat eases the men's guilt for causing marital dissolution.

TRANSFORMED PARTICIPATION

Respondents who reach this point on the continuum engage in homosexual behavior and have self-identities — and to a limited extent, public identities —
that reflect acceptance of their behavior. These men generally have come out as
gay and left their wives.

Acculturation into the gay world involves three areas of concern for respondents: (1) disadvantage of advanced age and late arrival on the scene, (2) the
necessity of learning new gay social definitions and skills, and (3) the need to
reconcile prior fantasies to the realities of the gay world. Once respondents no
longer live with wives and children, they begin to increase their contacts with
the gay world and their marginality to it decreases. They may now subscribe
to gay publications, join gay religious congregations, and go to gay social and
political clubs and private gay parties. They experience a rapid expansion of
gay consciousness and skills and take steps to form close friendships with others
of their sexual orientation.

Moving out of the closet, these men report a stabilization of self-concept and
a greater sense of psychological well-being. Their attitudes toward homoerotic
behavior become more relaxed and better integrated into their everyday lives.
Most experience a change in body image, exemplified by improved physical
fitness and increased care with their appearance. Many report the elimination
of nervous and psychosomatic disorders such as ulcers, excessive fatigue, and
back aches, as well as substance abuse.

These respondents' sexual orientation tends to be known by significant others
with two exceptions: their employers and children. Secrecy sometimes exists
with employers since respondents believe the legal system does not protect their
interests should they be dismissed for being gay (Levine, 1981).

Relatively little openness about homosexuality also exists with these respondents' children. Typically, only older children (if any) are told, and it is not considered a topic for general discussion. There is fear that, if the man's gayness
becomes known in the community, his employer might find out or his ex-wife
might become irked and deny him child visits. Successful legal appeal for gay
people in such matters is difficult, a situation these men perceive as legally
sanctioned blackmail.

In line with this, most respondents, rather than living with their children,
have visiting schedules with them. They do not have the financial resources
either to persuade their ex-wives to relinquish the children or to hire care for
them while devoting time to their own careers.

Men who are able to terminate marriages without their spouse's discovering
their homosexuality avoid this problem. However, fear of subsequent exposure
and loss of children through a new court order remains and prompts some men
to stay partially closeted even after marital dissolution. In spite of these fears,
the degree of passing and compartmentalization of gay and nongay worlds is
much less for men at this point on the continuum than for those who are Covert
and Marginal.

OPEN ENDORSEMENT

Respondents who reach this point on the continuum not only engage in homosexual behavior and have a self-identity reflective of the behavior but also

openly champion the gay community. Although they come from the full range of economic backgrounds, they tend to have high social and occupational resources. Some have tolerant employers; some are full-time gay activists; others are self employed, often in businesses with largely gay clienteles.

Proud of their newfound identity, these men organize their world, to a great extent, around gay cultures. Much of their leisure, if not occupation, is spent in gay-related pursuits. They have experienced unhappy marriages and divorce, the struggle of achieving a gay identity, and now feel they have arrived at a satisfactory adjustment. These men, consequently, distinguish themselves in ideology from respondents in other categories. For example, what the others refer to as "discretion," men in this category call "duplicity" and "sneaking around." Moreover, what closeted men see as "flaunting," openly gay respondents call "being forthright" and "upfront."

Respondents' efforts in constructing this new life are helped not only by having a gay love relationship, but by the Gay Liberation Movement (Humphreys and Miller, 1980b). Parallel processes are at work whereby the building of a personal gay identity is facilitated by the larger cultural context of increasing gay pride and diversification of gay institutions and heritage (Adam, 1987; Harry and DeVall, 1978; Murray, 1979). Still, coming out is not easy or automatic. This is partly due to the fact that there is no necessary conjunction among sexual behavior fantasy, self-identity, and object of affectional attachment. Although there is a strain toward consistency for most people among these components of sexuality, this is not invariably so. The ways these components change over time and the combinations in which they link with each other are multiple (Miller 1983; Simon and Gagnon, 1969).

Men who reach the Open Endorsement point often have fears that their father and ex-husband statuses could distance them from single gays. Sometimes respondents fear that single gays, similar to nongays, regard them with confusion, curiosity, or pity. Integrating gay and father roles requires patience, since it is often difficult for respondents to find a lover who accepts him and his children as a "package deal," and the gay father may feel he has not enough time and energy to attend to both children and a lover. Selecting a lover who is also a gay father is a common solution to this situation.

Most respondents who have custody of their children did not experience court custody battles but gained custody because the mother did not want the children or because the children, being allowed to choose, chose to live with their fathers. Respondents who live with their children are more likely to have a close circle of gay friends as their main social outlet, rather than participating primarily in gay commercial establishments (McWhirter and Mattison, 1984).

Men at this point on the continuum have told their children about their homosexuality. They report children's reaction to be more positive than expected and, when there is a negative reaction, it generally dissipates over time (Miller, 1979). Children's negative reactions centered more on the parent's divorce and subsequent household changes than on the father's homosexuality per se. Daughters tend to be more accepting of their father's homosexuality than sons, although most children feel their father's honesty brings them closer together. Children report few instances of neighborhood homophobia directed against them, possibly because the children try to disclose only to people they know will react favorably. There is no indication that the children of gay fathers are disproportionately homosexual themselves although, of the children who turned out to be gay, there were more lesbian daughters than gay sons. Wives and relatives sometimes worry that gay men's children will be molested by him or his gay friends. Evidence from this study supports earlier research findings that indicate such fears are unwarranted (Bozett, 1987).

DISCUSSION

The general tendency is for the Covert Behavior respondents to move toward Open Endorsement. There are several caveats, however, about this movement. For example, the continuum should not be construed as reifying transient states into types. Additionally, movement out of marriage into an openly gay identity is not unilateral. There are many negotiations back and forth, in and out of the closet. There is not a finite number of stages; not everyone becomes publicly gay and not everyone passes through every step. Few respondents move easily or accidentally through the process. Rather, each level is achieved by a painful search, negotiating with both oneself and the larger world.

The event most responsible for initiating movement along the continuum and reconstructing gay fathers' perceptions of the gay community is the experience of falling in love with another man. By contrast, factors hindering movement along the continuum include inability to percieve the gay world as a viable alternative as well as perceived lack of support from other gays, economic difficulty, family pressure, poor health, wives dependence, homophobia in respondents or community, and moral/religious scruples.

This study has several findings. Gayness and traditional marital relationships are perceived by the respondents as discordant compared to relationships established when they move into the gay world. Although respondents perceive gayness as incompatible with traditional marriage, they perceive gayness as compatible with fathering. Highly compartmentalized life-styles and deceit sometimes repress open marital conflict, but unresolved tension characterizes respondents' marriages. In contrast, men who leave their spouses and enter the gay world report gay relationships to be more harmonious than marital relationships. They also report fathering to be more salient once having left their marriages. Men who come out perceive less discrimination from family, friends, and co-workers than those who are closeted anticipate. Wives tend to be upset by their husbands' revelations, but respondents are typically surprised by the positive reactions of their children and their parents.

Future prospects for gay fathers hinge largely on the success of the gay liberation movement. If these men can politicize their status, if they can see their difficulties stemming from social injustice and society's homophobic conditioning rather than personal inadequacy, and if they can redefine themselves, not as deviants, but as an oppressed minority, self-acceptance is improved. This helps lift their depression and externalize anger — anger about prejudice and about wasting their precious early years in the closet. Further, it minimizes their guilt and eases adjustment into the gay community (Miller, 1987).

As the gay liberation movement makes alternatives for fathering available within the gay community, fewer gays are likely to become involved in heterosexual marriages and divorce. Adoption, surrogate parenting, and alternative fertilization are some of the new ways single gays can now experience fatherhood (Miller, 1988). If current trends continue, there will be a proliferation of family life-styles so that parenthood becomes available to all regardless of sexual orientation.

REFERENCES

Adam, B. (1987). *The rise of a gay and lesbian movement*. Boston: Hall.

Bozett, F. W. (1987). *Gay and lesbian parents*. New York: Praeger.

Harry, J. & DeVall, W. (1978). *The social organization of gay males*. New York: Praeger.

Hays, D. & Samuels, A. (1988). Heterosexual women's perceptions of their marriages to bisexual or homosexual men. In F. W. Bozett (Ed.), *Homosexuality in the family*. New York: Haworth.

Humphreys, L. & Miller, B. (1980a). Keeping in touch: Maintaining contact with stigmatized respondents. In W. Shaffir, R. Stebbins & A. Turowetz (Eds.), *Field work experience: Qualitative approaches in social research*. New York: St. Martin's.

Humphreys, L. & Miller, B. (1980b). Identities in the emerging gay culture. In J. Marmor (Ed.), *Homosexual behavior: A modern reappraisal*. New York: Basic.

Levine, M. (1981). Employment discrimination against gay men. In P. Stein (Ed.), *Single life*. New York: St. Martin's.

Libby, R. & Whitehurst, R. (1977). *Marriage and alternatives*. Glenview, IL: Scott, Foresman.

McWhirter, D. & Mattison, A. (1984). *The male couple*. Englewood Cliffs, NJ: Prentice-Hall.

Miller, B. (1979). Gay fathers and their children. *Family Coordinator* 28:544–552.

Miller, B. (1983). Foreword. In M. W. Ross (Ed.), *The married homosexual man*. London: Routledge & Kegan Paul.

Miller, B. (1987). Counseling gay husbands and fathers. In F. W. Bozett (Ed.), *Gay and lesbian parents*. New York: Praeger.

Miller, B. (1988). Preface. In F. W. Bozett (Ed.), *Homosexuality in the family*. New York: Haworth.

Miller, B. & Humphreys, L. (1980). Lifestyles and violence: Homosexual victims of assault and murder. *Qualitative Sociology*. 3:169–185.

Murray, S. (1979). The institutional elaboration of a quasi-ethnic community. *International Review of Modern Sociology*. 9:165–177.

Pearson, C. (1986). *Good-bye, I love you*. New York: Random House.

Schulenberg, J. (1985). *Gay parenting*. New York: Doubleday.

Simon, W. & Gagnon, J. (1969). On psychosexual development. In D. Goslin (Ed.), *Handbook of socialization theory and research*. New York: Rand McNally.

Perry Garfinkel

GRANDFATHERS AND MENTORS:
BRIDGES TO THE OUTSIDE WORLD

"I expected to be coached by men
after the images of my heroes.
Men, Ladies and Gentlemen, who one

could depend on, look up to, believe
in. I wanted what I had coming."
                            —Mark Medoff,
                            "The Locker Room Kid,"
                            Esquire, October 1975

Fathers — absent or present — are not enough. Nor should they be. Throughout their lives men pick up valuable pointers from other men about the basics
of the masculine connection, about how men act with each other. A boy needs
and gets messages from elsewhere about the mysteries of masculinity; and while
each new man in his life may add new depth and breadth to his understanding
of himself in relation to other men, he also begins to recognize familiar lessons
learned at his father's feet. These are lessons about power and control, the male
hierarchy, and closeness and distance between men.

    As a boy begins to look around in his life for other male role models, he finds
two men — his grandfather and his mentor — who contribute in significant
ways to his development. In his grandfather, and later in his mentor, he finds
two men whose partial appeal is that they are devoid of the emotional entanglement and competitiveness that arises with his father — at least at first.

GRANDFATHERS: THE SOFT SPOT

If we have learned anything, it is that the source of male power and empowerment comes down to us from the father. The man above him — the father's
father — must, we can only assume, have manifold power. We are pulled to
grandfathers as a connection to our male lineage, and as a key to understanding
our fathers and ourselves. They are drawn to grandsons as perhaps their final
opportunity to assure the continuation of their names or at least their wisdom.
In grandfathers we see our past. In grandsons we see our future. The link between the two was explained in a gripping fashion in a dream told to me by a
thirty-two-year-old Boston attorney:

> In the dream my grandfather had just died. We were at the funeral, except
> my grandfather was still alive; I guess it was that state before the soul is
> supposed to leave the body. Anyway, he was dressed in a white tuxedo
> sitting in a white wheelchair, surrounded by white walls and clouds. My
> father was pushing the wheelchair and I was walking next to it at my
> grandfather's arm; we were dressed in white tuxedoes too. My grandfather
> directed my father to a door and into a room that looked like the basement
> of my grandfather's house. My father used to haul winter storm windows
> up from there for my grandfather when Grandpa got too old to do it
> himself. He told my father to start bringing the windows upstairs. Then
> my grandfather turned to me — and I'm not sure here whether he actually
> said it or told me with his eyes — but the message was clearly, "You're
> the one." It was a strong image and a strong message. I was the inheritor
> of the family chalice, the family name; he was passing the family reputa-
> tion down to me. I felt my father was bypassed.

Memories of grandfathers frequently came up in interviews as the soft spot in
their man-to-man relationships. This, I realized, was quite possibly one of the

very few men in a man's world with whom you were practically guaranteed to be free of power struggles, competitiveness, and ego-clash. Why? The difference in generations accounts for a relative lack of assumptions and expectations of what constitutes success in the world — two factors that engender conflict between father and son. . . . Lower expectations produce higher satisfaction; they allow for emotional interchange but with a lot less static.

Also contributing to the relative emotional neutrality of the grandson–grandfather bond is the old man's power position in the world at large at a time when the boy is growing up and watching him intently. While the boy's father struggles to define and maintain his power/position at work, the grandfather may well be into the power years of his life — those 50s and 60s in which he is part of the command generation — in which he has clearly established his domain. But apart from his position in the outside world, his unquestioned role as the elder male in the family hierarchy may be enough to assure his superior position, both to himself and his grandson, rendering competition out of the question.

On the other hand, when the grandfather is "past his prime," retired, physically weak, and viewed by the rest of the family as a dependent figure, the boy may feel no threat of being overpowered and may be, therefore, much freer to open his heart, fears, and hopes to his grandfather.

So though the boy may be drawn to the grandfather's power, it is exactly the lack of competition for power that makes this such a rewarding conflict-free relationship. For both people it is distance that affords closeness.

This distance/closeness theme was reinforced in the two most commonly recalled images that surfaced when I asked men to tell me about their grandfathers. In both, the grandfather appears as a less-than-real, remote figure.

One view came in romantic sepia tones and diffused lighting, in an oval cameo, blurry at the edges. Here was the man with the largest, most inviting lap in the world, with all the time in the world. A warm man full of deep laughs, deep personal contentment, and always those deep sparkling eyes gazing adoringly at us. Clearly out of focus, it was the vision of a man so loved, so idolized, that I suspected these young boys never really got to know the man in a clear objective light. He remained a distant and distorted image — his own kind of stranger.

The other picture of the grandfather was quite different but no less distant. In cold, dark lighting we now see a dour, grumpy man with a long gray beard, speaking perhaps in a foreign language — a man who smelled funny, and never seemed to be paying full attention to us. He was the tyrannical patriarch whom everyone feared. When this man turned his attention to us — for however briefly — a shiver went up our spines. He too was a stranger.

Here again — as we learned from our fathers — we find built-in distance and separateness in one of our closest male–male relationships. With all its richness and warmth, the grandfather–grandson relationship brands us with that message. . . . And this lesson gets retaught and relearned. Nonetheless, a deep longing for closeness that all humans share draws men to each other, urges them to break down those barriers.

Closeness to one's grandfather also holds out the hope of closeness to one's father — though, ironically, sometimes the man who may attempt to block that hoped for connection is the father himself. These are the first words of Herbert Gold's *Fathers*:

My father has never spoken his father's name. "He hit me for whistling like a peasant, he brought home a carp for the holiday, he took me to the rabbi, but I didn't want to go." *He* did this or that. What my father has left me of my grandfather is a silent old man with a long white beard, a horse, a cart, a cow, a mud-and-log house — an old country grandfather fixed in my mind like the memory of a painting. That's not enough, of course. This stylization of images does not satisfy the craving for history. I must tempt out the truth.

A father's attempt to thwart his son's knowledge of the grandfather may reflect the father's own unresolved anger, pain and frustration with *his* father. Boys watching their fathers for clues as to how to relate both to father and all men pay careful attention to the interaction of grandfather and father. What they may find is a mirror of what they're encountering themselves. These observations were offered by two men from what appear to be diametrically opposite backgrounds, one an upper-class older white Anglo-Saxon Protestant (WASP), the other a working-class black man of twenty-two. First the WASP:

By the time I came along things were pretty hostile between Dad and his father. One reason was that Grandfather was financially dependent on my father. And my grandfather was a man of tremendous pride. And my father also resented some of my grandfather's earlier successes that my father never lived up to even though their roles were reversed by the time I can remember. My father and grandfather were up against it most of the time they were together. My father and his argued a lot.

Now the young black:

I think grandaddy had a real wicked temper but only with his sons, not his grandsons. I guess I figured my father must have done something bad to warrant my grandaddy's anger, because all the rest of the time with us he was so gentle. But I sensed my father and his had their own thing going, and I sensed myself as very much on the outside of it.

Feeling ostrasized from the interaction of father and grandfather only adds more confusion and a sense of inferiority — a feeling of being the outsider — in the shadow of "grown-up men." But, as Gold also implies, a boy craves to understand himself through understanding his own history — and in most cases that understanding comes through the lineage of men in his family — so he pushes through father to reach grandfather. Even when the grandfather has been long gone when the boy arrives, his craving is so strong he will find out about the man — if not from his own father, then from other relatives, (usually the women). Charles, a twenty-two-year-old computer programmer from western Massachusetts, told me about his grandfathers:

I never knew either of my grandfathers. One died when I was three, the other at four. In the last couple of years I've started to hear more about my father's father. I hear it all from my grandmother. My father never talks about him. You can't ask him or he gets evasive. They didn't have a relationship, as far as I could tell. I don't think he had much contact with his father except in what they always referred to as "projects." Like the time my grandfather bought a ton of grain and didn't know what to do with it, so my father started a chicken farm to get rid of it. And it's the same with me and my father. My only contact with him has been over these "projects," when I was building something with him. My grandfather was apparently the source of a lot of energy in our family. His philosophy was, "Don't just stand there — do something, even if it's wrong." He built a boat in the basement and then had to pull down part of the house to get it out. There's a story about my grandfather coming into the shoe factory he owned one winter day and telling the workers huddled around the hot steam pipes, "Get to work, you get warm that way." Knowing these stories bolsters a lot of fantasies I have about being the third in a line of driven men, men who get things done, who accomplish tasks quickly.

There was a swelling sense of pride in this young man's voice as he related these cherished family tales about his grandfather, a significantly different voice than when he talked about his father. It made me realize how much our grandfathers can mean to us — especially in light of disappointments with a father. Into them we can pour all the love we may have had trouble giving to our own fathers. They are our fathers once removed.

A fifty-five-year-old banking investor from San Francisco looked to his grandfather for an image when he rejected his father as one:

> With my father I developed an attitude of I-don't-give-a-damn-what-he-thinks, mainly because he never approved of anything I did anyway. I think my father meant well but he suffered from being the son of a well known vaudeville song-and-dance man when vaudeville was in its heyday. He performed in Europe and Japan and all over the world. I never knew him but my aunts told me stories about him. He had a powerful presence, I was told; he was elegant and arrogant. On his death bed, in his 90s, he propped himself up on his bed deciding in what pecking order the relatives could come in and visit him. He was probably a horrible person to know but a remarkably self-assured son-of-a-bitch, from what I could gather.

It was clear after sitting with this gentleman two hours that he had followed in his grandfather's footsteps. He was a short, stocky, self-assured son-of-a-bitch who savored army stories in which he put superior officers to shame. His employees, I was told before I left his office, called him Napoleon.

OTHER GRANDFATHERS

There are some men whose grandfathers made more than brief appearances, or came in dreams or retold stories. In the last century and early in this one, men left their families for months or years for jobs that would make them enough money to send for the rest of their families or retire early back to their homeland. The education of the man's young son, left at home with his mother, fell to the grandfather. I was told of such a relationship by a sixty-three-year-old Greek restauranteur living in New York City. I asked him, "What was the most important thing your father gave you?" "My grandfather," he answered. He explained:

> I didn't spend much time with my father because people at that time, in that area of the world [Greece], migrated or went to sea, or wherever there was work. Sometimes I wouldn't see him for a few years. It was kind of

strange. Since my mother was rather young and busy raising the family, it was my grandfather who really brought me up. He had the time, he had the interest and he knew so much. I was in awe of him, held him in the highest regard. I remember how people from different villages would come to talk to him, seeking advice. My grandfather would take me for walks and inject me with his philosophy of life. He talked about religion and war and Greek history. I admired him so much.

When I asked this man what he learned from his grandfather, he emphasized three points. The first was discipline. The second was what he called "worldly wisdom — he gave me a sense of the scope of the world, and what I had to know to be in it." And the third was the importance of lineage: "Our family structure is based on patriarchy. Everything is spelled out quite precisely. I understood that anything my grandfather told me came from the same source as my father."

Another kind of relationship between grandfather and grandson emerged through the interviews — a type of bridging relationship that helps the son who is revolting against his father nonetheless maintain contact with the men in his family. The young man, usually in his early or mid-twenties, is looking for a friend and approaches his grandfather for solace, camaraderie, conversation, and intimacy, and as a means of staying in touch with his own lineage. The grandfather, somewhat more dependent, himself lonely with his children preoccupied making a living and his own peers slowly dying off, appreciates an "ear." A thirty-six-year-old Los Angeles school administrator, Craig, described such a relationship:

My grandfather's 87 years old. I wasn't that close to him when I was a kid. He was your basic immigrant who killed himself working. He started with nothing and built up a pretty successful business. I really have a great deal of respect for him for that. Our closeness started about six or seven years ago, just after my grandmother died. I used to walk him to the dentist and he and I would walk and talk. It was beautiful. He talked about his childhood. He was so generous with his feelings, in a way that I couldn't be. And I was so responsive to that. I started to feel so open to him. We became very close, a deep friendship — without any regard for the older–younger thing or the fact that he was supposed to be my superior. He never moralized like my father. I couldn't share with him many of my contemporary experiences but we maintained a good level on lots of things and personal issues. I just spoke with him the other day on the phone for 45 minutes. It was heaven. I feel very lucky to have contacted him again.

"He never moralized like my father." Here is a key to the grandfather's role in a young boy's life — he can reminisce with, love, and *enjoy* the boy without feeling, as the father does, the need to create a fledgling man who reflects well on himself as masculine standard bearer. Through the old man the boy tastes the freedom to relate to a grown man on his own terms while still remaining anchored safely to the family.

◆◆◆

PART ELEVEN

Men and the Future

Q: Why did you decide to record again?
A: Because *this* housewife would like to have a career for a bit! On October 9, I'll be 40, and Sean will be 5 and I can afford to say "Daddy does something else as well." He's not accustomed to it — in five years I hardly picked up a guitar. Last Christmas our neighbors showed him "Yellow Submarine" and he came running in, saying, "Daddy, you were singing . . . Were you a Beatle?" I said, "Well — yes, right."

— John Lennon, interview
Newsweek, 1980

Are men changing? If so, in what directions? Can men change even more? In what ways should men be different? We posed many of these questions at the beginning of our exploration of men's lives, and we return to them here, in the book's last section, to examine the directions men have taken to enlarge their roles, to expand the meaning of masculinity, to change the rules.

Several of the articles in this section address the possibility of expanding the role option open to men and becoming more responsive to women and to other men. The selections by Connell, Radican, and Martin and by Cooper Thompson address, in different ways, the way men are changing and the ways in which men might continue to change. In the next article, Joseph H. Pleck addresses the possibility of men expanding their roles to include more domestic and child-centered tasks. Other men see the possibility of men changing as a political process that involves men organizing themselves into a political movement for change. The "Statement of Principles" of the National Organization for Changing Men provides a political program, and the article by Harry Brod provides its underlying rationale.

We began this book with a description of men's confusion. Men's confusion often makes men anxious, and some have said that men are experiencing a "crisis of masculinity." This confusion or "crisis" is beautifully captured by the Chinese character for the word "crisis," which is a combination of the characters for the words "danger" and "opportunity." If masculinity is in crisis, if men are confused, it is both dangerous and an exciting opportunity.

The danger is a danger of retreat. Confusion is often a frightening experience; one feels unsettled, problems are unresolved, and identity is off-center. Some people, when they are confused, will retreat to older, familiar ideas — ideas that may have once been appropriate but now are only safe anachronisms that will offer temporary solace from the confusion. Some men are therefore seeking a resolution to their confusion by the vigorous reassertion of traditional masculinity.

But many of us can recognize the opportunity that is presented by confusion. Feeling unsettled, restless, and anxious, confusion pushes us to wrestle with difficult issues, confront contradictory feelings and ideas, and challenge the ways in which our experiences do not fit with the traditional rules and expectations we have inherited from the past. Confusion opens the opportunity to change, to push beyond the traditional norms of masculinity. And with change comes the possibility to become more loving and caring fathers, more emotionally responsive lovers, and more reliable and compassionate friends, and to live longer and healthier lives. It is toward these changes that we hope this work has contributed.

Reprinted with permission by Matt Groening © 1988. Acme Features Syndicate.

Bob Connell, Norm Radican, and Pip Martin

THE CHANGING FACES OF MASCULINITY

THE PROBLEM OF CHANGE

"One is not born, but rather becomes a woman." Simone de Beauvoir's insight applies equally well to men: one is not born, but rather becomes a man. Men's bodies become masculine according to the way society interprets them. Dean C, a bus driver we interviewed, put it simply:

> I've always been brought up that the man is the breadwinner and that the man serviced the woman. They had children. She stayed at home and cooked.

History and anthropology tell us that this familiar, apparently "natural" arrangement is historically recent and culturally specific. In other times and places the arrangements about work, the family, and economic responsibility are very different. What a man believes to be "masculine" or "manly," the way he expresses his sexuality and identity, depends mainly on when and where he was born.

Masculinity, then, is produced by historical processes. To understand the way it works and its effects in the world we must study the way it changes. It can easily be shown that these changes are not trivial. In Renaissance Europe, for instance, the dominant form of masculinity made no sharp distinction between heterosexual pleasure and homosexual pleasure. A powerful man, such as a prince or a famous artist, could and would enjoy himself both with boys and with women. By the late nineteenth century the homosexual and heterosexual components had been split apart. The dominant form of masculinity was now defined as strictly heterosexual. "Homosexual" became the label for a minority whose whole social being was defined as criminal. Oscar Wilde was one of the men whose lives were destroyed in this process.

We are plainly living through another phase of change now, though its shape is not well understood. Since the rise of the new feminism in the early 1970s there has been a good deal of interest in "men's liberation," masculinity, and men's social position. Around 50 books on the subject have been published in English in the last 15 years. Unfortunately the volume of output has not been matched by quality. The research base of most of the "books about men" is slight. They have also been plagued by theoretical hangovers from a basically conservative sociology of "roles." Most authors have taken one dominant form of masculinity for granted, as a definition of the "male sex role," and have concerned themselves with where the shoe pinches — where men do and don't fit into their "role."

As a way of understanding the realities of men's lives, this is very limiting. It stimulates little curiosity about other forms of masculinity, especially those that are marginalized or stigmatized. It plays down the issue of sexual choice; most discussion of "sex roles" conspicuously avoids the experience of homosexuality. Equally it avoids the issue of social power, whether of men over women or of

Parts of this article appeared in *The New Internationalist* (September 1987, No. 175, pp. 18–20) under the title "The Evolving Man."

men over men. In consequence, the social acquisition of masculinity is presented as a rather bland process of learning sex role "norms."

But consider this account of a boy's first day at secondary school:

> The boarding school master and my mother were there and they handed me over to this guy named Anthony who was a charming young chap in Third Form, good family and all that. Anthony was supposed to show me around and look after me. But as soon as we left the office, it was "biff bam" and I was hanging upside down by my legs with rope. It was quite cruel actually.
>
> (Matthew B, student)

Violence is a vivid childhood memory for many men, from all social backgrounds. (It is worth noting that Matthew B came from an affluent background and is talking about an elite private school.) The making of masculinity cannot be understood without taking close account of the patterns of social power.

Power, in turn, cannot be understood abstractly. It is about relationships, and can be understood only by looking at how men live their lives on a practical day-to-day basis in their personal and historical context.

A RESEARCH PROJECT

To improve on the "sex role" approach we need research methods that are sensitive both to personal and to historical context. One important option is the "life history" method. Personal histories have been collected by psychologists and sociologists since the time of Freud. They have proved a basic research tool in studying psychosocial issues ranging from the causes of neurosis to the experience of migration.

Our research on changes in masculinity adapted this traditional method in the light of recent work on the theory of gender.[1] Our interviews move through the familiar stages of childhood, adolescence, and adulthood. In each stage we raise issues about three key structures of gender: power and authority, the division of labor, and sexuality and emotional attachment. We rarely ask for "attitudes" or beliefs. Rather the interviews concentrate on a person's practices and day-to-day strategies for dealing with gender issues, both in the workplace and in interpersonal relationships. Gender relations and sexual politics are approached as a "lived experience."

This method is intensive compared with paper-and-pencil surveys, so large samples are not possible and a statistical cross section of a whole population is an unrealistic goal. Instead we have focused on particular social contexts in which conventional models of masculinity are under pressure and the social dynamic of change may be thrown into relief. Most of our interviews have been done among four groups: men in "new" professions and technical jobs, working-class youth affected by structural unemployment, men involved in the counter-culture or in environmental politics, and men engaged in countersexist politics, both heterosexual and homosexual.

SOCIAL STRUCTURE AND MASCULINITY

The life-history approach gives abundant evidence of the social pressures operating in childhood. A boy growing up encounters rules, rituals, and symbols that define "masculinity" in its dominant form. Conforming may not be easy. Adam S, now an architect, offers an early memory:

> How a man throws a ball is different from how a woman throws a ball. I didn't want to throw a ball in front of my Dad because I wouldn't look right. It wouldn't be the way a good strong boy would throw it. And once, I remember, I was brave enough to throw it. And he made for me and said I threw it like a girl.

The insult by Adam's father points directly to the main social basis of the dominant form of masculinity: the subordination of women. In white Australian society (and many others) men are supposed to be stronger and more powerful than women. Broadly, men are supposed to have authority over women. To be "like a girl" is to be weak, to be in danger, to have a flawed masculinity.

In a patriarchal society, popular culture is permeated by the belief that men are superior to women. The assumption is often unstated or only half conscious, and generally contradicts official, legal, and religious declarations of equality. But it is still constantly assumed in practice that men rather than women are the people who matter, as a simple content analysis of the daily newspaper will show. Accordingly, to become a man is to acquire a position of social power. To "be a man" is to show the qualities needed to sustain power — courage in the face of threat or conflict, command over resources, etc. These qualities define an admired, socially dominant form of masculinity.

But this does not settle the everyday reality of men's lives, for most men cannot or will not live according to the ideal pattern. Rather, it defines a basic *tension* in masculinity. The tension about power may be built into an individual life, as is clear in the case of Adam S. At a collective level, it marks out relationships between the dominant — better, *"hegemonic"* — form of masculinity and less honored forms. There are subordinated or marginalized kinds of masculinity. In contemporary European cultures these include homosexual men, effeminate heterosexual men, very young men (i.e., boys), and a broader spread of adult men who simply do not live up to the dominant pattern.

Differences in resources or in prestige may become bitter experiences of subordination, even when they are transient. Peter G, a journalist, recalls such an experience at the age of 15:

> I had another scene with a girl at that stage. But she started going with one of the guys there — about 18, and had his own car, his own income and everything . . . I don't think my life really started until I started work about the age of 17, and had an income and was independent. That was the first time ever in my life that I felt good. I had a motor-bike, and I had a job, and I had lots of money . . . and I could get girls.

In Peter's story the relationship between masculinities is mediated through women. This illustrates a general point. Masculinity never exists by itself. It exists in relation to femininity, in the context of an overarching structure of gender relations. To understand that structure is a complex proposition. The structure includes — at least — the social organization of production, the structure of power and authority, and the social organization of emotion. A recognition that structural change is important is nevertheless a key to understanding what is happening to masculinity as a form of personal character.

TWO MEN "IN TRANSIT"

Let us explore this through two case studies drawn from our "new professions" group, a journalist and an architect. The changing social organization of work creates problems for conventional masculinity, for instance about whether a high degree of technical competence can give a livable social identity outside the recognized professions.

Peter G, whose teenage memories were just quoted, started his working life as a wool-classer. The wool industry in Australia has a heavily masculine identity. His new status as an adult man meant a lot to him:

> I went and lived in a tent down at the beach. . . . and I had lots of money . . . and I used to spend about eighty percent of it on beer.

But he wanted to get on in the world, and wool-classing was a dead-end job. So he shifted into journalism. He learned that profession the hard way, starting on country newspapers — being sacked from one for fucking the editor's daughter on the office floor. Peter rose rapidly to become a top reporter/photographer on a metropolitan daily by the time he was 30. He was "first [cab] off the rank" when a new story broke. He was often sent by his employers across the continent, and was given the most difficult issues, such as gangsterism, to chase up.

He was leading "a really fast lane kind of life," with a lot of prestige and a lot of pressure. Suddenly he saw it all as absurd. His technical skills as a journalist had not given him a stable social identity. Indeed, they probably provoked the crisis in his perception of himself. Peter threw in his job, bought a farm on an island, and swept his wife and five children off to a rural idyll:

> We walked out of the hotel at 9 o'clock in the morning, and at 4 o'clock in the afternoon we were standing on a beach watching the plane taxi away. My wife was wearing high heels and a suit, and we waved. We had a truck, and climbed into that, and drove to our little shack. We didn't have any electricity. And that was the beginning of a whole new world.

Not an easy world, as it turned out. They lost their money in the farm; they later set up a health food shop, but that eventually collapsed. The family broke up and Peter found himself living alone in a caravan. He began to wander from household to household, with few possessions or money, "relishing" his new found freedom. He would get up at 4 in the morning, roll a joint, and go off on an "adventure" in the bush for a day.

Peter's rejection of mainstream masculinity was itself a masculine gesture, assertive and self-dramatizing. He did not consult his wife and children first. But he has followed through its logic, as far as voluntary poverty. The rural counterculture, which is strong in his part of the country, provides support for people dropping out of a middle-class life-style. It does not provide a clear alternative sexual politics. So Peter is caught in a politics of personal gesture, and remains emotionally dependent on women. After leaving his wife he moved through a series of short-term relationships, starting a new one as soon as he broke off the last. It is perhaps not surprising that he is now building a nuclear-family household with a second wife.

A second problem in conventional masculinity concerns the convention of "toughness." The admired image in Western culture, from John Wayne and Jack Kennedy to Sylvester Stallone, is constructed in such extreme terms that most men cannot live up to it. Tension about this toughness deficit is likely to be at its worst in adolescence and early adulthood. Not by chance, this is the age group when men are most likely to be killed in car accidents or industrial accidents.

Adam S, whose childhood memory about throwing a ball was quoted above, recalls from his adolescence the moment when he saw himself as having a spoiled masculinity:

> We were running around on the beach, tackling and playing around. And my image, as I looked down at my legs and I saw that my thighs were fat — I was tackling or something — and they'd wobble like jelly. And I'd never noticed them like that before, and that's something I've still got embarrassment about. That also went along with being bigger in the hips than other boys, and smaller in the chest. Made me feel underconfident as a male.

As this illustrates, the male body is a canvas on which masculine social images are painted. In gender, social relations — such as dominance between groups of men — operate *through* body images and bodily responses.

Adam's memory also illustrates the self-criticism that is common among men whose form of masculinity is socially marginalized. He is bisexual, in the sense that he has kept up long-term sexual relations with both men and women.

Being "bisexual" is not a clear-cut social or personal identity and Adam's picture of gender is strikingly ambivalent. He dislikes dominant men, football, motorbikes, and the rest of the cult of machismo. But he likes "big muscly men" as sexual objects and approves of athletics. He admires women, and was introduced to politics and cultural life by women. But he keeps his women lovers in a subordinate place in his private life.

A university-trained expert with a job in a large bureaucracy, Adam S's working life is in the mainstream of technological modernism. But his experience of this work is alienating and he finds no personal base or public identity in his workplace. His response has been to search for meaning and fulfilment in personal relationships, especially relationships that combine sexual excitement with a social or artistic stimulus.

In a very different context, therefore, Adam's practice has something in common with Peter's. Both needed to break with conventional masculinity, Adam because he couldn't begin to inhabit it, Peter because his success in inhabiting it became unbearable. Both moved toward a private resolution of the tension. And both are dissatisfied with the result, without having any serious alternative in view.

SOURCES OF CHANGE

What are the prospects of a major alternative emerging? The "men's movement" of the 1970s proclaimed a great transformation, but had no clear idea of where it might come from. Our research, taken together with recent theoretical work, points to several distinct sources of change in masculinity. They do not necessarily move in the same direction.

The first source is tension within the "social construction" of masculinity.

Contradictions emerge in relation to power, in the realm of production, and in sexuality.

The dominant form of masculinity in Western culture embodies men's social power over women. It emphasizes force, authority, and aggressiveness. But to sustain this cultural ideal, the majority of men as actual living people must be put down. Some fail to match up: their legs are too flabby, their chests not hairy enough, their glance insufficiently flinty. Others are actively oppressed, gay men and effeminate men most obviously. Gay men are still sometimes beaten to death on the streets of a city like Sydney.

Rabbit S — young, working class, unemployed, and as tough as they come — ran into this contradiction full on:

> Gays I have trouble putting up with. That's half the reason I don't see my brother as much as I'd like. I used to go up to the Cross and poofter-bash and all the rest of it.* When my brother turned queer I ended up stopping it anyway. So long as they stay out of my way. I just have to remember he's my brother first, a queer second, makes it a bit easier to handle.

The economy produces another contradiction. Traditional masculinity is constructed around traditional authority: landlord over peasant, boss over worker, husband over wife, old over young. The restless development of capitalism disrupts such authority as it disrupts all other cultural patterns. Even in the heartland of industry, and within the ruling class, traditional authority is challenged by technocracy, the rough old-style manager by the smooth Harvard MBA. Clyde W, a computer systems analyst, pokes fun at his managers' ignorance:

> Like this computer for example, they [managers] have no idea what they are going to get. Actually I had very little problem persuading them because they don't know what I am persuading. They said "why have you made these decisions" — and I had most of the answers. It's probably not good to have all the answers; they want to know that they have done something.

But the rise of technical rationality challenges patriarchy itself. The subordination of women is economically irrational. It means a loss of labor and of talent, as "equal opportunity" campaigns in the rich countries point out, and as development agencies argue in the third world. The computer industry itself, highly sexist, though its ideology promotes pure rationality, shows this contradiction in a strong form.

A third contradiction arises in sexuality. The dominant form of sexuality is heterosexual, focused on the genitals and on erotic performance. Greg B, another computer specialist, reflects wryly on his sexual life in these terms:

> I fell flat on my face . . . not being successful in getting it up, so to speak, because my mind was just turning me off. It's difficult to know if I'm going to perform properly or not. If it doesn't happen, it doesn't happen. It doesn't happen frequently. And they say, "What's wrong?" And you go, "Oh well, I'm not at my peak at the moment."

---

*"The Cross'" (King's Cross), the main red-light district in Sydney, borders on the main social center for Sydney's gay men. "Poofter-bashing" means gang attacks on gay men.

The hegemonic form of sexuality has been socially constructed by tabooing other forms of sexuality. But as Freud showed, what is tabooed is not abolished. On the contrary it is likely to be given new symbolic and emotional power. Homosexuality haunts the masculine world, as endless jokes about football teams illustrate. Beyond flashy genital performance is a world faintly sensed by many men and actively explored by some (such as Peter G) of relaxed, mutual, whole-body pleasure. In this direction (though very much in the future) lies a form of sexuality in which gender would cease to be one's social fate and would become mainly a means of play.

These contradictions are emerging within the structure of masculinity. There are also pressures from outside. The most obvious is the demand for change from women. "Women's liberation" as a political movement has lost some impetus. But modern feminism must not be underestimated as a cultural force. Every man we interviewed has been conscious of it. Some are receptive and some hostile, all feel the mobilization of women as a presence. In the lives of some men it is a decisive presence. A case in point is Barry R, who describes his encounter with feminism thus:

> I didn't really understand very much about sexism, like I just sort of knew there was something wrong about sexism . . . And I read some pretty heavy stuff which made me feel terrible about being male, for a long time. And I remember I found it really hard because there were these conflicting needs. I needed sex and I needed relationships, and then again I needed to set aside my ideals and my own sexism, and I couldn't reconcile these. So I went through lots and lots of guilt.

Guilt does seem to be a common experience for men who take feminism seriously; it can be paralyzing, as it was for a time for Barry R. But he has worked through it to some purpose, and is exploring some new paths in his own life; among other things he has taken the unusual step, for a man, of training as a nurse.

General economic change also puts pressure on masculinity, as might be expected from the importance of "work" in most men's self-images. There are now 30 million officially unemployed in the OECD countries, and much more hidden unemployment than that. Traditional work-based masculinity can survive quite radical changes in technology, as Cynthia Cockburn's wonderful study of British printing workers, *Brothers*, has shown.[2] But structural change is now eliminating whole industries and categories of workers. What does it mean to be brought up a "breadwinner," as Dean C was, if the bread is not there to be won? Young working-class men like Rabbit S — for all the media hype about unemployed managers, unemployment is mainly concentrated in working-class areas — face a lifetime of at best intermittent casual employment.

STRATEGIES

The pressures just sketched will certainly generate change in and around masculinity, but they do not by themselves settle the shape that change will take. That is a matter of social action, of collective choices about strategy.

Among those men who have become conscious of the politics of masculinity, the main reaction has been to try to remake themselves in a new image, moving as far away as possible from mainstream "macho" images.

This has meant new codes of conduct: leaving space for women, not pushing for control within families, not demanding the initiative in sex. It has meant trying to build new relationships: caring for children, opening up emotionally to other men. It has meant shifting the focus of life from careers and money to human relationships, from the mechanical world to the natural world, from computers and cars to people and trees. Peter G is one of the men who have consciously taken that track.

This effort is important in producing new models of masculinity, showing how men might live more peaceably with each other and with women. But there are also dangers in this strategy. Both Peter G and Adam S became inward-looking and individualized. Even a shared politics, if focused on "masculinity" alone, can go astray. Parts of the "men's movement" come to the quite false conclusion that men and women were "equally oppressed" by their sex roles. Changing masculinity in these terms may be therapeutic and comforting but does nothing about the issue of equality.

In the final analysis it is equality that is central. In an "advanced" country such as Australia, the average income of a woman is 45% of the average income of a man. All the major centers of power are substantially controlled by men: the state, finance, media, industry, unions. That is broadly true across the world. Women are less likely to own their own houses or land, are more likely to be in poverty, and rarely control major institutions.

To reconstruct masculinity in a way that acknowledges its social dimension means men tackling those kinds of inequality. Partly it means quite conventional politics, in unions, parties, and workplaces. On the other hand it means an unconventional politics of households. In particular it means changing the mundane, and often unspoken, arrangements that require women to do most of the housework and virtually all the care of young children.

This is a collective enterprise more than an individual one. As it develops, the diverse sources of change in masculinity may become an asset rather than a source of confusion. For it will not be a change brought about by dramatic revolution. Rather it will mean complex alliances, many small gains and losses, and twists and turns. It will be important for different groups of men to learn from each others' experience, as well as from the experience of women. Attempts to share experience, like this book, are a hopeful sign.

REFERENCES

1. See R. W. Connell, *Gender and Power*. Polity Press, 1987.
2. C. Cockburn, *Brothers*. Pluto Press, 1983.

Cooper Thompson

A NEW VISION OF MASCULINITY

I was once asked by a teacher in a suburban high school to give a guest presentation on male roles. She hoped that I might help her deal with four boys who exercised extraordinary control over the other boys in the class. Using ridicule and their status as physically imposing athletes, these four wrestlers had succeeded in stifling the participation of the other boys, who were reluctant to make comments in class discussions.

As a class we talked about the ways in which boys got status in that school and how they got put-down by others. I was told that the most humiliating put-down was being called a "fag." The list of behaviors which could elicit ridicule filled two large chalkboards, and it was detailed and comprehensive; I got the sense that a boy in this school had to conform to rigid, narrow standards of masculinity to avoid being called a fag. I, too, felt this pressure and became very conscious of my mannerisms in front of the group. Partly from exasperation, I decided to test the seriousness of these assertions. Since one of the four boys had some streaks of pink in his shirt, and since he had told me that wearing pink was grounds for being called a fag, I told him that I thought he was a fag. Instead of laughing, he said, "I'm going to kill you."

Such is the stereotypic definition of strength that is associated with masculinity. But it is a very limited definition of strength, one based on dominance and control and acquired through the humiliation and degradation of others.

Contrast this with a view of strength offered by Pam McAllister in her introduction to *Reweaving the Web of Life:*

> The "Strength" card in my Tarot deck depicts, not a warrior going off to battle with his armor and his mightly sword, but a woman stroking a lion. The woman has not slain the lion nor maced it, not netted it, nor has she put on it a muzzle or a leash. And though the lion clearly has teeth and long sharp claws, the woman is not hiding, nor has she sought a protector, nor has she grown muscles. She doesn't appear to be talking to the lion, nor flattering it, nor tossing it fresh meat to distract its hungry jaws.
>
> The woman on the "Strength" card wears a flowing white dress and a garland of flowers. With one hand she cups the lion's jaws, with the other she caresses its nose. The lion on the card has big yellow eyes and a long red tongue curling out of its mouth. One paw is lifted and the mane falls in thick red curls across its broad torso. The woman. The lion. Together they depict strength.

This image of strength stands in direct contrast to the strength embodied in the actions of the four wrestlers. The collective strength of the woman and the lion is a strength unknown in a system of traditional male values. Other human qualities are equally foreign to a traditional conception of masculinity. In workshops I've offered on the male role stereotype, teachers and other school personnel easily generate lists of attitudes and behaviors which boys typically seem to not learn. Included in this list are being supportive and nurturant, accepting one's vulnerability and being able to ask for help, valuing women and "women's work," understanding and expressing emotions (except for anger), the ability to empathize with and empower other people, and learning to resolve conflict in non-aggressive, non-competitive ways.

LEARNING VIOLENCE

All of this should come as no surprise. Traditional definitions of masculinity include attributes such as independence, pride, resiliency, self-control, and physical strength. This is precisely the image of the Marlboro man, and to some extent, these are desirable attributes for boys and girls. But masculinity goes beyond these qualities to stress competitiveness, toughness, aggressiveness, and power. In this context, threats to one's status, however small, cannot be avoided or taken lightly. If a boy is called a fag, it means that he is perceived as weak or timid — and therefore not masculine enough for his peers. There is enormous pressure for him to fight back. Not being tough at these moments only proves the allegation.

Violence is learned not just as a way for boys to defend allegations that they are feminized, but as an effective, appropriate way for them to normally behave. In "The Civic Advocacy of Violence" Wayne Ewing clearly states:

> I used to think that we simply tolerated and permitted male abusiveness in our society. I have now come to understand rather, that we *advocate* physical violence. Violence is presented as effective. Violence is taught as the normal, appropriate and necessary behavior of power and control. Analyses which interweave advocacy of male violence with "SuperBowl Culture" have never been refuted. Civic expectations — translated into professionalism, financial commitments, city planning for recreational space, the raising of male children for competitive sport, the corporate ethics of business ownership of athletic teams, profiteering on entertainment — all result in the monument of the National Football League, symbol and reality at once of the advocacy of violence.

Ultimately, violence is the tool which maintains what I believe are the two most critical socializing forces in a boy's life: *homophobia*, the hatred of gay men (who are stereotyped as feminine) or those men believed to be gay, as well as the fear of being perceived as gay; and *misogyny*, the hatred of women. The two forces are targeted at different classes of victims, but they are really just the flip sides of the same coin. Homophobia is the hatred of feminine qualities in men while misogyny is the hatred of feminine qualities in women. The boy who is called a fag is the target of other boys' homophobia as well as the victim of his own homophobia. While the overt message is the absolute need to avoid being feminized, the implication is that females — and all that they traditionally represent — are contemptible. The United States Marines have a philosophy which conveniently combines homophobia and misogyny in the belief that "When you want to create a group of male killers, you kill 'the woman' in them."

The pressures of homophobia and misogyny in boys' lives have been poignantly demonstrated to me each time that I have repeated a simple yet provocative activity with students. I ask them to answer the question, "If you woke up tomorrow and discovered that you were the opposite sex from the one your are now, how would you and your life be different?" Girls consistently indicate that there are clear advantages to being a boy — from increased independence and career opportunities to decreased risks of physical and sexual assault — and eagerly answer the question. But boys often express disgust at this possibility and even refuse sometimes to answer the question. In her reports of a broad-based survey using this question, Alice Baumgartner reports the following responses as typical of boys: "If I were a girl, I'd be stupid and weak as a string;" "I would have to wear make-up, cook, be a mother, and yuckky stuff like that;" "I would have to hate snakes. Everything would be miserable;" "If I were a girl, I'd kill myself."

THE COSTS OF MASCULINITY

The costs associated with a traditional view of masculinity are enormous, and the damage occurs at both personal and societal levels. The belief that a boy should be tough (aggressive, competitive, and daring) can create emotional pain for him. While a few boys experience short-term success for their toughness, there is little security in the long run. Instead, it leads to a series of challenges which few, if any, boys ultimately win. There is no security in being at the top when so many other boys are competing for the same status. Toughness also leads to increased chances of stress, physical injury, and even early death. It is considered manly to take extreme physical risks and voluntarily engage in combative, hostile activities.

The flip side of toughness — nurturance — is not a quality perceived as masculine and thus not valued. Because of this boys and men experience a greater emotional distance from other people and fewer opportunities to participate in meaningful interpersonal relationships. Studies consistently show that fathers spend very small amounts of time interacting with their children. In addition, men report that they seldom have intimate relationships with other men, reflecting their homophobia. They are afraid of getting too close and don't know how to take down the walls that they have built between themselves.

As boys grow older and accept adult roles, the larger social costs of masculinity clearly emerge. Most women experience male resistance to an expansion of women's roles; one of the assumptions of traditional masculinity is the belief that women should be subordinate to men. The consequence is that men are often not willing to accept females as equal, competent partners in personal and professional settings. Whether the setting is a sexual relationship, the family, the streets, or the battlefield, men are continuously engaged in efforts to dominate. Statistics on child abuse consistently indicate that the vast majority of abusers are men, and that there is no "typical" abuser. Rape may be the fastest growing crime in the United States. And it is men, regardless of nationality, who provoke and sustain war. In short, traditional masculinity is life threatening.

NEW SOCIALIZATION FOR BOYS

Masculinity, like many other human traits, is determined by both biological and environmental factors. While some believe that biological factors are significant in shaping some masculine behavior, there is undeniable evidence that cultural and environmental factors are strong enough to override biological impulses. What is it, then, that we should be teaching boys about being a man in a modern world?

- Boys must learn to accept their vulnerability, learn to express a range of emotions such as fear and sadness, and learn to ask for help and support in appropriate situations.
- Boys must learn to be gentle, nurturant, cooperative, and communicative, and in particular, learn non-violent means of resolving conflicts.
- Boys must learn to accept those attitudes and behaviors which have traditionally been labeled feminine as necessary for full human development — thereby reducing homophobia and misogyny. This is tantamount to teaching boys to love other boys and girls.

Certain qualities like courage, physical strength, and independence, which are traditionally associated with masculinity, are indeed positive qualities for males, provided that they are not manifested in obsessive ways nor used to exploit or dominate others. It is not necessary to completely disregard or unlearn what is traditionally called masculine. I believe, however, that the three areas above are crucial for developing a broader view of masculinity, one which is healthier for all life.

These three areas are equally crucial for reducing aggressive, violent behavior among boys and men. Males must learn to cherish life for the sake of their *own* wholeness as human beings, not just *for* their children, friends, and lovers. If males were more nurturant, they would be less likely to hurt those they love.

Leonard Eron, writing in the *American Psychologist*, puts the issue of unlearning aggression and learning nurturance in clear-cut terms:

> Socialization is crucial in determining levels of aggression. No matter how aggression is measured or observed, as a group males always score higher than females. But this is not true for all girls. There are some girls who seem to have been socialized like boys who are just as aggressive as boys. Just as some females can learn to be aggressive, so males can learn *not* to be aggressive. If we want to reduce the level of aggression in society, we should also discourage boys from aggression very early on in life and reward them too for other behaviors; in other words, we should socialize boys more like girls, and they should be encouraged to develop socially positive qualities such as tenderness, cooperation, and aesthetic appreciation. The level of individual aggression in society will be reduced only when male adolescents and young adults, as a result of socialization, subscribe to the same standards of behavior as have been traditionally encouraged for women.

Where will this change in socialization occur? In his first few years, much of a boy's learning about masculinity comes from the influences of parents, siblings and images of masculinity such as those found on television. Massive efforts will be needed to make changes here. But at older ages, school curriculum and the school environment provide powerful reinforcing images of traditional masculinity. This reinforcement occurs through a variety of channels, including curriculum content, role modeling, and extracurricular activities, especially competitive sports.

School athletics are a microcosm of the socialization of male values. While participation in competitive activities can be enjoyable and healthy, it too easily becomes a lesson in the need for toughness, invulnerability, and dominance.

Athletes learn to ignore their own injuries and pain and instead try to injure and inflict pain on others in their attempts to win, regardless of the cost to themselves or their opponents. Yet the lessons learned in athletics are believed to be vital for full and complete masculine development, and as a model for problem-solving in other areas of life.

In addition to encouraging traditional male values, schools provide too few experiences in nurturance, cooperation, negotiation, non-violent conflict resolution, and strategies for empathisizing with and empowering others. Schools should become places where boys have the opportunity to learn these skills; clearly, they won't learn them on the street, from peers, or on television.

SETTING NEW EXAMPLES

Despite the pressure on men to display their masculinity in traditional ways, there are examples of men and boys who are changing. "Fathering" is one example of a positive change. In recent years, there has been a popular emphasis on child-care activities, with men becoming more involved in providing care to children, both professionally and as fathers. This is a clear shift from the more traditional view that child rearing should be delegated to women and is not an appropriate activity for men.

For all of the male resistance it has generated, the Women's Liberation Movement has at least provided a stimulus for some men to accept women as equal partners in most areas of life. These are the men who have chosen to learn and grow from women's experiences and together with women are creating new norms for relationships. Popular literature and research on male sex roles are expanding, reflecting a wider interest in masculinity. Weekly news magazines such as *Time* and *Newsweek* have run major stories on the "new masculinity," suggesting that positive changes are taking place in the home and in the workplace. Small groups of men scattered around the country have organized against pornography, battering and sexual assault. Finally, there is the National Organization for Changing Men which has a pro-feminist, pro-gay, pro-"new man" agenda, and its ranks are slowly growing.

In schools where I have worked with teachers, they report that years of efforts to enhance educational opportunities for girls have also had some positive effects on boys. The boys seem more tolerant of girls' participation in co-ed sports activities and in traditionally male shops and courses. They seem to have a greater respect for the accomplishments of women through women's contributions to literature and history. Among elementary school aged males, the expression of vulnerable feelings is gaining acceptance. In general, however, there has been far too little attention paid to redirecting male role development.

BOYS WILL BE BOYS

I think back to the four wrestlers and the stifling culture of masculinity in which they live. If schools were to radically alter this culture and substitute for it a new vision of masculinity, what would that look like? In this environment, boys would express a full range of behaviors and emotions without fear of being chastized. They would be permitted and encouraged to cry, to be afraid, to show joy, and to express love in a gentle fashion. Extreme concern for career goals would be replaced by a consideration of one's need for recreation, health, and meaningful work. Older boys would be encouraged to tutor and play with younger students. Moreover, boys would receive as much recognition for artistic talents as they do for athletics, and, in general, they would value leisure-time, recreational activities as highly as competitive sports.

In a system where maleness and femaleness were equally valued, boys might no longer feel that they have to "prove" themselves to other boys; they would simply accept the worth of each person and value those differences. Boys would realize that it is permissable to admit failure. In addition, they would seek out opportunities to learn from girls and women. Emotional support would become commonplace, and it would no longer be seen as just the role of the female to provide the support. Relationships between boys and girls would no longer be based on limited roles, but instead would become expressions of two individuals learning from and supporting one another. Relationships between boys would reflect their care for one another rather than their mutual fear and distrust.

Aggressive styles of resolving conflicts would be the exception rather than the norm. Girls would feel welcome in activities dominated by boys, knowing that they were safe from the threat of being sexually harassed. Boys would no longer boast of beating up another boy or of how much they "got off" of a girl the night before. In fact, the boys would be as outraged as the girls at rape or other violent crimes in the community. Finally, boys would become active in efforts to stop nuclear proliferation and all other forms of military violence, following the examples set by activist women.

The development of a new conception of masculinity based on this vision is an ambitious task, but one which is essential for the health and safety of both men and women. The survival of our society may rest on the degree to which we are able to teach men to cherish life.

Joseph H. Pleck

THE CONTEMPORARY MAN

Critical analyses of the limitations of the male role, for both men and women, began appearing a little over 15 years ago (Berkeley Men's Center, 1971; Sawyer, 1970). Men developing this critical perspective were at first dismissed as inadequate in their masculinity, guilt-ridden dupes of feminism, or discontented homosexuals. (This statement is based on personal experience.) In spite of this initial response, a growing number of books, articles, media reports, conferences, courses, and organizations over the last 15 years have continued the development of this new awareness about and among men.

Today, the examination of male roles has become established, even fashionable. There is now so much being written and said about men that the problem for one interested in the subject is no longer finding relevant material, but de-

Reprinted from *Handbook of Counseling and Psychotherapy for Men*, Scher et al., ed. Newbury Park, CA: Sage Publications, 1987. © 1987 by Sage Publications. Reprinted by permission.

termining what is important and true in all that is available. This chapter addresses this need by first presenting two findings from current research that appear especially helpful in identifying key parameters of contemporary male experience: men's increasing time in family roles, and men's increasing rates of psychological distress relative to women. The chapter concludes by analyzing the current cultural debate about the extent and nature of change in men, examining in particular Barbara Ehrenreich's *The Hearts of Men* (1983).

MEN'S INCREASING TIME IN FAMILY ROLES

In *Women's Two Roles: Home and Work* (1956), Alva Myrdal argued that women in industrial societies were, to an increasing degree, adding a new role in paid work to their traditional family role. The phrase "women's two roles" caught on as a description of this change in women's lives. A decade later, Myrdal developed her argument a step further: Women having two roles could not succeed in the long run unless men developed two roles as well. For men, having two roles meant adding a greatly enlarged family role to their customary responsibility as family economic breadwinners (Myrdal, 1967).

From this perspective, data on trends in time spent by men in their family roles provide a key social indicator of change in men. By examining data on this variable, one can objectively determine whether men are really changing. Time in the family is, in effect, the social indicator for men analogous to labor force participation for women. A surprisingly large number of studies have investigated how men's participation in family life has changed in the United States over the twentieth century (see detailed review in Pleck, 1985). This research in fact documents that men's family role has increased. Two analyses provide particularly valuable evidence.

In one of the classic American community studies, Robert and Helen Merrill Lynd investigated "Middletown" (Muncie, Indiana) in the mid-20s. Caplow and Chadwick (1979; Caplow, Bahr, Chadwick, Hill, & Williamson, 1982) replicated the study in 1978 with a similarly drawn sample from the same city. About 10% of all fathers were reported by their wives to spend *no* time with their children in 1924; in 1978, the parallel figure was 2%. Thus the proportion of completely uninvolved fathers dropped from 1 in 10 to 1 in 50. (The proportion of fathers spending more than 1 hour per day, the highest reported category of involvement reported by the researchers, rose from 66% to 76%.)

Most who ask whether men are really changing are thinking not of the last 60 years, but of only the last 10 or 20, that is, since the rise of the contemporary women's movement. Juster (1985) provides data on the time spent by adult males in the United States in family work (housework and child care combined) from time diary surveys conducted with national representative samples in 1965 and 1981. Men's time in these activities rose from about 1.6 hours per day in 1965 to slightly under 2.0 hours per day in 1981, an increase of somewhat over 20%. Taking into account women's decreasing time in these activities, men's proportion of all housework and child care (that is, the total performed by the average man and the average woman combined) rose from 20% to 30% over this 16-year period.

Thus, on a key social indicator, men show clear evidence of change in their role, and to more than a trivial degree. This change is not, of course, necessarily occurring to an equal degree among all men. Aggregate figures such as these probably conceal subgroups of men who have not changed or who are doing even less family work than they used to, men who have changed only a little, and men who have changed a great deal. But if an overall generalization is needed, it must be that American men have markedly increased their family participation over the last 60 years. Further, the pace of change over the last two decades (men's proportion of total family work rising from 20% to 30%) seems substantial when one considers that these data describe the U.S. population as a whole, not just the young, the highly educated, residents of college towns, or the large East and West Coast cities. This rate of change is in fact comparable to the increase in the average woman's proportion of the paid work performed by her and the average man combined, which rose from 27% to 35% during this same period (calculated from Juster, 1985).

The most important qualification to be made about these data is that they concern only the amount of time men spend in family roles, and not the degree of responsibility men take. Analyses of how spouses divide family tasks underline the importance of the distinction between simply performing an activity and being responsible for the task being done (Lein, 1984). The extent to which men are *responsible* for family work is much lower than their participation, and has probably not increased as much.

Nonetheless, men's increase in family participation is socially significant. In a similar way, women's increasing labor force participation has had tremendous social consequences, in spite of the fact that women's average earnings relative to men's have not changed. Many would argue today that any woman who aspires to, or actually has, a higher-level job than women have traditionally held (or who has a job, when traditionally she would not have) shows the effects of the changed consciousness among women stimulated by feminism. In the same way, any man who is doing more in the family than he used to, or than his father did, likewise demonstrates the effects of broader cultural change in the male role.

MEN'S INCREASING RATES OF PSYCHOLOGICAL DISTRESS RELATIVE TO WOMEN

One of the research results giving impetus to the women's movement during the 1970s was the finding that women have higher rates of mental health disorders, especially depression, than men, and that this gender difference could not be accounted for by biological factors (Chesler, 1972; Guttentag, Salasin, & Belle, 1980). Recent research, however, has documented a significant change over the last three decades in the relationship between gender and psychological distress.

Kessler and McRae (1981; see also McLanahan & Glass, 1985) analyzed five national surveys conducted between 1957 and 1976 that included measures of psychophysiological symptoms such as sleep difficulty, nervousness, headaches, and dizziness. These surveys also included items assessing symptoms such as "times you couldn't take care of things because you just couldn't get going" and "times when personal worries got you down physically." While women reported a higher rate of these stress indictors than did men in all five surveys, the average difference between women and men became steadily smaller between 1957 and 1976. Detailed analyses showed that women's rates of such symptoms increased slightly over these two decades (about four-tenths of a point on the symptom scale, which had a standard deviation of about 5.5). But men's rates increased about three times more (1.1 points). As a result, the "gender gap" in symptoms was 38% smaller at the end of the period than it was at the beginning. Over these two decades, men's mental health deteriorated relative to women's.

It is possible that men's increased reports of psychological distress may not reflect an increase in its actual frequency, only an increasing willingness to acknowledge it. Undoubtedly, this factor contributes to some degree. However, it cannot be the only explanation, since exactly the same trend is evident in data on attempted suicide from 1960 to the present: Women still do it more, but men are catching up. Generalizing across a large group of studies, the ratio of females to males attempting suicide dropped from about 2.3 to 1 in 1960, to about 1.3 to 1 in 1980 (Kessler & McRae, 1983). (Men show substantially higher rates of successful suicide than women.)

Kessler and McRae (1982) further analyzed the 1976 survey (the Americans View Their Mental Health Re-Study) to identify factors associated with greater psychological distress in men that might account for the decline in men's mental health relative to women since the late 1950s. One of the main changes since the 1950s is, of course, that today more men have employed wives. The increase in wives' employment did account for some of the change in men's psychological symptoms. In the 1976 data, men with employed wives reported significantly more depression and lower self-esteem than sole-breadwinning husbands, though the size of the difference was not great. It is interesting to note that this pattern did not hold true for the youngest group, men in their twenties.

Several factors that the investigator thought might explain exactly *how* wives's employment diminished husband's mental health were not validated. For example, husbands of employed wives did not appear to experience more symptoms because the money their wives made rendered their own breadwinner role less important. In fact, among husbands with employed wives, those with higher-earning wives reported less distress. Likewise, the problem did not seem to be that husbands of employed wives performed more housework and child care. In fact, among husbands with employed wives, those who performed more family tasks showed less, not more, distress.

Pleck (1985) found parallel results in a study focusing specifically on the impact of men performing more family work on their family satisfaction and overall well-being. Pleck's interpretation of this latter, initially puzzling finding is that husbands whose wives are employed, but who do *not* contribute significantly to household and family tasks, exhibit "learned helplessness" behavior (Seligman, 1974). Most two-earner families face considerable demands in maintaining the household and arranging for child care. If housework needs doing and the children need to be cared for, but the husband does not have any behavior in his repertoire that will help meet these needs, he will experience low control and increased stress.

It is sometimes asked whether men actually show signs of hurting as a result of the limitations of the traditional male role, or because relationships between the sexes are changing. The question is sometimes put more pointedly: What is the evidence that men today are actually feeling pain, and are not simply happily enjoying their male privilege? Kessler and McRae's data in fact show that men as a group are experiencing more psychological distress than they did three decades ago, both absolutely and relative to women.

From one point of view, the research discussed earlier about men's increased family participation is the "good news" about contemporary men, while the data about men's increasing psychological symptoms are the "bad news." Some might interpret the two trends together as suggesting that men experience increased stress *because* of the ways they are changing their role. Actually, the data suggest the exact opposite: The increased discomfort occurs predominantly among the men whose own role (as reflected by their family behavior) is *not* changing. Current research suggests that having a nontraditional role, in the sense of an enlarged family role, is good for men's mental health.

BROADER SOCIAL TRENDS AMONG MEN

Today, there is a cultural debate going on about what is happening among men. Are men not changing at all? Are men changing only superficially, or even getting worse? Or are men actually getting better? The answer to each of these questions is yes, for at least some men. That is to say, three broad social trends are evident among American men: continued traditionalism; superficial or negative change; and genuine, positive change. Current cultural debate about men is thus largely about these trends' relative strength. The debate also focuses in part on whether particular phenomena (e.g., men's new family role, men's search for their own fathers, and the men's movement) are examples of genuine, positive change or illustrate only superficial, even negative change.

The statement on these matters that more than any other has come to frame today's debate in feminist and intellectual circles is Barbara Ehrenreich's *The Hearts of Men: American Dreams and the Flight from Commitment* (1983; see also Ehrenreich, 1984). Ehrenreich develops a variant of the "superficial/negative change" argument. She first analyzes the instability in the husband–wife relationship inherent in the husband being the sole or primary breadwinner. She then notes several cultural phenomena, beginning in the 1950s, that encouraged male abdication of the family breadwinner role: *Playboy's* philosophy and advertising, the beatnik movement, and the "counterculture" of the 1960s. Ehrenreich then concludes that men are indeed changing, but only in that (1) men are fleeing the breadwinner role, often abandoning ex-wives and children to poverty, and (2) they are increasingly pursuing narcissistic consumer gratification.

While some evidence supports Ehrenreich's interpretation, parts of it are overstated, and contrary evidence is ignored. As an example of the former, Ehrenreich (1983, p. 11) cites a study finding that only 25% of the women who are awarded child support by the courts actually receive it, and 60% of these receive less than $1500 a year. However, national data (for 1981) actually show that 72% of mothers awarded child-support orders receive child support. Roughly two-thirds of these are receiving the full amount awarded, and the average support received was $2220 a year (U.S. Bureau of the Census, 1983).

While some men fit Ehrenreich's portrait of men fleeing the breadwinner role to pursue consumer gratification, the breadwinner still has a strong hold on the majority. The *Wall Street Journal*, for example, analyzed the impact of Pittsburgh's loss of 100,000 jobs in steel and related industries (equivalent to 60% of its current manufacturing workforce) in the last five years. Faced with imminent foreclosure on his home after six months of unemployment, a 39-year-old man killed himself by jumping in the Monongahela River. "I knew we needed help, but Henry was too proud to ask for it.' says his widow, Betty, who paid off the mortgage with $9,000 in insurance benefits" (Hymowitz & O'Boyle, 1984, p. 1).[1] These male "breadwinner suicides" did not occur only during the Great Depression; they are still happening today.

Another article portrays the despair resulting from the loss of unionized jobs in the "Rust Belt" industries of the Midwest (Richards, 1986). Loss of these jobs has meant the loss of what male workers called "the ladder," the progression of increasing seniority and wages that traditionally provided advancement into the middle class for generations of blue-collar workers. Even when alternative jobs are available, they are dead ends. Men's occupational suffering is not unique or worse than women's (women, of course, never had access to "the ladder"). But it does reveal the continuing hold of a male breadwinner ideology that Ehrenreich seems too ready to believe has largely disappeared among men.

Yet other reports show that, contrary to the popular stereotype of the consumption-oriented, "yuppie" baby-boomers, this generation is actually less well-off economically and has less discretionary income than the generation before it, particularly when increased income and social security taxes are taken into account (Levy & Michel, 1984). While the narcissistic male consumption patterns Ehrenreich describes may exist among an elite group, they do not seem accurate as a description of the dominant trend among adult males today.

In light of today's economic and labor market dislocations, it seems likely that far more men are being pushed out of the breadwinner role involuntarily than are fleeing it for selfish reasons. Even if rejected by some, fulfillment of the family breadwinner role remains a central objective for the majority of adult men in the United States. Future social historians may well conclude that economic changes undermining the male breadwinner role had equal or even greater impact on men during the last half of the twentieth century than did feminism.

What Ehrenreich argues is that the dominant change among contemporary men is probably better regarded as only one of several trends of relatively equal importance. While men today are changing in some ways that are superficial or potentially negative for women, contemporary males are also manifesting continued traditionalism in other respects, and demonstrating authentic, positive change in yet others. The challenge facing those who wish to foster positive change is to acknowledge and support it where it exists, and to respond creatively to the forms of traditionalism and only superficial change also so apparent today.

NOTE

1. Reprinted by permission of the *Wall Street Journal*, copyright Dow Jones & Company, Inc. (1984). All Rights Reserved.

REFERENCES

Berkeley Men's Center Manifesto. (1971). [Reprinted 1974 in J. H. Pleck & J. Sawyer (Eds.), *Men and masculinity* (pp. 173–174). Englewood Cliffs, NJ: Prentice-Hall].

Caplow, T., Bahr, H., Chadwick, B., Hill, R., & Williamson, M. H. (1982). *Middletown families: Fifty years of change and continuity*. Minneapolis: University of Minnesota Press.

Caplow, T., & Chadwick, B. (1979). Inequality and life-styles in Middletown, 1920–1978. *Social Science Quarterly, 60* 367–390.

Chesler, P. (1972). *Women and madness*. Garden City, NY: Doubleday.

Ehrenreich, B. (1983). *The hearts of men: American dreams and the flight from commitment*. Garden City, NY: Anchor Press/Doubleday.

Ehrenreich, B. (1984, May 20). A feminist's view of the new man. *New York Times Sunday Magazine*, pp. 36–39.

Guttentag, M., Salasin, S., & Belle, D. (Eds.). (1980). *The mental health of women*. New York: Academic Press.

Hymowitz, C., & O'Boyle, T. F. (1984, Aug. 21). Pittsburgh's evolution from steel to services sparks a culture clash. *Wall Street Journal*, p. 1.

Juster, F. T. (1985). A note on recent changes in time use. In F. T. Juster and F. Stafford (Eds.), *Time, goods, and well-being* (pp. 313–332). Ann Arbor, MI: Institute for Social Research.

Kessler, R., & McRae, J. (1981). Trends in the relationship between sex and psychological distress: 1957–1976. *American Sociological Review, 46*, 443–452.

Kessler, R., & McRae, J. (1982). The effect of wives' employment on the mental health of married men and women. *American Sociological Review, 47*, 216–227.

Kessler, R., & McRae, J. (1983). Trends in the relationship between sex and attempted suicide. *Journal of Health and Social Behavior, 24*, 98–110.

Lein, L. (1984). *Families without villains*. Lexington, MA: D. C. Heath.

Levy, F., & Michel, R. C. (1984). *Are baby-boomers selfish?* Washington, DC: Urban Institute.

McLanahan, S. S., & Glass, J. L. (1985). A note on the trend in sex differences in psychological distress. *Journal of Health and Social Behavior, 26*, 328–335.

Myrdal, A. (1967). Foreword. In E. Dahlstrom & E. Liljestrom (Eds.), *The changing roles of men and women* (pp. 9–15). London: Duckworth.

Myrdal, A., & Klein, V. (1956). *Women's two roles: Home and work*. London: Routledge & Kegan Paul.

Pleck, J. H. (1981). *The myth of masculinity*. Cambridge, MA: MIT Press.

Pleck, J. H. (1985). *Working wives, working husbands*. Newbury Park, CA: Sage.

Richards, B. (1986, March 12). Down the ladder: They have jobs again in LaPorte, but work doesn't pay so well. *Wall Street Journal*, p. 1.

Sawyer, J. (1970). On male liberation. [Reprinted 1974 in J. H. Pleck & J. Sawyer (Eds.), *Men and masculinity* (pp. 171–172). Englewood Cliffs, NJ: Prentice-Hall.]

Seligman, M. (1974). Depression and learned helplessness. In R. Friedman & L. Katz (Eds.), *The psychology of depression: Contemporary theory and research* (pp. 218–239). Washington, DC: Winston.

U.S. Bureau of the Census. (1983). *Current population reports* (Series P-23, No. 124). *Child support and alimony: 1981* (Advance Report). Washington, DC: Government Printing Office.

Statement of Principles

NATIONAL ORGANIZATION FOR CHANGING MEN

The National Organization for Changing Men is an organization supporting men as they undergo the process of change so evident in men's lives today. NOCM reflects a pro-feminist and gay-affirmative perspective, is open to men and women, and is committed to a broad goal of social and personal change.

We believe that the great changes now taking place in the roles and opportunities of women and men will be positive for men as well as women. By questioning the old-fashioned rules of masculinity, which came along with the assumption of male superiority, men have the opportunity to be freer, happier, and more fulfilled as human beings. Traditional masculinity includes many positive qualities in which we take pride and find strength (independence, courage, self-reliance, etc.). But is also contains qualities which have limited and harmed us: excessive involvement with work, isolation from our children, discomfort in expressing emotions, lack of close friendships, excessive competitiveness and aggressiveness, and many others. We believe that men can help one another to unlearn the traditional masculine lessons that have limited our options and caused so many problems for ourselves and others.

As an organization of changing men, we strongly support the continuing struggle of women for full equality. We acknowledge the insights and positive social changes that feminism has stimulated in our society for both women and men. We oppose such injustices to women as economic and legal discrimination, rape, domestic violence, sexual harassment, and many others. We also support reform of policies that may affect men unfairly, such as child custody laws. Women and men can and should work together as allies to change the injustices that have so often made men and women see one another as enemies.

One of the strongest and deepest anxieties of most American men is their fear of homosexuality. This "homophobia" is a major cause of exaggerated masculine behavior. It is a debilitating burden to heterosexual men, and contributes directly to the many injustices experienced by gay, lesbian, and bisexual persons. We call for an end to all forms of discrimination based on sexual orientation, and for the creation of a gay-affirmative society.

We acknowledge, too, that many people are victimized today because of their race, social class, age, religion, and physical condition. We believe that such injustices are vitally connected to patriarchy, with its fundamental premise the unequal distribution of power. Our goal is to change not just ourselves or other men as individuals, but to society as a whole, including institutions which have perpetuated inequality.

We welcome any person who agrees in substance with these principles to membership in . . . THE NATIONAL ORGANIZATION FOR CHANGING MEN.

Harry Brod

FRATERNITY, EQUALITY, LIBERTY

"Fraternity, Equality, Liberty." Those familiar with European history will recognize this as an inversion of the slogan of the French Revolution: "Liberty,

An earlier version of this paper was presented at The First Annual Northwest Conference on Men and Masculinity, University of Oregon, Eugene, Oregon, January 18–20, 1985.

Equality, Fraternity." The ordering of these principles by the ideologists of the revolution was not coincidental, but rather reflected a certain conceptual scheme. To their minds, the first order of business was to secure liberty, by which they meant freedom from restrictions imposed upon them by others. Having won this liberty, they would then proceed to establish a society of equality. Subsequently, once men were living in this new society, feelings of fraternity for the brotherhood of man would emerge among all men. From our contemporary vantage point, we recognize that this fraternity excluded women in principle, and in practice excluded or limited the participation of a great number of men who were not of the prescribed class, race, national origin, etc.

What would happen if we were to reverse this progression? Specifically, what would happen if we were to proceed by focusing first on real fraternity, that is, real commonality of interest *as men*? Could such an approach possibly lead to equality between and among men and women, and to real liberty for all?

At first glance this approach would seem to have little hope for success. Would not any identifiable interests men have *as men* be precisely those interests which separate them from and pit them against women? How then could furthering these interests lead to any kind of universal equality and liberty? I believe, however, that these objections pose a false dichotomy. The interests men have in banding together in a fraternal way are interests in overcoming the limitations of the male sex role. And it is precisely this same male sex role which sets women and men at odds. I believe men's interests *as men* lie in overcoming sexism. I believe men have needs for separate strategies and tactics against sexism because we are coming to the project of eliminating sexism with different backgrounds, issues, and perspectives than women, but not ultimately different goals.

If one believes that men have common fraternal interests in ending sexism — a sexism that offers very real material rewards to men, but at too high a personal cost — then one has a *positive* basis upon which to work with other men. I, for example, do not regard men as "the enemy," nor do I believe I am opposing another man or violating his individual rights in moving against his sexism. When I intervene against a man's sexism I am doing him — and myself — a favor, because trapped inside destructive and self-destructive behavior is an individual who would be relieved to be rid of this mode of being if he had a free choice. If one shares my starting assumption that nurturing, intimacy, and support are real human needs, then it follows that it is essential that men establish *real* friendships with each other. Not the implicit, contract of traditional male camaraderie, in which we mutually agree to keep our defenses up but not to mind it, and to keep our prejudices intact while validating each other's masculinity; rather, a shared intimacy in which feelings, including fears and joys, flow freely. Otherwise, men will continue to turn to women to fulfill these needs. And while women's abilities to nurture are clearly admirable, the necessity that they do so is equally clearly oppressive. Furthermore, such friendships with men are essential for supporting men in making and sustaining the needed long-term changes.

I would like to take the idea of finding a positive approach to working with men against sexism a significant step further. I suggest that we stop looking for the "original sin" on the basis of which men can be said to have erected patriarchy. Many aspects of male psychology are put forth as candidates for "original sin" status. We are said to have innate aggressive instincts, to have dominating sex drives, to have obsessive desires for immortality so that we force women to have our children, to have a need to create a despised "Other" in order to establish our own identities, to have a need to compensate for our "womb envy" of women's creative and regenerative powers, to either love or fear each other so much, depending on the theory, that we have institutionalized oppressive heterosexuality, and so on.[1] I propose that we stop looking for the fatal flaw in male psychology which is responsible for sexism. Instead, I will make the seemingly preposterous suggestion that sexist attitudes can be understood as stemming from inherently positive aspects of male psychology, aspects which are, however, distorted by an oppressive social order.

Let me explain how I reached this position, and then go on to specify exactly what I have in mind.[2] As a general rule of social analysis, I try to give people, men specifically included, credibility for integrity and insight. Thus, when I observe a group of people acting in what seem to me irrational ways, the question I pose is not "What's wrong with them?" but rather "What are the distorted and distorting features of their situation which make these actions appear rational to them?" Until I have satisfied myself that, if I were in their shoes, their seemingly outrageous or inexplicable actions would also appear as legitimate options to me, I consider myself not to have succeeded in understanding or explaining anything. Applying this methodology to male sexist attitudes, I have obtained the following results. I believe that as we are growing up, in our early childhood years of attitude formation, we are socialized with a crucially important belief, namely the belief that in our society people get what they deserve. While this belief, in its usual interpretations, as applied to material success or social prestige, for example, is blatantly false and can be seen to be so upon reflection, it is nonetheless a principle of justice deeply inculcated in children as they are being raised. Children are also very observant. Specifically, they will observe and note that women are universally treated as less than fully human, in contrast to men. The conjunction of this principle and this observation can be expressed as a logical syllogism:

> People get what they deserve.
> Women are treated inhumanly.
> Women are less than fully human.

I offer the above not as a historical account of the genesis of sexist attitudes and beliefs, but rather as a phenomenological description of the development of sexist beliefs and attitudes in contemporary consciousness. In this light, sexist beliefs and attitudes can be seen to result from an attempt to preserve a belief that the world is justly ordered in the face of observing the existence of gross inequality. Children are faced with a choice: either women really are less deserving than men in some fundamental way, or a basic structuring principle of their world is false, and their world loses coherence and credibility. Everything around them, as well as their own insecurities, impel children to affirm the former, sexist beliefs.

But precisely therein, I would argue, lies the hope for change. If my proposed reconstruction of the genesis of sexist consciousness is correct, then, paradoxically enough, sexist attitudes may be said to be rooted in the child's sense of justice. But as adults, we can now take the bad news that the world is indeed unjust and not reasonably ordered. That same sense of justice, the belief that people should be treated as they deserve, coupled with the belief that people really should have equal rights and freedoms regardless of such factors as the shape or color of their skin, can now be called upon to mobilize men to rectify sexist injustices.

Listen to sexist men defend their attitudes today, listen with a comprehending ear, and you will hear the pleas of someone trying to make sense of a world they never made: "There *must* be *some* reason why the world is this way," "That's just how it is," "It's always been like this, hasn't it," "You just can't change some things." This is the voice of confusion and fear, not a dominating will to power. I propose, then, that we not focus our attention on the search for an ultimate cause for sexism in the nature of the male psyche or body, but rather that we work with men in the here and now to undo the damage sexism does to all of us. While there is some need for a general explanatory theory of patriarchy so that we can properly direct our efforts for change and not pursue the wrong targets, I believe the search for such a theory is, for most of us, a misplaced emphasis.

I think we need to emphasize moving on from here, and worry less about how we got here. This is not simply a pragmatic retreat made because we happen not to have a fully satisfactory theory about the origins of patriarchy or what a future non-patriarchal utopia would look like. The search for such a blueprint for the future is misguided, an all too typically masculine attempt to impose a rigidly constructed plan upon the world. Rather, let us do the more intimately involved work of nurturing that new world to growth with our given materials. If it is true that fundamental change must be positively self-motivated and not merely reactive, then the priority must be to seek positive approaches which will enable men to make revolutionary feminist changes. The direction of these changes, as they emerge, will clearly enough show us what our new society is to look like. This is how I envisage fraternity developing. It is not simply a means to some pre-fabricated goal. To adopt a slogan from the peace movement: there is no way to fraternity, fraternity is the way.

Which brings me to the next of the three guiding concepts, equality. I believe all men are equal. Let me make that more directly relevant by making a statement that I expect some will find terribly false, and others will find trivially true. I hope to show that it is very significantly true. The statement is this: no group of men in our society is any more or less sexist than any other group of men. Gay or straight, black or white, rich or poor, we are all equal in this regard.

Let me proceed by articulating the point of view I take myself to be arguing against. It is fashionable in some circles to characterize our society as one dominated by white males. Fashionable, but inadequate, as many feminists are aware. Socialist feminists, for example, would insist that we are plagued not only by sexism and racism, but also by capitalism.[3] So the description of the dominating group has to be widened to ruling class white males. But why stop there? Our society also systematically discriminates against the old and the young, so one would need to specify the age bracket of the ruling group, and so on. By the time one was finished, one would have constructed a description which fits at most a relative handful of men, who, according to this theory, are somehow oppressing all the rest of us, usually in multiple ways. I regard such a result as untenable for a coherent social theory and practice. It is a mistake, and a serious one, to attempt to reduce the multiple systems of oppression which characterize our society into one matrix.

Let me give a personal example. Some people have attempted to commiserate with my wife, who is Greek, about how sexist Greek or Mediterranean men are. They thought they were practicing international feminist solidarity. What they were really practicing was Anglo-Saxon cultural imperialism. Mediterranean patriarchy is qualitatively different from Anglo-Saxon patriarchy. Each has distinctive features, which are more or less taken for granted within each culture and look more or less objectionable to others. To try to assess these qualitative differences on the same quantitative scale is, as the old saying has it, like trying to mix apples and oranges.[4]

It makes more sense to say that we live in a patriarchy, and under patriarchy men oppress women. Period. We also live under capitalism. Under capitalism, the ruling class, men and women, oppresses the working class. Period. And so on with regard to racism, etc. I am aware that the situation is in reality more complex than this. Patriarchy also orders men into hierarchies and capitalism divides the genders. However, the fundamental point I wish to make is that just as, for example, ruling class women's gender does not excuse them from accountability for their class privileges, so too their lack of class privileges does not excuse working class men from accountability for the exercise of their male privileges. These, and all other forms of oppression, are overlapping and interrelated but distinct systems. While it is true that, because they suffer from other forms of oppression, men from oppressed groups do not reap the material rewards of patriarchy to as great an extent as men from dominant groups, one should not therefore conclude that men from oppressed groups are to be held less accountable for their sexism.

I propose therefore that we abandon all discussions and debate about whether gay men, or working class men, or Hispanic men, or any other group of men, are more or less sexist or patriarchal than any other group. I propose instead that we realize that all sexism is simply wrong and unsupportable, and that to attempt to establish some sort of graduated scale is at best meaningless and at worst oppressive in some other form. And I propose further that men go back to their respective communities and get on with the task of instituting the specific and specifically different kinds of fraternities within each community which will enable us to move towards equality and liberty for all people.

Which brings me to the concept of liberty, the last of the triumvirate. Liberty is the most expressly political of the three concepts. I believe it is essential for men to retain a perspective which is self-consciously political, and not merely personal or psychological, regarding the tasks of overcoming male role restrictions. Correspondingly, we must also expressly link our efforts to the feminist movement. Personal freedom, of whatever kind, requires the securing of political liberty.

Let me give one example, drawn specifically from an aspect of the male role many are struggling with. Many men are trying to undo the damage done them by male role restrictions against showing their emotions. In these struggles, they are often joined and offered assistance by women, partly out of sympathy and partly — and this is the point I wish to stress — because women suffer from this aspect of the male role, not merely sympathetically, but in their own right as well. Our male dominated society confers real power on those who are skilled at withholding their emotions in many ways. Again, let us look not to flawed individual psyches but to broader social realities to understand male sexist behaviors and attitudes. Patriarchy draws to itself those who will seek its powers. No matter how much we raise men's consciousness about the value of expressing emotion, as long as patriarchy remains intact it impels men to adopt those emotional masks which give them power. Men's and women's roles cannot be simply conceptualized as complementary and equally restrictive roles, as some men's rights advocates would have us believe. Men's roles do carry real power with them. Any attempt to give up male role restrictions on an individual or apolitical basis is doomed to failure because existing power structures simply reproduce these roles, and exert enormous pressure on individuals to re-assume them. The male sex role maintains itself not because men are either evil or stupid, but because it confers benefits and maintains men's distance from those who bear the brunt of the system: women. That is to say, men who are competing to be less emotional are competing to be less womanlike. I believe the same sort of analysis applies not only to emotional expressiveness but to all the other aspects of the male sex role. Male problems are the other side of the coin and are inseparable from male privileges. Hence men aware of the personal drawbacks of the male role should also be drawn to a feminist political identity for themselves.

I think it is important that men claim title to be considered feminist for several reasons. I say this knowing that many men and women whom I would count among my allies on the relevant political questions would disagree. Many men and women sincerely committed to the fight against sexism insist that the label "feminist" can only be applied to women.[5] To refer to feminism as a movement consisting exclusively of women is, I believe, not a sign of radicalism but of misplaced liberalism. It relegates men to a position of sincere support, but from a distance, of women "doing their thing." One of the obstacles all liberation movements have faced is the liberal spirit of abstract tolerance from afar — e.g., it's good that women or blacks are now moving on and I wish them well, but of course this doesn't directly involve me. All too often the ideology of support by granting "autonomy" ends up being a kind of "benign neglect" where real critical thinking and support are withheld for fear of treading where one does not belong. Men should by no means dominate in women's activities of a political or personal nature, but too often a "hands off" kind of support, whose intent may be to create unity and support, may end up creating fragmentation and feelings of abandonment.

I respect the autonomy of the women's movement, but I take this stand as a feminist. My support for women's autonomy is based on a feminist political analysis which demonstrates that this autonomy is necessary, rather than basing it on a desire for a lesser degree of involvement with the movement. Perhaps an analogy from Marxist theory will be helpful here. One can be a Marxist without being a member of the proletariat, despite the fact that Marxism assigns the key role in revolutionary struggles to the proletariat. For example, being a Marxist and a member of the middle class would simply mean that I have a theory and practice of social change in which I recognize that the struggles of my own group will not play the determining role in bringing about the new society. It means that when organizing within my own group — an important task despite the fact that my political analysis tells me that this will not be the dominant force in revolutionary activity — I orient some of my efforts towards support for more key sectors. As a Marxist, I would also see the necessity for there being a working class party in which members of my class should not hold leadership positions. What I want to stress here is that I would be taking these positions *as a Marxist* — my politics is determined by how I act in my social position, not simply by seeing what class I belong to. The latter view is an example of the most crudely reductionist, determinist sort of analysis.

The relevance of this analogy to the question of men as feminists should be clear. As a male feminist, I see that my activities as a man will not be the determining ones in the struggle for a nonsexist society, and I see the need for an autonomous women's movement of which I would not be a part. But I take these positions *as a feminist*.

Why is this important? In the first place, it affirms the character of the feminist movement as essential for a qualitatively better society, and not just as the concern of a particular interest group (women) within this society. Secondly, it helps to keep in mind the difference between one's life-style and one's politics. All of us are deeply indebted to the women's movement for bringing to popular consciousness the idea that "the personal is political," but the radical importance of this slogan is trivialized and lost if it is taken to mean that everything I do in my life *is* in politics. Politics must be more than life-style, it must involve public, organized political action, and insistence that one need not be a woman to be a feminist restores this dimension to the movement. While I cannot live a woman's life or feelings, being a man, I can however live her politics.

Perhaps most importantly, any stand other than the insistence that men can be feminists betrays the most radical potential of the movement. Under the slogan "Biology is not Destiny," the feminist movement challenged the regressive idea that one's biological make-up should have a role in determining one's social/political/economic role. The stance that men cannot be feminists is a regression back to a standpoint which feminism has surpassed.

Furthermore, part of the oppressive ideology of society is the myth that the divisions between groups have been total and absolute, that there has been all-out warfare between women and men, blacks and whites, Jews and Gentiles, etc. While acknowledging the overwhelming reality of oppression, it must nonetheless be said that this is a falsification of our history and a denial of our strengths. The support which the early feminists received from their husbands and male friends *is* part of the history of feminism. The fact that approximately one third of the signatories to the 1848 Seneca Falls Declaration of the Rights of Women were men is as important a part of the history of feminism as the exploits of John Brown are part of the history of Abolitionism in the same century.

I have no doubt that the process of building male–female feminist alliances will be difficult. At times, men will more or less unconsciously continue to play out old patterns of domination and step on the toes of the women they are attempting to assist. When this occurs, I hope and trust it will be corrected. But how many opportunities to support feminist growth will be lost if we do not make efforts to establish such alliances?

I believe a male feminist theory and practice which can have any hope of success in mobilizing men in a politically effective way behind the clear moral imperatives supporting feminism must always remain simultaneously focused on both aspects of the personal/political dialectic. Men as a group benefit from the social powers which correlate with the male sex role. They reap the material rewards the society has to offer. But men individually pay too high a price for these benefits, and it is in their real personal interest to overthrow the system which creates and grants these privileges.[6] The male sex role is both unsatisfying and dangerous. The combination of breadwinner pressures, which make us neurotic, isolated competitors, and the restrictions on male emotional release for these pressures which are also part of the male role is a prescription for the earlier deaths and higher rates of tension-related health problems — heart attacks, ulcers, high blood pressure, suicides — we daily see men suffering from. Though not all men are aware of the source of their difficulties, I believe all men suffer from sexism. These are the disadvantages of the advantages men receive from a sexist system.

In these ways, the call for "Fraternity, Equality, and Liberty" presents us with the beginnings of a positive political analysis of and for changing men. I hope this becomes part of ongoing discussions of how to further feminist brotherhood.

NOTES

1. These hypotheses are among many popular in feminist theory, and one finds them in such frequently used women's studies texts as *Feminist Frameworks*, ed. Alison M. Jaggar and Paula S. Rothenberg (2nd edition McGraw-Hill, 1984) and *The Longest War*, by Carol Tavris and Carole Wade, (2nd edition, Harcourt Brace Jovanovich, 1984). See also the articles by Azizah al-Hibri, Eva Feder Kittay, Iris Marion Young, Pauline Bart, and Ann Ferguson in *Mothering: Essays in Feminist Theory*, ed. Joyce Trebilcot (Rowman & Allanheld, 1984).

2. Though he might will reject the analysis in this section, it is inspired by Albert Memmi's analysis of racism. See, for example, the section on "Racism and Oppression" in *Dominated Man*, Beacon, 1968.

3. See *Capitalist Patriarchy and the Case for Socialist Feminism*, ed. Zillah R. Eisenstein (Monthly Review Press, 1979).

4. I am indebted to Maria Papacostaki for clarifying discussions on this topic.

5. See Jon Snodgrass, *For Men Against Sexism: A Book of Readings*, Times Change Press, 1977, p. 9.

6. These points are developed in two brief articles of mine: "Feminism for Men: Beyond Liberalism," *Brother: The Newsletter of the National Organization for Changing Men* 3 : 3, 1985, and a review of Leo Kanowitz's *Equal Rights: The Male Stake* and William and Laurie Wishard's *Men's Rights* in *M.: Gentle Men for Gender Justice* 12, Spring 1984.

NOTES ON CONTRIBUTORS

Alan Alda is an actor, writer, and director, who is concerned about gender issues.

Anthony Astrachan is the author of *How Men Feel: Their Response to Women's Demands for Equality and Independence* (Doubleday, 1985).

Maxine Baca Zinn is in the department of sociology at the University of Michigan–Flint. She has written widely in the areas of family relations, Chicano studies, and women's studies, including most recently (with D. Stanley Eitzen), *Diversity in American Families*.

Tim Beneke a writer living in the San Francisco Bay area, is the author of *Men on Rape*.

Jessie Bernard, a sociologist at Penn State University, has written and lectured widely on gender and family issues. Her influential writings include *The Female World*.

Robert Bly is a poet and a leader of the mythopoetic wing of the men's movement. He writes and speaks about men and masculinity.

√ **Harry Brod** is Associate Professor of Philosophy and Gender Studies at Kenyon College. He is the editor of *The Making of Masculinities: The New Men's Studies* and *A Mensch Among Men: Explorations in Jewish Masculinity*. He was the Founding Editor of the *Men's Studies Review* and Founding Chair of the National Men's Studies Association.

Susan Brownmiller is the author of numerous articles and books which examine feminist issues, including *Against Our Will: Men, Women, and Rape* and *Femininity*.

John Ceeley lives in Madison, Wisconsin. He is the author of a book of poems, *The Country is Not Frightening*.

James Chin is a clinical psychologist at the Holliswood Hospital, a clinical research consultant to the NYS Office of Mental Health and in private practice. His areas of specialization include the prevention and treatment of addictive disorders, behavioral medicine, and health psychology.

Chris Clark graduated from New York University in 1985 and currently lives in New York.

Bob Connell is professor of sociology at Macquarie University in Sydney, Australia. His most recent works include *Gender and Power* and *Staking a Claim: Feminism, Bureaucracy, and the State*, co-authored with Suzanne Ranzway and Dianne Court.

Edward Donnerstein is Professor and Chair of the Communication Studies Program at the University of California, Santa Barbara. His major research interest is in mass-media violence and he has published widely in this area. His most recent books include *The Question of Pornography: Research Findings* *and Policy Implications* (with Dan Linz and Steve Penrod), and *Pornography and Sexual Aggression.*

Martin Duberman is Distinguished Professor of History at Herbert Lehman College of the City University of New York. Among his many books and plays are *In White America, About Time: Exploring the Gay Past*, and *Paul Robeson.*

Barbara Ehrenreich has written widely on gender issues, including her books, *The Hearts of Men: American Dreams and the Flight from Commitment* and *Re-Making Love.*

Wayne Ewing is Assistant Dean, Loretto Heights College, Denver, CO. He is author of *Violence Works/Stop Violence.*

Thomas J. Ficarrotto is a research associate with the Department of Psychiatry and Langley Porter Psychiatric Institute at the University of California in San Francisco. His areas of specialization include social psychology and health psychology. He writes on cross cultural aspects of homophobia and sex differences in mortality and health behaviors.

Jules Fieffer is a syndicated cartoonist and regular contributor at *The Village Voice.*

Bruce Feirstein is the author of *Real Men Don't Eat Quiche.*

Gary Alan Fine is in the department of sociology at the University of Minnesota. His most recent book is *With the Boys: Little League Baseball and Preadolescent Culture.*

Ben Fong-Torres is a journalist in the San Francisco Bay Area.

Jeffrey Fracher is a psychotherapist who practices in Metuchen, New Jersey, specializing in the treatment of sexual disorders. He is adjunct assistant professor of psychology at Rutgers University.

Clyde W. Franklin II is in the department of sociology at The Ohio State University. His research focuses largely on black masculinity. His numerous publications include *The Changing Definition of Masculinity.*

Perry Garfinkel is a journalist who lives in Oakland, California. He has published numerous articles on psychology and social trends and a book, *In a Man's World: Father, Son, Brother, Friend, and Other Roles Men Play.*

Barry Glassner is the chairman of the department of sociology at the University of Connecticut. He is the author of *Bodies: Why We Look the Way We Do (and How We Feel About It)*, among other books.

William J. Goode is professor of sociology and senior research fellow, Hoover Institution, Stanford University.

Matt Groening is a cartoonist based in Los Angeles. He is the author of *School is Hell, Work is Hell* and *Childhood is Hell.*

Alan E. Gross is former Professor and Chair of the Department of Psychology at the University of Maryland. He currently lives in New York City.

Jeffrey P. Hantover is a freelance writer and consultant living in New York City. He has published articles on photography, film, and social issues. He is presently working on a novel.

James Harrison is a clinical psychologist and codirector of Harrison Associates, a holistic psychological consultation center in New York City. He currently writes and produces videos on psychological issues with a particular interest in gender studies.

Joe Jackson is a singer/songwriter who lives in New York City. His records include *Body and Soul, Look Sharp* and the soundtracks to *Tucker* and *Mike's Murder.*

Franz Kafka was a German philosopher and novelist whose works include *The Trial, The Castle,* and *Metamorphosis.*

Ed Koren is a cartoonist at *The New Yorker.*

Gayle Kimball is director of women's studies at California State University, Chico. She is the author of *The 50/50 Marriage.*

Michael S. Kimmel is in the department of sociology at the State University of New York at Stony Brook. He is editor of *Changing Men: New Directions in Research on Men and Masculinity* (Sage Publications) and *Men Confronting Pornography* (Crown Books). He is currently editing *Against the Tide,* a documentary history of pro-feminist men in American history and writing *Gender and Desire,* on the relationship between sexuality and gender.

Gary Kinsman is an activist in the gay liberation and socialist movements in Toronto and is a member of the collective that publishes *Rites,* a magazine for lesbian and gay liberation. He is the author of *The Regulation of Desire.*

Seymour Kleinberg is the author of *Alienated Affections: Being Gay in America* and teaches at the Brooklyn Center of Long Island University.

John Krich is a writer whose books include *A Totally Free Man: An Unauthorized Autobiography of Fidel Castro* and a novel, *One Big Bed.*

Barbara Kruger is a graphic artist in New York City.

Gregory K. Lehne is the author of "Homophobia Among Men: Supporting and Defining the Male Sex Role." He is Assistant Professor of Medical Psychology in the Department of Psychiatry and Behavioral Sciences at The Johns Hopkins School of Medicine.

Martin P. Levine is Associate Professor of Sociology at Bloomfield College, New Jersey, and Adjunct Associate Professor of Urban Studies at Queens College. He is currently working as a Research Associate on a study of sexual decision making at Memorial Sloan Kettering Cancer Research Center. He has published extensively on the sociology of AIDS, sexuality, and homosexuality.

Charles J. Levy is the author of "ARVN as Faggots: Inverted Warfare in Vietnam."

Daniel Linz does research on the effects on males of exposure to various forms of media violence against women and other images of women. He currently teaches in the Department of Psychology at UCLA Center for the Study of Women.

John Lippert is the author of "Sexuality as Consumption."

Peter Lyman is Director of the Center for Scholarly Technology at the University of Southern California. His research on computing began when he was looking for a good field site to study anger, and a friend suggested the computer center. He is currently working on a study of how technical knowledge and hardware are "gendered," that is, founded in a masculine epistemology.

Richard Majors is a National Institute of Health Postdoctoral Fellow at Kansas University in the Department of Human Development and Family Life. His research interests focus on the psychosocial development of the black male, masculinity and gender development, coping processes, adolescent behavior, and nonverbal behaviors and communication styles among ethnic groups.

Pip Martin is a psychologist who has also worked as an activist in the Australian environmental movement.

Michael Messner is in the program for the study of women and men in society and the department of sociology at the University of Southern California. He has written widely on masculinity and sports, including his forthcoming book, *Masculinity and Sport: The Lives of Male Athletes*. He is also currently editing a book (with Don Sabo) entitled *Sport, Men, and the Gender Order: Critical Feminist Perspectives*.

Brian Miller has a private psychotherapy practice in West Hollywood and writes a regular mental health column for the Los Angeles magazine, *Edge*. His Ph.D. dissertation, completed at the University of Alberta, is a longitudinal study of the identity development of gay husbands and fathers and he has published widely on the subject.

John Moreland is the author of "Age and Change in the Adult Male Sex Role."

Geof Morgan is singer-songwriter who is active in the pro-feminist men's movement. His most recent album is *Talk It Over*.

Joseph H. Pleck is Henry R. Luce Professor of Families, Change and Society at Wheaton College. He is the author of numerous articles and books on men and masculinity, including *The Myth of Masculinity*, and (with Elizabeth H. Pleck) *The American Man*.

Norm Radican has a background in public health education and in counseling about sexuality. He is active in The Australian Men's Movement.

Rex Reece is the author of "Coping With Couplehood."

M. Rochlin is the author of "The Heterosexual Questionnaire."

Ebet Roberts is a photographer in New York City.

Lillian B. Rubin is a writer and therapist in the San Fransico Bay area. She is the author of *Intimate Strangers: Men and Women Together*, and various other books about gender issues.

Don Sabo is in the department of sociology at D'Youville College in Buffalo, NY. He writes and speaks widely about gender and sport. He is editor (with Ross Runfola) of *Jock: Sports and Male Identity*, and is currently editing a book (with Michael Messner) entitled *Sport, Men, and the Gender Order: Critical Feminist Perspectives*.

Jack Sattel is in the department of sociology of Normandale Community College in S. Bloomington, MN. He was among the first people to research male inexpressivity.

Ruth Sidel is Professor of Sociology at Hunter College of the City of New York. She studies the role of women, the care of preschool children, and the provision of human services. Her books include *Women and Childcare in China: A Firsthand Report*, *Families of Fengsheng: Urban Life in China*, and *The World of Working Class Women*.

Robert Staples is in the department of sociology at the University of California, San Francisco. He has written widely on black families and gender issues, including his book, *Black Masculinity*.

Gloria Steinem is a feminist leader and founding editor of *Ms* magazine.

John Stoltenberg is a writer and magazine editor living in New York City. He is co-founder of Men Against Pornography in New York City, and lobbied for the civil rights antipornography ordinance when it was before the Minneapolis City Council in May, 1984.

Cooper Thompson lives in Cambridge, Massachusetts, where he develops anti-sexist curricula for schools. He writes and speaks widely on this topic and is also active in the National Organization for Changing Men.

Barrie Thorne is Streisand Professor of Intimacy and Sexuality in the program for the Study of Women and Men in Society and the department of sociology at the University of Southern California. She has written widely on feminist theory and gender issues, especially with respect to children. Her works include *Rethinking the Family: Some Feminist Questions* (edited with Marilyn Yalom).

Robert S. Weiss is Professor of Sociology and Director of the Work and Family Research Unit at the University of Massachusetts, Boston.

Edmund White is a writer and novelist. His works include *States of Desire: Travels in Gay America*, *A Boy's Own Story*, and *The Beautiful Room is Empty*. He lives in Paris.

Robert Zussman is in the department of sociology at the State University of New York, Stony Brook. He is the author of *Mechanics of the Middle Class*.